S0-DZO-241

1980
NEWS
DICTIONARY

1980 NEWS DICTIONARY

Editor
Donald Paneth
Managing Editor
Stephen Orlofsky
Foreign Affairs Staff
Hal Kosut, Chris Larson,
Melinda Maidens
H. Martyn Williams
National Affairs Staff
Joseph Fickes,
Raymond Hill,
Marjorie Bank, Marguerite Karter,
Jeff Shapiro, Sheryl Lynn Presser

Production Manager
Robin Smith
Staff Artist
Andrew Elias

Production Assistant
Fran M. Fishelberg

Facts On File
460 Park Avenue South
New York, New York 10016

1980 NEWS DICTIONARY

Library of Congress Cataloging in Publication Data
Main entry under title:
News Dictionary. 1964-
New York, Facts on File.
v. 23 cm. annual. (A Facts on File publication)
Supersedes News year.
Editors: 1964- L.A. Sobel and H.M. Epstein
1. History—Yearbooks. I. Sobel, Lester A., ed. II. Epstein Howard M., ed. III. Facts on File, inc., New York
D410.N44 65-17649
ISBN 0-87196-111-3 (cloth-bound)

PHOTO CREDITS: *Wide World Photos* pages 6, 7, 9, 10, 11, 13, 16, 20, 21, 24, 25, 28, 30, 32, 33, 35, 36, 39, 53, 55, 62, 64, 67, 71, 73, 74, 82, 85, 88, 89, 93, 97, 99, 101, 104, 105, 111, 113, 115, 119, 126, 128, 130, 139, 145, 148, 154, 160, 161, 166, 168, 170, 171, 172, 177, 179, 185, 188, 194, 196, 200, 202, 205, 209, 210, 211, 212, 215, 217, 225, 229, 231, 235, 244, 257, 269, 270, 277, 279, 294, 299, 305, 307, 310, 320, 326, 337, 343, 344, 349, 362, 375, 379, 381, 383, 385, 389, 392

Introduction

News Dictionary 1980 records the historical events of an extraordinary year.

It is a unique enterprise. Here, from A to Z, is a look back at the developments and personalities that made history in the previous year. The subjects covered are as various as the world itself.

Specific entries include Abscam, Afghanistan, boxing, Canada, defense, earthquakes, elections, El Salvador, horse racing, Iran, Iraq, John Lennon, medicine and health, Middle East, Nobel prizes, Northern Ireland, nuclear energy, Poland, press, refugees, religion, soccer, Turkey, South-West Africa, Zimbabwe.

As a reference work, News Dictionary provides the researcher and student with an encyclopedic summary of every significant news event. As a history, it offers the general reader an opportunity to ponder the diverse currents of human affairs. To the best of our ability we have made this record accurate, unbiased and balanced; reports are proportionate. The unity of complex, worldwide events is demonstrated. News Dictionary thus places in the reader's hands a topography of contemporary events and a key to understanding them.

Otherwise fragmentary news reports are pulled together into a coherent form. This perspective is as significant as the material presented. One's viewpoint of events in time is essential to interpreting them. As a journalist, the editor observes that the way in which we experience time is changing. Television, supersonic air travel, space flights, contemporary art and literature are changing it. We not only pass through time and space at a greater rate, but in our minds are able to span epochs from at least 35,000 B.C. to 1 million years into the future. Two examples. Ice age cultures of France and northern Spain are made accessible to us in museum exhibitions. Macfarlane Burnet, the Nobel laureate and microbiologist, in his book, *Endurance of Life,* speculates about the long-term future of the human species.

The idea of time has evolved historically. The Greeks thought in terms of cyclic alternations of opposing forces. Christianity disputed the cyclic view. It propounded a linear sense of time, salvational history. Einstein measured time through the velocity of light. Today, many kinds of time are available to us. There is rotational time, based on the earth's rotation about its axis. There is ephemeris time, the earth's motion about the sun. There is atomic time, counting microwave cycles. There is local, standard and universal time, sidereal and mean solar time. There are light-cones, the backward cone converging from the past, the forward cone directed towards the future. The range in which we may view and try to understand events has expanded.

Yet, our daily newspapers, television and radio continue to report events as occurrences of the moment, in isolation from all that has preceded or might reasonably be expected to follow them. There is little attempt to integrate events, to study the sequences and patterns of events. Understanding is inhibited. On the other hand, a change in the time unit within which events are viewed would enhance it. Past, present and future might be studied simultaneously. A significant barrier to a longterm perspective of events would be eliminated.

Looking at the comprehensive nature of such publications as FACTS ON FILE (weekly world news digest) and NEWS DICTIONARY, it seems as if further steps in journalistic development might be forthcoming. These are the underlying premises: a longterm view is necessary if human problems of considerable duration and intensity are to be solved; new information and new types of information, presently available but still not widely circulated, are required to enable each and all to consider, debate and work on these problems; the information is accumlating at a rapid rate in the great libraries, research institutes, government agencies, the United Nations; it exists in at least six areas, 1) economics, 2) social, 3) technical, 4) scientific, 5) esthetic and 6) historical. If news events of the moment were compressed in the daily newpaper a good deal of this information could be imparted to the reader. Meanwhile, the daily event could be recorded at length in an expanded weekly digest – and a new course of information distribution by the press would have begun.

This is the 17th edition in the FACTS ON FILE series of news annuals. It is illustrated by some 125 photographs plus maps, charts and diagrams. The reader will find that it is as convenient to use as the WEBSTER'S that stands beside it on the bookshelf. The editors of FACTS ON FILE designed NEWS DICTIONARY to overcome the shortcomings of the typical yearbook, which are a complicated index, nine-month coverage and an eclectic choice of material. Here the reader will find a self-index, coverage from January 1 through December 31, a synthesis of all news on each subject.

The principle of NEWS DICTIONARY is the alphabet. To find the facts of an event, the reader-researcher simply looks up – as in a dictionary – the subject, the country concerned or the name of a key person or organization involved in the event; if the story is not found in the first place he looks, an explicit cross-reference will direct him to the proper location. Thus, the question of inflation is located under ECONOMY (U.S.) but the reader would be referred to it from cross-references under MONETARY DEVELOPMENTS and other headings.

A useful feature of NEWS DICTIONARY is the system of numbering paragraphs. The paragraphs are numbered consecutively. The cross-references refer the researcher to the category and in addition usually to the specific paragraph(s) in which the desired information is to be found. For example, a researcher seeking material on Mexico's fishing dispute with the U. S. would find under MARITIME AFFAIRS the reference "See MEXICO [6-11]." This refers him to paragraphs 6 to 11 of the MEXICO entry. The numbering system permits the use of NEWS DICTIONARY in the widest possible way.

DONALD PANETH

ABORTION

[1] **Medicaid Funding Limits Upheld.** The Supreme Court ruled, 5-4, June 30 that neither the federal government nor the state were consitutionally required to fund abortions for the poor. The decision upheld the so-called "Hyde Amendment," used since 1976 by Congress to limit Medicaid abortions, as well as similar state restrictions. The cases, consolidated for judgement, were *Harris v. McRae, Williams v. Zbaraz, Miller v. Zbaraz and U.S. v. Zbaraz.*

[2] The Hyde Amendment, named after Rep. Henry J. Hyde (R, Ill.), prohibited the Department of Health, Education and Welfare (now the Department of Health and Human Services) from using Medicaid funds for abortions except in instances of pregnancies that were the result of incest or rape or if the life of the mother would be endangered by carrying the fetus to term. At least 40 states also had restricted or banned the use of Medicaid fund for abortion. (Medicaid was funded jointly by the federal government and the states.)

[3] Decisions by two federal district judges, John F. Dooling Jr. in New York City and John F. Grady in Chicago, had found the funding limits unconstitutional. The Supreme Court overturned those judgements, holding, among other things, that it was not province of courts to "decide whether the balance of competing interests reflected in the Hyde Amendment is wise social policy."

ABSCAM (ARAB SCAM)

[1] Seven members of Congress and a number of other persons were indicted during 1980 on charges growing out of a corruption probe by the Federal Bureau of Investigation. Ten persons were tried and found guilty, though two convictions later were set aside. One member of the House of Representatives was expelled following his conviction; four lost their bids for reelection [see Elections 93].

[2] **Congressmen Linked to Bribery & Corruption.** Federal Bureau of Investigation agents posing as Arab businessmen seeking political favors had been gathering evidence against members of Congress in a two-year bribery and corruption investigation code-named Abscam – a contraction of "Arab scam."

[3] Details of the investigation surfaced Feb. 2 on the National Broadcasting Co.'s televised evening news and the Feb. 3 editions of *Newsday,* the *New York Times* and the *Washington Post.*

[4] The operation reportedly involved meetings between undercover FBI agents and public officials that were secretly videotaped and recorded. Agents were said to have paid bribes of as much as $50,000. The payments were said to have totaled hundreds of thousands of dollars. The FBI agents sought help from the officials in making investments, obtaining permission for Arab businessmen to reside in the U.S., and building hotels and gaining a

casino license in Atlantic City, N.J.

[5] Among those named by law enforcement authorities as subjects of the investigation were: Sen. Harrison A. Williams, Jr. of New Jersey, Rep. John M. Murphy of New York, Rep. Frank Thompson Jr. of N.J., Reps. Michael J. Myers, Raymond F. Lederer, and John Murtha of Pennsylvania, Rep. John W. Jenrette Jr. of South Carolina and Rep. Richard Kelly of Florida. All of the legislators, except Kelly, were Democrats. Other public officials probed were: Camden, N.J. Mayor Angelo J. Errichetti, N.J. Casino Control Commission member Kenneth N. MacDonald, and other state and local officials in New Jersey and Pennsylvania.

[6] At least one legislator, Sen. Larry Pressler (R, S.D.) was reportedly approached by undercover agents and flatly refused to consider financial favors in exchange for his legislative influence.

[7] The Abscam operation began in February 1978, when Melvin Weinberg, an FBI informer who had helped recover stolen paintings in return for a reduction in his sentence, introduced agents to allegedly corrupt public officials. The FBI invented an Arab sheik named "Kambir Abdul Rahman," and a false business, "Abdul Enterprise Ltd." FBI agents pretended to work for him and paid hundreds of thousands of dollars to officials who promised to use their influence to help the sheik. The agents met the targets of the probe throughout 1979 at New York hotels, a rented townhouse in Washington, a yacht off the coast of Florida, and in several other locations.

[8] The Abscam operation was run out of the FBI resident office in Hauppauge, N.Y. under the supervision of the head of the FBI's New York division and the chief of the Justice Department's Organized Crime Strike Force for the eastern district of New York. U.S. attorneys in other states cooperated.

[9] ***Congressional Reaction***—Members of Congress were stunned by the allegations. The Senate and House moved to conduct their own investigations.

[10] On Feb. 3, Rep. Charles Bennett (D, Fla.), chairman of the House Committee on Standards of Official Conduct (ethics committee), said his panel had been investigating for months charges of misconduct against some of the congressmen implicated in the FBI probe. He said his panel would broaden its probe.

[11] On Feb. 5, Attorney General Benjamin R. Civiletti asked congressional leaders to delay House and Senate investigations of the Abscam allegations. According to congressional sources, Civiletti said any probes started by Congress could prejudice any criminal cases brought by the Justice Department.

[12] But in a closed session Feb. 6, the Senate ethics committee voted unanimously to conduct a "preliminary inquiry" of Sen. Williams and to allow Williams a chance to defend himself. Also in closed session, the House ethics panel moved ahead with its probe by discussing candidates for a special counsel to aid in their inquiry.

[13]***Tactics, Disclosures Questioned***—The tactics of the FBI and the Justice Depatment during the Abscam operation and the premature disclosures that followed were sharply criticized.

[14]Some observers questioned the ethics of offering unsolicited bribes to members of Congress and other public officials. Haynes Johnson, in a Feb. 6 *Washington Post* column, quoted John Shattuck of the American Civil Liberties Union as commenting, "This raises very serious questions about the scope of FBI undercover operations. It appears government agents have been in the field for over a year, building a case from nothing, a case that does not appear to be focused on anyone . . . ."

[15] Other questions were raised about the possibility of entrapment and method of choosing the targets in the

probe. Assistant Attorney General Philip B. Heymann appeared before the Senate and House ethics panels Feb. 6 and told them the Abscam operation did not begin as a probe targeted against Congress but was a "relatively natural evolution" of a case that began with a search for stolen paintings. "There was never a decision to target any member," he said.

[16]Heymann said that informers declared themselves able to sell political influence and "the federal government did not step back." He added: "Anybody caught in the mesh of this investigation was brought into the mesh by those selling influence."

[17] If public officials were indicted on charges stemming from the Abscam operation, they would find it difficult to use the defense of entrapment, government and private lawyers told the *New York Times* Feb. 3. The lawyers pointed out that an entrapment defense implicitly assumed an admission of guilt but claimed the crime was committed because of illegal law enforcement conduct. The lawyers asserted that the FBI agents would have had to originated the idea of the crime and induced the targets to commit the crime when the targets were not otherwise disposed to do so.

[18] On another issue, the ACLU and consumer activist Ralph Nader criticized leaks of FBI and Justice Department documents implicating congressmen, the *Wall Street Journal* reported Feb. 8. The ACLU blasted the disclosures as "outrageous," and Nader contended, "In the minds of millions of people these guys are guilty, and they haven't even been charged."

[19] The appointment of Richard Blumenthal, U.S. attorney for Connecticut, to investigate leaks of confidential information about the Abscam probe was announced Feb. 11 by Attorney General Benjamin R. Civiletti. At a news conference Feb. 12 Blumenthal said he might subpoena reporters and their notes if necessary to find the source of the unauthorized disclosures.

[20] Reporter Jan Schaffer of the Philadelphia *Inquirer* was cited for contempt July 10 when she refused to testify about a confidential source of information in the Abscam investigation.

[21] Judge John P. Fullam of the U.S. District Court in Philadelphia ordered Schaffer imprisoned for six months or until she purged herself of contempt by saying whether she had spoken on Feb. 2 with Peter F. Vaira, a U.S. attorney, about the Abscam probe.

[22] Judge Fullam delayed her imprisonment pending an appeal. The contempt citation came as a result of the efforts of three Philadelphia city councilmen and a lawyer to have their trial dismissed on the grounds that preindictment publicity had destroyed their right to a fair grand jury hearing and trial.

[23] **Probe Involves N.J. Casinos.** New allegations surfaced Feb. 5 in the Abscam investigation linking Sen. Harrison A. Williams Jr. (D, N.J.) and other officials to a casino project in Atlantic City, N.J.

[24] Newspaper reports said that videotapes made by FBI investigators showed Williams boasting of having used his influence with the N.J. Casino Control Commission to aid Ritz Associates. Ritz Associates had applied to build a casino in Atlantic City. The president of Ritz Associates, John Murray, said he had met with Williams and the senator had recommended a long-time friend, who subsequently helped Ritz Associates win a variance from the state gambling commission. Williams' wife, Jeanette, formerly served as a Ritz board director and was a consultant to the company.

[25] A member of the Casino Control Commission, Kenneth N. MacDonald, who had been linked to a $50,000 bribe, resigned Feb. 4, although he denied any wrongdoing.

[26] On Feb. 11, Gov. Brendan Byrne and leaders of the New Jersey legislature proposed legislation to

Figures Linked to Abscam

Sen. Harrison A. "Pete" Williams Jr. (D, N.J.), 60: served in the House of Representatives from 1953 to 1957. Elected to the Senate in 1958, 1964, 1970, 1976. Compiled one of the most liberal voting records in the Senate (in 1978, 80% rating by Americans for Democratic Action, 89% by the AFL-CIO Committee on Political Education). Drew heavy support from labor in reelection campaigns, and from securities industry. Chairman of Senate Human Resources Committee, subcommittee of Senate Banking Committee. In 1970, he publicly admitted drinking problem, but said he had conquered it.

Rep. Frank Thompson Jr. (D, N.J.), 61: First elected in 1954, a leading backer of liberal and labor causes. His district, the 4th, occupied central position in state around Trenton. Former minority leader of the N.J. General Assembly. Chairman of House Administration Committee, and head of labor-management relations subcommittee of House Education and Labor panel.

Rep. John M. Murphy (D, N.Y.), 53: First elected to the House from the 17th District (Staten Island) in 1962. An honor graduate of West Point and a Korean war veteran. Friend of deposed Nicaraguan strongman Anastasio Somoza and the shah of Iran. Considered a conservative Democrat. Chairman of the Merchant Marine and Fisheries Committee.

Rep. John P. Murtha (D, Pa.), 47: The first Vietnam veteran to be elected to Congress, in 1974; a former Marine major who won a Bronze Star and two Purple Hearts. His district, the 12th, comprised the industrial areas northeast of Pittsburgh. Considered close to the Democratic leadership in the House. A member of the House Appropriations Committee and Ethics panel.

Rep. Michael J. "Ozzie" Myers (D, Pa.), 36: First elected in 1976 from the 1st District, the sourthern end of Philadelphia. A former longshoreman and solid backer of former Philadelphia Mayor Frank Rizzo. In early 1979 pleaded no contest to one count of disorderly conduct after an altercation in a Washington-area cocktail lounge. A member of the House Education and Labor, and Merchant Marine Committees.

Rep. Raymond F. Lederer (D, Pa.), 41: First elected in 1976 from the 3rd District, which took in Center City Philadelphia and North Philadelphia. A high school football coach and city probation officer. Considered a consistent liberal Democratic vote. A member of the House Ways and Means Committee.

Rep. John W. Jenrette (D, S.C.), 43: First elected in 1974 from the 6th District, which took in the northeastern corner of South Carolina. Hurt by stories about his personal life; married a young woman fired by the Republican National Committee for dating him. Implicated in a drug-smuggling ring by a friend who later recanted. Under Justice Department investigation in an obstruction of justice case. Member of the Appropriations Committee.

Rep. Richard Kelly (R, Fla.), 55: First elected in 1974 from the 5th District, which included part of Orlando and part of Seminole County, as well as Sumter County. An anti-labor, right-wing Republican with a reputation as a maverick and a loner. In 1979 it was discovered he had overspent his office expense allowance and had to repay the House clerk. A member of the Argriculture Committee and the Banking panel.

dissolve the five-member part-time Casino Control Commission and replace it with a full-time panel. Byrne said a restructuring of the commission was needed to restore public confidence in N.J.'s regulation of the gambling industry.

[27] **Indictments.** A series of indictments were handed up in the Abscam probe.

[28] In Philadelphia, a federal grand jury May 22 indicted three Philadelphia City Council members and an attorney on racketeering and conspiracy charges. The indictment named City Council President George X. Schwartz; Councilmen Harry P. Jannotti and Louis C. Johanson, all Democrats, and lawyer Howard L. Criden.

[29] Rep. Michael J. Myers (D, Pa.) was indicted May 27 by a federal grand jury in Brooklyn N.Y. for allegedly agreeing to trade his influence in Congress for $50,000. Charged along with Myers were Johanson, Criden and Camden, N.J. Mayor Angelo J. Errichetti. The grand jury May 28 indicted Rep. Raymond F. Lederer (D, Pa.) on charges of influence peddling, bribery and conspiracy. Errichetti, Johanson and Criden were indicted with Lederer.

[30] A federal grand jury in Washington, D.C., June 13 indicted Rep. John W. Jenrette Jr. (D, S.C.) on charges of bribery and conspiracy. Rep. Frank Thompson Jr. (D, N.J.) and John M. Murphy (D, N.Y.) were indicted June 18 by a federal grand jury in Brooklyn, N.Y. Named with them were Criden and New Jersey businessman Joseph Silvestri.

[31] Rep. Richard Kelly (R, Fla.) was indicted July 15 by a federal grand jury in Washington. Kelly denied any wrongdoing. He had said he had taken $25,000 as part of his own investigation into "shady characters" he thought were organized criminals.

[32] Sen. Harrison A. Williams Jr. (D, N.J.) and three associates were indicted Oct. 30 in Brooklyn, N.Y. on bribery, conspiracy and related charges for allegedly seeking a loan and stock in a titanium mine in exchange for political favors. Also charged with Williams were Alexander Feinberg, a lawyer and long-time friend of Williams, George Katz, a businessman, and Angelo J. Errichetti, the mayor of Camden, N.J.

[33] **Rep. Myers, Co-defendants Convicted.** Rep. Michael J. Myers (D, Pa.) and three co-defendants were convicted Aug. 31 of bribery and conspiracy in the first of the Abscam trials.

[34] Video tapes used during the trial showed Myers taking $50,000 from an undercover agent. Other trial evidence indicated that Myers' co-defendants shared the payoff money. U.S. District Judge George C. Pratt presided at the trial in Brooklyn, N.Y.

U.S. Apologizes to Arabs for Abscam Term

The State Department apologized Feb. 12 to Arab countries and Americans of Arab decent for the FBI's use of the term Abscam (from "Arab scam") in its probe of official corruption.

State Department spokesman Hodding Carter noted that Arab representatives in the United Nations had protested the use of the term. He said it "was an internal designation for what was intended as an unpublicized investigation." He admitted the term was "clearly offensive," and added, "It is not acceptable to slur any group of people as a matter of policy."

The term was redefined Aug. 20 by U.S. District Court Judge George C. Pratt. Presiding in Brooklyn, N.Y., at the trial of Rep. Michael J. Myers (D, Pa.) and three co-defendants, Pratt said that "Abscam" was a contraction of "Abdul scam." Abdul scam referred to Abdul Enterprises Ltd., the fictitious business that FBI undercover agents used as their front.

Rep. John W. Jenrette Jr. (D, S.C.) and his wife, Rita, outside courtroom following his conviction Oct. 7.

[35] ***Myers Expelled from House*** —Myers was expelled from the House of Representatives Oct. 2 by a vote of 376 to 30. It was the first expulsion of a member of the House since 1861, when three representatives were ousted for supporting the Confederacy during the Civil War.

[36] The Supreme Court Oct. 14 allowed the three commercial television networks to broadcast video tapes that had been the principal evidence in the first Abscam bribery and conspiracy trial. The court, in a one-sentence order, refused a petitition to stay a TV airing of the tapes. The case was *Myers, et al v. NBC, et al.*

[37] **Other Convictions.** George X. Schwartz, president of the Philadelphia City Council, and Councilman Harry P. Jannotti were convicted in Philadelphia Sept. 16 on extortion-conspiracy charges stemming from the government's Abscam investigation. Schwartz was also convicted on a racketeering-conspiracy charge. Their convictions were set aside Nov. 26 by federal district Judge John P. Fullam who said that the defendents had been victims of entrapment.

[38] Rep. John W. Jenrette Jr. (D, S.C.) and a co-defendant, John R. Stowe, were found guilty Oct. 7 of bribery and conspiracy charges related to the Abscam probe. Jenrette Dec. 10 resigned from the House to avert expulsion proceedings against him.

[39] Reps. Frank Thompson Jr. (D, N.J.) and John M. Murphy (D, N.Y.) were found guilty Dec. 3 of charges arising from the Abscam investigation.

AFFIRMATIVE ACTION—*See* Civil & Constitutional Rights [5-8]

AFGHANISTAN

[1] The Soviet invasion of Afghanistan in late December 1979 had widespread repercussions. President Carter

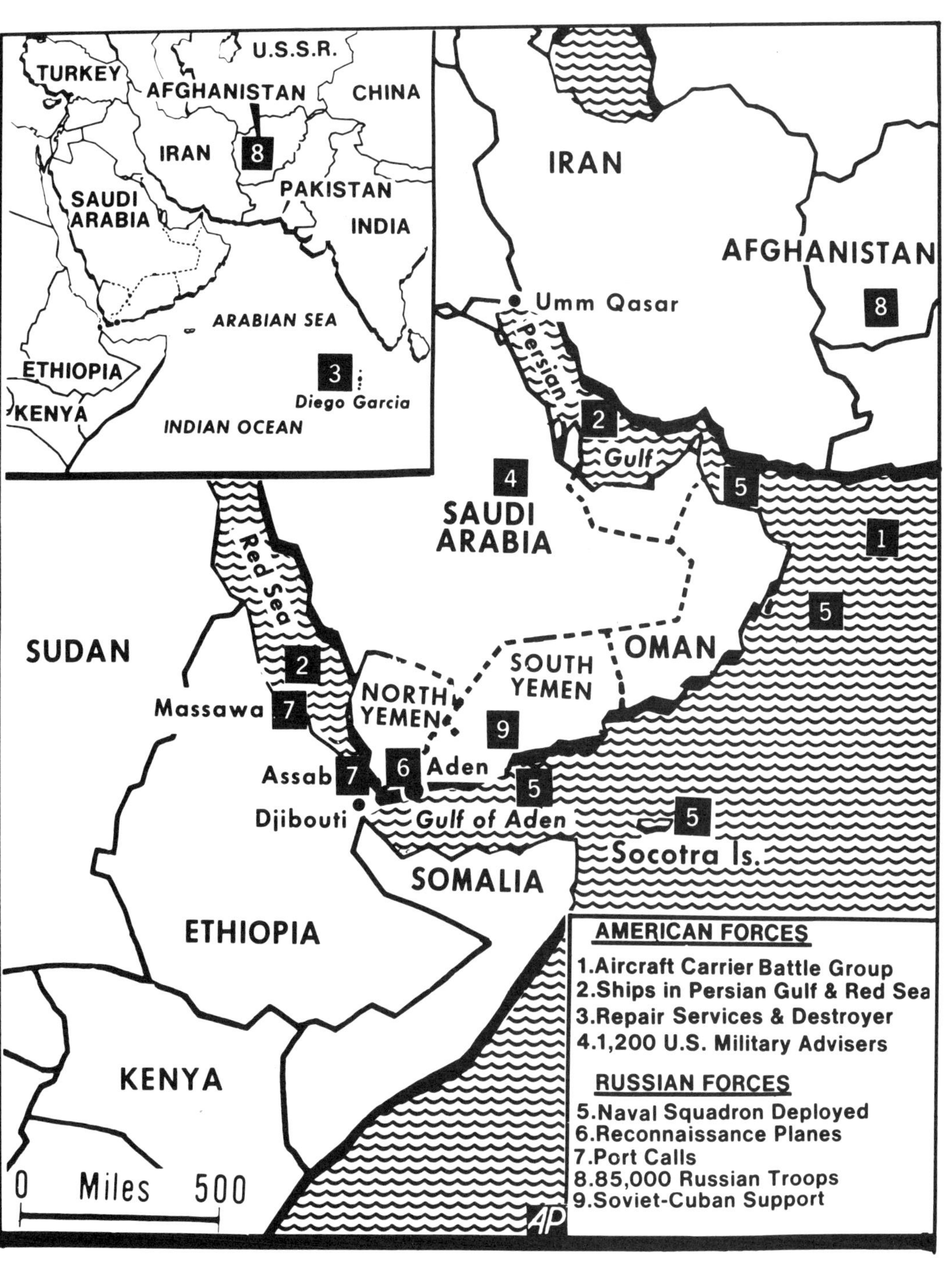

Line-up of U.S. and Soviet forces from Persian Gulf to Western Asia.

denounced the invasion as a threat to peace and imposed economic and cultural sanctions against the U.S.S.R. The U.N. General Assembly passed a resolution deploring the invasion. Some 95,000 Soviet troops were reported in Afghanistan. They encountered strong resistance from Moslem rebels at the beginning of the year, but fighting later diminished. Soviet units appeared to be in control of most of the major cities and towns.

[2] **Carter Denounces Soviet Invasion.** The Soviet invasion of Afghanistan was denounced Jan. 4 by President Carter in a nationwide television address as "an extremely serious threat to peace." He said "a Soviet-occupied Afghanistan threatens both Iran and Pakistan and is a stepping stone to possible control over much of the world's oil supplies."

[3] Carter announced several retaliatory measures by the U.S. They were:

Seventeen million metric tons of grain ordered by Moscow for use in building up livestock herds would not be delivered. Exempt were eight million metric tons the U.S. would deliver to the Soviets in 1980 under terms of a 1976 agreement.

The sale of high technology equipment would be suspended until further notice. Among the items were advanced computers and oil-drilling equipment.

Soviet fishing privileges in American waters would be severely curtailed depriving the Soviets of 350,000 tons of fish in 1980, according to White House estimates.

The opening of new American and Soviet consular facilities would be delayed indefinitely and any new cultural and economic exchanges would be deferred.

[4] In order to ease the impact of the grain embargo on the American farmer, the President pledged to remove the undelivered grain from the market through government storage and price-support programs, with the grain to be purchased at market prices.

[5] The U.S. took further retaliatory action Jan. 8. Washington ordered the withdrawal of an advance party of seven U.S. consular officials from Kiev; at the same time, it directed the expulsion of 17 diplomats from a projected Soviet consulate in New York. U.S. Coast Guards ships and planes were ordered to keep track of the 24 Soviet fishing trawlers in the Bering Sea and the Gulf of Alaska to make certain they did not exceed their catch limits. The Civil Aeronautics Board reduced to two from three the weekly round-trip flights of the Soviet state-owned Aeroflot airline would be permitted to operate between the U.S. and the U.S.S.R.

[6] President Carter Feb. 25 ordered a halt to exports of phosphate products to the U.S.S.R. Carter's decision "forcefully demonstrates our refusal to do business as usual with the Soviets," declared Commerce Secretary Philip Klutznick. U.S. phosphate sales to the Soviet Union had totaled $97 million in 1979, and the 1980 figures had been expected to reach as much as $400 million.

[7] **American Journalists Expelled.** The expulsion of all 50-60 American correspondents from Afghanistan on the grounds of biased reporting and "interference" in its internal affairs was ordered Jan. 17 by the Kabul government.

[8] **Islamic Parley Condemns Invasion.** The Soviet invasion of Afghanistan was condemned by the Conference of Islamic States, meeting in emergency session.

[9] The parley, held in Islamabad, Pakistan Jan. 27-29 and attended by foreign ministers of 36 Moslem nations, also criticized Iran for continuing to hold the 50 American hostages in Teheran.

[10] The Conference suspended Afghanistan from membership and called on all Islamic nations "to withhold recognition from the illegal regime in Afghanistan and sever diplomatic rela-

tions with that government until the complete withdrawal of Soviet troops." Afghanistan boycotted the meeting. Six other members of the Conference did not attend: Syria, South Yemen, Uganda, Upper Volta, Guinea Bissau and Egypt. The Palestine Liberation Organization also stayed away.

[11] **U.S. Seeks Western Support.** Secretary of State Cyrus Vance visited Bonn, Rome, Paris and London Feb. 20-21 in an effort to improve coordination of the response of the U.S.' four Western allies to the Soviet military intervention in Afghanistan.

[12] **NATO Denounces Afghan Invasion.** Foreign and defense ministers of the North Atlantic Treaty Organization took a firm stand May 14 against the Soviet invasion of Afghanistan. The meeting signaled a shift in NATO policy on Afghanistan. In the early stages of the invasion, NATO had conclued that Afghanistan was not crucial to the alliance.

U. N. Action

[13] **Soviets Veto U.N. Resolution.** A U.N. Security Council resolution condemning the Soviet invasion of Afghanistan and demanding the withdrawal of its troops from that country was vetoed Jan. 7 by the Soviet Union. The resolution had been approved by the Council 13-2; the other negative vote was cast by East Germany.

[14] ***General Assembly Deplores Invasion***— A resolution deploring the Soviet invasion of Afghanistan and calling for "the immediate, unconditional and total withdrawal of the foreign troops" in that country was approved Jan. 14 by the U.N. General Assembly. The Afghan issue had been shifted to the Assembly Jan. 10 after a Soviet veto had blocked action in the U.N. Security Council. The veto did not apply in the Assembly.

[15] The Assembly resolution was

In cartoon in Soviet newspaper, *Sovetska Rossiya,* Uncle Sam lowers Statue of Liberty barrier to block U.S. participation in Moscow Olympics. Sign on Miss Liberty says, "Boycott of 22nd Olympiad."

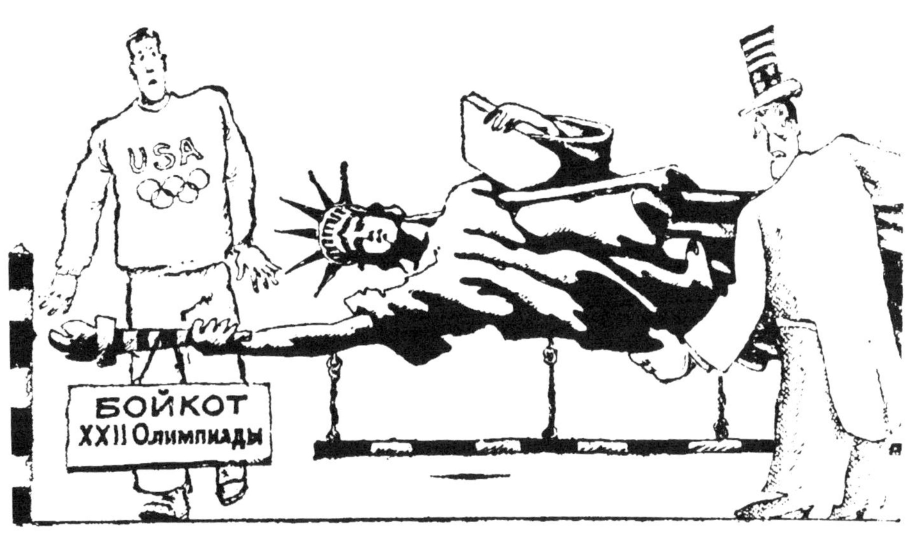

Антиолимпийский шлагбаум. Рис. Н. Щербакова.

Soviet battery of 122mm howitzers dug in along Jalalabad road near Kabul.

adopted by a vote oi 104 to 18, with 18 countries abstaining and 12 absent. It did not mention the Soviet Union by name. Nevertheless, the large number of nations supporting the resolution reflected the widespread disapproval of the Soviet action among Third World countries in Asia, Africa and Latin America. Many of these states normally voted with Moscow on U.N. issues.

[16] The General Assembly Nov. 20 approved a resolution renewing its appeal of the Soviet union to pull its troops out of Afghanistan. The vote was 111-22, with 12 abstentions and nine countries either absent or not voting.

Moscow Olympics' Boycott

[17] **Boycott Weighed.** Secretary of State Cyrus R. Vance Jan. 14 warned the Soviet Union to withdraw its troops from Afghanistan by mid-February or face the possibility of an American boycott of the 1980 Summer Olympics.

[18] **Carter Urges Site Shift.** President Carter Jan. 20 proposed that the 1980 Summer games be removed from the Soviet Union, postponed or canceled unless the U.S.S.R. withdrew its troops from Afghanistan within one month. Failing any of these changes, Carter called for an international boycott.

[19] ***Soviets Ignore Pullout Deadline***—The Soviet Union ignored President Carter's demand that it pull its forces out of Afghanistan by Feb. 20.

[20] **Carter Stand Gains Support.** The executive board of the U.S. Olympic Committee voted unanimously Jan. 26 to ask the International Olympic Committee to move, postpone or cancel the 1980 Summer Olympics.

[21] ***IOC Endorses Games***—The International Olympic Committee Feb. 12 announced that the 1980 Summer Olympics would take place in Moscow as scheduled. White House officials expressed "regret" at the IOC decision and indicated that the U.S. would lead a boycott of the summer games.

Rebels in mountains northwest of Herat near Soviet border.

[22] **Carter Adamant on U.S. Boycott.** President Carter told members of the Athletes Advisory Council of the U.S. Olympic Committee March 21 that his decision not to send a U.S. contingent to the 1980 Olympic Games in Moscow was irreversible.

[23] **European Olympic Panels Rebuff U.S.**—Representatives of the Olympic committees of 16 European nations March 22 voted against a boycott of the Moscow games. The action came during a meeting in Brussels.

[24] Moreover, delegates from eight nations indicated that their athletes would go to Moscow even if their governments joined the U.S. led boycott. They represented Olympic committees of Sweden, Finland, France, Italy, Ireland, Belgium, Spain and Great Britain.

[25] **IOC Sees 85 Nations Going to Moscow.** At least 85 nations would compete in the 1980 Summer Olympics in Moscow, according to the International Olympic Committee May 27. Twenty-nine countries had rejected invitations.

[26] Both the Soviet Union and the U.S. disputed the list. The U.S.S.R. predicted that at least 100 nations would compete in the Summer Olympics, while the U.S. estimated that at least 60 countries would boycott. Final figures: 81 countries took part; 65 nations did not attend.

Military Developments

[27] **Invasion Resisted.** Soviet troops in Afghanistan encountered heavy resistance by Moslem rebels.

[28] Western European sources in Kabul Jan. 2 said fighting was raging northwest of Kabul and in the eastern city of Herat. In the northwest, in Bamian province, forces clashed with Soviet Hazara tribesmen, one of the several insurgent groups opposed to the Marxist government in Kabul.

[29] Pakistani newpapers Jan. 2 told of the launching of a Soviet Drive against insurgents in northeastern Kuna and Nuristan provinces near the Pakistani border. One newpaper said the rebels

had captured a military base on the Pakistani frontier near the Khyber Pass, after a three-day battle.

[30] The United Nations High Commissioner for Refugees reported Jan. 6 that 15,000 Afghan refugees had fled to Pakistan in the last two weeks of December 1979. This raised the number of Afghan refugees in Pakistan to an estimated 402,000.

[31] **Soviet Troops Control Major Towns.** Soviet forces had secured control of all major towns and highways in mid-January, while the Moslem rebels were said to have increased their domination of the countryside in the northeast provinces of Takhar and Badakhshan.

[32] By Jan. 16, the Soviet invaders were reported to have deployed nearly half of their estimated 85,000-man force in the western regions near the Iranian border, and were continuing their military buildup between Herat in the west and Kandahar in the south. Winter snows along the eastern frontier with Pakistan had forced a considerable drop in clashes between the Soviets and the rebels. The decrease in fighting also was attributed to the fact that Soviet and Afghan army soldiers had not moved very far from their encampments in towns and along major roads.

[33] The Soviet Union Jan. 19 launched a new airlift to Afghanistan bringing in more troops. Heavy military transports landing at Kabul also were ferrying in new supplies of food and equipment. Many of the fresh troops were said to have come from Soviet garrisons in Eastern Europe.

[34] Western diplomats in Kabul estimated Feb. 20 that the U.S.S.R. had 95,000 troops in the country.

[35] **U.S. Arms Rebels.** The U.S. had started to supply light infantry weapons to Afghan insurgents in mid-January, White House officials said Feb. 15.

[36] According to a *New York Times* report, the officials said the decision had been made by the Special Coordination Committee of the National Security Council and was subsequently approved by President Carter. The Central Intelligence Agency was reportedly handling the covert mission by shipping weapons to the rebels through Pakistan. The arms were said to be largely of Soviet design.

[37] The story was refuted Feb. 16 by a spokesman for the NSC. There had been several "contradictory reports," which "we neither confirm or deny," the spokesman said.

[38] In the fighting, Moslem insurgents had launched new attacks against Soviet troops in the northeast, Western diplomats in New Delhi, India reported Feb. 5. The insurgents were said to have taken control of all approaches to Jalalabad, Afghanistan's fourth largest city by Feb. 20. The Soviet news agency Tass Feb. 5 confirmed Western reports of rebel attacks in Badakhshan province as well as in two other eastern provinces, Nangarhar and Paktia, but made no mention of Soviet troop involvement.

[39] A combined force of Soviet and Afghan troops Feb. 29 launched a major assault against Moslem insurgent strongholds in eastern Afghanistan's Kunar province.

[40] A rebel report on the fighting March 4 said the insurgents in the province were routed. He said the Afghan-Soviet offensive had been preceded by several days of artillery and air strikes, which had killed more than 1,000 civilians and rebels and leveled several villages. Up to 200 Soviet tanks and more than 50 helicopters and other aircraft spearheaded the drive.

[41] The rebel spokesman accused the Soviets of carrying out a "scorched-earth policy" by using napalm, incendiary devices and poison gas in subduing the rebels in Kunar province.

[42] (The Pakistani government announced March 1 that the number of Afghan refugees in Pakistan now totaled 513,116. This did not include about 50,000 who had not registered in government refugee camps and were

Afghan landscape of rebels, village and terraced fields.

being supported by relatives. The number of refugees was reported Dec. 1 to have risen to 1,309,505.)

[43] **Anti-Soviet Strike, Violence in Kabul.** A general strike began in Kabul Feb. 21 in response to a Moslem rebel call to protest the Soviet military presence. The walkout of shopkeepers, civil servants and laborers triggered street fighting between the civilians and rebels and Afghan and Soviet troops. At least 300 civilians and an undertermined number of Soviet and Afghan soldiers were reported killed.

[44] The violence prompted the Afghan government to impose martial law in Kabul Feb. 22, placing Afghan government rule in the hands of the Soviet military commander. Soviet and Afghan troops were put under a joint command.

[45] In a crackdown, Afghan forces Feb. 26 carried out widespread arrests in Kabul of Shiite Moslems suspected of having instigated the anti-Soviet disturbances. The Shiites included members of the Hazara ethnic group, which made up 10% to 20% of Afghanistan's 15 million people. The Hazaras traditionally had faced social and religious discrimination at the hands of Afghanistan's dominating Pathan ethnic group, which was Sunni Moslem.

[46] The anti-Soviet violence that had swept Kabul for a week had subsided, it was reported Feb. 28. Almost all merchants who had closed their shops reopened them and civil servants who had walked off their jobs were back at government offices. Most of the Afghan army tanks had been withdrawn from key intersections and strategic points around the capital. However, Afghan and Soviet forces were back on the streets Feb. 29 in anticipation of an expected antigovernment demonstration that day that failed to materialize.

[47] The official Afghan radio reported June 8 that 140 persons had been killed and 30 schools destroyed in renewed

anti-Soviet and anti-Afghan government rioting by students in Kabul in April-May.

[48] **Soviet-Afghan Drive in Paktia.** A combined Afghan-Soviet force had launched a major drive against Moslem rebels in eastern Paktia province, it was reported in Pakistan March 10.

[49] Meanwhile, there were further allegations of Soviet use of poison gas in their Kunar offensive. An observer of the International Federation of the Rights of Man, a Paris-based human rights organization, interviewed Afghan refugees in Peshawar, Pakistan. The observer said that Soviet forces March 4 had "destroyed" Kunar villages, and that "poison gas was used." The Afghan radio March 5 denied that poison gas had been employed and insisted that only Afghan troops, not Soviet soldiers, were fighting the rebels in Kunar province.

[50] **U.S. Reports Fighting Impasse.** U.S. government officials reported April 4 that fighting between Soviet and Afghan rebel forces had reached an apparent stalemate. The major cities, towns and lines of communication remained under Soviet control, while the countryside was still dominated by the insurgents, the officials said.

[51] **Rebels, Soviets Clash Near Kabul.** Soviet troops and Afghan rebel forces engaged in severe fighting around Kabul, it was reported June 7. The rebels were said to have suffered high casualties in the closest fighting to the Afghan capital since the Soviet invasion.

[52] Heavy fighting raged between Moslem rebels and Soviet and Afghan forces in the Panjshir Valley, about 50 miles (80 kilometers) north of Kabul, diplomatic sources in New Delhi reported Sept. 13.

[53] **Soviets Withdrawing Some Troops.** The Soviet Union announced June 22 that it would be withdrawing some of its troops from Afghanistan. A summit meeting in Venice of seven major industrialized democracies—the U.S., West Germany, Japan, Great Britain, Canada, France and Italy—reacted by urging a total Soviet withdrawal from Afghanistan. A further report by Moscow radio June 23 said the Soviet withdrawal would involve a division (anywhere from 7,000 to 14,000 men) and 108 tanks.

[54] The U.S.S.R. said it would not withdraw any more of its troops from Afghanistan until foreign interference in Afghan affairs stopped, it was reported June 27.

[55] Despite claims that it was withdrawing some troops from Afghanistan, the Soviet Union was dispatching fresh forces into the country, sources in Kabul reported July 3. The units were said to consist of specially trained antiguerrilla fighters equipped with new combat gear to press the war against the Afghan rebels.

[56] In addition, the report said, the Soviets showed signs of planning a long stay in Afghanistan. They were said to be carrying out more construction at their main military base in Kabul, building six-story apartment houses for families of Soviet personnel, laying down new tarmac at their air base adjacent to the airport in Kabul and resurfacing the main road from Kabul to the Soviet border.

[57] **Rebels Attack Soviet Base.** Afghan rebels July 6 attacked a Soviet military camp 15 miles (24 kilometers) north of Kabul, inflicting heavy casualties. The Soviet forces counterattacked and in a three-day operation killed hundreds of Afghans, including civilians, and forced thousands of others to flee their homes, according to an Associated Press dispatch from Kabul July 9. The Soviet force consisted of 400 tanks and personnel carriers, heavy artillery, jet fighters and helicopter gunships.

[58] **Soviet Troops Battle Army Rebels.** Soviet forces had launched an offensive against Afghan army troops

who mutinied and seized a garrison at Ghazni, 75 miles (120 kilometers) southwest of Kabul, it was reported July 28. The Soviet soldiers recaptured the garrison after 4,500 of the 5,000 Afghan troops there deserted or joined Afghan rebels, it was reported Aug. 3.

[59] Soldiers of an Afghan army garrison in Kabul fought with Soviet troops for almost a week, Western diplomats in Islamabad, Pakistan reported Oct. 15. Soviet tanks finally sealed off the post, which housed two Afghan armored brigades, the reports said.

[60] **Soviets Annexing Vital Border Area.** Soviet forces had moved into the largely uninhabited Wakhan salient in northeastern Afghanistan and were gradually annexing it, a Pakistani news agency reported Nov. 4.

Government

[61] **Karmal Consolidates Power.** Afghan President Babrak Karmal had carried out a major shakeup of his government, centralizing power under his control, Kabul radio reported July 20.

[62] A former Afghan official in exile in New Delhi said the government shift appeared to be "the beginning of a purge" of members of the Khalq faction of the ruling People's Democratic Party. The two groups had been engaged in a bitter struggle, often violent.

[63] **Soviets Renew Support.** The Soviet Union Oct. 16 reaffirmed its support for the Afghan government and said it would maintain its troops in the country to help fight the Moslem rebellion. The Soviet position was outlined in a joint communique signed after a meeting in Moscow that day between Presidents Leonid Brezhnev and Babrak Karmal.

Defections

[64] **Soccer Team.** Seven members of Afghanistan's national soccer team defeated to West Germany March 26 and asked for political asylum.

[65] ***Olympic Athletes***—Seven member of Afghanistan's national basketball team and seven members of its wrestling team scheduled to take part in the Moscow Olympics had defected to Pakistan, it was announced June 20 and July 6, respectively.

[66] **UNESCO Delegate Defects to West.** Akhtar Mohammad Paktiawal, Afghanistan's chief delegate to a conference in Belgrade of the United Nations Educational, Scientific and Cultural Organization defected to West Germany Oct. 25 after denouncing the Soviet invasion of his country and assailing his own government.

See also China, People's Republic of [26-27]; Pakistan [1-6]

AFRICA

[1] **OAU Holds Summit.** The 17th annual summit conference of the Organization of African Unity held July 1-4 in Sierra Leone was marked by sharp debate over the conflict in the Western Sahara between Morocco and the Algerian-based Polisario Front. (Polisario guerrillas were fighting to establish an independent country in the former Spanish colony.)

[2] Mozambique's president, Samora Machel, and Prime Minister Robert Mugabe of Zimbabwe both denounced Morocco's four-year war against the Polisario. Further discord was generated by the guerrilla group's application for admission to the OAU as the Sahara Arab Democratic Republic. Despite the backing of 26 member states, which constituted the simple majority required for passage in the 50-member OAU, resolution of the question was postponed when eight dissenting members threatened to withdraw from the organization if the Polisario was admitted.

[3] Other matters dealt with at the summit included:

The U.S. base on Diego Garcia was

denounced as "a threat to Africa and the concept of a zone of peace in the Indian Ocean," and the conferees demanded that the British-owned island be ceded to Mauritius.

The delegates called for the total withdrawal of Western investment in South Africa.

[4] Chairman Siaka Stevens, president of Sierra Leone, July 4 closed the meeting by expressing concern over the OAU's failure to end the civil war in Chad. He said the failure exemplified the organization's "tragic shortcomings."

See also Human Rights [9]

AGRICULTURE

Crop Support Increase. President Carter July 28 ordered a $1 billion increase in federal price support loan rates to help grain farmers survive what Carter called "a serious cost-price squeeze" that had decreased their profits. The loans allowed farmers to borrow from the federal government by using their crops as collateral.

See also China [23]; El Salvador [4-7]; Grain; Union of Soviet Socialist Republics (U.S.S.R.) [16]

AIR POLLUTION—*See* Environment [2-3, 6-7, 15]

ALABAMA—*See* Death Penalty [5-6]

ALASKA—*See* Wildlife [1-2]

ALGERIA—*See* Earthquakes [10-12]; Iran [108]

ALIENS, Illegal

[1] **14 Rescued, 13 Die in Ariz. Desert.** A group of 14 illegal aliens—12 Salvadorans and two men hired to smuggle them into the U.S.—was rescued near death July 5 in Arizona's Organ Pipe National Monument. The bodies of 13 others, including one

Illegal alien is nabbed by U.S. Border Patrol agent in river bottom four miles north of boundary between Mexico and California.

thought to be a smuggler, were subsequently found by Arizona police officers. They had succumbed to heat and thirst.

[2] ***22 Stowaways on Freighter Drown***—Twenty-two persons who had hidden inside the ballast tanks of a Panamanian freighter in an apparent attempt to gain illegal entry into the U.S. were found drowned Sept. 5. Twelve others were rescued by sailors who pulled them to safety shortly before the tanker was scheduled to depart from Santo Domingo for Miami.

[3] **Schooling Ordered.** U.S. District Judge Woodrow Seals July 21 struck down as unconstitutional a Texas law barring the use of state funds for the schooling of the children of illegal aliens. Seals ordered the state to begin enrolling uncounted thousands of such children for the 1980-81 school year.

[4] The ruling came in a challenge to a 1975 Texas law that prohibited state reimbursement of local school districts for the costs of educating illegal aliens. Many schools barred the children outright, others imposed high tuitions. Seals said the children had a right to a free public school education under the equal protection clause of the 14th Amendment.

AMNESTY INTERNATIONAL —*See* Chile [8]; Colombia [10-11]; Iran [148-150]

ANCHORAGE—*See* City & State Affairs [5]

ANDERSON, JOHN B.—*See also* Black Americans [6]; Elections [21-23, 63-68, 76]

ANTITRUST ACTIONS

[1] **MCI Wins $1.8 Billion AT&T Suit.** A federal district court jury in Chicago June 13 awarded MCI Inc. a record $1.8 billion in its antitrust case against American Telephone & Telegraph Co.

[2] MCI, a Washington, D.C.-based provider of long distance telephone service, first brought suit against AT&T in 1974, claiming the Bell System used its dominance in local telephone services to prevent MCI's growth. The company specifically charged AT&T with unfairly denying it access to specialized long distance calling service.

[3] The case went to trial before the seven-woman, five-man jury in the Chicago court in February 1980. After hearing the closing arguments and final instructions from Judge John Grady, the jury deliberated for two days before finding AT&T guilty on 10 of 15 charges of antitrust practices. The jury awarded MCI $600 million of the $900 million it had orginally sought. A provision of the Sherman Antitrust Act automatically tripled the amount of the award.

[4] According to lawyers for both sides, MCI had to prove four issues to win the case: the existence of a market for both companies, AT&T possession of monopoly power in the market, AT&T's deliberate attempt to perserve the monopoly, and whether or not MCI had been damaged by AT&T actions.

[5]**Gypsum Price-Fixing Case Settled.** Four major manufacturers of gypsum board agreed to pay the government an estimated $6 million in taxes rather than face retrial on criminal price-fixing charges.

[6] An agreement between the companies and the Justice Department was accepted by U.S. District Judge Hubert I. Teitelbaum in Pittsburgh on March 3. The companies—U.S. Gypsum Co., Georgia Pacific Corp., National Gypum Co. and Celotex Corp. (a unit of Jim Walter Corp.)—had been convicted in 1975 of fixing prices, conditions of sale, and handling of some $4.8 billion worth of gypsum board over a 14-year period. A retrial had been ordered by the Supreme Court in 1978.

[7] **Key Ingredient Monopolies Backed.** The Supreme Court ruled 5-4 June 27 that companies could legally monopolize the crucial ingredient of a patented scientific process, even if the

ingredient itself was not patented. The case was *Dawson Chemical Co. v. Rohm & Haas Co.*

[8] The decision allowed Rohm & Haas Co. to control the market for propanil, an unpatented chemical weed killer that was the central ingredient in a process patented by the company for protecting rice crops. Led by Justice Harry A. Blackmun, the majority interpreted a 1952 amendment to federal patent law to mean that Congress intended to encourage technological growth through economic incentives, despite the possible suppression of "competition in the market for an unpatented commodity." Justice Stevens, Byron R. White, Thurgood Marshall and William J. Brennan Jr. dissented.

APPOINTMENTS & RESIGNATIONS (U.S. Government)

[1] **Dickenson Parks Director.** Russell E. Dickenson became director of the National Park Service May 1. Dickenson, 57, had joined the service in 1947 as a park ranger in the Grand Canyon. He succeeded William J. Whalen, who was dismissed April 24 by Secretary of the Interior Cecil D. Andrus.

[2] **New White House Chief of Staff.** Jack Watson Jr. was appointed White House chief of staff June 11, replacing Hamilton Jordon who was taking a leave of absence to direct President Carter's reelection campaign. Watson, 42, had been serving as secretary to the Cabinet. Jordon would officially become deputy chairman of the Carter reelection committee. Robert Strauss was committee chairman.

[3] **Carnesale Named as NRC Chief.** Albert Carnesale, a nuclear engineer, was named July 9 as chairman of the Nuclear Regulatory Commission by President Carter. Carnesale, 44, professor of public policy at Harvard University, succeeded John F. Ahearne, interim chairman.

[4] **Clausen Picked to Head World Bank.** A.W. Clausen, president and chief executive officer of BankAmerica Corp., was nominated Oct. 30 by President Carter to become the next president of the World Bank. Clausen would succeed President Robert S. McNamara, who had announced his intention to resign as of June 1981.

ARGENTINA

[1] **Banking System Shaken.** Argentina's private banking system was shaken April 25 by the bankruptcy of the country's two biggest commercial banks and the near insolvency of many smaller financial institutions.

[2] The crisis had been touched off March 28 by the forced closing of the country's second largest private bank, Banco de Intercambio Regional, which had about $1 billion in deposits. The failure of Banco de Intercambio Regional had come about after central bank auditors had discovered that its bad debts totaled 150% of its assets.

[3] The action caused a stampede by depositors who began withdrawing their funds from the private bank and depositing them in state-owned or foreign banks. By April 25, the equivalent of $1.7 billion in peso deposits had been withdrawn from 100 of Argentina's 496 private banks. Banco do Los Andes, the country's largest private bank, lost $700 million of its $1.2 billion in peso deposits. On April 25, the government took over the bank's operations and ordered the arrest of Hector Grecco, head of the family that owned Banco de Los Andes.

[4] In an effort to restore confidence in the banks, the government April 25 announced that it had raised the central bank's guarantee for peso deposits in savings accounts to the equilvalent of $56,000, from $675. Deposits of more than that were 90% guaranteed in the event of bankruptcy.

[5] **Fiscal Plan.** Jose Alfredo Martinez de Hoz, Argentina's minister of finance, made a nationally broadcast

speech, July 11 in which he announced a series of fiscal measures designed to restore confidence in the country's economy.

[6] Martinez stressed that the measures did not represent a change in Argentina's four-year economic program. He spent a large part of his speech defending his policies and refuting critics, who had become increasingly vocal. Since the banking crisis, interest rates in Argentina had been climbing steadily. Argentina's central bank had had to pour more than $2 billion into banks to prevent further collapses, and the nation's reserves of money had been sharply reduced.

[7] To offset these developments, Martinez said that restrictions on foreign currency deposits would be eliminated. By allowing inflows of foreign capital. Martinez hoped interest rates would go down as capital became more available. This in turn would reduce the rate of inflation, which had hit 107% in the past twelve months. Martinez resisted pressure from farmers and industrialists for a major devaluation of the peso, now trading at 1,870 to the U.S. dollar. Instead, he offered a reduction in taxes on some agricultural goods, promised employers that social security payments would be reduced and hinted to workers that personal income taxes might be abolished.

[8] **Viola Named Next President.** The military junta Oct. 3 named Roberto Eduardo Viola, a former commander in chief of the army, as the next president of Argentina. Viola would replace President Jorge Rafael Videla, who was to step down March 29, 1981.

See also Human Rights [8, 18]

ARIZONA—*See* Weather [1-3]

ARKANSAS—*See* Cuba [15, 17-20]

ARMAMENTS (International)

[1] **'70 Nuclear Explosions Totaled.** A total of 421 underground nuclear explosions were set between 1970-79, the Swedish National Defense Research Institute reported Jan. 17. The institute, which monitored underground nuclear blasts throughout the world, said the U.S.S.R. had set off the most, 191. The U.S. was second with 154 nuclear explosions during the decade. The other figures were: France, 55; China, 15; Great Britain, five, and India, one.

[2] **Israel Protests Iraqi A-Deal.** Israeli Foreign Minister Yitzhak Shamir July 28 called in the French envoy to protest a French-Iraqi agreement under which Paris would supply enriched uranium to Iraq. Israel was concerned that the French aid would permit Iraq to acquire atomic weapons that it might use against Israel.

[3] **NPT Review Conference.** The 75-nation review conference of the 1968 nuclear nonproliferation treaty ended Sept. 7 in Geneva without issuing a final declaration.

[4] Non-aligned and developing nations said the inconclusive outcome was a warning to nuclear powers that their obligations, including the reduction of their atomic weapons arsenals, must be kept. They argued that they had accepted NPT limitations and safeguards in the understanding they would receive access to technology on peaceful uses of nuclear fission. They said they had also renounced acquisition of nuclear weapons in hopes the arms race would be slowed.

[5] However, the three major nuclear power among the NPT signatories, the U.S., Soviet Union and United Kingdom, were farther from negotiating curbs on the nuclear arms race than they were when the treaty took effect, according to Sri Lankan Ambassador M.I.B. Fonseka.

See also Afghanistan [35-37, 42]; China, People's Republic of [27-28, 30-31]; Foreign Aid; France [25-27]; Germany, West [5-11]; Great Britain [42-52]; Israel [12]; Union of Soviet Socialist Republics [25-28]

ART

[1] **New York Auctions Set Many Records.** Sales of Impressionist, modern and contemporary works at New York City's two largest art auction houses virtually rewrote the record books May 12-16. The auctions were conducted by Sotheby Parke Bernet and Christie, Manson & Wood.

[2] A total of $55.8 million in art was sold by the two houses during the week, more than double the record $29.6 million brought in New York art auctions during a week in November 1979. Of the $55.8 million figure, Christie's sales totaled $30 million and Sotheby's $25.8 million.

[3] The dispersal of 10 paintings from the collection of Henry Ford 2d accounted for $18.3 million of Christie's $30 million for the week. Sotheby's sold 40 works from the estate of the late Edgar William and Bernice Chrysler Garbisch for $14.8 million of the $25.8 million weekly sum.

[4] The jewel of the Garbisch collection was Pablo Picasso's *Saltimbanque (Acrobat) Seated with Arms Crossed,* which had been painted in 1923 during the modern master's "classical" period. The painting was sold May 12 for $3 million – the highest price ever paid for a 20th-century work sold at auction and a record for a painting by Picasso. The Picasso work was bought by Susumu Yamamoto, a Japanese dealer, for the Bridgestone Museum of Fine Art in Tokyo.

[5] Several other personal records for artists were set May 12 at Sotheby's during the dispersal of the Garbisch collection. However, all of the personal marks except Picasso's were eclipsed by the subsequent auction of the Ford works at Christie's. One such personal record was the $1.8 million bid for Paul Gauguin's *Tahitian Woman Under the Palms.* The painting was bought by a private collector in Argentina.

[6] The auction was crowned by the sale of Vincent Van Gogh's *Le Jardin du Poete, Arles* (The Garden of a Poet in Arles) for $5.2 million, a record for a modern work and the highest price (with buyer's commission) for a painting sold at auction. The commission brought the true cost of Van Gogh's painting to $5.72 million. It was purchased by telephone by an anonymous collector.

[7] The previous world auction record was set in 1970, when a painting by the Spanish master Velazquez, entitled *Portrait of Juan de Pareja,* went for $5.5 million. However, the practice of tacking on a 10% buyer's commission was not in effect that year.

[8] In other record sales:

One of the world's rarest postage stamps, the 1856 British Guiana one-cent magenta, was sold for a record $850,000 in New York City April 5. The stamp had been owned by a Pennsylvania collector, Irving Weinberg, who had purchased it for $280,000 in 1970. The buyer wished to remain anonymous.

The most valuable object on earth for its size—the British Guiana one-cent postage stamps—was sold for $850,000 April 5.

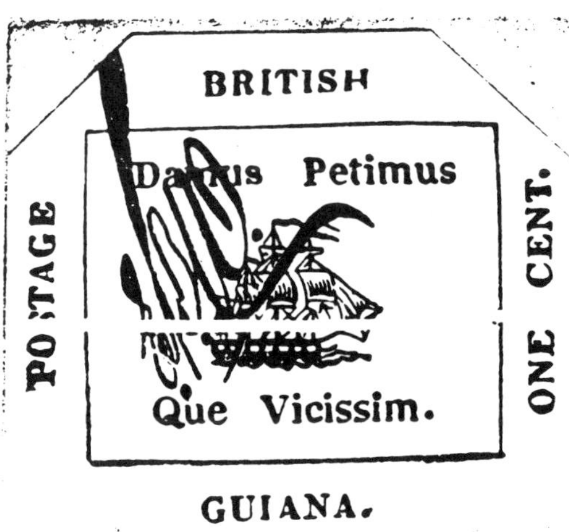

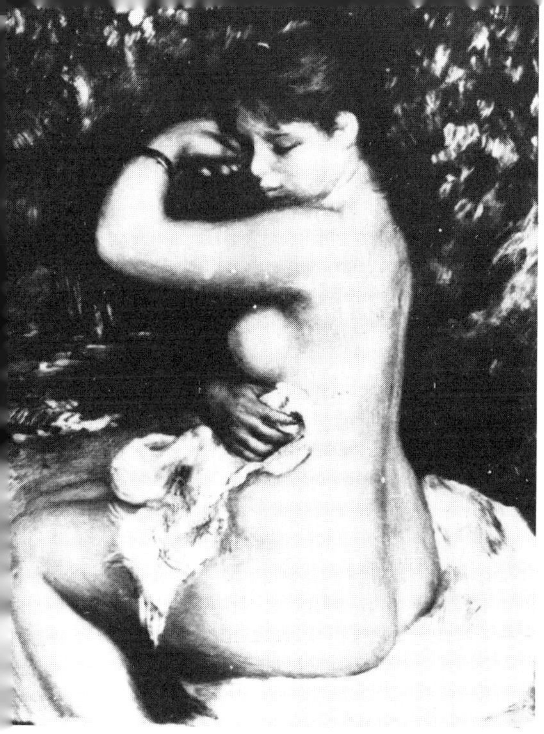

Renoir's *Baigneuse*, the famous painting of a young girl drying herself beside a pool, sold Dec. 3 for $1,198,500 at auction in London. A Tokyo gallery was the purchaser.

The stamp, which was about half the size of a U.S. first-class stamp, depicted a black sailing ship on a magenta background and had the motto "Damus Petimus Que Vicissim ("We give and we seek in return"). Experts regarded it as the most valuable object on earth for its size and weight.

A set of 11 gold coins designed by American artist August Saint-Gaudens was sold in New York to the New England Rare Coins Galleries of Boston for $1 million April 10. It was the first time that a set of coins had been sold for a seven-figure sum. The set consisted of seven $20 gold pieces and four $10 gold pieces, all minted in Philadelphia between 1907 and 1908.

[9] **Crack Found in 'Last Supper.'** Electronic devices had detected a long crack in *The Last Supper,* Leonardo da Vinci's masterpiece, it was reported June 16. The Renaissance fresco was painted on a wall of the Church of Santa Maria delle Grazie on Milan.

[10] The Italian government had begun a new restoration of the painting in 1979. Electronic monitoring devices had been installed as part of the effort. The device found a crack about six feet (1.8 meters) long and the width of a finger running vertically an inch and a half (3.6 centimeters) to the right of the finger of the Apostle Simon. Simon was the disciple seated farthest to right in the fresco. Milan's superintendent of art, Carlo Bertelli, said the crack posed "no immediate danger to the fingers in the painting or the wall as a whole." However, the church had been closed to visitors since the crack's discovery.

[11] ***Leonardo Notebook Sells for $5 Million***—A Leonardo da Vinci notebook, *Of the Nature, Weight and Movement of Water,* was sold at Christie's in London Dec. 12 for $5.1 million to Armand Hammer, president of the Occidental Petroleum Co. The price was the highest ever paid for a manuscript at auction.

ASTRONOMY

[1] **'Superbubble.'** Data from the orbiting High Energy Astronomical Observatory suggested that there was a "superbubble" in a huge interstellar gas cloud known as the Great Rift of Cygnus, *Science News* reported Jan. 26. The bubble—a rarefaction in the interstellar matter—had a tremendous amount of energy associated with it: 10 to 21 times the energy output of the sun since it was formed about 5 billion years ago. The astronomers who discovered the bubble theorized that it was formed by several generations of supernovas (violent explosions of stars), and speculated that such bubbles might be important in the processes of star formation.

[2] **Immense Quasar Reported.** Radio astronomers using a fully steerable radio telescope in West Germany discovered what they claimed was the

largest object in the Universe, the *New Scientist* reported April 10. The object was a quasar (an acronym for quasistellar object), labeled 3C 345. It emitted radio waves across a region of space calculated to be 78 million light years long.

[3] **Soviets Monitor Outer Space, Hear Nothing.** Soviet scientists, after over a decade of monitoring outer space for radio signals, had concluded that there were probably no civilizations in outer space, the Soviet news agency Tass reported April 25.

[4] **A Pattern of Evolution for Galaxies?** Scientists at Ravishankar University, Raipur, India, found that a statistical survey of different categories of astronomical objects suggested a pattern of evolution for galaxies, the *New Scientist* reported Aug. 14. The astronomers plotted the red shift (the movement of spectral lines toward the infrared end of the spectrum, indicative of the speed with which an object was receding from the observer) of five kinds of objects: quasars, compact N-galaxies, Seyfert galaxies, radio galaxies and normal galaxies. The red shift progressively decreased, in the order listed above. Since the red shift was taken to correspond to distance and so to earlier eras of the universe (since the light or radio signal took time to reach the Earth), an evolutionary progression could be set up, starting with quasars and gradually developing into normal galaxies.

AUSTRALIA

[1] **Fraser Wins National Elections.** Prime Minister Malcolm Fraser's ruling coalition of the Liberal and National Country parties won reelection in national balloting Oct. 18, but with a reduced majority.

[2] The victory for Fraser – his third in a row – came despite polls that indicated a vote swing to Labor. Fraser hailed the outcome as "a very substantial victory even though some seats have been lost." When asked whether the reduction in the government's majority might signal voter dissatisfaction, he replied, "We've heard that message, and I understand that message." William Hayden, leader of the Labor opposition, was generally given credit for running a strong campaign.

[3] **Long Drought Broken.** Southeast Australia benefited from heavy rains that ended an 18-month drought described as the worst for parts of the country since 1902, the National Bureau of Meterology said April 24.

[4] The agency said that as much as 4.5 inches (11 centimeters) of rain had fallen over the past week on Tasmania, South Australia, Victoria and New South Wales. The rainfall was especially welcome to farmers in New South Wales, where there had been little sustained rain since the start of 1978.

[5] **Wheat Sales to Soviet Increase.** The amount of wheat sold to the Soviet Union had risen dramatically over the past nine months, according to official figures released June 17. For the nine months ending March, 1980 Australia had sold 1,700,000 metric tons of wheat to the Soviet Union, more than 11 times the amount – 157,000 tons – sold in the same period the year before.

[6] **Island Trade Pact.** Australia and New Zealand signed a trade agreement with several small island neighbors providing better access for the island nations to markets in Australia and New Zealand, it was reported July 24.

[7] The agreement, which revoked duties on a wide range of goods, was signed at a meeting of the South Pacific Forum, but not by all the members of the forum. (In addition to Australia and New Zealand, the forum included the Cook Islands, Fiji, Kiribati, Nauru, Niue, Papua New Guinea, the Solomon Islands, Tonga, Tuvalu, Western Samoa and the New Hebrides.)

[8] The pact was not reciprocal: it did not apply to exports to the islands

from Australia and New Zealand. The aim of the accord was to improve the islands' commercial prospects and so ultimately render them less dependent on Australia and New Zealand.

[9] **U.S. B-52 Base Planned.** Defense Minister James Killen said Sept. 9 that the government would begin talks with the U.S. about permitting U.S. B-52 bombers to land in Australia. Heretofore, the planes had only been allowed to fly over northern Australia during training flights from Guam.

[10] ***Articles on U.S. Ties Censored***—The High Court Nov. 8 barred two newspapers from publishing articles on Australia's defense and foreign policy ties with the U.S. The next day the court granted a government request for an order blocking publication of the book from which the newspaper articles were excerpted.

[11] The press injunctions were the first such action since World War II. The two newpapers involved were the Sydney *Morning Herald* and *The Age* of Melbourne. The book from which the articles were drawn was titled *Documents on Australian Defense and Foreign Policy, 1968-75,* and was written by George Munster and Richard Walsh.

AUTOMOBILES

Chrysler

[1] **Carter Signs Aid Bill.** President Carter signed into law Jan. 7 a bill granting $1.5 billion in federal loan guarantees to financially troubled Chrysler Corp. The legislation had cleared Congress in December 1979.

[2] Chrysler Corp. posted a $375.8 million loss in the fourth quarter of 1979, bringing its losses for the year to nearly $1.1 billion, believed to be a record for American business, it was reported Feb. 7.

[3] **Fraser Elected to Chrysler Board**—Douglas A. Fraser, president of the United Automobile Workers, union, was elected to Chrysler's board of directors May 13. He became the first union leader elected to the board of an American company.

[4] Chrysler management had agreed to nominate Fraser for a board seat as part of a favorable labor agreement in which the UAW gave up some $642 million in wages and benefits. The concessions were needed to allow the auto maker to qualify for federal financial help.

[5] **Chrysler Receives First $500 Million.** Chrysler Corp. June 24 received the first government aid it had been seeking as the beleagured auto maker, with a crucial federal guarantee, borrowed $500 million by selling notes priced to give investors a yeild of 10.35%.

[6] The Chrysler Corp. Loan Guarantee Board set up by Congress to administer the aid approved the first $500 million installment of debt guarantees for Chrysler and reaffirmed its intention to support up to $1 billion more. An hour after that approval, Chrysler marketed the $500 million of notes.

[7] Chrysler Corp. reported July 31 it had lost $536.1 million from April through June, the largest quarterly operating deficit ever suffered by a U.S. corporation. The Chrysler Loan Guarantee Board July 31 gave approval to $300 million in additional federal loan guarantees for the auto maker. The new guarantee brought the total amount of federally backed loans to $800 million.

[8] On Dec. 23 Chrysler asked the federal government for guarantees for up to $400 million in new loans. That move would increase the government's commitment to the company to $1.2 billion.

[9] **UAW Votes to Reopen Chrysler Contract.** The Chrysler Council of the United Automobile Workers union Dec. 22 agreed to negotiate $600 million in possible wage concessions to Chrysler Corp. over the next 20 months.

Auto workers listen intently as plans to layoff some 2,700 of nearly 6,000 employes at General Motors plant in Janesville, Wisc. are presented April 15.

Labor & Plant Issues

[10] **Production Cuts Lead to Plant Closings.** U.S. auto makers responded to the slide in domestic car sales by cutting production and closing car assembly plants. By mid-April, over 240,000 American auto workers had been laid off, with about 170,000 on indefinite layoff status.

[11] Ford Motor Co. April 15 announced major cutbacks in its workforce designed to slash the auto maker's operating costs $1.5 billion a year. Ford eliminated 15,000 jobs, with many of the cuts coming among Ford executives and white-collar salaried employees. It permanently closed three plants, including its big Mahwah, N.J. assembly plant, which employed over 3,500 workers and produced Ford Fairmont and Mercury Zephyr compact cars. A foundry in Dearborn, Mich. and a casting plant in Windsor, Ont. were also shut.

[12] General Motors Corp. announced April 16 that it was scheduling major production cutbacks at seven of its 26 U.S. car and truck assembly plants, indefinitely idling 12,000 hourly workers. It was GM's sixth such cutback since the summer of 1979. A total of some 82,000 GM workers had been indefinitely laid off. Chrysler had indefinitely laid off a total of 40,600, it was reported April 3. Ford had indefinitely laid off some 43,000 workers, it was reported April 15.

[13] ***Carter Proposes Aid Package*** – President Carter visited Detroit July 8 with a package of proposals to help the automobile industry recover from its severe economic slump. Carter described his proposals as "a first step" in a "permanent partnership" between Washington and Detroit.

[14] His package included steps to ease federal regulation on car-exhaust emissions and safety, to extend credit to car dealers, to speed depreciation of tax write-offs and to accelerate action by the U.S. International Trade Commission on whether the industry had been injured by foreign imports.

[15] **Car Sales Decline.** U.S. new car sales in January rose 3.2% above January 1979, then dropped during the rest of the year. In March, sales declined sharply, despite showroom price cuts and heavy sales promotions. Domestic slippage, coupled with lower foreign car deliveries caused by dealer shortages, pulled down March sales some 16% from a year earlier. Both domestic and foreign car sales plunged in May. Dealers of domestic and foreign makes retailed about 694,000 new cars in May, down 33% from about 1,041,000 in May of 1979. Car sales dropped 22% in August compared to the same month of the previous year. The drop was attributed to a slip in sales of imported makes. U.S. officials of foreign car makers cited recent price increases and a shortage of the smallest, most fuel-efficient models as reasons. U.S. car sales fell 5.1% in October from year-earlier levels. The trend continued with sales off 22% in the Dec. 11-20 period compared to the same period of 1979.

Other Developments

[16] **Pinto Trial: Ford Acquitted.** A jury in Winamac, Ind., March 13 found Ford Motor Co. not guilty of three charges of reckless homicide in connection with the 1978 deaths of three young women in a crash in its subcompact Pinto car.

[17] It was the first time an American corportation had stood trial on criminal charges in a product defects case. Only monetary penalties were involved. The charges arose after sisters, Judy and Lyn Ulrich, 18 and 16 years old respectively, and their cousin Donna Ulrich, 18, were killed when their 1973 Pinto burst into flames after it was struck from behind by a van near Goshen, Ind. in August 1978. The jury deliberated for 25 hours over a four-day period before ending the 10-week trial with the not guilty verdict.

[18] The chief issue in the trial was whether Ford knew there were serious safety problems with the Pinto's fuel system but decided against design changes to save money. (Ford had recalled 1.5 million of the Pinto cars in 1978 after federal officials concluded that they were susceptible to bursting into flames even in relatively low-speed rear-end collisions.)

[19] ***Few Cars Pass Crash Tests***– Only five cars among 48 imported and domestic models tested in a special study passed all safety categories in 35 miles-per-hour crash tests, the Transportation Department reported Feb. 28.

[20] The five cars, all American-made, were: the mini-compact Chevrolet Chevette; the subcompact Plymouth Horizon; the intermediate compacts Chevrolet Citation and Ford Mustang; and the full-size Dodge Magnum-Chrysler Cordoba.

See also Japan [3-4]; Mexico [2]

AUTO RACING

[1] **Rutherford Wins Indy 500.** Johnny

Johnny Rutherford May 25 wins his third Indianapolis 500.

Rutherford, driving the Pennzoil Chaparral of car owner Jim Hall, won the 64th Indianapolis 500-Mile Race at the Indianapolis Motor Speedway May 25. It was Rutherford's third victory in the Indy 500.

[2] Ten drivers led during the course of the race, and 13 caution flags kept the contenders tightly bunched for most of the distance. The only serious casualty was Bill Whittington, who suffered a broken leg in an accident early in the race. Rutherford won a record $318,020 from the speedway's first $1.5 million purse. Tom Sneva, who had started dead last in 33rd place, finished second. He picked up $128,945. Gary Bettenhausen finished third and won $86,945. He had started in 32d place. Rutherford ran the race at an average speed of 142.862 miles per hour, covering the 200 laps around the 2.5 mile oval track in 3 hours, 29 minutes and 59.56 second.

[3] **French Team Wins LeMans—**The French team of Jean Rondeau and Jean-Pierre Jaussaud overcame rain and tough competition from the Porches to win the 48th 24 Hours of LeMans endurance race June 15. Rondeau became the first driver in the 57-year history of the race to win the event in a car he had built.

[4] The pair managed to hold off a late charge by Jacky Ickx of Belgium and Reinhold Jost of West Germany in a Porche 908. Third place went to a team of brothers, Jean-Michael and Philippe Martin, also in a Rondeau-built car. The winners covered 338 laps (2,859.7 miles or 4,601 kilometers) at an average speed of 119.169 miles (191.7 kilometers) per hour. Despite two spins in the rain, Rondeau's car finished 14 miles (22 kilometers) ahead of Ickx. Only 25 of the 55 starters finished the race. Last year's winners, Don and Bill Whittington, dropped out with a broken differential. Mark Thatcher, son of the British prime minister, crashed near dawn.

[5] **Baker Wins Daytona 500—**Buddy Baker won the Daytona 500 Grand National stock car race Feb. 17 on his 18th try. In doing so, he drove the fastest 500-mile stock car event ever, averaging 177.606 miles per hour at the Daytona Beach (Fla.) International Speedway.

[6] Baker won $102,275 out of the $660,000 purse. He finished 12 seconds ahead of Bobby Allison. Neil Bonnet came in third. Baker's victory was not without drama. On his last pit stop, he decided to take on only 24 gallons of fuel instead of 44, reasoning that he would not need more and could run faster with less weight. He barely made the finish line before running out.

[7] **Jones Wins World Title.** Alan Jones of Australia clinched the world driving title Sept. 28, with a victory in the Canadian Grand Prix near Montreal.

[8] Jones capped his first world championship Oct. 5 by winning the U.S. Grand Prix at Watkins Glen, N.Y., the final race on the Grand Prix circuit. The Watkins Glen win gave him a final total of 71 points. In addition to taking the Montreal and upstate New York races, Jones also won the Grand Prixs in Argentina (Jan. 13), Spain (June 1), France (June 29) and Great Britain (July 13).

AVIATION

[1] **International Deregulation Bill Signed.** President Carter Feb. 15 signed into law the International Air Transportation Competition Act.

[2] The bill reduced statutory barriers against the entry of individual air carriers into new international markets. It granted airlines greater flexibility, permitting them to adopt fares 5% above or 50% below standard foreign fare levels.

[3] The measure also gave the Civil Aeronautics Board new powers to suspend or revoke permits of foreign air carriers whose governments placed unreasonable restrictions on the operations of U.S. carriers. The Senate had passed the bill Jan. 31 and the House, Feb. 4, both by voice vote.

[4] ***Domestic Fare Increases***

Allowed—In a major step toward deregulation of air fares, the Civil Aeronautics Board May 13 gave airlines authority to raise domestic ticket prices essentially without CAB approval. The CAB ruled that airlines could boost fares by unlimited amounts on routes of as many as 200 miles (320 kilometers) long; could raise fares by up to 50% above the basic CAB-set fare level on routes of 201 to 400 miles (322 to 640 kilometers), and could boost fares by 30% on flights of more than 400 miles (640 kilometers).

Disasters & Inquiries

[5] **No Defects Found in DC-10 Pylon.** The Federal Aviation Administration announced Jan. 23 that it had found "no fundamental shortcomings in the design" of the DC-10 engine support pylon.

[6] After a six-month study of the structure of the jumbo jet's engine mount, or pylon, the FAA said minor changes were needed to prevent the sort of maintenance demage that led to the American Airlines DC-10 crash in Chicago that killed 273 persons in 1979. The FAA's findings were based on a study performed by McDonnell Douglas Corp., the builder of the DC-10, supervised by the federal agency and reviewed by the Air Force.

[7] In a separate development, the FAA said Jan. 23 that McDonnell Douglas had agreed to pay $300,000 in civil penalties to settle charges in defective quality control in the production of DC-10 pylons. The FAA said the allegations did not involve the Chicago crash. McDonnell Douglas agreed to pay the penalties without admitting any violations.

[8] **U.S. Boxing Team Killed in Air Crash.** A Polish jet liner crashed March 14 near Warsaw killing all 87 persons aboard, including 22 boxers and officials of a U.S. amateur boxing team.

[9] The LOT Airlines Soviet-built Ilyushin 62 jet was on a scheduled flight from New York to Warsaw and was attempting to make an emergency landing after developing engine trouble.

[10] Among the dead were 14 boxers—some as young as 16—representing the U.S. Amateur Athletic Union, and eight team officials and aides. The team had been scheduled to compete against the Polish national team. The team had included two of the top amateur boxers in the U.S.—Lemuel Steeples, a light welterweight from St. Louis, and Andre McCoy, a middleweight from New Bedford, Mass. Also on board was Tom (Sarge) Johnson of Indianapolis, coach of the boxing team, who had guided the U.S. squad to five gold medals at the 1976 Summer Olympics. Another victim was identified as a popular Polish singer, Anna Jantar, who was returning from a tour of Polish communities of the U.S.

[11] **146 Killed in British Jet Crash.** A chartered British jetliner carrying vacationers enroute from Manchester crashed April 25 into a mountain in the Canary Islands killing all 146 persons aboard.

[12] **Brazil Air Crash Kills 54.** A Transbrasil Airlines jet crashed April 12 in a rainstorm near the southern port city of Florianopolis, killing 54 of the 58 persons aboard. The Boeing 727, on its approach to the airport, slammed into a wooded hillside and burst into flames. It was Brazil's worst air disaster in 20 years.

[13] **81 Killed in Italian Jet Crash.** An Italian DC-9 jetliner crashed June 28 in the Tyrrhenian Sea west of Naples, killing all 81 persons aboard.

[14] **301 Die in Saudi Jet Fire.** A Saudi Arabian Airlines jetliner attempting an emergency landing Aug. 19 at Riyadh (Saudi Arabia) Airport burst into flames on the runway. All 301 persons aboard died. Officials believed the fire to have been caused by a Moslem pilgrim who had lit a portable butane stove to brew tea.

AZORES—*See* Earthquakes [13]

B

BANI-Sadr—*See* Iran [34, 41-43, 85, 115-117, 124]; Iraq [9, 13]

BANKS & BANKING

[1] **Prime Rate.** The prime rate ascended, descended and ascended during 1980. It finished the year at a record peak that varied between 20.5% and 21.5%.

[2] (The prime was the rate banks charged their most creditworthy corporate customers. Many other interest rates were scaled higher based on the prime.)

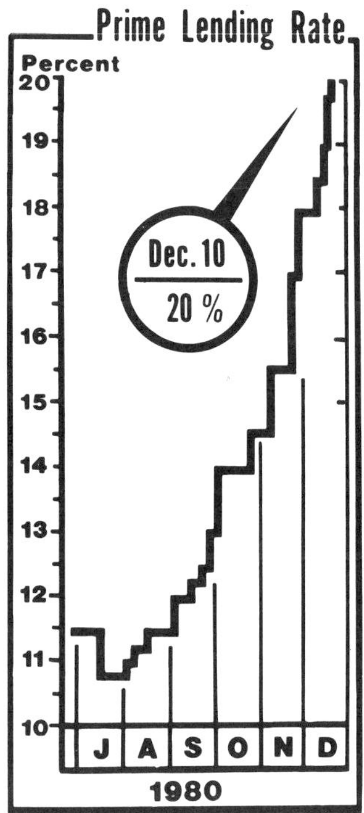

[3] The prime, which had stood at a split rate of 15% to 15.25% at the end of 1979, moved up Feb. 19 to 15.75%. It continued climbing bit by bit to 20% April 2, and then declined in the same fashion to 10.75% July 24. Heading back up, it rose gradually to 21.5% Dec. 19. At least one major bank cut its prime rate to 20.5% Dec. 22.

[4] Banks blamed the rise in the prime on heavy loan demand from corporations and on an increase in the rates they had to pay for their own funds.

[5] **Major Changes Enacted.** Banking legislation, called the most significant in 50 years, was signed March 31 by President Carter.

[6] The law made two major changes: it established a universal system of banking reserves and effected a series of reforms designed to favor the consumer.

[7] The first change gave the Federal Reserve System the authority to require reserves from both member and nonmember financial institutions.

[8] Under the law's provisions, during a phase-in period of eight years, all depository institutions would have to post reserves with the Federal Reserve System. Only Federal Reserve member banks had been required to keep reserves in the past. After eight years, the requirement would be 12% of all transaction balances over $25 million. (The current rules made large banks keep reserves of 16.25% on those balances, but that requirement would be also reduced to 12% over four years.) Some 40 institutions that had left the Fed since July 1, 1979 would

again have to post reserves at the rate that applied to Fed members. The moves were intended to solve the problem of declining membership in the Federal Reserve System. To help the consumer, the law gradually raised the ceiling on interest paid to small savers, authorized the payment of interest on checking accounts and increased to $100,000 from $40,000 the amount of bank savings insured by the federal government.

[9] The provision to allow new interest ceilings was designed to improve the nation's rate of savings, which fell to 3% in 1979, the lowest in 30 years. Banks were offering a maximum of 5.25% on regular passbook accounts, while savings and loans could give up to 5.5%. Under the new law, interest ceilings would be phased out over six years. There would probably be a .25 percent-age point increase in the first-18 months, a .5 percentage point increase in the following year and a half, and then half percentage point increase every year until 1986, when the controls would end.

[10] The House had voted, 380-13, March 27 to approve the bill. The Senate, on a voice vote, followed suit on March 29.

[11] **First Penn Bailout Set.** The Federal Deposit Insurance Corp. and a group of banks had assembled a $500 million assistance package for the financially troubled First Pennsylvania Bank, it was announced April 28.

[12] Under the plan, the FDIC would provide $325 million in loans and a syndicate of 22 banks would loan First Penn $175 million. The loans were for five years. In addition, other banks had agreed to furnish First Pennsylvania with a $1 billion line of credit. First Penn was the 23rd largest bank in the country.

[13] **Foreign Acquisitions of Banks Debated.** The General Accounting Office recommended Aug. 28 that Congress enact legislation temporarily banning foreign acquisitions of large and medium size U.S. banks.

[14] The GAO said that such legislation should be enforced until the government resolved "a basic unfairness" in U.S. banking and antitrust laws that prohibited U.S. banks from competing with foreign banks in many acquisition cases.

[15] Congress had ordered a three-month moratorium on foreign purchases of U.S. banks as part of the comprehensive banking legislation signed by President Carter March 31. But the moratorium had expired July 1, and pending acquisitions, such as that of the Crocker National Bank in San Francisco by London's Midland Bank Ltd. and of Financial Bankshares Inc. in Washington by a group of Arab investors, were again moving toward completion.

[16] U.S. banks were currently prohibited from buying banks incorporated in other states. To make the restriction applicable to foreign-owned banks, the Federal Reserve Board Sept. 17 issued new rules designed to limit the interstate banking activities of foreign-owned banks. Under the rules, each foreign bank would be allowed to select one "home state" in the U.S. to be its center of operations. Then the foreign bank's activities in other states would be limited in the same manner that domestic banks currently were. The rules, however, would allow the foreign banks to switch home states one time. This provision had caused controversy among the Fed's directors, some of whom had argued that an unlimited amount of moves should be allowable.

[17] The GAO released figures on assets of foreign investors in U.S. banks. They showed that as of December 1979, foreigners held $202.5 billion in U.S. banking assets. That represented 13.7% of total U.S. banking assets of nearly $1.4 trillion at the time. The agency said that the pending acquisitions of Crocker National and Financial General would increase those assets controlled by foreign investors

Jerry Ruess of Los Angeles Dodgers hurled 8-0 no-hitter against San Francisco Giants June 28.

to around 15%.

See also Argentina [1-4, 6]; Credit, Consumer [1-9]; Crime [13-16]; Lance, Thomas Bertram (Bert) [1-4]; Silver [14-17]

BASEBALL

[1] **Phillies Win World Series.** The Philadelphia Phillies of the National League won their first world championship Oct. 21, when they defeated the Kansas City Royals of the American League in the sixth game of the 1980 World Series.

[2] The Phillies took the best four-of-seven series by winning the first two and the last two games. Kansas City captured the third and fourth games. It was the Phillies' third appearance in a World Series. They had lost to the Boston Red Sox, four games to one, in 1915 and had been swept in four games by the New York Yankees in 1950. (The 1950 Phillies were known as the "Whiz Kids" because of their youth and gutsy play.) In the 1970s, Philadelphia had gained a reputation as a talented but undisciplined club that usually folded under pressure. This trend changed with the 1979 hiring of Dallas Green as manager. Green's hardnosed, no-nonsense approach gained the club the pennant, although it also alienated several of his players.

[3] Philly third baseman Mike Schmidt was voted the most valuable player of the 1980 World Series. Schmidt batted .381 in the series, the second-best of any Philadelphia player, had two of the club's three home runs and led his team with seven runs batted in. A total of 324,516 fans attended the six games in the two home cities.

[4] **Royals, Phillies Clinch Pennants**—The Kansas City Royals and Philadelphia Phillies clinched pennants in the American League Oct. 10 and the National League Oct. 12 respectively. Kansas City swept three games from the New York Yankees in the best-of-five AL playoffs. Philadelphia defeated the Houston Astros in a dramatic playoff series that

went all five games.

[5] **NL All-Stars Win Again.** The National League continued its domination of the All-Star game, defeating the American League all-stars by a 4-2 score in Dodger Stadium in Los Angeles July 8. The victory in the 51st All-Star game was the ninth in a row for the National Leaguers and the 17th out of the last 18 games.

[6] **Reuss Pitches No-Hitter.** Jerry Reuss of the Los Angeles Dodgers pitched a no-hitter June 28 in an 8-0 victory over the Giants in San Francisco. Reuss retired the last 25 batters in a row and would have had a perfect game but for a first-inning throwing error by Dodger shortstop Bill Russell. The error allowed Jack Clark to become the only Giant to reach first base in the game.

[7] **Strike Averted.** A threatened strike by major league baseball players was averted May 23 when negotiators for the players and owners agreed to defer settlement of the controversial freeagent compensation issue until 1981.

[8] Under an agreement that had expired Dec. 31, 1979, a team that lost a free agent to another team received in return a choice from the draft of high school, college and other amateur players held the following June. (A free agent was any player who had been in major leagues for at least five years and had elected to play out his contract with his team and enter a free-agent pool, from which 13 teams, plus one former one, could select negotiating rights to him.)

[9] The owners insisted that they needed more equitable compensation than a draft selection and demanded in addition a major and minor league player in return for losing what they called a "premier" free agent (a player who rated in the top half statistically at his position and was drafted by at least eight teams). The players opposed the idea, contending that increased compensation would dilute the attractiveness and lucativeness of free agency and eventually lead to a reduction in salaries for all players.

[10] A committee of two players and two general managers was to study the free agent system, and submit joint or separate reports no later than Jan. 1, 1981.

[11] **Snider, Kaline Join Hall of Fame.** Duke Snider, the hard-hitting Brooklyn Dodger outfielder, and Al Kaline of the Detroit Tigers became the 134th and 135th players inducted into the hall of Fame in Cooperstown, N.Y. Aug. 3.

[12] Snider batted .295 in 18 seasons, most of them with the Dodgers in Brooklyn and Los Angeles. He slugged 407 home runs, and enjoyed a five-year string (1952-57) in which he hit at least 40 each year. His 11 home runs in World Series play were a National League record.

[13] Kaline played his entire 22-year career with the Tigers. He compiled a career batting average of .297 with 399 home runs, and had 3,007 hits. In 1955 at the age of 21, he became the youngest batting champion in American League history with a .340 average.

[14] Chuck Klein, a former Philadelphia Phillie slugger, and Tom Yawkey, a past owner of the Boston Red Sox, were also inducted posthumously.

[15] **Winfield Signs for Record Sum.** Outfielder Dave Winfield became the highest-paid player in the history of baseball Dec. 15, when he signed as a free agent with the New York Yankees. According to varying figures, Winfield's 10-year contract with the Yankees would pay him at the start between $1.3 million to $1.5 million a year. At the close of the pact he could be earning as much as $3.3 million a year, due to a cost-of-living escalator in the contract. The total pact, including the escalator, was estimated in excess of $22 million.

BASKETBALL

[1] **Louisville Wins NCAA Title.** The

Los Angeles Lakers center Kareem Abdul-Jabbar shoots over top of Philadelphia 76er center Caldwell Jones (11) May 4 in first game of NBA championships. Abdul-Jabbar had game high 33 points as Lakers defeated 76ers 109-102.

University of Louisville won the national championship of college basketball March 24, with a 59-54 victory over the University of California at Los Angeles in the 42d National Collegiate Athletic Association tournament. The game was played before 16,637 fans at Market Square Arena in Indianapolis.

[2] ***Virginia Captures NIT***—The University of Virginia edged the University of Minnesota, 58-55, March 20 to win the 43rd National Invitation Tournament in New York City. The title game was watched by 13,598 fans in Madison Square Garden.

[3] **Lakers Win NBA Title.** The Los Angeles Lakers won the championship of the National Basketball Association May 16 by defeating the Philadelphia 76ers, 123-107, in the sixth game of the best-of seven final playoff series. The victory gave L.A. an edge of four games to two in the series. Philadelphia had reached the final round by beating Washington, two games to none, Atlanta, four games to one, and Boston, four games to one. Los Angeles had dropped Phoenix, four games to one, in the quarterfinals and downed defending NBA champion Seattle four games to one, in the semifinals.

BEAUTY CONTESTS

Miss America 1980. Susan Powell of Elk City, Okla. won the annual Miss America beauty pageant in Atlantic City, N.J. Sept. 6.

BEGIN, MENACHEM—*See* Israel [4-5, 7, 9-10, 12]; Middle East [5, 10, 77]

BIOLOGY—*See* Patents [1-9]

BLACK AMERICANS

[1] **'70s Economic Decline Reported.** The decade of the 1970s was a "time of retreat, retrenchment and lost opportunities" for blacks, according to the National Urban League Jan. 22. That

was the assessment of the league's annual report, entitled, "The State of Black America."

[2] On the political front, league President Vernon E. Jordan Jr., said he saw, in this presidential election year, "the center of political gravity moving to the right, with no candidate fashioning a platform of reform, activism and social justice.

[3] The report concluded that racism was "alive and well in the American body politic." "We enter the 1980s with an enormous gap between black and white America and with the black condition deteriorating," it said.

According to its data:

The average income of the black family declined to 57% of white income by 1979, from a 60% level in 1970.

The percentage of black families in the middle class declined to 9% of all black families, from a 12% level at the start of the decade.

Shawn Weatherly of Sumter, S.C., won bathing suit competition at Miss Universe contest in Seoul July 2.

Black unemployment increased to 11.9% from 8.2% during the decade, compared with an increase to 5.2% from 4.5% for whites.

On the positive side, black enrollment in colleges rose to 9.3% of total enrollment, almost up to the 11.5% population level of blacks within the U.S. Also, the number of blacks owning their own homes increased to 43.6% by 1977 from a 41.6% figure in 1970.

[4] ***Urban League Hears Candidates***—The National Urban League's annual conference, in New York Aug. 3-6, drew appearances by four presidential candidates. More than 15,000 people attended the conference, which was the 70th annual national meeting of the civil rights organization. "The black vote is up for grabs this year," John E. Jacob, the league's executive vice president said in opening the conference Aug. 3. "The black vote that elected Jimmy Carter in 1976 isn't in anybody's pocket in 1980," he said. President Carter, Sen. Edward M. Kennedy (D, Mass.), Ronald Reagan and Rep. John B. Anderson (R, Ill.) addressed the conference.

See also Census (U.S.) [3]; Civil & Constitutional Rights [5-8]; Civil Disorders

BOLIVIA

[1] A military coup d'etat extinguished the electoral process in Bolivia. Former leftist President Hernan Siles Zuazo failed to gain the required majority in presidential elections June 29. The election was thrown into Congress, but before it could meet the armed forces took over the government. The U.S. cut off most aid to the country.

[2] **Coup Rumors.** Rumors that Bolivia's military officers were planning a coup d'etat before the upcoming presidential elections gained credence June 9. On that day, the armed forces issued a statement calling on the government of interim President Lidia Gueiler Tejada to put off the elections

for one year "to reorganize the nation before the citizens go to the polls."

[3] On May 30, at least eight bombs had exploded in La Paz in what one report characterized as an attempt on the part of some right-wing military officers to create the illusion that chaos was approaching so that a military coup would be justified.

[4] **Siles Leads in Vote for President.** Former President Siles and his left-wing Democrate Popular Union appeared to be leading in Bolivia's presidential election June 29, but returns indicated he had failed to achieve the 50% total needed to victory. Congress was scheduled to meet to choose a new president.

[5] **Armed Forces Seize Power.** Bolivia's armed forces seized control of the government July 17 to prevent Hernan Siles Zuazo, a leftist, from being selected president by the Congress. Some resistance to the military coup developed.

[6] The Congress was to have met Aug. 4 to elect a new president from the top vote getters in the June 29 election. In a broadcast July 17, a military spokesman said that the decision to take control of the government had been made "for the dignity of Bolivia, to reject the results of the general elections and to declare the Congress and its actions unconstitutional."

[7] The coup began in the northern town of Trinidad, where military forces seized government offices and arrested a number of leftist politicians. At midday, a group of 20 "civilians" with automatic weapons forced their way into the presidential palace in La Paz and placed interim President Lidia Gueiler Tejada and members of her Cabinet under arrest. The military then ordered the disbanding of Congress and declared the country a military zone. Gen. Luis Garcia Meza, the commander of the army, was identified as the leader of the uprising, along with the air force commander, Gen. Waldo Bernal Pereira, and the navy chief, Adm. Ramiro Tarrazas.

[8] Resistance was reported July 20 in the tin and zinc mining district of Santa Ana, some 400 miles (640 kilometers) southeast of La Paz. An unconfirmed broadcast said that miners in the region had clashed with troops, resulting in "many casualties." Marcelo Quiroga Santa Cruz, the Socialist Party I candidate for president, who had won 10% of the vote, was killed in La Paz July 17 in a gun battle with military forces. Sporadic gunfire in La Paz continued through July 20.

[9] U.S. Ambassador Marvin Weissman arrived in Santiago, Chile July 20 after being recall by Washington July 17 to protest the coup. The U.S. suspended all military aid to Bolivia when news of the uprising reached Washington.

[10] The most serious opposition to the takeover had come July 23 when miners and peasants in Catavi near Lake Poopo in the southeast stormed the amy barracks. A five-hour battle ensued before the attackers were beaten off. Assaults on mining camps by the army had left more than 50 persons killed and some 300 captured. Most of the countryside was in control of the military forces with only towns in the mining districts still under seige. In La Paz, roundups of political suspects continued. Over 20 Bolivian news reporters had been detained, and a number of foreign correspondents had either been arrested or had left the country after receiving death threats.

[11] U.S. Secretary of State Edmund S. Muskie July 25 announced a cutoff of virtually all U.S. aid to Bolivia. Only humanitarian food aid programs administered by private or international aid organizations to some 200,000 Bolivian peasants remained unaffected by the action.

[12] **Compulsory Service Decreed.** Bolovia's new military leader, Gen. Luis Garcia Meza, decreed Aug. 1 that all Bolivians were eligible for compulsory "patriotic government service." The decree authorized the government

to make citizens work at whatever projects were deemed appropriate for a period of up to two years.

[13]Meanwhile, more than 1,000 persons remained unaccounted for since the coup. Many labor leaders and intellectuals were in hiding, and deposed interim President Lidia Gueiler Tejada had sought asylum in the residence of the papal nuncio in La Paz. Gueiler left the country Oct. 4 on an airliner bound for Paris, where her daughter lived.

BOOKS

[1] **American Book Awards.** The first annual American Book Awards were announced May 1 at a ceremony in New York City.

[2] The honors, sponsored by the Association of American Publishers, were the successor to the National Book Awards, which had been presented for 30 years.

[3] In creating the American Book Awards, the publishers' association made some radical changes that were opposed by segments of the literary community. The new format raised the number of award categories to 34 from seven. Paperbacks were honored for the first time. And, also for the first time, librarians, booksellers, publishers and editors joined authors and critics in picking the winners. Opponents charged that books nominated for the American Book Awards were selected for their commercial appeal, rather than their literary or artistic merit. Several writers whose works had been nominated boycotted the awards ceremony. They included William Styron, Norman Mailer and Calvin Trillin.

[4] Styron's *Sophie's Choice* won the award for general hardcover fiction. Other fiction winners included *Birdy* by William Wharton (Alfred A. Knopf) for first novel and *The World According to Garp* by John Irving (Pocket Books) for general paperback fiction. (Irving's novel had been nominated for the 1979 National Book Award. Tom Wolfe's *The Right Stuff* (Farrar, Straus & Giroux) took the honor for general hardcover nonfiction. The award for general paperback nonfiction went to *The Snow Leopard* by Peter Matthiessen (Bantam Books). The prestigious National Medal for Literature was given to Eudora Welty, a novelist and short-story writer known for her evocative stories of Southern life.

The other recipients were:

Art/Illustrated (hardcover collection): *Drawings and Digressions* by Larry Rivers with Carol Brightman; Hermann Strohbach, designer/art director (Clarkson N. Potter).

Art/Illustrated (hardcover original): *The Birthday of the Infanta* by Oscar Wilde; Leonard Lubin, illustrator; Barbara Hennessy, art director (Viking Press).

Art/Illustrated (paperback): *Anatomy Illustrated* by Emily Blair Chewning; Dana Levy, designer; Frank Metz, art director (Fireside/Simon & Schuster).

Autobiography (hardcover): *By Myself* by Lauren Bacall (Alfred A. Knopf).

Autobiography (paperback): *And I Worked at the Writer's Trade* by Malcolm Cowley (Penguin Books).

Biography (hardcover): *The Rise of Theodore Roosevelt* by Edmund Morris (Coward McCann & Geoghegan).

Biography (paperback): *Max Perkins: Editor of Genius* by A. Scott Berg (Pocket Books).

Eudora Welty wins National Medal for Literature.

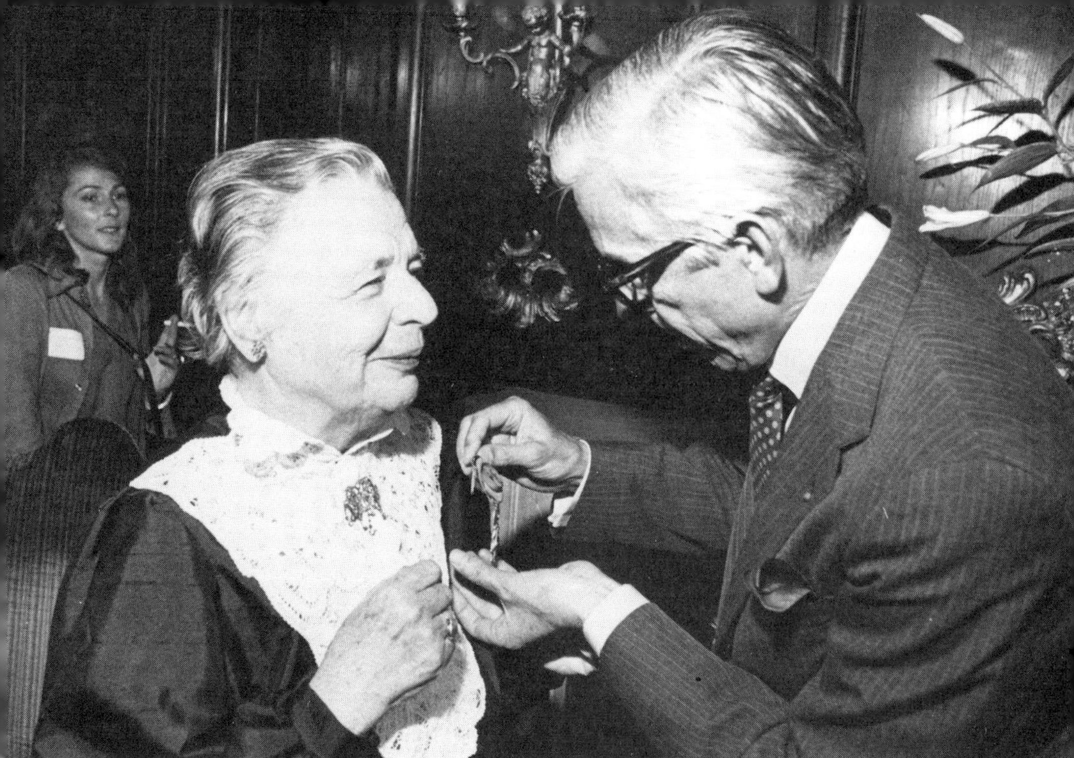

Novelist Marguerite Yourcenar receives medal of Legion of Honor in Boston June 5 from French Ambassador to U.S., Francois de Laboulaye. Yourcenar March 6 became first woman elected to French Academy.

Book Design: *The Architect's Eye: American Architectural Drawings from 1799-1978* by Deborah Nevins and Robert A. M. Stern; R. D. Scudellari, art director (Pantheon Books).

Children's Books (hardcover): *A Gathering of Days: A New England Girl's Journal, 1830-32* by Joan W. Blos (Charles Scribner's Sons).

Children's Books (paperback): *A Swiftly Tilting Planet* by Madeline L'Engle (Dell).

Cover Design: *Famous Potatoes* by Joe Cottonwood; David Myers, designer, Ann Spinelli, art director (Delta/Seymour Lawrence).

Current Interest (hardcover): *Julia Child and More Company* by Julia Child (Alfred A. Knopf).

Current Interest (paperback): *The Culture of Narcissism* by Christopher Lasch (Warner Books).

General Reference (hardcover): *Congressional Quarterly's Guide to the U.S. Supreme Court* edited by Elder Witt (Congressional Quarterly Inc.)

General Reference (paperback): *The Complete Directory to Prime Time Network TV Shows: 1946-Present* by Tim Brooks and Earle Marsh (Ballentine Books).

History (hardcover): *White House Years* by Henry Kissinger (Little, Brown & Co.)

History (paperback): *A Distant Mirror: The Calamitous 14th Century* by Barbara W. Tuchman (Ballentine Books).

Jacket Design: *Birdy* by William Wharton; Fred Marcellino, designer; Lidia Ferrara, art director (Alfred A. Knopf).

Mystery (hardcover): *The Green Ripper* by John D. MacDonald (J.B. Lippincott).

Mystery (paperback): *Stained Glass by William F. Buckley Jr. (Warner Books).*

Poetry: *Ashes* by Philip Levine (Atheneum).

Religion/Inspiration (hardcover): *The Gnostic Gospels* by Elaine Pagels (Random House).

Religion/Inspiration (paperback): *A Severe Mercy* by Sheldon Vanauken (Bantam Books).

Science (hardcover): *Godel, Escher, Bach: An Eternal Golden Braid; A Metaphorical Fugue on Minds and Machines in the Spirit of Lewis Carroll* by Douglas Hofstadter (Basic Books).

Science (paperback): *The Dancing Wu Li Masters: An Overview of the New Physics* by Gary Zukav (William Morrow & Co.).

Science Fiction (hardcover): *JEM* by Frederik Pohl (St. Martin's Press).

Science Fiction (hardcover): *The Book of the Dun Cow* by Walter Wangerin Jr. (Pocket Books).

Translation: Osip E. Mandelstam's *The Complete Critical Prose and Letters* translated by Jane Gary Harris and Constance Link (Ardis Publishers).

Western: *Bendigo Shafter* by Louis L'Amour (Bantam Books).

[5] ***Book Awards Revised***—Extensive changes in the American Book Awards were announced Oct. 19.

[6] The number of prize categories were reduced to 18 from 33 to placate critics who felt that the 1980 awards had had too many categories and too many nominees. The board also dropped the method of choosing winners by a poll of 2,000 volunteers in publishing and related fields. The 1981 winners—with the exceptions of the awards for translation and technical achievement—would be picked by 11 professionals: three authors, two critics or reviewers, two editors or

publishers, two librarians and two booksellers.

[7] **Yourcenar Elected to French Academy.** Novelist Marguerite Yourcenar March 6 became the first woman ever to be elected to the French Academy, the 345-year-old overseer of French intellectual and cultural life.

[8] Yourcenar, 76, who had written a number of distinguished historical works, including the novel *Hadrian's Memoirs,* was a poet, playwright, classicist and translator of ancient Greek poetry.

[9] **Tax Ruling Upsets Book Publishers.** The book publishing industry was upset over an inventory tax ruling that could force significant changes in its operations, it was reported Oct. 5.

[10] The ruling, issued by the Internal Revenue Service in February, prohibited publishers from writing down (depreciating) the value of their inventories for tax purposes. The IRS directive was based on a case that came before the Supreme Court in 1979, *Thor Power Tool Co. v. Commissioner of Internal Revenue.* In that case, the high court upheld the authority of the IRS to refuse to allow a company to write down the inventory value of replacement tools based on the same accounting methods it used to keep its financial records. The IRS in February 1980 applied the court decision retroactively to 1979 and extended it to every kind of industry, including book publishing. Publishers kept millions of books in warehouses for extended periods and counted on inventory tax writeoffs to ameliorate the expense. As a result of the IRS ruling, it would be unprofitable for publishers to keep slow-selling books in print.

[11] Only a few months after the IRS ruling, some publishers were reported to have increased by 30% their sales of inventoried stock to remainder outlets, which sold the books at a discount. Other publishers were opting to drastically reduce their inventories by turning books to pulp. Congress was considering legislation that would prevent the Supreme Court decision from being applied retroactively to all industries, or would exempt the publishing industry from being included in the decision.

See also Nobel Prizes [4]; Pulitzer Prizes [3, 5]

BOSTON—*See* Census (U.S.) [4]

BOTSWANA

[1] **President Khama Dies.** Seretse Khama, president of Botswana since independence from Britain in 1966, died of cancer July 13 in Gaborone. He was 59.

[2] Quett Masire, vice president under Khama, was elected July 18 by the National Assembly to succeed him as president. Masire, like Khama, was a founding member of the Bechuanaland Democratic Party, now the Botswana Democratic Party. He had served on the tribal council of the minority Bangwaketse tribe before becoming a member of the Legislative Council and later the Executive Council under the British governor.

BOXING

[1] **Holmes Defeats Ali.** Larry Holmes, the World Boxing Council heavyweight champion, easily retained his title Oct. 2 by beating former three-time champion Muhammad Ali in Las Vegas. Holmes' triumph was cemented when Ali failed to answer the bell for the 11th round. The bout went into the books as an 11th-round knockout.

[2] ***Holmes Stops Zanon, Jones***—Larry Holmes, the World Boxing Council heavyweight champion, scored technical knockouts of Italy's Lorenzo Zanon Feb. 3 and Leroy Jones March 31. Both bouts were held in Las Vegas.

[3] **Weaver Takes WBA Heavyweight Title.** Mike (Hercules) Weaver took the World Boxing Association heavyweight title March 31, with a

15th-round knockout of "Big John" Tate in Knoxville, Tenn. It was Tate's first defense of the championship he had won in 1979.

[4] **Hagler TKOs Minter for Middleweight Crown.** Marvin Hagler of the U.S. Sept. 27 captured the undisputed middleweight title with a third-round technical knockout of Alan Minter of Great Britain in London's Wembly Stadium. Minter, who had taken the middleweight crown from Vito Antuofermo in March, was bleeding badly from the face when the referee stopped the fight.

[5] **Leonard Regains Title.** "Sugar Ray"Leonard Nov. 25 regained the World Boxing Council welterweight championship with a shocking 8th-round technical knockout of titleholder Roberto Durnan of Panama. Duran had taken the crown from Leonard June 20.

[6] No one could have predicted the manner in which the bout ended: Duran simply stopped fighting at 2 minutes 44 seconds of the eighth round. The rematch was held in the Louisana Superdome in New Orleans before a crowd of 35,000. It was broadcast to about 345 closed-circuit locations in North America.

[7] **5 Boxers Died from Matches.** Johnny Owen of Wales, the British and European bantamweight champion, died Nov. 3 as a result of injuries suffered in a title bout with World Boxing Council champion Lupe Pintor of Mexico. The bout had been held Sept. 19 in Los Angeles.

[8] Cleveland Denny, a former Canadian lightweight champion, died July 7 as a result of injuries suffered in a non-title bout with the current Canadian champion, Gaetan Hart. The contest was held June 20 in Montreal. (The bout was a preliminary to the first "Sugar Ray" Leonard-Roberto Duran confrontation.) Three other boxers also died in 1980 because of fight injuries: professionals Tony Thomas (Jan. 1) and Charles Newell (Jan. 17) and amateur Harlan Hoosier (Jan. 18). All three were Americans.

[9] **Gavilan Penniless.** Legendary Cuban welterweight Kid Gavilan was penniless and living in Miami, it was reported April 1. Gavilan, whose real name was Gerardo Gonzalez, had held the world welterweight title from 1952 to 1954 and had earned almost $2 million in his 143 professional fights. *See also* Aviation [7-9]

BRANDT, Willy—*See* Economy (International) [1-6]

BRAZIL—*See* Aviation [11]

BREZHNEV, Leonid—*See* Union of Soviet Socialist Republics–[1-5, 7-9, 32-33]

BROADCASTING—*See* Christians, Evangelican [9-12]

BUDGET (U.S.)

[1] **Fiscal '81 Budget Cleared.** Congress voted final approval Nov. 20 of a fiscal 1981 budget with a deficit of $27.4 billion. A spending total of $632.4 billion was projected for the fiscal year, which began Oct. 1. The revenue total was $605 billion.

[2] The House approved the final budget resolution by voice vote Nov. 20. Senate approval came on a 50-38 vote after a verbal assault by many Republicans. In general, the Republicans argued that a deficit of $27.4 billion was too large even as it was but that the actual deficit would in all probability be even higher. A real deficit of about $38 billion was estimated by Sen. Henry Bellmon (Okla.), ranking Republican on the Senate Budget Committee.

[3] As worked out by a House-Senate conference committee Nov. 19, the resolution called for increased outlays from the previous year only in the defense sector. These expenditures were estimated at $160.1 billion for defense in fiscal 1981, up from $135.7 billion in the fiscal 1980 budget. The budget measure was not a law, but a

At budget briefing Jan. 26 are (left to right) Treasury Secretary G. William Miller, Budget Director James McIntyre, Chairman of Council of Economic Advisers Charles L. Schultze.

concurrent resolution designed to impose budgetary discipline on Congress and its committees. Under the normal congressional schedule, work on the budget resolution was supposed to be completed by Sept. 15. But the election year had brought delays.

[4] **Carter's Budget Forecasts Mild Recession.** President Carter presented Congress Jan. 28 with a "prudent and responsible" $615.8 billion budget for fiscal 1981.

[5] The budget was built upon an unusual forecast that a mild recession would occur in the first half of 1980. According to Charles L. Schultze, chairman of the Council of Economic Advisers, it was "the first time any administration's budget had officially forecast a recession in advance of its actually occurring."

[6] The $615.8 billion spending level requested for fiscal 1981, which would begin Oct. 1, would represent a 9.3% increase from the previous year. Revenues of $600 billion were estimated. The $15.8 billion deficit would be the lowest deficit in seven years.

[7] Despite the outlook of a recession, and the fact that it was a presidential election year, the budget did not include a tax-cut proposal. "Budget restraint is essential in our efforts to control inflation," the President told Congress in his budget message.

[8] On a program basis, the budget called for a sizable 12% increase in defense spending. Spending on research was the only other sector of the budget to be favored with an increase above the inflation rate. A 13% rise to a $36.1 billion level was projected, to be spread among 31 federal agencies devoted to scientific research and technological development.

[9] Carter did avoid drastic cutbacks in social programs in an election year. Some increases were proposed—for low-income housing, training for umemployed youth, health care for the poor.

[10] ***Defense***—The fiscal 1981 defense request of $142.7 billion represented 23.2% of federal spending. The total

was a 12% increase from the projected fiscal outlay of $127.4 billion. After allowing for inflation, the proposed spending increase would be about 3.3%.

[11] The fiscal 1981 figure for total U.S. obligational authority was $158.7 billion, an increase of 13.9% (real growth 5.4%) from 1980. Obligational authority referred to funds Congress would be asked to appropriate in fiscal 1981, but that would not all be spent in that year. Money appropriated in previous years and not spent (often said to be "in the pipeline") was included in the total.

[12] One of the major elements in the fiscal 1981 budget was the beginning of a $9-billion five-year program to develop a quick-strike, or rapid deployment force, for use in trouble spots around the world. The fiscal 1981 budget also called for $6.12 billion for 17 new naval vessels and the modernization of two ships.

[13] ***Employment***—The new youth-jobs effort planned by the Carter Administration would need only a $100 million infusion in fiscal 1981 over the $4 billion currently spent on youth-jobs programs. By fiscal 1983, however, spending was projected to rise to $6 billion a year.

[14] The government's largest jobs program, the public-service jobs project, was left unchanged in the new budget at the old 450,000-jobs level.

[15] Overall employment and training outlays were expected to increase by 9.2% in the fiscal 1981 budget to a total of $12.3 billion, from $11.2 billion the previous year. The increase, while substantial, was not expected to do much more though than maintain pace with inflation.

[16] **Income Maintenance**—The Social Security System's budget for fiscal 1981 totaled $136.9 billion. The 16% rise over the previous budget reflected anticipated cost-of-living increases of 13% in June 1980 and 9.9% in June 1981.

[17] The President did not request a rollback in a schedule increase in Social Security payroll taxes to 6.65% in 1981 from 6.13%, although relief for the taxpayer had been under consideration.

[18] The President was proposing some inter-fund borrowing among the Social Security System's three separate trust funds in order to meet short-term cash needs. Specifically, the old-age and survivor benefits fund was in need of the cash, which could come from the disability or health insurance funds.

The Carter Budget
(as submitted Jan. 28)

BUDGET RECEIPTS AND OUTLAYS

RECEIPTS (in billion of dollars)	Fiscal 1979 Actual	Fiscal 1980 Estimate	Fiscal 1981 Estimate
Taxes on individual incomes	$217.8	$238.7	$274.4
Social Security taxes	117.9	136.2	158.7
Taxes on corporate profits	65.7	72.3	71.6
Excise taxes	18.7	26.3	40.2
Unemployment-insurance taxes	15.4	16.8	18.6
Estate and gift taxes	5.4	5.8	5.9
All other revenue	25.0	27.7	30.6
Total Receipts	$465.9	$523.8	$600.0

OUTLAYS

National defense	$117.7	$130.4	$146.2
Social Security benifits	102.6	117.9	136.9
Interest on public debt	59.8	73.3	79.4
Medicare, other health programs	49.6	56.6	62.4
Public assistance, food stamps, other aid	28.6	36.1	40.1
Education, manpower, social services	29.7	30.7	32.0
Aid to veterans	19.9	20.8	21.7
Aid to transportation, business	18.2	23.4	19.3
Civil-service retirement	12.2	14.3	16.7
Unemployment compensation	10.7	15.6	18.8
International affairs, economic and military aid	6.1	10.4	9.6
Energy	6.9	7.8	8.1
Aid to community, regional development	9.5	8.5	8.8
General revenue sharing	6.9	6.9	6.9
Rivers, dams, natural resources	7.4	7.9	7.7

Science, space, technology	5.0	5.9	6.4
Pollution control	4.7	4.9	5.1
Aid to agriculture	6.2	4.6	2.8
Payment to the Postal Service	1.8	1.7	1.6
All other spending	8.7	8.2	10.4
Rents and royalties on outer continental shelf	($3.3)	($4.8)	($6.0)
Interagency deductions listed as spending above	($15.2)	($17.5)	($19.1)
Total Outlays	$493.7	$563.6	$615.8
DEFICIT	-$27.7	-$39.8	-$15.8

[19] **Carter Revises Fiscal '81 Budget.** President Carter March 31 sent Congress a revised budget for fiscal 1981 that used spending cuts and increased revenues to project a surplus.

[20] The revised package projected receipts of $628 billion and outlays of $611.5 billion, with a resulting surplus of $16.5 billion. It was in sharp contrast to Carter's first fiscal 1981 budget which projected a $15.8 billion deficit based on spending of $615.8 billion and revenues of $600 billion.

[21] In his message to Congress, Carter said the budget proposal was the "center" of his five-point anti-inflation plan unveiled March 14. The revised budget contained $15 billion in proposed spending cuts, some $2 billion more than expected. The big increase in projected revenues ($28 billion) came from inflation-produced tax receipts of $11.6 billion and two new tax proposals. Carter proposed an import fee on petroleum that would net some $12.6 billion and a new withholding tax on interest and dividend income, which was expected to result in an additional $3.4 billion.

[22] ***Spending Cuts***—The principle cuts proposed by Carter hit most of the new or expanded programs in the fiscal 1981 budget. The Administration did not make cuts in benefit programs like Social Security. It instead focused on aid to states and cities and the disadvantaged.

Some of the specific cuts included:

Defense: Some $1.4 billion in cuts through "program reductions and operating efficiencies" and by calculating annually, rather than semi-annually, cost-of-living pay adjustments for military retirees. The overall level of defense spending was up, however, by about $4.3 billion from the January proposal.

Job Programs: $1.4 billion dropped for federally subsidized jobs and unemployment compensation. Included was $500 million cut from the CETA public service jobs program, which gave jobs to unemployed poor people to counter economic downturns, and $100 million from cutting 10,000 jobs from the Young Adult Conservation Corps.

New Programs: Some $4 billion cut by deferring or reducing new programs.

Transportation: Cuts in highway and mass transit spending of $1.1 billion.

Space: $224 million by delaying plans to send a spacecraft over the sun's polar regions and by postponing purchase of certain scientific apparatus to be flown on the space shuttle.

[23] **Fiscal 1980 Deficit Doubles.** The federal government finished the fiscal 1980 budget year Sept. 30 with a deficit of $58.96 billion, more than twice the gap reported at the end of fiscal 1979 and the second largest ever.

[24] The figures released Oct. 29 by the Treasury Department and the Office of Management and Budget indicated that federal outlays rose 17.3% during fiscal 1980 to $579.01 billion from $493.61 billion in fiscal 1979. Revenues increased 11.6% to $520.05 billion in fiscal 1980 from $465.96 billion in fiscal 1979.

See also City & State Affairs [6]; Congress (U.S.) [7-8]

BURMA

[1] **Former Premier Nu Returns.** Former Premier U Nu returned to Burma July 29 after 11 years of exile in India. He had been the major political

figure from independence in 1948 until a 1962 coup that brought President Ne Win to power.

[2] **Army Battles Communists.** The Burmese army was suffering heavy casualties in the course of a campaign aimed at eliminating a communist insurgency movement based in northeast Burma near the border with China, according to press reports Aug. 10 and 15.

[3] Tight censorship by the government made it difficult to acquire firm knowledge, but it appeared that army casualties since an offensive was launched in November 1979 were in the range of 4,000-5,000. The offensive—code-named King Conqueror—had called for the army to cross the Salween River and take control of the rugged mountainous terrain between the river and the Chinese border, which for decades had been the base area of the communists rebels.

BUSINESS

[1] **FCC Sets Phone Industry Deregulation.** The Federal Communications Commission voted, 5-2, April 7 in favor of sweeping rules to restructure and deregulate the telephone industry.

[2] While maintaining regulatory control over basic phone service and rates, the commission backed the expansion of phone companies into the field of computer-enhanced data processing, which would be unregulated and also supported free-market competition in the sale of phone equipment. The new rules, which were to take effect March 1, 1982, would mean significant changes in the operations of the nation's two largest phone companies, American Telephone & Telegraph Co. and General Telephone & Electronics Corp. AT&T began a far-reaching reorganization Aug. 20, when its board approved steps to establish separate subsidiaries within the company. One of the steps taken, effective Sept. 1, was a realignment of central management. AT&T President William M. Ellinghaus was given charge of all company activities that would remain regulated. Vice Chairman James E. Olson was assigned to oversee the creation of the separate unregulated subsidiary. The board also established a wholly owned subsidiary, AT&T International, Inc., to handle the conglomerate's international interests. These interests had previously been divided between two other units, Western Electric International Inc. and American Bell International Inc. AT&T International joined Western Electric Co., Bell Laboratories and 23 operating companies that would remain under government regulation.

[3] **Hardships for Small Business.** Several studies released in the first half of 1980 blamed Carter Administration credit policies for difficulties faced by small business in the United States.

[4] Rep. Henry J. Nowak (D, N.Y.), chairman of the House Small Business subcommittee on business opportunities, said small business was bearing more of the costs of the federal government's tight credit policies than big business. He submitted a report May 29 that claimed high interest rates caused the number of commercial loans between $1,000 and $99,000 to drop by 48% from November 1979 to February 1980. (Many small firms were dependent on the loans to meet payrolls and maintain inventories.)

[5] Nowak's report said the number of commerical loans between $100,000 and $499,000 dropped by 24% in the same period. At the same time, loans of $1 million and more, traditionally sought and received by large businesses, rose 16%. A Small Business Administration study reported May 15 said small business bankruptcies increased 48% after the Carter Administration began its tight money policy of raising interest rates in October 1979.

[6] The White House Commission on Small Business ended a two-year study

and sent a report with recommendations to President Carter May 15. The report made 60 proposals for reversing what the commission called the government's "double tilt" against small business. The chief proposals included the reduction of corporate tax rates for lower earning firms and the granting of tax credits for investment in new small businesses.

[7] A study by the National Center for Economic Alternatives said Jan. 13 that small business was becoming "an endangered species in America." The report said the Carter Administration's tight money policies were only part of the reason 80% of small businesses failed before their fifth year of operation.

[8] It focused on regulatory policies that led to the dominance of an industry by large firms, declaring small businesses carried a disproportionate share of responsibility for complying with government regulations.

[9] ***Small Business Aid Bill Signed***—President Carter Sept. 19 signed the Regulatory Flexibility Act.

[10] The act required the federal government to anticipate and reduce the impact of rules and paperwork requirements on small businesses. Specifically, agencies were to publish semiannually an agenda of new regulations that affected small business, analyze in detail new rules, and systematically review all rules that had an "adverse" impact on small business. The bill was passed in the Senate Aug. 6 and the House Sept. 9.

[11] **Utilities' Free Speech Upheld.** The Supreme Court June 20 ruled in two New York cases that public utilities had the right to communicate with their customers through inserts attached to the customers monthly bills. The decisions extended the doctrine of "corporate free speech" established in *First National Bank of Boston v. Bellotti* (1978).

[12] In one case June 20, *Central Hudson Gas & Electric Corp. v. Public Service Commission,* the high court ruled, 8-1, that the state could not prevent a utility from including promotional advertising with its bills. In the other case, *Consolidated Edison v. Public Service Commission,* the court ruled, 7-2, that New York could not prohibit a utility from issuing policy statements with its bills.

[13] Both decisions, with Justice Lewis F. Powell writing for the majorities, held that even though utilities were state-regulated monopolies, states had only limited authority to interfere with the free speech of utilities. The high court however did back the power of state regulatory agencies to prevent utilities from passing along to their customers the cost of their advertising or policy statment inserts.

Mergers

[14] **Pan Am-National Merger.** Pan American World Airways completed its merger with National Airlines Jan.7.

[15] **Newhouse Acquires Random House.** RCA Corp. said Feb. 6 that it agreed in principle to sell Random House Inc., its book publishing subsidiary, to Newhouse Publications for between $65 million and $70 million. Newhouse, a communications conglomerate, said Random House would have editorial autonomy.

[16] **Sun Bids $2.3 Billion for Seagram Unit.** Seagram Co. Ltd., the world's largest liqour producer, April 11 said it had accepterd a $2.3 billion offer from Sun Co. for the bulk of U.S. oil and gas properties of Texas Pacific Oil Co., a little-known Seagram subsidiary.

[17] **3 Railroads File to Merge.** Union Pacific, Missouri Pacific and Western Pacific Sept. 15 filed joint applications with the Interstate Commerce Commission to merge into a 22,800-mile (36,480-kilometer) rail system. Such a system would span 21 states in the western two-thirds of the U.S.

See also Antitrust Actions

CABINET (U.S.)—*See* Ronald Reagan [3, 6-13]

CALIFORNIA—*See* Civil & Constitutional Rights [1]; Disasters & Accidents]17-18]; Water [1-3]; Weather [1-3]

CAMBODIA

Famine

[1] **Disaster Averted.** An international relief effort had prevented a disastrous famine in Cambodia, at least for the next few months, a U.N. official announced Feb. 10.

[2] The assessment was made by James Grant, who had taken over Jan. 1 as executive director of the United Nations International Children's Emergency fund (UNICEF), which was in charge of a joint relief operation in Cambodia with the Red Cross. Grant, who had just returned from a week-long visit to Cambodia, said thousands of tons of food and medicine piled up in warehouses in Cambodia were finally reaching the countryside.

[3] UNICEF and the Red Cross Feb. 7 had temporarily halted operations at Nong Chan, a Thai border feeding station north of Aranyaprathet. The shipment of aid to as many as 200,000 Cambodians was suspended following reports that the supplies reaching Cambodian territory were being expropriated by Vietnamese troops. Food deliveries from Thailand to Cambodia were continuing elsewhere along the frontier.

[4] **Famine Resurgent.** Only a month after optimistic reports on the food situation had reached the West, U.N. officials in March warned that Cambodia faced a serious famine.

[5] The U.N. International Children's Emergency Fund concluded March 21 that "the prospect of famine has significantly increased." The rapid change in the situation was caused by two harvest failures and a shortage of rice seed. Also, U.N. officials reported, port facilities at Pnompenh and Kompong Som were so badly neglected that they could not handle relief cargoes. The docks had fallen apart, according to relief officials, and could handle only 4,000 tons of cargo a month, down from a normal capacity of 18,000 tons a month.

[6] The U.N. called an emergency one-day conference in New York March 26 to seek an additional $260 million in aid. But the 43 nations that attended the meeting came up with only $20 million, of which $8 million was pledged by the U.S. Most nations pointed to conflicting figures by different relief organizations as the reason for holding back contributions.

[7] A second U.N. meeting on providing more aid to Cambodia was held May 26-27 in Geneva. The need for Cambodia and Vietnam to remove any obstacles to delivery and distribution of relief supplies was stressed by the president of the 59-nation parley, Australian Foreign Minister Andrew Peacock. The conference pledged $116 million of the $181 million required to continue the relief operation through 1980.

[8] **Aid Halted, Resumed.** Officials of the Thai government and international relief agencies agreed in Bangkok July 27 to resume food shipments to hungry Cambodians along Thailand's eastern border. The dispatch of supplies south of the Thai border two of Aranyaprathet had been suspended June 17 by the Red Cross following reports that some of the aid was being diverted to the Khmer Rouge guerrillas, who were fighting Cambodian government forces.

[9] **Red Cross Ends Cambodia Food Aid.** The Red Cross Dec. 16 ended its distribution of food across the Thai-Cambodian border. The need of such relief assistance for Cambodian refugees in the region had eased, an agency official said.

[10] The official said the Red Cross would restrict is operation to providing medical care for the estimated 90,000 refugees residing in camps on the Thai side of the frontier. UNICEF would terminate its relief operation in the area early in 1981, he added.

[11] U.N. relief agency officials in Pnompenh said more than 300,000 Cambodian refugees had returned to their homeland from Thailand. Laos and Vietnam, it was reported Nov. 13. About 175,000 of them had come from the Thai-Cambodian border region.

Vietnam Conflict

[12] **Border Battle.** Heavy fighting raged near the Thai-Cambodian border Jan. 25-31 between combined Vietnamese and Cambodian forces and guerrillas of the ousted Cambodian government of Pol Pot. Many of the clashes occurred in an area close to Cambodian refugee camps straddling the Thai-Cambodain frontier, the U.S. State Department reported Jan. 30.

[13] **China Promises to Help Guerrillas.** Chinese Premier Hua Kuo-feng March 9 promised his country's full support for Cambodian guerrillas fighting the Vietnamese-backed Cambodain government forces. Hua's pledge was made at a Peking banquet in honor of Khieu Samphan, premier of the ousted Cambodian government.

[14] At a news conference March 11 before leaving China, Khieu said, "all peace-loving and justice-loving countries ought to realize that it is in their interest to stop Vietnamese and Soviet expansionism" in Afghanistan and Cambodia.

[15] **U.N. Asks Vietnam to Quit Cambodia.** The U.N. General Assembly Oct. 22 approved a resolution calling on Vietnam to withdraw its troops from Cambodia. The vote was 97 to 23 with 22 abstentions. The assembly had approved a similar resolution in 1979.

[16] The latest resolution urged that the Cambodian people decide their own political future through U.N.-supervised elections. It proposed the holding of an international conference to bring the parties together to end the fighting in Cambodia. Vietnam Oct. 23 rejected the proposal for an international conference on Cambodia.

See also United Nations [28]; Vietnam, Socialist Republic of [4]

CANADA

[1] **Trudeau Reelected.** Pierre Elliott Trudeau was reelected prime minister of Canada Feb. 18 in a remarkable comeback. The Liberal party, defeated only nine months before, captured a firm majority of 146 seats in the 282-member House of Commons.

[2] The Progressive Conservatives were reduced to 103 seats from the 136 they held when Parliament was dissolved. The New Democratic Party increased its standing to 32 seats. The Social Credit Party, whose five members had been instrumental in bringing down former Prime Minister Joe Clark's government, was com-

pletely wiped out of Parliament. (One Quebec seat was not filled because of the death of a candidate. A Liberal was elected March 24 in a by-election to give Trudeau's party a total of 147 House seats.)

[3] With their popularity in opinion polls rising steadily since the May 1979 election, the Liberals, received 46.2% of the popular vote Feb. 18. The PC share of the popular vote was 31.7%, and the NDP received 19%. Other parties took the remaining 3.1%. Voter turnout was more than 70% despite the fierce Canadian winter. Of the 15.4 million persons eligible to vote, 10.8 million cast ballots.

[4] Clark's defeat was attributed mainly to his proposal to increase energy costs. The campaign was popularly referrred to as the "18-cent election" because of the PC plan to increase the excise tax on gasoline by 18 cents Canadian (15 U.S. cents). (A gallon of Canadian gasoline cost an average of 84 U.S. cents.) Another factor that harmed Clark according to observations in the press, was his image as an indecisive leader. His party had been hurt by changes of policy on tax reductions and a controversy over moving Canada's embassy in Israel to Jerusalem from Tel Aviv.

[5] **Trudeau's Policies**—In his post victory speech Feb. 19, Trudeau gave several indications of his general policies. He pledged to increase Canadian ownership of the countrys oil industry to 50% from 25% by 1990 and to increase the activities of Petro-Canada, the government-owned petroleum corporation. He said his government would seek to establish more control over foreign investors in Canada and keep close watch on the activities of foreign-owned enterprises.

[6] Trudeau's remarks seemed to indicate that "Canada is geographically situated between the two superpowers and. . . .is very much interested in the preservation of peace" between the U.S. and the U.S.S.R.

Breakdown of Canadian Vote by Provinces

	Liberals	PC	NDP
Newfoundland	5	2	–
Prince Edward Island	2	2	–
Nova Scotia	5	6	–
New Brunswick	7	3	–
Quebec*	73	1	–
Ontario	52	38	5
Manitoba	2	5	7
Saskatchewan	–	7	7
Alberta	–	21	–
British Columbia	–	16	12
Yukon Territory	–	1	–
Northwest Territories	–	1	1
Total	**146**	**103**	**32**

*The election in one riding (district) was postponed because of the death of a candidate.

[1] **Trudeau Sworn In, Names Cabinet.** Trudeau was sworn in March 3 as Canadian prime minister, formally assuming his fourth term in office. He also announced his Cabinet appointments, which included many of his close colleagues in past Liberal governments.

[8] The Cabinet had a distinctly left-of-center and nationalist tone, according to observers cited in press reports. Especially indicative of Trudeau's intentions was the appointment of Herbert Gray as minister of industry, trade and commerce. Gray had been the creator in 1974 of the legislation that established the Foreign Investment Review Agency, which examined all proposed foreign takeovers of Canadian industry.

[9] Trudeau faced a significant political problem in balancing his Cabinet among the provinces. No Liberals had been elected to the House of Commons from either Saskatchewan, Alberta or British Columbia, Canada's increasingly affluent and dissatisfied western provinces. The prime minister was forced to pick Cabinet member from the Senate, an appointed body with little power, in order to get Cabinet representation for those three provinces. (The three senators were: Bud Olson of Alberta, Raymond Perrault of British Columbia and Hazen Argue of Saskatchewan.)

[10] Another development was the return of Francis Fox to the Cabinet. Fox, formerly solicitor general, had been forced to resign in 1978 for secretly obtaining an abortion for a woman he had an affair with. Fox was named secretary of state and minster of communications.

[11] **Parliament Opens; Throne Speech Read.** Prime Minister Trudeau April 14 pledged to increase Canadian control over business and resources. The objectives of the Liberal government were read to the opening session of Canada's 32nd Parliament by Governor General Edward Schreyer, representative of Queen Elizabeth II, Canada's official head of state.

[12] Trudeau's program indicated that the federal government would play a more active role in shaping Canada's economy than previously. But the prime minister promised at the same time to reduce Ottawa's budget deficit. Ottawa's $11.23 billion deficit would be reduced gradually, Trudeau pledged, not by immediate and massive cuts.

[13] A Liberal shift to the left was evident in Trudeau's pledge to seek more Canadian control of business. He said Ottawa would double Canadian ownership of the oil industry to 50% from 25% by 1990, a pledge he had made during his election campaign. The Foreign Investment Review Agency, which examined takeovers of Canadian businesses by foreign companies would be given more power, and approval of foreign takeovers would be harder to obtain than in the past.

[14] **Constitutional Talks End in Failure.** Prime Minister Pierre Elliott Trudeau and the premiers of Canada's 10 provinces Sept. 13 ended six days of constitutional discussions without reaching agreement on any point.

[15] Trudeau, who reminded his colleagues that "Canada is the only independent country in the world that cannot amend its own constitution," had vowed to "go to London" to claim the document. (Canada's constitution,

[16] (Canada's constitution, the British North America Act, was an act of the British Parliament, which had technical sovereignty over it and sole authority to amend it, usually done at the request of Canadian governments. It had never been brought to Canada, or "patriated," because federal and provincial leaders traditionally differed over how authority was to be shared between them.)

[17] Federal officials had earlier called the Ottawa meeting – the culmination of a summer-long series of discussions on the constitutional question – "a last chance" to change the Canadian constitutional system. They argued that the federal government, with the support of many provincial premiers, had promised quick and decisive action on a new federal structure in their successful campaign for a "no" vote in Quebec province's May referendum on sovereignty/association.

[18] At the Ottawa gathering, all the provincial leaders seemed in favor of the principle of patriating the constitution. However, several of them, including Quebec's Rene Levesque and Newfoundland's Brian Peckford, argued that patriation would be a meaningless gesture if unaccompanied by substantial power-sharing arrangements between the central government and the provinces.

[19] At issue were several points of disputed authority, including questions of fisheries, resources, communications, marriage and divorce laws, and responsibility-sharing for national affairs and institutions. The most controversial points were Trudeau's proposals for a U.S.-style bill of rights and for strengthening the country's economic unity, which in effect meant greater economic centralization.

[20] Seven of the 10 provincial premiers Sept. 10 objected to putting basic human rights, which both the federal and provincial governments already provided for in ordinary legislation, into documents that would make them

strictly the responsiblity of the courts. The provincial leaders said that would effectively strip the population of its voice in social issues by depriving elected representatives of any responsibility. Chief among the proposed rights was a provision guaranteeing language rights for minorities.

[21] Trudeau also proposed restrictions on the provinces' economic powers particularly over actions that hindered the free movement of persons, goods, services and capital throughout the country. Only one province, Ontario, supported the prime minister, it was reported Sept. 12, while the leaders of the other nine asserted their rights to legislate and administer in favor of their residents for preferences in jobs, contracts and pricing of natural resources.

[22] The Ottawa talks were originally scheduled to last five days. After four days of televised negotiations that were often heated, the Canadian leaders Sept. 12 moved behind closed doors in the hopes privacy would make agreement easier. In a last-minute attempt to forge agreement, the talks were extended to a sixth day, and the session was televised. Some of the participants at the Sept. 13 session insisted the week's meeting had not been a failure and pointed to the near agreement reached by both sides on certain points. However, Prime Minister Trudeau, indicating he was not prepared to make light of the differences and the threat he perceived to national interests, said, "The provinces agreed to ask for more power from the federal government and thought the federal government should give in. This is what I was asked to do and this is what I cannot do."

[23] **Budget, Energy Plan Introduced.** Finance Minister Allan MacEachen Oct. 28 introduced the government's budget for 1981 and a package of proposals for a drastic restructuring of the Canadian energy industry.

[24] The budget, the Liberals' first since reattaining power in February, was presented in pessimistic tones by the minister. He forecast a drop in the production of goods and sevices in the country as well as an overall inflation rate of 10%. He also predicted an 8.5% unemployment rate in 1981. MacEachen presented an anti-inflation package that included restraints on federal government spending and continued tight money policies. He also pledged to reduce the budget deficit, which was projected at C$13.7 billion for the year.

[25] The National Energy Program, as the energy proposals were called, was aimed at developing Canadian self-sufficiency in energy by 1990. At the same time, it was designed to increase Canadian ownership of oil and natural gas assets in the country. Canada currently imported approximately one-quarter of its total oil requirement and owned or controlled eight of the 25 largest oil and natural gas companies operating in the country.

[26] **Heated Opposition Provoked**—The federal budget and energy proposals sparked heated parliamentary debate and a chorus of opposition from provincial leaders.

[27] Both opposition parties in the federal parliament Oct. 29 criticized the energy proposals and tabled motions for a vote of no-confidence. They also deplored what they said was the absence of budget measures for adequately dealing with inflation and unemployment.

Economy

[28] **1979 Corporate Profits Up.** Corporate profits had increased by 40.4% during 1979, according to a survey of 115 Canadian companies published Feb. 7. The increase over 1978 was larger than anticipated.

[29] Total profits of the 115 companies were C$6.1% billion. Economists had expected an increase of only 20% during 1979. (For 1978, corporate profits rose 24.6% over 1977.) Mining and chemical companies surveyed led the

list of profit-making companies. The six base metals companies surveyed had a total profit that was 159.9% higher than in 1978. The four chemical companies in the report had increased their profits by 168.5% over 1978.

[30] **Minimum Wage to Increase.** The minimum wage covering workers in industries under federal jurisdiction would rise C60¢ an hour by May 1981, it was reported Aug. 11. It was the first minimum wage hike in four years.

[31] The wage hike was to be implemented in two stages: the current minimum wage of C$2.90 would rise to C$3.25 an hour as of Dec. 1, and to C$3.50 an hour effective May 1, 1981. The minimum wage for employees 17 and under would rise to C$3.00 and C$3.25 from C$2.65. Industries subject to the federal increase included air, interprovincial highway and rail transport, banking, broadcasting and telephone operations.

[32] **GNP Grows Slightly.** Canadian economic output, as measured by gross national product, grew .4% in the quarter ending Sept. 30, according to Statistics Canada figures reported Dec. 6.

[33] Real (inflation-adjusted) GNP for the July-September quarter rose to a seasonally adjusted annual rate of C$129.94 billion. The .4% increase, the first rise in Canadian GNP in three quarters, followed successive declines of .6% and 1.1%.

[34] ***Umemployment.*** The number of persons unemployed declined in November to 853,000, approximately 7.3% of the Canadian workforce, according to Statistics Canada figures reported Dec. 10. The seasonally adjusted November rate was the lowest reported for any month since December 1979, when it was 7.1%.

[35] **Dollar Hits 47-Year Low.** The Canadian dollar Dec. 16 dropped to 82.69 U.S. cents, its lowest value relative to U.S. currency since the Depression of the 1930s.

[36] By the end of the month, however, the Canadian dollar had climbed back to 84 U.S. cents, the lower end of its normal trading range. The Canadian dollar hovered around the 84 cent level for over a week, finishing the year on Dec. 31 at 83.77 U.S. cents.

Separatism

[37] **Quebec Votes 'No.'** Quebec voters May 20 rejected by a margin of 58.2% to 41.8% a proposal to make Quebec independent from Canada.

[38] An estimated 54% of French-speaking Quebecers joined 80% of the English Canadians and other ethnic groups in the province to defeat the referendum. Turnout was high, at 84.3% of the 4.3 million voters, reflecting the intense passions aroused by the separation debate.

[39] THe referendum was defeated in 96 of the province's 110 electoral districts. The final (unofficial) vote was 2,140,814 opposed and 1,475,509 in favor. Conceding defeat at 9:30 that evening, Quebec Premier Rene Levesque said the Parti Quebecois "must accept" the federalists' victory. He warned Ottawa against "imposing changes on Quebec that are not in harmony with what Quebecers have been demanding for the past 40 years." The provincial government, he continued, "will be extremely careful to safeguard its rights and powers."

[40] Prime Minister Pierre Elliot Trudeau issued a low-keyed response to the referendum results. "We have all lost a bit as a result of this referendum," he said in Ottawa. "Having fought for Canada for so long, I should be extremely happy with the results, but I can't help thinking of those who voted 'yes,' who fought with such conviction and who must give up their dreams and bow to the will of the majority tonight."

[41] Trudeau said the result "signals the end of a long period of uncertainty, of doubt, of strained relations between Quebec and other provinces and French and English-speaking Canadians." Now, he added, "we must not

delay in rebuilding our house and responding to the new needs of the family of Canadians." (Quebec's dispute with Ottawa was the most visible of the federal-provincial quarrels, but it was not the only one. Oil-rich western provinces like Alberta and Saskatchewan feuded with Ottawa over control of resource prices, while poorer provinces like Newfoundland and Nova Scotia wanted a greater share of federal benefit and job-creation programs.)

[42] **Bilingualism Still Not Working.** The Canadian government was still failing to promote bilingualism, Official Languages Commissioner Maxwell Yalden charged. He presented his annual report to Parliament April 22.

U.S. Relations

[43] **Acid Rain Pact.** An agreement to try to curb the acid rain that had destroyed fish, crops, and forests on both sides of the border was signed August 5 in Washington by U.S. Secretary of State Edmund Muskie and Canadian Ambassador Peter Towe.

[44] The agreement called for vigorous enforcement of existing anti-pollution standards, and established five work groups to prepare a new air quality treaty.

[45]**New Tax Treaty**—Finance Minister Allan MacEachen and U.S. Treasury Secretary G. William Miller Sept. 26 signed a new bilateral tax treaty, concluding eight years of negotiations.

[46] Both countries agreed to reduce withholding tax (applied by one country on domestically-generated income earned by residents of the other one) from 15% to 10%. They also agreed for the first time to split withholding taxes on pensions paid to cross-border residents.

[47] **Canadians, Americans Compared.** Significant differences between Canadians and Americans were disclosed in a study released July 16 by Statistics Canada.

[48] The study showed that the median annual income of Canadians passed that of Americans in 1976, leveling off at slightly above US$15,000, an increase of 55% from 1965. American income grew only 19% during the same period, to just less than US$15,000.

[49] Canadians were found to be younger on the average than Americans due to a higher birth rate and a larger number of immigrants. (Immigrants tended to be younger than the average age of a population.) The median age of Canadians in 1976 was 27.8 years old, compared with the American median of 29 years. The study showed that there were proportionally more immigrants in Canada than the U.S., and many of the immigrants in Canada had emigrated from the U.S.: 5% of the American population of 218.5 million in 1970 was foreign-born, compared with 15% of Canada's 1971 population of 23.5 million.

In the study Canadians were also found to:

Have a divorce rate half the American rate: 2.4 divorces per 1,000 people, compared with 4.8 in the U.S.

Have a lower infant mortality rate: 15 deaths per 1,000 births compared with 16 per 1,000 in the U.S.

Be safer than Americans: murder and rape rates were three times higher in the U.S.

Have a higher suicide rate since 1971.

Have fewer opportunities for higher education: in 1976, 19% of all Canadians between the ages of 18 and 24 were enrolled in higher education. For the same group in the U.S., the rate was 24%.

Consume less than their American counterparts: in 1974, Americans bought cars and TVs at a rate twice that of Canadians.

Other Developments

[50] **'O Canada' Named National**

Anthem. Parliament June 27 declared *O Canada* the official national anthem despite a dispute over its English lyrics.

[51] Parliament passed the National Anthem Bill in time for Dominion Day, July 1. On that day, Canadians all over the country stopped at noon to sing the song, which had been the unofficial anthem for years.

[52] *O Canada* was orginally a French song written in 1880, with music by Calixa Lavallee of Quebec and French lyrics by Sir Adolphe Routhier. The French lyrics were not disputed. The English lyrics, written by Robert Stanley Weir of 1908, were in question because of the four opening lines. Weir's lyrics were not a translation of the French.

O Canada! Our home and native land,
True patriot love in all thy sons command.
With glowing hearts we see thee rise,
The true North strong and free!

[53] The reference to "native land" was disputed by immigrants for whom Canada was not a native land; "sons" was labelled sexist by women's rights groups; western Canadians felt sighted by "the true North," and easterners demanded equal space with westerners. Another group of Canadians preferred *God Save the Queen* as a national anthem. Officially, *O Canada* would be the national anthem and *God Save the Queen* the royal anthem.

[54] **Thomson Wins Control of FP Chain.** Thomson Newspapers Ltd. Jan. 11 bought FP Publications Ltd. for C$164.7 million after a hectic round of bidding. The victory gave Thomson, a leading owner of North Americn and British newspspers, control of eight daily Canadian papers, including the influential Toronto *Globe and Mail.* With the acquisition of FP, Thomson owned 127 newspapers, among them the *Times of London* and its sister publication the *Sunday Times.*

[55] **Two Major Newpapers Closed**—Two of Canada's most important daily newpapers shut down permanently Aug. 27.

[56] The Ottawa *Journal,* with 375 employees, ceased publication shortly after midnight, leaving the federal capital with only one English-language newspaper. The 95-year-old *Journal,* owned by Thomson Newspapers Ltd., had been losing money since 1976. The 77,000-circulation daily had lost C$3.4 million in 1979, and had incurred an equally large deficit in the first eight months of 1980. The 90-year-old Winnipeg, *Tribune,* owned by Southam Inc., also closed down Aug. 27. The 106,000-circulation daily, employing 370 persons, had lost more than C$13 million between 1975 and 1979.

See also Economy (International); Iran [8-12]; Ku Klux Klan (KKK) [3-4]

CANCER—*See* Environment [11]

CARIBBEAN—*See* Immigration

CARTER, Billy

[1] The Billy Carter affair of 1980 was not quite a scandal. The President's brother registered as an agent of Libya. A Senate subcommittee held hearings in the case and issued a report critical of President Carter and leading member of the Administration. However, the panel found no evidence of illegal activity. The President's conduct also was criticized by the Justice Department in another report released a few days before the election.

[2] **Billy Carter Files as Libyan Agent.** Billy Carter, the President's brother, July 14 registered with the Justice Department as an agent of Libyan government. He disclosed he had received more than $220,000 in payments from the North African country in 1980.

[3] Carter had been ordered to register by the U.S. District Court in Washington. The Justice Department had charged that Carter had violated the Foreign Agents Registration Act

by failing to report activities he had undertaken on behalf of the Libyans since 1978.

[4] Carter acknowledged receiving $220,000 in two installments from the Libyans. He termed the money a loan, but his lawyers said no repayment plan had been arranged.

[5] **Senate Panel to Investigate.** A Senate subcommittee was established July 24 to investigate Billy Carter's role as a paid agent for Libya. Sen. Birch Bayh (D, Ind.) was named chairman of the panel, which would consist of five Democrats and four Republicans. A White House statement issued later that day pledged full cooperation with the probe.

[6] The move for a Senate inquiry had gained impetus after the disclosure July 22 that the White House had used Billy Carter as a liaison to the Libyans in an effort to gain release of the U.S. hostages in Iran.

[7] **Controversy Grows.** Information about the Billy Carter case continued to come out in bits and pieces July 25-30, each bit seemingly more damaging to President Carter.

[8] These were among the developments:

Attorney General Benjamin Civiletti, despite repeated prior statements to the contrary, disclosed July 25 that he had spoken to President Carter about his brother Billy Carter's case on June 17. That was after the department had learned of the $220,000 payment to Billy Carter by the Libyan government but before Billy Carter had registered as an agent of that government.

President Carter, who had described his brother's dealings with the Libyans as inappropriate, acknowledged July 30 he had discussed with Billy Carter classified State Department cables concerning Billy's Libyan trip in 1978.

A Justice Department official, Joel Lisker, said July 30 that Billy Carter had lied about payments he had received from Libya and the "veracity" of his registration declarations, therefore, had been called into question.

[9] In his first public remarks on the situation, the President July 29 said he had no doubt the "complete disclosure of the facts" would show that his brother had not influenced him in his decisions toward Libya and that no one had tried to interfere with the Justice Department inquiry.

[10] **Billy Did Get Cable from Carter—**Billy Carter had received a copy of a State Department cable concerning his visit to Libya in 1978, it was disclosed Aug. 1. Originally Billy had claimed, then denied, having ever received a cable. The denial had been supported by the White House.

[11] Lawyers of Billy, however, came up with a copy of a cable. It was marked "confidential" and bore a note from President Carter saying, "To Billy, you did a good job under the 'dry' circumstances!" It was signed, "Jimmy."The note was a reference to Libyan prohibition on alcoholic beverages and to the content of the cable, which reported that there had been "no negative fallout" from Billy's visit to Libya.

[12] **President's Report.** President Carter denied Aug. 4 any wrongdoing, aside possibly from bad judgment, in his relationship with his brother, Billy Carter, and Billy's dealing with the Libyan government.

[13] The President sent a 13,000-word report to the Senate panel investigating the controversy. The report also was made public and President Carter spent a greater part of a televised new conference Aug. 4 fielding tough questions on the subject. The report to the Senate included items from the President's personal diary and subsidiary statements from several top aides.

[14] In his effort to lay the Billy Carter case to rest, the President made these points:

The President tried repeatedly to have Billy mute his contract with the Libyans and he opposed Billy's second trip to Libya, in September 1979.

He had not known of the Libyan

payments to Billy until after Billy filed as a foreign agent on July 14. Carter conceded, in reply to a query, that "it occurred to me" that his brother might seek financial benefit from his Libyan connection. In his report, the President denied that any of the Libyan money would find its way to him or the trust that operated the Carter family business.

There had been nothing reprehensible about a brief conversation he had with Attorney General Benjamin Civiletti on June 17. Civiletti had told him it was "foolish" for Billy not to register as a foreign agent, since if he did there would be no punishment or prosecution. The President insisted the conversation stopped there, that he had not repeated it to Billy or anyone else.

The President made the decision, on a suggestion from his wife, Rosalynn, to use Billy to set up a meeting with a Libyan representative to help gain release of the American hostages in Iran. That "may have enhanced Billy's stature in the minds of the Libyans," the President conceded, and therefore it "may have been bad judgement."

Billy was a "colorful personality" who was "thrust into the public limelight when I was elected." The President, it was clear from his personal notes, was concerned about his brother's health and personal problems throughout this period. He was close to his brother, he said, and they loved each other.

[15] **Senate Probe Opens.** The Senate subcommittee investigation of Billy Carter and his role as a Libyan agent opened uneventfully with background hearings Aug. 4 and 6 on U.S.-Libyan relations and U.S. policy concerning foreign agents.

[16] Billy Carter testified Aug. 21-22. He assured the panel he had never attempted to influence U.S. policy on behalf of Libya nor had he been asked to do so by the government of Libya.

[17] The major points of his testimony Aug. 21 were that:

Billy Carter (left) confers Aug. 22 with his attorney, Henry S. Ruth (right) during appearance before Senate Judiciary subcommittee.

The $220,000 he received from the Libyans was an advance on a $500,000 loan he was hoping to get. There was no formal loan agreement made for the money. He had spent much of the money, mostly to pay off debts.

The election of his brother to the presidency had changed his own life drastically. He could no longer live the life of "a typical small-town businessman." His mounting financial problems has forced him to cast about for a source of income, such as from the Libyan connection.

He had never discussed with the Libyans or anyone in the U.S. government the Lockheed C-130 cargo airplanes the Libyans purchased from the U.S. The planes had never been delivered because of a U.S. proscription against such sales to countries abetting terrorism.

[18] Billy Carter received some stern advice from subcommittee members during his appearance Aug. 22. It was clear, Sen. Max Baucus (D, Mont.) told him, "that a loan to the brother of a

President from a radical country does potentially compromise the President." Sen. Strom Thurmond (R, S.C.) could not understand, rhetorically, how "you became in debt to this government which has engaged in terrorism and assassination." "A lot of people went out to use you," Sen. Patrick Leahy (D, Vt.) summed up. "Quite frankly, you could have stopped it and didn't."

[19] The Senate investigation of Billy Carter's ties to Libya continued Sept. 4-17 with testimony from Justice Department officials and President Carter's counsel and national security adviser.

[20] **Senate Group Issues Critical Report.** The Senate subcommittee Oct. 2 issued a report critical of President Carter and top Administration members in their handling of the Billy Carter case. But the panel found no illegal or clearly unethical activity by federal officials.

[21] Billy Carter's activity "was contrary to the interests of the President and the U.S. and merits severe criticism," the panel concluded. President Carter was faulted for having failed to make clear to Libya that it "should not expect to gain any influence in the United States by cultivating" a relationship with his brother. The panel expressed "significant concern" about the transmission of intelligence information during the case by Attorney General Benjamin Civiletti, National Security Adviser Zbigniew Brzezinski and Central Intelligence Agency Director Stansfield Turner.

[22] ***Justice Department Report Criticizes President***—An internal Justice Department report critical of the response made by President Carter to the department's probe of his brother Billy's ties with Libya was circulated a few days before the election.

[23] News accounts of the report appeared after it was sent to Congress Oct. 29. The White House replied to the criticism Oct. 30 and again Nov. 1 when it was officially released by the Senate subcommittee that investigated the matter. Administration officials said there had been no attempt to delay the probe.

[24] The report contended that the President had not cooperated fully with the department's probe. It said requests for access to his diary and personal notes had not been granted and several interviews with the President had been canceled. The report also accused Attoney General Benjamin Civiletti of "dissembling" on the case and Billy Carter of withholding information and of lying.

CARTER, Jimmy (James Earl Jr.)

[1] **State of Union Address: Carter Warns Soviet Union.** President Carter gave warning Jan. 23 that the U.S. was prepared to go to war if necessary to protect the oil-supply routes of the Persian Gulf region. The warning, directed at the Soviet Union, was contained in a State of the Union address to a joint session of Congress.

[2] "An attempt by any outside force to gain control of the Persian Gulf region will be regarded as an assault on the vital interests" of the U.S., Carter declared. "And such an assault will be repelled by use of any means necessary, including military force."

[3] The President said he was planning to have the Selective Service System "revitalized" so that national registration for the draft could begin and future mobilization needs could be met rapidly "if they arise." He believed that the volunteer forces were adequate for current defense needs, and he hoped that it would not become necessary to impose the draft. But "we must be prepared for that possibility" he said.

[4] The President also asked Congress to remove "unwarranted restraints" on U.S. intelligence-gathering capabilities. He called for "quick passage of a new charter to define the legal authority and accountability of

President Carter Jan. 23 delivers State of the Union message to a joint session of Congress. Vice President Walter F. Mondale is behind the President, House Speaker Thomas P. O'Neill Jr. at right.

our intelligence agencies."

[5] Carter touched on domestic issues, notably the need to strengthen the economy, but the address was dominated by the world scene. He concentrated his view of the world scene upon the Soviet attempt "to subjugate" Afghanistan and the "terrorism and anarchy" in Iran where 50 Americans were being held hostage. He stressed that the "Iranian quarrel with the United States" was "unwarranted" and that "the real danger to their nation lies to the north in the Soviet Union and from the Soviet troops now in Afghanistan."

[6] **Reaction**—Arab nations in the Persian Gulf area were almost unanimously critical of Carter's pledge to protect Western interests in the region. His State of the Union address was widely interpreted as a pretext for U.S. interference in the region's internal affairs.

[7] "The people of this region are perfectly capable of preserving their own security and stability," remarked Kuwaiti Minister of State of Cabinet Affairs Abdel Aziz Hussein Jan. 25. "The gulf must remain aloof from conflicts between superpowers and free from superpower military presence."

[8] Iraq charged that the U.S. policy was meant to "justify and pave the way for military interference" in the Persian Gulf. The Palestine Liberation Organization added that the speech was an example of "American arrogance, hegemony and gunboat policy."

[9] Only Saudi Arabian Crown Prince Fahd expressed approval of Carter's stand. In an interview published Jan. 26, he said the President "has understood the Arab cause. . . ." He expressed hope that this understanding would lead Carter to support the Palestinians.

[10] The Soviet Union Feb.2 denied that it had any intentions of seeking control of the Persian Gulf. A commentary in *Pravda*, the Soviet Communist Party newspaper, declared that the "Soviet Union has never had and does

not have now any intention to push its way to warm seas."

[11] **U.S. Needs Allied Help, Carter Says.** The U.S. alone could not protect the Persian Gulf region from a Soviet take-over, President Carter admitted Jan. 29. Speaking to visiting editors in the White House, he said, "I don't think it would be accurate for me to claim that at this time or in the future we expect to have enough military strength and enough military presence there to defend the region unilaterally."

[12] Carter stressed that it was important for the nations in the Persian Gulf area to take the initiative in opposing Soviet expansion. He also indicated that Western Europe and Japan were expected to coordinate their policies with U.S. interests in the region.

[13] **U.S. Envoy Cautions Soviets.** Former Defense Secretary Clark Clifford warned the Soviet Union Jan. 31 that it would provoke a war by moving toward the Persian Gulf. Clifford made the remark in New Delhi, where he had been sent by President Carter to reassure Indian officials about the Administration's plans to resume military aid to Pakistan.

[14] Clifford said he was sending the Soviets a "message" from President Carter, that "they must know that if part of their plan is to move toward the Persian Gulf that means war."

[15] Clifford's statement was challenged Feb. 1 and 2 by Secretary of State Cyrus Vance and U.S. Senate Majority Leader Robert Byrd (D, W.Va.). Testifying before a Senate Appropriations subcommittee, Vance said Clifford's words were "more dramatic than I would have used." Sen. Byrd said that Clifford had gone beyond Carter's warning to the U.S.S.R. The senator said he didn't think Clifford would "find very many here on the [Capitol] Hill who would agree with that statement. . . I don't think there's any good purpose to be served by escalating in advance on hypothetical courses of action."

Other Developments

[16] **Carter's Net Worth Declines.** President Carter's net worth declined to $893,304.35 as of Dec. 31, 1979 from just above $1 million a year earlier, according to a White House statement released April 15. A trust, formed around assets from the Carter family farm and peanut warehouse operation in Plains, Ga., had dropped in value from $784,345.45 to $529,332.10.

[17] **Carter Looks to Memoirs, Fishing.** President Carter said Nov. 12 he would return to his home town of Plains, Ga. after leaving office on Jan. 20, 1981 and begin writing his memoirs. Another thing he intended to do, he said, was "to become a good fly-fisherman."

[18] **Carter Breaks Collar Bone.** President Carter broke his collar bone Dec. 27 while skiing near Camp David, Md.

See also Afghanistan [2-6, 18-20, 22]; Agriculture; Appointments & Resignations [2-4]; Automobiles [1, 11-12]; Aviation [1]; Banks & Banking [1]; Black Americans [6]; Budget [1, 4, 9, 17-22]; Business [11]; Carter, Billy; China [24-25, 33]; Civil Disorders [6-7]; Congress (U.S.) [8]; Cuba [11-13]; Defense (U.S.) [1-5, 30, 38]; Disarmament [4-6]; Draft Registration [1-10]; Economy (U.S.([1-2, 4, 19-20,. 23-25, 27-32]; Education [6]; Elections [3-7, 10, 12, 14-16, 18-19, 31, 42-43, 47-53, 55-58, 66, 69-73, 75-76, 80-82]; Energy [1-5, 19, 11-12]; Environment [8]; Foreign Aid; France [27]; Germany, West [5]; Housing [8-10]; India [32-34]; In- 27-28, 44, 51, 53-54, 56, 63-65, 68-70, 83, 104]; Iraq [19-21]; Middle East [47-51, 56-57]; Oil [7-10, 19, 21-27]; Poland [40-41, 45, 73]; Press [11-15]; Railroads [1-4]; Refugees [1, 6]; Steel [8-10]; Thailand [3-4]; Trade & Tariffs [2]; Trucking [2]; Veterans' Affairs [2, 4]; Volcanos [10]; Weather [3]; Wildlife [1-3]

CASTRO, FIDEL—*See* Cuba [3]

CATHOLIC CHURCH,

ROMAN—*See* El Salvador [13-16, 31-33]; Poland [23, 44, 51, 82]; Religion

CENSUS (U.S.)

[1] **Court Orders Adjustments.** U.S. District Judge Horace Gilmore of Detroit ruled Sept. 25 that the 1980 census had undercounted the nations's population, particularly minorities. He ordered that the figures be adjusted upward before release of the date.

[2] The ruling was made on a suit brought by the city of Detroit. The suit was supported by dozens of other cities, all of which also stood to lose Congressional representation and billions of dollars of federal aid as a result of undercounting.

[3] The Census Bureau admitted that a certain amount of undercounting occurred in its decennial population counts. It put the undercount at 3.3% of the total 1950, 2.7% in 1960 and 2.5% in 1970. The undercount in 1970, some 5.1 million persons, affected only 1.9% of the nation's whites but 7.7% of its blacks, the bureau reported. The disproportion was cited in Gilmore's ruling. The undercount "results in dilution of plaintiff's vote relative to the votes of whites," he said.

[4] Other suits against the census count had been filed by New York, Chicago, Philadelphia and Newark, N.J. New York City was contending that 800,000 of its residents were missed in the current count. Cook County, which included Chicago, claimed an undercount of 200,000, Philadelphia 150,000, Cleveland 43,000 and Boston 140,000.

[5] **1980 Figures Reported.** The Census Bureau reported the 1980 population figures to President Carter Dec. 31. The final national population count was 226,504,825. It was 11.4% more than the 1970 figure of 203,302, 031.

[6] A congressional reapportionment based on the 1980 count would shift 17 seats in Congress to states in the South and West from states in the Northeast and Midwest. Official certification of the 1980 census, which was required by law to be done by Dec. 31, had been held up by a federal court ruling that there had been a "disproportionate undercount" in New York's population. Judge Henry Werker, who made the ruling Dec. 23, ordered an adjustment of the figures for city and state.

[7] The Census Bureau was appealing the decision of the U.S. Court of Appeals for the Second Circuit in New York. The bureau also sought relief from the U.S. Supreme Court. It asked Justice Thurgood Marshall for an emergency order to allow the census count to be certified. Marshall opposed granting the order. He took the issue to the full court, which ruled, 7-1, Dec. 30 that the bureau could report the final count to the President while Judge Werker's order was under appeal. Marshall was the dissenter. Justice John Stevens did not participate in the ruling. (A similar federal court ruling in Detroit against the 1980 census court also was under a Supreme Court stay, granted by Justice Potter Stewart.)

Official Census Figures
Dec. 31, 1980

Below are results of the 1980 census as submitted to President Carter Dec. 31. Population is listed first, then the number of representatives each state will have in the 98th Congress, which will be elected in 1982, and on the right the number of representatives gained or lost as a result of the 1980 census:

Alabama	3,890,061	7	
Alaska	400,481	1	
Arizona	2,717,866	5	+1
Arkansas	2,285,513	4	
California	23,668,562	45	+2
Colorado	2,888,834	6	+1
Connecticut	3,107,576	6	
Delaware	595,225	1	
D.C.	637,651	0	
Florida	9,739,992	19	+4
Georgia	5,464,265	10	
Hawaii	965,000	2	

Idaho	943,935	2	
Illinois	11,418,461	22	-2
Indiana	5,490,179	10	-1
Iowa	2,913,387	6	
Kansas	2,363,208	5	
Kentucky	3,661,433	7	
Louisiana	4,203,972	8	
Maine	1,124,660	2	
Maryland	4,216,446	8	
Massachusetts	5,737,037	11	-1
Michigan	9,258,344	18	-1
Minnesota	4,077,148	8	
Mississippi	2,520,638	5	
Missouri	4,917,444	9	-1
Montana	786,690	2	
Nebraska	1,570,006	3	
Nevada	799,184	2	+1
New Hampshire	920,610	2	
New Jersey	7,364,158	14	-1
New Mexico	1,299,968	3	+1
New York	17,557,288	34	-5
North Carolina	5,874,429	11	
North Dakota	652,695	1	
Ohio	10,797,419	21	-2
Oklahoma	3,025,266	6	
Oregon	2,632,663	5	+1
Pennsylvania	11,866,728	23	-2
Rhode Island	947,154	2	
South Carolina	3,119,208	6	
South Dakota	690,178	1	-1
Tennessee	4,590,750	9	+1
Texas	14,228,383	27	+3
Utah	1,461,037	3	+1
Vermont	511,456	1	
Virginia	5,346,279	10	
Washington	4,130,163	8	+1
West Virginia	1,949,644	4	
Wisconsin	4,705,335	9	
Wyoming	470,816	1	
TOTAL	226,504,825	435	

CENTRAL INTELLIGENCE AGENCY (CIA)

[1] **CIA Disclosure Limits Upheld.** The Supreme court ruled, 6-3, Feb. 19 that a Central Intelligence Agency regulation prohibiting unauthorized publication by employees was legal. The case was *Snepp v. U.S.*

[2] The ruling came in a government suit against Frank W. Snepp, a former CIA agent who had contravened the regulation by writing a book about CIA operations in Vietnam, *Decent Interval.*

[3] A U.S. district court in 1978 had ruled in favor of the CIA and ordered Snepp to turn over to the government all profits from the book. The U.S. 4th Circuit Court of Appeals in 1979 had also upheld the CIA rule, but overturned the damage award on the ground that the government was not entitled to the profits because Snepp had not disclosed classified data in his book. (The CIA had made no such claim.)

[4] The Supreme Court upheld both the regulation and the award. In doing so, the high court did not address the First Amendment issue in the case. Snepp had maintained that the CIA rule violated his right of free speech through prior restraint. Instead, the high court, in an unsigned opinion, held that the regulation constituted a judicially enforceable contract that applied to the unsanctioned publishing of "any information," whether classified or not. Justices John Paul Stevens, Thurgood Marshall and William J. Brennan Jr. dissented.

[5] **Court Permits U.S. to Sue Agee.** U.S. District Court judge ruled April 1 that the U.S. Justice Department could sue Philip Agee, author of the two books exposing Central Intelligence Agency activities and employees. The Justice Department was seeking to recover all of Agee's profits from the books, *Dirty Work I* and *Dirty Work II.*

[6] Agee was living in West Germany, immune from prosecution by the U.S. government. But Judge Gerhard Gesell held that the former CIA agent lost his immunity when he filed suit with the Justice Department for the release of government documents under the Freedom of Information Act.

[7] ***Another Ex-Agent Sued***—The Justice Department March 3 started legal proceedings against John Stockwell, another former CIA agent. The department was seeking Stockwell's earnings from his book *In Search of Enemies: A CIA Story,* which was about CIA involvement in Angola in 1975-76.

[8] Stockwell had been a CIA agent from 1965-77. He had signed the pledge not to publish material about the agency without first obtaining CIA approval.

[9] Stockwell June 25 agreed out of court to pay the federal government all future profits from his book. The

government's suit originally sought all profits Stockwell had made from its publication. But the government agreed to forgo its claims, according to Stockwell's lawyer, because the author no longer had the $40,000 he had earned and because sales had tapered off.

[10] **CIA Admits Press, Clergy Use.** Central Intelligence Agency Director Stansfield Turner Feb. 21 testified that "in very limited occasions," he had waived his 1977 policy directive and allowed the use of journalists, clergymen and academics as CIA operatives.

[11] Turner revealed the CIA's use of individuals from the restricted groups in testimony before the Senate Select Committee of Intelligence. Turner and the CIA were opposing an attempt to place such prohibitions into law, arguing that some circumstances might warrant the use of journalists, clergymen, or professors, or their institutions.

[12] **Alleged CIA Agents Exposed.** *Covert Action Information Bulletin,* an anti-U.S. intelligence periodical, March 7 listed the names and "covers" of more than three dozen alleged Central Intelligence Agency agents it said were stationed overseas.

[13] *Covert Action,* which listed former CIA agent Philip Agee on its board of advisers, gave names and biographical information on 16 alleged CIA chiefs of station and 23 other alleged senior officers in numerous countries, including the Soviet Union and China. The publication claimed its material was researched from public documents. The Carter Administration had been joined by some congressmen in calling for the CIA charter to make such disclosures criminal acts.

See also Intelligence Issues [1-4]

CHAD

[1] **Heavy Fighting Shatters Truce.** An uneasy truce among Chad's warring factions ended March 22 as fighting erupted in Ndjamena. The death toll was estimated at more than 700 by March 25, according to reports from Westerners who had hurriedly left the capital.

[2] Forces loyal to President Goukouni Oueddei and Premier Hissene Habre fought each other with artillery and rocket fire. It was the most serious violence since August 1979, when the rival groups had agreed to form a government and end their continuous battles.

[3] About 400 whites were evacuated from Ndjamena March 24 by French military aircraft. They included all of the American personnel at the U.S. Embassy, including the ambassador. Other evacuees included West Germans, Dutch, French and Lebanese.

[4] Three French soldiers stationed in Chad were reported killed in fighting. The 1,200-men French force had been in the country since early 1979, but it did not intervene in the renewed strife. A Congolese peacekeeping unit had been in Chad since January, but it too stayed out of the conflict.

[5] **Factional Fighting Intensifies.** Factional fighting in Ndjamena grew more intense during April, as five separate cease-fire agreements failed to take hold. The latest cease-fire attempt April 8 lasted less than 24 hours.

[6] The truce was negotiated with the help of Gnassingbe Eyadema, president of Togo. He flew to Ndjamena April 5 and shuttled between President Goukouni Oueddei and Premier and Defense Minister Hissene Habre. After signing the agreement, Oueddei admitted that he had little hope that the truce would hold.

[7] Fighting resumed April 9, after 18 hours of peace. By the next day, more troops had reached Ndjamena. Vice President Wadal Abdelkadar Kamougue joined his troops to Oueddei's forces. Oueddei had received help March 31 from Foreign Minister Ahmat Acyl, whose faction was supported by Libya. Habre's guerrillas

were reinforced by more of his men from the north.

[8] (Kamougue was from the south, which was largely Christian and animist. Oueddei, Acyl and Habre were Moslems from Chad's barren north. The major factors in Chad's conflict were religious strife and personality clashes.)

[9] **French Troops Withdraw.** French troops completed their withdrawal from Chad May 16. They had been ordered to leave April 17, after helping evacuate Europeans from the war-torn country. The battle for control of Ndjamena continued despite efforts by other nations to achieve a truce.

[10] **Peace Parley Fails.** A peace conference aimed at ending the Chadian civil war was held in Togo Oct. 18-19 but failed to bring results. Held under the auspices of the Organization of African Unity, the conference brought together President Goukouni Oueddei and his opponent, Premier and Defense Minister Hissene Habre. The parley also was attended by representatives of Sierra Leone, Guinea and the People's Republic of the Congo.

[11] **Libyan Troops Occupy Capital.** Libyan tanks and troops Dec. 16 entered the Chadian capital of Ndjamena on behalf of the country's president after a week of intense fighting in the nation's civil war.

[12] The Libyan troops, supporting the forces of President Goukouni Oueddei, used heavy artillery and air power to force troops loyal to Hissene Habre, premier and defense minister, to abandon the city. Habre fled to the neighboring country of Cameroon, where he signed "with reservations" a cease-fire agreement worked out Nov. 28 under the auspices of the Organization of African Unity.

[13] The Libyan troops first entered the country in June but did not actually participate in the hostilities until Dec. 12. An estimated 2,500 Libyan troops, half of the Libyan force reported in Chad, took part in the push for the capital.

See also Africa [4]

CHATTANOOGA, TENN—*See* Civil Disorders [13-14]

CHEMISTRY—*See* Nobel Prizes [5-6]

CHICAGO—*See* Census (U.S.) [4]; City & State Affairs [10]; Women's Rights [6-7]

CHILE

[1] **High-Ranking Army Officer Assassinated.** Lt. Col. Roger Vergara Campos, 43, the director of Chile's army intelligence school, was shot to death in Santiago July 15 by four men disguised as workers. The assassins escaped. Chilean security forces attributed the murder to the clandestine Revolutionary Left Movement, led by Andres Pascal Allende, a nephew of the late President Salvador Allende Gossens.

[2] **Opposition to Pinochet Surfaces.** Opposition to the seven-year military rule of Chilean President Augusto Pinochet Ugarte surfaced in Santiago Aug. 27 when thousands of persons paraded through the streets shouting slogans against the general and the military government. It was the first open demonstration of opposition since Pinochet came to power in a coup Sept. 11, 1973.

[3] The demonstration in Santiago began when police refused to allow a large crowd to join 8,000 other persons attending a rally sponsored by former Chilean President Eduardo Frei. In a fiery speech, Frei denounced a forthcoming plebiscite to endorse a proposed constitution, which would allow Pinochet to retain the presidency until at least 1989. Frei called the military government a "fraud." On Aug. 8, Pinochet had announced that the vote on the proposed charter would be held

Sept. 11, the anniversary of the coup. A majority of votes in favor of the charter would mean that Pinochet would remain as president until 1989, after which he could conceivably be reelected for another eight years, until 1997.

[4] Further opposition to Pinochet's rule came from within the military Sept. 2, when air force Gen. Gustavo Leigh Guzman, a former member of the ruling junta, said that he would vote against the proposed constitution. He said that it would institutionalize military rule. Leigh pointed out that a person 18 years old would have to wait until he was 42 before he would gain the right to vote.

[5] ***Voters OK New Charter***—Voters in Chile Sept. 11 approved by a margin of more than two to one a new constitution that would allow Pinochet to remain president until 1989.

[6] Before casting his ballot in the nationwide plebiscite, Pinochet had said he would step down in 1989, even though the constitution provided that the first elected president could serve another six-year term. Approximately 68% of the electorate endorsed the proposed charter. Some 30% voted against it, and 2%, or about 165,000 votes were listed as void. The blank votes were counted as votes in favor of the new constitution.

[7] The new constitution replaced the 1926 charter, which Pinochet had suspended after coming to power in a coup Sept. 11, 1973. An eight-year "transition" period was to begin in March 1981. In 1989, the junta was to nominate a president whose candidacy would be voted on in a national referendum.

[8] **Rights Violations Seen Increasing.** Amnesty International, the London-based human rights organization, reported Sept. 8 that instances of arbitrary arrests and systematic torture in Chile had increased dramatically since the assassination July 15 of a high-ranking army officer. A detailed AI report said that since July 15, as many as 1,000 and possibly 2,000 persons had been arrested by the Chilean secret police.

Letelier Case

[9] **Court Overturns Letelier Convictions.** The U.S. Court of Appeals for the District of Columbia Sept. 15 overturned the convictions of three Cubans in the 1976 car-bombing deaths of former Chilean Foreign Minister Orlando Letelier and his colleague, Ronni K. Moffit, in Washington D.C.

[10] The court ordered new trials for two of the men, Guillermo Novo Sampol and Alvin Ross Diaz, because it said their convictions had been based on evidence given by jailmates who were acting as government informants. The court ruled that the evidence should not have been admissible in the trial. Its decision was based on a ruling June 16 by the U.S. Supreme Court that the government's use of jail informants violated a defendant's right to have a lawyer present while being questioned by the government.

[11] The court also found that Judge Barrington D. Parker should have granted the request of the third defendant, Ignacio Novo Sampol, for a separate trial because he had faced lesser charges—perjury and concealing information from prosecutors.

[12] **Letelier, Moffit Kin Awarded $5 Million.** A federal judge in Washington Nov. 5 awarded $4.9 million to the families of Letelier and Moffit.

[13] The judge said in a 15-page ruling that the Chilean government should pay $2.9 million of the damage award because the assassinations had been carried out by agents of the Chilean secret police, DINA. The remaining $2 million was to be paid by Juan Manuel Contreras, the former head of DINA, two of its agents, two Cuban exiles and an American, Michael Vernon Townley, who had planned and carried out the killings.

CHINA, People's Republic of

Government & Politics

[1] **Premier Hua Resigns.** Hua Guofeng (Kuo-feng) formally resigned Sept. 7 as premier of China but retained his post as chairman of the Communist Party. His intention to give up the premiership had been rumored for months and constituted a major shift in the country's leadership.

[2] Hua submitted his resignation to the National People's Congress, which had opened its annual session Aug. 30. In addition to the leadership change, a new policy regarding the economy and financial institutions was announced. [See below] In its closing meeting Sept. 10, the Congress accepted Hua's resignation and named Hua's choice of Deputy Premier Zhao Ziyang (Chao Chi-yang) as his successor. The appointment of Zhao, a former Communist Party chief of Sichuan (Szechwan) province, represented a victory for Deputy Premier Deng Xiaoping (Teng Hsiao-ping), China's supreme ruler and Zhao's mentor.

[3] In another major change, five deputy chairmen of the Standing Committee of Congress, whose ages averaged 84, resigned as part of the campaign to lower the age of the country's leaders. They were replaced by five men who averaged 65. Three new deputy premiers were appointed. They were Foreign Minister Huang Hua, 67, Zhang Aiping, 70, an army deputy chief of staff, and Yang Jingren, 62, a Chinese Moslem who headed the Nationalities Affairs Commission.

Among other actions taken at the final session:

■ Article 45 of the Constitution was abolished. The article, proclaimed by the late party Chairman Mao Tse-tung, had established the "four freedoms to speak out freely, air views fully, hold great debates and write" wall posters

Zhao Ziyang named Chinese premier Sept. 10.

criticizing government policy.

■ A new marriage law was enacted raising the minimum age to 22 for men and 20 for women, a two-year increase, in an effort to curb population growth. Requirements for divorce were eased.

■ Overseas Chinese were prohibited from holding both Chinese citizenship and citizenship of the country in which they resided.

■ A 33% tax was levied on foreign companies participating in joint ventures with the Chinese government in China.

■ China's first income tax law was instituted, but it would affect only foreigners in the country and about 21 Chinese artists and writers who earned high royalties.

[4] ***Profits, Local Control Stressed***— Finance Minister Wang Bingqain Aug. 30 announced the launching of a major program to revamp China's financial institutions and economic practices. The new policy was designed to promote economic growth by encouraging the profit motive.

[5] The program would be aimed primarily at individual entrepreneurs. Both farmers and workers were being encouraged to form cooperatives, business partnerships and individual enterprises such as family stores. Business tax laws, Wang said, were being changed to reduce tax burdens on such enterprises.

[6] On the basis of limited experiments in the previous two years, Wang continued, there would be an increased dispersal of economic authority by the central government to provinces, counties, communes and businesses. For example, banks would be operated independently and would be responsible for their own loans and cash flow. Also, investment in capital construction would have to be paid for in the form of interest on loans from banks, replacing interest-free financial assistance from the state.

[7] **Teng Yields Army Post.** Deputy Premier Teng Hsiao-ping, 77, had resigned as army chief of staff, the Foreign Ministry said Feb. 25. He was replaced by Yang Dechi, 70, formerly commander of the Kunming military region, bordering Vietnam.

[8] Teng had been named chief of staff in 1975, but was purged the following year, only to be reinstated in 1977. Teng had said in recent statements that he would like to give up some of his duties and be able to retire in five years.

[9] **Liu Shao-chi Rehabilitated.** The Chinese Communist Party's Central Committee had posthumously rehabilitated former chief of state Liu Shao-chi, it was announced Feb. 29 at the conclusion of a week-long meeting of the committee.

[10] Liu, who had been purged during the Cultural Revolution in the 1960s as Mao Tse-tung's chief rival, was described in a committee communique as "a great Marxist." The statement said that charges made during the Culture Revolution that Liu was a "renegade, traitor and scab" were unjustified.

[11] **Public Portraits of Mao Removed.** The Chinese Communist Party Central Committee Aug. 11 issued a directive calling for the removal of all but a few of the public portraits, slogans and poems of Mao Tse-tung because the practice was "lacking in political dignity."

[12] A further indication of Chinese efforts to bring an end to the worship of individual leaders came Aug. 16 with a Chinese Foreign Ministry announcement that portraits of Joseph Stalin, Karl Marx, Friedrich Engels and V. I. Lenin would also be removed from Tien An Men Square in the center of Peking.

Gang of Four Trial

[13] **Trial Starts.** The Gang of Four and six other defendants went on trial in Peking Nov. 20 on charges arising from their alleged excesses while in office during the Cultural Revolution in the 1960s.

[14] The details of the indictment had

been released by Chinese authorities in four installments between Nov. 15 and 18. The first portion, made public Nov. 15 by the Hsinhua news agency, said the 10 defendants had persecuted large numbers of officials while in office, plotted to assassinate Communist Party Chairman Mao Zedung, attempted to overthrow the state and planned "an armed rebellion in Shanghai," once a stronghold of radicals. The alleged crimes were among "48 specific offenses" committed by the 10 during the Cultural Revolution and up to Mao's death in 1976, the report said.

[15] Another portion of the indictment, made public Nov. 16, said the defendants were responsible for "persecuting to death" 34,380 persons during the Cultural Revolution. The third part of the indictment, disclosed Nov. 17, said that Lin Biao, his wife, his son and five senior generals had plotted to assassinate Mao in 1971. Lin's son, Lin Liguo, a deputy director of operations of the air force, died in a 1971 plane crash along with his parents, after their plot was uncovered.

Jiang Qing, widow of Mao Zedung, Nov. 20 listens to proceedings as trial begins in Peking.

[16] The fourth and final part of the indictment, released Nov. 18, said three members of the Gang of Four had planned an armed uprising in Shanghai shortly after Mao's death in September 1976 in an attempt to seize power. The three were Zhang Chunqiao, Yao Wenyuan and Wang Hongwen. Jiang Qing, Mao's widow, was not mentioned as part of the plot.

[17] ***Trial Developments***—Two members of the Gang of Four, Wang Hongwen and Yao Wenyuan, Nov. 24 admitted they had attempted to prevent Deng Xiaoping from becoming deputy premier in 1974. They said they had tried to persuade Mao not to appoint Deng to the post by hinting that Deng and Premier Zhou Enlai were plotting against Mao.

[18] Testifying for the first time at her trial, Jiang Qing Nov. 26 denied that she had tried to stop Mao from naming Deng as deputy premier in 1974, as charged in the indictment. Jiang's denial was in response to the prosecution's query as to whether she had invited the three other Gang of Four members to her home to discuss blocking Deng's nomination.

[19] Three of the 10 defendants testified Nov. 25 that they had taken part in a plot by the late Defense Minister Lin Biao to assassinate Mao in 1971. Two of them Huang Yongsheng, then army chief of staff, and Lin Zuopeng, former political commissar of the navy—said they had pased on information about Mao to Lin. The third defendant, Jiang Tengjiao, then political commissar of the Nanjing military region, said he had been appointed head of the conspiratorial group by Lin's son, Lin Liguo, at a secret meeting. Lin Liguo was believed to have actually organized the plot.

[20] **Death Sentence Demanded for Jiang.** A Chinese special high court in Peking Dec. 29 concluded the treason trial of the Gang of 4 and six other

defendants. Sentences were expected to be handed down in January 1981.

[21] In the final court session, the chief prosecutor demanded that Jiang be sentenced to death.

Economy

[22] **'79 Economic Report Issued.** China issued a report on its economic performance in 1979 that was the most comprehensive and detailed in many years, the Associated Press said May 1.

[23] The report noted a marked increase in the grain harvest in 1979. The 1979 havest was 332.1 million metric tons, up 9% from 1978. The 1980 grain target was set at 335.8 million metric tons. (A metric ton equalled 36.7 bushels of wheat or 49 bushels of rice.) Agricultural output combined with industrial production grew 8.5% in 1979, down from the 12.3% rate of growth registered in 1978.

[24] The report said that salaried workers had received pay increases averaging 7.6% in 1979, while peasants earned an 11.2% boost in the money they had been paid by their collectives. Inflation in 1979 grew at a rate of 2.3% while the inflation-adjusted value of retail sales increased by 12.4% in the year. China's overall foreign trade in 1979 rose 28% because of large increases in imports of technology, equipment and consumer goods. As a result, China had a trade deficit equivalent to $2.07 billion in 1979.

[25] **IMF Admits China, Expels Taiwan.** The International Monetary Fund voted April 17 to admit the People's Republic of China. China's quota with the IMF was set at $693 million, the equivalent of 550 million Special Drawing Rights (SDRS).

[26] Although not specifically mentioned in the announcement following the vote, the entrance of China into the IMF implied the expulsion of Taiwan. Taiwan was known to have completed arrangements to settle its outstanding debt with the IMF, about $158 million.

Defense

[27] **Long-Range Missile Tested.** China announced May 18 that it had successfully conducted its first test launch of an intercontinental ballistic missile. The rocket was believed to have been launched from a site in northern China and to have descended 6,000 miles (9,600 kilometers) distant in the South Pacific.

[28] **Atmospheric A-Test Conducted.** China Oct. 16 set off a nuclear explosion in the atmosphere, its first such test since December 1978.

[29] The blast, estimated at between 200,000 and 1 million tons of TNT, occurred at the Lop Nor test site in northwestern China. U.S. officials said there were little health danger to Americans from the blast fallout, which began to pass over the coast of the western U.S. Oct. 20.

U.S. & Soviet Relations

[30] **Technology Sales Approved.** The Carter Administration had approved the sale of military-related equipment and technology to China, U.S. Defense Secretary Harold Brown announced May 29. Weapons, however, were not included in the agreement, Brown emphasized.

[31] Export licenses would be granted for such equipment as air-defense radar, helicopters and transport aircraft, communications units and computers, the Defense Department said.

[32] ***Grain Pact***—The U.S. and China Oct. 22 signed an agreement under which China would purchase at least six million metric tons of wheat and corn a year from the U.S. for 1981 through 1984.

[33] **Carter Meets Hua in Tokyo.** President Carter met with Chinese Premier Hua Kuo-feng in Tokyo July 10. Both men were in the Japanese capital to attend memorial services for the late Premier Masayoshi Ohira.

[34] ***Soviets See Destabilization***—Responding to the Carter-Hua meeting, the Soviet Union July 10 asserted that the talks were aimed "at advancing the process of creating a U.S.-Japan-China tripartite alliance." Such a grouping, Moscow warned, "can seriously destabilize the situation in Asia."

[35] **China Cancels Soviet Talks.** The Chinese government announced Jan. 19 that it would no longer hold talks with the U.S.S.R. on improving relations. A Foreign Ministry statement said further meetings had been called off because of the Soviet invasion of Afghanistan.

[36] Only one formal round of talks had been held, and no movement toward improved relations resulted. It had been hoped that the negotiations would reduce tension along the Sino-Soviet border.

[37] **New Chinese Ambassador Arrives.** Yang Shouzheng arrived in Moscow April 20 to assume his post as China's ambassador.

[38] Conciliatory statements by both sides appeared in the press in early April. *Pravda*, the Soviet Communist Party newspaper, said April 7 that "a constructive solution" to the two countries' problems was possible. The previous week, a Chinese magazine had reaffirmed the Soviet Union's position as "a basically socialist country," despite previous Chinese accusations that the U.S.S.R. had deviated from the socialist path.

[39] **Sino-Soviet Trade Declines.** An annual Sino Soviet trade agreement signed in Peking June 6 showed a 15% drop over the previous accord.

[40] China's Hsinhua news agency, which reported the signing of the agreements, gave few details, but Japan's Kyodo news agency said trade between the two countries in 1980 would amount to about $375 million, down from $500 million in 1979. In recent years trade had increased significantly between the two nations from a low of $41 million in 1970. The pact was believed to provide for the continuation of barter trade between the two countries. Under this arrangement, China supplied foodstuffs and other basic commodities to the Soviet Union in exchange for motor vehicles, aircraft parts, and other manufactured goods.

See also Armaments (International) [1]; Cambodia [13-14]; Disarmament [1-3]; Disasters & Accidents [5-6]; Grain [1]; Hong Kong [1-2]; Human Rights [11, 18]; Vietnam, Socialist Republic of [2-7]

CHINA, Republic of (Taiwan)

[1] **China vs. New U.S.-Taiwan Pact.** A new U.S.-Taiwan agreement was signed in Washington Oct. 2. The pact was criticized by China Oct. 4 as granting special privileges to Taipei's representatives in the U.S. in "violation of the agreement between the United States and China."

[2] A U.S. State Department official said the agreement provided "non-diplomatic immunity" to persons assigned to the American Institute in Taiwan and the Taiwan Coordination Council for North American Affairs in Washington, the nongovernmental bodies of the two countries that signed the pact. The institute and council were set up by Taiwan and the U.S. to maintain trade and cultural relations.

[3] China's Hsinhua news agency said the agreement granted officials of the two organizations immunity from taxation or legal action while stationed in each other's country. This made the Taiwan and U.S. representatives "official diplomats in everything but name," the agency charged.

CHRISTIANS, EVANGELICAL

[1] **A Political Force.** The 1980 presidential campaign saw the emergence of conservative and ultraconservative evangelical Christians as an active political force in the U.S. with a

potential for influencing elections across the country.*

[2] Spurred by the belief that a sharp moral and spiritual decline was threatening American society, fundamentalist Christian groups had begun to take an activist role in politics. That development marked the abandonment of a long tradition of shunning organized political action.

[3] Among the social forces cited in the growth of evangelical political action was an apparent belief that fundamentalist Christian values on such issues as abortion, women's rights, divorce, family life, homosexuality, pornography and religion in the schools were no longer reflected in public policy.

[4] Much of the impetus behind the organization of this movement came from well-financed television and radio evangelists who were purchasing large blocs of prime time in major broadcast markets. Among the most prominent of these evangelists were the Reverends Jerry Falwell of Lynchburg, Va., Pat Robertson of Virginia Beach, Va. and James Robison of Fort Worth, Texas, whose gospel sermons were reaching large national audiences, particularly in the urban Midwest, the Deep South and the West.

THE REV. JERRY FALWELL

[5] Overall, an estimated 30 million to 65 million Americans were considered evangelical Christians. These included Protestants and Catholics, as well as persons who did not hold any church membership but retained the "born-again" religious beliefs of fundamentalist Christianity. Among the key tenets of these Christians were the acceptance of Christ as a personal savior, the authority of the Bible and the need to evangelize the faith in Christ.

*New York *Times*, Aug. 17-20; *Newsweek*, Sept. 15; *Wall Street Journal*, July 11; *The New Right: We're Ready to Lead*, by Richard A. Viguerie, (the Viguerie Co., Falls Church, Va.), 1980.

[6] One of the most influential of the new evangelical organizations was the Moral Majority, a political lobby founded in 1979 by the Rev. Falwell. That lobby, which broadcast religious programming and sponsored rallies and seminars on how to use political power, had a membership of 400,000 nationally, including 72,000 ministers. The lobby group had raised $1.5 million in contributions in its first year and set up political action committees in some 48 states to raise campaign funds for candiates who espoused fundamentalist views. The Moral Majority opposed abortion, the proposed Equal Rights Amendment for women, homosexual rights and the strategic arms limitation treaty. It supported prayer in public schools, increased defense spending and strong U.S. backing for Israel.

[7] The Moral Majority, along with other evangelical political groups, formed the core of what was considered an ultraconservative "Christian New Right." That movement was viewed by many observers as a backlash against the social liberalism that had

characterized much of American society since the 1960s. Many evangelical Chrisitians were said to consider themselves "outsiders" in American society who must now fight the forces of "secular humanism" and atheism on such issues as abortion and religion in the schools.

[8] Politically, the evangelical Christian movement was credited with a key role in the 1980 presidential primaries and with shaping important sections of the Republican Party platform. The movement was also credited with helping to block passage of the ERA in 15 states, disrupting the White House Conference on the Family, impeding recent congressional efforts at criminal-code reform and forcing the Federal Communications Commission and the Internal Revenue Service to back down on challenges to religious organizations.

[9] **Airwave Evangelism Growing.** Television and radio gospel broadcasts spurred by a combination of fundamentalist preaching and mass media techniques were becoming a fast-growing industry, it was reported Feb. 25.

[10] According to the Los Angeles *Times,* evangelical broadcasts were becoming a billion-dollar business with a weekly audience of more than 129 million persons. In 1980, the *Times* said, TV broadcast ministries would spend an estimated $600 million to purchase air time. There were currently 1,400 radio stations, 36 TV stations and 66 cable systems in the U.S. that specialized in religious broadcasts.

[11] The broadcast ministries aired on the programs were mostly fundamentalist or Pentecostalist and often featured so-called Biblical "faith-healers." The rapid growth in radio and TV gospel broadcasts was largely aided by the sophisticated use of TV and communications satellite technology. Other contributing factors were the use of professional direct-mail, fund raising techniques and high-speed computers to process coded address lists of potential donors.

[12] The boom in the "electronic church" had stirred controversy and created friction between fundamentalist groups and established mainline religious denomiations. At a symposium Feb. 6-7 on the electronic church held in New York City, mainline critics charged that airwave evangelist were using hucksterism, slick commercials and simplistic theology to gain followers and raise money.

Broadcasting Revenues of Top TV Evangelists

Ministry	Annual Estimates (in $ millions)
Oral Roberts	$60
Pat Robertson (700 Club)	58
Jim Bakker (PTL Club)	51
Jerry Falwell	50
Billy Graham Assn.	30
Rex Humbard	25
Jimmy Swaggart	20
Robert Schuller	16

Source: Los Angeles *Times*

[13] **Conservative Christians Rally.** Some 200,000 evangelical Christians assembled for a "Washington for Jesus" rally marched and prayed April 29 in Washington D.C.

[14] Carrying Bibles, American flags and placards reading "America for Jesus" and "America Must Repent or Perish," the crowd gathered on the Washington Mall, prayed for God's intercession in what one of their leaders called "a world aflame in sin." The rally, sponsored by One Nation Under God, a coalition of mostly conservative church groups, featured 60 speakers, including well-known evangelist and broadcast preachers. Many of the speakers warned of the moral and military deterioration of the United States and denounced, among other things, abortion, divorce, pornography and homosexuality.

[15] A group of Christian, Jewish and

secular leaders charged April 29 that the organizers of the evangelical rally were "right-wing" with "a hidden political agenda" for the United States.

[16] **Reagan Talks to Fundamentalists.** Ronald Reagan appeared before a gathering of thousands of fundamentalist Christian leaders, preachers and "born-again" followers in Dallas Aug. 22 and urged them to get involved in politics.

[17] Reagan deplored a "morally neutral" antichurch attitude in government and said church people "have not just a right to vote but a duty to vote." He said: "When I hear the First Amendment used as a reason to keep traditional moral values away from policymaking, I am shocked. The First Amendment was written not to protect the people and their laws from religious values, but to protect those values from government tyranny."

[18] At a news conference before his speech, Reagan was questioned in reference to the beliefs of the fundamentalists. He remarked at one point that in his view there were "great flaws" in the theory of evolution and he suggested that along with the scientific approach public schools should be teaching the Biblical story of creation.

[19]**Baptist's Remarks on Jews Stir Dispute.** A statement by the president of the Southern Baptist Convention Aug. 22 that God did not hear the prayers of Jews belatedly set off a controversy, it was reported Sept. 19.

[20] The statement was made by the Rev. Dr. Bailey Smith in August at a national conference on evangelical Christianity and politics in Dallas, but went largely unnoticed at the time. Smith said: "It's interesting to me at great political battles how you have a Protestant to pray and a Catholic to pray and then you have a Jew to pray. With all due respect to those dear people, my friends, God Almighty does not hear the prayer of a Jew.... No one can pray unless he prays through the name of Jesus Christ."

[21] Smith's remarks, apparently missed by reporters, were condemned by Jewish and Baptist leaders. Smith, of Del City, Okla. denied his remarks were anti-Semitic. Said Smith: "I am pro-Jew. I believe they are God's special people, but without Jesus Christ they are lost." Smith had been elected in June as president of the 13.4 million-member denomination, which had been wracked in recent years by divisions between theological moderates and fundamentalists.

[22] ***Falwell Reverses Position on Jews***—In a related controversy, broadcast evangelist Jerry Falwell said Oct. 11 that he believed God heard the prayers of Jews, reversing an earlier position.

[23] In a statement released by the American Jewish Committee, Falwell, who headed the Moral Majority, said, "God is a respecter of all persons. He loves everyone alike. He hears the cry of any sincere person who calls Him." Falwell had said in a press conference a week earlier, "I believe God . . . does not hear the prayers of unredeemed gentiles or Jews." That assertion was regarded as an apparent endorsement of the views expressed by the Rev. Dr. Bailey Smith, president of the Southern Baptist Convention. [See above]

CHRYSLER—*See* Automobiles [1-9, 12]

CITY & STATE AFFAIRS

[1] **Nebraska Rejects D.C. Amendment.** Nebraska's unicameral legislation Feb. 11 rejected the proposed constitutional amendment giving the District of Columbia full voting representation in Congress.

[2] A resolution urging rejection of the amendment was approved in the state Senate by a vote of 13 to 9. State Sen. Rex Haberman, who sponsored the resolution, argued that the nation's founding fathers wanted the District of

Columbia to be nonpolitical, and said that reasoning was still valid. Seven states had ratified the amendment since it was passed by Congress in 1978. Nebraska was the 12th state to reject the amendment.

[3] **Bond Issues Canceled in Wary Market.** Falling prices and rising interest rates had caused many cities and states to postpone or cancel their long-term borrowing plans, it was reported by the *Wall Street Journal* Feb. 28.

[4] Municipalities that had hoped to raise money in the bond market at interest rates of 6% or 7%, were now forced to offer investors interest rates of 8%, 9% or higher, according to the *Journal*. At the same time, underwriters were being forced to cut the prices of bonds in order to sell them to investors. The high rates, coupled with declining prices, were making the bond market increasingly unattractive to borrowers.

[5] Three U.S. cities, St. Paul, Minn., Anchorage, Alaska and Sarasota, Fla. on Feb. 26 dropped plans to issue bonds. The *Journal* noted that North Carolina had called off the planned sale of $100 million in state bonds during the same week.

[6] **New York Approves Balanced Budget.** The government of New York City June 16 approved a $13.6 billion balanced budget for the 1981 fiscal year, beginning July 1. It was the city's first balanced budget in over a decade.

[7] ***Wayne County, Michigan***—Some 3,000 county workers were hit with their second "payless payday" of the year Sept. 19, when the county fell about $2 million short of meeting its $2.5 million payroll. Elected officials and judges were among the unpaid employees.

[8] Detroit, Wayne County's largest city, continued to have fiscal woes of its own, including a projected 1980 budget deficit of more than $50 million and a separate school budget deficit of $37 million. Lowered state and federal aid, coupled with decreased tax revenues, contributed to the city's problems. The lower tax revenue reflected the city's growing unemployment. (Detroit had a jobless rate of 18.5% in July.) By Sept. 8, the city government had sent layoff notices to 690 police officers, and more than 700 teachers were slated to be put out of work.

[9] In an earlier development, Standard & Poor's Corp. Aug. 6 lowered its rating on Detroit's general obligation bonds to BB from BBB. BBB bonds were regarded to be investments wtih an "adequate capacity to pay interest and repay principal." BB had "some quality and protective characteristics" that were overshadowed by "large uncertainties or major risk exposures to adverse conditions."

[10] ***Other Cities***—Chicago Sept. 10 authorized emergency borrowing of up to $50 million to cover its bills. The city gained a new line of credit through an agreement with five banks, which were to meet Chicago's borrowing needs at a loan rate fixed at 60% of the prime interest rate.

[11] Washington, D.C. ended its 1980 fiscal year Sept. 30 with an estimated total cumulative debt of $409 million, not including an estimated $2 billion in municipal employee pension liabilities for which the city had no source of funds.

See also Census (U.S.)

CITIZENSHIP

[1] **Revocation Law Backed.** The Supreme Court ruled, 5-4, Jan. 15 that the government could revoke a person's citizenship if a "preponderance of evidence" indicated that the person intended to give up his citizenship. The ruling in *Vance v. Terrasas* upheld federal law governing the loss of citizenship as well as State Department policy.

[2] The case concerned Laurence J. Terrazas, a U.S. national with dual U.S. and Mexican citizenships. In

1970, Terrazas swore allegiance to Mexico in an application to become a Mexican national. The U.S. State Department subsequently lifted his American citizenship.

CIVIL DISORDERS

[1] **16 Die in Miami Rioting.** An outburst of racial rioting in the Liberty City area of Miami, Fla. May 17-19 left at least 14 persons dead, more than 300 persons injured, nearly 1,000 arrested and an estimated $100 million in damage to property, buildings and businesses burned out. By May 26, the death toll reached 16.

[2] It was the worst racial rioting to hit an American city in more than a decade.

[3] The rioting erupted May 17 only hours after an all-white jury in Tampa had acquitted four former Miami police officers who had been accused of the fatal beating of Arthur McDuffie, 33, a black insurance executive from Miami. McDuffie had died Dec. 21, 1979, four days after having been held for a traffic violation.

[4] Rock throwing and bottle throwing gained momentum and spread rapidly into arson, looting, beatings and shootings. Three whites were dragged from an automobile and beaten to death. A black was killed by police after allegedly firing a pistol at a patrol car. Two others were shot and killed, reportedly, while looting. Some 3,600 National Guardsmen were rushed to the area by Gov. Bob Graham. A dawn-to-dusk curfew was imposed.

[5] U.S. Attorney General Benjamin Civiletti announced May 20 that a federal team of prosecutors and agents had been assigned to the area to investigate alleged civil rights abuses by local law enforcement officers.

[6] President Carter visited the riot-torn area of Miami June 9. His visit

Smoke billows behind National Guardsman summoned to duty during Miami rioting May 17-19.

was marred by booing from an angry crowd of several hundred demonstrators as he left a meeting with black and white local leaders. Several bottles were thrown at his motorcade.

[7] At the meeting, Carter promised to meet private business "at least halfway" to help rebuild the riot-torn area. But he advised the leaders that the rebuilding initiative "must come from the community" itself. "It cannot come from Washington," he said, and the federal government could not be expected to pay the entire cost.

[8] Violence flared anew July 15-17. At least 40 persons were injured during the unrest, including five police officers who were shot.

[9] **Racial Tension in Georgia.** A scuffle between black demonstrators and a group of whites broke out in front of the county sheriff's office in Wrightsville, Ga. April 8. Nine persons reportedly were injured.

[10] Black demonstrators reported that a group of 100 or more whites, including sheriff's deputies, charged into the group of about 75 demonstrators. Johnson County Sheriff Rowland Attaway denied that the charge had occurred or that he or other police officers were involved. The blacks had gathered to protest what they considered employment discrimination and lack of political representation. State troopers were sent to the central Georgia town after the incident, on orders of Gov. George D. Busbee.

[11] Three persons – a white policeman, a white firefighter and a black bystander – were wounded by gunfire in an outbreak of shootings May 19, when a fire broke out in the black section of Wrightsville. Police arrested 38 blacks that night. There were charges that the deputies entered private homes and churches and made arrests "indiscriminately." A black man was shot and seriously wounded on a deserted Johnson County road early May 22.

[12] **4 Black Women Shot.** A shotgun blast from a car wounded four black women in Chattanooga, Tenn. April 19. Three Ku Klux Klan members were arrested in connection with the incident.

[13] ***Disorders Erupt***—Racial disorders erupted in Chattanooga, Tenn. July 22-24 after the acquittal of two Ku Klux Klan members in the shooting of the four women.

[14] An all-white jury acquitted two of the Klansmen and gave a third a reduced sentence of nine to 20 months in the county workhouse. Protest against the verdict eventually grew into firebombings, lootings and stone-throwing incidents. A curfew was imposed July 24 by Mayor Pat Rose. There was occasionl sniper fire, and seven police officers were wounded by birdshot fired from ambush July 24. More than 50 persons had been arrested in the disorders by July 25.

[15] **Wichita Riot.** A group of about 200 blacks raged through Wichita, Kan. April 22 burning cars and breaking windshields following an incident in a coin-operated laundry between a black man and a white police officer. About 300 officers were called out eventually, armed with tear gas. A number of arrests were made and minor injuries treated.

[16] **Black Leader Wounded by Sniper.** Black civil rights leader Vernon E. Jordan Jr. was shot and critically wounded in a motel parking lot in Fort Wayne, Ind. May 29.

[17] Jordan, who was president of the National Urban League, underwent a four-and-a-half-hour operation and was removed from the hospital's critical list later May 29 but remained in "very serious" condition. "The shooting was not accidental," Federal Bureau of Investigation Director William Webster said.

[18] A 30.06-caliber shell was found in a grassy area near the motel, where police also found a padded-down section that could have been caused by a gunman lying in ambush. The bullet that struck Jordan was the type that fragmented on impact. Jordan, who was struck in the back between the

Vernon E. Jordan Jr. (left), president of the National Urban League, was shot and critically wounded May 29 in Fort Wayne, Ind.

chest cavity and the pelvis, had just returned to his motel with a female companion about 2:05 a.m. He apparently got out of the car and was walking around the back when he was hit.

[19] The woman was Martha C. Coleman, 36, a white divorcee. She was a member of the board of the Fort Wayne Urban League, whose annual dinner Jordan had addressed the night of the shooting. After the meeting, and a reception, Jordan and Mrs. Coleman went to her home for coffee, along with some other people, before returning to his motel.

[20] Police and FBI agents were reported June 12 to have no suspects and few leads in the case.

CIVIL & CONSTITUTIONAL RIGHTS

[1] **Shopping Center Petitioning Backed.** The Supreme Court ruled unanimously June 9 that states can require privately owned shopping centers to provide access to citizens wishing to circulate petitions. The court in *PruneYard Shopping Center v. Robins* upheld a California Supreme Court decision that the personal property rights of the shopping center owner were not violated when the state ordered him to allow high school students to circulate petitions.

[2] **Right to Sue States Broadened.** The Supreme Court ruled, 6-3, June 25 that private citizens could collect damages from state or local authorities for non-constitutional violations of their civil rights. The case was *Maine v. Thiboutot.*

[3] The case involved a couple who sued Maine under the Civil Rights Act of 1871 over the state's refusal to increase their welfare benefits. The state's Supreme Judicial Court awarded the couple increased benefits and reimbursement of attorney's fees. In doing so, the Maine court rejected the state's argument that the civil rights law did not pertain to the deprivation of rights not contained in the Constitution. (The nation's welfare system, jointly administered by the federal and state governments, had been established by an act of Congress and did not explicitly involve constitutional rights.)

[4] The Supreme Court affirmed the Maine court through a broad interpretation of Section 1983 of the civil rights law. The section allowed private citizens to collect damages from states or localities for "the deprivation of any rights, privileges or immunities secured by the Constitution and laws" of the nation.

[5] **Racial Quotas Uphelp in Federal Contracts.** The Supreme Court ruled, 6-3, July 2 that Congress had the authority to redress past racial discrimination through the use of quotas in government contract awards. The case *Fullilove v. Klutznick* (formerly *Fullilove v. Kreps).*

[6] The Fullilove ruling joined the Bakke decision (1978) and the Weber

Rosa Parks (right), who touched off historic Montgomery, Ala. bus boycott almost 25 years ago when she refused to give up her seat at the front of a bus to a white rider because she was tired, received Martin Luther King Jr. Nonviolent Peace Prize from Mrs. King in Atlanta Jan. 14.

judgment (1979) as the third major case dealing with affirmative action to be decided by the high court in recent years.

[7] The Fullilove case concerned a challenge to a provision of the Public Works Employment Act of 1977 that required the Department of Commerce to set aside 10% of federal public works contracts for construction companies owned by minorities. The provision specified "minorities" as blacks, American Indians, Spanish-speaking Americans, Eskimos, Aleuts and Oriental-Americans. Two lower federal courts had upheld the law in the face of opposition that characterized it as "reverse discrimination" against whites. The Supreme Court, too, upheld the statute. It was the first time that high court has expressly backed the awarding of federal funds based on the race of the recipients.

[8] Legal experts noted that the decision explicitly involved congressional power. It appeared to leave open the question of whether federal agencies or departments could on their own mandate contract quotas.

[9] **'Wilmington 10' Convictions Reversed.** A federal appeals court Dec. 4 unanimously reversed the 1972 arson and conspiracy convictions of the "Wilmington 10," whose inprisonment had prompted an international civil rights controversy.

[10] A three-judge panel of the 4th U.S. Circuit Court of Appeals in Richmond, Va. held that the North Carolina civil rights workers were denied their constitutional right to a fair trial in 1972 because their attorneys were not given full access to contradictory testimony by a key prosecution witness. The appeals court sent the case back to the federal trial court for further action.

[11] The Wilmington 10, who included the Rev. Ben Chavis and eight high school students, had pleaded not guilty to firebombing a grocery store in Wilmington, N.C. in 1971 and conspiring to assault firefighters who answered alarms for the blaze. That incident occurred against a backdrop of

racial violence in which two men, one black and one white, were shot to death. After one mistrial, all 10 defendants were convicted and sentenced to long prison terms.

CLARK, JOSEPH—*See* Canada [2, 4-5]

CLEVELAND—*See* Census (U.S.) [4]

COFFEE

[1] **Coffee Glut: Price Slides.** With a glut in supplies of raw coffee beans on world markets, the price of coffee had been in a steep slide since June. On Oct. 7, the price of a pound of coffee was about $1.30, down from close to $2 in June.

[2] To stabilize the price of coffee, the International Coffee Organization, a group of 67 coffee-producing and consuming nations, announced Oct. 3 that price limits would be established for coffee at between $1.15 and $1.55 a pound during the next year. Exports by producing nations would be limited to 57,370,000 bags of coffee a year. A bag contained 132 pounds.

See also El Salvador [4-7]

COLOMBIA

[1] **Leftists Seize Envoys from 16 Nations.** Leftist guerrillas seized the embassy of the Dominican Republic in Bogota Feb. 27, taking the U.S. ambassador and diplomats from 15 other countries and the Vatican hostage.

[2] The terrorists numbered about 25 men and women. They were members of the guerrilla group April 19 Movement, or M-19, which had been the target of a massive government anti-terrorist campaign since the beginning of 1979. The leftists demanded a ransom of $50 million to be raised by the hostages' countries, the release of 311 leftists facing charges of terrorism and the publication of a manifesto in the main newspaper of the hostages' countries.

[3] In addition to the U.S ambassador, Diego C. Asencio, the other ambassadors being held were from Austria, Brazil, Costa Rica, the Dominican Republic, Egypt, El Salvador, Guatemala, Haiti, Israel, Italy, Switzerland, Uruguay, the Vatican and Venezuela. The Bolivian and Paraguayan charges d'affaires were also taken. Other hostages included Colombian officials, secretaries, and cooks and waiters hired for the reception.

[4] ***Takeover Ends***—a 61-day occupation of the Dominican Republic's embassy in Bogota ended peacefully April 27.

[5] Sixteen guerrillas and 18 hostages who were still being held captive left the embassy an hour before dawn in a caravan of three Red Cross ambulances and two buses. At Bogota's international airport, 12 of the hostages boarded a Cuban jetliner and, as arranged, the guerrillas handed over their grenades. Six of the hostages were released. On board the jet with the guerrillas went the U.S. ambassador, Diego C. Asencio, the papal nuncio, Msgr. Angelo Acerbi, the ambassadors from Brazil, Guatemala, Haiti, Mexico and Switzerland, the charges d'affaires of Bolivia and Paraguay, and diplomats from Guatemala, Peru and Venezuela.

[6] Although government negotiators had met 24 times with a female representative of the guerrillas during the two-month takeover, a break in the standoff did not come until the Cuban government offered to help with "private" negotiations, and the Inter-American Human Rights Commission of the Organization of American States entered the talks. The "private" negotiators were Jose Manuel Rivar Sacconi, a former Colombian foreign minister, and Victor Sasson Taeil, a

local businessman. They allegedly paid the guerrillas a ranson of $2.5 million. However, no leftist prisoners were released.

[7] The 12 remained hostages were set free upon the jetliner's arrival in Havana.

[8] **2 Key M-19 Guerrillas Escape Prison.** Ivan Ospina and Jose Marin, members of the high command of the guerrilla April 19 Movement (M-19), escaped June 25 from Colombia's La Picata prison outside Bogota, where they were being tried by a military tribunal for subversive activities.

[9] Ospina and Marin were among some 300 imprisoned guerrillas whose release had been demanded by the M-19 guerrillas who seized the Dominican Embassy in Bogota Feb. 27. Colombia's minister of justice, Felio Andrade Manrique, personally took charge of an investigation of the escape and ordered the arrest of all prison guards who had been on duty at the time of the breakout.

[10] **Government Accused of Torture.** Amnesty International, the London-based human rights organization, said Sept. 22 that "conclusive evidence" showed that the government systematically used beatings, drugs, electric shock, rape and other forms of torture on political prisoners.

[11] A 258-page report issed by AI identified 35 military centers throughout the country where the alleged torture had taken place. Six hundred individual cases of torture were cited. The report noted that most of the victims were "peasants, Indians and trade unionists," although professionals such as doctors, lawyers and "others who tried to uphold professional codes of conduct" had also been seized and tortured.

See also Disasters & Accidents [1]; Immigration; United Nations [3]

COMMODITIES

[1] **CFTC Tightens Trading Rules.** The Commodity Futures Trading commission Nov. 25 adopted a new rule that shortened the amount of time a trader had to settle a margin call when the value of a futures contract declined.*

[2] A second new rule doubled the amount of cash brokerage companies were required to have on hand when they engaged in commodity futures trading.

[3] The two rules were adopted to prevent a recurrence of the near collapse in commodity trading caused when the price of silver dropped precipitously in March, resulting in huge losses for Nelson Bunker Hunt and his brother Herbert, whose silver trading activities became one of the most widely publicized business events of the year.

*Margin is cash or collateral deposited with a broker to secure him against loss on a contract made on behalf of a trader. Margin often constitutes a partial payment of the purchase. For example, a trader who bought a $10,000 contract on 50% margin would put up $5,000 (the margin) and borrow the remaining $5,000 from the broker at prevailing interest rates. If the value of the contract fell or if the value of collateral used for margin fell, the broker would call for additional margin.

CONGO, PEOPLE'S REPUBLIC OF—*See* Chad [10]

CONGRESS (U.S.)

[1] **Michel Elected House GOP Leader.** House Republicans Dec. 8 elected Rep. Robert H. Michel (Ill.) minority leader for the 97th Congress. He succeeded Rep. John J. Rhodes (Ariz.), who declined to continue in the post.

[2] Michel, 57, had been minority whip since December 1974. Rep. Trent Lott (Miss.) was elected minority whip to replace Michel.

[3] ***Foley Named Democratic Whip***—House Democrats Dec. 8 picked Rep. Thomas S. Foley (Wash.), as majority whip. Rep. John Brademas (Ind.), who held the post in the current

Congress, had been defeated for reelection.

[4] There were no contests for the top Democratic posts. Rep. Thomas P. O'Neill Jr. (Mass.) was redesignated speaker. Rep. Jim Wright (Tex.) was reelected majority leader.

[5] ***Senate Democrats Retain Leaders***—Senate Democrats, preparing for their new minority role, confirmed their current leadership Dec. 4.

[6] Majority Leader Robert C. Byrd (W. Va.) was elected minority leader and chairman of the Democratic Conference. Majority Whip Alan Cranston (Cal.) was unopposed for minority whip.

[7] **96th Congress Adjourns.** The 96th Congress adjourned Dec. 16 after a five week post-election session. The lame-duck session became necessary because Congress had failed to pass the 1981 budget and many important appropriations bills before the November elections.

[8] The adjournment followed the approval of compromise legislation providing funds for many key government agencies whose funding had officially ended at midnight. Other measures approved included:

Nov. 17 (H), Nov. 19 (S)–The Gasohol Competition Act, which was designed to facilitate the sale of gasohol and other synthetic motor fuels. The measure was an amendment to the Clayton Antitrust Act. President Carter signed the bill Dec. 2.

Dec. 2–The authorization of $1.12 billion for the National Science Foundation in fiscal 1981. Of that sum, $30 million was to be used to promote the participation of women and minorities in scientific careers. Carter signed the bill Dec. 12.

Dec. 5–The third military pay and benefits bill of 1980. Military pay was to increase by an estimated $130 million in each of the years 1981-1984. Higher bonuses for Navy personnel on sea duty accounted for about two-thirds of the increase. Carter signed the bill Dec. 23.

Other Developments

[9] **Diggs Resigns Seat.** Rep. Charles C. Diggs Jr. (D, Mich.) June 3 resigned from the House of Representatives.

[10] His resignation came after the Supreme Court June 2 refused to review his 1978 conviction for taking kickbacks from his staff. The Detroit Democrat, the senior black member of Congress, faced a three-year prison sentence.

[11] **Justice Drops Talmadge Probe.** The Justice Department, closing a 22-month investigation, said May 30 that it would not prosecute Sen. Herman E. Talmadge (D, Ga.) for alleged financial misconduct.

[12] Talmadge had been "denounced" by the Senate in 1979 for mishandling his office and campaign finances. After reviewing the evidence, Justice Department officials reportedly concluded that they probably could not obtain a conviction.

[13] **Wilson Censured by House.** The House of Representatives June 10 censured Rep. Charles H. Wilson (D, Calif.) for violating House rules by converting campaign funds to his own use and for accepting money from a person with direct interest in legislation before Congress.

[14] Wilson, who had repeatedly denied any guilt, was roundly defeated in the California Democratic primary on June 3. He was the third member of Congress to be censured in the 20th century.

See also Abscam; Automobiles—[1]; Banks & Banking [7, 10-12]; Billy Carter [5-6, 15-21]; Budget [1-4]; Defense (U.S.) [37-39]; Draft Registration [7-10]; Education [6-8]; Elections [86-96]; Energy [1-5, 8-12]; Housing [1-10]; India [32-35]; Indians, American [2-3]; Intelligence Issues [1-4]; Middle East [53]; Nicaragua [20-21]; Oil [22-27]; Press [11-15]; Railroads [1-4]; Refugees [1-8]; Silver [14]; Taxes (U.S.) [1-5]; Trucking [1-2]; Union of Soviet Socialist Republics [19]; Veterans' Affairs [6-9]; Wildlife [1-5]

CONNECTICUT—*See* Ku Klux Klan (KKK) [5-7]

COPPER—*See* Labor [34-7]

COURTS—*See* Labor [5-15]; Steel [1-6]; Supreme Court; Women's Rights [6-7]

CREDIT, Consumer

[1] **Lenders Tighten Policies.** Banks, retailers and credit card issuers had made major changes in their credit policies in the wake of new Federal Reserve Board credit guidelines, the *New York Times* reported March 27.

[2] On March 14, as part of President Carter's anti-inflation plan, the Fed had called upon lenders to hold the total amount of credit to the level of that day. Lenders who increased the amount of credit outstanding above March 14 levels had to set aside 15% of the increase in a noninterest bearing account in a federal reserve bank.

[3] The Fed did not tell lenders how to hold credit to the target level. But among the methods used so far, the *Times* reported, were: requiring larger purchases for installment payments, increasing interest charges, imposing fees for many of the bank cards (Visa, MasterCard), and refusing to issue any new bank cards or make new installment loans.

[4] **Credit Controls Modified.** The Federal Reserve Board April 2 modified its anti-inflation credit restrictions in an attempt to protect consumers from sudden changes in the terms of repayment of existing balances on credit cards.

[5] The Fed clarified regulations for tightened credit announced March 14. By a 5-0 vote, the Fed made several modifications:

■ Credit card holders had to be given 30 days notice of new terms for repayment imposed by creditors, such as additional charges or increased minimum monthly payments.

■ Consumers had to be given the option of repayment of their existing credit card balances under their original repayment terms. To take that option, however, a consumer would have to stop using his or her credit card.

■ Consumers who continued to use their cards would be considered to have "implicitly" accepted new repayment terms. Those terms would apply to existing and new balances.

[6] The new Federal Reserve regulations applied to credit cards issued by banks, retailers, oil companies and other forms of credit that continued indefinitely with no fixed date for final repayment.

[7] The Federal Reserve Board, responding to signs that the nation was heading into a recession, May 22 further relaxed the restraints it had imposed on credit to fight inflation.

[8] **Fed Ends Controls.** The Federal Reserve Board July 3 announced it was phasing out the remaining credit controls imposed in March to fight inflation.

[9] "Recent evidence indicates that the need for these extraordinary measures has ended," the Fed said. "For the year to date, credit expansion, particularly at banks, is clearly running at a moderate pace. In recent months, there has been apparent contraction in consumer borrowing, indications are that anticipatory and speculative demands for credit have subsided and funds have been in more ample supply."

CRIME

Government Officials

[1] **Flood Pleads Guilty.** Former Rep. Daniel J. Flood (D, Pa.) Feb. 26 pleaded guilty to a single count of conspiracy to violate federal campaign laws and was placed on probation for a year. In return for the guilty plea, the Justice

Department dropped more serious charges of bribery and perjury against the 76-year-old Pennsylvania Democrat. Flood had resigned his seat in the House Jan. 31.

[2] **Illinois Attorney General Convicted.** Illinois Attorney General William J. Scott was convicted March 19 of federal tax fraud in a U.S. District Court in Chicago.

[3] A jury found Scott guilty of one-count of a five-count indictment. According to government estimates, Scott had underreported his income by a "bare minimum" of $52,252 for 1972-75. The verdict came one day after Scott had lost a bid for the Republican nomination for the U.S. Senate.

[4] Scott was sentenced July 29 to a year and a day in prison.

Bribery, Fraud & Extortion

[5] **Dock Union Leaders Sentenced.** Seven officials of the International Longshoremen's Association and five businessmen were sentenced to prison terms and fined Jan. 11 for their part in waterfront racketeering in five Southeastern states.

[6] Federal Judge William Hoeveler in Miami, Fla. handed down sentences ranging from simple probation to 15 years in prison and imposed fines up to $10,000 on nine persons. They were convicted in 1979 of conspiring to corrupt waterfront commerce through a system of payoffs and intimidation. Also sentenced were three others who had pleaded guilty to charges connected with the conspiracy.

[7] The sentencing brought to a close the major portion of a four-year investigation by the Federal Bureau of Investigation and the U.S. Justice Department's organized crime strike force of waterfront corruption in the ports of Miami, Mobile, Ala., Savannah, Ga., Charleston, S.C. and Jacksonville, Fla.

[8] ***Scotto & Anastasio Sentenced***—Anthony M. Scotto, general organizer of the International Longshoremen's Association, was sentenced Jan. 22 to five years in prison and fined $75,000 on federal racketeering charges. He had been convicted in 1979 of receiving more than $200,000 in cash payoffs.

[9] Co-defendant Anthony Anastasio, an executive vice-president of Brooklyn ILA local 1814, was sentenced Jan. 23 to two years in prison and fined $5,000. He had been found guilty of accepting more than $50,000 in kickbacks. The sentences were handed down by U.S. District Judge Charles E. Stewart Jr. in New York.

[10] **Phila. 'Bust-Out Scam' Indictments.** Twenty-one defendants were indicted Feb 12 by a federal grand jury in Philadelphia on charges of operating a business scheme that defrauded creditors of at least $5 million.

[11] According to the indictment, the defendants had used a network of 10 separate companies to operate a "bust-out scam," an increasingly popular form of white-collar fraud, to confuse and thwart creditors. One of the companies, actually a merger of two of the others, was called Rekcus Consolidated Inc. Rekcus was sucker spelled backward.

[12] A "bust-out scam," in essence, involved purchasing goods on credit from various manufacturers without the intention of paying for them and then selling the goods for cash, often at a substantial discount, to colleagues in the scheme. The bust-out companies would then go bankrupt or cease operations without paying for the goods.

[13] **Sindona Convicted of Bank Fraud.** Michele Sindona, the Sicilian-born financier involved in the Franklin Bank failure of 1974, was convicted by a federal court jury in New York March 27 on 65 counts of fraud, conspiracy, false bank statements and perjury. Sindona was sentenced June 13 by U.S. District Court Judge Thomas G. Griesa to 25 years in prison.

[14] The trial, originally scheduled for September 1979, had been postponed

after Sindona disappeared from his residence in New York.

[15] Sindona, 59, rose from poverty to build a huge but frail financial empire of $500 million. He became involved with the Franklin Bank in 1972, when he bought one million shares, or 21.6% control, of Franklin New York Corp., parent of the bank, for $40 million. He was found guilty of fradulently removing back to Italy $15 million through improper foreign currency speculation in order to salvage two of his own banks there. This caused a loss of $30 million to Franklin Bank and its eventual collapse in 1974. It was the largest bank failure ever recorded in this country.

[16] At the start of the trial, Feb. 6, the presiding judge, Thomas P. Griesa, revoked the $3 million bail that had allowed Sindona to remain out of jail. Sindona had said that his disappearance was the result of being kidnapped by left-wing Italian terrorists. However, the prosecution rejected his claim and presented a U.S. customs form and an airline ticket as evidence that Sindona had flown to Vienna on Aug. 2, 1979 and returned from Frankfurt, West Germany to New York two months later. The supposed kidnapping was not mentioned during the trial itself.

[17] **Vesco Grand Jury Dissolved.** A federal grand jury investigating an alleged attempt by fugitive financier Robert Vesco to bribe members of the Carter Administration was dissolved without bringing indictments against anyone, according to a government lawyer April 1.

[18] **Deliverers Union Head Sentenced.** Douglas LaChance, president of the independent Newspaper and Mail Deliverers Union of New York, was convicted May 15 by a federal court jury of extorting more than $300,000 from companies that delivered newspapers in the New York metropolitan area. LaChance was sentenced June 26 by U.S. District Judge Milton Pollack to 12 ¼ years in prison and a fine of $100,000.

[19] **Illegal 'Pyramid' Schemes Growing.** An epidemic of illegal pyramid-type investment schemes that had defrauded many thousands of investors was spreading across the United States, it was reported May 17.

[20] Law enforcement officials and fraud investigators said that the investment schemes, with their promises of easy money, were flourishing in at least a dozen states, including California, Oregon, New Mexico, Colorado, Missouri, Iowa, Illinois, and Ohio.

[21] Some officials said that there had not been such a surge nationwide of get-rich-quick schemes since the Great Depression, when many desperate Americans invested in chain letters and similar schemes in the hope of making a big financial bonanza. That practice had led many states to outlaw pyramid games and other "endless chains" as frauds.

[22] The scheme was called a pyramid because, if it worked according to plan, it would grow with an ever-widening base of new investors. Each new investor was expected to bring in two more investing participants. Investors thus moved up the pyramid with those at the top getting rich as new participants put in money. But if no new players could be found, then the progression stopped and the investors would then end up losing money.

[23] Police officials, who expressed concern at the extent of fad, said that the vast majority of investors were losing money in the fast-moving schemes. Despite warnings, many pyramid participants were bitterly protesting police crackdowns in raids on pyramid parties, arguing that it was their prerogative to invest their money in the pyramids if they chose.

[24] **FBI Bribery Plot Convictions.** Two crime kingpins were convicted July 3 by a federal jury in Cleveland on charges of bribing a file clerk for the Federal Bureau of Investigation to obtain secret documents on underworld activities.

[25] Convicted on two counts of bribery were Anthony D. Liberatore and Thomas Lanci. Liberatore, once on the FBI's list of 10 most wanted criminals, had been a major political appointee of former Cleveland Mayor Ralph Perk. Acquitted were James T. Licavoli, onetime member of Detroit's Purple Gang, and John P. Calandra Sr., a reputed lieutenant in organized crime. The defendants had been accused of participating in a plot to bribe Geraldine Rabinowitz, a former FBI file clerk and her husband, to steal secret documents on underworld activities. The Rabinowitzes, who had testified as key witnesses in the three-week trial, had pleaded guilty two years earlier to two counts of accepting nearly $16,000 in bribes for the documents.

Homicides

[26] **Suspect Held in Adamson Murder.** A discharged employe was charged Feb. 2 with the murder of Joy Adamson, author of the best-selling book, *Born Free.*

[27] Adamson, 69, Austrian-born, was an internationally known figure in the wildlife conservation movement. In *Born Free,* she had told the story of Elsa, a lion cub reared as one of her family into a full-grown lioness.

[28] Adamson's body was found Jan. 3 outside her Shaba Game Reserve campsite, 175 miles (280 kilometers) north of Nairobi; she had been stabbed to death. The suspect, Paul Nakware Ekai, 23, reportedly had worked briefly for Adamson at the campsite. She had fired him following a dispute.

[29] **Bolles Killers Convictions Overturned.** The Arizona state Supreme Court Feb. 25 unanimously reversed the first-degree murder convictions of two men under sentences of death for the bomb slaying of newspaper reporter Don Bolles.

[30] The court ruled that the trial judge had unconstitutionally frustrated efforts by defense attorneys to cross-examine a key prosecution witness and ordered that the two defendants be retried.

[31] The defendants, Max Dunlap, 50, a millionaire Phoenix contractor, and James Robison, 57, a plumber, had been sentenced to death Jan. 10, 1977 for killing Bolles. Bolles, an investigative reporter for the *Arizona Republic,* had written articles linking organized crime and powerful business interests in the state. He died in June 1976 after a bomb exploded beneath his car in the parking lot of a Phoenix hotel.

[32] ***Adamson Found Guilty***—John Harvey Adamson was convicted Oct. 17 by a Superior Court jury in Tucson, Ariz. of first-degree murder in the Don Bolles slaying

[33] Adamson was accused of planning the killing, luring Bolles to a Phoenix hotel and then planting a bomb under his car in a parking lot. It was the second time he had stood trial on the charges in the murder-for-hire case.

[34] During his first trial in January 1977, Adamson, 36, had pleaded guilty to a charge of second-degree murder under a plea bargain agreement and was sentenced to 20 years in prison. In exchange, he testified against Dunlap Robison. When state prosecutors moved to retry them after their convictions were reversed, Adamson balked at testifying again unless his sentence was further reduced. The state claimed that Adamson had breached his plea bargain agreement and filed the first-degree murder charge against him.

[35] Adamson was sentenced Nov. 14 to die in the gas chamber.

[36] **Defectors from Cult Murdered.** Two of the earliest defectors from the Rev. Jim Jones's Peoples Temple were murdered at their home in Berkeley, Calif. Feb. 26.

[37] Al and Jeannie Mills were found shot to death by his mother. Also found shot in the head was Daphene, the couple's daughter. She was pronounced dead Feb. 27 after tests had shown that she was neurologically dead, and her life support systems had

been disconnected.

[38] The Millses had joined the temple in 1970 under the name of Elmer and Deanna Mertle when the temple was based in northern California. They had become leaders of the organization before leaving in 1975. They changed their names out of fear that Jones would retaliate for their disloyalty. In 1977, the couple filed suit against Jones and other officers of the temple, contending that they had been defrauded of almost all their property and been kept virtual prisoners in the church by "threats of force and coercion."

[39] **'Scarsdale Diet' Doctor Killed.** Dr. Herman Tarnower, 69, a prominent physician and author of the best-selling *The Complete Scarsdale Medical Diet,* was shot and killed March 10 in his secluded country home in suburban Purchase, N.Y.

[40] Jean S. Harris, 56, a long-time friend and headmistress of the Madeira School, a prestigious private high school for girls in Virginia, was charged March 11 with second-degree murder in the slaying. Harris, who had been divorced 15 years ago, had reportedly been romantically involved with Tarnower, often traveling with him, but was said to have been rejected by the doctor in favor of a younger woman, Lynne Tryforos, who worked on his medical staff.

[41] **Allard K. Lowenstein Slain.** Former U.S. Rep. Allard K. Lowenstein, 51, was fatally shot March 14 in his New York City law office.

[42] The gunman was identified as Dennis Sweeney, 37, a former associate of Lowenstein in the civil rights movement in the South in the 1960s. Sweeney, who had a history of treatment for mental disorders, was indicted March 18 on a charge of second-degree murder.

[43] Police said that Sweeney, a carpenter who lived in New London, Conn., had blamed Lowenstein for family problems that had led to the death of his stepfather after a heart attack in Oregon in February. Lowenstein, who had met Sweeney at Stanford University in the early 1960s, was reported to have recently said that he was "seriously worried" about Sweeney's mental condition.

[44] Lowenstein was elected in 1968 to a term as a Democratic representative from New York and later served in various United Nations posts. He was best known as the main architect of the 1968 anti-Vietnam War movement to block the renomination of President Lyndon B. Johnson.

[45] **Mafia Chief Shot to Death.** Angelo Bruno, 69, reputed chief of organized crime in Philadelphia and southern New Jersey, was shot to death March 21 in an apparent gangland execution in Philadelphia.

[46] **180 Years For Haitian Drownings.** Jeffrey Hastings, convicted of manslaughter April 18 for the drownings of a Haitian women and her five children in an aborted attempt to smuggle them into the U.S., was

Pallbearers carry casket with body of reputed Mafia chief Angelo Bruno outside church in south Philadelphia. Bruno was shot and killed March 21.

sentenced to 180 years in prison June 24. The sentence was double the normal term of 15 years for each manslaughter count because Hastings was a habitual offender who had been convicted of murdering his wife in 1973 and had been a prison escapee.

[47] **Violinist Slain in N.Y. Opera House.** A woman violinist was found slain July 24 at the Metropolitian Opera House at Lincoln Center in New York City.

[48] The body of Helen Hagnes, 30, was found nude, bound and gagged in a ventilation shaft at the opera house 11 hours after she had disappeared from the orchestra pit during an intermission between ballets. Police said that Hagnes had been hurled from the Met's sixth-floor roof into the air shaft.

[49] Hagnes, a freelance violinist hired to play for a two-week run of the Berlin Ballet, had been last seen in a lounge during the intermission when she told a colleague that she was going to see ballet star Valery Panov, a Soviet emigre dancer who had been starring in the show. However, police said, she did not see Panov and instead apparently encountered her killer somewhere in the Met's backstage area, which was a labyrinth of corridors, dressing rooms, stairwells and elevators.

[50] Police detectives questioned more than 1,300 persons, including performers, musicians, stagehands and others who had access to the backstage area of the 3,400-seat opera house. The Canadian-born violinist, who had made her professional debut at age 13, was married to Janis Mintiks, a sculptor.

[51] A Met stagehand was indicted Sept. 7 by a New York grand jury in the slaying. Craig S. Crimmins, 21, of the Bronx, N.Y., had been arrested Aug. 30, and charged with second-degree murder and attempted rape.

[52] **Doctor's Murder Convictions Voided.** The murder convictions of Dr. Jeffrey R. MacDonald, a former Green Beret captain, in the 1970 slayings of his wife and two daughters were overturned July 30 by a federal appeals court in Richmond, Va.

[53] The Fourth U.S. Circuit Court of Appeals in a 2-1 opinion held that "sheer bureaucratic indifference" and the "government's calloused and lackadaisical attitude" had led to a violation of MacDonald's constitutional right to a speedy trial and caused a two-year delay between an Army investigation and his murder indictment in 1975. MacDonald had been convicted in 1979, and sentenced to three consecutive life terms.

[54] **'Playmate of Year' Slain in Los Angeles.** *Playboy* magazine's 1980 "playmate of the year" and her estranged husband were found shot to death Aug. 15 in Los Angeles.

[55] The bodies of Dorothy Stratten, 20, and Paul Snider, 29, were found nude in Snider's West Los Angeles home in an apparent murder-suicide. Police theorized that Snider had killed Stratten with a single blast from a 12-guage shotgun and then turned the weapon on himself. Friends of the couple said that Snider, a promoter, had been distraught over a nude picture layout of his wife published in *Playboy* in August 1979. The couple, married in 1979, had separated in May. Stratten, a statuesque blonde, had appeared in several films, including *Skatetown U.S.A.*, *Galaxina* and *They All Laughed.*

[56] **6 Blacks Slain in Buffalo, N.Y.** The slayings of six blacks in Buffalo, N.Y. and the surrounding area within a three-week period, had alarmed the city's black population and prompted an intensive investigation by law enforcement officials, it was reported Oct. 13.

[57] The slayings left public officials and residents worried that the killings would lead to mounting racial tension. There was a growing belief that the killings were racially motivated.

[58] The first four victims, who ranged in age from 14 to 71, were killed within a 36-hour period from Sept. 22 to Sept. 24. They were found with shots to the left side of the head. The two other vic-

tims, both taxi drivers, slain separately in another three-day period, were found beaten to death and their hearts cut out.

[59] **Prominent Physician Slain in Wash., D.C.** A nationally known physician, journalist and author, Dr. Michael J. Halberstam, was shot and killed Dec. 5 in Washington, D.C.

[60] Halberstam was shot twice in the chest after he and his wife surprised a burglar in their northwest Washington home. After he was shot and was attempting to drive to a hospital, Halberstam saw his alleged assailant fleeing in the street, swerved his car and struck him, police said. Charged with the shooting Dec. 6 was Bernard Charles Welch Jr. of Great Falls, Va., a convicted burglar and escapee from the Clinton Correctional Facility in Dannemora, N.Y. Welch, 40, had been serving a 10-year sentence on burglary charges when he escaped in 1974.

[61] News accounts Dec. 7 reported that Welch had lived quietly in an affluent Washington suburb with his wife and three children under the alias of "Norm Hamilton." He drove a $39,000 Mercedes-Benz automobile and told neighbors he was in stocks and real estate. A police search of Welch's home turned up hundreds of thousands of dollars worth of stolen goods. Meanwhile, police in Duluth, Minn., where Welch maintained a second home, reported seizing 61 items, mostly antiques, valued at a minimum of $50,000. The slain physician was a brother of David Halberstam, an author and Pulitzer Prize-winning former *New York Times* correspondent.

Organized Crime

[62] **FBI Probes Southwest Corruption.** A major federal undercover investigation of political corruption in the Southwest turned up evidence of bribery involving political officials, labor leaders and a leading organized crime figure, government documents released Feb. 8 by a federal judge in Los Angeles indicated.

[63] State and local public officials had accepted bribes from a government informer and agents of the Federal Bureau of Investigation in a nine-month "sting" operation, the documents suggested.

[64] Federal law enforcement officials Feb. 9 identified the following political figures as targets of the investigation: Jimmy Fitzmorris, Democratic lieutenant governor of Louisiana and an unsucessful gubernatorial candidate; Louis Lambert, a Louisiana Democrat who lost a gubernatorial race in 1979 and now governor-elect, and Billy Wayne Clayton, speaker of the Texas House of Representatives.

[65] Another major figure in the investigation was Carlos Marcello of New Orleans, who had for years been considered by federal agents and prosecutors head of organized crime in the Gulf Coast area.

[66] Federal officials said that each of the three political figures had accepted $10,000 from undercover agents in an insurance kick-back scheme. They said that Marcello received money from undercover agents and provided introductions to politicians for the undercover agents.

[67] The federal probe in the Southwest, begun in the spring of 1979, was codenamed Brilab by the FBI for "briberylabor." The operation, coordinated by the U.S. Justice Department's Organized Crime Strike Force and FBI agents, was aimed initially at union corruption in California. But the undercover probe quickly spread to Arkansas, Louisiana, Texas and Oklahoma.

[68] ***Texas House Speaker & Marcello Indicted***—Indictmnets growing out of the Brilab probe were returned in Texas and Louisiana. The speaker of the Texas House of Representatives was indicted June 12 by a federal grand jury in Houston on fraud, conspiracy and racketeering charges. The six-count indictment named Billy

Underworld figure Angelo Sica hides his face and covers TV cameras lens as he approaches county courthouse in Freehold, N.J. March 10.

Wayne Clayton, the speaker of the Texas House; and two Austin, Texas lawyers, Donald W. Ray and Randall B. Wood. Clayton, Ray and Wood were found not guilty Oct. 23 by a federal court jury.

[69] Reputed crime leader Carlos Marcello was indicted June 17 by a federal grand jury in New Orleans. The 12-count indictment also named I. Irving Davidson, a Washington, D.C. public relations man; Charles E. Roemar 2d, a former Louisiana state official, and Vincent A. Marinello, a New Orleans lawyer.

[70] **N.Y. 'La Cosa Nostra' Boss Convicted.** Frank (Funzi) Tieri, reputedly one of the top leaders of organized crime in the U.S., was indicted June 30 in New York City on charges of being "the boss of one of the five New York City 'families' of La Cosa Nostra." He was convicted Nov. 21, and sentencing set for Jan. 6, 1981.

[71] The four-count indictment, returned in U.S. District Court, contained charges of racketeering, racketeering conspiracy, fraud conspiracy and tax evasion. Tieri was found guilty of all but the tax evasion charge.

[72] Federal prosecutors said that it was the first time that anyone had been convicted on a charge of heading a "crime family." The indictment defined Tieri's alleged "crime family" as an enterprise engaged in activities that "affected interstate commerce through a pattern of racketeering."

[73] According to Nathaniel H. Ackerman, the prosecutor in charge of the case, Tieri headed the Genovese "crime family" and was the "senior member" of a commission that supervised organized crime in the U.S. "He is the boss of the largest crime family in La Cosa Nostra in the United States," Ackerman said, adding that Tieri "received tribute" from activities that included extortion, gambling, fraud, narcotics and murder.

[74] Federal authorities said that the indictment stemmed from an investigation of the bankrupt Westchester Premier Theatre in Tarrytown, N.Y. The fraud conspiracy charge alleged that Tieri had participated in a scheme to defraud creditors of the bankrupt theater. In the racketeering conspiracy charge, Tieri was alleged to have engaged in extorting loans, receiving $25,000 stolen from Korvettes Inc. and of having participated in an alleged murder scheme.

[75] **Mafia, Pizza Industry Ties Probed.** Investigations in New York, New Jersey and Pennsylvania reported Aug. 24 that organized crime had gained extensive control of the mozzarella cheese and pizza industries.

[76] The Pennsylvania Crime Commission said organized crime had gained "unbroken control" of the pizza industry in that state from manufacturers of mozzarella cheese through distributors to corner pizza shops. The pattern was seen as part of an effort by organized crime to gain nationwide control of the lucrative business.

[77] The commission study alleged that

organized crime had tried to stifle competition in the pizza industry, using such tactics as arson, death threats and start-up loans to shops. In addition, the study charged that some Mafia-linked cheese and pizza companies had "skimmed" an estimated $25 million in cash a year to avoid taxes.

[78] **Joe Bonanno Convicted.** Reputed Mafia leader Joseph (Joe Bananas) C. Bonanno Sr., and a nephew were convicted Sept. 2 by a federal judge of conspiracy to obstruct justice by interfering with a grand jury investigation of possible money-laundering schemes in his family's business. Bonanna's nephew Jack DiFilippi, a San Jose, Calif. commodities broker was also found guilty of perjury.

[79] The convictions were handed down in San Francisco by U.S. District Judge William Ingram, who heard the case without a jury during a 14-week trial. The defendants had waived a jury trial. It was the first felony conviction for Bonanno, 76, who was reputedly the chief of one of the five original Mafia "families" organized in New York City in the 1930s. He left the East Coast in the early 1960s following an alleged organized crime feud known as the "Banana Wars" and settled in Arizona.

Tax Evasion

[80] **Studio 54 Owners Sentenced.** Studio 54 owners Steven Rubell and Ian Schrager were sentenced Jan. 18 in a New York City federal court to 3½ years in prison and fined $20,000 each on charges of corporate and personal income tax evasion.

[81] U.S. District Judge Richard Owen imposed the sentences and chastised the two defendants for "tremendous arrogance" in skimming cash from their popular discotheque and evading $366,000 in corporate taxes and more than $50,000 in personal taxes. Rubell and Schrager had pleaded guilty last year to charges of personal and corporate tax evasion. In exchange, government prosecutors agreed to drop additional charges including conspiracy to obstruct justice. The defendants also agreed to pay the taxes owed to the government.

[82] Judge Owen Dec. 31 reduced the prison sentences he had imposed on Rubell and Schrager to 20 months because of their cooperation with an investigation of tax fraud in the discotheque industry.

See also Abscam; Civil & Constitutional Rights [9-11]; Death Penalty; Lance, Thomas Bertram (Bert) [1-4]; Lennon, John [1-17]; Obscenity & Pornography [1-3]; Police [1-3]; Radicals [1-9]; Ronald Reagan [15-6]; Prisons [1-7]; Steel [6-7]

CUBA

[1] An extraordinary exodus brought 125,000 Cuban refugees to the U.S. in 1980. The refugees arrived in a "freedom flotilla" of small fishing boats, landing for the most part in Key West, Fla. The exodus took place during a five-month period, from late April to late September.

[2] **Thousands Seek Asylum.** Six Cubans April 1 crashed a bus through the gates of the Peruvian Embassy compound in Havana to gain asylum. A Cuban guard was killed. By April 6, a crowd of some 7,000 persons seeking refuge and safe passage out of Cuba had gathered inside the compound.

[3] Cuba April 4 had withdrawn its guards from outside the compound. The Cuban authorities April 7 began supplying food and water to the refugees, and President Fidel Castro personally went to the embassy to assure those inside that they would be granted safe passage out of Cuba as soon as another country signaled a willingness to take them.

[4] Cuban exiles took to the streets in Miami April 7 to rally in support of those seeking asylum. For more than 24 hours, thousands of the

demonstrators waved flags, blew horns and paraded in the southern Florida city, the home of the largest number of Cuban exiles in the U.S. A Spanish-language radio station, WQBA, reported that it had collected more than six planeloads of food and medicine for the refugees and about $70,000 for use in chartering aircraft to feery them from Havana to Florida.

[5] A U.S. State Department spokesman said April 10 that the U.S. was prepared to accept "a fair share of the Cubans and a fair share of the costs" of resettling them, but that the U.S expected Latin American countries to take the lead in offering asylum. One estimate put the total number of Cuban exiles who had been granted asylum in the U.S. since Castro came to power in 1959 at 800,000

[6] **U.S. Flotilla Picks Up Refugees.** About 50 small fishing boats set sail for the Cuban port of Mariel April 21 to pick up refugees hoping to escape to the U.S.

[7] While the U.S. continued to insist that it would enforce the law and impose penalties to curb the boat traffic, high-ranking U.S. officials in Florida conceded April 24 that it would be very difficult to halt the flow of refugees into Key West. One estimate put the number of refugees already picked up and in Key West or on their way at 2,000. The Cubans were being admitted "conditionally" for 60 days, during which time they could file claims for political asylum. Under the Refugee Act of 1980, which took effect April 1, up to 18,000 Cuban refugees could be admitted into the U.S. every year. However, immigration officials said that the refugees arriving in Key west were being let in under the President's emergency parole power and not the new law.

[8] **Refugees Pouring into the U.S.** Despite U.S. warnings of $1,000 fines for each refugee brought into the country, the flotilla of boats waiting in Port Mariel, Cuba had grown to 3,000 May 1, and more boats were sailing to Cuba every day.

[9] Immigration officials in Key West said that they had identified 55 common criminals among the 6,000 refugees processed to date. The suspected criminals were being detained, although it appeared doubtful that they would be forced to return to Cuba.

[10] A fierce storm with winds up to 100 miles per hour (160 K.p.h.) whipped through the Gulf of Mexico April 25-28, churning the ocean to swells up to 15 feet (4.5 meters). The Coast Guard estimated that some 30 boats feerying refugees had capsized during the storm, and four of those aboard were known to have drowned.

[11] **U.S. Offers Warm Reception.** President Carter pledged May 5 that the U.S. would "provide an open heart and open arms" to the thousands of Cuban refugees pouring into Florida from Cuba. Carter's remarks came on a day when 3,500 more Cuban refugees arrived in Key West, and the flood of Cuban exiles into the U.S. showed no sign of abating.

[12] Carter May 6 declared a state of emergency in regions of Florida affected most by the refugees and authorized $10 million to be sent to help community organizations provide relief. By May 6, an estimated 17,636 refugees had reached Florida since mid-April.

[13] ***New Policy Announced***— In a dramatic shift of policy on the Cuban refugee exodus to the U.S., President Carter May 14 abandoned his offer of "open arms" in favor of a five-point program designed to reduce the influx of Cuban refugees to a more manageable level.

The five-point program:

An orderly airlift and sealift of qualified refugees would be provided by the U.S. government as soon as Cuba accepted the offer.

All persons wishing to leave Cuba would have to be screened by U.S. and international authorities prior to their departure. In the meantime, the U.S. would formulate a quota system to determine how many Cubans would be permitted to enter the U.S. on a monthly and yearly basis.

The Coast Guard would act to halt the flotilla of private boats carrying refugees from Cuba to Florida.

A family registration center was to be opened in Miami to begin receiving the names of persons in Cuba who were eligible for immigration.

Persons already in the U.S. who had been imprisoned in Cuba for non-political crimes would be excluded from consideration for emigration to the U.S. By May 15, some 400 suspected criminals had been detained by U.S. authorities, and proceedings were under way to have them returned to Cuba.

[14] By May 15, more boats had arrived in Key West with some 2,600 refugees, bringing the total for the three-week exodus to nearly 46,000.

[15] The Cubans were being processed in four centers around the country. Eglin Air Force Base in the Florida panhandle and Fort Chaffee in Arkansas were near capacity by May 21, with 10,000 and 19,000 Cubans, respectively. Fort Indiantown Gap, in Pennsylvania, had a capacity of 20,000 and started receiving refugees May 18. Another processing center opened May 25 at Fort McCoy, Wis.

Young Cuban refugee plays with her dolls May 19 at temporary housing facility in Key West, Fla.

[16] Hundreds of Cuban refugees, frustrated and angry over the delays in thier processing, threw stones and scuffled with military police at the refugee processing center at Eglin Air Force Base in Florida May 24. Eglin officials said that between 20 and 100 of the refugees fled during the distubance, but that by early May 25, most had been returned to the camp.

[17] **Refugees Riot at Fort Chaffee.** Some 200 Cuban refugees burst through the front gate at the Fort Chaffee processing center in Arkansas June 1.

[18] The Cubans were forced back inside the military compound by police officers and soldiers who used tear gas and clubs in an attempt to subdue the refugees. Thirty-five Cubans were arrested. Forty persons were injured in the melee, and four buildings were burned to the ground.

[19] The Fort Chaffee center had been the scene of numerous confrontations in the previous week. As many as 1,000 of the 18,000 refugees awaiting relocation at the base had gathered to demand their freedom. On June 2, about 300 Army troops and 2,000 National Guardsmen were called in to maintain calm.

[20]President Carter directed the Justice Department June 7 to move to expel any Cuban refugees who had committed "serious crimes" in Cuba and to prosecute or expel those found responsible for the June 1 rioting at the Fort Chaffee, Ark. refugee camp.

[21] **Refugees Hijack Jets to Havana.** Seven Cuban refugees hijacked an Air Florida jet with 74 persons aboard after takeoff from Key West Aug. 13

Cuban refugee is handcuffed June 1 after rioting at Fort Chaffee, Ark.

and forced the pilot to fly to Havana.

[22] Three hihackings to Cuba took place Aug. 16. An Eastern Air Lines jet with 52 passenagers on a flight from Miami to Orlando, Fla. was commandeered by six men and forced to fly to Cuba. A Republic Airlines jet bound to Orlando from Miami was hijacked to Cuba by three men, and a Delta Air Lines jet was forced to Cuba by a single man.

[23] **'Freedom Flotilla' Ends.** The Cuban government Sept. 26 closed the harbor at Mariel, thus ending the five-month-long boatlift of Cubans to the United States known as the "freedom flotilla." The boatlift had brought 125,000 Cuban refugees to the U.S. since it began April 21. About 16,000 of the refugees remained in resettlement camps around the U.S. and 2,000 who had been found to have committed serious crimes were in federal prisons undergoing expulsion hearings.

See also Immigration; Refugees [6-8]; United Nations [3, 22-23, 30]; Yemen, People's Democratic Republic of [1-3]

CYCLING

[1] **Zoetemelk Wins Tour de France.** Joop Zoetemelk, a 31-year-old Dutchman, July 20 won the Tour de France, the world's most prestigious bicycle endurance race.

[2] The race, which began June 28, covered 2,436 miles (3,896 kilometers), starting in the Dutch city of Leiden and ending in Paris. It was run in 22 stages of about 110 miles (176 kilometers) each.

[3] Zoetemelk won with an overall time of 109 hours 19 minutes 14 seconds. It was his first victory in the race in 12 attempts. Hennie Kuiper of the Netherlands was second overall and Raymond Martin of France, third. France's Bernard Hinault, winner of the 1978 and 1979 tours, dropped out of the 1980 race July 9, citing tendinitis in his right knee.

CYPRUS

[1] **Intercommunal Talks Resume.** Negotiations between the Greek Cypriot and Turkish Cypriot communities resumed in Nicosia Aug. 9 after a break of 14 months. The United Nations-sponsored talks dealt with certain preliminary issues in the first session; the two sides agreed to begin discussion of substantive issues related to the restoration of an over-all island government.

[2] An opening statement from U.N. Secretary General Kurt Waldheim said that it was his "understanding" that both communities favored "a federal solution of the constitutional aspect and a bizonal solution of the territorial aspect of the Cyprus problem." In permitting the use of the word "bilzonal" in Waldheim's statement, the Greek Cypriots had made a concession. However, Greek Cypriot leader President Spyros Kyprianou said that if the Turkish Cypriots tried to interpret "bizonal" in such a way as to justify

partition of the island, then there would be "no room for progess or negotiation." Turkish Cypriot leader Rauf Denktash said he considered that the question of refugees and persons displaced by the 1974 Turkish invasion of Cyprus had been "settled" and the matter should be forgotten. Kyrianou took issue with this.

CZECHOSLOVAKIA

[1] **Unofficial Lectures Suppressed.** Police broke up several informal lectures at private homes in March and April. Prof. Julius Tomin, a noted dissident philosopher, was detained briefly March 19 and April 2 as a result.

[2] Tomin conducted regular discussions in his apartment in Prague. Other informal gatherings were broken up by police in Brno. The lectures were similar to the "flying universities" organized by dissident Polish scholars.

[3] At a lecture by Tomin March 9, police detained Prof. William Newton-Smith, a philosophy professor at Oxford University. After several hours of questioning, Newton-Smith was deported to West Germany. The British professor's visit to Tomin had been sponsored by Oxford.

[4] **Charter '77 Founder Expelled.** Czech journalist Jiri Lederer, a co-founder of the Charter '77 human rights movement in Czechoslovakia, arrived in West Germany Sept. 2 after being expelled from him homeland.

See also Human Rights [13]

DEATH PENALTY

[1] **Gacy Sentenced to Death.** John Wayne Gacy was sentenced by a jury in Chicago March 13 to die in the electric chair for the sex slaying of 33 boys and young men. Gacy, 37, had been convicted by the same jury March 12 of 33 counts of murder. Illinois law provided that a defendant convicted of a capital crime could choose to have his death penalty hearing before a jury or the trial judge. Gacy's attorneys had asked that the hearing be held before a jury. An automatic appeal was filed.

[2] **Ga. Death Law Application Narrowed.** The Supreme Court voted, 6-3, May 19 to overturn the death sentence of a convicted Georgia murderer, Robert Franklin Godfrey. In doing so, the high court signaled its apparent intention to monitor the application of death penalties by the states.

[3] Godfrey had been found guilty of the 1977 shotgun slaying of his wife and mother-in-law. He had been sentenced to die under a provision of the Georgia capital punishment law that permitted the death sentence for "outrageously or wantonly vile, horrible or inhuman [crimes that involve] torture, depravity of mind or an aggravated battery."

[4] The Supreme Court reversed Godfrey's sentence but did not nullify the law itself. The court had specifically upheld the constitutionality of the stature in 1976. Four members of the majority–Potter Stewart, Harry A. Blackmun, John Paul Stevens and Lewis F. Powell Jr.–held that the "depravity" provision had been too broadly applied in Godfrey's case. Wrote Stewart: "There is no principled way to distinguish this case, in which the death penalty was imposed, from the many cases in which it was not." States had to make such a distinction, he said, to prevent the imposition of a death sentence from being unconstitutionally "arbitrary or capricious."

[5] **Alabama Statue in Limbo.** The status of Alabama's death penalty law was in doubt due to a ruling Oct. 15 by a three-judge panel of the U.S. 5th Circuit of Appeals in New Orleans. The tribunal overturned the death sentence of John Louis Evans 3rd and ordered retrials for him and 44 other prison imates facing execution.

[6] The U.S. Supreme Court had held in June, in the case *Beck v. Alabama*, that the state's capital punishment law was invalid because defendants tried under the statute could not be found guilty of a lesser offense not punishable by execution. It was left up to the Alabama Supreme Court to determine if any other sections of the law were constitutional, and if some or all the state's death row immates were entitled to new trials. The Alabama Supreme Court had not yet handed down a ruling on the capital punishment law.

[7] **Massachusetts Law Struck Down.** The Massachusetts Supreme Court Oct. 28 ruled, 6-1, that capital punishment was "impermissibly cruel" and "brutalizes the state that imposes it." The court voided a 1979 state law that reinstated the death penalty.

DEFENSE (U.S.)

Nuclear Policy

[1] **New Strategy.** President Carter had adopted a new strategy that the United States would use in fighting a nuclear war with the Soviet Union, government officials said Aug. 5.

[2] The strategy, detailed in President Directive 59, gave priority to attacking military targets in the Soviet Union, and lessened a previous emphasis on all-out retaliation against Soviet cities and industrial complexes.

[3] Administration officials asserted the chance of nuclear war would decrease if U.S. forces had the capacity to initiate limited nuclear strikes against Soviet military targets. They believed the Soviets would be less inclined to launch "pinpoint nuclear attacks" if the U.S. could deny them eventual victory in a nuclear war by destroying vital Soviet military capability.

[4] Government specialists felt the Soviet Union's nuclear strategy had long been aimed at developing the kind of capability, known as "counterforce," the U.S. now sought. They also believed the U.S. now had sufficiently accurate weapons – such as the Navy's submarine launched Trident I ballistic missile, the new MK 12A warhead, for the Minuteman III force, and the soon-to-be-deployed cruise missile – to fight the prolonged but limited nuclear war they felt the Soviets would try to wage.

[5] The new nuclear doctrine reflected changes in the thinking of senior Administration officials, who as late as January 1979 believed the U.S.'s massive nuclear arsenal, with its potential to destroy every large and medium-sized city in the Soviet Union, sufficed to deter any threat of nuclear war. The officials, reportedly including Defense Secretary Harold Brown and National Security Adviser Zbigniew Brzezinski, had come to think the Soviets did not believe in the concept of "mutually assured destruction," as Washington did, and that the Soviets did believe a nuclear war could be fought and won.

[6] ***Muskie Unaware of Strategy Shift***—Secretary of State Edmund S. Muskie Aug. 8 said he had not been informed of President Carter's decision to revise U.S. nuclear war strategy. Muskie said he first learned of the shift by reading newspaper accounts. Muskie's chief concern was not as much with the substance of the policy revision, as with "being frozen out of discussions of it." The Pentagon Aug. 1 sent a senior official to brief Muskie at his Maine home.

[7] ***Soviets Condemn Stretegy Change***—The official Soviet news agency Tass Aug. 11 condemned the revision of U.S. nuclear war policy as "insanity," conceived by persons "who have lost all touch with reality and are prepared to push the world" into nuclear war.

[8] **Brown Discusses Policy.** Defense Secretary Brown Aug. 20 discussed the new nuclear strategy adopted by the U.S. with the signing of Presidential Directive 59.

[9] In a speech at the Naval War College in Newport, R.I., Brown claimed the policy revision "is not a new strategic doctrine, not a radical departure from U.S. strategic policy over the last decade or so." But in a surprising and unexpected change, Brown said that America's landbased nuclear Minuteman missile force might already be vulnerable to a Soviet first strike.

[10] That was seen as a major reassessment of U.S. vulnerability. In his annual report on defense preparedness, Brown had predicted that the Soviets would attain the capabiltiy to destroy many or most of America's 1,000 Minuteman missiles "within a year or two." In his prepared text for the Newport speech, in a paragraph that Brown did not read, he conceded, "That potential has been realized, or close to it."

Titan 2 missile silo was destroyed in explosion Sept. 19.

Mishaps

[11] **One Killed in Misille Silo Blast.** A fuel explosion rocked an underground Titan 2 nuclear missile silo Sept. 19 near Damascus, Ark., sending flames 500 feet (150 meters) into the air and injuring 22 Air Force personnel, one fatally.

[12] The explosion forced a 12-hour evacuation of about 1,400 residents within a five-mile (eight-kilometer) radius of the missile site. However, Defense Department officials said that there was no evidence of damage to the missile's 10-megaton nuclear warhead or of any radiation leaks caused by the explosion.

[13] The blast shattered the 750-ton concrete door atop the silo, leaving a crater about 25 feet (8 meters) deep. The nuclear warhead atop the 103-foot-long (31 meters) intercontinental ballistic missile was hurled by the explosion out of the silo, landing about 250 yards (225 meters) away in nearby woods. Military officials said that the warhead had been "unarmed" because the detonation sequence to arm it had not been set off. Officials said that "fail-safe" devices prevented the command sequence that led to detonation from occurring in the event of an accidental explosion.

[14] The accident was triggered when an Air Force maintenance technician, who was working at the third level of the missile, dropped a three-pound (1.5-kilogram) wrench socket that fell 70 feet (21 meters) puncturing the missile's first stage fuel tank. The rupture caused toxic vapors to escape and the workmen evacuated the silo. A fire flared in the engine, triggering an automatic sprinkler system that poured 100,000 gallons (450,000 liters) of water into the 146-foot-deep (44 meters) silo. However, the water failed to cover the engine or the fuel tank. The explosion occurred about six and a half hours after the fuel tank rupture, just as an emergency action team of the Strategic Air Command was leaving the silo's access chamber. The fuel

was a mixture of hydrazine and unsymetrical dimethylhydrazine, which could ignite upon contact with the oxident, nitrogen tetroxide.

[15] The Air Force said that among the 22 injured, 18 required hospitalization. The sole fatality, Sgt. David Livingston, of Heath, Ohio, died in Little Rock, after undergoing surgery for shrapnel wounds in the face and stomach. The missile silo explosion was the third fatal accident since 1965 involving missile fuel leaks.

[16] **Computer Errors Trigger Alerts.** Errors in the U.S. air defense network's computer system sent out false signals that Soviet land-based and submarine-based nuclear missiles had been launched against the U.S. twice during the week of June 6.

[17] In both cases the false alarm was quickly discovered, but not before American's nuclear forces had been ordered to a higher state of readiness. It was the third time in seven months that a computer malfunction in the Wimex system had falsely indicated a Soviet attack.

[18] The first false alarm came June 3, it was disclosed June 5, and originated from the North American Air Defense Command headquarters in Colorado Springs. While the engines of bombers were started and communications with U.S. missile crews intensified, commanders checked other sensors and concluded that the warnings were false. The error was detected within three minutes. Neither President Carter nor Defense Secretary Harold Brown was notified of the "possible threat," but the White House situation room was contacted.

[19] The second error occurred June 6, but as with the previous malfunction, it was caught within three minutes. Although the engines of some Strategic Air Command planes were turned on, U.S. forces did not go "on alert." According to defense experts, it would take about nine minutes for missiles launched by Soviet submarines to hit U.S. bomber bases and 30 minutes for intercontinental ballistic missiles fired from within the Soviet Union to strike targets in the U.S.

[20] **Cruise Missile Problems.** Air Force tests of two types of air-launched cruise missiles had revealed serious problems in their guidance systems, according to a report in the Jan. 14 issue of *Newsweek* magazine. The missiles, which were supposed to be able to correct their course during flight, had crashed into mountains or other natural barriers in seven out of 16 test firings since July 1979.

[21] General Dynamics Corp. and the Boeing Co. were competing for an Air Force contract worth $2 billion for 3,418 cruise missiles. Three Boeing and four General Dynamics misilles had crashed in tests. None of the missiles was armed, and none of the crashes caused property damage or injuries.

[22] The Boeing Co. was named March 25 by the Defense Department as the prime contractor to build the weapon.

Other Developments

[23] **Brown: 'Mobility Required.'** Defense Secretary Harold Brown, in his annual assessment of the U.S. military posture, Jan. 29 said the U.S. had to improve its military forces' ability to move with great power and speed on a worldwide basis" to protect American interests.

[24] Brown said the growth of Soviet military power and the danger of conflict in the Middle East or Southeast Asia made it imperative that the U.S. augment its ability to reinforce its own troops, or its allies, with air and ground support. "We have never fully acquired the agility and the mobility required by such a reinforcement strategy," said he.

[25] In his 300-page posture statement, Brown outlined Soviet threats to the sea lanes of the world, a particular area of danger because Western oil supplies were dependent upon their safety. He claimed the Soviet arms buildup went

beyond any reasonable national security need. He said the U.S.S.R. might be planning to field enough forces to fight on three fronts at once.

[26] Brown and Air Force Gen. David C. Jones, chariman of the Joint Chiefs of Staff, appeared before the House Armed Services Committee to explain the Carter Administration's request for an increase in the defense budget to $142.7 billion in fiscal 1981.

[27] **U.S. Gets Bases in Oman, Kenya, Somalia.** The U.S. announced April 21 that it had reached military and economic agreements with Oman and Kenya giving American forces access to air and naval bases in those two countries.

[28] The U.S. and Somalia Aug. 21 signed an agreement providing the U.S. with military facilities in the East African country in return for American military aid.

[29] **MX System Revised.** The Defense Department said May 6 that it had discarded the controversial "race track" basing plan for the long-range MX missile and had opted for a "straight-track" deployment system. The racetrack concept had been opposed by many Utah and Nevada residents who felt it would take vast amounts of lands unnecessarily.

[30] As first envisioned, and approved by President Carter, 40 MX installations were to be built. Each would consist of five oval-shaped "race tracks" for a total of 4,600 underground shelters and 20,000 miles (16,000 kilometers) of roadway. Each race track would have one missile and 23 shelters. Such a deployment system would allow the nuclear-armed MX missiles to be shuttled quickly from one shelter to another in a "shell game" meant to confuse a possible Soviet first strike.

[31] Defense officials said the change to a linear track system could reduce the miles of road built by 20%.

[32] **'Stealthy Aircraft' Said to Evade Radar.** A new U.S. plane that could evade detection by Soviet radar had been developed, it was revealed Aug. 20.

[33] Defense Department officials said the radar-evading experimental aircraft had been tested secretly at Nellis Air Force Base in Nevada for two years. The plane, nicknamed the "stealthy aircraft," was built in a shape designed to eliminate the sharp corners that produced maximum radar reflection. In addition, the plane was coated with a special material that diffused radar waves.

[34] Officials said that the technology designed for the new aircraft, which was developed by Lockheed Aircraft Corp., could be used in designing a new manned strategic bomber to penetrate the Soviet Union's air defense network.

[35] Some congressional staff defense experts were quoted by the *New York Times* as suggesting that the disclosure of the "stealthy aircraft" was made by the Carter Administration in response to criticism by Ronald Reagan, the Republican presidential candidate. Reagan had attacked President Carter for canceling production of the proposed B-1 bomber. Carter claimed the manned long-range bomber was obsolete and vulnerable to Soviet defenses. The revelation of an "invisible" aircraft was seen as a way of proving the Carter contention that there were more technically sophiscated weapons than the B-1 available.

[36] Ronald Reagan Sept. 4 accused the Carter Administration of "a cynical misuse of power and a clear abuse of the public trust" by disclosing the develpment of the so-called "stealth" aircraft. Reagan contended that the leaks were a political ploy to disguise Carter's "dismal defense record."

[37] **Defense Bill.** The House Dec. 5 voted, 321 to 36, in favor of a $160.1 billion defense appropriation bill. Shortly afterward, the Senate followed suit with a vote of 73 to 1. (Sen. Mark Hatfield [R, Ore.] was the Senate's lone dissenter.)

[38] The bill, approved by a House-

Senate conference committee Dec. 4, appropriated $5.6 billion more than President Carter had requested. The final measure included $300 million for development of a manned bomber, $35 million for development of the CX cargo plane, $1.2 billion for increases in military compensation and up to $3.4 billion for Pentagon contracts awarded in areas of high unemployment.

[39] The $19 million appropriated in the House version of the bill for the development of nerve gas production facilities was dropped. The conferees agreed to let Ronald Reagan decide whether to resume nerve gas production, which had been halted in 1969 by President Richard Nixon.

See also Armaments (International) [1]; Australia [9-11]; Budget [3, 8, 10-12, 22]; Congress [8]; Egypt [8-11]; Germany, West [5-11]; Union of Soviet Socialist Republics (U.S.S.R.) [20-33]

DELAWARE—*See* Weather [11-12]

DENG XIAOPING (Teng Hsiao-ping)—*See* China, People's Republic of [2, 7-8]

DENMARK—*See* Economy (International) [7-8]

DETROIT—*See* Census (U.S.) [1-3]; City & State Affairs [7-9]

DISARMAMENT

[5] **China Joins Geneva Conference.** China attended the Feb. 5 opening of the 1980 session of the Conference of the Committee on Disarmament (the Geneva disarmament conference) for the first time since the conference was created in 1962. Chinese Deputy Foreign Minister Zhang Wenjin used the session to deliver a sharp attack on the U.S.S.R.

[2] Zhang charged that detente was a pretext for Soviet expansionism. He asserted that the Soviet Union and the U.S. were about equal in nuclear arsenals. The Soviets, he continued, had "obvious superiority" in conventional armed forces. The Soviet military intervention in Afghanistan, he declared, extended Moscow's "practice of military aggression and occupation to the Third World and Islamic countries."

[3] Turning to specific problems of disarmament, Zhang said his country favored drafting arms control treaties with the CCD as a whole. Usually, draft treaties were drawn up by the U.S. and the U.S.S.R. in bilateral discussions and then presented to the CCD for debate. Zhang added that it was up to the two superpowers to take the first step in reducing their nuclear arsenals. Only then could the rest of the world be expected to agree to arms reduction programs, he declared.

[4] **U.S. Might Renounce SALT II: Carter.** At a White House news conference March 14, President Carter left open the possibility that the U.S. might renounce the second strategic arms limitation treaty with the Soviet Union if, in consultations with the Senate leadership, it was decided that the SALT treaty and U.S. interests did not coincide.

[5] This was the first time that Carter had stated publicly that the U.S. might renounce the treaty.

[6] Carter said that the U.S. would continue to comply with the terms of the treaty, even though it had not been formally ratified by the Senate, as long as the Soviets did the same. Carter added that because of the Soviet moves in Afghanistan, "it is obvious that we would not be successful in ratifying the SALT II treaty at this time."

[7] The U.S.S.R. informed the U.S. March 19 that it would not discuss implementation of the strategic arms limitation treaty as long as the pact had not been ratified by the U.S. Senate. Moscow's statement did not

say whether the Soviet Union would abide by the treaty's terms even though it was not in force.

[8] ***Vance Urges SALT Approval—*** Former Secretary of State Cyrus Vance called on the Senate to approve the U.S.-Soviet treaty limiting nuclear arms. Vance spoke June 5 at Harvard University's commencement exercises in his first public appearance since he resigned his office April 28.

[9] Vance called the SALT II treaty "the very heart of a sensible and far-seeing American foreign policy," and said the Senate should approve it by the end of 1980, despite the Soviet invasion of Afghanistan. He said that further delay would be "a profound mistake" with serious consequences for U.S.-Soviet relations in the 1980s and for the future of the arms control process.

[10] **Percy 'Confident' of Early Talks.** Sen. Charles H. Percy (R, Ill.), the incoming chairman of the Senate Foreign Relations Committee, Dec. 12 said he was "confident" that the U.S. and Soviet Union were willing to begin talks on arms control early in the administration of Ronald Reagan.

[11] **MBFR Discussions End in Deadlock.** The 22nd round of European force reduction talks between the North Atlantic Treaty Organization and the Warsaw Pact ended in Vienna Dec. 19 with no progress achieved on key issues.

See also Union of Soviet Socialist Republics [29-30]

DISASTERS & ACCIDENTS

[1] **222 Killed in Colombia Bullring Collapse.** At least 222 persons were killed, and more than 500 were injured, Jan. 21 when rain-soaked wooden bleachers collapsed at a bullring in the northern Colombian city of Sincelejo.

[2] **31 Killed in South African Mine.** Thirty-one South African miners were killed March 27 when the cable of a

RESCUE DRAMA: Boston fireman Johnnie Green March 17 saves cat from fire.

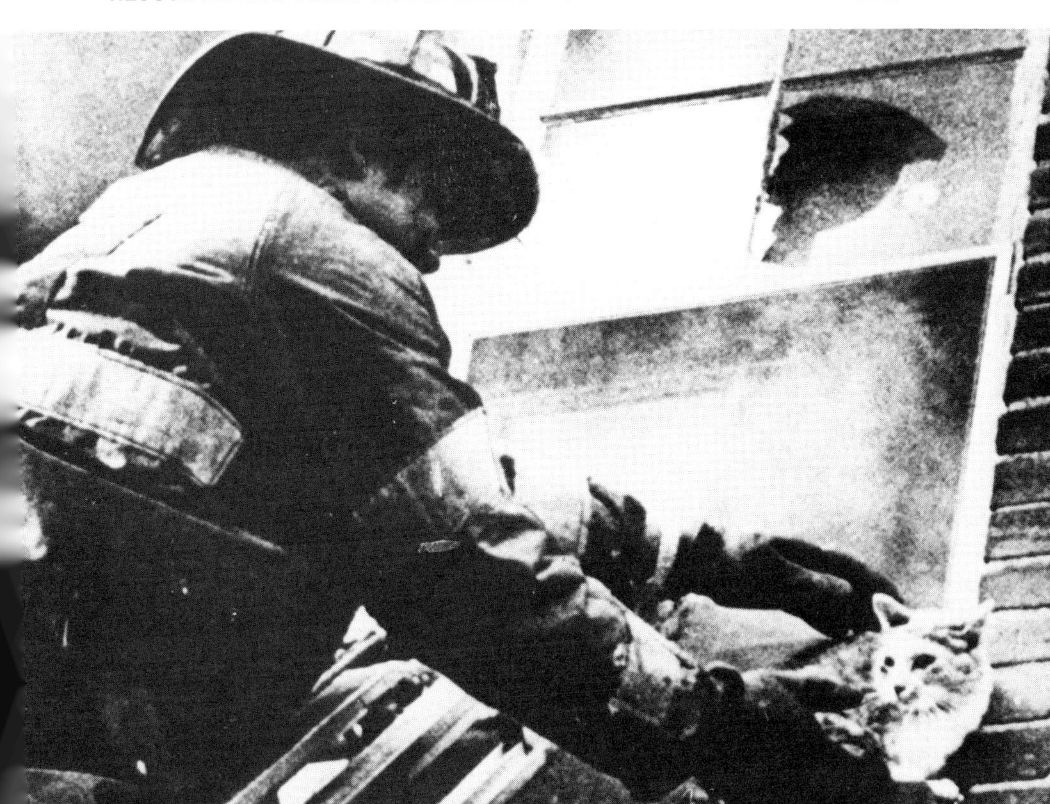

mineshaft elevator snapped, plunging the miners more than a mile to their deaths.

[3] The 12-foot-high double-decker elevator cage carrying the miners fell for more than 30 seconds as it reached a speed of more than 160 miles per hour (250 k.p.h.) The elevator cage was compressed to a height of less than 12 inches (30 centimeters) at impact. The accident occurred at the Vaal Reefs mine, the world's largest gold mine, about 100 miles (160 kilometers) southwest of Johannesburg.

[4] **Oil Platform Capsizes.** A total of 123 persons died when a North Sea floating oil field platform capsized March 27 in turbulent seas. The five-legged, 10,105-ton (9,165-metric ton) platform had been used as a floating dormitory for oil workers in the Ekofisk (Norwegian) oil field of the North Sea.

[5] ***Chinese Oil Rig Collapses***—Seventy persons were believed to have been killed in the collapse of a Chinese offshore oil drilling rig in Bo Hai Gulf, it was reported July 6.

[6] The oil rig collapse was said to have occurred Nov. 25, 1979. However, it was not disclosed until a joint investigation by the Communist Party newspaper *Jenmin Jih Pao* and the Hsinhua news agency. According to the press accounts, the accident occurred after a Communist Party official in charge of the rig had ordered it moved to a new drilling site despite warnings of a major storm in the area. Engineers aboard the rig had reportedly opposed the move as too dangerous, but were overruled. The accounts also said that the officials in charge were so heedless of safety that they did not bother to translate the operating instructions of the Japanese-made rig until after the accident.

[7] **35 Killed in Fla. Bridge Accident.** At least 35 persons were killed May 9 when a ship rammed a bridge over Tampa Bay in Florida. In the accident, a Greyhound bus and several other vehicles plunged 140 feet (about 40 meters) into the water.

[8] Most of the dead were passengers aboard the bus, which was bound from Chicago to Miami. The collision tore away a 1,200-foot (365-meter) section of the bridge's south-bound span, tumbling it into the bay.

[9] The accident occurred when the ship, a Liberian freighter, the *Summit Venture,* struck the Sunshine Skyway Bridge as it was heading into port in a blinding rainstorm. The *Summit Venture,* a 606-foot (185-meter), 35,000-ton phosphate freighter, suffered extensive damage. The accident was the third involving the Sunshine Skyway in 1980. On Jan. 28, the Coast Guard cutter *Blackthorn* collided with an oil tanker, the *Texas Capricorn,* near the same bridge, killing 28 Coast Guardsmen, the worst peacetime disaster in Coast Guard history.

[10] On May 10, Coast Guard officials were reported to have disclosed that Capt. John Lerro, the harbor pilot who was guiding the *Summit Venture* when it hit the bridge, was also at the helm when the Liberian freighter *Jonna Dan* struck the bridge March 8, causing $40,000 damage. In all, Lerro was said to have been involved in seven previous collisions or groundings. Tampa was the seventh busiest port in the U.S. and the busiest in the state. According to the state records, Tampa was also the scene for more nautical accidents – 120 – in the past five years than all other ports in the state combined.

[11] **67 Killed in S. Africa Bus Accident.** At least 67 persons were killed and 18 injured June 7 when a high-speed train and bus collided at a rail crossing near Empangeni, South Africa.

[12] **470 Flee Fire on Dutch Ocean Liner.** A Dutch luxury liner on a 30-day cruise to the Orient caught fire Oct. 4 in the Gulf of Alaska, forcing 470 persons to abandon the ship in stormy seas.

[13] Some 320 passengers, mostly elderly Americans, and 150 crew

Fire Nov. 21 killed 84 persons at MGM Grand Hotel in Las Vegas, Nev.

members were lowered into lifeboats 180 miles (290 kilometers) southwest of Sitka, Alaska. About 40 crew members remained aboard the listing 427-foot (130 meter) *Prinsendam* to fight the spreading flames. Ships and helicopters, responding to the ship's pre-dawn distress call, converged on the vessel within three hours. No deaths or injuries were reported.

[14] **84 Die in Las Vegas Hotel Fire.** A fire swept through the MGM Grand Hotel in Las Vegas Nov. 21 killing 84 persons and injuring at least 500 others.

[15] Most of the victims, apparently trapped between the 19th and 24th floors of the 26-story luxury hotel and casino, died of smoke inhalation in the second worst hotel fire in U.S. history.

[16] ***26 Die in N.Y. Hotel Fire***—An electrical flash fire swept through conference rooms at the Stouffer Inn, a suburban hotel complex in Harrison, N.Y. Dec. 4, killing 26 persons and injuring at least 40 others. Among the dead were 13 executives of the Arrow Electronics Corp. of Greenwich, Conn. and 11 executives of Nestle Co.

[17] **Brush Fire Blaze in Southern California.** Brush and timber fires, fanned by hot, dry winds of up to 100 miles an hour, laid waste to more than 86,000 acres (34,400 hectares) in five Southern California counties, in a 15-day period, starting Nov. 15.

[18] The rampaging brush fires swept over tinder-dry hillsides and grasslands, destroying small communities perched along the foothills north and south of Los Angeles. At least 11 major fires blazed in the region, destroying more than 300 homes and 150 other buildings and causing an estimates $82 million in property and watershed damage. Four persons were killed. By Nov. 30 most of the fires had been brought under control.

See also Aviation [8-14]; Earthquakes; Volcanos [1-15]; Weather

DISTRICT OF COLUMBIA—

See City & State Affairs [1-2, 11]

DOMINICAN REPUBLIC—*See* Colombia [1-7]; Immigration

DRAFT REGISTRATION

[1] A controversial draft registration law was proposed by President Carter and enacted by Congress in 1980. The President asked that women as well as men be registered, but Congress rejected this provision of the plan. Registration of men only was held unconstitutional by a federal court panel in Philadelphia; Supreme Court Justice William F. Brennan ruled that registration could proceed, pending a review of the law by the entire high court. Some four million 19- and 20-year old men were required to register at post offices across the nation under the program. Protests against registration were mostly peaceful. A 93% rate of registration was announced by the Selective Service System, but antidraft groups challenged the accuracy of the figure.

[2] **Administration Plan.** A plan for draft registration was announced Feb. 8 by President Carter. It called for registration of women as well as of men.

[3] Registration was needed, he said, "to increase our preparedness and as a further demonstration of our resolve as a nation." The President stressed anew, as he had in his State of the Union Address, that "the Soviet invasion of Afghanistan poses a serious threat to a region that is vital to the long-term interests of the United States and our allies."

[4] His decision to register women was "a recognition of the reality that both women and men are working members of our society," Carter said.

[5] Registration of women for the draft, which had never been done in the U.S., required congressional authority. The

President already had the authority to start registration of men. The Administration's plan called for registration in 1980 of 19 and 20 year olds, those born in 1960 and 1961. They would register at post offices by completing a form with their name, address, date of birth and Social Security number.

[6] The following year, people born in 1962 would register and from thereafter registration would be required when a person became 18. Draft cards were not to be issued under the Administration's plan. The Selective Service System was to send out letters confirming the registration information and requesting notification of address changes. The date on registrants was to be kept in computers for ready mobilization if necessary. A return to a draft, which the Administration stressed it did not intend at this point, would require congressional action. As part of the President's plan, local citizens were to be selected and trained for potential draft-board service.

[7] **Female Draft Registration Rejected.** President Carter's proposal to register women for the draft was defeated by a 8 to 1 vote March 6 in the House Armed Services military personnel subcommittee. Only Guam's delegate to the House, Antonio Won Pat, voted for female registration.

[8] **Registration Bill Passed & Signed.** President Carter June 27 signed a controversial draft-registration measure, opening the way for the July registration of some four million young men aged 19 or 20.

[9] The House voted 234-168 on June 25 for $13.3 million in funds to put the registration program into effect. The penalty for failing to register would be up to five years in prison, and/or a fine of up to $10,000.

[10] The Senate had passed the bill on June 12 by a 58-34 vote. Senate action on the bill came after opponents ended

Students at Princeton University demonstrate Feb. 12 against draft registration.

a week of efforts to kill the proposal by a filibuster. Sen. Mark O. Hatfield (R, Ore.), led the opposition. The Senate voted 62-32 June 10 to invoke cloture, which limited debate tactics in exchange for a vote on a final amendment. Hatfield's amendment attempted to get the Senate to vote for funds to set up the registration machinery but not for actual registration. That amendment was defeated, 59-35.

[11] **Brennan OKs Registration.** Supreme Court Justice William F. Brennan Jr. July 19 ruled registration for the draft could begin. He lifted a day-old prohibition by three federal judges that barred the government from carrying out registration.

[12] A special three-judge panel in Philadelphia July 18 ruled that draft registration that excluded women was unconstitutional. In their 41-page ruling, Judges Max Rosen, Joseph Lord and Edward Cahn held the government had not proven the "exclusion of women is substantially related to an important governmental function."

[13] Justice Brennan, acting from his vacation home, agreed with the Justice Department's contention that the panel's ruling left the country without the means of drafting an army and undercut the president's ability to conduct foreign policy. Brennan granted the government's request to stay the effect of the panel's decision until the entire Supreme Court could review it.

[14] **Registration Takes Place.** The nation's first draft registration program since 1975 took place between July 21 and Aug. 2, with government officials claiming success and antidraft organizers maintaining the program had failed. Nearly four million 19- and 20-year-old men were required to register at post offices across the nation.

[15] Selective Service Director Bernard D. Rostker July 31 said his agency would enforce the law against those who failed to register.

[16] Protests marked the beginning of registration July 21. The protests were mainly peaceful. No serious incidents were reported in Washington, D.C. or New York, where the largest anti-registration demonstrations were staged.

[17] ***93% Compliance***—Bernard D. Rostker, the director of the Selective Service System, said Sept. 4 that 93% of the men subject to draft registration had registered.

[18] The 93% figure was far higher than the figures given out by some antidraft groups. The Committee Against Registration and the Draft (CARD) Aug. 26 said that, according to its survey of postmasters, a fifth to a third of draft-age youths in some communities had failed to register.

DROUGHT—*See* Weather [6-10]

DRUGS & NARCOTICS

[1] **Jordan Cleared.** A special grand jury concluded that there was insufficient evidence to support allegations that Hamilton Jordan had used cocaine, Arthur H. Christy announced May 28. Christy was a special federal prosecutor appointed to investigate the allegations.

[2] Jordan, White House chief of staff to President Carter, had been accused of cocaine use during a 1978 visit to New York's Studio 54 discotheque.

[3] **Miami Banks Linked to Drug Money.** In testimony before the Senate Banking, Housing and Urban Affairs Committee June 5, Miami bankers and government officials said that they had uncovered evidence linking several Miami banks to the drug trade.

[4] The Senate hearings, chaired by Sen. William Proxmire (D, Wis.), were called following a Treasury Department crack-down June 3 on the activities of the banks in South Florida. Richard J. Davis, assistant treasury secretary for enforcement, told the committee that some of the banks had

shown "unusual deposit patterns" with the Federal Reserve System involving large amounts of cash that were "clearly identified with drug trafficking."

[5] Davis said that steps had been taken to tighten the requirements for reporting large cash deposits to the Treasury. Under the Bank Secrecy Act of 1970, banks did not have to report cash deposits over $10,000 into the Federal Reserve System if the deposits were made by established customers. The new rule made it mandatory that all such deposits be reported to the Treasury unless the depositor was both an established customer of the bank and an American citizen running a legitimate large cash-flow business.

[6] According to some government narcotics officials, the drug trade was now South Florida's biggest business, worth some $7 billion in 1979. According to figures from the Federal Reserve Board, the currency surplus in southern Florida had grown to $3.9 billion in 1979 from $3.3 billion in 1978, while banks in the rest of the U.S. had suffered a deposit shortage. Proxmire said that one bank in the Miami area had deposited $600 million into the Federal Reserve in 1979 when it had been expected to deposit only about $13 million. None of the suspect banks was named.

[7] **Cocaine Use Reported Widespread in NBA.** Between 40% and 75% of the players in the National Basketball Association used cocaine, reported the Los Angeles *Times* Aug. 19.

[8] Frank Layden, general manager of the Utah Jazz told the *Times* that there was "not a team in the league you can confidently say does not have a drug problem. Every team could benefit from a rehabilitation program. I had two [drug] cases out of 11 players last year."

[9] Layden referred to forward Bernard King and guard Terry Furlow. King, a former New Jersey Net, had pleaded guilty June 4 to two counts of forcible sexual abuse involving a Salt Lake City woman. He had been arrested for the offenses Jan. 2 at his apartment. During the arrest, police confiscated a small amount of white powder, believed to be cocaine. King, who had been suspended indefinitely by the Jazz, June 4 was given two suspended one-year jail terms and a $2,000 fine. Furlow, 25, had been killed May 23 near Cleveland, when the car he was driving veered off the highway and smashed into a utility pole. An autopsy later disclosed the presence of Valium and cocaine in his system.

[10] Michael Gearon, president of the Atlanta Hawks, said he believed as many as half the players in the NBA used cocaine and as many as 10% might use free base. (Free base was a cocaine derivative that was smoked, rather than snorted, by the user.) A former player contended: "Coke is rampant in the league. I mean, 75% use it. Its like drinking water. You 'hit the blow' (snort cocaine) to be sociable. Coke didn't start in the NBA, but its now the drug of the money culture. It has taken the place of alcohol in the league." A current player said, "It's really scary. Some of the best players in the league, players who don't even drink, are into free base, and they are spending some very big sums of money." Cocaine cost between $90 and $125 a gram. The average salary in the NBA was about $180,000 a year.

The village of Balvano, Italy was devastated by earthquake Nov. 23.

E

EARTHQUAKES

[1] **Quake Devastates Southern Italy.** An earthquake struck southern Italy Nov. 23, causing wide devastation to dozens of villages, towns and cities and leaving hundreds of thousands homeless.

[2] Official figures released Dec. 8 from relief headquarters in Naples said that 3,105 persons had been killed, 1,575 were missing and presumed dead and 7,671 were injured.

[3] The earthquake, the strongest to hit Italy in 70 years, measured 6.8 on the Richter scale. It was followed by a wave of 32 aftershocks that were felt from the island of Sicily in the south to Trieste in the northeast along the Yugoslav border. The epicenter of the quake was Eboli, a town near the Bay of Salerno about 30 miles (48 kilometers) southeast of Naples. The earthquake damage was spread over a 10,156 square mile area that included the cities of Naples and Salerno, the volcano Mt. Vesuvius and the ancient cities of Pompeii and Herculaneum.

[4] Among the hardest hit regions were the provinces of Naples, Salerno, Potenza and Avellino, where the quake devastated at least 97 towns and villages, destroyed bridges and roads and toppled high buildings. In Balvano, a mountain village west of Potenza, 100 persons were reported killed, half children, when the facade of a medieval church crumbled during an evening mass. In Sant' Angelo de Lombarde in Avellino province, 300 persons were killed, incluing 27 children and two nuns, when an orphanage collapsed. In Naples, where the first jolt struck, the earthquake leveled dozens of buildings, including a 10-story apartment bulding where 11 persons were killed.

[5] Efforts to reach many of the stricken towns and villages in the mountain areas east of Naples were hampered by blocked roads, downed telephone lines and heavy fog. The Italian government Nov. 24 declared a "state of natural calamity" and mobilized army soldiers, truck convoys and helicopters to bring in tents, set up field hospitals and distribute medical supplies. Pope John Paul II Nov. 25 flew by helicopter to visit the area and pray with survivors. The earthquake was the worst to hit Italy since Dec. 28, 1908 when a quake killed about 75,000 persons at Messina, Sicily.

[6] The earthquake gave rise to political controversy, as the press and political figures charged that government relief efforts had been slow and inadequate, resulting in the loss of lives that could have been saved.

[7] President Sandro Pertini, after visiting the disaster area, appeared on television Nov. 26 and criticized the rescue efforts. Pertini said that 48 hours after the earthquake occurred some towns had still not received any official help. He praised the dismissal of one local official who had been slow to respond to the situation. He urged that all other officials found negligent be punished.

[8] Premier Arnaldo Forlani insisted Dec. 2, speaking to parliament for the first time since the earthquake, that

Wide World

Epicenter of earthquakes that devastated southern Italy was near Eboli.

"everything possible was done and is being done."

[9] The unsettled conditions in the disaster area led to an outbreak of crime, with local factions of the Mafia reportedly taking over relief supplies, through theft or fraud. According to a report Dec. 11, a convoy that arrived in the region with 44 trailers for the homeless had 16 trailers stolen by the time it reached a mountain town that was its final destination.

[10] **Thousands Killed In Algerian Quakes.** A double earthquake Oct. 10 struck the northwestern city of Al Asnam, killing thousands of persons and destroying hundreds of buildings.

[11] The first quake, registering 7.5 on the Richter scale, struck the city of 125,000 just after midday. The second, registering 6.5, hit three hours later on a fault line 100 miles (160 kilometers) southwest of the capital city of Algiers. Aftershocks continued for at least 72 hours.

[12] A hugh international aid effort was under way by Oct. 11, with medical teams and emergency supplies reaching Algeria from North American, Africa, the Middle East and Europe. Red Crescent officials Oct. 14 estimated casualties at 20,000 dead and 60,000 injured. Government officials said some 200,000 were homeless.

[13] **Azores Quake Kills 52.** An earthquake struck Portugal's Azores Islands Jan. 1, toppling buildings, killing at least 52 persons and injuring more than 300 persons.

ECONOMY (International)

[1] **Brandt Study Urges More Aid to Poorer Countries.** An international panel headed by former West German Chancellor Willy Brandt Feb. 12 called for the institution of universal taxation to fund increased aid for poorer countries.

[2] The group—the Independent Commission on International Development—said that the rich countries should provide $8 billion a year in new food aid. Development aid and loans should be increased to total $50 billion to $60 billion annually over the next five years, the commission said.

[3] To diminish the control of national legislatures over aid decisions, the panel recommended that a form of universal taxation be instituted, with the amount of a country's contribution determined by the size of its national income. A start could be made, the commission said, by creating a World Development Fund that would collect taxes on foreign trade, particularly the arms trade, and on sea-bed mining.

[4] The commission also recommended the convening of a North-South summit conference. At a press conference Feb. 12, Brandt conceded that the elevated tensions created by the Soviet invasion of Afghanistan put problems in the way of such a meeting. But the commission nevertheless urged the summit because it believed that "the present deadlock is so serious, and the

need to break through is so evident, that nothing should delay discussion and negotiation at the highest level."

[5] The commission was made up of prominent persons from government or public affairs around the world. They were not responsible to their respective national governments, thus making it easier to achieve a consensus for their report.

[6] **Western Labor Costs Compared.** Belgium, Sweden, the Netherlands and West Germany had the highest unit labor costs per hour in 1979 in the manufacturing sector of the economy, a study of the major non-communist industrialized nations disclosed Aug. 12. The study, carried out by the Cologne-based Institute of the German Economy, showed major changes in relative costs since 1970.

[7] The top six countries on the list–which included Switzerland and Denmark as well as those listed above–were fairly close in total labor costs per hour: all were in the range of $11.30 to $12.10. Next came the U.S., with average total labor costs of about $9.50 per hour, then, Italy, Canada and France, all with average labor costs of about $8.50 per hour. Austria followed at about $8 per hour, while in Japan the average cost came to about $6.60 per hour. Britain and Spain both had average labor costs of approximately $5.70 per hour, and Ireland's figure was about $5 per hour. Greece had the lowest average labor cost figure reported: about $3.50 per hour.

[8] In 1970, by contrast, the U.S. had had the highest overall costs of all the countries compared, with Canada next. Belgium's labor costs, the highest in 1979, were well behind those of both Sweden and West Germany in 1970, and Dutch labor costs had also increased more than most others in Europe. In 1970, Japan had been considerably behind Britain, now labor cost more in Japan.

[9] **World Bank: Outlook Is Bleak.** In a survey of the world's economic prospects, the World Bank Aug. 17 predicted declining economic growth rates, higher inflation and more poverty in the first half of the 1980s.

[10] The survey, the bank's third, was more pessimistic than its reports in 1979 and 1978. A major reason for the gloomy forecast was the expectation that the price of oil and other energy resources would continue to climb. It was estimated that oil prices would rise from $29.80 a barrel in early 1980 to $78.30 in 1990.

[11] The report noted that the impact of the oil-price increases would be felt most in African and South Asian countries that had to import all their oil. This area contained most of the 800 million people living in what the bank called "absolute poverty." The economic report saw growth rates in these areas dropping to the levels of the 1960s or below, or about 1.8% to 2.4% a year. Inhabitants of sub-Saharan Africa were expected to be poorer in 1990 than they were in 1980.

[12] **IMF Revises SDR Valuation Method.** The board of directors of the International Monetary Fund voted Sept. 17 to change the method of calculating the value of Special Drawing Rights–the form of money it distributed to its 140 member nations.

[13] At present, the value of one Special Drawing Right (SDR) was determined by the composite value of 16 of the world's leading currencies. One SDR was worth about $1.31 at present exchange rates. Over the past 10 years, some 17 billion SDRS, worth $22 billion, had been distributed to member nations.

[14] Under the new plan, which was to be put into effect Jan. 1, 1981, the value of one SDR was to be calculated using just five currencies–the U.S. dollar, the West German mark, the French franc, the Japanese yen and the British pound.

[15] One consequence of the change was that the weight of the dollar in the currency "basket" would be reduced to 42% from just under 50%. The weight of the mark would rise to 19% from

12½% and the franc, yen and pound would each determine 13% of the value of an SDR instead of 7½% each.

The SDR would be based on this new basket of five currencies on Jan. 1, 1981:

U.S. dollar	42%
West German mark	19%
French franc	13%
Japanese yen	13%
British pound	13%

[16] **World Bank, IMF Meet in Washington.** The 35th annual joint meeting of the World Bank and the International Monetary Fund took place in Washington, D.C. Sept. 30–Oct. 3.

[17] Robert S. McNamara, the president of the World Bank, and Jacques de Larosiere, managing director of the IMF, delivered the principal speeches to the 3,500 finance ministers, central bank governors and monetary officials who attended.

[18] In an emotional speech, McNamara, who had announced June 9 his plan to retire from the bank in June 1981 after 13 years as president, said that the bank had "only begun to develop its potential for service" to poor nations. McNamara said that the bank's current plans called for increased lending to developing nations to boost the collective output of their economies to $30 billion in 1985 from $12 billion in the year ended June 30, 1980.

[19] Larosiere, in contrast, focused his speech on the industrialized nations, cautioning that an abandonment of austerity programs and tight fiscal policies could lead to "unmanageable strains on the international financial system." He pointed out that three problems currently dominated the world economic situation: inflation, energy and the "plight of the non-oil exporting developing countries."

See also Nobel Prizes [12-13]

ECONOMY (U.S.)

[1] **Key Reports Predict Recession.** The Carter Administration said Jan. 30 that the U.S. economy would continue to be plagued by high inflation and would experience a recession and higher unemployment in 1980.

[2] The grim outlook came in two key reports issued by the White House–the President's economic report to Congress and the annual report of the President's Council of Economic Advisers. Carter and his economic advisers argued that fiscal and monetary policies had to restrain demand over an extended period of time, a position that supported the Federal Reserve Board's tight money policy.

[3] **U.S. Reported in Recession.** The National Bureau of Economic Research, an academic group that tracked business cycles, said June 3 that the U.S. was in an economic recession that had begun in January. The bureau, a nonprofit research group based in Cambridge, Mass., was generally accepted as the authority on when recessions began and ended.

[4] The Carter Administration's midyear budget review July 21 projected rising unemployment, high inflation and continued sluggish output. "The economy is experiencing a deeper recession than expected earlier this year," the Administration reported.

[5] **'Real' GNP Up in '79 4th Quarter.** The nation's "real" gross national product rose at a 1.3% seasonally adjusted rate during the fourth quarter of 1979, according to the Commerce Department Jan. 18.

[6] That followed a third quarter in 1979 in which there was a 3.1% annual rate of growth, which meant the U.S. economy had expanded 2.3% in 1979. That was far below 1978's growth rate of 4.4%, but it was considered satisfactory in a year during which a recession had been expected. Real GNP was a measure of the economy's total output of goods and services, adjusted for inflation.

[7] The inflation rate for all of 1979 was 8.8%, up from 7.3% in 1978 and 6% in 1977.

[8] ***GNP Growth Up in 3rd Quarter of '80***—The 'real' GNP grew at a seasonally adjusted annual rate of 1% in the third quarter of 1980, the Commerce Department reported Oct. 17. It had declined at a rate of 9.1% in the second quarter, while increasing at a rate of 1.1% in the first quarter.

[9] The GNP deflator, or price index, which indicated the impact of inflation, rose to an adjusted 9.1% annual rate in the third quarter, following a 10.7% rise in the second quarter and a 9.5% rise in the first quarter.

Inflation

[10] **Consumer Prices Up 13.3% in 1979.** The government's consumer price index rose 13.3% during 1979, the largest annual increase in 33 years, the Labor Department reported Jan. 25.

[11] The inflation rate in 1979 was the fifth highest since the government began compiling statistics in 1913. Only in 1946, when President Harry S Truman lifted wartime price controls, and during the war years of 1917-1919, had there been higher inflation.

[12] The 13.3% rise in the CPI in 1979 brought the index to 229.9% of the 1967 base average. That meant goods and services that had cost $100 in 1967, the base year, cost $229.90 at the end of 1979. (The year-to-year index calculation, based on comparison with 1967 prices, was not adjusted for seasonal variations.)

[13] ***Prices Continue to Rise***—The consumer price index rose by 1% for the third consecutive month in November 1980, the Bureau of Labor Statistics reported Dec. 23.

[14] The CPI for November stood at 256.2% on a 1967 base of 100. That meant it took $250.62 to buy goods and services costing $100 in 1967. The November CPI was 12.6% higher than a year earlier.

[15] **Business Calls for Controls.** Influential members of the business community were for the first time calling for wage and price controls as part of the solution for double-digit inflation.

[16] Henry Kaufman, a partner in Salomon Bros., the New York investment banking firm, and one of the most widely respected Wall Street economists, Feb. 21 called for a temporary "wage and price freeze or a simple mandatory controls program." Kaufman, speaking to the American Bankers Association meeting in Los Angeles, said that the Carter Administration should declare a national emergency to deal with inflation.

[17] He said credit in the economy had to be limited by restricting the lending ability of all major financial institutions, not only commercial banks. His call for wage and price controls was tied to adoption of other policy innovations including a limit to growth of nondefense expenditures to 6% to 7% a year and a commission to revitalize economic growth in the U.S.

[18] *Business Week* magazine, in its March 3 issue, editorially supported a six-month freeze on wages and prices that would be part of "a comprehensive attack that focuses primarily on eliminating the basic causes of inflation." *Business Week* proposed a sharp reduction of dependence on foreign oil, the restraint of monetary growth, a cutback in government spending and the stimulation of growth and productivity. The magazine, read by businessmen across the nation, warned: "The U.S. is in danger of becoming another Brazil, with an intolerably high rate of inflation institutionalized. The result will be an end to the democratic system."

[19] ***Carter Resists Controls***—President Carter, in remarks to a group of magazine editors made public Feb. 25, stated that inflation had reached "a crisis stage." He attributed the high rate of inflation to the inability of Congress to pass the administration's energy program.

[20] More of his remarks to the editors were released Feb. 27, and Carter was

quoted as saying the administration's basic anti-inflation policies "suit me fine." He indicated that they might be adjusted a bit, but reiterated his strong opposition to wage and price controls, claiming they "were out of the question for me."

[21] **Fiscal 1980 Pay Guidelines.** A wage increase ceiling of 7.5% to 9.5% for fiscal 1980 was endorsed March 13 by the Carter Administration.

[22] Acceptance of the voluntary standard recommended by the presidential Pay Advisory Committee was announced by Alfred E. Kahn, chairman of the Council on Wage and Price Stability. Kahn said that "under normal circumstances, wage and salary increases should average 8.5%." Businesses with more than 1,000 employees that granted pay increases in excess of 8.5% would be asked to report to the council along with their reasons for agreeing to such increases.

[23] **New Carter Anti-Inflation Plan.** President Carter March 14 unveiled a new five-point anti-inflation program that included cutting federal spending by $13 billion to achieve a balanced budget in fiscal 1981. It was Carter's fourth anti-inflation plan since taking office.

Inflation rate is bound to creep upwards, Alfred Kahn, the Carter Administration's chief inflation fighter, says Jan. 25. He testified before Joint Congressional Economic Committee.

[24] Carter proposed the plan before more than 200 government officials, business and labor leaders and other spectators at an afternoon meeting in the White House East Room. That evening he answered questions on the proposals in a nationally televised news conference.

The five major elements of the Carter package were:

■ Budget Discipline: balancing the fiscal 1981 budget by making $13 billion in cuts in government spending by canceling some new programs and restricting existing ones. (Some $2 billion in cuts would also be made in the fiscal 1980 budget.) Carter aides said the administration was committed to a 3% real growth rate in defense spending in fiscal 1981. Cuts were unspecified, but believed aimed at revenue-sharing programs for states and cities ($1.7 billion), welfare reform ($860 million), capital grants for mass transit ($265 million) and a reduction in the federal work force of 20,000 civilian employees.

■ Credit Restraints: restraining spending by individuals by curbing the use of credit cards, check overdraft plans and other forms of consumer credit. The Federal Reserve would also place restraints on banks and money market mutual funds.

■ Wage-Price Action: reaffirming "absolute opposition" to wage-and-price controls and accepting the recommendation of the Pay Advisory Committee, which permitted pay increases in the range of 7.5% to 9.5%. The staff of the Council on Wage and Price Stability was to be increased to expand the monitoring of wages and prices.

■ Oil-Import Fee: imposing a $4.62 fee on each barrel of imported oil, which would eventually be replaced by a 10-cents-per-gallon (2.6-cents-perliter) increase in the federal gasoline tax. The import fee was expected to raise the price of gasoline by 10 cents a gallon in the interim.

■ Productivity Measures: encouraging structural changes to promote productivity, savings and research. Congress was called upon to pass comprehensive legislation to deregulate the banking, trucking, railroad and communications industries, as well as pass the Financial Institutions Reform Act, which Carter said would gradually increase interest rates for small savers. A future tax reduction was proposed, but only after a balanced budget had been achieved.

[25] Carter also suggested that more than $3 billion in federal revenues could be raised by having financial institutions withhold taxes on interest and dividend payments to customers. A standard withholding rate of 15% would be applied across the board, with the tax apparently handled like federal withholdings from paychecks.

[26] Separately, the Federal Reserve announced March 14 an additional surcharge of 3 percentage points on the discount rate to large banks borrowing from the Fed on a frequent basis. With the discount rate at 13%, such a surcharge brought the discount rate to 16% for those banks. The Fed left the 13% basic discount rate unchanged for smaller banks and large banks that only borrowed occasionally. The action was meant to restrain business borrowing.

[27] In his comments on the anti-inflation plan at the new conference, Carter said he could "guarantee" that there would be a balanced budget in fiscal 1981. He also predicted "a substantial reduction" in the 1980 inflation rate, and added, "I believe that we'll be under the double-digit inflation next year."

[28] ***Domestic Reception Tepid***—President Carter's anti-inflation program was not well-received on Capitol Hill.

[29] Democrats and Republicans alike criticized the Carter proposals as too hesitant and too vague. Sen. Edward M. Kennedy (D, Mass.) March 14 called the program, "too little, too late and too unfair." Sen. Alan Cranston (D, Calif.), the majority whip, and Sen. Edmund S. Muskie (D, Me.), chairman of the Senate Budget Committee, indicated March 14 that Congress would vote more funds for defense than Carter had asked.

[30] Republican leaders March 17 accused Carter of attempting to balance the budget through taxation. The Republicans contended that Carter's proposed fiscal 1981 budget would involve an $87 billion tax increase. The increase revenues would come from Carter's tax proposals and from "bracket creep" as taxpayers were pushed into higher income tax brackets by the impact of inflation on their paychecks.

[31] Many of the nation's leading business executives were unconvinced that President Carter's proposals would be effective, the *Wall Street Journal* reported March 15. Economic experts were questioning whether the Carter policy was strong enough to battle inflation, the *Journal* reported March 17. The reaction of most executives interviewed could be summed up in the words of Loral Corp. Chairman Bernard L. Schwartz, who said, "The administration overpromised and underdelivered."

[32] ***Favorable Reaction Abroad***—For the most part, the new Carter anti-inflation package was applauded as stronger than expected by the international community.

[33] A West German government spokesman said March 15, "These are steps in the right direction." Japanese and British government officials also expressed agreement with the package.

[34] **Kirkland Sees No Restraint**—AFL-CIO President Lane Kirkland said May 6 he had "not noticed any restraint" at the bargaining table because of the guidelines. Kirkland recommended

that unions seek the best possible settlements for their members regardless of the federal wage standard.

[35] **Emergency Action Considered.** President-elect Ronald Reagan was considering the possibility of declaring a national economic emergency shortly after assuming office, James A. Baker, who was slated to become Reagan's White House chief of staff, said Dec. 17.

[36] ***Emergency Unlikely***—Edwin Meese, Reagan's designated White House counselor, said Dec. 28 that Reagan had decided against declaring a national "economic emergency" upon assuming office.

See also Trade and Tariffs [1-2]

ECUADOR—*See* Immigration

EDUCATION

[1] **College Faculty Unions Curbed.** The Supreme Court ruled, 5-4, Feb. 20 that most of the faculty unions at private colleges and universities were not protected by federal labor law. The ruling affirmed a decision by the U.S. 2d Circuit Court of Appeals. The cases consolidated for judgment, were *National Labor Relations Board v. Yeshiva University* and *Yeshiva University Faculty Association v. Yeshiva University.*

[2] **N.Y. Private School Aid Backed.** The Supreme Court ruled, 5-4, Feb. 20 that New York State could reimburse private and parochial schools for the costs of carrying out state-mandated testing and other activities. The case was *Committee for Public Education and Religious Freedom v. Regan.*

[3] **College Endowment Earnings Increase.** College and university endowment fund earned a higher rate of return on investments in 1979 than at any other time since 1975, it was reported March 24.

[4] According to the results of an in-

COUNTRY IDYLL: Amish children leaving school near Middlefield, Ohio April 7.

vestment survey published in the *Chronicle of Higher Education*, endowment funds showed a 10.8% total rate of return in the 12-month period ending June 30, 1979. The performance was an improvement over previous years, according to the survey. Rates of total return in the six-year period studied were as follows: 1974, down 11.43%; 1975, up 12.00%; 1976, up 9.93%; 1977, up 5.07%; 1978, up 2.49%, and 1979, up 10.80%.

[5] The larger endowments were said to have relied more heavily on common stocks and less on bonds than did the smaller funds. Those with a market value of more than $50 million had an average of 60% invested in stocks, 25.3% in bonds and 11.5% in cash. Endowments of $10 million or less invested an average of 42.3% in stocks, 38.4% in bonds and 17.2% in cash. The annual survey was conducted by the National Association of College and University Business Officers (NACUBO) and based on a study of 147 institutions.

University and College Endowments

1979 Rank	Institution	Market Value ($ millions) 6/30/78	6/30/79
1.	Harvard	$1,393	$1,458
2.	Texas	N.A.	1,054
3.	Yale	545	578
4.	Columbia	478	504
5.	Princeton	523	474
6.	California	360	385
7.	MIT*	330	374
8.	Rochester	305	324
9.	Chicago	283	311
10.	Cornell	265	288
11.	New York U.	261[1]	273[2]
12.	Rice	235	271
13.	Northwestern	241	257[2]
14.	Washington U.	227	221
15.	Rockfeller U.	N.A.	202
16.	Dartmouth	146	174
17.	U. of Penn.	153	168
18.	Johns Hopkins	152	165
19.	Cal. Tech**	155	164
20.	Notre Dame	116	138

*Massachusetts Institute of Technology
**California Institute of Technology
[1]As of Aug. 31, 1978
[2]As of Aug. 31, 1979

Source: *Chronicle of Higher Education*, National Association of College and University Business Officers.

[6] **Carter Signs Higher Education Bill.** President Carter Oct. 3 signed the Higher Education Amendments of 1980, extending the authorization for federal higher education programs through fiscal 1985.

[7] A House–Senate conference committee, in its second round of negotiations, cut $1.4 million from the bill, including $378 million in student loan programs in fiscal 1981, to make spending consistent with the ceilings set in the fiscal 1981 budget. The House then passed the $48.4 billion bill by a voice vote Sept 18, and the Senate Sept. 25 cleared it by a vote of 83-6.

[8] Major provisions of the bill included an increase in interest rates on Guaranteed Student Loans (to 9% from 7%), a reduction in authorization levels in 11 higher education programs, and the strengthening of congress's authority to utilize a new cost-saving mechanism for financing National Direct Student Loans. The latter would use money borrowed from the Federal Financing Bank instead of direct appropriations.

See also Veterans' Affairs [6-9]

EGYPT

[1] **Anti-Sadat Front Formed.** The formation of an exile Egyptian group whose aim was to overthrow President Anwar Sadat was announced in late March in Damascus by Saad Eddin al-Shazli, former Egyptian chief of staff.

[2] Shazli said in Beirut April 2 that he had been chosen secretary general of the organization and that it would be based in Syria. The front had been recognized by Syria, Libya, South Yemen and the Palestine Liberation Organization, all of which strongly opposed Sadat's peace moves with Israel. Its manifesto had been signed by four factions of Egyptain exiles: a Nasserite group backed by Libya, the outlawed

Egyptian Communist Party, a coalition of left-wing Egyptian expatriates residing in Beirut and a Moslem fundamentalist group.

[3] **Sadat Revamps Cabinet.** President Sadat May 15 carried out a major reshuffling of his Cabinet in which he took full personal control of Egypt's internal affairs by assuming the additional post of premier. Sadat carried out the change in an urgent effort to solve the country's chronic economic problems – inflation, unemployment and an acute housing shortage.

[4] **Voters Approve Charter Change.** Egyptian voters overwhelmingly approved major changes in the nation's 1971 Constitution in a referendum May 22.

Among the amendments to the charter:

The presidential two-term limit was lifted, permitting President Anwar Sadat to be reelected indefinitely. Under the previous Constitution, Sadat would have been required to step down from office when his second six-year term expired in 1982.

The Sharia, Egypt's Islamic code, was recognized as the principal source of law. In effect, this amendment reaffirmed Islam as the nation's religion and Arabic as its official language.

Sadat's establishment of a multiparty system was declared official and the Arab Socialist Union, formed by his predecessor, President Gamal Abdel Nasser, was formally abolished. (The country's three active parties were the governing National Democratic Party and the opposition Socialist Labor Party and the leftist Union Progessive Party.

[5] The final results of the referendum, announced May 23: 10.3 million persons voted yes and only 108,657 voted no.

[6] **Egypt Bolsters Border with Libya.** Egypt announced June 16 that martial law was to be reimposed June 18 along the Libyan border.

[7] An Egyptian government

F-4E fighters pass over pyramids near Cairo.

spokesman said that the action was being taken in response to threats by the Libyan leader, Muammer el-Qaddafi. The official Libyan news agency Jana had quoted Qaddafi as saying June 11 that he would support a coup d'etat against Sadat.

U.S. Relations

[8] **U.S. Jets Deployed.** A squadron of U.S. Air Force F-4E jet fighters landed at a Cairo air base July 10 for 90 days of joint training exercises with the Egyptian air force. Nearly 400 support personnel, including operations, intelligence, technical and supply staffs, had arrived earlier.

[9] **U.S. Forces Maneuver.** A 1,400-member U.S. Rapid Deployment Force conducted air and ground exercises in the Egyptian desert northwest of Cairo Nov. 18-28. The troops trained separately at first and then jointly with Egyptian forces.

[10] The objective of the maneuvers, termed Operation Bright Star, was to familiarize American airmen and ground troops with Middle East terrain for the possible deployment of a U.S. force to the Persian Gulf area in an emergency strategy called for delivering a combat-ready battalion to the gulf region within 48 hours, followed by a brigade-sized force within a week, and two divisions within 30 days.

[11] One of the C-154 transports ferrying troops and equipment from the U.S. for the exercises Nov. 13 had crashed on landing at the Cairo airport, killing all 13 Americans aboard.

See also Foreign Aid; Iran [131-139]; Human Rights [9]; Middle East [1-21]

ELECTIONS

[1] Ronald Reagan was elected President of the United States. The sweeping Republican vote that ousted the Carter Administration and brought the GOP into control of the Senate stunned the Democratic Party. Its coalition of support since Franklin Delano Roosevelt's day lay in ruins; the blue-collar vote, the ethnic vote, Roman Catholics, Jews and the South all deserted to Reagan.

[2] Standing almost alone among the debris, Democratic House Speaker Thomas O'Neill called the election results a "disaster for the Democrats." Although they lost 33 seats to the Republicans, the Democrats retained their majority in the House. The GOP also picked up four governorships, for a total of 23. The liberal Democratic ranks in the Senate were decimated. George McGovern (S.D.) was gone, as was Birch Bayh (Ind.), Frank Church (Idaho), John Culver (Iowa), Gaylord Nelson (Wis.), Warren Magnuson (Wash.) and John Durkin (N.H.). Election victims in the House including Majority Whip John Brademas (Ind.), Ways & Means Committee Chairman Al Ullman (Ore.), Public Works committee Chairman Harold Johnson (Cal.) and such House veterans as James Corman (Cal.), Bob Eckhardt (Texas) and Thomas Ashley (Ohio), among others.

[3] President Carter graciously extended total cooperation for a smooth transition. He felt that Iran's intrusion, a few days before the election, of terms for release of the American hostages, plus ever-intractable inflation, had led to his defeat. President-elect Reagan said he wanted the world to know that "there is no political division that affects our foreign policy." He intended to move "as swiftly as possible," once in office, to carry out an economic overhaul – tax cuts, a federal hiring freeze and a spending reduction.

Primary Highlights

[4] **Candidates.** President Carter and Sen. Edward M. Kennedy (Mass.) were the leading contenders for the Democratic presidential nomination; Gov. Edmund G. (Jerry) Brown Jr. of California withdrew April 1. On the

republican side, Ronald Reagan led the field. George Bush, his nearest rival, bowed out May 26. Other Republicans who withdrew were Sen. Larry Pressler (S.D). Jan. 8; Sen. Howard H. Baker Jr. (Tenn.), March 5; John B. Connally, March 9; Sen. Bob Dole (Kan.), March 15; Meldrim Thomson, a former governor of New Hampshire, April 14; Rep. Philip M. Crane (Ill.), April 17. Former President Gerald Ford said March 15 that he would not be a candidate for the nomination. Rep. John B. Anderson (Ill.) April 24 quit the GOP race and announced he would run as an independent for the presidency.

[5] **Carter & Reagan Top the Primaries.** The incumbent Democratic president, Jimmy Carter, and the Republican challenger, Ronald Reagan, each won enough delegate support in state primaries and caucuses to assure their nominations. Carter chalked up a delegate court of 1,964, with 1,666 needed for nomination; Reagan garnered 1,420, with 998 required.

[6] Carter and Reagan won primaries in New Hampshire (Feb. 26), Florida, Georgia and Alabama (March 11), Illinois (March 18), Wisconsin and Kansas (April 1), Louisiana (April 5), Texas (May 3), Tennessee, Indiana and North Carolina (May 6), Maryland and Nebraska (May 13), Oregon (May 20), Kentucky and Nevada (May 27), Montana, Ohio and West Virginia (June 3).

[7] Carter also captured primaries in Puerto Rico (March 16) and Arkansas (May 27). Reagan also took primaries in South Carolina (March 8), New York (March 25), Idaho (May 27), California, New Jersey, New Mexico, Rhode Island and South Dakota (June 3).

[8] Sen. Edward M. Kennedy (D, Mass.) won primaries in Massachusetts (March 4), New York and Connecticut (March 25), Pennsylvania (April 22), District of Columbia (May 6), California, New Jersey, New Mexico, Rhode Island and South Dakota (June 3). George Bush prevailed in primaries in Puerto Rico (Feb. 17), Massachusetts (March 4), Connecticut (March 25), Pennsylvania (April 22), District of Columbia (May 6) and Michigan (May 20).

[9] **New Hampshire.** Ronald Reagan was a big winner in the New Hampshire Republican presidential primary Feb. 26. On the Deomcratic side, President Carter won a clear victory over Sen. Edward M. Kennedy (Mass.).

[10] Carter won 49% of the Democratic vote, to capture 10 delegates for the party's nominating convention. Kennedy won 38% and nine delegates. Gov. Edmund G. Brown Jr.'s (Calif.) third place finish with 10% of the vote was less than the 15% required for a share of the state's 19 convention delegates.

[11] Reagan emerged from the crowded Republican field of seven candidates with 50% of the total vote. He defeated his nearest rival, George Bush, by more than 2-1 although their race had been rated a toss-up. The delegate count was 13 for Reagan, five for Bush and two for Rep. John B. Anderson (Ill.).

[12] **New York, Connecticut.** Sen. Kennedy upset President Carter by winning both the New York and Connecticut presidential primaries March 25.

[13] The Republicans had two victors – George Bush in Connecticut and Ronald Reagan in New York. Bush was on home turf, of sorts. He grew up in Connecticut, where his father had been a popular U.S. senator.

[14] **Pennsylvania.** Sen. Kennedy narrowly beat President Carter in the Pennsylvania presidential primary April 22, and Republican George Bush scored an upset win over front-runner Ronald Reagan.

[15] But Carter and Reagan continued on their way to nomination by picking up during the day more delegates than their closest competitors in election with caucuses across the nation. At this point, Carter had amassed 1,137 of the 1,666 Democratic delegates needed for nomination, according to a *New*

York Times count. Kennedy had 592 delegates, including 93 from his Pennsylvania win (Carter won 92 Pennsylvania delegates). For the Republicans, Reagan's delegate total climbed to 607 of the 998 needed to be nominated. Bush had 176.

[16] **Final Primary Day.** On the final primary day of the election year June 3, President Carter achieved a clear majority of the number of delegates necessary to win the presidential nomination at the Democratic Party's convention in August.

[17] But Sen. Kennedy had his best day of the campaign. He won five of the eight Democratic primaries held, including the prizes of California and New Jersey.

[18] Kennedy won 372 delegates for the day, to bring his total to 1,239 of the 1,666 needed for nomination. The President, however, won 321 delegates for the day to elevate his total to 1,964, or 298 more than the number needed for nomination. Carter won three of the June 3 primaries. "It's over," Carter campaign chaiman, Robert S. Strauss, told reporters that night. ". . . We're thinking about the fall campaign."

[19] Kenndey won in California, New Jersey, New Mexico, Rhode Island and South Dakota. Carter won in Ohio, Montana and West Virginia.

[20] Reagan won in those eight states and in Mississippi as well. He won 416 of the 423 delegates at stake, although the count had become academic; he had picked up a total of 1,004 delegates by May 26 with 998 needed for nomination.

Ronald Reagan: the Basic Speech

Excerpts from Ronald Reagan's "basic speech" follow. The material represented the gist of the candidate's views as he presented them in hundreds of speeches throughout the primary campaign. It was compiled by the *New York Times* and appeared in its issue of Feb. 29.

. . .Despite the protests about all the problems he inherited, Jimmy Carter came into office with the economy expanding, with inflation reduced to less than 5%, and with the dollar a relatively stable measure of value. In 36 months he has tripled the rate of inflation; the prime interest rate has risen to the highest level since the Civil War; the price of gold has risen. . .to more than $600 and fluctuates up there at that level, which measures the extent to which international confidence in the dollar has fallen. And that is the indication of the collapse of confidence of economic policies in the Carter Administration.

After last summer's Cabinet massacre, the departing secretary of the Treasury confessed that the Carter Administration did not bring with it to Washington any economic philosophy of its own. . .

Together Mr. Carter, his Democratic Congress and . . . the Federal Reserve proceeded on the premise of . . . national prosperity, federal deficits and easy money. Pursuing the course together, they made a shambles of our national economy, wiping out in three years' time tens of billions of dollars of value in our private pensions, savings, insurance, stocks and bonds.

But. . .the damage done to the national economy is insignificant alongside the damage done to our national security. In May of 1977, five months after he took the oath of office, President Carter declared . . . we are now free . . . of that inordinate fear of communism which led to moral poverty in Vietnam.

Now. . .it may. . .be true that Vietnam was the wrong war, in the wrong place, at the wrong time. But 50,000 Americans died in Southeast Asia. They were not engaged in some racist enterprise, as candidate Carter charged in 1976.

And when 50,000 Americans make the ultimate sacrifice to defend the people of a small, defenseless country in Southeast Asia from communist tyranny, that, my friends, is a collective act of moral courage, not an example of moral poverty.

Since Mr. Carter dismissed his fear of communism as inordinate, he has set about systematically to diminish and dismantle what one of his predecessors called the great arsenal of democracy.

He junked the B-1 bomber program. . .

[He] killed the neutron warhead. . .

[He] delayed or postponed the cruise missile program, the MX and the Trident submarine.

And after all these unilateral concessions,. . .[the Administration] brought home from Europe the SALT II treaty. The Senate has so far refused to ratify, as well it should refuse.

Mr. Carter described the agreement as fair, as just, and for the security interests of the U.S. . . . . The President said we must ratify the SALT II treaty because no one will like us if we don't. He said we should give away the Panama Canal because no one would like us if we didn't. It is time to tell the President: We don't care if they like us or not. We intend to be respected throughout the world.

We want arms limitation. We want arms control. But the United States should never place a seal of approval on an unfair, unequal, dangerous document which legitimizes American strategic inferiority to a hostile, imperial power whose ambitions extend to the ends of the earth.

. . .It is time for the Republican Party to come to the rescue of this country. . . .

The American people are prepared for large and definite purpose. It is many-faceted:

It is to restore. . .this society of high principle, of equality for all and special privilege for none. . . .

It is to care, shelter, and protect the least protected among us and that includes especially the unborn.

It is to conserve the environment . . . without shackling the free enterprise system that has made a poor backward agricultural country the greatest nation on earth.

It is to set aside forever the discredited dogma. . .that an endless string of federal deficits is the path to national prosperity.

It is, lastly, to begin the moral and military rearmament of the United States for the difficult, dangerous decade ahead, and to tune out those cynics, pacifists, and appeasers who tell us the Army and Navy of this country are nothing but the extensions of some malevolent military-industrial complex.

If there is one message that needs to be sent to all the nations of the world by the next President, it is this: "There will be no more Taiwans, and no more Vietnams, regardless of the price or the promise, be it the oil of Arabia or an ambassador sitting in Peking, there will be no more abandonment of friends by the United States of America." I want very much to send that message.

[21] **Anderson runs as Independent.** Rep. John B. Anderson (R, Ill.) announced April 24 he would run for the presidency as an independent. At the same time he said he was withdrawing his bid for the Republican nomination.

[22] The nation needed a choice in November, Anderson said at a press conference in Washington, D.C. "Not just a choice among candidates," he said. "I mean a choice, of course, for the nation. I want to offer that choice."

[23] "Too many people in our nation are disillusioned with the prospective choices our party structures are offering," Anderson said. "The result is frustration, apathy and despair." He disputed the argument that he would only function as a spoiler in the race, a contention frequently voiced by the White House. "It doesn't 'spoil' the political process when I seek to involve in that process young people" or "to provide the American people with new and alternative ideas," he said.

John B. Anderson, independent candidate for President.

[24] ***Citizens' Party Selects Ticket***—"Move over" became the rallying cry of the newly organized Citizens' Party April 13.

[25] Barry Commoner, nominated by the party as its presidential candidate, coined the slogan in an attack on big business and the established political parties. Commoner was an environmental scientist at Washington University in St. Louis. LaDonna Harris, a Comanche Indian and the wife of former Sen. Fred Harris (D, Okla.), was named Commoner's running mate.

[26] ***Clark on Ballot in All 50 States***—Ed Clark, the Liberatarian candidate for president was on the ballot in all 50 states and the District of Columbia, it was reported Oct. 28. Clark, a 50-year-old antitrust attorney with Atlantic Richfield Co., was the first third-party candidate to accomplish that feat. Libertarian idelology borrowed from both conservative and liberal viewpoints, with a goal of protecting the freedom of the individual.

[27] **Open Convention Move.** Gov. Hugh Carey (D, N.Y.) May 5 urged President Carter and Sen. Edward M. Kennedy to release their delegates to vote freely at the Democratice convention.

[28] Carey, saying the nation was "in trouble" under President Carter's leadership, claimed that a "totally open" convention with "an element of genuine risk" would be the best way to unite Democrats behind one candidate. Carey listed the "events" since the New Hampshire primary that might have changed the minds of elected

delegates: "The interest rates, the discharge of auto workers, the near collapse of the economy on the housing side, unemployment raging upwards, skyrocketing inflation unchecked, a lack of consistency and total uncertainty in foreign policy."

[29] An effort to open the Democratic convention to a presidential candidae other than President Carter of Sen. Edward Kennedy (D, Mass.) began to take shape in the midst of the continuing controversy over the President's brother Billy Carter [See Billy Carter]

[30] The effort gained impetus from the President's lowly poll status and mounting fears among Democratic members of Congress about the prospect of running with an unpopular President at the head of the ticket. "What we're looking for is an alternative to both," said Rep. Jerome Ambro (N.Y.), one of about 40 Democratic members of Congress who met July 25 to consider the possibility of an open convention, Senate Democratic leader Robert C. Byrd (W. Va.) endorsed the idea Aug. 2.

[31] President Carter, meanwhile, was adamant in his opposition. Carter told 400 of his delegates at the White House Aug. 1: "It's almost incomprehensible how a brokered, horse-trading, smoke-filled convention can be labled open, and a decision made by 20 million Democrats in the open primaries and open caususes could be called closed. To violate that commitment and that rule would be a travesty, in my opinion. . . . "

Conventions

[32] **Republican National Convention.** Ronald Reagan was named as the Republican Party's presidential candidate at its 32d national convention in Detroit July 14-17.

[33] A conservative platform was adopted. Harmony and unity extended in all directions. Reagan's choice of a running mate was the only real surprise before the convention. Momentum built up behind former President Ford for a "dream ticket," only to be deflated by the actual choice of George Bush, the second-place finisher behind Reagan all season in the primaries.

[34] But unity was restored the final night, when Ford joined Reagan and Bush on the rostrum for all to accept the ovation of the delegates, roused by Reagan's call for Americans to "recapture our destiny" and "make America great again." Reagan promised to cut taxes, bolster defenses and reduce the federal role by transferring many governmental functions to the state and local level.

[35] Reagan gained the presidential nomination in balloting by the convention July 16. The vote was 1,939 votes, to 37 for Rep. John B. Anderson (Ill.), who was running currently as an independent candidate. Bush, who had released his delegates shortly after arriving at the convention, received 13 votes. Anne Armstrong, former ambassador to Britain, received one vote, and there were four abstentions.

[36] Bush was put in the vice presidential spot by 1,832 of the 1,994 votes on the convention July 17. Sen. Jesse Helms (N.C.), a leader of the GOP's conservative forces, received 54 votes in the balloting. Rep. Jack Kemp (N.Y.) received 42 votes. Rep. Philip Crane (Ill.), a presidential candidate at one time, received 23 votes. Some 43 other votes were scattered among seven other names or were recorded as abstentions.

[37] ***The Running Mate Question***—The Republican convention July 16 focused on former President Gerald Ford as a possible vice presidential nominee.

[38] There were meetings between his representatives – former Secretary of State Henry Kissinger and former chairman of the Council of Economic Advisers Alan M. Greenspan – and the Reagan camp. Ford met with Reagan twice during the six-hour period preceding the final decision. Ford also expressed his views on the subject in a

New York Times interview July 16 and to Walter Cronkite on the CBS Evening News July 16. The expectation of a "dream ticket" of Reagan and Ford swept the convention that night and was anticipated by delegates and media. The rumor was that Ford had demanded, and apparently received, promises of authority and power not normally associated with the vice presidency. Ford had asserted on television that he would not go to Washington to be "a figurehead vice president." (A former president running for vice president was unprecedented in American history.)

[39] Reagan broke precedent that night by going to the convention hall, past midnight, soon after winning the nomination. "It is true that we have gone over this and over this and he and I have come to the conclusion that he believes he can be of more value campaigning his heart out, as former President, as he has promised to do, than as a member of the ticket," Reagan said. "I respect his decision." Then Reagan disclosed he had chosen "a man who has wide experience in government, a man who told me that he can enthusiastically support the platform across the board" – George Bush.

[40] ***GOP Platform***—The Republican National Convention July 15 adopted the longest party platform in American history. The document, entitled "Family, Neighborhood, Work, Peace, Freedom" ran to 40,000 words. It was considered in large part a reflection of the views of the Republican nominee, Ronald Reagan. The platform took no position on the ratification of the Equal Rights Amendment, breaking with a party tradition of support dating from 1940. It also called for a constitutional ban on abortion and the appointment of judges who opposed abortion. The platform's major innovation was its commitment to stimulating the national economy. The document favored tax cuts as the most effective stimulant, mentioning them 46 times. The document's other major commitment was in pledging American military superiority over the Soviet Union. Such a stand repudiated policies of the recent Republican administrations of Richard Nixon and Gerald Ford.

[41] The platform committed the Republicans to increase the nation's energy supply by expanding production and down-playing conservation and environmental controls. It criticized federal election spending limits and federally financed elections, promoted transportation deregulation, supported the death penalty, opposed gun control, and called for the return of voluntary nondemoninational prayer in public schools.

[42] **Democratic National Convention.** President Carter won renomination for a second term at the 38th Democratic National Convention in New York Aug. 11-14, but Sen. Edward Kennedy was the star performer. After refusing to concede months ago, despite Carter's attainment of a winning majority of delegates for the nomination, Kennedy abruptly ended his candidacy only hours into the convention. He acted after losing one last fight over a rule that bound Carter's majority to him for a certain first-ballot victory. The Kennedy fight continued on platform issues and as part of it Kennedy delivered a powerful speech on Democratic Party ideals and commitment. Kennedy left his imprint on the platform, but Carter balked on the key Kennedy plank for a $12 billion jobs program. He came half-way, endorsing the spirit if not the $12 billion. Kennedy balked then on Carter's repeated overtures for support. But he came half-way, too. After Carter delivered a savage attack on the Republican nominee, Ronald Reagan, in his acceptance speech, Kennedy joined him on the podium. His reserve was noticeable; he left after three minutes, and the convention closed.

[43] ***Kennedy Withdraws***—Sen. Kennedy ended his bid for the presidency Aug. 11 less than five hours after the

convention opened in Madison Square Garden. After losing the rules fight, on which a last stand had been made to try to turn the tide of defeat, Kennedy telephoned President Carter, who was at Camp David, Md., and then publicly announced his withdrawal.

[44] The rule–Rule F3(c)–over which the fight was waged bound the delegates to vote on the first convention ballot for the presidential candidate they were elected to support in the primary or caucuses in their home states, unless released in writing by their candidate. Delegates trying to violate the rule could be replaced with alternates. The Kennedy side proposed that the delegates be free to vote as they pleased on the first ballot for the nomination. But "we cannot take from a man what he has rightfully won," Sen. Abraham A. Ribicoff (D, Conn.) said on the other side of the issue. "It is not fair to change the rules now," Ribicoff said. "It is not fair to the 19 million Democrats who voted. It is not fair to the candidate who won the most delegates." The Kennedy forces lost on the roll-call vote, 1,390.6 to 1,936.4, with 1,666 votes needed to win.

[45] ***His Speech Rouses Convention***—Kennedy brought the convention to life Aug. 12 with a stirring call for the party to reaffirm its commitment to economic justice.

Kennedy stated his "fundamental Democratic principles":

■ That unemployment, high interest rates and human misery would never be misused "as false weapons against inflation."

■ That employment would be the first priority of economic policy.

■ That there would be security for those at work and jobs for those out of work.

[46] The speech set off a 35-minute spate of cheering and dancing in the aisles and a frenzy of support for Kennedy, although it was extracted now for a cause rather than a candidacy.

[47] ***Economic Planks Approved***—After Kennedy spoke, the convention shouted approval of several of his economic planks opposed by the Carter Administration.

[48] The major Kennedy plank adopted called for a $12 billion jobs program. Another voice vote approved a Kennedy plank pledging the Democrats to abjure a policy of high interest rates and unemployment to curb inflation. Still another plank opposed by President Carter was adopted. It pledged the Democrats not to support any program that would increase unemployment. A major Kennedy plank calling for wage and price controls was defeated.

[49] President Carter put his seal of approval, in general, on the platform Aug. 13. Much of the convention day was spent in speculating what position the President would take on the key Kennedy economic plank calling for a $12 billion jobs program to stimulate revival from the recession. Carter had expressed misgivings about the economic planks put into the platform by Kennedy. Carter's final position, seen as conciliatory by some and insufficient by others, was: "I accept and support the intent behind this . . . (plank) and plan to pursue policies that will implement its spirit and aims. The amounts needed to achieve our goals will necessarily depend on economic conditions, what can be effectively applied over time, and the appropriate concurrence by Congress."

[50] ***Carter Renominated***—President Carter won renomination to a second term on the first ballot in the early hours of Aug. 14. The vote was 2,129 to 1,146 for Sen. Edward Kennedy (D, Mass.).

[51] Kennedy had released his delegates before the roll-call to "vote their consciences." All but 100 stayed with him. After the roll-call, Kennedy's suggestion that the renomination be made by acclamation, "in the interest of harmony and unity," was relayed to the convention, which shouted approval.

[52] Carter accepted renomination with

a scathing attack Aug. 14 on his Republican opponent Ronald Reagan as an advocate of dangerous policies. Republicans "have promised to launch an all-out nuclear arms race" in which "all the people on earth could be the losers," Carter warned. Reagan advocated "abandoning arms control policies" supported by every president since Harry Truman, he said, and "this radical and irresponsible course would threaten our security – and could put the whole world in peril."

[53] Looking elsewhere, Carter called Reagan's proposals "an attack on almost every achievement in social justice and decency we have won in the last 50 years." A Reagan administration, he said, would bring "surrender of our energy future to the merchants of oil . . . massive tax cuts for the rich, massive service cuts for the poor and massive inflation for everyone." They offered "a fantasy America" of "simple solutions," he said, "simple and wrong."

[54] Walter Mondale was renominated as Carter's vice presidential running mate earlier in the evening. Mondale also delivered a sharp attack on Reagan and the Republicans in his acceptance speech.

The Campaign

[55] **Major Statements:** ***Carter***— President Carter Aug. 28 unveiled a series of proposals he called "an economic program for the eighties." The centerpiece of the plan was tax reductions for individuals and industry amounting to $26.7 billion in 1981. The program aimed at stimulating economic growth through investment and productivity without, in the President's words, "reigniting inflation." The plan called for an increase in federal spending – about $4.29 billion during the 1981 and 1982 fiscal years. The spending increase represented a reversal in Administration policy. Carter had called for spending cuts in March, when he had introduced a five-point plan to fight inflation.

[56] Carter contended Sept. 22-23 that election of his Republican rival Ronald Reagan could lead to war. (Reagan denounced the attack Sept 23 as "beneath decency.")

[57] In Chicago Oct 6, Carter was greeted by one of the biggest crowds of his campaign at Daley Bicentennial Plaza. Mayor Jane Byrne (D) appeared with him at the rally. That evening, at a party fund-raising event, Carter combined the racial issue with the war-and-peace issue. He told the party workers, "You'll determine whether or not this American will be unified or, if I lose the election, whether Americans might be separated, black from white, Jew from Christian, North from South, rural from urban – whether this nation will be guided from a sense of long-range commitment to peace and broad consultation; whether we'll have a feeling of community and consultation with our allies, whether our adversaries will be tempted to end the peace for which we all pray."

[58] Carter conceded Oct. 8 that he had been "carried away on a couple of occasions" in attacking Reagan. He and Reagan both had made comments that were "probably ill-advised," he said in an ABC-TV interview with Barbara Walters. He intended to get his presidential campaign "back on track," Carter said. Carter campaign aides also asserted the President's intention to soften his attack and put a more positive stamp on his campaign.

[59] ***Reagan***— Ronald Reagan sounded his "peace through strength" theme in appearances before veterans' groups. In Chicago Aug. 18, before the Veterans of Foreign Wars convention, Reagan said the nation's defense was "in shambles" while the Carter Administration was "totally oblivious" to the grand Soviet design. Reagan addressed the American Legion convention in Boston Aug. 20. "Since when has it been wrong for America to aim to be first in military strength?" he asked its delegates.

[60] Reagan proposed Sept. 9 a five-

year economic plan designed to "balance the budget, reduce tax rates and restore our defenses." The federal budget would be balanced within three years, under his plan. Federal income tax rates would be reduced 10% a year over three years. Tax rates would be indexed to prevent inflation from pushing taxpayers into higher brackets. Business would receive accelerated depreciation allowances to stimulate investment and job creation. On defense, the goal would be to increase the defense budget about 6% annually.

[61] Carter was "reaching a point of hysteria," Reagan said Oct. 7 in reaction to the President's campaign themes. The President "owes the country an apology," he said. There was "absolutely no evidence to substantiate such terrible claims as he has made," Reagan said.

[62] At a news conference in Los Angeles Oct. 14, his first in almost a month, Reagan denied that he was "somehow opposed to full and equal opportunities for women." If elected, he said, he would name a woman to fill "among the first Supreme Court vacancies in my administration." Reagan declared his total commitment Oct. 19 to peace and pledged to undertake arms negotiations and to restore bipartisanship in American foreign policy. He addressed the country in a paid half-hour telecast.

[63] ***Anderson***—John B. Anderson announced Aug. 25 that he had selected Patrick J. Lucey, a Democrat, as his running mate on his independent presidential ticket. Lucey, 62, was governor of Wisconsin in 1971-77 and ambassador to Mexico in 1977-79.

[64] Anderson and his running mate, Aug. 30 issued a "National Unity Platform" and said that it would require "a patriotism greater than party." The platform charged that President Carter had "failed to rally the nation" and its allies, that he had reneged on 1976 campaign commitments and that he "failed to provide coherent and creditable leadership." It also accused Republican presidential candidate Ronald Reagan of "simplicity" and of advocating a tax-cut policy that would give "a bonanza to the rich, crumbs to the middle class and nothing at all to the poor." The proposals in the 317-page platform were considered somewhat more conservative on social programs than those advocated by the Democrats—lower spending and less government involvement—and more liberal than Republican proposals—greater emphasis on individual rights, energy and the environment. On foreign policy and military matters, the *New York Times* said Aug. 31, the platform was closer to the traditional "liberal" bipartisan approach than that of either the Democrats or Republicans. The platform called for restraint in weapons systems, a greater effort to limit strategic arms and more accommodation with the Soviet Union.

[65] **Debates: Reagan-Anderson**—Ronald Reagan and John B. Anderson disagreed on most issues in a nationally televised debate Sept. 21.

[66] President Carter refused to participate in the debate, which was sponsored by the League of Women Voters. Carter insisted that his first appearance in a campaign debate be with Reagan alone, without Anderson. Reagan and Anderson duly remarked on the absence of the President. "The man who should be here tonight to answer those questions chose not to attend," Anderson remarked in reply to a question about the economy.

[67] Reagan said that he and Anderson differed more with the President than with each other on military policy. A part of military policy was about the only thing Reagan and Anderson agreed upon. They both opposed reimposition of a peacetime draft. They were in disagreement on virtually every other topic raised, including tax reduction, energy policy, the MX mobile-missile project, revitalization of the cities, abortion and separation of

church and state. Generally, Reagan was on the conservative side of the issues, Anderson, on the liberal side.

[68] The debate itself was undramatic. But neither man stumbled or made any major gaffes. Anderson performed with aplomb, even eagerness, and handled the national issues with all the assurance expected of a major presidential candidate. Reagan delivered a polished performance, by all accounts, marked by amiability and sincerity. The 60-minute debate was held in Baltimore, Md., at the Convention Center.

[69] ***Carter-Reagan***— President Carter and Ronald Reagan condensed their presidential campaigns into an hour-and-a-half confrontation in a nationally televised debate Oct. 28.

[70] Both candidates focused on their main campaign themes of the past eight weeks. For Carter, it was nuclear arms control and the risk of war. His challenger had an "extremely dangerous and belligerent" attitude on the issue, he said, and it was "the most important crucial difference in this election campaign." For Reagan the big issue was the economy. "Are you better off than you were four years ago?" was the question electorate should be asking, he said.

[71] The President also stressed his incumbency. He considered himself "much wiser and more experienced" than four years ago because of the "thousands of lonely decisions" he had made in the Oval Office. Reagan spoke of the national "humiliation" of Iran's holding of the 52 American hostages. Once they were safely home, he said, in maybe the only new proposal of the evening, a congressional investigation should be undertaken to look into the diplomatic handling of the situation.

[72] Throughout, the debate was sprinkled with charges and denials and counter-charges. Carter called Reagan's arms control position "very dangerous and disturbing," his tax-cut proposal "ridiculous" and minimum-wage approach "heartless." Reagan fended off the President's attacks. He questioned a figure, one remark was a "distortion," another a "mis-statement" and another "just not true." "There you go again," he genially began at one point.

[73] And that was the pattern. The incumbent President with a vulnerable record on the attack and the challenger maintaining composure, reasonableness and pleasantness. When it was over, he was the one who walked over to shake hands with the President, who remained cool and collected, cold even, some said, throughout the debate, which was held at the Cleveland Convention Center Music Hall.

Elections

[74] **Reagan Defeats Carter.** Ronald Wilson Reagan was elected 40th President of the United States Nov. 4 by an outpouring of support from across the nation. Elected along with him as vice president was his running mate, George Bush.

[75] Incumbent President Jimmy Carter won only six states and the District of Columbia. His concession, at 9:50 p.m. election night, was the earliest concession since 1904 when Alton B. Parker bowed to Theodore Roosevelt. He became the first elected incumbent President since Herbert Hoover in 1932 to be defeated.

[76] Independent presidential candidate John B. Anderson took 7% of the vote, which made him eligible for federal election subsidies. His support was not a factor in the outcome. Reagan won 43,201,220 votes, or 51% of the total cast, to 34,913,332, or 41%, for Carter. Anderson drew 5,581,379 votes. The electoral count was more sweeping—489 to 49 in favor of Reagan, whose mandate was nationwide in scope. He captured most of Carter's native South, all the West and almost all of the Midwest and much of the East. Carter's home state of Georgia was the largest state, elec-

PRESIDENT JIMMY CARTER

torally, won by the President. His other victories were in Maryland, Rhode Island, Minnesota, Hawaii and West Virginia, in addition to the District of Columbia. The rest was Reagan country. The decisive turn to Reagan apparently came within two or three days of the election and thus was not indicated by the polls, which took longer to prepare. Up to that point, most of them were pointing to a toss-up vote, although Reagan was leading in electoral counts. "Exit" polls of voters leaving the voting booths showed a dissatisfaction with Jimmy Carter as a major ingredient of the Reagan sweep. The biggest irritant was the state of the economy, especially inflation. Dissatisfaction also was voiced against Carter's "weak" handling of foreign policy. This apparently grew in intensity just prior to the voting with Iran's demands of concessions by the U.S. for release of the 52 American hostages, whose first anniversary of capture fell on Election Day.

[77] ***Political Breakthrough***—A *New York Times*-CBS News poll Election Day showed a large loss of traditional support for the Democrats among blue-collar workers, Roman Catholics and Jews. These segments of support, plus the South, had formed the traditional coalition of strength for Democrats since New Deal days.

[78] "We cracked the unions, blue-collar voters, ethnics, Catholics and the South, just as we had planned," Reagan pollster Richard Wirthlin commented. "This could be the breakpoint election in bringing about a party realignment," said Republican National Chairman Bill Brock. "In this election we have brought together the elements of a new coalition."

[79] "The cementing of that coalition depends on our performance in office." The turnout–52.3% of the nation's 160,491,000 eligible voters–was the lowest in a presidential election since 1948, when 51.1% voted in President Harry Truman's win over Thomas E. Dewey.

[80] ***Carter Pledges 'Fine Transition'***—President Carter congratulated Reagan on "a fine victory" and pledged to work closely with him for "a very fine transition period."

[81] The President reported on his telephone call to Reagan in his concession statement at a Washington hotel at 9:50 p.m. Nov. 4. "I promised you four years ago that I would never lie to you," he told a crowd of supporters, "so I can't stand here tonight and say it doesn't hurt." He continued:

[82] "I've not achieved all I set out to do, perhaps no one ever does, but we have faced the tough issues." He did not feel that his landslide loss was "a personal turning against me." He thought the voters had expressed frustration over Iran, the economy and America's diminished position in world affairs. What was next for him? He intended to go back to Georgia and begin on his memoirs.

[83] **President-Elect Meets Press.** In his first press conference in Los Angeles Nov. 6 as President-elect, Ronald Reagan said that he was "not going to intrude" while the Carter Administration was still in office.

[84] Reagan stressed the point especially in reference to foreign affairs. "Foreign leaders must be aware that the President is still the president," he said. Insisting that he did not want to appear "to be trying to invade the province of the President," Reagan cautioned Iran not to "have any ideas that there will be profit to them in waiting any period of time" in release of the American hostages. "We want those people home," he said.

[85] On several other foreign affairs issues, Reagan indicated a departure from current policies. With regard to the Soviet Union, he revived a theory of "linkage" associated with former Secretary of State Henry A. Kissinger during the Nixon Administration. "I don't think you simply sit down at the table with the Soviet Union to discuss arms limitation, for example, but you

RONALD REAGAN

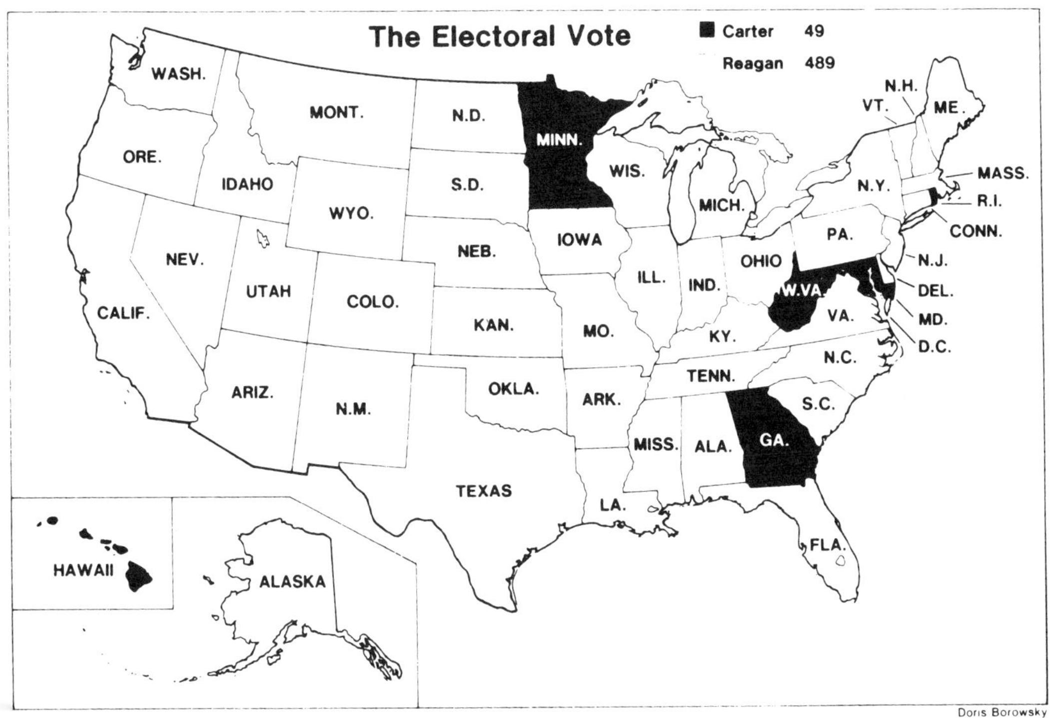

Doris Borowsky

discuss the whole attitude—world attitude—as to whether we're going to have a world at peace or whether we're simply going to talk about weaponry and not bring up these other subjects," Reagan said. "In other words, I believe in linkage." On the issue of human rights, Reagan recommended consistency. He opposed punishing countries "basically friendly" to the U.S. while ignoring the issue with other countries "where human rights are virtually nonexistent."

Senate

Membership: 53 R, 46 D, 1 Independent
Pre-election lineup: 41 R, 58 D, 1 Independent

[86] The Senate experienced a major turnaround, with Republicans gaining a majority. There were changes in party control for 12 of the 34 seats that were at stake Nov. 4. All went from Democrat to Republican. Seven of the Senate's leading liberals were ousted, and most replaced by extremely conservative Republicans.

[87] Ten out of 26 incumbents lost their seats, including Jacob K. Javits, who switched his party affiliation in New York from Republican to Liberal after losing the Republican nomination. GOP victories over Democratic incumbents came in Georgia, where Mack Mattingly upset Herman E. Talmadge; in Idaho, where Steven D. Syms beat Frank Church; in Indiana, where Dan Quayle defeated Birch Bayh; in Iowa, where Charles E. Grassley beat John C. Culver; in New Hampshire, where Warren Rudman beat John A. Durkin; in North Carolina, where John P. East defeated Robert Morgan; in South Dakota, where James Abdnor beat George McGovern; in Washington, where Slade Gorton defeated Warren G. Magnuson, and in Wisconsin, where Robert W. Kasten defeated Gaylord Nelson. Senators defeated in their state primaries were: Donald Stewart (D, Ala.), Mike Gravel (D, Alaska), Richard Stone (D, Fla.), and Javits. In

each of those states, the Republican candidate won. Jeremiah Denton was elected to represent Alabama, Frank H. Murkowski to represent Alaska, Paula Hawkins to represent Florida and Alfonse M. D'Amato to represent New York.

[88] **Senators of the 97th Congress.** The 100 members who make up the Senate of the 97th Congress are listed below. Each senator is described according to his party affiliation (D = Democrat, R = Republican), the date of his birth or age, the year in which he entered the Senate (date in parentheses) and his election status (* designates an incumbent, *italics* indicate that the senator was elected or reelected in November 1980 for term ending 1987 unless otherwise specified, and † indicates that the senator's service began in the year shown but has not been continuous).

Sen. Edward M. Kennedy (D, Mass.), President Carter's major rival for the Democratic presidential nomination.

Ala.	Howell T. Heflin (D) term ends 1985; b. June 19, 1921 (1979)
	Jeremiah Denton (R) age 56
Alaska	Ted Stevens (R) terms ends 1985; b. Nov. 18, 1923 (1968)
	Frank H. Murkowski (R) age 47
Ariz.	**Barry M. Goldwater* (R) b. Jan. 1, 1909 (1953)†
	Dennis DeConcini (D) term ends 1983; b. May 8, 1937 (1977)
Ark.	**Dale Bumpers* (D) b. Aug. 12, 1925; (1975)
	David Pryor (D) term ends 1985; b. Aug. 29, 1934 (1979)
Calif.	**Alan Cranston* (D) b. June 19, 1914 (1969)
	Samuel Ichiye Hayakawa (R) term ends 1983; b. July 18, 1906 (1977)
Colo.	William L. Armstong (R) term ends 1985; b. March 16, 1937 (1979)
	**Gary W. Hart* (D) b. Nov. 28, 1937 (1975)
Conn.	Lowell P. Weicker Jr. (R) term ends 1983; b. May 16, 1931 (1971)
	Christopher J. Dodd (D) b. May 27, 1944
Del.	William V. Roth Jr. (R) terms ends 1983; b. July 22, 1921 (1971)
	Joseph R. Biden Jr. (D) term ends 1985; b. Nov. 20, 1942 (1973)
Fla.	Lawton Chiles (D) term ends 1983; b. April 30, 1930 (1971)
	Paula Hawkins (R) age 53
Ga.	Sam Nunn Jr. (D) term ends 1985; b. Sept. 6, 1938 (1973)
	Mack Mattingly (R) age 49
Hawaii	Spark Masayuki Matsunaga (D) term ends 1983, b. Oct. 8, 1916 (1977)
	**Daniel K. Inouye* (D) b. Sept. 7, 1924 (1963)
Idaho	James A. McClure (R) term ends 1985; b. Dec. 27, 1924 (1973)
	Steven D. Symms (R) b. April 23, 1938
Ill.	Charles H. Percy (R) term ends 1985; b. Sept. 27, 1919 (1967)
	Alan J. Dixon (D) b. July 7, 1927
Ind.	Richard Green Lugar (R) term ends 1983; b. April 4, 1932 (1977)
	Dan Quayle (R) b. Feb. 4, 1947
Iowa	Roger Jepsen (R) term ends 1985; b. Dec. 23, 1928 (1979)
	Charles E. Grassley (R) b. Sept. 17, 1933
Kan.	**Robert Dole* (R) b. Jan. 22, 1923 (1969)
	Nancy Landon Kassebaum (R) term ends 1985; b. July 29, 1932 (1979)
Ky.	Walter Huddleston (D) term ends 1985; b. April 15, 1926 (1973)
	**Wendell H. Ford* (D) b. Sept. 8, 1924 (1975)
La.	**Russell B. Long* (D) b. Nov. 3, 1918 (1948)
	J. Bennett Johnston Jr. (D) term ends 1985; b. June 10, 1932 (1973)
Maine	William S. Cohen (R) term ends 1985; b. Aug. 28, 1940 (1979)
	George J. Mitchell (D) term ends 1983; b. Aug. 20, 1933 (1980)
Md.	**Charles McC. Mathias Jr.* (R) b. July 24, 1922 (1969)
	Paul Spyros Sarbanes (D) term ends 1983; b. Feb. 3, 1933 (1977)
Mass.	Edward M. Kennedy (D) term ends 1983; b. Feb. 22, 1932 (1963)
	Paul Tsongas (D) term ends 1985; b. Feb. 14, 1941 (1979)
Mich.	Donald Wayne Riegle Jr. (D) term ends 1983; b. Feb. 4, 1938 (1977)
	Carl Levin (D) term ends 1985; b. June 28, 1934 (1979)
Minn.	Rudy Boschwitz (R) term ends 1985; b. Nov. 7, 1930 (1979)

Dave F. Durenberger (R) term ends 1985; b. Aug. 19, 1934 (1978)

Miss. John C. Stennis (D) term ends 1983; b. Aug. 3, 1901 (1948)
Thad Cochran (R) term ends 1985; b. Dec. 7, 1937 (1978)

Mo. **Thomas F. Eagleton* (D) b. Sept. 4, 1929 (1969)
John Clagett Danforth (R) term ends 1983; b. Sept. 5, 1936 (1977)

Mont. John Melcher (D) term ends 1983; b. Sept. 6, 1924 (1977)
Max S. Baucus (D) term ends 1985; b. Dec. 11, 1941 (1978)

Neb. Edward Zorinsky (D) term ends 1983; b. Nov. 11, 1928 (1977)
J. James Exon (D) term ends 1985; b. Aug. 9, 1921 (1979)

Nev. **Paul Laxalt* (R) b. Aug. 2, 1922 (1975)
Howard W. Cannon (D) term ends 1983; b. Jan. 26, 1912 (1959)

N.H. Gordon J. Humphrey (R) term ends 1985; b. Oct. 9, 1940 (1979)
Warren Rudman (R) age 49

N.J. Harrison A. Williams Jr. (D) term ends 1983; b. Dec. 10, 1919 (1959)
Bill Bradley (D) term ends 1985; b. July 28, 1943 (1979)

N.M. Pete V. Domenici (R) term ends 1985; b. May 7, 1932 (1973)
Harrison Hogan Schmitt (R) term ends 1983; b. July 3, 1935 (1977)

N.Y. Daniel Patrick Moynihan (D) term ends 1983; b. March 16, 1927 (1977)
Alfonse M. D'Amato (R) age 43

N.C. Jesse A. Helms (R) term ends 1985; b. Oct. 18, 1921 (1973)
John P. East (R) age 49

N.D. Quentin N. Burdick (D) term ends 1983; b. June 19, 1908 (1960)
Mark Andrews (R) b. May 19, 1926

Ohio **John H. Glenn Jr.* (D) b. Dec. 18, 1921 (1975)
Howard Morton Metzenbaum (D) term ends 1983; b. June 4, 1917 (1974)†

Okla. David L. Boren (D) term ends 1985; b. April 21, 1941 (1979)
Don Nickles (R) age 31

Ore. **Robert W. Packwood* (R) b. Sept. 11, 1932 (1969)
Mark O. Hatfield (R) term ends 1985; b. July 12, 1922 (1967)

Pa. Henry John Heinz III (R) term ends 1983; b. Oct. 23, 1938 (1977)
Arlen Specter (R) age 50

R.I. Claiborne Pell (D) term ends 1985; b. Nov. 22, 1918 (1961)
John Chafee (R) term ends 1983; b. Oct. 22, 1922 (1977)

S.C. Strom Thurmond (R) term ends 1985; b. Dec. 5, 1902 (1955)
**Ernest F. Hollings* (D) b. Jan. 1, 1922 (1967)

S.D. Larry Pressler (R) term ends 1985; b. March 29, 1942 (1979)
James Abdnor (R) b. Feb. 13, 1923

Tenn. Howard H. Baker Jr. (R) term ends 1985; b. Nov. 15, 1925 (1967)
James R. Sasser (D) term ends 1983; b. Sept. 30, 1936 (1977)

Texas John G. Tower (R) term ends 1985; b. Sept. 29, 1925 (1961)
Lloyd M. Bentsen Jr. (D) term ends 1983; b. Feb. 11, 1921 (1971)

Utah **Jake Garn* (R) b. Oct. 12, 1932 (1975)
Orrin G. Hatch (R) term ends 1983; b. March 22, 1934 (1977)

Vt. **Patrick J. Leahy* (D) b. March 31, 1940 (1975)
Robert T. Stafford (R) term ends 1983; b. Aug. 8, 1913 (1971)

Va. John W. Warner (R) term ends 1985; b. Feb. 18, 1927 (1979)
Harry E. Byrd Jr. (Independent) term ends 1983; b. Dec. 20, 1914 (1965)

Wash. Henry M. Jackson (D) term ends 1983; b. May 31, 1912 (1953)
Slade Gorton (R) b. Jan. 8, 1928

W. Va. Robert C. Byrd (D) term ends 1983; b. Jan 15, 1918 (1959)
Jennings Randolph (D) term ends 1985; b. March 8, 1902 (1958)

Wis. William Proxmire (D) term ends 1983; b. Nov. 11, 1915 (1957)
Robert W. Kasten Jr. (R) b. June 19, 1942

Wyo. Malcolm Wallop (R) term ends 1983; b. Feb. 27, 1933 (1977)
Alan K. Simpson (R) term ends 1985; b. Sept. 2, 1931 (1979)

The House

Membership: 242 D, 192 R, 1 Independent.

Pre-election Lineup: 273 D, 159 R (Three formerly Democratic seats were vacant.)

[89] Republicans made a net gain of 33 seats in House races Nov. 4. Overall, the GOP picked up 37 seats held by Democrats and lost four.

[90] Even though the Republicans failed to win a majority in the House, the new members that were elected were overwhelmingly conservative and, in most cases, replaced liberal Democrats. Conservatives were expected to exert far greater influence in the House than any time within recent memory. The infusion of New Right representatives was coupled with some startling upsets of Democratic House leaders. Rep. John Brademas (D, Ind.), a member of Congress for 22 years and the third-ranking Democrat in the House as majority whip, was upset by Republican John P. Hiler. Rep. Al Ullman (D, Ore.), a 12-term congressman and chairman of the powerful House Ways and Means Committee, fell to Republican Denny Smith. Rep. Harold T. (Bizz) Johnson

(D, Calif.) in his 21st year in Congress and chairman of the House Public Works Committee, was knocked off by Republican Eugene A. Chappie.

[91] Other Democratic House leaders who lost to Republicans included: Thomas L. Ashley (Ohio), chairman of the Banking, Finance and Urban Affairs subcommittee on housing and community development; Lionel Van Deerlin (Calif.), chairman of Interstate and Foreign Commerce subcommittee on communications; Bob Eckhardt (Texas), chairman of the Interstate and Foreign Commerce subcommittee on oversight and investigations; K. Gunn McKay (Utah), chairman of the Appropriations subcommittee on military construction, and James C. Corman (Calif.), chairman of the Ways and Means subcommittee on public assistance and unemployment compensation.

[92] The lone major upset involving a House Republican leader was the defeat of Rep. Samuel L. Devine of Ohio, third-ranking in the GOP leadership, by Democrat Bob Shamansky.

[93] The Federal Bureau of Investigation's Abscam bribery probe apparently took its toll on most of those representatives who were implicated. Of the five Democratic representatives touched by the scandal, only Raymond Lederer (Pa.) won reelection. Reps. Frank Thompson Jr. (N.J.) and John M. Murphy (N.Y.), both under indictment, lost their races. Two others who had been convicted, Rep. John Jenrette (S.C.) and former Rep. Michael J. Myers of Pennsylvania, failed in their reelection bids.

[94] Minorities and women made slight gains in the House. Black candidates won 17 House seats, two more than they presently held. All 13 black incumbents who stood for reelection won. Four blacks won congressional elections for the first time, two of them taking seats that had previously been held by blacks. The four new representatives were Harold Washington, an Illinois state senator who had defeated Rep. Bennet Steward (D, Ill.) in the Democratic primary; Marvyn Dymally, a native of Trinidad and former lieutenant governor of California, who defeated Rep. Charles Wilson (D, Calif.) in the Democratic primary; Gus Savage, a publisher in Chicago, and George Crockett, a retired judge from Detroit. All of the new black House members were Democrats. Dymally became the second black to represent a congressional district with a white majority. (The other was Rep. Ronald Dellums, a Democrat from California's eighth district.) Other minorities just held thier own. The five Hispanic representatives seeking reelection all won. Three Japanese-American incumbents also won reelection.

[95] The number of women in the House rose to 19, a net gain of three. The four new women members, all Republicans, were Lynn Martin (Ill.), Claudine Schneider (R.I.), Marge Roukema (N.J.) and Bobbi Fiedler (Calif.)

[96] **Congressmen of the 97th Congress.** The 435 members who make up the House of Representatives of the 97th Congress are listed below. Each representative is described according to his party affiliation (D = Democrat, R = Republican), the date of his birth or age, the year in which he entered the House (date in parentheses) and his election status (*designates an incumbent and † indicates that the representative's service began in the year shown but has not been continuous).

Alabama: 4 D, 3 R [4 D, 3 R]

1. *Jack Edwards (R) b. Sept 20, 1928 (1965)
2. *William Louis Dickinson (R) b. June 5, 1925 (1965)
3. *William Nichols (D) b. Oct. 16, 1918 (1967)
4. *Tom Bevill (D) b. March 27, 1921 (1967)
5. *Ronnie G. Flippo (D) b. Aug. 15, 1937 (1977)
6. Albert Smith (R) age 49
7. *Richard C. Shelby (D) b. May 6, 1934 (1979)

Alaska: 1 R [1 R]

At Large: *Donald E. Young (R) b. June 9, 1933 (1973)

Arizona: 2 D, 2 R [2 D, 2 R]

1. *John J. Rhodes (R) b. Sept. 18, 1916 (1953)
2. *Morris K. Udall (D) b. June 15, 1922 (1961)
3. *Bob Stump (D) b. April 4, 1927 (1977)
4. *Eldon D. Rudd (R) b. July 15, 1920 (1977)

Arkansas: 2 D, 2 R [2 D, 2 R]

1. *William Vollie "Bill" Alexander Jr. (D) b. Jan 16,

1934 (1969)
2. *Edwin R. Bethune Jr. (R) b. Dec. 19, 1935 (1979)
3. *John Paul Hammerschmidt (R) b. May 4, 1922 (1967)
4. *Beryl F. Anthony Jr. (D) b. Feb. 21, 1938 (1979)

California: 22 D, 21 R [25 D, 18 R]

1. Eugene Chapple (R) age 60
2. *Don H. Clausen (R) b. April 27, 1923 (1963)
3. *Robert T. Matsui (D) b. Sept. 17, 1941 (1979)
4. *Vic Fazio (D) b. Oct. 11, 1942 (1979)
5. *John L. Burton (D) b. Dec. 15, 1932 (1974)
6. *Phillip Burton (D) b. June 1, 1926 (1964)
7. *George Miller (D) b. May 17, 1945 (1975)
8. *Ronald V. Dellums (D) b. Nov. 24, 1935 (1971)
9. *Fortney H. Stark (D) b. Nov. 11, 1931 (1973)
10. *Don Edwards (D) b. Jan. 6, 1915 (1963)
11. Tom Lantos (D) age 52
12. *Paul N. "Pete" McCloskey Jr. (R) b. Sept 29, 1927 (1967)
13. *Norman Y. Mineta (D) b. Nov. 12, 1931 (1975)
14. *Norman D. Shumway (R) b. July 28, 1934 (1979)
15. *Tony Coelho (D) b. June 15, 1942 (1979)
16. *Leon E. Panetta (D) b. June 28, 1938 (1977)
17. *Charles "Chip" Pashayan Jr. (R) b. March 27, 1941 (1979)
18. *William Thomas (R) b. Dec. 6, 1941 (1979)
19. *Robert J. Lagomarsino (R) b. Sept. 4, 1926 (1974)
20. *Barry M. Goldwater Jr. (R) b. July 15, 1938 (1969)
21. Bobbi Fiedler (R) age 43
22. *Carlos J. Moorhead (R) b. May 6, 1922 (1973)
23. *Anthony Charles Beilenson (D) b. Oct. 26, 1932 (1977)
24. *Henry A. Waxman (D) b. Sept. 12, 1939 (1975)
25. *Edward R. Roybal (D) b. Feb. 10, 1916 (1963)
26. *John H. Rousselot (R) b. Nov. 1, 1927 (1961)†
27. *Robert K. Dornan (R) b. April 3, 1933 (1977)
28. *Julian C. Dixon (D) b. Aug. 8, 1934 (1979)
29. *Augustus F. Hawkins (D) b. Aug. 31, 1907 (1963)
30. *George E. Danielson (D) b. Feb. 20, 1915 (1971)
31. Mervyn Dymally (D) b. May 12, 1926
32. *Glenn M. Anderson (D) b. Feb. 21, 1913 (1969)
33. *Wayne Grisham (R) b. Jan. 10, 1923 (1979)
34. *Daniel E. Lungren (R) b. Sept. 22, 1946 (1979)
35. Dave Dreier (R) age 28
36. *George E. Brown Jr. (D) b. March 6, 1920 (1963)†
37. *Jerry Lewis (R) b. Oct. 21, 1934, (1979)
38. *Jerry M. Patterson (D) b. Oct. 25, 1934 (1975)
39. *William Dannemeyer (R) b. Sept. 22, 1929 (1979)
40. *Robert E. Badham (R) b. June 9, 1929 (1977)
41. Bill Lowery (R) age 32
42. Duncan Hunter (R) age 32
43. *Clair W. Burgener (R) b. Dec. 5, 1921 (1973)

Colorado: 3 D, 2 R [3 D, 2 R]

1. *Patricia Schroeder (D) b. July 30, 1940 (1973)
2. *Timothy E. Wirth (D) b. Sept. 22, 1939 (1975)
3. *Ray P. Kogovsek (D) b. Aug. 19, 1941 (1979)
4. Hank Brown (R) age 40
5. *Ken Kramer (R) b. Feb. 19, 1942 (1979)

Connecticut: 4 D, 2 R [5 D, 1 R]

1. *William R. Cotter (D) b. July 18, 1926 (1971)
2. Samuel Gejdenson (D) age 32
3. Lawrence J. DeNardis (R) age 42
4. *Stewart B. McKinney (R) b. Jan. 30, 1931 (1971)
5. *William R. Ratchford (D) b. May 24, 1934 (1979)
6. Toby J. Moffett (D) b. Aug. 18, 1944 (1975)

Delaware: 1 R [1 R]

At Large: *Thomas B. Evans Jr. (R) b. Nov. 5, 1931 (1977)

District of Columbia (non-voting)

*Walter E. Fauntroy (D) b. Feb. 6, 1933 (1971)

Florida 11 D, 4 R [12 D, 3 R]

1. *Earl D. Hutto (D) b. May 12, 1926 (1979)
2. *Don Fuqua (D) b. Aug. 20, 1933 (1963)
3. *Charles E. Bennett (D) b. Dec. 1, 1910 (1949)
4. *William V. Chappell Jr. (D) b. Feb. 3, 1922 (1969)
5. Bill McCollum (R) age 36
6. *C. W. Young (R) b. Dec. 16, 1930 (1971)
7. *Sam M. Gibbons (D) b. Jan. 20, 1920 (1963)
8. *Andrew P. Ireland (D) b. Aug. 23, 1930 (1977)
9. *Bill Nelson (R) b. Sept. 29, 1942 (1979)
10. *L. A. Bafalis (R) b. Sept. 28, 1929 (1973)
11. *Dan Mica (D) b. Feb. 4, 1944 (1979)
12. Clay Shaw (R) age 40
13. *William Lehman (D) b. Oct. 5, 1913 (1973)
14. *Claude Denson Pepper (D) b. Sept. 8, 1900 (1963)
15. *Dante B. Fascell (D) b. Mar. 9, 1917 (1955)

Georgia: 9 D, 1 R [9 D, 1 R]

1. *Ronald B. Ginn (D) b. May 31, 1934, (1973)
2. Charles Hatcher (D) age 41
3. *Jack Thomas Brinkley (D) b. Dec. 22, 1930 (1967)
4. *Elliott H. Levitas (D) b. Dec. 26, 1930 (1975)
5. *Wyche Fowler (D) b. Oct. 6, 1940 (1977)
6. *Newt Gingrich (R) b. June 17, 1943 (1979)
7. *Lawrence P. McDonald (D) b. April 1, 1935 (1975)
8. *Billy Lee Evans (D) b. Nov. 10, 1941 (1977)
9. Edgar L. Jenkins (D) b. Jan. 4, 1933 (1977)
10. *D. Douglas Barnard (D) b. March 20, 1922 (1977)

Hawaii: 2 D [2 D]

1. *Cecil Heftel (D) b. Sept. 30, 1924 (1977)
2. *Daniel Akaka (D) b. Sept. 11, 1924 (1977)

Idaho: 2 R [2 R]

1. Larry Craig (R) age 35
2. *George V. Hansen (R) b. Sept. 14, 1930 (1965)†

Illinois: 10 D, 14 R [10 D, 14 R]

1. Harold Washington (D) age 58
2. Gus Savage (D) age 54
3. *Martin A. Russo (D) b. Jan. 23, 1944 (1975)
4. *Edward J. Derwinski (R) b. Sept. 15, 1926 (1959)
5. *John G. Fary (D) b. April 11, 1911 (1975)
6. *Henry J. Hyde (R) b. April 18, 1924 (1975)
7. *Cardiss W. Collins (D) b. Sept. 24, 1931 (1973)
8. *Dan Rostenkowski (D) b. Jan. 2, 1928 (1959)
9. *Sidney R. Yates (D) b. Aug. 27, 1909 (1949)†
10. *John E. Porter (R) age 44 (1980)
11. *Frank Annunzio (D) b. Jan. 12, 1915 (1965)
12. *Philip M. Crane (R) b. Nov. 3, 1930 (1969)
13. *Robert McClory (R) b. Jan. 31, 1908 (1963)
14. *John N. Erlenborn (R) b. Feb. 8, 1927 (1965)
15. *Tom Corcoran (R) b. May 23, 1939 (1977)
16. Lynn Martin (R) age 40
17. *George M. O'Brien (R) b. June 17, 1917 (1973)
18. *Robert H. Michel (R) b. March 2, 1923 (1957)
19. *Thomas F. Railsback (R) b. Jan. 22, 1932 (1967)
20. *Paul Findley (R) b. June 23, 1921 (1961)
21. *Edward R. Madigan (R) b. Jan. 13, 1936 (1973)
22. *Daniel B. Crane (R) b. Jan. 10, 1936 (1979)
23. *Charles Melvin Price (D) b. Jan. 2, 1905 (1945)
24. *Paul Simon (D) b. Nov. 29, 1928 (1975)

Indiana: 6 D, 5 R [7 D, 4 R]

1. *Adam Benjamin Jr. (D) b. Aug. 6, 1935 (1977)
2. *Floyd J. Fithian (D) b. Nov. 3, 1928 (1975)
3. John Hiler (R) age 27
4. Dan Coats (R) age 37
5. *Elwood Hillis (R) b. March 6, 1926 (1971)
6. *David W. Evans (D) b. Aug. 17, 1946 (1975)
7. *John Thomas Myers (R) b. Feb. 8, 1927 (1967)
8. *H. Joel Deckard (R) b. March 7, 1942 (1979)
9. *Lee Herbert Hamilton (D) b. April 20, 1931 (1965)
10. *Philip R. Sharp (D) b. July 15, 1942 (1975)
11. *Andrew Jacobs Jr. (D) b. Feb. 24, 1932 (1965)†

Iowa: 3 D, 3 R [3 D, 3 R]

1. *James A. S. Leach (R) b. Oct. 15, 1942 (1977)
2. *Tom Tauke (R) b. Oct. 11, 1950 (1979)
3. Cooper Evans (R) age 56
4. *Neal Smith (D) b. March 23, 1920 (1959)
5. *Tom Harkin (D) b. Nov. 19, 1939 (1975)
6. *Berkley Bedell (D) b. March 5, 1921 (1975)

Kansas: 1 D, 4 R [1 D, 4 R]

1. Pat Roberts (R) age 44

2. *Jim Jeffries (R) b. June 1, 1925 (1979)
3. *Larry Winn Jr. (R) b. Aug. 22, 1919 (1967)
4. *Dan Glickman (D) b. Nov. 24, 1944 (1977)
5. *Roger Whittaker (R) b. Sept. 18, 1939 (1979)

Kentucky: 4 D, 3 R [4 D, 3 R]

1. *Carroll Hubbard Jr. (D) b. July 7, 1937 (1975)
2. *William H. Natcher (D) b. Sept. 11, 1909 (1953)
3. *Romano L. Mazzoli (D) b. Nov. 2, 1932 (1971)
4. *Marion Gene Snyder (R) b. Jan. 26, 1928 (1963)†
5. Harold Rogers (R) age 42
6. *Larry J. Hopkins (R) b. Oct. 25, 1933 (1979)
7. *Carl D. Perkins (D) b. Oct. 15, 1912 (1949)

Louisiana: 6 D, 2 R [6 D, 2 R]

1. *Robert L. Livingston (R); b. April 30, 1943 (1977)
2. *Corinne C. "Lindy" Boggs (D) b. March 13, 1916 (1973)
3. *William J. Tauzin (D) b. June 14, 1943 (1980)
4. Charles Roemer (D) age 37
5. *Jerry Huckaby (D) b. July 19, 1941 (1977)
6. *W. Henson Moore 3rd (R) b. Oct. 4, 1939 (1975)
7. John B. Breaux (D) b. March 1, 1944 (1973)
8. *Gillis W. Long (D) b. June 16, 1928 (1963)†

Maine: 2 R [2 R]

1. *David F. Emery (R) b. Sept. 1, 1948 (1975)
2. *Olympia J. Snowe (R) b. Feb. 21, 1947 (1979)

Maryland: 7 D, 1 R [6 D, 2 R]

1. Royden Dyson (D) age 31
2. *Clarence D. Long (D) b. Dec. 11, 1908 (1963)
3. *Barbara Ann Mikulski (D) b. July 20, 1936 (1977)
4. *Marjorie S. Holt (R) b. Sept. 17, 1920 (1973)
5. *Gladys N. Spellman (D) b. March 2, 1918 (1975)
6. *Beverly Byron (D) b. July 27, 1932 (1979)
7. *Parren J. Mitchell (D) b. April 29, 1922 (1971)
8. *Michael Barnes (D) b. Sept. 3, 1943 (1979)

Massachusetts: 10 D, 2 R [10 D, 2 R]

1. *Silvo O. Conte (R) b. Nov. 9, 1921 (1959)
2. *Edward P. Boland (D) b. Oct. 1, 1911 (1953)
3. *Joseph D. Early (D) b. Jan. 31, 1933 (1975)
4. Barney Frank (D) age 40
5. *James Shannon (D) b. April 4, 1952 (1979)
6. *Nicholas Mavroules (D) b. Nov. 1, 1929 (1979)
7. *Edward J. Markey (D) b. July 11, 1946 (1977)
8. *Thomas P. "Tip" O'Neill, Jr. (D) b. Dec. 9, 1912 (1953)
9. *John Joseph Moakley (D) b. April 27, 1927 (1973)
10. *Margaret M. Heckler (R) b. June 21, 1931 (1967)
11. *Brian J. Donnelly (D) b. March 2, 1946 (1979)
12. *Gerry E. Studds (D) b. May 12, 1937 (1973)

Michigan: 12 D, 7 R [13 D, 6 R]

1. *John J. Conyers, Jr. (D) b. May 16, 1929 (1965)
2. *Carl D. Pursell (R) b. Dec. 19, 1932 (1977)
3. *Howard Wolpe (D) b. Nov. 2, 1939 (1979)
4. *David A. Stockman (R) b. Nov. 10, 1946 (1977)
5. *Harold S. Sawyer (R) b. March 21, 1920 (1977)
6. Jim Dunn (R) age 36
7. *Dale E. Kildee (D) b. Sept. 16, 1929 (1977)
8. *Bob Traxler (D) b. July 21, 1931 (1974)
9. *Guy Adrian Vander Jagt (R) b. Aug. 26, 1931 (1966)
10. *Donald Albosta (D) b. Dec. 5, 1925 (1979)
11. *Robert Davis (R) b. July 31, 1932 (1979)
12. *David E. Bonior (D) b. June 6, 1945 (1977)
13. George Crockett (D) age 70
14. Dennis Hertel (D) age 31
15. *William David Ford (D) b. Aug. 6, 1927 (1965)
16. *John D. Dingell (D) b. July 8, 1926 (1955)
17. *William M. Brodhead (D) b. Sept. 12, 1941 (1975)
18. *James J. Blanchard (D) b. Aug. 8, 1942 (1975)
19. *William S. Broomfield (R) b. April 28, 1922 (1957)

Minnesota: 3 D, 5 R [4 D, 4 R]

1. *Arlen Erdahl (R) b. Feb. 27, 1931 (1979)
2. *Tom Hagedorn (R) b. Nov. 27, 1943 (1975)
3. *William E. Frenzel (R) b. July 31, 1928 (1971)
4. *Bruce Frank Vento (D) b. Oct. 7, 1940 (1971)
5. *Martin Olav Sabo (D) b. Feb. 28, 1938 (1979)
6. Vin Weber (R) age 28
7. *Arlan Stangeland (R) b. Feb. 8, 1930 (1977)
8. *James L. Oberstar (D) b. Sept. 10, 1934 (1975)

Mississippi: 3 D, 2 R [3 D, 2 R]

1. *Jamie L. Whitten (D) b. April 18, 1910 (1941)
2. *David R. Bowen (D) b. Oct. 21, 1932 (1973)
3. *Gillespie V. Montgomery (D) b. Aug. 5, 1920 (1967)
4. *Jon Hinson (R) b. March 16, 1942 (1979)
5. *Trent Lott (R) b. Oct. 9, 1941 (1973)

Missouri: 6 D, 4 R [8 D, 2 R]

1. *William L. Clay (D) b. April 30, 1931 (1969)
2. *Robert A. Young (D) b. Nov. 27, 1923 (1977)
3. *Richard Andrew Gephardt (D) b. Jan. 31, 1941 (1977)
4. *Ike Skelton (D) b. Dec. 20, 1931 (1977)
5. *Richard Bolling (D) b. May 17, 1916 (1949)
6. *E. Thomas Coleman (R) b. May 29, 1943 (1977)
7. *Gene Taylor (R) b. Feb. 10, 1928 (1973)
8. Wendell Bailey (R) age 40
9. *Harold L. Volkmer (D) b. April 4, 1931 (1977)
10. Bill Emerson (R) age 42

Montana: 1 D, 1 r [1 D, 1 R]

1. *Pat Williams (D) b. Oct. 30, 1937 (1979)
2. *Ron Marlenee (R) b. Aug. 8, 1935 (1971)

Nebraska: 3 R [1 D, 2 R]

1. Douglas K. Bereuter (R) b. Oct. 6, 1939 (1979)
2. Hal Daub (R) age 39
3. *Virginia Smith (R) b. June 30, 1911 (1975)

Nevada: 1 D [1 D]

At Large: *James Santini (D) b. Aug. 13, 1937 (1975)

New Hampshire: 1 D, 1 R [1 D, 1 R]

1. *Norman E. D'Amours (D) b. Oct. 14, 1937 (1975)
2. JUdd Gregg (R) age 33

New Jersey: 8 D, 7 R [10 D, 5 R]

1. *James J. Florio (D) b. Aug. 29, 1937 (1975)
2. *William J. Hughes (D) b. Oct. 17, 1932 (1975)
3. *James J. Howard (D) b. July 24, 1927 (1965)
4. Christopher H. Smith (R) age 27
5. *Millicent Fenwick (R) b. Feb. 25, 1910 (1975)
6. *Edwin B. Forsythe (R) b. Jan. 17, 1916 (1971)
7. Marge Roukema (R) age 50
8. *Robert A. Roe (D) b. Feb. 28, 1924 (1969)
9. *Harold C. Hollenbeck (R) b. Dec. 29, 1938 (1977)
10. *Peter Wallace Rodino Jr. (D) b. June 7, 1909 (1949)
11. *Joseph George Minish (D) b. Sept. 1, 1916 (1963)
12. *Matthew J. Rinaldo (R) b. Sept. 1, 1931 (1973)
13. *James A. Courter (R) b. Oct. 14, 1941 (1979)
14. *Frank Guarini (D) b. Aug. 20, 1924 (1979)
15. Bernard Dwyer (D) age 59

New Mexico: 2 R [1 D, 2 R]

1. *Manuel Lujan Jr. (R) b. May 12, 1928 (1969)
2. Joe Skeen (R) age 53

New York: 22 D, 17 R [26 D, 13 R]

1. *William Carney (R) b. July 1, 1941 (1979)
2. *Thomas J. Downey (D) b. Jan. 28, 1949 (1975)
3. Greg Carman (R) age 42
4. *Norman F. Lent (R) b. March 23, 1931 (1971)
5. Raymond McGrath (R) age 38
6. John LeBoutillier (R) age 27
7. *Joseph Patrick Addabbo (D) b. March 17, 1925 (1961)
8. *Benjamin S. Rosenthal (D) b. June 8, 1923 (1962)
9. *Geraldine Ferraro (D) b. August 26, 1935 (1979)
10. *Mario Biaggi (D) b. Oct. 26, 1917 (1969)
11. *James H. Scheuer (D) b. Feb. 6, 1920 (1965)†
12. *Shirley Anita Chisholm (D) b. Nov. 30, 1924 (1969)
13. *Stephen J. Solarz (D) b. Sept. 12, 1940 (1975)
14. *Frederick W. Richmond (D) b. Nov. 15, 1923 (1975)
15. *Leo C. Zeferetti (D) b. July 15, 1927 (1975)
16. Charles Schumer (D) age 28
17. Guy Molinari (R) age 51

18. *S. William Green (R) b. Oct. 16, 1929 (1978)
19. *Charles B. Rangel (D) b. June 11, 1930 (1971)
20. *Theodore S. Weiss (D) b. Sept. 17, 1927 (1977)
21. *Robert Garcia (D) b. Jan. 9, 1933 (1978)
22. *Jonathan Brewster Bingham (D) b. April 24, 1914 (1965)
23. Peter A. Peyser (D) b. Sept. 7, 1921 (1971)†
24. *Richard L. Ottinger (D) b. Jan. 27, 1929 (1965)†
25. *Hamilton Fish Jr. (R) b. June 3, 1926 (1969)
26. *Benjamin A. Gilman (R) b. Dec. 6, 1922 (1973)
27. *Matthew F. McHugh (D) b. Dec. 6, 1938 (1975)
28. *Samuel S. Stratton (D) b. Sept. 27, 1916 (1959)
29. *Gerald B. Solomon (R) b. Aug. 14, 1930 (1979)
30. David Martin (R) age 36
31. *Donald J. Mitchell (R) b. May 8, 1923 (1973)
32. George Wortley (R) age 53
33. *Gary A. Lee (R) b. Aug. 18, 1933 (1979)
34. *Frank Horton (R) b. Dec. 12, 1919 (1963)
35. *Barber B. Conable Jr. (R) b. Nov. 2, 1922 (1965)
36. *John J. LaFalce (D) b. Oct. 6, 1936 (1975)
37. *Henry J. Nowak (D) b. Feb. 21, 1935 (1975)
38. *Jack F. Kemp (R) b. July 13, 1935 (1971)
39. *Stanley N. Lundine (D) b. Feb. 4, 1939 (1976)

North Carolina: 7 D, 4 R [9 D, 2 R]

1. *Walter B. Jones (D) b. Aug. 19, 1913 (1966)
2. *L. H. Fountain (D) b. April 23, 1913 (1953)
3. *Charles Whitley (D) b. Jan. 3, 1927 (1977)
4. *Ike F. Andrews (D) b. Sept. 2, 1925 (1973)
5. *Stephen L. Neal (D) b. Nov. 7, 1934 (1975)
6. Eugene Johnston (R) age 44
7. *Charles G. Rose 3rd (D) b. Aug. 10, 1939 (1973)
8. *W. G. "Bill" Hefner (D) b. April 11, 1930 (1975)
9. *James G. Martin (R) b. Dec. 11, 1935 (1973)
10. *James Thomas Broyhill (R) b. Aug. 19, 1927 (1963)
11. Bill Hendon (R) age 35

North Dakota: 1 D [1 R]

At large: Byron Dorgan (D) age 38

Ohio: 10 D, 13 R [10 D, 13 R]

1. *Willis D. Gradison Jr. (R) b. Dec. 28, 1928 (1975)
2. *Thomas A. Luken (D) b. July 9, 1925 (1974)†
3. *Tony P. Hall (D) b. Jan. 16, 1942 (1979)
4. *Tennyson Guyer (R) b. Nov. 29, 1913 (1973)
5. *Delbert L. Latta (R) b. March 5, 1920 (1959)
6. Bob McEwen (R) age 30
7. *Clarence J. Brown (R) b. June 18, 1927 (1965)
8. *Thomas N. Kindness (R) b. Aug. 26, 1929 (1975)
9. Ed Weber (R) age 49
10. *Clarence E. Miller (R) b. Nov. 1, 1917 (1967)
11. *John William Stanton (R) b. Feb. 20, 1924 (1965)
12. Bob Shamansky (D) age 53
13. *Donald James Pease (D) b. Sept. 26, 1931 (1977)
14. *John F. Seiberling, Jr. (D) b. Sept. 18, 1918 (1971)
15. *Chalmers Pangburn Wylie (R) b. Nov. 23, 1920 (1967)
16. *Ralph S. Regula (R) b. Dec. 3, 1924 (1973)
17. *John Milan Ashbrook (R) b. Sept. 21, 1928 (1961)
18. *Douglas Applegate (D) b. March 27, 1928 (1977)
19. *Lyle Williams (R) b. Aug. 23, 1942 (1979)
20. *Mary Rose Oakar (D) b. March 5, 1940 (1977)
21. *Louis Stokes (D) b. Feb. 23, 1925 (1969)
22. Dennis Eckart (D) age 30
23. *Ronald M. Mottl (D) b. Feb. 6, 1934 (1975)

Oklahoma: 5 D, 1 R [5 D, 1 R]

1. *James R. Jones (D) b. May 5, 1939 (1973)
2. *Mike Synar (D) b. Oct. 17, 1950 (1979)
3. *Wesley Watkins (D) b. Dec. 15, 1938 (1977)
4. Dave McCurdy (D) age 30
5. *Marvin H. Mickey Edwards (R) b. July 12, 1937 (1977)
6. *Glenn English (D) b. Nov. 30, 1940 (1975)

Oregon: 3 D, 1 R [4 D]

1. *Les AuCoin (D) b. Oct. 21, 1942 (1975)
2. Denny Smith (R) age 42
3. Ron Wyden (D) age 31
4. *James Weaver (D) b. Aug. 8, 1927 (1975)

Pennsylvania: 12 D, 12 R, 1 I [15 D, 10 R]

1. Thomas Foglietta (I) age 51
2. *William H. Gray III (D) b. Aug. 20, 1941 (1979)
3. *Raymond F. Lederer (D) b. May 19, 1938 (1977)
4. *Charles F. Dougherty (R) b. June 26, 1937 (1979)
5. *Richard T. Schulze (R) b. Aug. 7, 1929 (1975)
6. *Gus Yatron (D) b. Oct. 16, 1927 (1969)
7. *Robert W. Edgar (D) b. May 29, 1945 (1975)
8. James Coyne (R) age 33
9. *E. G. Shuster (R) b. Jan 23, 1932 (1973)
10. *Joseph Michael McDade (R) b. Sept. 29, 1931 (1963)
11. James Nelligan (R) age 51
12. *John P. Murtha (D) b. June 17, 1932 (1975)
13. *Lawrence Coughlin (R) b. April 11, 1929 (1969)
14. William Coyne (D) age 44
15. *Don L. Ritter (R) b. Oct. 21, 1940 (1979)
16. *Robert S. Walker (R) b. Dec. 23, 1942 (1977)
17. *Allen E. Ertel (D) b. Nov. 7, 1936 (1977)
18. *Doug Walgren (D) b. Dec. 28, 1940 (1977)
19. *William F. Goodling (R) b. Dec. 5, 1927 (1975)
20. *Joseph M. Gaydos (D) b. July 3, 1926 (1969)
21. *Don Bailey (D) b. July 21, 1945 (1979)
22. *Austin J. Murphy (D) b. June 17, 1927 (1977)
23. William F. Clinger Jr. (R) age 49
24. *Marc Marks (R) b. Feb. 12, 1927 (1977)
25. *Eugene V. Atkinson (D) b. April 5, 1927 (1979)

Rhode Island: 1 D, 1 R [2 D]

1. *Fernand Joseph St. Germain (D) b. Jan. 9, 1928 (1961)
2. Claudine Schneider (R) age 33

South Carolina: 2 D, 4 R [4 D, 2 R]

1. Thomas Hartnett (R) age 38
2. *Floyd Spence (R) b. April 9, 1928 (1971)
3. *Butler C. Derrick Jr. (D) b. Sept. 30, 1936 (1975)
4. *Carroll Campbell (R) b. July 24, 1940 (1979)
5. *Kenneth L. Holland (D) b. Nov. 24, 1934 (1975)
6. John Napier (R) age 33

South Dakota: 1 D, 1 R [1 D, 1 R]

1. *Thomas Daschle (D) b. Dec. 9, 1947 (1979)
2. Clinton Roberts (R) age 45

Tennessee: 5 D, 3 R [5 D, 3 R]

1. *James H. "Jimmy" Quillen (R) b. Jan. 11, 1916 (1963)
2. *John James Duncan (R) b. March 24, 1919 (1965)
3. *Marilyn Lloyd Bouquard (D) b. Jan. 3, 1929 (1975)
4. *Albert Gore Jr. (D) b. March 31, 1948 (1977)
5. *Bill Boner (D) b. Feb. 14, 1945 (1979)
6. *Robin L. Beard Jr. (R) b. Aug. 21, 1939 (1973)
7. *Ed Jones (D) b. April 20, 1912 (1969)
8. *Harold E. Ford (D) b. May 20, 1945 (1975)

Texas: 19 D, 5 R [20 D, 4 R]

1. *Sam B. Hall Jr. (D) b. Jan. 11, 1924 (1976)
2. *Charles Wilson (D) b. June 1, 1933 (1973)
3. *James M. Collins (R) b. April 29, 1916 (1968)
4. Ralph Hall (D) age 56
5. *James Alabon Mattox (D) b. Aug. 29, 1943 (1977)
6. *Phil Gramm (D) b. July 8, 1942 (1979)
7. *W. R. "Bill" Archer (R) b. March 22, 1928 (1971)
8. Jack Fields (R) age 28
9. *Jack Brooks (D) b. Dec. 18, 1922 (1953)
10. *J. J. "Jake" Pickle (D) b. Oct. 11, 1913 (1963)
11. *Marvin Leath (D) b. May 6, 1931 (1979)
12. *James C. Wright Jr. (D) b. Dec. 22, 1922 (1955)
13. *Jack Hightower (D) b. Sept. 6, 1936 (1975)
14. William Patman (D) age 53
15. *E. Kika de la Garza (D) b. Sept. 22, 1927 (1965)
16. *Richard Crawford White (D) b. April, 29, 1923 (1965)
17. *Charles W. Stenholm (D) b. Oct. 26, 1938 (1979)
18. *Mickey Leland (D) b. Nov. 27, 1944 (1979)
19. *Kent Hance (D) b. Nov. 14, 1942 (1979)
20. *Henry B. Gonzalez (D) b. May 3, 1916 (1961)

21. *Thomas Loeffler (R) b. Aug. 1, 1946 (1979)
22. *Ron Paul (R) b. Aug. 20, 1935 (1979)
23. *Abraham Kazen Jr. (D) b. Jan. 17, 1919 (1967)
24. *J. Martin Frost (D) b. Jan. 1, 1942 (1979)

Utah: 2 R [1 D, 1 R]

1. James Hansen (R) age 48
2. *David Daniel Marriott (R) b. Nov. 2, 1939 (1977)

Vermont: 1 R [1 R]

At large: *James M. Jeffords (R) b. May 11, 1934 (1975)

Virginia: 1 D, 9 R [4 D, 6 R]

1. *Paul S. Trible Jr. (R) b. Dec. 29, 1946 (1977)
2. *G. William Whitehurst (R) b. March 12, 1925 (1969)
3. Thomas Bliley (R) age 48
4. *Robert W. Daniel Jr. (R) b. March 17, 1936 (1973)
5. *W. C. "Dan" Daniel (D) b. May 12, 1914 (1969)
6. *M. Caldwell Butler (R) b. June 22, 1925 (1973)
7. *James Kenneth Robinson (R) b. May 14, 1916 (1971)
8. Stanford E. Parris (R) b. Sept. 9, 1929 (1973)†
9. *William Creed Wampler (R) b. April 21, 1926 (1953)†
10. Frank Wolf (R) age 41

Washington: 5 D, 2 R [6 D, 1 R]

1. *Joel M. Pritchard (R) b. May 5, 1925 (1972)
2. *Al Swift (D) b. Sept. 12, 1935 (1979)
3. *Don Bonker (D) b. March 7, 1937 (1975)
4. Sid Morrison (R) age 45
5. *Thomas Stephen Foley (D) b. March 6, 1929 (1965)
6. *Norman D. Dicks (D) b. Dec. 16, 1940 (1977)
7. *Mike Lowry (D) b. March 8, 1939 (1979)

West Virginia: 2 D, 2 R [4 D]

1. *Robert M. Mollohan (D) b. Sept. 18, 1909 (1953)†
2. Cleve Benedict (R) age 45
3. Mick Staton (R) age 40
4. *Nick Joe Rahall (D) b. May 20, 1949 (1977)

Wisconsin: 5 D, 4 R [6 D, 3 R]

1. *Les Aspin (D) b. July 21, 1928 (1971)
2. *Robert William Kastenmeier (D) b. Jan. 24, 1924 (1959)
3. Steven Gunderson (R) age 29
4. *Clement J. Zablocki (D) b. Nov. 18, 1912 (1949)
5. *Henry S. Reuss (D) b. Feb. 22, 1912 (1955)
6. *Thomas Petri (R) b. May 28, 1940 (1979)
7. *David R. Obey (D) b. Oct. 3, 1938 (1969)
8. *Toby Roth (R) b. Oct. 10, 1938 (1979)
9. *F. James Sensenbrenner (R) June 14, 1943 (1979)

Wyoming: 1 R [1 R]

At Large: Richard Cheney (R) b. Jan. 30, 1941 (1979)

Governorships In control: 27 D, 23 R Pre-election lineup: 31 D, 19 R

[97] Republicans won seven of the 13 gubernatorial elections Nov. 4, for a net gain of four statehouses.

[90] Republicans gained governorships in Arkansas, Missouri, North Dakota and Washington. In Arkansas, Frank D. White, a conservative banker, defeated Gov. Bill Clinton, at 34 years old, the youngest governor in the U.S. In Missouri, Christopher S. Bond, a former governor defeated for reelection in 1976, defeated Gov. Joseph P. Teasdale. In North Dakota, Allen I. Olson, the state attorney general, defeated Gov. Arthur A. Link. In Washington, John Spellman, King County executive, defeated state Sen. James A. McDermott.

[99] **State Governors.** The governors of the 50 states are listed below. Each governor is described according to his party affiliation (D = Democrat, R = Republican), the year in which he became governor (date in parentheses) and his election status (*designates an incumbent, *italics* indicate elected or reelected in November 1980 and † indicates that service began in the year shown but has not been continuous). Unless indicated, the governor serves four years.

Ala.	Forrest James Jr. (D) term ends 1983; b. Sept. 15, 1934 (1979)
Alaska	Jay S. Hammond (R) term ends 1983; b. July 21, 1922 (1975)
Ariz.	Bruce Babbit (D) term ends 1983; b. June 27, 1938 (1978)
Ark.	*Frank D. White* (R) term ends 1983; age 46
Calif.	Edmund G. Brown Jr. (D) term ends 1983; b. April 7, 1938 (1975)
Colo.	Richard D. Lamm (D) term ends 1983; b. Aug. 3, 1935 (1975)
Conn.	Ella T. Grasso (D) term ends 1983; b. May 10, 1919 (1975)
Del.	**Pierre Samuel duPont IV* (R) term ends 1985; b. Jan 22, 1935 (1977)
Fla.	Robert Graham (D) term ends 1983; Age 44 (1979)
Ga.	George Busbee (D) term ends 1983; b. Aug. 7, 1927 (1975)
Hawaii	George R. Ariyoshi (D) term ends 1982; b. March 12, 1926 (1975)
Idaho	John V. Evans (D) term ends 1983; b. Jan. 18, 1925 (1977)
Ill.	James Robert Thompson (R) term ends 1983; b. May 8, 1936 (1977)
Ind.	*Robert D. Orr* (R) term ends 1985; age 62
Iowa	Robert D. Ray (R) term ends 1983; b. Sept. 28, 1928 (1969)
Kansas	John W. Carlin (D) term ends 1983; b. Aug. 3, 1940 (1979)
Ky.	John Y. Brown (D) term ends 1983; age 46 (1979)
La.	David C. Treen (R) term ends 1984; b. July 16, 1928 (1980)
Maine	Joseph E. Brennan (D) term ends 1983; Nov. 2, 1934 (1979)
Md.	Harold R. Hughes (D) term ends 1983; b. Nov. 13, 1926 (1979)
Mass.	Edward J. King (D) term ends 1983 b. May 11, 1925 (1979)
Mich.	William J. Milliken (R) term ends 1983; b. March 26, 1922 (1969)
Minn.	Albert H. Quie (R) term ends 1983; b. Sept. 18, 1923 (1979)
Miss.	William Winter (D) term ends 1984; b. Feb. 21, 1923 (1980)

Mo.	*Christopher S. Bond* (R) term ends 1985; b. May 6, 1939 (1973)†
Mont.	*Ted Schwinden* (D) term ends 1985; b. Aug. 31, 1925
Neb.	Charles Thone (R) term ends 1983; b. Jan. 4, 1924 (1979)
Nev.	Robert List (R) term ends 1983; b. Sept. 1, 1936 (1979)
N.H.	**Hugh Gallen* (D) term ends 1983 b. July 30, 1924 (1979)
N.J.	Brendan T. Byrne (D) term ends 1982; b. April 1, 1924 (1974)
N.M.	Bruce King (D) term ends 1983; b. April 6, 1924 (1971)†
N.Y.	Hugh L. Carey (D) term ends 1983; b. April 11, 1919 (1975)
N.C.	**James Hunt* (D) term ends 1985; b. May 16, 1937 (1977)
N.D.	*Allen I. Olson* (R) term ends 1985; b. Nov. 5, 1938
Ohio	James A. Rhodes (R) term ends 1983; b. Sept. 13, 1909 (1963)†
Okla.	George Nigh (D) term ends 1983; b. June 9, 1927 (1979)
Ore.	Victor Atiyeh (R) term ends 1983; b. Feb. 20, 1923 (1979)
Pa.	Richard L. Thornburgh (R) term ends 1983; b. July 16, 1932 (1979)
R.I.	**John Joseph Garrahy* (D) term ends 1983; b. Nov. 26, 1930 (1977)
S.C.	Richard W. Riley (D) term ends 1983; b. Jan. 2, 1933 (1979)
S.D.	William J. Janklow (R) term ends 1983; b. Sept. 13, 1939 (1979)
Tenn.	Lamar Alexander (R) term ends 1983; age 40 (1979)
Texas	Bill Clements (R) term ends 1983; April 13, 1917 (1979)
Utah	**Scott M. Matheson* (D) term ends 1985; b. Jan. 9, 1929 (1977)
Vt.	**Richard Arkwright Snelling* (R) term ends 1983; b. Feb. 18, 1927 (1977)
Va.	John Dalton (R) term ends 1982; b. July 11, 1931 (1978)
Wash.	*John Spellman* (R) term ends 1985; age 53
W. Va.	**John D. Rockefeller IV* (D) term ends 1985; b. June 18, 1937 (1977)
Wis.	Lee S. Dreyfus (R) term ends 1983; b. June 20, 1926 (1979)
Wyo.	Ed Herschler (D) term ends 1983; b. Oct. 27, 1918 (1975)

[100] **Referendum Issues.** The Nov. 4. ballots contained a wide variety of referendum issues ranging from property tax cuts to restrictions on nuclear power and bilingualism.

[101] Massachusetts voters approved a measure calling for a major reduction in property taxes. The measure, called Proposition 2½, would roll back property taxes to 2½% of assessed valuation, for a 40% tax cut. The issue was bitterly contested by the state and local officials, who contended that the proposition would lead to cutbacks and users fees for such services as garbage collection and public libraries. However, proponents said it would stimulate growth and stop business from leaving the state for regions with lower taxes. The measure was approved with a 60% majority. Other tax relief measures were approved in Iowa, South Dakota, Utah, Arizona, Nevada, Oregon, Montana, Arkansas and Ohio. Proposals to restrict the use of nuclear power were on the ballot in five states. Missouri and South Dakota voters rejected restrictions on nuclear power plants and Montanans turned down a and Montanans turned down a measure to severely limit uranium mining. However, in Washington, voters approved strong limits on nuclear waste storage, and in Oregon, voters barred construction of nuclear plants without federally licensed dump sites for radioactive waste. In a controversial Florida referendum initiative, Dade County voters approved a measure that would end six years of bilingualism by banning mandatory governmental use of Spanish or any language other than English. The measure was seen largely as a backlash against Miami's 600,000 Cuban immigrants.

See also Carter, Billy [22]

EL SALVADOR

[1] **Leftists Form Coalition.** Three of the most powerful leftist organizations in El Salvador formed a coalition Jan. 10 to coordinate their struggle against the civilian-military junta.

[2] The coalition included the Popular Revolution Bloc (BPR), the United Popular Action Front and the 28th of February Popular Leagues (LP-28). Diplomatic sources estimated that the combined total of the three factions was 75,000 persons. Each group contained a militant guerrilla wing.

[3] ***Moderates Back Leftists***—A broad-based coalition of moderate and center-leftist groups called the Democratic Front announced its formation April 2 and endorsed the

military Revolutionary Coordinating Committee, formed Jan. 10. Professionals and technicians, previously nonaligned unions, the social democratic National Revolutionary Movement and dissident Christian Democrats who had opposed their party's participation in the civilian-military junta were represented in the new group.

[4] **Political Turmoil Hurts Economy.** The political unrest in El Salvador was having a profound affect on the country's economy especially the coffee crop, on which El Salvador relied for 70% of its gross national income, the *Wall Street Journal* reported Jan. 17.

[5] Leftist guerrila groups had vowed to undermine the nation's economy, and the government, through a series of strikes and armed confrontations. Because of this, the *Journal* said, many nervous coffee growers had already harvested 80% of the 1979-80 October-to-March crop, about 20% more than normal. This had caused an increase in the cost of processing the beans and an accompanying decrease in the quality of the coffee.

[6] Equally damaging was the fact that the new military junta had suspended coffee sales shortly after it came to power Oct. 15, 1979 to give the government control over the marketing of the coffee. By Jan. 17, when 50% of the crop would normally have been sold, the *Journal* said, only 3% of the year's crop was sold. During the suspension of sales, the price of coffee dropped to $174 per 100 pound bag from $212.

[7] The result was that the expected coffee yield for the 1979-80 October-to-March growing season would be worth $550 million, instead of the $900 million previously forecast. Suspension of coffee exports had also resulted in an increase in unemployment to about 15% during a time of year when employment was usually close to 100%. Coffee production employed about 40% of El Salvador's 4.8 million people during the harvest season.

[8] ***Junta Seeks Aid for Failing Economy***—The Salvadoran government was actively seeking aid from abroad to help bolster the failing economy, but its requests had not been successful because of the junta's image as a repressor of human rights, the *New York Times* reported Oct. 15.

[9] Some $90 million in economic aid provided by the U.S. had been criticized by human rights groups in U.S. and Social Democratic movements in Europe and Latin America because of the junta's repression of leftist groups, especially in rural areas. The junta had made requests for some $400 million in emergency aid from the World Bank, the Inter-American Development Bank, but so far none of the aid had been granted, according to the *Times.*

[10] On Oct. 13, two major Salvadoran business groups published statements in newspapers calling for resignation of the U.S.–backed junta and a return to constitutional rule. In making the appeal, the two groups–the Salvadoran Industrialist Association and the Salvadoran Chamber of Commerce–defied a law prohibiting criticism of the government. Their rationale for the announcement was the "true economic crisis in the country."

[11] **Junta Reforms.** El Salvador's ruling civilian-military junta Feb. 11 announced a series of economic reforms.

[12] Junta member Col. Adolfo Arnoldo Majano said in a radio broadcast that all the nation's banks were to be nationalized, government controls were to be placed on foreign trade and an agrarian reform program would be carried out.

[13] **Archbishop Romero Assassinated.** Roman Catholic Archbishop Oscar Arnulfo Romero y Galdamez, one of the most outspoken and respected figures in strife-torn El Salvador, was assassinated March 24. Romero was killed by a single bullet, as he said mass in a small chapel in San Salvador. The assassin escaped.

[14] Romero had often taken stands on human rights and aid for the poor and

Bodies of four persons killed March 30 at funeral of murdered Archbishop Oscar Arnulfo Romero lie in San Salvador cathedral.

oppressed in his weekly sermons at the Metropolitan Cathedral. Above all, Romero had preached peace and prayed for an end to the violence between the left and right in El Salvador.

[15] Romero's death heightened fears that the turmoil in El Salvador would lead to civil war. During the early morning hours of March 25, a series of 30 bomb blasts caused heavy damage to banks and other businesses in San Salvador and in other towns around the country. The U.S. Department of State March 25 evacuated all 21 dependents of 25 diplomats working in the U.S. Embassy in San Salvador.

[16] On March 26, the body of the slain prelate was carried through the city's streets. About 5,000 persons joined in the silent procession, led by four bishops and 400 priests and nuns. Heavily armed police enforced an uneasy truce along the 15-block route to the Metropolitan Cathedral. One priest said that the crowd was not larger because the people were "now too scared to appear in public." More than 600 deaths from political violence had been recorded so far in 1980.

[17] Bomb blasts, sniper fire and panic set off a stampede in San Salvador March 30 during Romero's funeral. About 30 persons were killed in the melee, many of them crushed as some 75,000 sought safety.

[18] **Death Toll Mounts.** The Salvadoran Human Rights Commission estimated that some 2,065 persons had died in El Salvador as a result of political violence between January 1 and May 31 1980, according to *Latin American Weekly Report* June 13. At least 503 deaths were attributed to leftist violence against the government figures and wealthy landowners. The rest were persons killed by army, police and rightist groups.

[19] **Guerrilla Leader Captured.** Julian Espinoza, the leader of the leftist-guerrilla Popular Liberation Forces (FPL), was captured by troops in El Salvador June 23.

[20] **Troops Storm National University.** A force of 500 government troops

supported by armored cars stormed the campus of the National University in San Salvador June 26, triggering a fierce battle with leftist gunmen that left some 50 persons dead. Scores of civilians were arrested. The invasion of the university was unprecedented in that police were legally barred from entering the campus.

[21] **Guerrillas Fought in Northeast.** More than 170 peasants and leftist guerrillas were killed in the country's northeast July 29-Aug. 1.

[22] The operation involved 3,500 troops and included the use of helicopter gunships to bomb and strafe villages suspected of harboring the guerrillas. Battles were reported as close as 20 miles (30 kilometers) to San Salvador with the heaviest fighting near the town of Perguin, 71 miles (114 kilometers) northeast of the capital. Government officials said that at least 60 soldiers had been wounded in the fighting around Perguin, but no figures on the number of soldiers killed were released.

[23] A major offensive by 5,000 Salvadoran troops with heavy artillery, helicopter gunships, tanks and armored cars had dislodged some 25,000 peasants from their homes in northern El Salvador, it was reported Oct. 25. Many of the peasants fleeing the violence in the north had traveled to San Salvador and to refugee camps in other areas of the country. Some had moved across the border into Honduras, and others had sought refugee in Mexico, the U.S. and other countries.

[24] **2 Rights Activists Slain.** Maria Magdalena Henriquez, a spokeswoman for El Savador's Human Rights Commission, was found murdered Oct. 7 in the Pacific Coast town of La Libertad, 20 miles (32 kilometers) south of San Salvador.

[25] The commission, a private organization, had recently reported that 7,000 civilians had been killed in the violence in El Salvador in 1980, and that more than 3,000 persons had disappeared after being arrested.

[26] Ramon Valladares, the administrator of the commission, was assassinated Oct. 26 while driving his car in Sal Salvador.

[27] **Christian Democratic Spokesman Slain.** The chief spokesman for the Christain Democratic Party in El Salvador was assassinated near his home in San Salvador Oct. 10. Melvin Rigoberto Orellana was killed instantly when his car was ambushed. Witnesses said that members of the Popular Liberation Forces, a leftist terrorist group, had done the shooting.

[28] **6 Prominent Leftists Slain.** Six prominent leftist leaders were kidnapped Nov. 27 during a clandestine meeting in San Salvador. Their bullet-riddled bodies were later found on roadsides around the capital. Twenty-three others who attended the meeting at a Jesuit-run high school, were also abducted by a force of some 200 uniformed gunmen. It was feared that they too had been murdered.

[29] The dead men were identified as Enrique Alvarez Cordoba, the leader of the Democratic Revolutionary Front (FDR), Juan Chacon, leader of the Popular Revolutionary Bloc, Manuel Franco of the Communist National Democratic Union, Enrique Barrera of the National Revolutionary Movement, Humberto Mendoza of the Popular Liberation Movement and Donoteo Hernandez, the leader of a labor union.

[30] On Nov. 28, a right-wing paramilitary group, the Maximiliano Hernandez Brigade, claimed responsibility for the killings. But a spokesman for the FDR charged that the government had helped plan and carry out the killings and that soldiers and helicopters had been used to surround the school in downtown San Salvador during the attack.

[31] **4 American Women Found Slain.** The bodies of three American nuns and one lay worker were found Dec. 4 in a crude grave near San Salvador.

[32] The women had been missing since

Dec. 2. Police said that they had apparently died from gunshot wounds and strangulation. The women were identified as: Dorothy Kazel, 40, of the Ursiline Order, and Jean Donovan, 27, the lay worker, both from Cleveland, Ohio, Sister Ita Ford, 40, of Brooklyn, N.Y., and Sister Maura Clarke, 46, of Queens, N.Y., both of the Maryknoll Order.

[33] At least 10 Roman Catholic priests, including San Salvador's archbishop, Oscar Arnulfo Romero, had been assassinated in El Salvador in the last two years. Many in El Salvador reportedly felt that the deaths of the American women were the work of extremists operating with the covert permission of El Salvador's military authorities.

[34] **Duarte Named President.** Jose Napoleon Duarte, the leader of the Social Democratic Party, who had joined the civilian-military junta in March, was named president of El Salvador Dec. 13.

[35] **Leftist Offensive Stalled.** The commander of the army in northern Chalatenango Province, near the Honduran border, said Dec. 28 that troops had surrounded some 400 guerrillas in the town of Dulce Nombre de Jesus and that "a large number of guerrillas had died."

[36] Some 1,000 guerrillas had launched simultaneous attacks on police stations and military posts in at least eight towns in Chalatenango Dec. 26.

[37] On the same day, one of El Salvador's top guerrilla commanders, Ferman Cienfuegos, said that the leftist revolutionaries would embark on a final offensive against the military-civilian junta to shift the balance of power before U.S. President-elect Ronald Reagan took office in 1981. Cienfuegos, who commanded the Armed Forces of National Resistance, was one of five members of the Farabundo Marti National Liberation Front's executive directorate. The front took its name from the leader of a peasant uprising in El Salvador in 1932.

See also Aliens, Immigration [1]; Human Rights [18]

EMPLOYMENT—*See* Budget [9, 13-15, 22]

ENERGY

[1] **Synthetic Fuels Bill Passed.** Congress completed one of the last two major elements of the Carter energy plan, the synthetic fuels bill, legislation which created the U.S. Synthetic Fuels Corp. to speed development of alternate energy sources.

[2] The House approved the synfuels development bill June 26 by a 317-93 vote. The Senate had passed the $20 billion program on June 19 by a 78-12 vote. President Carter signed the measure June 30.

[3] The bill aimed at reducing dependence on imported oil by boosting American production of synfuels to 500,000 barrels daily by 1987 and two million barrels daily by 1992. The measure created solar-energy bank and authorized a $1.45 billion alcohol fuel production program.

[4] The seven-member U.S. Synthetic Fuels Corp. was authorized in the bill to spend $20 billion in fiscal 1981. The federal corporation was also authorized to seek as much as $68 billion more in future years. As incentives, the corporation could build three government-owned plants.

[5] The final element of the Carter energy program, the Energy Mobilization Board, which would be established by separate legislation, was still being drafted in Congress.

[6] ***3 Nations to Build Synfuel Plant—*** President Carter July 31 signed an agreement with Japan and West Germany for the construction of a $1.4 billion synthetic fuels plant in West Virginia.

[7] The Japanese and West German

governments each agreed to pay 25% of the costs of the project, designed to produce the equivalent of 20,000 barrels of oil a day by 1984. The joint operators of the plant, Gulf Oil Corp., two German concerns and a group of Japanese companies, were scheduled to contribute a total of $100 million toward the costs of the project, which would use a Gulf Oil-developed process known as solvent refined coal to produce oil for gasoline, home heating oil and industrial boiler fuel. The U.S. Department of Energy was responsible for the bulk of the costs, approximately $600 million, for the Morgantown, W. Va. plant.

[8] **House Downs Energy Mobilization Board.** Liberal Democratic environmentalists and conservative Republicans in the House joined to defeat a bill to create an Energy Mobilization Board June 27, by a 232-131 vote.

[9] The proposed legislation, backed by President Carter, was a compromise version of separate bills passed by the House and Senate in 1979. The measure, called the Priority Energy Act of 1980, was returned to House-Senate conference, but supporters acknowledged that it was probably dead for this session of Congress.

[10] The Energy Mobilization Board would have had the power to override environmental and safety laws blocking key energy projects. Liberals viewed the board as a threat to existing environmental law, while Republican conservatives opposed it as a incursion on state rights.

[11] **Fusion Development Bill.** President Carter Oct. 7 signed into law a bill whose goal was to accelerate the development of fusion research so that a commercial demonstration plant would be operating in the U.S. by the year 2000.

[12] Fusion was a process that released energy by combining, or fusing, hydrogen atoms. Present commercial nuclear plants utilized fission, or the process of releasing energy by splitting uranium atoms. The legislation had been passed by the House Aug. 25 and by the Senate in an amended version Sept. 23. The House agreed to the amendments Sept. 24, thus clearing the bill. The bill did not increase specific funds to be spent on fusion development, but called for doubling of the current spending within seven years. (Carter had signed an appropriations bill for energy Oct. 1 appropriating $393 million for fusion programs in fiscal 1981.)

See also Congress [8]; Oil; Solar Energy

ENVIRONMENT

[1] **Water Pollution the Big Problem.** The nation's water and allied resources were "in trouble," the President's Council on Environmental Quality warned Feb. 19 in its 10th annual report.

[2] "We can no longer expect an endless supply of cheap, clean water at the twist of a faucet," council Chairman Gus Speth said.

The report outlined a number of environmental problem areas. Among them:

- Ninety percent of hazardous wastes produced in the U.S. were not being disposed of properly.
- Americans were producing 1,400 pounds of trash and junk per person every year, of which only 1% was being burned and only 7% was being recycled.
- Noise pollution levels were to the point that one in every 10 Americans was subjected to the possibility of damaged hearing.
- In New York and Los Angeles, two of every three days in 1977 were rated "unhealthful" in air quality.

[3] However, other major metropolitan areas showed improvement in air quality, according to the report. The improvement was attributed largely to more general use of emission controls on automobiles.

[4] The nation's water problems ranged

from the recurrent cycles of shortages and floods in the West to acid rain in the East. "As a result of this increased acidity, many lakes in the northeastern part of the United States and Canada now can no longer support fish and other life," the report said. It also found that more than one-third of the country's commercial shellfishing waters had been closed because of pollution.

[5] ***EPA Clean Water Enforcement Backed***—The Supreme Court ruled, 8-0, Dec. 2 that the Environmental Protection Agency did not have to consider the cost of compliance when requiring a company to meet federal water pollution standards. The decision in *EPA v. National Crushed Stone Association* reversed a ruling by the U.S. 4th Circuit Court of Appeals.

[6] **N.J. Chemical Dump Burns.** A chemical waste dump in Elizabeth, N.J. exploded into a raging fire April 22 that took nearly 10 hours to bring under control.

[7] Black smoke and ash from the fire extended over a 15-square-mile area and a precautionary health alert was imposed on parts of New Jersey and New York City. The site of the fire was along the Arthur Kill, separating New Jersey from Staten Island, N.Y. The dump had been closed in 1979 under pressure from the state of New Jersey, which then removed some 10,000 barrels of what were considered the most hazardous chemicals. Another 24,000 barrels of chemicals remained in the dump at the time of the explosion and fire.

[8] **Love Canal: A State of Emergency.** President Carter declared a state of emergency at the Love Canal in Niagara Falls, N.Y. May 21 as plans were made to evacuate 710 families from the chemically contaminated site.

[9] Under the emergency order, the federal government would pay for the evacuation and temporary housing of the families until it was determined whether the area was safe for a return. Some families left the area that day.

[10] In 1978, a total of 239 families had abandoned homes in the area because of the existence and threat of health problems from leaking toxic chemicals. The Love Canal had been used as a chemical dump site for many years by the Hooker Chemicals and Plastics Corp.

[11] Results of a study, reported May 16, indicated that 30% of the residents of the area had suffered chromosome damage. Preliminary results showed that 11 of 36 persons tested on Jan. 18 and 19 possessed rare chromosomal aberrations, changes that frequently were linked to cancer, as a forerunner of the disease, and that also could lead to genetic damage in offspring. A second study of Love Canal residents had turned up "results suggestive of peripheral nerve damage" among the residents, the Environmental Protection Agency disclosed May 21.

[12] ***Second Love Canal Suit Filed***—New York State filed a $635 million damage suit April 28 against the Occidental Petroleum Corp. and its Hooker Chemical unit over the dumping of toxic chemical wastes in the Love Canal area.

[13] The state action charged that 21,000 tons of chemicals had been dumped in the area between 1942 and 1953 and that Hooker had failed to warn the public or those who lived in the region about "the hazardous nature of the chemicals disposed of" or about "the danger to people and the environment of exposure to such chemicals." It was the second major suit filed in the case. A $124 million federal suit against Occidental and Hooker had been filed in 1979.

[14] **OSHA Rebuffed on Benzene Standard.** The Supreme Court voted 5-4, July 2 to uphold a lower court decision that voided the federal government's work safety standard on exposure to the chemical benzene. The case was *Industrial Union Department v. American Petroleum Institute.*

[15] Benzene, which was suspected of causing leukemia, was widely used as a

gasoline additive in paints, solvents and other products. In 1978, the Occupational Safety and Health Administration had issued rules reducing the allowable airborne exposure at a work place to one part benzene per million parts of air, from 10 parts benzene per million parts of air, over an eight-hour period.
[16] The U.S. 5th Circuit Court of Appeals struck down the new standard, primarily because OSHA had failed to weight the cost to businesses of complying with the standard against the expected benefits. The Supreme Court backed the appeals court, but by and large avoided the much-disputed cost-benefit issue. Instead the majority ruled that OSHA had arbitrarily adopted the new standard.

Oil Spills

[17] **Spill Must Be Reported.** The Supreme Court ruled, 8-1, June 27 that federal law required an individual or company responsible for an oil spill to report the spill, even though the report could be used to impose a civil fine against the polluter. The case was *U.S. v. Ward.*
[18] **Runaway Well Capped.** The runaway Ixtoc 1 offshore oil well in the Gulf of Mexico had finally been capped, Mexican officials said March 24.
[19] The well, which blew out June 3, 1979, had spilled oil into the Gulf at a rate of about 30,000 barrels a day. It had confounded efforts by U.S. and Mexican technicians to cap it. On Oct. 14, 1979, the flow of oil had been cut in half after a cone was placed over the well head to collect the escaping oil.
[20] Drilling on two relief wells was then started to equalize the pressure inside the reservoir of oil. The first was completed Jan. 10. When the second well was ready, mud and thickening substances were pumped into the blown well, reducing the flow to negligible amounts. Finally the hole was plugged with about 200 sacks of cement, which hardened into a 685 feet- (200 meter) deep plug. A final 500 sacks of quick-drying cement applied March 24 shut off the flow entirely.
[21] The Ixtoc spill was the worst ever recorded. An estimated 3.1 million barrels of oil were lost before the spill could be contained. Officials of Pemex, the Mexican state oil company, now estimated that the oil field beneath Ixtoc contained at least 800 million barrels of oil.
See also Canada [43-44]; Energy [10]; Union of Soviet Socialist Republics [17-20]; Wildlife [1-2]

ENVIRONMENTAL PROTECTION AGENCY (EPA)—*See* Environment [5, 11]

EQUAL RIGHTS AMENDMENT (ERA)—*See* Women's Rights [10-15]

ESPIONAGE

[1] **Satellite Spy Escapes.** Christopher Boyce, convicted in 1977 of selling U.S. satellite secrets to the Soviets, escaped from the federal prison in Lompoc, Calif., officials reported Jan. 22.
[2] The 26-year-old son of a former Federal Bureau of Investigation agent was discovered missing at a 10 p.m. bedcheck on Jan. 21. Officials said searchers found wirecutters and a makeshift wooden ladder near a guard tower at the rear of the maximum security institution. Lompoc was on the Pacific coast about 100 miles (160 kilometers) northeast of Los Angeles. Boyce had been serving a 40-year sentence.
[3] **French Catch Soviet Spy.** French security agents in Marseilles caught a Soviet consular official Feb. 9 as he was accepting delivery of confidential documents relating to the Mirage 2000 combat aircraft.
[4] The official, Gennady Travkov, departed France for Moscow Feb. 10.

French security officials said Feb. 14 that Travkov had tried to infiltrate the aircraft manufacturer building the Mirage 2000, which was intended to replace the Mirage 3 fighter in the French air force by 1984. Several additional persons were reported to have been arrested in connection with the Travkov affair.

[5] **200 Soviet Spies in Switzerland.** About 200 of the 650 Soviet officials and diplomats attached to United Nations offices in Switzerland worked for the Soviet Union's various intelligence agencies, a Swiss government spokesman said Feb. 18.

[6] A Lausanne newspaper report had claimed that Switzerland was the only country other than the U.S. in which the Soviets maintained two offices of their military intelligence agency GRU. This was confirmed by Ulrich Hubacher, spokesman for the federal Justice and Police Department. One office was in Berne and the other in Geneva.

[7] **Soviet Industrial Spy Sentenced.** A Belgian businessman accused of being an industrial spy for the Soviet Union was sentenced Aug. 1 to four months in prison.

[8] Marc Andre DeGeyter pleaded guilty in an Alexandria, Va. federal district court to two misdemeanor charges. In return, the federal government agreed to dismiss an eight-count felony indictment against him. Federal prosecutors had charged that DeGeyter was part of an industrial espionage operation that attempted to get computer trade secrets from a Virginia computer company for a Soviet foreign trade company. DeGeyter had been arrested May 18, after giving an undercover Federal Bureau of Investigation agent a $500,000 check for computer tapes that he believed contained the information.

[9] **Ex-CIA Agent Pleads Guilty.** David H. Barnett, a former U.S. intelligence agent, Oct. 29 pleaded guilty to a federal court in Baltimore, Md. to a charge of selling to the Soviet Union information concerning a covert operation conducted by the Central Intelligence Agency.

[10] Barnett had worked for the CIA for 12 years before resigning in 1970. In January 1979 he returned to conduct training programs until March 1980. He was indicted Oct. 24 on a charge of espionage. Barnett's guilty plea was a result of plea bargaining between him and his lawyer and the Justice Department.

See also United Nations [10-12]

ETHIOPIA

[1] **Ogaden War Rekindled.** Fighting intensified in Ethiopia's southern Ogaden region at the beginning of 1980. After several months of isolated attacks in 1979, ethnic Somali guerrillas reported March 18 that 2,200 Ethiopian soldiers were killed in clashes at Babile and Jijiga, two prin-

A starving child weeps May 7 at Ethiopian refugee camp near the Kenyan border.

cipal towns in the area. The guerrillas were fighting to join the Ogaden to Somalia.

[2] Constant warfare in the region had driven more than one million ethnic Somalis from Ogaden into Somalia, according to international relief reports. Somali refugees charged that Ethiopia had mounted a deliberate campaign to drive the entire Ogaden population out of the country. Two U.S. representatives April 6 called Somalia's refugee problem greater than Cambodia's. Reps. Patricia Schroeder (D, Colo.) and Andrew Maguire (D, N.J.) made their statement after touring a Somali refugee camp. The two representatives said conditions at the camp were catastrophic. The camp was one of 21 that held 1.3 million ethnic Somalis from Ethiopia, most of them women and children.

[3] Ethiopian troops killed 1,300 Somali soldiers and wounded 2,000 others in an ambush of a Somali military convoy in the disputed Ogaden region, the official Ethiopian radio announced Aug. 8.

EUROPE—*See* Human Rights [12]

EUROPEAN COMMUNITY (EC) (Belgium, Denmark, France, Great Britain, Ireland, Italy, Luxembourg, Netherlands, West Germany)

[1] **Britain OKs Budget Compromise.** British Prime Minister Margaret Thatcher June 2 approved a proposal for reducing Britain's net contribution to the European Community budget. The compromise plan had been finalized May 30 after a marathon negotiating session in Brussels of EC foreign ministers.

[2] The budget dispute had absorbed the EC's attention since late 1979. London had demanded action on the budget because under the existing arrangements, Britain, although the third poorest member in the community, would make the largest net contribution to the budget in 1980. This was estimated at $2.5 billion, with a $3 billion net contribution in 1981. The Brussels compromise reduced Britain's net contribution to $865 million for 1980, and $1.03 billion for 1981.

[3] The EC's farm policy was the main reason why Birtian ended up making such heavy net contributions to the EC budget. The policy provided aid to inefficient food producers—primarily in other countries than Britain—and in effect penalized Britain for importing a large proportion of its food. The accord called for changes in the farm policy; if these could not be approved in time to affect the 1982 budget, then Britain would get relief that year too.

[4] Agreement on a 1980 EC budget was finally achieved July 9 in Strasbourg. The European Parliament adopted a budget of 17.3 billion units of account ($26.5 billion).

[5] **Nuclear Fusion Research.** EC foreign ministers, meeting in Brussels Feb. 5, approved funding of $2.06 billion for research into nuclear fusion over the period 1979-1983.

[6] **Steel Cuts.** The EC nations agreed in Luxembourg Oct. 30 to adopt a program calling for general reduction in steel production.

[7] The program was an attempt to end the price-cutting competition that had developed because of the weak international steel market. Under the program, companies would be required to reduce output by up to 18%, retroactive to Oct. 1. The plan could remain in effect through June 1981, although it might be ended earlier. In effect, the new plan amounted to establishment of a West European steel cartel. In order to take the action, foreign and industry officials of the EC nations were obliged to declare the steel industry "in manifest crisis" as defined by EC law. Currently, steel industry losses were

believed to be exceeding $3 billion annually.
See also Iran [74-76]

EVANGELICAL CHRISTIANS—*See* Christians, Evangelical

F

FAMINE—*See* Cambodia [1-11]

FASHION

[1] **Soft, Sophisticated Dressing for 1980.** A soft, sophisticated mood dominated the 1980 fashion scene. In Paris, Milan and New York, couture and ready-to-wear collections featured "smart," snappy clothes. This new chic shape was reported in the February 1-8 and August 1-8 issues of the fashion publication W.

Sonya Rykiel's soft, sexy sweater dressing made a major fashion statement in 1980. The short, side slit skirt, trimmed with ruffles, and the bi-colored knickers were paired with square shouldered sweater tops.

[2] Proportion and detail were key elements. Short skirt lengths just grazed the knee. Longer lengths fell from the lower calf to the top of the ankle. Shoulders were defined but softened by ruffles, bows and flounces.

[3] In Paris, Yves St. Laurent and Hubert de Givenchy created the "delightful dress," a basic waistless chemise accentuated by a long torso and a flippy or tiered skirt. Flounces, soft bowed collars and ribbon or ruffle trims completed the detailing. Flowered prints and geometrics, particularly in black and white silk, were favorite fabrics. In New York, Oscar de la Renta, Halston and Bill Blass offered their versions of the femine flowered "delightful dress."

[4] Coats had wide arms, lifted and slightly extended shoulders, full but not voluminoius shapes. Capes and capelets were also popular. Suits with knee length straight skirts were also fashion news. At St. Laurent, the Shakespearean-inspired suit with full sleeves and body-conscious fit looked newest. St. Laurent also reintroduced the blouson, soft and feminine in silk crepe de chine for day and lame and silk for evening. Pants were fuller with knickers, jodhpurs and Bermudas dominant. Sweater dressing soared to new popularity. Ralph Lauren updated the classic, preppy looks in New York, while Sonya Rykiel made Paris stare with ruffled, bows and sexy, see-through designs.

[5] For evening, the top coutures created rich, exotic clothes. St. Laurent translated his Renaissance theme in velvets and satins with

huge sleeves, simple draping and gem colors. Givenchy used iridescent, rich-colored taffetas with black velvet ribbon trim and intricate shirring. Oriental designs, venetian pleating, rich colors and exotic beading inspired clothes for evening.

FEDERAL BUREAU OF INVESTIGATION (FBI)

[1] **Two FBI Ex-Aides Convicted.** W. Mark Felt, former acting associate director of the Federal Bureau of Investigation, and Edward S. Miller, former chief of the FBI's intelligence division, were convicted Nov. 6. A jury in federal district court in Washington, D.C. found both men guilty of conspiring to violate the constitutional rights of American citizens by authorizing federal agents to break into homes and offices (without warrants) in search of fugitive members of the radical Weather Underground in 1972-73. (Such break-ins were also known as "black bag jobs.")

[2] Felt and Miller were sentenced Dec. 15 to pay fines of $5,000 and $3,500, respectively.

See Abscam; Civil Disorders [17, 20]; Crime [24-25]; Ku Klux Klan (KKK) [1-2]; Obscenity & Pornography [1-3]

FEDERAL COMMUNICATIONS COMMISSION—*See* Business [1-2]

FEDERAL RESERVE SYSTEM

[1] **Membership Exodus Feared.** Membership in the Federal Reserve System was continuing to decline and could threaten the Fed's control over the nation's money supply, Paul A. Volcker, chairman of the Federal Reserve Board, said Feb. 4.

[2] Volcker told the Senate Banking Committee that 69 banks with total deposits of about $7 billion gave notice of withdrawal from the system's membership in the fourth quarter of 1979. Volcker urged legislative action. He warned that failure to act would mean "the stream of member banks withdrawing will reach flood proportions."

[3] (The Atlanta *Constitution* Jan. 23 estimated that of the 5,483 banks in the system, some 267 were certain or probable withdrawals and another 301 were considering such a move. [See chart])

[4] The Fed required member banks to place a proportion of their deposits in noninterest-bearing reserve accounts with the Federal Reserve System. The central bank, in turn, provided such services as check clearance and access to loans. A bank that dropped membership in the Federal Reserve System (and as a consequence its national charter) and switched to a state charter was able to invest a larger share of its required reserve, often in interest-bearing securities.

Defections of Member Banks From Federal Reserve System

District	Total Members	Certain, Probable Withdrawals	Possible Withdrawals
1	176	30	45
2	236	19	49
3	225	68	48
4	409	–	41
5	389	7	3
6	590	14	16
7	910	40	26
8	399	40	10
9	510	8	4
10	797	13	23
11	704	21	27
12*	138	7	9
Totals	5,483	267	301

*includes Hawaii and Alaska

Source: Atlanta *Constitution* 1/23/80

[5] **Discount Rate Fluctuates.** The discount rate fluctuated around the 13% level during much of the year. It fell to a low of 10% July 25 and then moved back up.

[6] (The discount rate was the interest charged to member commercial banks when they borrowed money from their district Fed banks.)

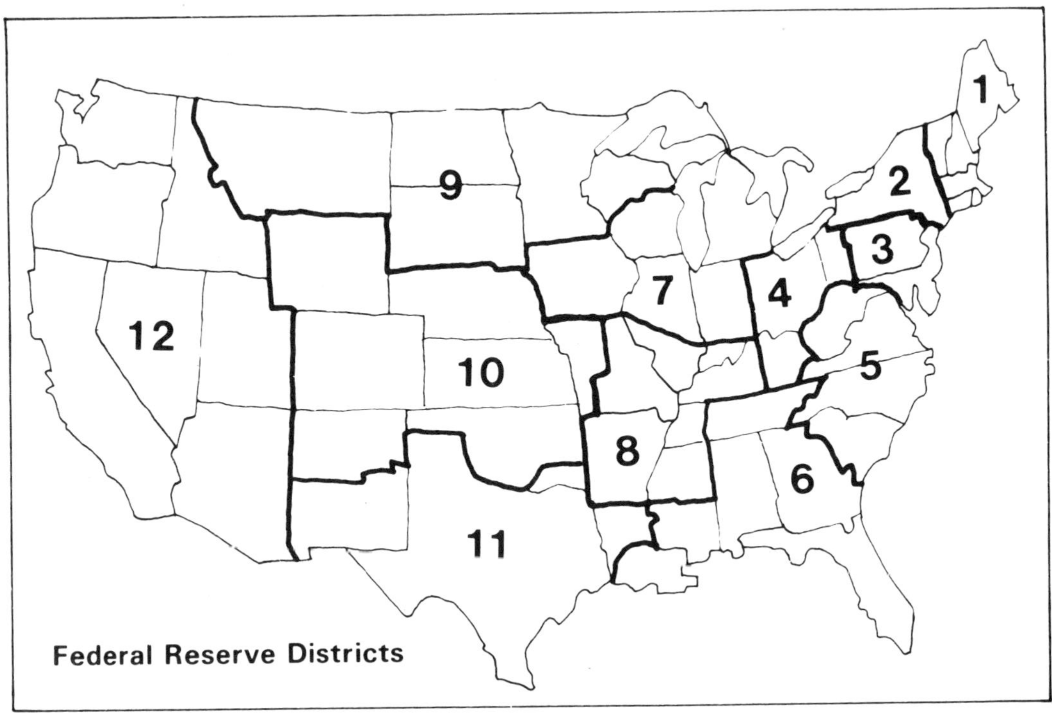

[7] The Federal Reserve moved Feb. 15 to increase the discount rate a full percentage point, to 13% from 12%. The rate was cut back to 12% May 28 and to 11% June 12. Subsequently, it was raised to 11% Sept. 25, to 12% Nov. 14, and to 13% Dec. 4.

[8] A surcharge of three percentage points on the discount rate was announced March 14 by the Federal Reserve for large banks borrowing from the Fed on a frequent basis. The surcharge was eliminated May 6. A surcharge of two percentage points was imposed Nov. 14, and raised to three percentage points Dec. 4.

See Banks & Banking [3-4, 13] Credit, Consumer [1-9]; Silver [14-15]

FLORIDA—*See* Cuba [1, 4, 7-9, 11-16, 21-22]; Disasters & Accidents [7-10]

FOOTBALL

[1] **Alabama Ranked No. 1.** The University of Alabama was chosen the national champion of college football Jan. 2 in separate polls conducted by United Press International and the Associated Press.

[2] Alabama had finished the season with a 12-0 won-lost record–including a victory in the 1980 Sugar Bowl [See below]–making it the only undefeated, untied major team in the nation. It was the ninth time the Crimson Tide had been picked No. 1, but the first time it had swept both polls. This was also the sixth national title for Alabama head coach Paul (Bear) Bryant.

[3] ***College Bowl Results***—Alabama rolled over Arkansas, 24-9, Jan 1 in the **Sugar Bowl** in the Louisiana Superdome in New Orleans. Major Ogilvie, the Crimson Tide's junior tailback, ran for two touchdowns in the first quarter.

[4] Southern Cal came from behind to edge Ohio State, 17-16, Jan. 1 in the **Rose Bowl** in Pasadena, Calif. Heisman Trophy winner Charles White rushed for 247 yards on 39 carries–a Rose

Bowl record—and dove into the end zone from one yard out with less than two minutes left in the game to give USC the victory.
[5] Oklahoma ripped previously undefeated Florida State, 24-7, Jan. 1 in the **Orange Bowl** in Miami. Billy Sims, the 1978 Heisman Trophy winner, gained 164 yards on 24 carries and scored one TD in his last game for the Sooners.
[6] The University of Houston nipped Nebraska, 17-14, Jan. 1 in the **Cotton Bowl** in Dallas. The Cougars won the game in the final 12 seconds of play, when Eric Herring snagged a tipped six-yard touch-down pass from quarterback Terry Elston.
[7] **Steelers Win 4th Super Bowl.** The Pittsburgh Steelers won the championship of the National Football League Jan. 20, with a 31-19 victory over the Los Angeles Rams in the Super Bowl XIV. The game was played in the Rose Bowl in Pasadena, Calif., before 103,985 fans—a Super Bowl record—and a national television audience. It was Pittsburgh's fourth Super Bowl triumph in as many attempts and the team's fourth title in six years.
[8] Terry Bradshaw, the Steeler's quarterback, completed 14 of 21 passes (three touchdowns) for 309 yards and two touchdowns. Bradshaw won his second consecutive most valuable player award and joined Green Bay quarterback Bart Starr as the only two-time Super Bowl MVP.

FORD MOTOR CO.—*See* Automobiles [9, 13-15, 17]

FOREIGN AID

[1] **Programs Funded.** Foreign aid programs were given $6 billion for fiscal 1981 in the omnibus continuing spending bill that cleared Congress Dec. 15. It was the second fiscal year in a row that Congress had failed to pass a regular foreign aid appropriations bill. President Carter signed the measure Dec. 16.
[2] The spending bill contained $40 million for Jamaica under the Economic Support Fund, an appropriation that *Congressional Quarterly* Dec. 20 said was a reward to that country for voting the Jamaican Labor Party of Edward Seaga into power. Under the authorization bill, Israel was to receive $1.4 billion in arms loans (including $500 million to be treated as a grant), and Egypt was to get $550 million in arms loans. In addition, Israel was to receive $785 million and Egypt $750 million in economic grants.
See also Bolivia [1, 10, 12]; El Salvador [8-10]; Nicaragua [20-1]; Pakistan [4-6]; Turkey [19-23]

FRANCE

Economy

[1] **Price Increases.** The government authorized price increases of up to 12% for a wide variety of goods and services, including gasoline, coal, rents, domestic airline fares and coffee and beer served in cafes, it was reported Jan. 2.
[2] The government in effect lifted price controls for most kinds of retail goods. It did this by declining to sign a decree that previously had been signed each year limiting the amount of profit shopowners could take. Controls would still remain, at least temporarily, on certain foods, including coffee, sugar, meat and some fruits and vegetables. The removal of price controls was a long-standing policy of the government headed by Raymond Barre.
[3] **Truckers Block French Border.** Spanish truck drivers blocked traffic for five days June 16-20 at the French border near La Junquera to protest the burning June 16 of nine Spanish trucks by militant French farmers.
[4] The French farmers had attacked the Spanish trucks in Perpignan, 20

miles (32 kilometers) from La Junquera, to protest the importation of cheaper Spanish produce into France. The dispute over entry into France of Spanish produce had been rekindled June 5 when French President Valery Giscard d'Estaing, reversing an earlier position, had suggested that Spain's entry into the Common Market be postponed. The blockade involved as many as 4,000 trucks on both sides of the border. One report estimated the losses from the tie-up at $60 million in perishable merchandise that had rotted inside the stationary trucks.

[5] **Fishermen Blockade Ports.** Fishermen Aug. 19 temporarily lifted a blockade of Cherbourg to let British tourists return home, but continued to seal off other ports on the Atlantic and Mediterranean coasts.

[6] The blockade had begun several weeks earlier in Boulogne in protest against job cuts on trawler crews caused by rising fuel costs and lower prices for fish. It had spread first to the Atlantic ports, and then had extended to some of the Mediterranean ports.

[7] While many tourists were able to make alternative arrangements—flying home or travelling to Belgium and leaving from there—the blockade also had trapped cargo vessels in port. At Le Havre, the third largest commercial port in Europe, some 30 ships were reported trapped in the port as of Aug. 19, with another 40 outside waiting to get in.

[8] Naval tugboats using water cannons and tear-gas were brought into action by the government Aug. 27 to open France's largest oil tanker terminal, at Fos near Marseilles. Four fishermen were injured.

[9] **Cabinet OKs Draft Budget.** The Cabinet Sept. 10 approved a draft budget for 1981 that included investment incentives for business and tight limits on government spending.

[10] President Valery Giscard d'Estaing, commented, "The 1981 budget has been most carefully prepared and calculated with two objectives in mind: underpinning productive activity in the economy and preserving the value of the franc." Union figures and the left-wing political opposition criticized the proposals, charging that they were orchestrated to improve Giscard's reelection chances in 1981.

[11] Overall, the budget mandated expenditures of $147.7 billion in 1981, a 16% increase over 1980. However, most government programs would operate on a tight budget, while the spending increases would be concentrated in four areas: defense, investment, research and family policy. The defense budget was scheduled to increase by 18% in 1981.

[12] The government hoped to bring inflation down to a 10.5% annual rate in 1981. For 1980, it was projected to come to 13.3%. The budget anticipated a deficit of $7.1 billion in 1981. This would amount to 0.95% of the projected gross economic product for 1981, a percentage that the government said compares favorably with that of most other industrialized nations. The government expected the economy to expand by 1.6% in 1981, down from 1980 growth of 2.2%.

[13] **Cabinet Approves 5-Year Plan.** The Cabinet Oct. 1 approved France's eighth five-year plan (1981-85). The plan stressed development of advanced technology, with the objective of making France one of the world's most technologically advanced countries.

[14] Over the five-year period, the government planned to devote about $23 billion to a wide range of technological fields, from the nuclear industry to aerospace to telecommunications and computers.

Government & Politics

[15] **PFC-Moscow Rapprochement Seen.** Georges Marchais, leader of the French Communist Party (PFC), left Paris Jan. 7 to visit Moscow. The visit—Marchais' first since 1974—and Marchais' endorsement Jan. 11 of the

Soviet military intervention in Afghanistan were generally seen as marking the completion of the French party's return to a pro-Soviet stance after several years in which the party had asserted some degree of independence from Moscow.

[16] Marchais' actions broadened the gulf between the PCF and the Communist parties in Italy and Spain, and was regarded as dealing a major blow to the concept of Eurocommunism.

[17] **Assembly OKs Crime Bill.** The National Assembly June 21 approved, by a 265 to 205 vote, controversial legislation to revise France's criminal code.

[18] The legislation, prepared by Justice Minister Alain Peyrefitte, expanded police powers, allowing police, among other things, to stop a person at any time to demand indentification. It also set minimum sentences for a number of crimes, including euthanasia, and increased punishment for many crimes.

[19] **Debre Declares Candidacy.** Michel Debre, mayor of Amboise and a former premier under the late Charles De Gaulle, announced June 30 that he was entering himself as a candidate in the 1981 presidential elections.

[20] The move threatened to split the Gaullist vote, and thus aid President Valery Giscard d'Estaing, who was expected to run for a second seven-year term, although he had made no formal announcement. A Gaullist meeting in March had rejected the idea of Debre's candidacy. Jacques Chirac, leader of the party and mayor of Paris, was expected to be the party's official candidate in the presidential election.

[21] Giscard was also seen as benefiting from a division among the Socialists. Francois Mitterrand, the Socialists' leader, was confronted with a dissident movement led by Michel Rocard, who had declared his candidacy for the presidency.

[22] ***Marchais Nominated—*** George Marchais, leader of the French Communist Party (PCF), was nominated by his party Oct. 12 to run for the presidency.

[23] **By-Elections Go Against Giscard.** Elections for seven seats in the National Assembly Nov. 30 produced a setback for the Union pour la Democratie Francaise (UDF), the coalition backing President Giscard.

[24] The UDF had entered the by-elections in control of three of the seven seats at stake; it emerged with none. The Gaullist Rassemblement Pour la Republique increased its number of seats from one to two, but the big gainers were the Socialists, who won four seats. Before the elections, the Socialists had held two of the seven. The other seat was won by the small left-wing Radical party, which had already held it.

Defense

[25] **Neutron Bomb Test Disclosed.** France had successfully tested a prototype neutron bomb, President Valery Giscard d'Estaing announced June 26. In two or three years, he said, France could be ready to decide whether to produce the weapon.

[26] The neutron bomb essentially was a hydrogen bomb modified to reduce blast effects while enhancing radiation. Advocates of the weapon claimed it would serve as an ideal means of neutralizing the Warsaw Pact's large edge in tanks. Exploded over an invading tank column, the bomb would kill the invaders while supposedly causing relatively little damage to surrounding countryside and towns.

[27] U.S. President Carter had announced in 1978 that he was deferring production of the weapon, saying that the U.S.'s ultimate decision would be "influenced by the degree to which the Soviet Union shows restraint in its conventional and nuclear arms programs and force deployment. . . ." Carter's announcement followed nearly a year of sharp controversy over the weapon.

Wreckage of cars destroyed by bomb outside Paris synagogue Oct. 3. Four persons were killed.

Terrorism

[28] **Synagogue Bomb Kills Four.** A bomb, apparently placed in a car parked outside a Jewish Reform synagogue on Rue Copernic in the Passy section of Paris, exploded Oct. 3, killing four persons and seriously injuring 10. The bombing followed a number of attacks on Jewish targets, none of which, however, had injured individuals.

[29] The bomb had apparently been intended to go off just as the worshippers left the synagogue after evening Sabbath services. In any event, it exploded a few minutes before the service ended. Of the four persons killed, two were non-Jews and one was a visiting Israeli. An anonymous telephone call received after the blast by Agence France-Presse said that the explosion was the work of a far-right group, European National Fascists, which was headed by Mark Frederiksen. However, a spokesman for the group denied any involvement Oct. 4.

[30] The bombing was condemned by leaders of all political parties, as well as union and religious figures. Christian Bonnet, the minister of the interior, met with a number of Jewish leaders as well as police officials Oct. 4 and it was announced that five companies of riot police would be assigned to protect Jewish synagogues and other establishments. (Formerly, only two companies had had this duty.) The Representative Council of Jewish Organizations issued a statement Oct. 4 criticizing the "indifference of our governors" and the "inexplicable impotence of the police." Part of the problem, government critics said, stemmed from the fact that the police had been infiltrated by extremist right-wing groups. Jose Deltorn, secretary-general for the plainclothes policemen's union, claimed that about one-fifth of the 150 known members of a banned neo-Nazi group, the Federation of National and European Action, were policemen.

[31] Several demonstrations were held

Oct. 4 to protest the bombing. A larger rally, in which 100,000 people took part, was held Oct. 7, with members of political parties of all persuasions turning out.

[32] **Terrorists Destroy Computers.** An extremist group called Direct Action claimed responsibility April 15 for the bombing of government buildings and a computer center in Paris.

[33] Three unidentified men fired rocket grenades against the Transport Ministry building and one of its annexes. Simultaneously, a powerful explosion rocked the government computer center that regulated holiday traffic. No one was injured during the incidents.

[34] The bombings were the latest in a series of terrorist actions against computer installations. On April 5 the terrorists raided Philips Data Systems Co. in Toulouse. Four days later it was the turn of C.I.I.-Honeywell Bull in the same city. In both cases, responsibility was claimed by Direct Action, though another terrorist group, Clodo, also took responsibility for the Philips Data System raid. Experts of C.I.I.-Honeywell Bull said the commercial loss was "incalculable." Most of the raiders were apparently computer experts and their sabotage actions were therefore particularly efficacious. In one instance, for example, they were able to destroy a computer program that had taken five years to elaborate.

[35] The apparent aim of these actions was to paralyze computer operations and programs on the ground that they were dangerous weapons in the hands of the government. ". . . Computers are the favorite instruments of the powerful," the terrorists wrote in a statement published by the Parisian press. "They are used to classify, to control and to repress. We do not want to be shut up in the ghettos of programs and organizational patterns."

[36] **Right-Wing Extremists Seized.** Police in Paris July 1 arrested 11 members of two right-wing extremist organizations that had claimed responsibility for attacks against left-wing and human rights organizations, as well as against the offices of the Soviet airline, Aeroflot.

[37] The two groups were the Federation of National and European Action (FANE) and the National Revolutionary Movement. FANE had referred to the World War II holocaust of the Jews as a "myth"; it had called for the expulsion from France of foreign workers, and had advanced as its goal the organization of the white race. Marc Fredriksen, the leader of FANE, was charged under a 1972 statute barring "apologia of war crimes and incitement to racial hatred."

[38] **Right-wing Extremist Group Banned.** The government Sept. 3 outlawed an extremist right-wing group called the Federation for National and European Action (FANE). The group had been linked to a number of terrorist attacks, some of them against Jews.

[39] The order was issued under a 1972 law forbidding private militias, and it brought to 22 the number of extremist organizations outlawed since the unrest of 1968. Most of them were far-left or regional separatist organizations.

[40] **Jewish Targets Attacked.** Unidentified gunmen sprayed four Jewish targets in Paris with machine-gun fire Sept. 26 just before sunrise, causing slight damage but not injuring anyone. Two days later, on Sept. 28, a synagogue in Paris was fired upon, again without causing any injuries.

Corsica

[41] **Separatist Unrest Hits Corsica.** Three persons were killed the night of Jan. 9 in Ajaccio, the capital of Corsica, victims of heightened tensions on the island stemming from an outbreak of separatist violence.

[42] **Separatist Bombs Hit Paris, Nice.** The Corsican National Liberation Front claimed responsibility for bomb attacks in Paris and Nice April 23. The

bombings–seven in Paris and two in Nice–damaged travel agencies, stores and government offices.

Other Developments

[43] **Charges Brought Against *Le Monde.*** Justice Minister Alain Peyrefitte Nov. 7 ordered charges brought against the editor of *Le Monde,* France's most respected newspaper, for allegedly seeking to discredit the country's legal system.
[44] In addition to the editor, Jacques Fauvet, the charges cited Philippe Boucher, a member of the editorial staff. The charges carried possible sentences of six months' imprisonment or fines of $7,000 or both. Fauvet responded to the charges by saying they were politically motivated and emanated from "afar or on high." The newspaper, Fauvet said, would continue to express its opposition to certain government policies and investigate suspected governmental wrongdoing.
See also Armaments [1-2]; Auto Racing [3-4]; Chad [3-4, 9]; Economy (International) [7]; Espionage [3-4]; Iran [76]

FREEDOM OF INFORMATION ACT

[1] **Access to Kissinger Records Blocked.** The Supreme Court ruled, 5-2, March 3 that government agencies were not obligated under the Freedom of Information Act to retrieve documents that had been removed from their possession. The case was *Kissinger v. Reporters' Committee for Freedom of the Press.*
[2] Specifically, the high court reversed two lower courts and held that the State Department was not required to recover transcripts and tape recordings of telephone conversations made by Henry A. Kissinger, a former secretary of state.
[3] Kissinger had served as both national security adviser (1968-77) and secretary of state (1973-77). In both offices, his telephone conversations had been recorded at his request. Before leaving Washington in January 1977, Kissinger had transferred his records to the Pocantico Hills, New York estate of former Vice President Nelson A. Rockefeller. Later, Kissinger donated the records to the Library of Congress with the condition that they not be made public for 25 years, or five years after his death.
[4] A group of journalists and historians had sought all of Kissinger's transcripts and tape recordings under the Freedom of Information Act. Lower federal courts subsequently held that his records as national secretary adviser were exempt from the information act, but that the State Department had to supply the foreign policy documents requested. (The Library of Congress, as an arm of the legislative branch, was not covered by the information law.)
[5] The Supreme Court upheld the lower courts with regard to the exemption of Kissinger's national security records. However, the high court reversed the lower courts with regard to the State Department documents. Writing for the majority, Justice William H. Rehnquist asserted that "Congress did not mean that an agency improperly withholds a document which has been removed from the possession of the agency prior to the filing of the FOIA request. . . . In such case, the agency has neither the custody or control necessary to enable it to withhold."
[6] Justices John Paul Stevens and William J. Brennan Jr. each issued separate dissenting opinions. Stevens argued that the ruling "creates an incentive for outgoing agency officials to remove potentially embarrassing documents from their files in order to frustrate future FOIA requests." Brennan held that if the information law were to be effective, "it must

necessarily incorporate some restraint upon the agency's power to move documents beyond the reach of the FOIA requester." Justices Thurgood Marshall and Harry A. Blackmun did not participate in the decision.

GAS, NATURAL—*See also* Germany, West [12]

GASOHOL—*See* Congress (U.S.) [8]

GEORGIA—*See* Civil Disorders [9-11]; Death Penalty [2-4]

GERMANY, EAST (German Democratic Republic)

[1] **Germanies to Increase Trade.** At a time of acute East-West tensions, the governments of the two Germanies agreed April 17 to expand trade between the two countries. The agreement came at the end of a two-hour long meeting between Gunter Mittag, East Germany's top economic planner and member of the Politburo, and West German Chancellor Helmut Schmidt.

[2] ***Transport Pact***—East and West Germany signed a five-year agreement in East Berlin April 30 to improve transportation between the two countries.

[3] The agreement—valued at $282 million—called for West Germany to finance work by East Germany to improve rail, water and road links between West Berlin and West Germany. The projects included a widening of the Mittelland Canal between East and West Germany and railroad reconstruction to expedite traffic to Berlin.

See also Skating [4]; Soccer [4]; United Nations [4, 11-12]; Yemen, People's Democratic Republic of [1-3]

GERMANY, WEST (Federal Republic of Germany)

[1] **3 Sentenced for WW II Crimes.** Three former members of the Nazi SS were found guilty Feb. 11 by a court in Cologne of taking part in the deportation and murder of French Jews during World War II.

[2] The three men, and their prison sentences, were: Herbert Hagen, 12 years; Kurt Lischka, 10 years, and Ernst Heinrichsohn, six years. Hagen, 66, had served as head of ss information service's Jewish section and commander of the Nazi policy in the Atlantic region of France. Lischka, 70, had been chief of the Gestapo in Paris, and Heinrichsohn, 59 had worked for the ss in Paris.

[3] All three had lived with ease and pursued careers in postwar West Germany. Their conviction was considered a triumph for Serge Klarsfeld, a French lawyer who led the effort to bring them to trial.

[4] **Pre-War Bonds Redeemed.** The government's Debt Administration Board said it was taking action to redeem a 50-year old issue of $300 million in 5.5% bonds, it was reported June 3. It was one of West Germany's last major pre-World War II debts to be redeemed.

[5] **Carter on A-Missiles.** West German Chancellor Helmut Schmidt was reported June 16 to have been urged by U.S. President Carter in a strongly

worded letter not to stray from Western policy on nuclear weaponry during his forthcoming talks with Soviet leaders in Moscow June 30-July 1.

[6] The contents of the letter, delivered the previous week, were not divulged, but reportedly dealt with the decision taken in December 1979 by the North Atlantic Treaty Organization to deploy medium-range nuclear missiles in Western Europe in response to recent increases in Soviet missile strength, particularly the deployment of the new SS-20 missiles. The U.S. was concerned about indications that Bonn might favor an East-West freeze on missiles, rather than going ahead with the NATO deployment plans.

[7] *Pravda*, the Soviet Communist Party newspaper, June 12 had called on West Germany to abandon its decision to station medium-range missiles on its soil.

[8] **Schmidt & Brezhnev Confer.** Chancellor Helmut Schmidt paid a two-day visit to Moscow June 30-July 1, meeting there with Soviet President Leonid Brezhnev and other top Soviet officials and urging the Soviet Union to withdraw its troops from Afghanistan.

[9] Schmidt also discussed the issue of medium-range nuclear missiles with the Soviets. At the end of his visit, July 1, he hinted that the Soviets were willing to negotiate about limitations on these missiles. But Schmidt refrained from disclosing the Soviet position in detail, or even informing his Cabinet about it, until the new Soviet statements could be relayed to Washington. West German Foreign Minister Hans-Dietrich Genscher was dispatched on this errand.

[10] U.S. officials said July 2 that Genscher told President Carter that the Soviets no longer insisted as a precondition for negotiations on the medium-range missiles that NATO abandon a decision taken in December 1979 to go ahead with deployment of the missiles. (In addition to the differences between the Soviets and NATO over the missiles, there had been friction within the NATO alliance itself on the issue. Some countries had voiced reservations about the planned deployment, and the U.S. at one point had appeared worried that Schmidt's visit to Moscow might mean he was wavering on the matter.)

[11] Schmidt July 15 called on the NATO allies to stick by a 1979 decision to deploy medium-range nuclear missiles. Delay in deployment by some of the smaller members of NATO was the source of considerable concern, Schmidt said. He was referring to Belgium and the Netherlands, although he did not mention them by name. Both had gone along with the NATO decision, but had put off action on the politically touchy issue.

[12] **Economic Pact**—Coinciding with Schmidt's visit, a long-term agreement calling for industrial and economic cooperation between the two countries was signed July 1. The two nations also said they supported the building of a $13.3 billion gas pipeline from western Siberia to West Germany.

[13] **Terrorist Given Life Sentence.** A court in Stuttgart July 31 sentenced Knut Folkerts to life imprisonment for his part in the 1977 murder of Siegfried Buback, then the chief federal prosecutor.

[14] Folkerts' sentencing came in a period of renewed antiterrorist activity, prompted by the discovery of Juliane Plambeck, one of the country's most wanted terrorist suspects. Plambeck and a companion named Wolfgang Beer were killed in an automobile crash near Stuttgart July 25. Weapons and a radio transmitter were found in the wrecked car. The police launched a major manhunt, saying that another terrorist attack apparently had been in preparation.

[15] **Oktoberfest Bomb Kills 13.** A bomb exploded Sept. 26 at the crowded main entrance to the Munich Oktoberfest, killing 12 persons and injuring more than 200. The death toll

Victim of Munich Oktoberfest bomb blast Sept. 26 is placed in coffin.

rose Oct. 1 to 13 when a 17-year-old boy died from his injuries.

[16] Federal Prosecutor Kurt Rebmann announced Sept. 28 that investigators thought that the bomb was planted by Gundolf Kohler, a 20-year-old member of a banned neo-Nazi organization, the Defense Sports Group. Kohler was killed in the blast.

[17] **Schmidt Coalition Wins Election.** Chancellor Schmidt's ruling coalition of Social Democrats (SPD) and Free Democrats (FDP) won an increased majority in national parliamentary elections Oct. 5. The voting assured Schmidt of another four years in office. The controversial candidate for chancellor of the opposition Christian Democrats/Christian Social Union, Franz Jose Strauss, was defeated.

[18] The election increased the SPD-FDP's majority in the Bundestag, the lower house of parliament, to 45 seats, up from 10. Most of the gain was accounted for by the junior partner in the coalition, the FDP, which raised its share of the vote to 10.6% from 7.9% in the 1976 election. This meant an increase to 53 seats from 39.

[19] Schmidt's own SPD increased its seat total to 218 from 214 in 1976, representing a vote share of 42.9%, compared with 42.6% in 1976. The opposition Christian Democrats/Cristian Social Union lost 17 seats—dropping to 226 from 243—as their vote share declined to 44.5% from 48.6% four years ago.

[20] The Greens, a grouping of environmentalist interests, won only 1.5% of the vote, far short of the 5% threshold required for representation in the Bundestag. A number of other small parties, including the Communist Party and the neo-Nazi National Democratic Party won about 0.5% of the vote all together.

[21] **Reichstag Fire Verdict Overturned.** A West Berlin court Dec. 15 canceled the 1933 verdict that found a Dutchman guilty of setting the fire that burned down the Reichstag (parliament) building in Berlin.

[22] The ruling, announced Dec. 29, posthumously acquitted Marinus van der Lubbe, a self-described communist

Chancellor Helmut Schmidt after winning reelection Oct. 5.

who was executed in 1934 for the crime. The ruling did not directly address the issue of van der Lubbe's guilt or innocence; instead it held that the 1933 trial had been a "serious perversion of justice" in which the judges had departed from the law in order to suit the Nazis.

See also Chad [3]; Economy (International) [1-6, 8]; Energy [7]; Germany, East; Iran [76]; Skating [4]

GHOTBZADEH, Sadegh—*See* Iran [34, 36, 38-39, 47, 126-128, 130, 134]; Iraq [4]

GISCARD D'ESTAING, VALERY—*See* France [4, 10, 20-21, 25]

GOLD

[1] The price of gold continued to rise in 1980, but its course was erratic. It spiralled upwards to more than $800 an ounce in January, plummeted below $500 an ounce in March, and then resurged to close the year near the $600 an ounce level.

[2] At the beginning of the year, gold soared on international markets in a frenzy of activity that culminated Jan. 18 in a price of $835 an ounce on the London market.

[3] Gold bullion—$524 an ounce at the close of trading in London Dec. 31, 1979—had begun its meteoric rise Jan. 2 when the International Monetary Fund held its monthly gold auction. The IMF sold 444,000 ounces of gold at a record average price of $562.85 an ounce. This was $136.48 an ounce higher than at the previous IMF auction Dec. 5, 1979.

[4] Spurred by a surge of prices in New York, the Hong Kong market Jan. 3 saw gold prices soar above $600 to $660 an ounce before falling in the afternoon to $615. The rise in price continued in Europe Jan. 3 where the London market closed at a record $634 an ounce in hectic trading. Later, in New York, the price fell to $621 Jan. 3. After a lull of about 10 days, the price of gold rose to record highs on every trading day of the week Jan. 14-18.

[5] Most dealers attributed the wild trading in gold to Middle Eastern investors and increased numbers of Americans worried about inflation and recent developments in the Middle East, Iran and Afghanistan. One gold and currency trader Jan. 17 termed the market a "thermometer of international anxiety."

[6] Gold prices plunged March 17 in reaction to President Carter's anti-inflation program. (See Economy [U.S.]) In London, the price of an ounce of gold fell $49 closing at $477.50. It was the first time in 1980 that the price of an ounce of gold had dropped below the $500 level. On Jan. 21, gold had closed on the New York Commodity Exchange at a record $875 an ounce. The March 17 close was 46% below that record high.

[7] On March 19, gold moved up $36.50 an ounce in London as ag-

gressive investors moved to take advantage of "bargain" prices. The price per ounce closed March 19 at $527.
[8] Gold declined Nov. 5 after an initial post-election increase because of President-elect Ronald Reagan's image as a hawk who might increase international political tensions. The price of an ounce of gold on the New York Commodity Exchange settled at $637, down $9 from the Nov. 4 price.
[9] The price of gold closed Dec. 31 in both Zurich and London at $589.50 an ounce.

Final 1980 PGA Money Winners
Oct. 12

Tom Watson	$530,808
Lee Trevino	385,814
Curtis Strange	271,400
Andy Bean	269,033
Ben Crenshaw	237,727
Jerry Pate	222,976
George Burns	219,928
Craig Stadler	206,291
Mike Reld	206,097
Ray Floyd	192,993

Final 1980 LPGA Money Winners
Oct. 12

Beth Daniel	$231,000
Donna Caponi Young	220,619
Amy Alcott	219,887
Nancy Lopez-Melton	209,078
JoAnne Carner	185,915
Pat Bradley	183,377
Sally Little	139,127
Jane Blalock	127,873
Jo Ann Washam	107,063
Sandra Post	102,822

GOLF

[1] **Ballesteros Wins Masters.** Severiano Ballesteros became the youngest player in history to win the Masters April 13 by shooting a par 72 in the final round at the Augusta (Ga.) National Golf Club.
[2] The 23-year-old Spaniard became only the second foreigner to wear the green blazer, after South African Gary Player, who had won the tournament in 1978, 1974 and 1961. Ballesteros fired a 13-under-par 275 for the four rounds, beating Gibby Gilbert and Jack Newton by four strokes. The victory was worth $55,000 to the hard-driving son of a Spanish dairy farmer.
[3] **Nicklaus Wins PGA Title, U.S. Open.** Jack Nicklaus Aug. 10 won the 62d Professional Golfer's Association championship in Rochester, N.Y. Nicklaus earned a $60,000 top prize by shooting a 72-hole total of 274, six under par. It was Nicklaus' fifth PGA title.
[4] Nicklaus captured his fourth U.S. Open June 15, with a two-stroke victory over Isao Aoki of Japan. The tournament was held at the lower course of the Balturol Golf Club in Springfield, N.J. The win was worth $55,000
[5] ***Alcott Takes U.S. Women's Open***—Amy Alcott won the U.S. Women's Open at Nashville July 13. Alcott shot a 72-hole total of 280, four under par, for the top prize of $20,047.
[6] **British Open Goes to Watson.** Tom Watson breezed to victory in the 109th British Open July 20 at Muirfield, Scotland. Watson took home $59,250 by shooting a 13-under-par 271 over the 72 holes.

GRAIN

[1] **Fears of Shortages Send Prices Up.** Grain futures prices rose sharply Oct. 28 on U.S. exchanges amid indications that a poor harvest in the Soviet Union would force that country to import more grains and recognition that the U.S.-China grain pact signed Oct. 22 would put a strain on available supplies in the U.S.
[2] The price of December delivery corn on the Chicago Board of Trade gained 7½ cents to $3.77¾ a bushel. December wheat rose 12 cents to $5.41½ a bushel. The prices were six-year highs. The price of soybeans for November delivery hit a three-year high of $9.14½ a bushel, rising the limit of 30 cents a bushel for the day's trading.

[3] The steep price jumps were attributed to agricultural experts' predictions that world grain stocks were expected to hit a five-year low in 1981 and that consumption would exceed production by 37 million metric tons, according to the *Wall Street Journal* Nov. 4.

[4] U.S. grain stockpiles in the fall of 1981 were expected to be down 39% from the levels in 1980, according to the U.S. Agriculture Department. The department predicted that world grain stocks would be down by 19% to 155.2 million metric tons in 1981. The lower grain yields were largely attributed to droughts in major grain producing countries this summer. But another factor was that world grain consumption in the last five years had risen by 15% while production had increased by only 12%.

[5] **Iowa Grain Elevator Scandal.** Iowa farmers were reported Feb. 25 to have lost at least $4.3 million in corn and soybean crops in a grain shortage scandal involving the worst financial collapse of a grain elevator in the state's history.

[6] Some 1.2 million bushels of corn and soybeans were reported missing at last count from the Prairie Grain Co. elevator in Stockport in a scandal that sent local farmers scrambling for cash to plant the spring crop and caused heavy losses to local businesses. More than 200 farmers had grain stored at the elevator and their losses were expected to range from a few thousand dollars to more than $100,000.

[7] The scandal began to unfold after the apparent suicide Jan. 31 of Raymond Heller, a co-owner and operator of the Stockport elevator and the town's leading businessman. Heller had shot himself a few hours after a state auditor had begun an inspection of the financial records of the grain elevator company. State investigators and auditors, reviewing the records, believed that Heller had apparently been speculating in the commodities market and was selling grain to make up for his losses. Heller was known to have been deeply in debt on nearly $2.1 million in bank loans that had been called for payment on Feb. 1. Following his death five other banks made claims for loans ranging from $65,000 to $450,000.

[8] An investigation by state authorities concluded that an embezzlement scheme had been going on for at least five years and had been aided unwittingly by its victims, it was reported May 14. But the probe of the now defunct Prairie Grain Co. was unable to determine what had happened to more than $10 million worth of grain.

[9] According to the investigators, the scheme carried out by Heller dated back to March 1975. It was a pyramid-type swindle in which Heller had to embezzle increasingly more grain and borrow heavily to continue to cover his losses. The investigators also disclosed that Heller was aided in concealing the fraud by his close relationship with local farmers. In some cases, grain storage sales with local farmers were not recorded by the issuance of warehouse receipts. In return, farmers were not charged a storage fee. But this procedure enabled Heller to embezzle grain without any record.

[10] Heller's scheme was apparently undone by President Carter's order Jan. 4 embargoing U.S. grain sales to the Soviet Union. Fearing a drop in price, many farmers sought immediate sale of the grain they had in storage. Heller couldn't move sufficient grain to meet the sell orders. The investigators said they were unable to determine what had happened to all the money earned from the embezzled grain. They did conclude, however, that it had not been lost in commodity trading, as had been first suspected. Final figures indicated that the grain elevator owed more than $10 million to farmers, banks and other businesses. It had assets of $2.5 million.

See also China [23, 32]; Union of Soviet Socialist Republics [16]

GREAT BRITAIN

Economy

[1] **Budget Presented.** A budget intended to curb inflation was presented March 26 to Parliament by Chancellor of the Exchequer Geoffrey Howe.

[2] The budget—which covered the year starting April 1—was not calculated to soften the impact of the recession that Britain appeared to be entering. It mandated $1.26 billion in cuts in government spending. This was aimed at reducing the budget deficit to $18.6 billion in the new fiscal year, compared with $19.7 billion in the year ending March 31.

[3] The cuts were concentrated mainly in housing, education, industrial aid and job training. Spending on defense and police service would go up, as would health expenditures. In an attempt to cut health service costs, however, health service prescription charges would rise to $2.20, a five-fold increase since the Conservatives took power in 1979.

[4] The reduction of the deficit, Howe said, was vital to the government's effort to control the money supply. Holding down growth in the money supply was, in turn, the main component in the government's anti-inflation strategy. Howe said that the government's target was for growth of 7%-11% in the money supply for the new year, with 6%-10% growth in the following year, 5%-9% in 1982-83 and 4%-8% in 1983-84.

[5] Howe announced some measures to raise revenues. The price of wine and beer would go up slightly; a bottle of whisky would increase more than $1 in price; a pack of cigarettes would cost more than 10¢ more, and gasoline prices would also increase, with the cost of a U.S. gallon rising to about $2.37 from about $2.19. A $22 increase in the annual car license fee would raise it to $132. The impact of these tax increases would be to raise the retail price index by about one percentage point, Howe admitted.

[6] A government minister described the budget package as "slightly austere." Labor Party leader James Callaghan labeled the budget message the "most depressing" he had ever heard, and a similar view was expressed by David Basnett, head of the General and Municipal Workers' Union. Basnett said the budget was "incomprehensibly divisive" and deflationary. An official of the Confederation of British Industry, on the other hand, said the package was "realistic and roughly the right budget."

[7] **BBC Cutbacks.** In a move designed to save at least £120 million ($275 million) over the next two years, the British Broadcasting Corp. said Feb. 28 that it would cut 1,500 jobs.

[8] The BBC economy measures included the disbanding of five of its 11 orchestras, including the Scottish Symphony Orchestra, the Northern Ireland Orchestra and the London Studio Players. Radio Three, a national network that chiefly played classical music, would face an earlier shutdown under the plan, and a popular daytime radio serial, *Waggoners Walk,* would be ended. Educational programming would also be pared.

[9] The BBC would keep in existence several orchestras that had earlier been slated for disbandment, it was reported July 31. The Scottish Symphony, the most prestigious of the orchestras scheduled to be disbanded, would be retained. The Northern Ireland Orchestra and the London Studio Players also would be kept in existence, but several radio orchestras would be disbanded.

[10] **Reports See Downturn.** Studies by four nongovernmental organizations March 3 predicted an economic turndown in Britain over the next two years and continuing high inflation.

[11] The reports generally agreed that industry would be hardest hit during the projected recession. Rising labor costs and the high exchange rate of the pound were damaging industry's com-

petitiveness, the reports said. Additionally, problems were created by the government's emphasis on assisting the production of new goods.

[12] The reports were prepared by the Organization for Economic Cooperation and Development, a grouping of 24 industrialized non-communist nations, the Keynesian-oriented National Institute of Economic and Social Research, the London Business School and the Confederation of British Industry.

[13] **Steel Strike Settled.** A 13-week strike against the state-owned British Steel Corp. came to an end April 1 when the executive bodies of the two largest unions involved voted to accept a pact providing a 15.5% pay increase.

[14] ***British Steel Reports Record Loss***—The state-controlled British Steel Corp. announced that it had suffered a record loss of £1.8 billion ($4.2 billion) for the fiscal year ending March 29, it was reported July 30.

[15] **Joblessness Hits Post-War High.** Unemployment increased by 49,400 in June, the biggest monthly rise in nearly five years, bringing the jobless total to 1,467,400, a post war record, according to official figures announced June 24.

[16] The figures, which were seasonally adjusted, meant that the underlying jobless rate was 6.2%. Unemployment had been increasing sharply since fall of 1979, and some economists projected that it would pass two million in 1981.

[17] **State Monopolies to Be Curbed.** Government ministers announced July 21 that legislation was being prepared to curb state monopolies in the production of electricity and the supply of telecommunication equipment. "We are determined to make nationalized industries more competitive," Energy Secretary David Howell said.

[18] Since 1909, it had been illegal for private companies to generate electricity for sale. A company or individual could generate electricity for private use; at present, about 17% of the electricity used by industry was produced privately. The government did not expect that ending the state monopoly would lead to a great demand for private generating plants, but it thought that some small plants might be set up to furnish electricity to industrial parks, farming cooperatives or similar establishments.

[19] The announcement on telecommunications was made by Industry Secretary Keith Joseph. He said that the Post Office's present monopoly would be relaxed to allow private companies to compete in the supplying of equipment for the telephone network.

[20] Joseph also had told Parliament July 16 that the goverment intended to reduce the Post Office's monopoly on mail distribution. While the Post Office would retain its monopoly for most mail, private firms would be permitted to compete for the handling of "time-sensitive, valuable" mail, provided they charged a minimum fee of £1 ($2.35).

[21] ***Docks Share to Be Sold***—The government planned to sell private investors a 49% share in the British Transport Docks Board, which operated about a quarter of Britain's ports, including Southampton and Hull, it was announced July 21. The board had been self-financing since 1972, and in 1979 had posted a pre-tax surplus of £27 million ($63.5 million). the government hoped to clear up to £50 million ($117.5 million) from the sale of the 49% share.

[22] **Interest Rate Cut.** Chancellor of the Exchequer Howe Nov. 24 announced a cut of two percentage points in the record 16% minimum lending rate and a new levy on North Sea oil, along with other measures intended to meet the worse-than-expected recession.

[23] **Job Protest in Liverpool.** Over 40,000 people marched in Liverpool Nov. 29 to protest Britain's rising unemployment and the austerity policies followed by Prime Minister Thatcher's government.

Prime Minister Margaret Thatcher reaffirmed government economic policies.

Government & Politics

[24] **Labor Censure Motions Defeated.** A motion of no confidence in the government's economic policies, put forward by the Labor Party opposition, was defeated Feb. 28 by a vote of 327-268.

[25] Speaking in support of the censure motion, Labor Party leader James Callaghan said that Prime Minister Margaret Thatcher had failed to keep a grip on prices, employment and earnings, and was starting to lose control of monetary policy. Callaghan said that the government's rigid adherence to strict monetary curbs was weakening the nation's industries, and added that the social atmosphere around Britain was beginning to deteriorate. Thatcher responded by insisting that the government would stick to its monetary policies. Curbing the growth of the supply of money, she said, was the only sure way to hold down inflation.

[26] The Labor Party opposition mounted a sharp attack on Prime Minister Thatcher's economic policies, but Thatcher July 29 easily defeated a vote of no-confidence by a 333-274 margin.

[27] Joblessness had steadily increased and inflation had jumped since Thatcher took office, but she insisted that it was "no good dreaming about U-turns [reversals in economic policy]—there aren't any available." Opposition leader James Callaghan observed that after 15 months of Conservative government, unemployment had reached a post World War II high of 7.8%, or approximately 1.9 million people. Inflation had doubled while the Tories were in office, reaching the 21% level, he said. Interest rates were 4% higher, manufacturing output had dropped by 8% and there were many more bankruptcies.

[28] **Left Advances at Labor Conference.** The Labor Party's annual conference, held in Blackpool Sept. 29-Oct. 3, was marked by sharp and occasionally tumultuous clashes between

the party's left and right wings, with the left generally prevailing.

[29] The antagonisms that surfaced at the conferece came close, at times, to breaking out into fistfights, forcing the conference chairman, Lena Jager, to shout at one point, "You're not at a football match, so either sit down or leave the hall." Peter Shore, a leading left-wing Laborite, described the activities as "absolute total bloody chaos."

[30] The question of how the party's leader – who would be prime minister, if Labor won a majority in Parliament – should be chosen aroused the most controversy. At present, the leader was voted on by the Labor MP's (the so-called Parliamentary Labor Party). The left-wing of the party favored adopting a system that would give local Labor Party constituency groups and labor unions a role in the election. This sort of broader franchise, the left-wingers argued, would be more democratic. Members of the labor right wing contended, however, that the constituency organizations had small memberships dominated by left-wing activists, and so were not representative; left-wing activists also exercised undue influence in union leadership, the right-wing argued. In any case, observers generally agreed that a broader franchise would give a left-wing candidate for party leader more chance of success.

[31] The conference Oct. 1 voted narrowly, 3,609,000 to 3,511,000, to broaden the electorate that chose the party leader. However, when several concrete proposals were put forward to specify what the new "electoral college" would be, each was voted down. The next day, the conference reaffirmed the decision to broaden the electorate for the party leader, but once again failed to agree on a precise formula. It was decided to deal with the issue in a special party conference to be held in January or February of 1981.

[32] The conference also Oct. 1 voted to commit the Labor Party to withdraw Britain from the European Community if it gained office. The vote was 5,042,000 to 2,097,000. By a show of hands, the conference Oct. 2 adopted a motion calling for the next manifesto to incorporate a commitment for Britain to undertake unilateral nuclear disarmament.

[33] ***Callaghan Quits***—Former Prime Minister James Callaghan resigned October 15 as leader of the Labor Party. Callaghan, 68, said he thought it was time for someone "with more vigor, new insight, a fresh eye" to take over.

[34] ***Foot Elected***—Labor Party MPS elected Michael Foot as leader of the party by a 139-to-129 vote Nov. 10. Foot, a leftist who had served in Parliament for 30 years, defeated Denis Healey, the former chancellor of the Exchequer.

[35] Foot, 67, was a firm supporter of the welfare state and expanded state ownership of industry. He also favored nuclear disarmament; in a recent television broadcast he had said he was opposed to stationing U.S. cruise missiles in Britain, and would "send them back" if he became prime minister. However, Foot indicated that his views did not call for Britain's withdrawal from the North Atlantic Treaty Organization. He also stressed that Labor's primary task at the moment was to put forward a united opposition to the government.

[36] **Tories Meet in Brighton.** The Conservative Party held its annual conference Oct. 7-10 in Brighton, with the government vowing to continue its economic policies despite high inflation and unemployment.

[37] While a few speakers at the meeting called upon the government to change its policies – in particular, lower interest rates – in an effort to deal with unemployment, both Prime Minister Margaret Thatcher and Chancellor of the Exchequer Geoffrey Howe insisted that there would be no reversals by the government. In a speech Oct. 10, Thatcher said, "You turn if you want to. The lady's not for turning." (This was a

Prince Charles views Winston Churchill poster at opening of Second World War museum exhibit in London.

word-play on the title of a play by Christopher Fry.)

[38] With 5,000 demonstrators outside the convention hall carrying on a "Right to Work" protest, Thatcher insisted on the depth of her concern for the unemployed. "If I could press a button and genuinely solve the unemployment problem, do you think I would not press that button this instant? Does anyone imagine that there is the smallest political gain in letting this level of unemployment continue?"

[39] **Queen's Speech.** Queen Elizabeth II opened a new session of Parliament Nov. 20 with a speech setting forth the government's legislative priorities and reaffirming the government's adherence to the aim of curbing inflation through strict control of spending and the money supply. The speech was written by Prime Minister Thatcher's Conservative Party government.

[40] Among the specific legislative plans listed by the queen were:

■ A new definition of British citizenship that would restrict it to people with "a close personal connection with the United Kingdom." This proposal, viewed with concern by many non-whites, was one of the government's more controversial initiatives.

■ Revision of the law to relax rules regarding press coverage of court cases.

[41] On the key issue of economic policy, the speech reaffirmed that Thatcher would stick by the policies she had campaigned on, despite rising unemployment. Thatcher said, however, in the debate following the queen's speech, that the government would expand a jobs program for youths. The program would be enlarged to provide 440,000 places in 1981, which was 180,000 more than in 1980.

Defense

[42] **Nuclear Weapons Plans Described.** Defense Secretary Francis Pym revealed to the House of Commons Jan. 24 that secret development work to modernize the warheads of the nuclear missiles carried by Britain's

four Polaris nuclear submarines was near completion.

[43]The £1 billion ($2.25 billion) developmental program–code-named Chevaline–was begun in secrecy by the Conservative government headed by Edward Heath and continued by the subsequent Labor government. The disclosure of the Labor government's role in continuing the program came as a shock to a number of Labor MPs. A significant part of the parliamentary Labor Party had frequently criticized Britain's nuclear strategy. In the 1974 general election campaign, the Labor Party manifesto had come out against production of a new generation of nuclear weapons.

[44] Pym said that the modernized warheads resulting from the Chevaline program would be able to penetrate Soviet antiballistic missile defenses into the 1990s. A number of successful flight trials had already been completed, he said, and the developmental stage would soon be concluded. "Deployment will begin soon thereafter," Pym said. The acquisition of new warheads for the Polaris missiles did not remove the necessity of coming to a decision "before long" on a new nuclear deterrent force to replace the Polaris system, Pym continued. The government was prepared to spend between £4 billion and £5 billion ($9 billion to $11.25 billion) over the next 10-15 years on a new generation of nuclear submarines and missiles.

[45] **Cruise Missile Storage Sites Chosen.** Defense Secretary Francis Pym told the House of Commons June 17 that the government had decided to station 160 ground-launched nuclear-tipped cruise missiles at the U.S. Air Force standby base at Royal Air Force Greenham Common, Berkshire, and at RAF Molesworth, an inactive airbase in Cambridgeshire.

[46] Disagreement within the Labor Party over cruise missiles surfaced when Pym made his announcement. William Rodgers, the Labor spokesman on defense, said that the government's arrangements were "in some ways satisfactory," although any divided responsibility (between the U.S. and Britain) would be dangerous. Labor backbenchers, however, criticized the government's plans as unacceptable, and called upon Rodgers to resign as defense spokesman.

[46] In an attempt to reduce opposition from residents near the storage sites, Pym said that no live missiles or warheads would be used on exercises, and there would be no test flying of the missiles in Britain. Since the missiles would not be jointly owned with the U.S., nor would the production costs be shared, there would be no dual key system employed to control their firing, Pym said. However, a decision to fire the weapons would only be made after Britain and the U.S. had jointly agreed on the step, he added.

[48] ***A-Weapons Protested—*** Thousands of people marched through London June 22 to protest nuclear weapons.

[49] Organizers of the rally said it was the largest such protest gathering since the ban-the-bomb marches of the 1960s. Police estimated the crowd at 15,000, but Labor Party organizers claimed the number was between 20,000 and 30,000. Michael Foot, Labor Party deputy leader, told the protesters that since the nuclear-tipped cruise missiles would not be deployed for two years, the time should be used to work for "multinational disarmament." Many of the speakers urged unilateral disarmament by Britain.

[50] **Trident Missiles Selected.** The government announced July 15 that it would modernize its nuclear deterrent force by acquiring the Trident system from the U.S.

[51] The Trident missiles would be deployed on four or five new British-built submarines, which were expected to enter service in the early 1990s. Britain would pay about $2.5 billion for approximately 100 Trident missiles and associated equipment, such as fire-

control systems. Overall, to purchase the submarines as well as the missiles, Britain expected to spend nearly $12 billion. The project would take 3% of the country's defense budget over the next 15 years.

[52] Britain's current submarine deterrent force consisted of four nuclear-powered vessels, each equipped with 16 Polaris missiles. These missiles each had three nuclear warheads (not independently targetable), and they had a range of about 2,800 miles (4,540 kilometers). The Trident missiles, by contrast, had ranges of better than 4,000 miles (over 6,400 kilometers), and each missile would carry eight to 10 independently targetable warheads.

Terrorism

[53] **Commandos Storm Iranian Embassy; 5 Terrorists Killed.** A British commando team stormed the Iranian Embassy in London May 5 and freed 19 persons held captive by Arab Iranian terrorists since April 30. The assault was ordered after the terrorists holding the building murdered a hostage and threw his body out onto the street. Five terrorists were killed by the assault force.

Commandos of Special Air Service regiment storm Iranian Embassy in London May 5.

[54] London police and members of the Special Air Service regiment, who had surrounded the embassy in London's Kensington section, mounted the attack. Two explosions shook the embassy as the British force moved in. The building burst into flames, and the troops penetrated inside behind a hail of gunfire. The fire completely destroyed the embassy.

[55] The gunmen had referred to themselves as citizens of Arabistan, the name given by dissidents to Arab-speaking Khuzistan province. They said they belonged to an organization called "Group of the Martyr," which was campaigning for autonomy.

[56] The murdered hostage was identified as Abbas Lavasani, the embassy press officer. The body of a second dead hostage, Ali Akbar Samadzadeh, an embassy employee, was found in the rubble.

[57] **Libyan Exiles Slain.** Two exiled opponents of Col. Muammer el-Qaddafi were assassinated in London, apparently on orders of the Libyan leader. Mohammed Mustafa Ramadan, a journalist, was shot April 11 as he left a London mosque, and Mahmoud Nafa, a lawyer, was slain by a gunman April 25 in his London office. Both men had been active with anti-Qaddafi Libyan exile groups. London police charged two Libyan students with Ramadan's death.

Other Developments

[58] **Film Strains U.K.-Saudi Relations.** A documentary drama broadcast on British commercial television April 10 raised tensions between Britain and Saudi Arabia. The program, titled *Death of a Princess,* was a dramatized reconstruction of the 1977 execution by the Saudi government of Princess Mishaal,* who had committed

Scene from British television film, *Death of a Princess*, depicting public executions of Saudi Arabian princess and her lover. Body of prince lies on ground at right.

adultery with a commoner.

[59] The program was viewed in advance by Saudi officials, who waged an unsuccessful campaign to prevent it from being broadcast. There were press reports that the Saudi government had threatened to sever diplomatic ties with Britain and was considering suspending oil exports and other business contracts. The British Foreign Office maintained, however, that it had not been informed of any such threats.

[60] The Foreign Office did consider the situation serious enough, however, to have the British ambassador to Saudi Arabia cut short a vacation in France to return to Riyadh. The British Foreign Office issued a statement April 10 saying, "We profoundly regret any offense which the program may have caused in Saudi Arabia. We have, of course, no power to interfere with the editorial content of programs, still less to ban them."

*The princess's name was reported in 1978 as Misha Abdul Aziz. The *Journal of Commerce* reported April 11 that the princess was not executed for adultery but her open admission of adultery. "The film suggested that wealthy but bored Arabian women pay only lip service to Islamic laws and regularly arrange to meet their lovers in the desert," the *Journal* said.

[61] ***The Times* Offered for Sale.** Thomson Organisation Ltd. announced Oct. 22 that it was offering the old and prestigious daily newspaper the *Times of London* for sale, along with its sister publication, the *Sunday Times,* and three weekly supplements. If no buyer was found by March 1981, the papers would be closed, the Canadian-based firm said.

[62] In the current year, according to a management statement, the papers were expected to suffer a pretax loss of about $36.5 million, The main problem with the papers, management said, was a continuing pattern of labor trouble that had led to overstaffing and production tie-ups. Publication had been suspended for 11 months in 1978 and 1979 in an effort to win union agreement to changes aimed at improving efficiency. However, continued difficulties barred implementation of the changes agreed upon, according to management spokesmen. In particular, it had not proved possible

Editor of *Times of London,* William Rees Mogg (center) informs staff Oct. 22 that *Times, Sunday Times* and three weekly supplements will shut unless a buyer is found by March 1981.

to make use of new technology that management saw as essential.

See also Armaments (International) [15]; Aviation [10]; Economy (International) [8]; European Community [1-4]; Iran [76]; Zimbabwe [9, 11-12, 14]

GRAMMY AWARDS—*See* Music [1-5]

GREECE

[1] **Caramanlis Elected President.** Premier Constantine Caramanlis May 5 was elected president of Greece in the third and final ballot in parliament. He was to succeed President Constantine Tsatsos, whose five-year term was to expire June 19. George John Rallis was selected May 8 to become premier.

[2] Rallis was named premier by a parliamentary caucus of the ruling New Democracy Party. Rallis, who had served as foreign minister under Caramanlis, won an 88-84 victory over Defense Minister Evanghelos Averof-Tossizza. Rallis said after his election that he was committed to bringing Greece back into full membership in the North Atlantic Treaty Organization. Greece had withdrawn from its military NATO obligations in 1974.

[3] **U.S. Cooperation Accord Signed.** Greece and the U.S. signed a five-year agreement April 22 calling for cooperation in the economic, scientific, technological, cultural and educational fields.

[4] No specific commitments by either party were included in the accord signed in Athens. Its main practical effect would be the creation of working groups to review economic and commercial relations between Greece and the U.S. and make recommendations for mutually beneficial programs.

GUATEMALA

[1] **39 Die in Embassy Sit-In.** Thirty-nine persons were killed Jan. 31 when a fire broke out in the Spanish Embassy in Guatemala City. The dead were Indian peasants who had occupied the embassy and taken the Spanish ambassador hostage.

[2] The Spanish ambassador, Maximo Cajal y Lopez, escaped with only minor

injuries. But a former Guatemalan vice president, Eduardo Caceras Lehnhoff, and a former Guatemalan foreign minister, Adolfo Molina Orantes, were said to have died in the fire. It was not clear how the fire began. Witnesses, contradicting earlier Red Cross reports that the fire started shortly after police had stormed the embassy, said the blaze already had started by the time the police rushed inside in an apparent attempt to save the victims.

[3] The peasants occupying the embassy were from the Quiche tribe. They had been demanding an audience with government officials to air their grievances of army repression.

[4] ***Indian Survivor Murdered***—The only Indian survivor of the fire at the Spanish Embassy in Guatemala City was abducted by a band of heavily-armed men from his hospital room Feb. 1. Gregaria Yuga Xona, who was badly burned in the fire, was found shot to death over the Feb. 2-3 weekend on the campus of the national university. His murder was blamed on a right-wing "death squad."

[5] ***Spain Severs Relations***—Spain broke diplomatic relations with Guatemala Feb. 1. A communique released in Madrid Feb. 1 said that relations between the two countries would cease until Spain received "a clear and acceptable explanation" of why the Guatemalan police had stormed the embassy despite repeated efforts on the part of the Spanish ambassador to prevent the assault.

[6] **Labor Unrest at Coca-Cola Plant.** An explosive labor dispute at the Coca-Cola franchise in Guatemala resulted in the murder May 27 of the secretary general of the plant's union. The union official was the fourth worker at the Coca-Cola plant killed in May and the third secretary general of the plant's union to be murdered in the past 18 months.

[7] Suppression of union activities at the beverage plant had become the focus of a church-backed international protest campaign by the New York-based Interfaith Center on Corporate Responsibility. The International Union of Food and Allied Workers Associations, based in Geneva, had launched protest strikes April 16 to denounce Coca-Cola for failing to replace its license holder in Guatemala, Texas businessman John Clinton Trotter, whom the IUF charged with "violent repression of trade unions" and anti-labor practices.

[8] Coca-Cola products in Scandinavia were boycotted April 16 and a plant in Sweden was closed for three days. A week-long production halt in Mexico was started April 24. A three-day stoppage of Coca-Cola production and a five-day consumer boycott were launched April 25, and a 10-day sales and consumer boycott in Spain began May 1.

[9] Trotter, the main target of the IUF's protests, had run the Coca-Cola plant in Guatemala for 20 years on behalf of its largest stockholder, Mary Hodge Fleming, a wealthy widow living in Houston. The union had charged Trotter with trying to bribe its officials in 1975 and later threatening to get the government to suppress the union after the officials had refused the bribe.

[10] On Dec. 12, 1978, the union's secretary general was murdered while on his delivery route. The next union secretary received so many death threats that on Jan. 31, 1979, after three attempts had been made on his life, he took asylum in the Venezuelan Embassy. On April 5, 1979, the next union secretary was beaten to death while on his delivery route.

[11] **Vice President Resigns in Protest.** Francisco Villagran Kramer resigned as vice president Sept. 2 and charged right-wing elements in the government with having "adopted a policy of violation of human rights."

[12] **10 Killed in Leftist Attack.** Nine guerrillas and one soldier were killed when a band of leftist rebels attacked an army post in the northern department of Quiche Sept. 6. The attackers were driven off.

GUINEA-BISSAU

[1] **Premier Ousts President in Coup.** Premier Joao Bernardo Vieira Nov. 14 seized power in a coup that ended President Luis de Almeida Cabral's plan to unify Guinea-Bissau with its sister republic of the Cape Verde Islands.

[2] Troops loyal to Vieira, a guerrilla leader during the 11-year war of independence against Portugal, which ended in 1974, met little resistance when they occupied the capital city of Bissau Nov. 15. Two government officials were reported killed. A curfew in the capital was lifted Nov. 16 and there were reports of spontaneous celebrations by the population.

[3] Vieira, who headed the new Council of the Revolution, opposed Cabral's plan to unite the West African country with the Republic of Cape Verde, an archipelago 400 miles (640 kilometers) off the coast. Former Portuguese colonies, both countries had until the coup had been ruled by the left-leaning African Party for the Independence of Cape Verde and the Guinea-Bissau. Vieira was a leader of the blacks in Guinea-Bissau who opposed unification with the mixed-race Cape Verdeans. Cabral was of mixed-race descent. Observers said that although Vieira had reportedly been trained as a rebel in communist countries, he was more of an African socialist than a Marxist.

See also Chad [10]

HAITI

[1] **New Law Stifles Press Criticism.** A new law announced by the government April 11 provided for jail sentences of up to three years for anyone convicted of criticizing President-for-life Jean-Claude Duvalier in the press. The law also stated that no journalist could operate in Haiti without a press card signed by the miniser of information, but the law did not explain how such a card could be obtained.
[2] **200 Alleged Agitators Arrested.** Between Nov. 28-30, Haitian police arrested some 200 journalists, politicians, human rights activists, doctors, teachers, medical students and writers in connection with alleged communist-inspired agitation.
[3] The arrests began Nov. 28 with the detention of more than 40 members of the Haitian press most outspoken in their criticism of the government's economic policies. Articles scoring the Duvalier regime had followed the much-publicized incident Nov. 13 in which over 100 stranded Haitians were forcibly removed from an island in the Bahamas and returned to Haiti. Among those held were Gregoire Eugene, leader of the Social Christian Party and publisher of the newletter *Fraternite,* Garcia Marcus, chief editor of Radio Metropole, Pierre Clitandre, editor of *Le Petit Samedi Soir,* Jean-Robert Herard, chief political writer for *Le Petit Samedi Soir,* and his brother, Gabriel.
[4] More arrests came Nov. 29 and included members of the family of Sylvio Claude, the leader of the Christian Democratic Party, who had been arrested Oct. 13, and Lafontant Joseph, a founding member of the Haitian Human Rights League.
See also Crime [46]; Human Rights [18]; Immigration [3-11]; Refugees [6-8]

HEALTH CARE—*See* Budget [9]

HELSINKI REVIEW CONFERENCE

[1] **Meeting Opens.** The 35-nation review meeting of the 1975 Helsinki accords on European security and cooperation opened Nov. 11 in Madrid although the participating countries had not agreed on an agenda for the discussions.
[2] Delegates from the 33 participating European nations and the United States and Canada had worked for two months prior to the conference opening to devise a calendar for the talks. Western representatives had pushed for a lengthy period for reviewing each country's compliance with the human rights provisions of the Helsinki accords. The Soviets had fought to limit the time.
[3] Several compromise formulas for allocating time had been proposed. However, none had been accepted. The delegates agreed to hear the opening speeches while a working group was created to find ways to prevent the procedural impasse from wrecking the whole conference.

[4] The head of the U.S. delegation, former Attorney General Griffin Bell, Nov. 13 attacked the Soviets for their invasion of Afghanistan. Bell also called attention to the "lamentable record of continued denial of human rights" in Eastern Europe. He spoke of Soviet jamming of Western radio broadcasts, the drop in Jewish emigration from the Soviet Union, travel restrictions, and the persecution of dissidents in Czechoslovakia who monitored that country's infringement of human rights.
[5] The U.S. and the Soviets Nov. 14 agreed to a compromise offered by the Austrian, Cypriot, Swedish and Yugoslav delegations. The compromise called for a six-week initial phase devoted to opening speeches and compliance examination. A second six-week phase would be solely devoted to consideration of new proposals for furthering detente in Europe.
[6] Relatives of Raoul Wallenberg, the Swedish diplomat supposedly imprisoned by the Soviets since 1945, came to Madrid Nov. 28 in an effort to stimulate interest on his behalf. Delegations from Jewish communities in Western European countries arrived Dec. 5, and requested meetings with the Soviets to discuss the problems of Jews in the Soviet Union.
[7] ***1st Phase Ends***—The first phase of the review conference closed Dec. 19. At the last session, the U.S. said that a Soviet invasion of Poland would sabotage detente and undermine the agreements being reviewed.
[8] Max M. Kampelman, co-chairman of the U.S. delegation said that the current "movements and preparations of sizable Warsaw Pact forces in Central and Eastern Europe were totally inconsistent" with the Helsinki provisions prohibiting the use or threat of force. Kampelman warned that if Soviet forces moved in violation of the Helsinki provisions, "East-West relations as we know them could not continue." He added that detente would be a "certain casualty of that disaster."
[9] The conference was scheduled to resume in late January 1981.

HOCKEY

[1] **Islanders Win Stanley Cup.** The New York Islanders won their first Stanley Cup May 24, with a 5-4 overtime victory over the Philadelphia Flyers in the sixth game of the National Hockey League playoffs. The triumph gave the Islanders a record of four wins and two defeats in the best-of-seven final round.
[2] It was the first NHL title for the eight-year-old club. They clinched the Cup before a crown of 14,995 fans at the Nassau Coliseum in Uniondale, N.Y., the team's home ice. The Islanders reached the finals by defeating the Los Angeles Kings, three games to one, and the Boston Bruins, four games out of five, in early playoff rounds. They triumphed over the Buffalo Sabres in the semifinal series, four games to two. The Flyers swept the Edmonton Oilers, three games to none, and beat the New York Rangers, four games to one, to reach the semifinals. Philadelphia then beat the Minnesota North Stars, four games to one, to gain the final round.
[3] **NHL Adopts Overtime, Brawl Rules.** The National Hockey League's Board of Governors voted June 23 to institute a five-minute sudden death overtime period for all preseason and regular season games, beginning with the 1980-81 season. The NHL had not had overtime play to break ties during the regular season since 1942.
[4] The new rules said that if a game was tied at the end of the regulation three periods, the teams were to change sides and resume the play after a two-minute intermission. If no winner emerged after five minutes of overtime, the game would end in a tie and each club would be awarded one point. The league's rules committee June 9 acted to curb fighting. New rules required all players to leave the area where a fight erupted and return to

Philadelphia Flyers' Bobbie Clarke scores in first game of Stanley Cup playoffs May 13. New York Islanders' goalie Bill Smith is on the ice. Islanders won game 4-3, and went on to take series.

their benches or a non-combat zone. Players who failed to do so would be penalized.

[5] ***Flames Sale, Transfer Approved—*** The NHL's Board of Governors June 24 approved the sale and transfer of the financially trouble Atlanta Flames to Calgary.

[6] **Howe Retires.** Gordie Howe announced his retirement from hockey June 4. Howe, 52, had played for 32 seasons, breaking into the National Hockey League in 1946 with the Detroit Red Wings. He was the league's all-time scoring leader, with 801 regular season goals, and also held the mark for the most assists (1,518) and the most games played (2,421).

See also Olympics [4, 11-13]

HONDURAS

[1] **Junta Cedes Power to Assembly.** The military junta in Honduras, led by Gen. Policarpo Paz Garcia, formally handed over the government to a new Constitutional Assembly July 20. The 71-seat Assembly, which had been formed in national elections April 20, met to draw up a new constitution and organize direct elections to choose a civilian president.

[2] Robert Suazo Cordova, the 53-year-old head of the Liberal Party, was named chairman of the Assembly. Suazo's party had scored an upset victory in the April 20 vote, and he was strongly favored to become Honduras' next president. The voting was to be held in April 1981. In the meantime, Gen. Paz would serve as provisional president. Although leftist parties had been excluded from the 1980 elections, the fact that Honduras had renewed its former two-party system, within which the Liberals and the Nationals would offer candidates, was viewed as significant. The National party had the support of the country's businessmen and the army, while the Liberals were favored by workers and peasants. Honduras had had a military government since 1963, with the exception of a one-year interval in 1972.

HONG KONG

[1] **Immigration Policy: A 'Radical' Change.** Sir Murray MacLehose, governor of Hong Kong, announced Oct. 23 a "radical" change in the British crown colony's immigration policy aimed at stopping the flood of immigrants entering Hong Kong illegally from China. MacLehose's proposals were rushed through the Legislative Council, Hong Kong's parliament, and were to take effect immediately.

[2] The new rules in effect abolished the old "touch base" policy, under which Chinese who succeeded in evading border patrols – both communist Chinese and Hong Kong – and contacting friends or relatives in the colony could then register for permanent resident status in Hong Kong. Under the new scheme, the authorities were empowered to arrest and repatriate illegal immigrants no matter where they were found in the colony. The new policy, MacLehose said, had been worked out in cooperation with authorities in China, where it had full support, he said. It would not affect the 150 immigrants arriving legally each day from China.

HORSE RACING

[1] **Triple Crown.** Each leg of the 1980 Triple Crown was won by a different horse. Genuine Risk, a filly, won the Kentucky Derby May 3. Codex beat Genuine Risk in a controversial race at the Preakness Stakes May 17. Temperence Hill, a 50-1 longshot, won the Belmont Stakes June 7.

[2] Genuine Risk became only the second female horse in history to win the Kentucky Derby. She beat a field of 12 males on the 1 1/4-mile Churchill Downs course. At odds of 12-1, she returned $28.60 for a first place bet of $2. Her time of 2 minutes 2 seconds was one of the fastest Derby times in the last 20 years. Rumbo finished second and Jaklin Klugman finished third. The winner's purse of $250,000 went to the filly's owners, Mr. and Mrs. Bert Firestone. Genuine Risk was trained by LeRoy Jolley and ridden by Jacinto Vasquez.

[3] Codex, a California-bred horse, won the Preakness with the third best time ever run in the 1 3/16-mile Pimlico racetrack classic in Maryland. But the victory was clouded by the assertion that he fouled the favorite, Genuine Risk, in the final turn. The filly's jockey, Jacinto Vasquez, claimed that Codex bumped the horse and that the colt's rider, Angel Cordero Jr., struck Genuine Risk with his whip. The race's stewards immediately ruled that "Codex went slightly wide, but in our opinion did not hinder the filly enough to warrant disqualification." The Maryland Racing Commission supported the steward's decision June 4. Codex, with odds of nearly 3-1, paid $7.40 for a $2 win bet, with a winning time of 1:54.2. Owned by Tartan Farm stables and trained by Wayne Lukas, the horse earned a winner's purse of $186,000. Colonel Moran finished third in the Preakness.

[4] Temperence Hill, a 50-1 longshot almost scratched from the race by his trainer, won the 1 1/2-mile Belmont Stakes at Elmont, N.Y., beating Genuine Risk by two lengths. Rockhill Native was third. Codex finished seventh. Temperence Hill's victory, with a time of 2:29.8, gave his owner, John Anthony a $176,220 purse. The horse was trained by Joe Cantey and ridden by Eddie Maple. He paid $108.80 on a $2 first place bet, the second-highest return in the race's history.

[5] ***Spectacular Bid Sets Money Marks***—Spectacular Bid, winner of the 1979 Kentucky Derby and Preakness, set a new high for career thoroughbred race winnings June 8. The new mark, $2,394,268, broke the figure set by Affirmed in 1979.

[6] The horse set another money mark earlier in 1980. He was syndicated for stud for $22 million on March 11, the

Temperence Hill (left), with Eddie Maple up, pounds through mud to win 112th Belmont Stakes June 7. Genuine Risk (second left), piloted by Jacinto Vasquez, was second, Rockhill Native (right) with John Oldham in the irons, third.

highest price ever paid for studding.

In other racing news:

■ Private Account won the $151,000 Widener Handicap at Hialeah, Florida March 1. The horse covered the 1 1/4-mile-track in 2:03.2. Jeffrey Fell was aboard.

■ Codex, a 25-1 shot, won the 43rd Santa Anita Derby March 30 in California. Codex, who returned $52.60 for a $2 win bet, ran the 1 1/8 miles in 1:47.4, just two-fifths of a second slower than the race record. He was ridden by Laffit Pincay Jr.

■ Ben Nevis, an American horse, won the Grand National Steeplechase in Great Britain by 20 lengths March 29. His rider Charlie Fenwick, was only the second American to win the race in 137 years.

■ Henbit, an American-bred horse, won the English Derby at Epsom Downs June 4, with Willie Carson aboard.

[7] **Ex-Jockey Convicted in Race Fixing.** Con Errico was found guilty May 19 of bribing jockeys to fix nine races at New York state race tracks in 1974 and 1975.

[8] Errico, who retired from racing in 1975, was the only man indicted after a federal investigation of New York horse racing. He was first implicated in race fixing in a November 1978 *Sports Illustrated* article in which convicted race fixer Anthony (Big Tony) Ciulla said that Errico had helped him bribe several jockeys.

[9] Jose Amy, a 26-year old Puerto Rican jockey, testified at the Errico trial that other jockeys and several trainers were involved in race fixing. Amy said Angel Cordero Jr. and Jacinto Vasquez, both two-time winners of the Kentucky Derby, as well as several others had fixed races. Amy said that Errico had paid him $1,500 per race to fix races at Aqueduct and Saratoga race tracks.

HOUSING

[1] **Mortgage Rates Soar.**

"Astronomical" mortgage rates were leading some analysts to predict the worst housing recession since World War II, the *Wall Street Journal* reported March 7.

[2] Kenneth Rosen, a real estate expert at the University of California at Berkeley, told the *Journal* a continuation of rates in the range of 14% to 16% "will end nearly all demand for housing and may produce a drop in house prices over 10% by late spring."

[3] According to economists, mortgage rates were being pushed up by the high interest rates that savings and loan associations, still the main source of mortgage money, had to pay their depositors. Six-month money market certificates, which accounted for about 30% of S&L deposits, were being offered at 14.792% on March 6. To make a profit at such rates institutions would have to relend the money at mortgage rates exceeding 16%.

[4] In California, American Savings & Loan Association, the nation's second largest thrift lender, March 19 raised its prime, or best, mortgage rate to 17.5%, the highest such rate in the U.S.

[5] **Flexible-Rate Mortgages OK'd.** The Federal Home Loan Bank Board April 3 unanimously approved final regulations allowing the nation's 2,000 federally chartered savings and loan associations to issue renegotiated-rate mortgages (RRM) with interest rates that could be raised or lowered every three to five years.

[6] The mortgages were a form of flexible-rate mortgages, also know as rollover mortgages. [See box for description of mortgages.] The FHLBB action allowed any federal S&L to offer the RRM instead of the traditional fixed-rate mortgage.

[7] At the same time, the bank board approved a $630 million infusion of funds into savings and loan associations. The money would be paid mostly in the form of increased dividends from the 12 regional Home Loan Banks to S&Ls that were members of the FHLBB system. The bank board's action was intended to aid savings and loan associations that were hard pressed because customers were shifting savings deposits to investments offering higher rates of return. According to the

Mortgages

A mortgage was a legal agreement that created an interest in real estate or tranferred title to personal property as security for an obligation. The most common mortgages were for home purchases. Normally a mortgage financed the major part of the purchase price of the home and was repayable over a specific period of time, generally from 10 to 30 years.

In the past, conventional home mortgages had been **fixed-rate mortgages.** The interest rate paid over the life of the mortgage remained the same. (Those rates had soared to 17% or 18% in the first months of 1980).

Under a **renegotiated-rate mortgage** (RRM), the interest rate could be raised or lowered over the life of the mortgage by no more than 5 percentage points. Rates could not fluctuate more than half a percentage point a year. Every three to five years, borrowers either could renegotiate rates or shop without penalty for a new mortgage.

Under a **variable-rate mortgage,** interest rates reflected changes in the cost of funds to savings and loan associations, but the fluctuations up or down could not exceed .5 percentage points a year, and the rate could not increase more than 2.5 percentage points over the life of the mortgage. In addition, mortgages could be renegotiated every six months. Variable-rate mortgages were allowed for federally chartered S&LS in 1979. In California, state-chartered banks had offered them since 1975.

FHLBB, 266 associations posted losses during the second half of 1979, up 42% from the first half.

[8] **Housing Bill.** The Housing and Community Development Act of 1980 was signed by President Carter Oct. 8.

[9] The $48 billion multiyear authorization bill was approved by voice vote in both the Senate and the House Sept. 30. Approval came only after two major issues were resolved. One controversial issue was whether to make the 1975 Home Mortgage Disclosure Act (HMDA) permanent. This antiredlining act required savings and loan associations and banks to make annual reports of the number, location and dollar amount of their mortgage and home improvement loans. The Senate had extended HMDA, but the House had not. Finally, Senate Banking Committee Chairman William Proxmire (D, Wis.) was persuaded to agree to concurrent resolution to sunset, or end, HMDA in five years. After the Senate and House approved the conference report, they both cleared the concurrent resolution.

[10] The other key issue was a House-passed program to subsidize mortgages for apartments for middle-income renters. According to one source, Proxmire withdrew his support because of press reports that middle class families earning up to $30,000 a year would be aided at the expense of the poor. As a result, the program was dropped. In exchange for scuttling the proposal, the Senate agreed not to cut to 65% from 80% of the average median income of families qualifying for Section 8 aid. Under Section 8, families whose incomes fell below 80% of the median for their area would pay between 15% and 30% of their incomes in rent, and the government would pay the landlord the difference.

HUA KUO-FENG—*See* Cambodia [10]; China, People's Republic of [1-2, 24-25]

HUMAN RIGHTS

[1] **U.S. Study.** In a report on the observance of human rights around the world, the U.S. State Department said Feb. 5 that the Soviet Union had created a situation of total "disregard for basic human rights" in Afghanistan.

[2] The annual report for the first time discussed rights in Communist countries. Previous reports had been confined to nations that received U.S. aid, but new congressional rules mandated reports on all countries.

[3] Much of the criticism in the report was directed at Soviet-bloc countries or other nations with which the U.S. had political differences. However, there was also criticism of U.S. allies and various counties with which the U.S. government was trying to improve relations in order to orchestrate a response to the Soviet invasion of Afghanistan. Pakistan and Argentina fell in this category. [See below]

[4] With regard to Afghanistan, the report said that "torture, arbitrary arrest, extended and unexplained imprisonment" were commonplace under the Moscow-influenced regimes of Nur Mohammad Taraki and Hafizullah Amin.

[5] In the Soviet Union itself, according to the report, dissenters were "subject to constant harassment and physical abuse . . . appear to have become less prevalent in the 1970s." There were, the report said, an estimated 10,000 political prisoners in the Soviet Union, some kept in mental hospitals where they were made to take drugs.

[6] By country or region, the other main findings of the report were:

[7] ***Pakistan***—Traditional Islamic punishments such as flogging were employed in Pakistan, the report noted. Political freedoms had been denied by the regime of Gen. Muhammad Zia ul-Haq, who, the report observed, had in October 1979 "indefinitely postponed national elections, dissolved all political parties, ex-

panded the jurisdiction of military courts and imposed formal censorship of newspapers." Zia had imprisoned many politicians associated with former Premier Zulfikar Ali Bhutto, who had been executed in 1979.

[8] ***Argentina***—There was evidence of the "systematic use" of torture, execution and imprisonment without due process against critics of the military regime, the report said. The number of unexplained disappearances of critics appeared to have declined in 1979 from former years, the report said, adding that this might reflect the regime's success in eliminating the leftist opposition. Political activity was barred and labor unions were subject to stringent curbs, the reports added.

[9] ***North Africa and the Middle East***—Iraq, Lebanon, Morocco and Syria were cited as frequent violators of human rights. Conditions had improved in Egypt and Saudi Arabia, the report said, while noting the lack of democracy in both countries.

[10] ***Israel***—Human rights were well observed within Israel itself, the report said, but the treatment of the Palestinians in the occupied West Bank and Gaza strip was open to criticism. The report noted that there continued to be charges of torture or improper treatment of Arab suspects, but it added that such allegations were promptly investigated and had resulted on occasion in punishment for Israeli wrongdoers.

[11] ***China***—Mainland China was said to be "a less oppressive place in which to live than it was three years ago." The report added, however, that the liberalization had "not yet broken entrenched patterns of harassment, arbitrary arrests and harsh punishment without free trial for political dissent."

[12] ***Europe***—The Communist nations of Eastern Europe practised repressive policies similar to those found in the Soviet Union, the report said. In Western Europe the governments exhibited a high regard for human rights, although terrorist activity had led some to adopt security measures that were controversial.

[13] **ILO Scores U.S.S.R., Czechoslovakia.** The International Labor Organization May 12 criticized the Soviet Union, Czechoslovakia, the Ukraine and Belorussia for their labor laws. The United Nations agency said some of their labor laws violated international agreements against forced labor.

[14] The ILO cited provisions in those countries that called work a "moral obligation" and mandated prison terms for persons considered "parasites"—those without visible means of support—and pointed out that the laws "may serve as a means of compulsion to work."

[15] **OAS Resolution.** Overcoming deep ideological differences, the Organization of American States Nov. 27 approved a resolution calling on six Latin American countries to improve human rights conditions.

[16] The motion was passed by a vote of 16-2, with four abstentions. Five countries boycotted the session. The vote followed a fiery all-night debate in which delegates to the OAS' 10th General Assembly had concentrated on the report of the Inter-American Human Rights Commission on abuses in Argentina.

[17] Following President Carter's opening remarks to the Assembly Nov. 19, in which he defended the emphasis on human rights in his administration's foreign policy, Argentina had mounted a campaign to discredit the policy in Latin America. On Nov. 20, Argentina's delegate to the assembly, Foreign Minister Carlos Washington Pastor, criticized the Carter Administration and threatened to withdraw from the OAS if debate centered on the issue of human rights.

[18] A compromise resolution gave backing to the Inter-American Human Rights Commission's work and in one article named six countries (without condemning them) for their poor performance on human rights. The six

countries cited were Argentina, Chile, El Salvador, Haiti, Paraguay and Uruguay.

[19] **Amnesty International Cites Abuses.** Amnesty International reported Dec. 10 that more than half the countries of the world imprisoned persons for political or religious beliefs and that torture, summary trials and execution were common.

[20] Jose Zalaquett, chairman of AI's executive body, called the 1980 death toll from executions and political murders "a matter of the gravest and most urgent concern." Zalaquett's remarks were in the preface of the group's country-by-country review of human rights in 110 nations.

[21] In the U.S. AI said, "police brutality is widespread and severe, resulting in death in many cases." The group said that the brutality was probably not official policy but added that it probably occurred to the degree documented because it was "officially tolerated."

See also Chile [8]; Colombia [10-11]; El Salvador [18, 24-26]; Helsinki Review Conference; Iran [148-150]; Union of Soviet Socialist Republics [31-51]

I

ICELAND

[1] **NATO Critic Elected President.** Vigdis Finnbogadottir, a leftist who opposed continued membership for Iceland in the North Atlantic Treaty Organization, won election June 30 as Iceland's president, a largely ceremonial position.
[2] Finnbogadottir was the first women to become Iceland's head of state. She defeated three men in a close election.

Vigdis Finnbogadottir wins election as president of Iceland June 30.

IMMIGRATION

[1] **Iranians Continue to Enter U.S.** A total of 11,079 Iranians had entered the U.S. since the U.S. Embassy in Teheran was occupied in November 1979, an offical of the U.S. Immigration and Naturalization Services reported March 12.
[2] Of the Iranians who had entered the U.S., some 5,000 – many of them Jews and Bahais – had done so because they feared religious persecution in Iran. They had arrived in the U.S. on student, business and visitors' visas or had applied for permanent resident status.
[3] **Haitians Win Class Action Suit.** A federal judge in Miami ruled July 2 that the Immigration and Naturalization Service had knowingly violated the "constitutional, statutory, treaty and administrative rights" of thousands of Haitian refugees seeking political asylum in the U.S.
[4] Judge James L. King, in a 164-page opinion, ruled that the INS's refusal to recognize the political nature of the refugees' claims showed "a profound ignorance, if not an intentional disregard of the conditions in Haiti." The ruling prevented the INS from taking any further action to deport the Haitians until the government had presented King with an acceptable plan for reconsidering their asylum claims. The decision concluded a class action suit filed in 1979 on behalf of some 5,000 Haitians in Florida.
[5] During the trial, testimony was presented by Haitian witnesses

Aboard 44-foot sailboat, Haitian refugees head for Miami.

cataloguing abuses they had suffered under the regime of President-for-Life Jean-Claude Duvalier. A 1979 State Department report had concluded that the Haitians were fleeing harsh economic conditions and that they were not trying to escape political repression. Judge King criticized the State Department report, calling it "unworthy of belief."

[6] ***Haitians Reach Fla. in Record Numbers***—Refugees fleeing economic deprivation and political oppression in Haiti were reaching Florida in record numbers in 1980.

[7] More than 1,300 Haitian refugees had arrived in Florida in March, a new monthly record. The previous high was 637, recorded in October 1979. Accurate estimates of the number of Haitians now living in the south Florida area were difficult to obtain. Immigration officials said that they had records of 12,000 Haitians living in the area. Dade County reported 23,000, but Haitian refugee leaders claimed as many as 30,000 of their countrymen lived in and around Miami.

[8] The U.S. Coast Guard reported Sept. 9 that four boats carrying hundreds of Haitians toward the U.S. had been sighted at sea. More than 400 Haitians arrived in the U.S. that day, apparently the highest one-day number ever.

[9] The unabated flow of Haitians trying to reach the U.S. in small wooden boats was creating a tragic drama. On Sept. 6, a small sail boat with more than 100 Haitians aboard capsized just as a Coast Guard cutter found the boat and was approaching to rescue its passengers. Three young Haitians drowned when the passengers accidently overturned the boat by rushing together to one side to hail the cutter. An immigration official in Key West, Fla. said these Haitians had left about two weeks before and that at least 20 other persons had died while making the crossing.

[10] ***Haitians Evicted***—A group of 102 Haitian refugees stranded on Cayo Lobos Island in the Bahamas for about 40 days were herded aboard a ship by club-wielding Bahamian police Nov. 13 and taken back to Haiti.

[11] The group included mostly young men and several pregnant women. They had been spotted on the tiny island by a U.S. patrol plane Oct. 9. Five persons starved to death on the island, and the survivors were suffering from malnutrition and dehydration. The miniscule island was situated 20 miles (32 kilometers) north of Cuba, and some 300 miles (480 kilometers) from Haiti.

See also Aliens, Illegal [1-4]; Cuba; Hong Kong [1-2]; Refugees [1-8]

Latins: the New Wave of U.S. Immigrants

Just as European immigrants in the 19th and early 20th century had a profound impact on the life and culture of the U.S., the influx of Spanish-speaking peoples in the 20th century was changing American life, according to a *New York Times* survey of Hispanic Americans May 11-14.

The influx of immigrants from Latin America and the Caribbean now constituted about half of all newcomers entering the U.S. each year. This was twice the number of persons arriving from Europe.

Though the Latin immigrants came to the U.S. from different countries with sometimes conflicting traditions and political systems, once in America, they shared one major characteristic—the Spanish language—which differentiated this wave of immigrants from those of the past.

In New York, where about a third of the 950,000 children enrolled in public schools were Hispanic, nearly half of the city's 7.8 million residents had a mother tongue other than English. Almost 15% of those claimed Spanish as their primary language, making Spanish twice as common as Italian, which ranked second. Nationwide, the 1976 census had found that about 28 million persons living in the U.S—including 5 million school-aged children—had mother tongues other than English. More than a third of the 28 million—and 60% of the school-aged children—spoke Spanish.

The 1976 federal survey also found that Hispanic persons living in the U.S. tended to keep using Spanish. Four out of five Hispanics lived in homes in which Spanish was spoken, and one-third of them spoke Spanish as their preferred language. Some 430 radio stations and 34 television stations in the U.S. broadcast all or most of the time in Spanish, and one organization was establishing a coast-to-coast Spanish television network. Such widespread use of Spanish was making it possible for Hispanics to choose which language they wished to use, giving rise to a bilingual way of life that had not existed in the U.S. before.

According to New York City Planning Commission estimates, 1.8 million Hispanic residents lived in New York. Of them, more than one million were from Puerto Rico. There were some 400,000 Dominicans, 300,000 Colombians, 170,000 Ecuadoreans and 107,000 Cubans. In addition, there was said to be a substantial number of illegal aliens from Latin America living in the New York area.

In Miami, Cubans made up about 25% of the population in Dade County. Since the Castro revolution Jan. 1, 1959, an estimated 800,000 Cubans had fled to the U.S., and at least 400,000 of them had settled in Miami.

As the influx of Latins continued to grow, the pressure to integrate into American society was seen to be dwindling, and the resentment of Latins by blacks and non-Hispanics was seen growing. A survey reported in the May 20 *Wall Street Journal* found that 68% of non-Latin whites and 57% of blacks in Florida thought that the new wave of Cuban refugees would hurt Dade County. The pressure on Latins to assimilate into American society also was lessened by their common desire to preserve the traditions of their homeland. Despite difficulties that Hispanic immigrants faced, statistics reported in the *Journal* indicated that conditions are improving. By 1978, the median income of Hispanic families in Dade County had reached $13,644, up 32% from 1975. But in New York, 30% of the Puerto Rican families received some welfare payments, and 40% lived in poverty. Statistics published in the *Times* May 12 indicated that homicide was the single greatest cause of death for Puerto Ricans in the 15-44 age group.

INCOMES—See Black Americans [4]

INDIA

Government & Politics

[1] **Gandhi's Congress-I Party Triumphs.** Indira Gandhi was returned to power in national elections Jan. 3 and 6. Gandhi's Congress-I Party took overwhelming command of the Lok Sabha, India's lower house of Parliament, capturing 350 of its 542 seats.

[2] None of the other parties won the total of 50 seats required to qualify as the official opposition party. The Janata Party, which had defeated Gandhi in 1977 and remained the power until the summer of 1979, won only 32 seats.

[3] The Lok Dal Party headed by caretaker Prime Minister Charan Singh gathered 41 seats. The two Communist parties, which had agreed not to run competing candidates, jointly won 45 seats—the pro-Soviet Communist Party of India winning 10 of those and the Communist Party-Marxist, which followed policies somewhat more distant from Moscow, taking 35. The faction of the Congress party opposed to Gandhi, headed by Devaraj Urs, won 13 seats.

[4] In additon to the strong majority enjoyed by her own party, Gandhi also received promises of support from a number of legislators elected as independents or members of regional parties.

[5] Other prominent members of the Congress-I (The "I" stood for Indira) Party to win election included Gandhi's son, Sanjay Gandhi, former Information Minister, Vidya Charan Shukla and former Defense Minister Bansi Lal. All had been with Gandhi during the unpopular period when her government ruled under a state of emergency, and all had been defeated in the 1977 elections.

[6] Gandhi was sworn in Jan. 14 as prime minister of India.

[7] **Janata Party Leader Resigns.** Jagjivan Ram resigned March 7 as leader of the opposition Janata Party and gave up his membership in the organization. He urged other Janata members to join him in forming a new opposition party.

Sanjay Gandhi (left) and his mother, India's Prime Minister Indira Gandhi. Sanjay was killed June 23 when the light plane he was flying crashed in New Delhi.

[8] In relinquishing his party leadership, Ram said it was better to separate "those who prefer to support communal and caste tendencies based on religious fanaticism from those who believe in secularism and equality." Ram, who was foremost among India's 100 million harijans (low-caste Hindus or untouchables), was referring to his opposition to the link between former leaders of the Jana Sangh wing of Janata and RSS (the Union of Selfless Servers), an upper-caste Hindu cadre.

[9] (India had been plagued by an outbreak of attacks on harijans. In the latest incident, 14 persons were killed Feb. 26 when an armed gang of about 500 attacked a village of harijans in Bihar state.)

[10] **Sanjay Gandhi Killed in Plane Crash.** Prime Minister Indira Gandhi's son, Sanjay, died June 23 when the light plane he was flying crashed in New Delhi.

[11] The death was expected to have a considerable impact on public affairs in the country, since Sanjay was considered one of the most powerful figures in India, although he held no formal post in the government. (He was, however, a member of Parliament.) On June 6, the ruling Congress-I Party in Uttar Pradesh elected Sanjay as its leader. This qualified him to be the state's chief minister, but Indira Gandhi ruled that her son could not take the job. She said that she could not do without his services in New Delhi.

[12] Sanjay, 33, had been handling the government's economic policy since his mother was elected prime minister.

Unrest

[13] **Caste Groups Clash.** Twelve persons were killed Feb. 7 when low-caste Hindus were attacked by upper-caste Hindus in a village in Bihar state. A thirteenth person died in a retaliatory raid Feb. 8.

[14] Similar caste violence had broken out in Tamil Nadu state Jan. 17, leav-

ing more than 40 persons injured; 29 were arrested.

[15] **Assam Hit by Rioting.** Troops patrolled parts of the northeastern state of Assam April 2 to keep order after rioting March 31. Two persons were killed.

[16] The violence stemmed from a student-led campaign to have several million people who had settled in Assam over the past three decades deported. The non-Assamese were Bengalis, mostly from Bangladesh and the neighboring Indian state of West Bengal. The campaign had resulted in the closing of schools and colleges and the cancellation of elections. It also had cut off the flow of crude oil from Assam to other parts of India. (Assam accounted for about half of India's domestically produced petroleum.)

[17] Indian troop reinforcements were sent to Assam and Tripura states to quell spreading violent protests against immigrants, mostly Bengalis, from neighboring Bangladesh, it was announced by New Delhi June 9.

[18] About 50 persons had been reported killed in clashes in May between Assamese and Bengalis in the state's northern districts. The unrest had spread June 5 to Tripura and left 20 dead in clashes between native residents of the state and Bengalis.

[19] ***Bengalis Massacred in Tripura***— Indigenous tribal residents in Tripura state killed at least 350 Bengali immigrants in the village of Mandai June 7-8 in another outbreak of violence against the former citizens of Bangladesh. An Indian army unit that arrived on the scene June 9 found no survivors.

[20] The latest outbreak of clashes brought to 700 the number of persons recently killed in two dozen places in Tripura, army sources said. Most of the victims were Bengalis. Nearly 20,000 persons had fled their homes and had been given haven in about 100 camps established by the central government.

[21] **86 Die in Mosque Riot.** A riot erupted near a mosque in Moradabad, Uttar Pradesh state, Aug. 13 and reportedly led to 86 deaths. Some worshippers apparently thought that police were permitting pigs—considered unclean animals by Moslems—to wander in the area of the mosque. The death toll in Moslem-Hindu fighting in Uttar Pradesh rose to 142 Aug. 17, the fifth day of communal voilence. The violence, initially directed by Moslems at local police, spread through the town, and turned into a confrontation between Moslems and Hindus. As news of the violence spread, intercommunal tension erupted into rioting throughout northern India, with its heavily concentrated Moslem minority. The army was called out to contain rioting in Ranpur, Kanpur and Meerut, and killings were reported in old Delhi.

[22] At least 10 persons died Sept. 8 in a renewal of clashes between Hindus and Moslems in Aligarh, Uttar Pradesh. Military forces were rushed into the city to maintain order.

[23] Political violence broke out Sept. 8 in Bihar state, where rebels fought police in Gua. Sixteen persons, including four policemen, were killed.

[24] **Security Law Decreed.** A national security law aimed at combating Hindu-Moslem violence and other disturbances was issued by the government Sept. 22. Violators of the decree could be jailed for a year without trial.

[25] An official statement said: "The need for the ordinance has arisen looking to the prevailing situation of communal disharmony, caste conflicts, social tensions, extremist activities, atrocities on minorities and other weaker sections of society. . . ." The statement added that "secessionist activities and regional movements pose a grave challenge to the lawful authority."

[26] Opposition parties expressed fears that the decree would bring a return to wholesale detentions carried out during Prime Minister Indira Gandhi's 1975-77 emergency rule.

[27] **Police Kill 12 Naxalites.** Police in India's southernmost state, Tamil Nadu, killed at least 12 members of the Naxalites, a Maoist extremist group committed to violent confrontation with government authorities, it was reported Oct. 11.

[28] The group was said to be organizing landless laborers and poor peasants in the agricultural villages in the western districts of the state. The laborers and peasants reportedly were being exploited by landlords and moneylenders said to have violated land reform and debt relief laws.

Nuclear Energy

[29] **U.S. Delays India A-Shipments.** U.S. State Department officials said March 13 that the U.S. had postponed shipping uranium fuel to India until the Indian government guaranteed that the fuel would not be used to produce nuclear explosives.

[30] **Uranium Sale to India Halted.** A proposed sale of nuclear fuel to India was blocked May 16 by a unanimous vote of the U.S. Nuclear Regulatory Commission. Specifically, the commission denied two export licenses for the shipment of 38 tons (38,000 kilograms) of enriched uranium destined for the Indian nuclear plant at Tarapur.

[31] The NRC rejected the licenses under the Nuclear Nonproliferation Act of 1978, which prohibited the sale of nuclear fuel to nations that refused international inspections of their nuclear facilities, or that had refused to sign the nonproliferation treaty banning the spread of nuclear weapons.

[32] **Carter OKs Uranium Sale to India.** President Carter June 19 signed an executive order approving the sale of 38 tons of enriched uranium to India. The order overruled a decision by the NRC in May.

[33] In a message to Congress defending his order, the President stressed the need for closer ties with India, especially in view of the strife in the Persian Gulf-Southwest Asia region. Despite the Administration's contention, more than 30 members of Congress co-sponsored a bipartisan resolution in opposition to the uranium sale. The resolution was introduced to the House June 19. The resolution would overturn Carter's executive order if passed by majorities of both houses within 60 days. Carter could not veto the resolution.

[34] ***U.S. Congress Fails to Block Sale***—The Carter Administration won an important foreign policy victory Sept. 24, when the Senate voted 48-46, to defeat a resolution that would have blocked the sale of 38 tons of enriched uranium to India.

[35] The House Foreign Affairs Committee and the Senate Foreign Relations Committee both passed the resolution Sept. 10. The full House voted, 298-98, in favor of the resolution Sept. 19. The issue then hinged on the Senate vote.

Other Developments

[36] **Dowry Murders.** More than 200 women in New Delhi were burned to death in 1979 by husbands or in-laws dissatisfied with the dowry brought by the women, according to the estimates of women's groups reported by the *Washington Post* April 9.

[37] The sucess of the feminist groups in focusing public attention on the dowry murders was one of their main achievements, according to the *Post*. The women's groups had succeeded in getting police departments, which previously had often refused to look into such cases, to investigate them, it was reported.

See also Armaments (International) [1]

INDIANS, AMERICAN

[1] **Maine Indians Settle Land Case.** Members of the Penobscot Indian tribe March 15 approved a proposed $81.5 million settlement of a land claims case

against the state of Maine.

[2] The settlement had been approved earlier, by the Passamaquoddy tribe, which, together with the Penobscots, had contended that 12.5 million acres (5 million hectares) of land, approximately the northern two-thirds of the state of Maine, had been taken from them in violation of the Indian Non-Intercourse Act of 1790. The act required congressional ratification of all transactions involving Indians. Maine had acquired the land from the Indian's by a 1794 treaty, which Congress had not ratified.

[3] Under an "agreement in principle" reached between Indian and state negotiators, the two tribes would receive a $27 million trust fund plus $54.5 million to purchase 300,000 acres (120,000 hectares) as a "permanent land base" for the tribes. The settlement would go next to the Maine Legislature and the U.S. Congress for approval. In preliminary action in 1978, Congress had agreed to pay the cost of a settlement and to underwrite a trust fund, but it committed itself only to $10 million extra to buy 100,000 acres (40,000 hectares).

[4] **Souix Win $122.5 Million.** The Supreme Court ruled, 8-1, June 30 that the Sioux Nation of Indians was entitled to $122.5 million in compensation and interest for the illegal seizure in 1877 by the federal government of their land in the Black Hills of South Dakota. The case was *U.S. V. Sioux Nation.*

[5] In 1979, the U.S. Court of Claims had ruled that Washington owed the Sioux $17.5 million, the market value of the land in 1877, plus $105 million in interest (calculated at a rate of 5% over 103 years). The government did not quarrel with the $17.5 million award, but asked the Supreme Court to void the part of the judgment requiring payment of back interest.

[6] The high court upheld the total award. Justice Harry A. Blackman, writing for the majority, held that the "subsistence rations" provided by the government to the Indians after taking their land "did not constitute adequate consideration for the Black Hills." Therefore, he said, the seizure violated the Fifth Amendment, which guaranteed "just compensation" for private property acquired for public use. Justice William H. Rehnquist dissented.

[7] A federal district judge in Omaha, Neb. Sept. 11 dismissed a suit by the Oglala Sioux Indian tribe that sought to block the federal government from paying the Sioux nation for the Black Hills of South Dakota.

INDONESIA

[1] **East Timor Rebels Battle Troops.** East Timor rebels were still battling government troops in the Indonesian province, it was reported from Lisbon July 23. The account, given by ethnic Chinese refugees from East Timor, also told of continued widespread starvation caused by the civil war.

[2] One report said a hospital in the capital city of Dili had regularly admitted Indonesian military casualties along with civilians, many of whom were suffering from malnutrition. The number of the Indonesian military wounded was estimated at 50-100 a week, with "many, maybe half" of them dying, it was said.

[3] The reports of continued fighting appeared to conflict with a statement June 10 by U.S. Assistant Secretary of State Richard Holbrooke. He told a House subcommittee that it "was not until late 1978 and early 1979 that centrally directed Fretilin [the rebel Timor National Liberation Front] armed activity was fully contained by Indonesia military activity and ceased to pose a significant problem."

INFLATION—*See* Economy (U.S.) [10-36]; Great Britain [4-5, 10, 25, 27, 39]; Israel [1-2]

INTELLIGENCE ISSUES

[1] **Oversight Bill Approved.** President Carter Oct. 14 signed into law legislation revising the way Congress oversaw U.S. intelligence agencies.

[2] The oversight legislation was included in a routine bill authorizing funds for U.S. intelligence agency operations in fiscal 1981. The appropriations part of the bill authorized undisclosed amounts of money for the Central Intelligence Agency as well as $11.4 million for Federal Bureau of Investigation counterterrorism operations in the U.S. The bill also authorized $17.8 million for staff support for the director of the CIA and $55.3 million for the CIA retirement and disability fund.

[3] The portion of the bill dealing with intelligence oversight repealed the Hughes-Ryan Amendment of 1974, which required that covert actions of the CIA be reported to Congress "in a timely fashion." As a result of the amendment, as many as eight controversial committees were receiving that information. Under the new law, notification of CIA actions would have to be made to only two congressional committees – the House and Senate Intelligence Committees. The bill required the executive branch to keep those committees "fully and currently informed" of all U.S. intelligence activities, and established that despite the required reports, the committees could not disapprove intelligence operations. The president could restrict prior notification of planned intelligence activities if he "determined it was essential to limit prior notice to meet extraordinary circumstances affecting vital interests of the U.S."

[4] The bill provided that if the president did not comply with the prior notice provision, he would have to report the operation in question "in a timely fashion" together with "a statement of the reasons for not giving prior notice." The president would also have to report "in a timely fashion . . . any illegal intelligence activity or significant intelligence failure and any corrective action that had been taken or was planned." The bill had cleared the Senate by voice vote Sept. 19 and had been approved by the House and cleared for the president Sept. 30 by a vote of 385-18.

INTERNATIONAL MONETARY FUND (IMF)—*See* China [25-26]; Economy (International) [12-16]; Pakistan [7]; Turkey 24-25]

INTERNAL REVENUE SERVICE (IRS)

[1] **Prosecution Guidelines.** The Internal Revenue Service had allegedly told its agents not to pursue criminal prosecution of most tax cheaters unless they underpaid the government for a minimum average of $2,500 for three consecutive years, according to a report Aug. 2.

[2] The information appeared in a classified July IRS directive obtained and scheduled for publication by the *National Law Journal,* a weekly publication for the legal profession. The guidelines set down amounts below which tax agents should not file criminal charges against suspected cheaters. The guidelines concerned only criminal cases of tax fraud. Most routinely discovered tax underpayments were handled as civil matters and were not affected by the new guidelines.

[3] According to the unsigned *Journal* article, the IRS had previously used an unwritten policy of not prosecuting cases involving less than $1,000. The *Journal,* which did not reveal how it obtained the confidential document, detailed the recommendations from Thomas J. Clancy, director of the agency's criminal investigation division, to IRS agents in charge of deciding which cases to prosecute.

[4] **IRS: Middle-Class Bears Tax Burden.** The American middle class was liable for 60.1% of federal income taxes, even though middle-income earners made up only 38.2% of the tax-paying population, according to a survey by the Internal Revenue Service made public Sept. 12.

[5] The survey was based on 90.9 million 1979 federal tax returns processed through the first seven months of 1980. Middle-income Americans were defined by the IRS as individuals, couples and families who earned in the range of $15,000-$50,000. In 1977, the IRS said, this group had filed 32.7% of the tax returns and had paid 60% of the taxes.

Among other income groups:

■ Those earning under $10,000 accounted for 43.9% of the 1979 returns filed. They were liable for 4.4% of the total taxes of $207 billion (In 1977, they had been 49.1% of the filers and paid 5.6% of the $159.8 billion in taxes.)

■ Those in the $10,000-$15,000 range were 15.5% of the tax-paying population and were liable for 8% of the taxes. (In 1977, they had filed 16.4% of the returns and paid 10.7% of the taxes.)

■ Those who earned more than $50,000 in 1979 were 2.4% of the processed returns and they paid 27.4% of the taxes. (In 1977, they had filed 1.8% of the returns and accounted for 23.7% of the taxes.)

IOWA—*See* Grain [5-10]; Women's Rights [8-9]

IRAN

[1] All efforts to free the U.S. hostages in Iran failed during 1980. These efforts included negotiations, United Nations action, a military rescue mission. U.S. Secretary of State Cyrus R. Vance resigned in the aftermath of the military mission. Meanwhile, the exiled shah died in Cairo. Iran elected its first president and a parliament. War broke out between Iran and Iraq [see Iraq].

[2] **U.S. Sees No Break in Crisis.** In briefings held Jan. 8 and 9, President Carter and Secretary of State Cyrus Vance expressed doubts about an imminent release of the American hostages. They believed the crisis could last for weeks and possibly months.

[3] Carter told a group of 80 congressmen Jan. 8: "The most powerful single political entity in Iran consists of the international terrorists or the kidnappers who are holding our hostages. Whenever there has been a showdown concerning the hostages between [Ayatollah Ruhollah] Khomeini and the Revolutionary Council versus the terrorists, the terrorists always prevailed." (It was the first time the President had publicly referred to the militants holding the U.S. Embassy in Teheran as terrorists.)

[4] **U.S Newsmen Ousted.** The ruling Revolutionary Council Jan. 14 ordered the expulsion of all American newsmen from Iran because of "biased reporting." More than 100 journalists and technicians working for American newspapers, news services and three major television networks were affected.

[5] Some U.S. journalists were permitted to reenter the country. Newsmen from ABC-TV began broadcasting from Iran March 7 for the first time since U.S. reporters were banished from the country in January. A news team from NBC-TV started work again in Iran that day. United Press International also sent a reporter back to Iran. Other reporters for *Time*, the *Washington Post*, the *New York Times* and *Newsweek* magazine had received visas for Iran.

[6] A second order, expelling U.S. newsmen from Iran, was issued by the government April 23.

[7] Iran announced Nov. 15 the lifting of restrictions on foreign journalists

AYATOLLAH RUHOLLAH KHOMEINI

wishing to cover the Iranian-Iraqi war. According to a government order, newsmen wishing to enter Iran would be able to obtain visas from Iranian embassies and consulates abroad.

[8] **Canada Helps 6 Americans to Escape.** Six U.S. Embassy employees not among the 53 known American hostages in Teheran had flown out of Iran Jan. 28 with the help of Canadian diplomats, the U.S. and Canada announced Jan. 29. They posed as Canadian diplomats and carried forged Iranian visas in passing through security checks at the Teheran airport.

[9] The six–four men and two women–returned to the U.S. Jan. 30 after a stopover at Frankfurt, West Germany.

[10] The Americans were said to have fled the embassy when it was first seized by Iranian militants Nov. 4, 1979. According to Canadian officials, they showed up at the Canadian Embassy in Teheran the following day and were given sanctuary. External Affairs Minister Flora MacDonald said the Americans lived in the Teheran residences of Canadian diplomats for most of the three months.

[11] U.S. and Canadian officials had wanted the matter of the escape kept quiet for fear of possible retaliation against the Americans still held in captivity. The officials, however, confirmed the affair after a Montreal newspaper, *La Presse,* published a report that the Canadian Embassy was closed to cover the escape. The embassy staff had been cut from 18 to four in November. The four remaining Canadian diplomats left Iran with the Americans.

[12] The Americans were identified as: Mark J. Lijek, consular officer; his wife, Cora A. Lijek; Robert C. Anders, consular officer; Henry Lee Schatz, agricultural attache; Joseph D. Stafford, consular officer, and his wife Kathleen F. Stafford, consular assistant.

[13] **U.S. Group Meets Militants.** A group of 49 Americans sympathetic to the Iranian revolution Feb. 10 met with the militants at the U.S. Embassy in Teheran but they were not permitted to visit the hostages.

[14] The group was headed by Norman Forer, a professor at the University of Kansas. The Americans had been invited to Iran by the militants to examine evidence of the shah's alleged crimes, a spokesman for the captors said Feb. 2.

[15] ***Parents Visit Hostage Son***—The mother and stepfather of Sgt. Kevin Hermening arrived in Teheran April 19 to visit their son, who was one of the hostages in the U.S. Embassy. Kenneth and Barbara Timm made the trip despite President Carter's April 17 ban on trips to Iran.

[16] Mrs. Timm was allowed to see her son April 21 in the U.S. Embassy compound. The militants permitted her to spend 45 minutes with the 20-year-old sergeant, the youngest hostage in the embassy. "We never quit holding hands," Mrs. Timm said afterward. "I kept telling him how strong he was, and he kept telling me how strong I was."

[17] **U.S. Cuts Ties with Iran.** The U.S. April 17 severed diplomatic relations with Iran, formally banned American exports to that country and ordered the ouster of Iranian diplomats from the U.S. The punitive steps, announced by President Carter, were in response to a statement by Ayatollah Khomeini that the hostages in the U.S. Embassy in Teheran would remain under control of the militants and would not be turned over to the Iranian government.

[18] The break in relations called for the immediate closing of the Iranian Embassy in Washington and consulate offices in five cities and for the departure of all Iranian diplomatic personnel by midnight April 8. The diplomats complied with the directive and more than 50 of them and their families left for Teheran April 8.

[19] (Thousands of students and other Iranians would be permitted to stay in the U.S. for months and perhaps for

In Hermitage, Pa., an American flag was raised for each day hostages were held in Iran. This photo was taken Feb. 28, the 117th day of their captivity.

several years until their visas expired, Administration officials explained April 8. All visas issued to Iranians for future entry to the U.S. were canceled.)

[20] The trade embargo, which did not apply to food and medical shipments, was largely symbolic, since the freeze on Iranian assets in the U.S. in November 1979 and other Administration actions had dramatically reduced American business and banking with Iran. Exports had dropped to $1.8 million in February.

[21] **Carter Warns U.S. Might Take Military Action.** President Carter warned April 17 that the U.S. might be compelled to take military action against Iran if economic and political sanctions failed to produce the early release of the American hostages. He set no deadline. Any military move, the President suggested, would be aimed at interrupting trade with Iran, rather than mounting an invasion or any other combat operation.

[22] Speaking at a televised news conference, Carter also disclosed the following new reprisals to be taken against Iran:

■ A ban against "all financial transfers by persons subject to the jurisdiction of the United States to any person or entity in Iran." Exempt from this order were American journalists in Iran and family remittances to the hostages.

■ A ban on all imports from Iran to the U.S.

■ Americans were prohibited from traveling to Iran, with the exception of newsmen. The journalists and news-gathering organizations, however, were asked "to minimize as severely as possibly their presence and their activities in Iran."

U.N. Actions

[23] **Waldheim Mission.** United Nations Secretary General Kurt Waldheim conferred with Iranian officials in Teheran Jan. 1-3 in an effort to obtain the release of the American hostages held at the U.S. Embassy.

Waldheim returned to New York Jan. 4 and told a news conference: "The situation is evidently more grave and serious than people believe." He expressed doubt about an early release of the captives.

[24] Waldheim was barred from visiting the hostages and was not permitted to meet with Iranian ruler Ayatollah Ruhollah Khomeini. The secretary general visited Iran under terms of a U.S.-sponsored resolution approved by the U.N. Security Council Dec. 31, 1979.

[25] ***Soviets Veto U.N. Call for Sanctions Against Iran***—A U.S.-sponsored U.N. Security Council resolution calling for economic sanctions against Iran was vetoed Jan. 13 by the Soviet Union. The sanctions were intended as part of the campaign to free the hostages.

[26] The Council vote was 10-2; East Germany cast the other negative vote and two countries abstained—Bangladesh and Mexico. China did not participate.

[27] **U.S. Backs Inquiry.** A proposal to send an international commission of inquiry to Teheran to investigate Iranian grievances received the support Feb. 13 of President Carter.

[28] The President told a Washington news conference that since November 1979 the U.S. had been discussing the proposed commission with Iranian officials and United Nations Secretary General Kurt Waldheim, who had suggested sending the body to Teheran.

[29] **Commission Formed.** United Nations Secretary General Kurt Waldheim Feb. 17 completed formation of a five-member commission to investigate Iran's grievances against Shah Mohammed Riza Pahlevi. The U.S. and Iran gave their approval of the body.

[30] The members of the commission were: Harry W. Jayewardene, 63, a lawyer from Sri Lanka and brother of President Junius R. Jayewardene; Louis-Edmond Pettiti, 64, of France, a judge on the European Court of Human Rights; Andres Aguilar Mawdsley, 55, who had served as Venezuela's ambassador to the U.S. (1972-74) and as his country's representative to the U.N.; Adib Daoudy, 57, a career diplomat from Syria, who was a political adviser to President Hafez al-Assad, and Mohammed Bedjaoui, 50, Algeria's chief delegate to the U.N. and a member of the U.N. Commission of International Rights.

[31] The U.N. commission of inquiry into Iran's grievances against deposed Shah Mohammed Riza Pahlevi arrived in Teheran Feb. 23 to begin its work.

[32] The panel's success, however, was cast in immediate doubt as Iranian officials continued to insist that there was no connection between the commission's probe and the release of the American hostages. The Iranians further stated that there was no chance that the U.S. captives would be set free before April or May.

[33] As the commission landed in Teheran Feb. 23, Ayatollah Khomeini indicated in a prepared statement that the hostages would not be let out before parliamentary elections to be held in April.

[34] ***U.N. Panel Promised Cooperation***—The U.N. commission of inquiry held preliminary meetings Feb. 24 with President Bani-Sadr and Foreign Minister Sadegh Ghotbzadeh, who promised to cooperate with the panel.

[35] The commission Feb. 26 heard testimony from five jurists and more than 140 invalids who said they had been torture victims of the shah's government. Many of them had lost eyes or limbs.

[36] At a rally outside the U.S. Embassy, a spiritual spokesman for the militants Feb. 27 said they were opposed to any visit by the commission to the hostages. The commission pressed for a meeting with the hostages at a conference with the Revolutionary Council Feb. 28. Foreign Minister Ghotbzadeh promised that a visit would be arranged but he did not say when or whether there would be condi-

tions. A spokesman for the Revolutionary Council said after meetings with the U.N. panel that it could see the American captives only if the hostages testified "on the crimes of the shah and the United States," a condition strongly opposed by the Carter Administration.

[37] The militants holding the American hostages announced March 6 that they would turn the captives over to the ruling Revolutionary Council because of "intolerable pressures" from Iranian authorities. No date for the transfer was set.

[38] Asked by newsmen about the future status of the Americans now that they were about to be transferred, Foreign Minister Ghotbzadeh said, "They are hostages, and they remain hostages." He said the U.N. commission of inquiry, which had been pressing to visit the hostages, would be able to do so "as soon as the first step is cleared up."

[39] The commission had been about to leave Iran March 6 after apparently giving up hope of seeing the hostages. At a final meeting that day with Ghotbzadeh on the way to the airport, the U.N. panel was said to have been asked to stay in Teheran for another two to three days to give the Revolutionary Council more time to arrange a meeting with the American hostages.

[40] **Khomeini Backs Militants; Commission Departs.** The U.N. commission suffered a severe setback March 10 when Khomeini gave full support to the militants holding the U.S. hostages. Khomeini imposed stringent conditions for the commission's proposed visit to the American captives, prompting the panel to leave the country and suspend issuing a report of its investigation.

[41] Asked by the ruling Revolutionary Council for clarification of the dispute, Khomeini overruled the efforts of Foreign Minister Ghotbzadeh and President Bani-Sadr to force the militants either to transfer the hostages to the council as they had promised or permit the commission to visit all of them.

[42] In his statement, Khomeini said the commission could only visit the embassy for the purpose of questioning those Americans accused by the militants of having been "involved in the crimes of the United States and Shah Mohammed Riza Pahlevi."

[43] Bani-Sadr was critical of both the militants and the Revolutionary Council. In an interview with the French newspaper *Le Monde* March 11, Bani-Sadr said, "Unfortunately, they [the militants] sometimes let themselves be influenced by certain political groups favorable to the U.S.S.R., such as the [Iranian] communist Tudeh Party, which wants to isolate Iran on the international scene." Bani-Sadr accused the Revolutionary Council of "weakness and indecision."

[44] President Carter had said March 8 that he would not yield to Teheran's demand that the U.S. apologize for its past actions in Iran to win release of the hostages. However, he said he was willing to issue an expression of concern to Iran.

[45] ***Commission Withholds Report***— U.N. Secretary General Waldheim said March 10 that the commission of inquiry would not issue its report on Iran's grievances against the deposed shah, although it had finished its "fact-finding" mission in Teheran. Waldheim inisited that the report was only half the panel's mandate. The other half provided for steps toward the release of the American hostages, including a visit with all of them, he said.

[46] In an interview with the *Washington Post* March 11, Waldheim praised the Iranian government's effort to resolve the crisis, but he regretted its failure to get the backing of the militants and Khomeini. "The whole thing boils down to this – the Iranian government couldn't deliver."

[47] **Renewed U.N. Hostage Mission Fails.** A member of the U.N. commission of inquiry, Adib Daoudy, June 16 ended a 27-day visit to Iran after fail-

ing in a renewed effort to end the stalemate over the 53 U.S. hostages. Iranian Foreign Minister Sadegh Ghotbzadeh told a news conference that neither Daoudy nor the entire commission had any "reason, as far as we are concerned, to return to Iran."

Rescue Mission

[48] **U.S. Rescue Mission Fails.** The U.S. April 24 launched an airborne attempt to free the American hostages in Teheran, but the mission was called off after one of the helicopters involved in the operation developed engine trouble in a staging area in the Iranian desert. Eight Americans were reported killed and several injured in the collision of two planes during the subsequent withdrawal of the U.S. force.

[49] The equipment breakdown was said to have occurred just as the rescue team was about to take off for the U.S. Embassy in Teheran.

[50] The White House announced the aborted rescue effort in the early morning hours of April 25. A further statement on the event was given by President Carter later in a nationally televised address.

[51] The White House statement gave few details. It said the President "has ordered the cancellation of an operation in Iran that was under way to prepare for a rescue of our hostages. The mission was terminated because of equipment failure." Carter added little additional information in his statement. He said planning for the rescue mission had started shortly after the U.S. Embassy had been seized in November 1979, "but for a number of reasons I waited until now to put those rescue plans into effect."

[52] An official report on the ill-fated U.S. mission to rescue the American hostages was first made public April 25 by Defense Secretary Harold Brown. A more detailed account was provided by Carter April 27 in a letter to House Speaker Thomas P. O'Neill (D, Mass.) and Sen. Warren G. Magnuson (D. Wash.), president pro-tempore of the Senate.

[53] The following is a composite description of the operation as given by Brown and Carter and subsequently by other U.S. officials:

[54] Carter gave the readiness order for the operation April 11 and the go-ahead signal April 14. Six U.S. C-130

White House Statement on Rescue Attempt in Iran

The President has ordered the cancellation of an operation in Iran that was under way to prepare for a rescue of our hostages.

The mission was terminated because of equipment failure. During the subsequent withdrawal, there was a collision between our aircraft on the ground at a remote desert location. There were no military hostilities but the President deeply regrets that eight American crewmen of the two aircraft were killed and others were injured in the accident.

Americans involved in the operation have now airlifted from Iran and those who were injured are being given medical treatment and are expected to recover.

This mission was not motivated by hostility toward Iran or the Iranian people and there were no Iranian casualties.

Preparations for this rescue mission were ordered for humanitarian reasons, to protect the national interests of this country and to alleviate international tensions.

The President accepts full responsibility for the decision to attempt the rescue.

The nation is deeply grateful to the brave men who were preparing to rescue the hostages.

The United States continues to hold the government of Iran responsible for the safety of the American hostages. The United States remains determined to obtain their safe release at the earliest possible date.

Body of U.S. serviceman lies in Iranian desert April 26 near wreckage of U.S. helicopter and transport plane.

Hercules transport planes and eight RH-53 helicopters "entered Iranian airspace" April 24. The transports carried 90 members of the commando team (dubbed "Operation Blue Light"). They also were loaded with communications-jamming equipment, helicopter fuel and 90 support personnel. The C-130s had taken off from Egypt and the helicopters left the aircraft carrier *Nimitz* in the Arabian Sea.

[55] All six C-130s but only six of the eight helicopters landed at the designated rendezvous at Dasht-i-Kavir (the Great Salt Desert), near the town of Tabas, 200 miles (320 kilometers) southwest of Teheran. The crews disembarked and began to prepare for the next phases of the operation.

[56] During the flight to the rendezvous point, two of the eight helicopters developed operating problems. One returned to the *Nimitz* and the second landed in the desert, where its crew was picked up by another helicopter and flown on to the landing site. One of the six helicopters that arrived at Dasht-i-Kavir "developed a serious hydraulic problem and was unable to continue with the mission." Since the plan called for a minimum of six helicopters to carry out the rescue, "it was determined not to proceed as planned." At this point, Carter said he had decided, on the recommendation of the force commander and his military advisers, to cancel the operation and ordered the American force to leave Iran.

[57] During the pullout, one helicopter collided with a C-130, which was about to take off, resulting in the death of eight men and injury to five others. All surviving members of the party then boarded the five C-130s and left; the remaining five helicopters were left behind as were the eight dead.

[58] Altogether, the U.S. force remained on the ground for about three hours. During the operation, the U.S. force at the landing site stopped a passing Iranian bus on a nearby road. Its 44 occupants were detained and

later released unharmed just before the Americans departed. In another brief encounter with Iranians, the Americans halted a passing truck by shooting into its headlights. The driver ran to a second truck accompanying his vehicle, which then escaped. Neither of the two incidents "affected the subsequent decision to terminate the mission."

[59] The eight dead Americans were identified as: Marine Cpl. George N. Holmes Jr., 22; Air Force Capt. Richard Bakke, 33; Marine Sgt. John Davis Harvey, 21; Marine Staff Sgt. Dewey L. Johnson, 31; Air Force Capt. Harold Lewis; Air Force Tech. Sgt. Joel C. Mayo, 34; Air Force Capt. Lynn D. McIntosh, 33, and Air Force Capt. Charles T. McMillan, 28.

[60] ***U.S., Iranian Agents Aided Mission***— An unknown number of U.S. paramilitary agents had infiltrated into Teheran earlier in the year to help prepare for the final phase of the rescue of the American hostages. Other agents involved were said to be Iranians opposed to the Khomeini government.

[61] The U.S. agents were reported to have purchased a warehouse in Teheran that was to serve as a staging area for the assault on the embassy. U.S. military officials said April 29 that the American agents, including Special Forces troops, had slipped out of Iran the same way they entered, by posing as European businessmen.

[62] ***Raid Leader Reports on Mission***—Col. Charles Beckwith, Army commander of the ground force of the ill-fated rescue mission, said May 1 he had personally suggested to the on-site commander that the operation be called off after three of the eight helicopters became disabled.

[63] At a meeting with reporters at the Pentagon, Beckwith denied reports

Participating in U.S. rescue mission were six C-130s and eight helicopters. The initial landing site was near Tabas, Iran. The C-130s reportedly came from a base in Egypt and the helicopters took off from the carrier *Nimitz* near the Strait of Hormuz. One of two helicopters that developed operating problems returned to the Nimitz; the second was forced down in Iran, abandoned and its crew picked up. A third helicopter became disabled at the landing site.

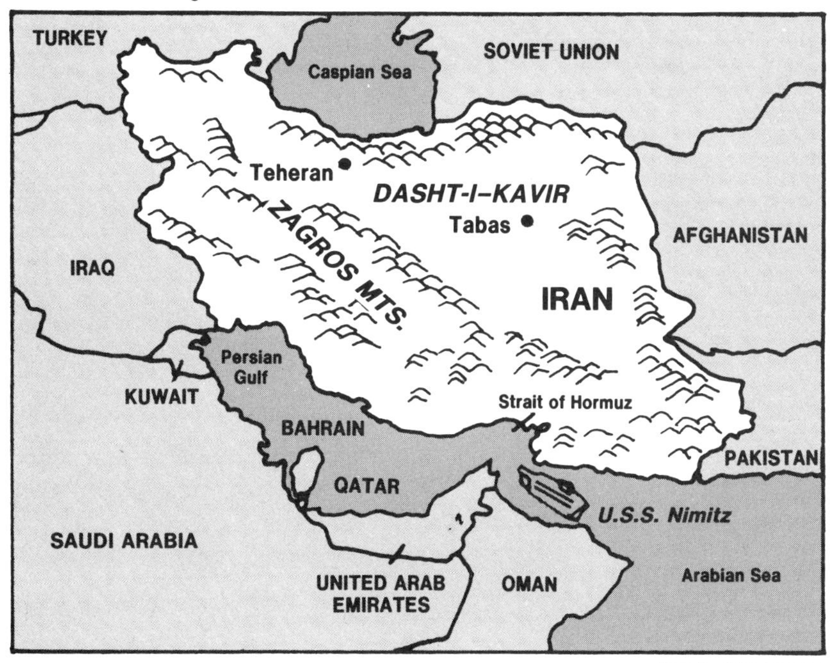

Map by Anita Fosman

Sen. Edmund Muskie of Maine (left), named as Secretary of State April 29. Cyrus Vance (right) resigned.

that he proposed that the mission go forward with the five remaining helicopters. The colonel said that in his discussions with the on-site commander, an Air Force colonel, he said he favored aborting the plan. The decision was then relayed to President Carter, who affirmed it.

[64] ***Carter Defends Mission***—All but a few questions at President Carter's news conference April 29 dealt with the aborted rescue mission. The President resolutely defended the effort and his decisions to go ahead with it and to call if off.

[65] He said he had "no doubt" that the attempt to rescue the 53 hostages was "the right decision." He had approved the undertaking after concluding that it would end the crisis if its goal of rescuing all of the hostages unharmed was achieved or even if it had ended "without complete success," he said.

[66] ***Hostages Moved***—The American hostages had been removed from the U.S. Embassy in Teheran to other cities in the country to prevent further rescue attempts, Iran state radio announced April 26. The militants who had been holding the embassy said that groups of the captives had been taken to such provincial cities as Qom and Tabriz.

[67] The Iranians holding the U.S. hostages announced July 6 that they had transferred some of them from three cities in Iran to "different parts of the country" because of U.S. threats against their lives. The three cities were identified as Arak, Mahallat and Nejafabad, about 250 miles (400 kilometers) south of Teheran. Three Americans were still being held in the Iranian Foreign Ministry in Teheran.

[68] **Secretary of State Vance Resigns.** Secretary of State Cyrus Vance resigned April 26 because he could not support the U.S. decision to attempt to rescue the hostages in Iran. President Carter April 28 accepted his resignation and the following day named Sen. Edmund S. Muskie (D, Me.) as his successor.

[69] Vance told the President he knew "how deeply you have pondered your decision on Iran." "I wish I could support you in it," he said. "But for the reasons we have discussed, I cannot." (Not since 1915—when William Jennings Bryan resigned rather than sign a note President Wilson had drafted in protest against the sinking of the *Lusitania* by Germany—had a secretary of state resigned as a result of a policy dispute with a president.)

[70] Vance was present at the White House ceremony when Muskie was named to the post. At a televised news conference the night of April 29, Carter explained that Vance's resignation was prompted by his opposition to any military action rather than disagreement with details of the particular mission undertaken. Earlier in the conference he had been asked whether his national security adviser, Zbigniew Brzezinski, was gaining influence at the expense of the secretary of state. "That's an erroneous report," Carter replied. "We have a very good and proper balance of advisers."

[71] The same issue came up at the White House ceremony that afternoon. "The President has left no doubt in my mind on that score," Muskie assured reporters. "I'll be the foreign policy spokesman."

[72] Muskie, 66, a member of the Senate since 1959, was a former Democratic vice presidential nominee and an unsuccessful presidential contender in 1972. He had a reputation as a dove, from his opposition to the Vietnam war.

[73] Vance resumed his law practice with the New York City firm of Simpson, Thacher & Bartlett June 11.

Post-Mission Developments

[74] **EC Nations Impose Limited Sanctions.** Foreign ministers of the nine-member European Community voted May 18 to impose limited economic sanctions against Iran, following a two-day meeting in Naples, Italy. The

EC move was a gesture of support for the U.S. effort to free the American hostages. The sanctions went into effect May 22.

[75] Under the adopted formula, EC member states would cancel all trade contracts signed with Iran since Nov. 4, 1979, when the U.S. Embassy in Teheran was seized. This fell far short of the EC's original decision April 22 to impose total economic sanctions, except for food and medicine. The more limited sanctions would permit billions of dollars in contracts negotiated before Nov. 4, 1979 to stand. An estimated $10 billion would have been lost to Western European countries trading with Iran if the deals contracted before Nov. 4 had been canceled.

[76] The French and West German cabinets approved the trade sanctions May 21. However, Britain had broken with the EC majority and decided May 19 to limit the trade ban to new contracts only. London's action was taken in the face of strong opposition in the British Parliament to the EC move. According to some Conservative and opposition MPs, sanctions would harm British traders, impede rather than promote the release of the hostages and be contrary to Britain's long-standing tradition against retroactive laws. (Current British trade with Iran totaled more than $100 million a month, nearly as high as before the Iranian revolution in February 1979.)

[77] **World Court Orders Iran to Free Hostages.** The International Court of Justice in The Hague May 24 handed down a six-point decision ordering Iran to release all 53 U.S. hostages, warning it not to put them on trial and holding Iran liable to reparations for its actions.

[78] The 15-member court voted unanimously on two points of the six-point decision – those dealing with the release of the American captives and the warning against trials. The Soviet member of the panel, Judge Platon D. Mazorov, voted against the four other points – those holding Iran responsible for violating international law and requiring it to make reparations to the U.S.

[79] The court's decision reviewed in detail all the actions taken by Iran, before, during and after the seizure of the American Embassy in Teheran. Its ruling was based on a case filed by the U.S. Nov. 29, 1979. The review also covered Iranian messages sent to the court Dec. 9, 1979 and March 16, stating that the court must examine what Teheran claimed was the U.S.'s oppressive record during its 25-year presence in Iran.

[80] **Clark Group Defies Travel Ban.** A delegation of 10 Americans headed by former Attorney General Ramsey Clark attended an Iranian-sponsored conference on U.S. "intervention in Iran" in Teheran June 2-5. The group went to Iran in defiance of a U.S. government travel ban to that country ordered by President Carter April 17.

[81] The Americans also ignored a warning May 30 by Attorney General Benjamin Civiletti that U.S. citizens who violated the travel ban faced "penalties of up to 10 years in prison and fines of up to $50,000 under the International Emergency Economic Powers Act."

[82] Among the other Americans in Clark's group: Dr. George Wald, corecipient of the 1967 Nobel Prize for medicine; Lennox S. Hinds, associate professor of criminal justice at Rutgers University; attorney Leonard Weinglass, defender of the Chicago Seven in 1969-70; Mary Anderson, lecturer in economics at the Massachusetts Institute of Technology; Kay Camp, president of Women's International League for Peace and Freedom, and John Gerassi, political science professor at Queens College in New York.

[83] President Carter told reporters June 10 he favored taking legal action against former Clark and the other Americans who defied his travel ban to Iran. However, no action was taken against them.

[84] **Hostage Crisis Called 'Insoluble'**—President Bani-Sadr had called the crisis over the American hostages "insoluble," it was reported June 28.

[85] Bani-Sadr, who previously had called for the release of the hostages, said "the hostage crisis is insoluble, the Americans feel that Iran is their private property."

[86] **U.S. Hostage Freed.** One of the 53 American hostages held in Iran was released July 11 because of deteriorating health. Richard I. Queen, 28, a vice consul at the Teheran embassy, was flown to Zurich, Switzerland July 12 for medical treatment. Queen was transferred later that day to a U.S. Air Force Base hospital in Wiesbaden, West Germany, where it was announced July 15 that he was suffering from multiple sclerosis. He left for the U.S. July 18.

[87] **U.S. Arrests, Frees Iranian Demonstrators.** Iranian demonstrators supporting and criticizing Ayatollah Khomeini clashed with each other and with U.S. citizens and police in Washington July 27, leading to the arrest of nearly 200 Iranians. The demonstrators were transferred to federal jails and deportation was considered, but ultimately federal authorities freed them Aug. 5.

Iranians release hostage Richard I. Queen, who arrived home in Lincolnville, Maine July 23. His mother, Jeanne, greets him.

[88] About 700 Iranian, Arab and American Moslems marched through downtown Washington, D.C. Aug. 8, expressing support for the Palestinians and for Iranian revolutionary leader Ayatollah Ruhollah Khomeini. Crowds gathered to yell insults and occasionally throw eggs and tomatoes at the marchers. Eight people were arrested, the *Washington Post* reported Aug. 9.

[89] Khomeini Aug. 6 had called for demonstrations around the world on Aug. 8, which was the last day of the Moslem holy month of Ramadan. In Rome, Iranians marched in St. Peter's Square in the Vatican. Police arrested 22. In Beirut, some two dozen Iranian students demonstrated in front of the U.S. Embassy, while in the Philippines, police in Manila broke up a protest by Iranian students and arrested 13. In London, 68 demonstrators were arrested Aug. 4 outside the U.S. Embassy.

[90] **U.S. Invasion Plan Reported.** Newspaper stories by syndicated columnist Jack Anderson published Aug. 16 asserted the Carter Administration had formulated a plan for a limited invasion of Iran, primarily aimed at freeing the 52 American hostages. White House spokesmen denied the charges.

[91] Anderson's allegation's were scheduled for publication in five articles beginning Aug. 18, but several newspapers printed excerpts from the columns two days early. Anderson wrote that a plan to invade Iran with "a powerful military force" had been prepared for the President. He indicated the invasion was set for mid-October, a few weeks before the November presidential election.

[92] White House officials Aug. 16

termed Anderson's charges "absolutely false," and said the suggestion that the Carter Administration would start hostilities "for political benefit is grotesque and totally irresponsible."

[93] **Khomeini Lists the Terms for Freeing Hostages.** Ayatollah Khomeini Sept. 12 listed four of six previously stated conditions for the release of the American hostages. In omitting the two other demands, a U.S. apology for its previous actions in Iran and a trial for the hostages, Khomeini raised speculation that Teheran was easing its terms for the freeing of the captives. However, other Iranian leaders later said the conditions for letting the hostages out remained unchanged.

[94] The four conditions stated by Khomeini: The U.S. turn over to Iran the property of the late Shah Mohammed Riza Pahlevi, cancel its claims against Iran, unblock Iran's assets frozen by President Carter and promise not to intervene politically or militarily in Iran.

[95] ***Muskie Sees Little Hope.*** Secretary of State Edmund Muskie Sept. 15 saw little hope for optimism.

[96] He told a news conference, "I think it is very important to be cautious in our reaction to statements coming out of Iran. We have read them before. As a matter of fact, we've been reading them over a period of weeks and months. It would be a mistake to raise expectations based on any specific statements."

[97] ***U.S. Apology Demanded***—The speaker of the Iranian parliament, Ayatollah Hasheimi Rafsanjani, Sept. 15 said Khomeini's failure to call for an American apology for its past actions in his Sept. 12 statement was an inadvertent ommission and that the demand remained a condition for the freeing of the hostages.

[98] Asked at a news conference whether the views of parliament, which was to debate the issue, coincided with those of Khomeini, Rafsanjani replied: "No. Definitely, there are more conditions. . . . What cannot be ignored is that America must comdemn its previous policy in Iran. This is a condition that parliament will insist on."

[99] ***Reagan's Reaction***—In Washington, Ronald Reagan said Sept. 13 that the U.S. should agree to most of Khomeini's demands for release of the American hostages.

[100] The U.S. "can and should" agree to free Iranian assets in this country, he said, and it should cancel claims against Iran and pledge nonintervention in Iran's domestic affairs. The fourth condition stated by Khomeini—return of assets of the late Shah Mohammed Riza Pahlevi—could not be met without "due process of law," Reagan said.

[101] President-elect Reagan denounced Iran in statements made Dec. 24 and 28. In his Dec. 28 remarks, Reagan assailed Iran's demands for billions of dollars in assets in exchange for the hostages. He said he was opposed to such a "down payment. No I don't think you pay ransom for people that have been kidnapped by barbarians."

[102] **Parliament Debates Hostage Issue.** The Iranian parliament met between Oct. 26 and 30 to discuss terms for the release of the American hostages but reached no conclusions.

[103] The Oct. 30 session at which the issue was to be debated in public was canceled for lack of quorum. (The previous meetings, held Oct. 26-27 and 29, were behind closed doors. No meeting was held Oct. 28 because of a Moslem holiday.) A majority of parliament's 228 members were said to favor a quick solution, but no more than 162, or 17 short of a quorum, showed up. Ayatollah Sadegh Khalkhali, the head of the Islamic courts and a member of parliament, rushed to the rostrum and denounced the absentees, accusing them of "blackmail" and "disruption." Khomeini had addressed the Oct. 29 session but made no mention of the hostage issue. His avoidance of the subject was regarded as an indication

of his willingness to permit the debate in parliament to run its course.

[104] ***Terms for Release Set***—The Iranian parliament Nov. 2 formally approved terms for the release of the 52 American hostages and agreed to negotiate the matter directly with the U.S. President Carter called the decision "a significant development."

[105] The terms were essentially the same as the four-point plan announced by Ayatollah Ruhollah Khomeini in September but contained clauses that added new details to Iran's demands. In general they called for a U.S. pledge not to interfere in Iran's internal affairs, the unfreezing of all Iranian assets in and outside the U.S., the dropping of economic sanctions against Iran and the return to Iran of the properties of the late shah.

[106] The following is the text of the four-point plan parliament approved by a voice vote:

[1]

Due to the interference of the United States in the internal affairs of Iran, political, military, economic, the U.S. must now make a firm commitment to avoid all direct or indirect political and military interference into the affairs of the Islamic Republic of Iran.

[2]

Unfreezing all Iranian assets in and outside the United States. These assets should be put at the disposal of the Iranian government in order that we may utilize them in every possible way. The presidential order of Nov. 14, 1979, that blocks our assets should be declared null and void by presidential order. Financial relations would continue as before this presidential order, with the removal of economic blocks and all consequent effects. All legal procedures must be taken to void the presidential order concerning the confiscation of Iranian properties by the United States courts. Guaranteeing the security and free transfer of these properties must be made. No private U.S. citizen or resident of the U.S. may make a claim against these properties.

[3]

Cancellation and annulment of economic and financial actions and measures against the Islamic Republic of Iran must be made. Legal procedures should be implemented to cancel and annul all claims against Iran. These claims might be presented by an official or unofficial citizen, an American company or the American government. In the case of any type of claim made against Iran or any Iranian citizen in any court of the United States in connection with the Islamic revolution of Iran and the seizure of the nest of spies and the arrest of U.S. citizens in Iran, the U.S. government should guarantee to answer and pay any consequent damage or expenses caused by the conviction of Iran or any Iranian citizen.

[4]

The properties of the deceased shah must be returned. The United States government should officially recognize the right of the Iranian government to the deceased shah's wealth and that of his close relatives. According to Iranian law, these properties belong to the Iranian nation and Iran should be able to control them. The President of the United States should issue a proclamation to this effect, and take all legal and administrative actions necessary to transfer these properties to Iran.

[107] A seven-member parliamentary commission, whose recommendations were approved by the full parliament, said in its report that the U.S. must not only accept the conditons but must carry them out before the hostages could be set free. If the conditions were not fulfilled all at once, the hostages should be released in stages as each term was complied with, the commission suggested.

[108] ***Algeria Acts as Go-Between***—A team of U.S. officials, led by Deputy Secretary of State Warren Christopher, arrived in Algiers, Algeria Nov. 10 with a detailed and secret response to the four demands made by the Iranian parliament for releasing the U.S. hostages. Algeria, which was acting as the intermediary between the two countries, delivered the U.S. response to Iranian officials in Teheran Nov. 12.

[109] U.S. officials said that the secret U.S. response was phrased in a "positive tone" and sought to go as far as it could, within the framework of U.S. law, toward meeting the Iranian demands. A U.S. official said that the response did not "reject anything out of hand," but rather described the limits on the U.S. government in meeting the Iranian demands.

[110] Reportedly, the U.S. did not see any problems in complying with two of the demands, those requiring a U.S. pledge not to interfere in Iranian affairs and that Iranian assets in the U.S. be unfrozen. However, the note reportedly indicated the U.S. might not have the legal powers to meet the other two demands: that claims against Iran by U.S. individuals and organizations be dropped and that the property of the late shah and his near relatives be handed over to Iran. (The issue of claims against Iran was tied up with those of Iranian assets in the U.S., since legal actions seeking damages from Iran asked that the Iranian assets in the U.S. be attached to pay the damages.)

[111] **U.S. Response Criticized.**The U.S. response to Iran's terms for freeing the hostages was described Nov. 22 by Iranian Premier Mohammed Ali Rajai's office as "neither explicit nor clear."

[112] The U.S. reply had not been made public. But the U.S. State Department Nov. 20 said that the U.S. had accepted Teheran's four conditions "in principle as a basis for resolution of the crisis." The department, however, stressed that both sides were still in disagreement on the details of the package currently being discussed.

[113] **Teheran Demands $24 billion.** Iran Dec. 19 demanded $24 billion of its frozen assets and the wealth of the late shah in exchange for the release of the American hostages. The U.S. rejected the demands as excessive.

[114] The Iranian demands were delivered to Washington by the Algerian intermediaries. A text of the demands was made public by Teheran Dec. 21. Iran, calling its terms final, demanded that the U.S. deposit $10 billion in identified Iranian assets in the Central Bank of Algeria, another $4 billion as a guarantee against assets that were yet to be identified and $10 billion in the form of a one-year bond against identification and recovery of the shah's property in the U.S. The frozen assets were in the hands of a number of American banks, other companies and the U.S. government. (There were more than 300 pending lawsuits brought by private U.S. individuals and companies making claims on the Iranian assets.)

Government Affairs

[115] **Bani-Sadr Elected President.** Iranian Finance Minister Abolhassan Bani-Sadr was elected Iran's first president in nationwide balloting Jan. 25.

[116] According to the official results announced Jan. 28, Bani-Sadr received 10,709,330 votes (75%), defeating six other official candidates. A handful of votes were cast for about 60 unofficial candidates.

"DOWN WITH REAGAN," "LONG LIVE KHOMEINI" were signs at the gates to U.S. Embassy in Teheran Dec. 3.

[117] Bani-Sadr was named head of the ruling Revolutionary Council Feb. 7 and supreme commander of the armed forces Feb. 19.

[118] **Parliament Convenes.** Iran's new parliament convened in Teheran May 28. Of the 241 seats of the 270-seat legislature filled thus far, about 130 were controlled by the fundamentalist Islamic Republican Party and its supporters. Elections for parliament had been held March 14 and May 9.

[119] **Khomeini: Country Faces 'Chaos.'** Ayatollah Khomeini June 10 warned that Iran faced "chaos" because of differences between competing political forces in the country.

[120] Khomeini said the principal danger to stability was the choice of premier and the American hostages. The opposing forces in this dispute were the supporters of President Abolhassan Bani-Sadr and the fundamentalist Islamic Republic Party. The party favored holding espionage trials for the hostages, while Bani-Sadr opposed the idea.

[121] **Plot Smashed.** The Iranian government announced July 10 that it had smashed a plot by the military to overthrow the government. About 300 alleged conspirators were arrested. At least seven persons were killed in the attempted uprising. The dissident forces were said by the government to have planned to restore exiled former Premier Shahpur Bakhtiar to power.

[122] **Premier Named.** Parliament Aug. 11 approved the appointment of Education Minister Mohammed Ali Rajai as premier.

[123] **Cabinet Approved In Part.** The Iranian parliament Sept. 10 approved 14 of the 21 Cabinet members appointed by Premier Mohammed Ali Rajai. Seven other posts were left temporarily vacant because President Bani-Sadr had refused to give his required assent.

[124] Bani-Sadr refused to agree to the seven others because of doubts about their qualifications. The ministries he would not certify were foreign, economics and finance, planning and

Abolhassan Bani-Sadr was elected president of Iran Jan. 25.

budget, labor and social affairs, oil and education and commerce. The president was known to have objected to the naming of journalist Hussein Moussavi as foreign minister to succeed Sadegh Gbotbzadeh. Moussavi was a member of the fundamentalist Islamic Republican Party and edited its newspaper, *Islamic Republic.*

[125] Parliament's approval of the 14 Cabinet members led to the dissolution Sept. 11 of the Revolutionary Council, which had ruled Iran since the ouster of the monarchy in 1979.

[126] **Ghotbzadeh Arrested, Released.** Former Foreign Minister Sadegh Ghotbzadeh was arrested in Teheran Nov. 7 by Iranian Revolutionary Guards, but released Nov. 10 by Khomeini's order.

[127] Ghotbzadeh was seized after he criticized the state broadcasting system, saying that it was falling under the censorship of Islamic fundamentalists and charging that unauthorized persons were imposing their views on it. He made his comments on Teheran television's local second channel, which had affiliated itself with President Bani-Sadr.

[128] Ghotbzadeh's arrest was ordered by Teheran Public Prosecutor Assadollah Lajevardi. The action unleashed a storm of protest from moderates, including Bani-Sadr and former Premier Mehdi Bazargan. Bani-Sadr contended that Lajevardi had acted improperly in ordering the arrest and charged that Islamic fundamentalists were seeking to censor the presidency. Bazargan criticized the arrest, asking, "When a militant of long record is arrested so simply and scandalously and insulted, what honor will be left for Islam, the revolution and Iran."

The Shah

[129] **Panama Denies Arrest of Shah.** Panama Jan. 23 denied an Iranian claim that Shah Mohammed Riza Pahlevi was under house arrest. A cablegram sent to Iran by President Aristedes Royo Sanchez also said the deposed Iranian monarch "remains under the care of the security authorities of Panama."

[130] The Panamanian statements were in response to an assertion earlier Jan. 23 by Foreign Minister Sadegh Ghotbzadeh that Royo had informed him by telephone that the shah had been arrested and was being held for return to Iran to stand trial.

[131] **Shah Leaves Panama for Egypt.** The deposed shah March 23 left his exile in Panama and arrived the following day in Cairo, where Egyptian President Anwar Sadat granted him permanent asylum. The former Iranian monarch's departure was seen as complicating efforts to obtain the release of the American hostages in Teheran.

[132] The shah left his home on Contadora island as Iran prepared to submit formal papers to the Panamanian government March 24 for his extradition to stand trial in Teheran.

[133] White House Chief of Staff

Iranian woman, wearing traditional chador, looks over parliamentary election campaign posters in Teheran March 13.

Hamilton Jordan had flown to Panama March 21 to persuade the shah not to leave the country. He sought to assure him that a dispute between American and Panamanian doctors over treatment of his medical problems had been resolved, and that it was doubtful that Panama would grant Iran its request for extradition. (The dispute between the U.S. and Panamanian doctors concerned an alleged remark by an aide to the shah casting aspersion on Panama's ability to provide the shah with proper medical attention.)

[134] Iranian Foreign Minister Sadegh Ghotbzadeh March 22 had accused former Secretary of State Henry Kissinger and Chase Manhattan Bank head David Rockefeller of planning to block Iran's extradition proceedings against the shah. He offered no evidence to support his charges that both men were plotting to take the shah out of Panama before the March 24 filing deadline.

[135] The shah underwent surgery in Cairo March 28 to remove his enlarged spleen. The operation was performed by a team of U.S. and Egyptian surgeons headed by Dr. Michael DeBakey, a Houston heart surgeon.

[136] The former monarch was reported to be in good condition following the surgery. He was taken off the intensive care list three days later. Doctors reported March 31 that they had found signs of cancer in the former shah's liver. He would go back to taking anticancer drugs, they said.

[137] The ex-shah's presence in Egypt prompted violent demonstrations March 28 and 31 by university students in Asyut, 235 miles (390 kilometers) south of Cairo. Police used tear gas to disperse the protesters, and several students were reported injured. Protests against the shah's arrival in Egypt also took place at Cairo University March 25.

[138] **Shah Dies.** The shah died July 27 in an Egyptian military hospital near Cairo. Doctors attributed his death to the effects of a lymphatic cancer. He was 60 years old.

Egyptian President Anwar Sadat (left) welcomes exiled shah (right) to Cairo. Shah died July 27.

[139] A state funeral for the shah was held in Cairo July 29. With Egyptian President Anwar Sadat leading the procession, a cortege bore the shah's coffin to the Al Rifai Mosque, where a tomb was prepared in a mausoleum containing Egypt's two last kings. The shah's father, Riza Khan, had been buried briefly in the same mosque in World War II before the return of his body to a shrine in Iran. The only prominent foreigners to attend the funeral were former President Richard Nixon and former King Constantine of Greece.

[140] **Shah's Son Takes Title.** Crown Prince Riza, the eldest son of the late shah, Oct. 31 laid claim to his father's throne. In ceremonies held in Kubbeh Palace in Cairo on his 20th birthday, the prince assumed the title of Shah Riza II.

Executions and Assassinations

[141] **Executions Renewed.** After several months in which large-scale executions were abandoned, close to 60 persons were executed in Iran May 21-26. Over half were accused of crimes related to drug trafficking, while others were charged with taking part in insurrection movements in Iran's provinces.

[142] Controversial religious judge Sadegh Khalkhali, who had gained notoriety by publicly displaying the charred remains of U.S. servicemen who died in the failed rescue mission, started off the new batch of executions when he ordered 20 alleged drug dealers put to death May 21.

[143] The next day, two leaders of the proscribed Moslem People's Republican Party of Azerbaijan were executed. They were accused of taking part in the demonstrations seeking more home rule for the Turkish-speaking provinces. Also on May 22, five individuals charged with sabotaging an oil pipeline in Khuzistan were executed.

[144] Seventeen persons had been executed July 3 for drug dealing, sexual offenses and murder. In the southwest town of Kerman, four persons convicted of sexual offenses were buried up to their chests and stoned to death.

[145] Iranian firing squads July 14 executed 26 persons. Another 15 were put to death July 20-21. One of those executed July 14 was Lt. Gen. Hushang Hatam, who had been convicted of widespread killings during the final days of Shah Mohammed Riza Pahlevi's rule. Hatam had served as deputy chief of staff.

[146] **Bakhtiar Escapes Assassination.** Three armed men July 18 burst into the Paris home of former Premier Shahpur Bakhtiar in an attempt to assassinate him. He escaped unhurt, but two other persons were killed and four wounded.

[147] Another exiled opponent of the Iranian government, Ali Akbar Tabatabai, was shot to death July 22 by an unknown assailant at his home in Bethesda, Md.

[148] **Rights Group Scores Execu-**

tions. Amnesty International said Aug. 28 that 1,000 persons, and possibly as many as 1,200, had been executed in Iran during the first 18 months of the Islamic revolution.

[149] In a letter sent to Premier Mohammed Ali Rajai, the London-based human-rights group pleaded for an end to the executions and the jailing of persons for their beliefs and origins. The letter recalled Amnesty's similar protests to Iran prior to the revolution when it had "appealed time and time again to the late shah for a stop to the executions, torture and the imprisonment of prisoners of conscience."

[150] The Amnesty statement came within hours of a Teheran radio report that seven persons had been executed by firing squad in Ahwaz for their alleged role in the July plot to overthrow the government. Another 11 convicted plotters were executed Aug. 30 in Teheran.

See also Immigration [1-2]; Iraq [1-48]

IRAQ

[1] Border clashes erupted into a major war between Iraq and Iran in September 1980. Iraqi forces advanced into Iran's oil-producing province of Khuzistan and besieged the refinery center of Abadan. Both the U.S. and the Soviet Union declared their neutrality in the conflict. However, the U.S. stressed the necessity of maintaining the freedom of oil shipments through the Persian Gulf.

[2] **Armies on Full Alert.** Iran and Iraq placed their armies on full alert April 7 as tensions increased over a long-standing border dispute between the two countries. The latest crisis was marked by a series of frontier clashes and the ouster of diplomatic representatives. At the same time, 7,000 Iranians moved back to their country after being expelled from Iraq.

[3] Iranian-Iraqi tensions hightened April 8 as Ayatollah Khomeini appealed to the Iraqi army and people to overthrow the government of President Saddam Hussein.

[4] Iranian Foreign Minister Sadegh Ghotbzadeh said, "We have decided to overthrow the Baathist regime of Iraq. Any country supporting America in practice must face action similar to the one Iran has taken against America." (Although the U.S. had no diplomatic relations with Iraq, trade between the two nations had been increasing.)

[5] Baghdad was permitting armed Iranian exiles in Iraq to form military groups aimed at overthrowing Khomeini's government, U.S. officials said April 9. The anti-Khomeini groups were said to be affiliated with supporters of former Iranian Premier Shahpur Bakhtiar, who left Iran at the time of the Islamic revolution and now lived in Paris.

[6] **Border Clashes.** Iranian and Iraqi forces clashed along their mutual border between Sept. 6 and 11.

[7] **Baghdad Cancels Border Pact.** Iraqi President Saddam Hussein Sept. 17 declared that his country's 1975 border agreement with Iran was "null and void." The proclamation was made amid intensified frontier clashes between the two countries.

[8] In an address to the National Assembly (parliament), Hussein charged that since the ouster of Iran's monarchy in 1979, the country's Islamic rulers had been "violating good-neighborly relations." The Shatt al-Arab, the estuary that separated the two countries, was "from here on in . . . totally Iraqi and Arab," the president said.

[9] Iranian President Abolhassan Bani-Sadr Sept. 17 acknowledged that Iran had not completely fulfilled the terms of the border treaty. Agence France-Presse quoted him as saying in an interview: "Who signed the agreement? Even the shah's regime did not apply it, and furthermore, from the start Iraq had adopted a hostile attitude toward the Islamic revolution." Bani-Sadr charged that Iraq was planning a "massive attack" against Iran's oil-rich

Khuzestan province.

[10] Teheran Radio Sept. 13 quoted the governor of the Iranian border town of Qasr-i-Shirin as saying that Iranian troops had "recovered three Iranian frontier outposts which had been taken by Iraq forces." Iraq Sept. 17 claimed its forces had repulsed Iranian attempts to retake positions occupied by Baghdad's troops in fighting the previous week.

[11] **Dispute Erupts into Open Warfare.** The simmering border dispute between Iraq and Iran flared into open warfare Sept. 22 as both sides launched heavy attacks against each other's territory with planes and heavy artillery. The targets included major cities and oil fields of both countries.

[12] On the diplomatic front, the United Nations Security Council Sept. 23 appealed to Iran and Iraq to stop the fighting. President Carter pledged that the U.S. would remain neutral in the conflict. While blaming U.S. policy for the crisis, the Soviet Union also avowed its neutrality. The U.S. emphasized the need for continued shipment of oil through the gulf.

[13] After weeks of sporadic clashes along the Iraqi-Iranian border, fighting stepped up Sept. 20. Assuming personal control of his country's military operations, Iranian President Bani-Sadr ordered a call-up of several thousand military reservists. Further escalation of the conflict was reflected in an Iraqi claim Sept. 21 that its forces had shot down an Iranian F-4 Phantom jet fighter and sunk eight Iranian gun-boats in the Shatt al-Arab.

[14] ***Conflict of Major Proportions***—The fighting assumed major proportions Sept. 22 as Iraqi planes struck 10 Iranian airfields, including Teheran's. The principal targets of the air strikes were an air base and oil refinery at Kermanshah. A blackout was imposed in Teheran.

[15] Among the other targets hit by Iraqi planes were the Iranian cities of Shiraz, Dizful and Ahwaz in Khuzistan

Major warfare erupted between Iran and Iraq. Both sides carried out air strikes against each other's oil centers at Abadan, Kirkuk, Basra and Mosul, forcing a halt to oil shipments. Iraqi troops pushed into Iran, capturing Qasr-i-Shirin and surrounding the major oil production center at Abadan. Iran threatened to block the strategic Strait of Hormuz.

In Dizful, Iran Oct. 13, a woman sits disconsolately amid ruins of her home destroyed by Iraqi rocket attack.

and the Omid base near the oilfield town of Agha Jari. Iraq claimed the raids caused extensive damage and loss of life.

[16] The hostilities widened further Sept. 23 as Iraqi planes attacked Iran's oil refineries at Abadan and Iraqi troops crossed into Iran at several points, surrounding Abadan and the neighboring port of Khurramshahr. The Abadan strike set oil and gas tanks ablaze. A second Iraqi crossing into Iran occurred 300 miles (480 kilometers) north of Abadan and led to the Iraqi capture of Qasr-i-Shirin and the nearby Sumar district.

[17] Iranian planes struck deep into Iraq, hitting the center of Baghdad three times. The capital's military and civilian airports were bombed. Iranian planes also attacked the northern Iraqi oil centers of Kirkuk and Mosul and petrochemical complexes near Basra and at Zubair, killing an estimated 50 persons, according to Iraqi accounts. Twenty-nine of the fatalities occurred at Zubair and included two British and four American workers at the facility.

[18] Iraq and Iran Sept. 24 again carried out air attacks against each other's oil installations. One of the principal Iranian targets was Kharg Island, the oil-loading terminal in the Persian Gulf. The installation was set afire, forcing Iran to halt shipments. Iraq temporarily stopped the shipment of oil as its installations at Basra, Kirkuk and Mosul came under Iranian air strikes.

[19] ***U.S. Stresses Oil Access***—President Carter Sept. 24 said the U.S. was consulting with other nations on plans to assure the continued shipment of oil through the Persian Gulf.

[20] Speaking to newsmen after a meeting of the National Security Council, Carter said the oil cutoff from Iran and Iraq posed no current danger of shortages or undue high prices because of inventories in the major consuming countries remained high. However, "a total suspension of oil exports from the other nations who ship through the Persian Gulf would create a serious threat to the world's supplies and consequently a threat to the economic

health of all nations," the President warned.

[21] "Freedom of navigation in the Persian Gulf is of primary importance to the whole international community," Carter stressed. "It is imperative that there is no infringement of that freedom of passage of ships to and from" the waterway, he added. The U.S., directly or indirectly, received about 100,000 barrels of oil a day from Iraq.

[22] **Iran Rejects Peace Bids.** As the war between Iraq and Iran intensified Sept. 25-Oct. 1, international attempts were undertaken to end the conflict. The principal moves included a new U.S. Security Council call for an end to the fighting and mediation, and the dispatch of an Islamic mission to Teheran and Baghdad. Iraq offered to end its military operations on certain conditions. Iran rejected all of these peace bids and vowed to continue the struggle.

[23] In the fighting, Iraqi forces advanced 50 miles into Iran and besieged the vital Khuzistan province centers of Abadan, Ahwaz and Khurramshahr. Oil installations of both nations continued to come under heavy air attack, leading Iraq to curtail drastically its petroleum exports. Iran pledged to keep open the strategic Strait of Hormuz at the entrance to the Persian Gulf. Saudi Arabia's fears of possible Iranian air strikes against its oil installations prompted it to ask the U.S. for air defense assistance. The request was granted and four American radar planes arrived in Saudi Arabia Oct. 1. The aircraft, AWACS (Airborne Warning and Control Systems), were accompanied by 300 personnel.

[24] The U.S. was sending more defense equipment to Saudi Arabia, Defense Secretary Harold Brown disclosed Oct. 5. Brown said the U.S. was dispatching a mobile ground radar station and another 96 airmen to Saudi Arabia to strengthen its air defenses. The U.S. Oct. 7 offered other Perisan Gulf states similar assistance if they stayed out of the Iranian-Iraqi war.

[25] **Jordan Aids Iraq.** Jordan became the first Arab state to openly support Iraq in its war with Iran. The support, in the form of material assistance, followed a visit to Baghdad Oct. 4-5 by King Hussein of Jordan.

[26] After the monarch's return to Amman, the Jordanian government Oct. 6 ordered mobilization of all transport vehicles in the country to carry food and supplies to Iraq, which bordered Jordan. Jordan made available its Red Sea port of Aqaba (directly opposite the Israeli port of Eilat) to ships of other nations carrying military equipment and other material for Iraq. The foreign vessels, prevented by the fighting from entering Iraqi ports, were diverted to Aqaba. These included vessels from the Soviet Union, East European countries, India and Lebanon. Soviet weapons stored in South Yemen and Ethiopia were being sent to Iraq via Aqaba, the Associated press reported Oct. 6

[27] ***Syria Blames Iraq for War***—Syria Oct. 7 assailed Iraq for its war on Iran, becoming the first Arab nation to take sides against Baghdad in the conflict.

[28] An article in the newspaper of Syria's ruling Arab Baath Socialist Party described Iraqi President Saddam Hussein as "an agent of imperialism and reaction who wants to play the role of the shah" as the predominant power in the Persian Gulf.

[29] Libyan leader Col. Muammer el-Qaddafi Oct. 10 declared his country's support for Iran in its war with Iraq.

[30] ***Iran Gets Arms from North Korea***—U.S. Treasury Secretary G. William Miller Oct. 8 disclosed that Iran had been purchasing military and medical supplied from North Korea in recent days and using military cargo planes to bring the material to Teheran.

[31] **Gulf Nations to Increase Oil Exports.** Saudi Arabia's oil minister, Sheik Ahmed Zaki Yamani, said Oct. 5

Oil pipelines afire Oct. 16 near the Abadan-Teheran highway.

that major oil-producing states in the Persian Gulf would boost their oil exports to offset losses caused by the war between Iraq and Iran.

[32] A further report Oct. 6 from Saudi Arabia confirmed that Saudi Arabia, Kuwait and the United Arab Emirates had jointly agreed to increase their oil exports to offset the estimated 2.9 million barrels of oil a day lost to the world's oil markets as a result of the stoppage of Iran and Iraq's oil exports. No exact figures on how much the three countries would increase their production were given. Saudi Arabia was currently producing 9.5 million barrels a day. The country had facilities capable of producing 10.5 million barrels a day. Kuwait produced 1.5 million barrels a day, and the UAE 1.7 million.

[33] **Iraqi Drive to Capture Abadan.** Iraqi forces Oct. 10 launched a major drive to capture Abadan. By Oct. 16 they had advanced to within one mile of the burning Iranian oil-refinery center. Its defenders began digging trenches in the streets "in preparation for hand-to-hand fighting," the Iranian press agency said.

[34] At the same time, heavy combat continued in Khurramshahr, north of Abadan, whose northern port area had been taken by Iraqi troops earlier in the week. The capture of Khurramshahr and Abadan would achieve Iraq's aim of gaining full control of the Shatt al-Arab, which formed the border between the two countries at the head of the Persian Gulf.

[35] The push for Abadan started with the Iraqis throwing pontoon bridges across the Karun River in the Shatt al-Arab area. On Oct. 11 a "big Iraqi force" of tanks and troops crossed the river and started moving south from Khurramshahr toward Abadan, Baghdad military sources said.

[36] **U.S. Sends Cruiser to Gulf.** The U.S. Defense Department announced Oct. 11 that it was dispatching a guided-missile cruiser to the Persian Gulf.

[37] The ship, a department spokesman

said, would replace a destroyer so that the total number of U.S. naval vessels in the Gulf would remain at five. The U.S. also was sending two KC-135 aerial refueling tanker planes to Saudi Arabia to enable the AWACS planes sent earlier by the U.S. to stay in the air longer.

[38] **Iran Ends U.N. Boycott.** Iran Oct. 15 ended its boycott of the United Nations Security Council by sending its representative to attend a meeting on the war.

[39] Iran had been staying away from council meetings since its revolution in February 1979.

[40] At the Oct. 15 session, Iraqi Foreign Minister Saadun Hamadi called his country's invasion of Iran an act of "self-defense." He accused Iran and its leader, Ayatollah Khomeini, of attempting to export the Iranian revolution "by inciting religious, sectarian strife."

[41] Addressing the Security Council, Iranian Premier Mohammed al Rajai Oct. 17 ruled out any truce in his country's war with Iraq and charged that Iraq's invasion of Iran was inspired by the U.S.

[42] **Iraq Says Khuzistan Cut Off.** Iraq said Oct. 22 that its military forces had isolated Iran's oil-rich province of Khuzistan from the rest of the country.

[43] The statement followed an Iraqi leader's announcement Oct. 21 that his country's "ultimate aim" was to capture Iran's oil fields and cities in Khuzistan, the focus of the war, and hold them until Teheran agreed to negotiate. On the military front, fighting continued through Oct. 22 for Abadan and Khurramshahr, Iraq's two principal targets in Khuzistan. House-to-house combat raged inside Khurramshahr and Iraqi troops maintained a tight hold around Abadan although Iranian defenders mounted heavy resistance.

[44] Iraq Oct. 24 claimed its forces that day had captured Khurramshahr.

[45] Iraqi forces Nov. 14 launched a major drive to capture Susangird, the Iranian city northwest of Ahwaz, the capital of Khuzistan province. Heavy casualties were suffered by both sides in fighting for the city through Nov. 18.

[46] **Iran's Oil Minister Captured.** Iranian Oil Minister Mohammed Jawad Baqir Tunguyan and five senior aides were captured by Iraqi troops Oct. 31 near Abadan.

[47] **Iran Announces Austerity Measures.** Shortages caused by the war prompted Iran Nov. 9 to announce a series of austerity measures. Gasoline prices for private cars would be tripled starting Nov. 15, sugar would be rationed effective Nov. 22 and electricity would be conserved.

[48] **Fighting Spreads to Kurdistan.** Iraq extended its war with Iran by invading Kurdistan province, Iraqi President Saddam Hussein announced Dec. 25. As a result, the war front now stretched 550 miles (880 kilometers), nearly the entire length of the Iranian-Iraqi border.

See also Armaments (International) [2]; Carter, Jimmy [8]; Human Rights [9]

IRELAND, Northern (Ulster)

[1] **Stormont Talks.** The government-sponsored talks on Northern Ireland's future system of government began as scheduled Jan. 7 at Stormont, Belfast, with three of Northern Ireland's four main political parties in attendance. The discussions quickly bogged down as the different parties appeared committed to contradictory objectives.

[2] The largest Protestant-based party – the Official Unionists, headed by James Molyneaux – boycotted the conference. The three parties attending it were: the largly Catholic Social Democratic and Labor Party (SDLP) headed by John Hume; the Protestant Ulster Democratic and Unionist Party, led by Rev. Ian Paisley, and the nonsectarian Alliance Party, headed by Oliver Napier.

[3] Part of the difficulty at the Stormont conference arose from the question of whether Northern Ireland's relations to the Republic of Ireland should be made a topic of discussion. The SDLP–which backed eventual unification with the republic–pressed for discussion of the "Irish dimension," while Paisley's Unionist Party firmly opposed "any discussion whatsoever on ways and means to bring about a united Ireland."

[4] Another point of controversy at the talks was whether, in whatever form of local government Northern Ireland adopted, a guarantee should be included requiring the Protestant majority to share the power with the Catholic minority. The SDLP favored such a guarantee; Paisley's party was opposed to it.

[5] The government decided March 19 to adjourn the Stormont talks. The talks had been unable to resolve a deadlock over power-sharing. SDLP representatives said they saw no point in continuing to meet in the absense of progress on this issue.

[6] **Home Rule Plan.** The British government July 2 released a "white paper" sketching out a governmental structure for restoring a measure of local rule to Northern Ireland. For the past six years, Northern Ireland had been ruled directly from London.

[7] The proposal called for a single-chamber 80-member legislature, elected by proportional representation. On the controversial issue of executive power, Britain set forth two alternatives:

■ Under one system, any party obtaining a certain percentage of the popular vote would be guaranteed a place in the executive (i.e., a party winning 25% of the popular vote would get a quarter of the executive). In effect, this was equivalent to the power-sharing arrangement tried in 1973, which the Protestants had rejected.

■ The other option allowed a majority party to form an executive by itself. The executive, however, would be supplemented by a second body called a Council of the Assembly, made up of chairmen and deputy chairmen of departmental committees. These offices (and hence the council) would be divided evenly between those supporting the executive and those opposing it. For a measure to gain approval in the council, it would need 50% plus one vote. The council would have the power to delay and possibly even block legislation put forward by the executive.

[8] Northern Ireland's sectarian division–a Protestant majority and Catholic minority–made the question of how the executive would be formed a controversial one. The Protestants by and large insisted that the governmental framework not permit the wishes of the majority to be frustrated by a minority. The Catholics insisted on guarantees that home rule would not mean a return to a pattern of oppression by the majority.

[9] The white paper, titled "Proposals for Further Discussion," called for the government in Northern Ireland to have jurisdiction over such areas as education, housing, employment, agriculture, commerce, and the environment. Law and order, finance and foreign affairs would remain under the control of the national government in London.

[10] ***Reaction***—Political leaders in Northern Ireland were guarded in their initial response to the government's proposals, but generallly refrained from outright condemnation. Protestant leaders, however, voiced opposition to any arrangement resembling power-sharing.

[11] Rev. Ian Paisley, head of the Protestant Democratic Unionist Party, remarked July 2 that "quite a bit of this document is constructive." Paisley labeled as "totally unworkable" the proposed scheme for an executive that guaranteed a role in the body to all parties gaining a certain percentage of the vote.

[12] **New Talks.** Humphrey Atkins, secretary of state for Northern Ireland, met Sept. 22 with Ian Paisley for discussions of how to restore at least some local rule to Northern Ireland. Atkins planned to meet separately with leaders of the other main political groups in the province.

[13] **Violence Continues.** The new year brought no respite to the sectarian voilence in Northern Ireland. Two British soldiers were shot dead Jan. 1 by members of their own unit who had mistaken them for Irish guerrillas. The shooting occurred at Tullydonnell, near south Armagh's border with the Irish Republic.

[14] Other developments related to the conflict included:

■ Anne Maguire, the mother of the three children whose deaths prompted the formation of the Community of Peace People, committed suicide Jan. 21. The peace movement was awarded the 1976 Nobel Peace Prize.

■ One youth was killed and two others wounded March 31 when they tried to crash a car through a checkpoint manned by British troops.

■ Members of the Provisional Irish Republican Army machine-gunned to death one policemen and wounded three others in Belfast April 9. The gunmen had situated themselves in a house, where they held a woman and child captive overnight, and then lured police into firing range by a telephone call reporting a break-in.

■ A Protestant politican was shot dead June 4 in his car a few miles from his home at Carnlough. The politician, John Turnley, was one of the few Protestants to favor unification of Northern Ireland with the Irish Republic; police said they suspected the murder was the work of terrorists who wanted Northern Ireland to remain under British control.

■ A car bomb exploded in June 21 in the center of the village of Fintona in co Tyrone, damaging scores of shops in and homes. There were no casualties; residents of the area had been evacuated minutes before the explosion went off.

■ Two policemen in the Republic of Ireland were killed July 7 while giving chase to bankrobbers thought to belong to the Irish National Liberation Army, a terrorist organization that sought to have Northern Ireland unified with the republic. One of the six-man gang of robbers was wounded and captured.

■ Four persons were slain during the weekend of Aug. 9-10 as protests and unrest marked the ninth anniversary of the introduction of internment without trial.

[15] The controversial statute had been abandoned earlier in 1980, but a protest demonstration organized by the Provisional Sinn Fein, the political wing of the Irish Republican Army, still went forward. A march was held in the predominantly Catholic area of West Belfast, and a crowd of about 2,000 gathered to hear speeches calling for the withdrawal of British forces from Northern Ireland and describing conditions of IRA prisoners held in the Maze and Armagh prisons.

■ Two men, both members of the Irish Republican Socialist Party, were murdered by gunmen in an attack in Belfast Oct. 15. One of the men—at whose home the attack took place—was the son of a former Protestant leader. The son had converted to the cause of Irish republicanism and had been jailed in 1971. The son's wife was also wounded in the attack.

[16] **Prison Hunger Strike.** Seven inmates of the Maze Prison near Belfast, all convicted Irish Republican Army terrorists, began a hunger strike Oct. 27 to press their demand to be treated as political prisoners, not ordinary criminals. The hunger strikers were supported by scores of other IRA prisoners, who followed a policy of noncooperation with prison authorities.

[17] The noncooperation took the form of refusing to wear standard issue prison garments—the prisoners covered themselves with blankets in-

stead – and smearing their cells with excrement rather than using toilets.

[18] By asking for "political" status, the prisoners meant they wished to be allowed to wear civilian clothes, refrain from prison duties and meet together whenever they wished. The government Oct. 23, after the hunger strike had been threatened, offered a concession on the clothing question. All male prisoners would be issued civilian clothing to wear. However, at the same time, the government reiterated its position that it would not distinguish the IRA prisoners as "political."

[19] The prisoners who had vowed to fast until they died unless the government treated them as political prisoners ended their 53-day-old hunger strike Dec. 18, even though the government had not acceded to their demands. The next day, 33 other prisoners who had joined the hunger strike about a week earlier, also called off their fast.

[20] Humphrey Atkins, the minister for Northern Ireland in the British government, said in a statement Dec. 18, that no secret concessions had been offered to the hunger strikers. "The government position was clearly set out before this hunger strike started, and we haven't moved since the very beginning." Speaking Dec. 19 in Parliament, Atkins said, "The hunger strike could not achieve its object, and the strikers finally realized that."

IRELAND, Republic of

[1] **Ulster: Haughey Calls for Action.** Charles J. Haughey, the new prime minister of the Republic of Ireland, said Feb. 16 that his country and Great Britain should "face the reality that Northern Ireland, as a political entity, has failed, and a new beginning is needed."

[2] Haughey, who was speaking before the annual convention of his Fianna Fail party, stressed that the situation was "urgent," adding, "The time for a solution is now, and that solution can only come through political action." Haughey said that "a declaration by the British government of their interest in encouraging the unity of Ireland, by agreement and in peace, would open the way towards an entirely new situation in which peace – real, lasting peace – would become an attainable reality."

[3] Talking to reporters Feb. 17, Haughey proposed that an international parley be convened to address the problems of Northern Ireland. In addition to Great Britain and the Irish Republic, the U.S. and the Common Market countries should take part, he said.

[4] **Haughey Meets Thatcher.** Prime Minister Haughey met in London May 21 with British Prime Minister Margaret Thatcher to discuss Northern Ireland. Both sides described the talk as productive, but fundamental differences remained in the way the two sides envisioned Northern Ireland's political future.

[5] While Haughey favored ultimately incorporating Northern Ireland in the Irish Republic, Thatcher reportedly told him that her government intended to grant Northern Ireland only a measure of regional government while retaining it as a part of the United Kingdom.

[6] **Haughey Attacks U.S. Groups Aiding IRA.** Prime Minister Haughey, speaking July 27 at a meeting of the Fianna Fail party in Cork, condemned a U.S. organization – the Northern Ireland Aid Committee (Noraid) – for providing support for violence in Northern Ireland.

[7] Haughey called on "all Americans who have the interests of Ireland at heart not to give this body any support, financial or moral." Noraid was based in New York City. Haughey also cited the Irish National Caucus, which was based in Washington, D.C., as having a similar role. Intelligence sources estimated that Noraid and other organizations had contributed more than $2 million to the Irish Republican

Army, which used terrorist tactics in an effort to drive the British out of Northern Irland and unify the island.

ISRAEL

Economy & Politics

[1] **'79 Inflation a Record 111.4%.** Israel registered the highest inflation rate in its history during 1979. According to figures released Jan. 15, prices rose by 111.4% during the year.

[2] Leading factors in the price spiral were housing, for which prices rose 159.4%; food, 135.6%; clothing, 66.4%; health care, 94%; furniture, 75.9%, and household maintenance, 124.8%.

[3] **New Foreign Minister Named.** The appointment of Yitzhak Shamir as foreign minister of Israel was announced by the government March 9.

[4] Shamir replaced Moshe Dayan, who had resigned in October 1979 in opposition to the government's handling of the Palestinian issue. Premier Menachem Begin had served as acting foreign minister in the interim. A member of Begin's Herut Party, Shamir was speaker of the Knesset (parliament). He was a strong supporter of Jewish settlements in occupied Arab territories and had abstained on several Knesset roll-call votes on the Camp David agreements in 1978. Shamir reportedly felt that Begin had conceded too much to Egypt in the Camp David accord.

[5] ***Weizman Quits Cabinet***—Ezer Weizman resigned May 25 as defense minister of Israel. Prime Minister Begin announced July 1 that he would temporarily hold the defense portfolio himself.

[6] Weizman had long opposed the government's policy of settlements on the ground that it jeopardized Palestinian automony negotiations. His actual resignation was provoked by government efforts to cut the defense budget. A government order issued the previous week by Finance Minister Yigal Hurvitz to freeze all military contracts because of a jump in the inflation rate was defied by Weizman, who continued to sign such contracts. Hurvitz threatened to bring the government down over the issue and Weizman backed off after finding little support even within his own Herut Party.

[7] **Begin Survives No-Confidence Vote.** The Israeli Knesset (parliament) Nov. 19 defeated, by a 57-54 vote, a motion of no-confidence in Begin's government.

[8] Separate motions submitted by the opposition Labor Party, the Communist Party and the small right-wing Renaissance party assailed the government's handling of the economy. The roll call on the three motions was combined into one vote.

[9] According to Israel's Central Bureau of Statistics, the cost of living between October 1979 and October 1980 had risen by 138.4%. Other economic developments were equally disturbing: real wages in January-June had fallen by 14%, the largest decline in the country's 32 years; private consumption had dropped by 8% during the same period, and unemployment had increased to 5% in July-September, the highest since Begin took office in 1977.

[10] In the Knesset vote, two men who had served in Begin's Cabinet—former Defense Minister Ezer Weizman and former Foreign Minister Moshe Dayan—joined the opposition. Passage of the no-confidence motion would have led to the dissolution of the Knesset in preparation for early elections. Regularly scheduled elections for the renewal of Begin's term of office were to be held in November 1981.

[11] ***Herut Ousts Weizman***—Former Defense Minister Weizman was expelled Nov. 23 from the Herut Party, one of the political groups in the ruling Likud coalition. He was ousted for voting against the government on a no-confidence motion Nov. 19. His expul-

sion deprived the government of a parliamentary majority, leaving it in control of only 60 of the Knesset's 120 seats.

[12] **Peres to Run Against Begin in '81.** Former Defense Minister Shimon Peres Dec. 18 was reconfirmed as chairman of the opposition Labor Party and thus won the party's nomination to oppose Prime Minister Begin in parliamentary elections in 1981.

[13] Peres turned back a challenge to his leadership by Yitzhak Rabin, receiving 2,123 votes to 875 cast for the former prime minister at the party's annual convention in Tel Aviv.

Other Developments

[14] **Israel Linked to Atomic Blast.** CBS News claimed Feb. 21 that a mysterious blast that occurred off the Atlantic coast of South Africa in 1979 was the test of a nuclear bomb by Israel with the "help and cooperation" of the South Africans. The report was denied by the governments of both Israel and South Africa. U.S. officials said they had evidence to confirm the report.

[15] **Israel Plans Dead Sea Canal.** The Israeli Cabinet Aug. 24 authorized a canal to be dug between the Mediterranean and the Dead seas.

[16] The canal–which would be about 65 miles (100 kilometers) long and cost about $700 million–would be used to generate power. The Dead Sea lay some 1,300 feet (400 meters) below sea level, so the water passing through the canal could be used to turn hydroelectric turbines and generate 600 megawatts of power. Current plans called for the canal's Mediterranean terminus to be in the Gaza Strip near Deir el Balah. The canal, which would run through a tunnel for the greater part of its length, would pass south beneath Beersheba and then hook back to the Dead Sea near Masada. It would be between 30 and 50 feet (9 to 15 meters) wide.

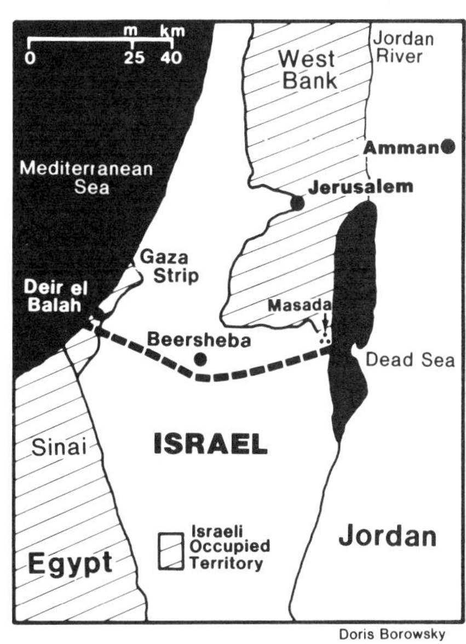

Doris Borowsky

Israel planned Mediterranean-Dead Sea canal to generate hydroelectric power.

[17] The project was politically controversial, with critics complaining that the Israeli government was taking a unilateral decision on a matter that affected the Gaza Strip–occupied territory previously under Egyptian control–and the Dead Sea, which Israel shared with Jordan.

[18] **U.S.-Israeli Oil Agreement.** The U.S. would supply Israel with oil in times of shortage or soaring prices under an accord announced Oct. 15 by Vice President Walter F. Mondale. The U.S. had committed itself to provide Israel with such guarantees after the Israelis withdrew from the Sinai oil fields as part of their peace treaty with Egypt. The agreement was signed Oct. 17.

See also Armaments (International) [2]; Foreign Aid; Human Rights [10]; United Nations [27, 31]

ITALY

Government & Politics

[1] **Cossiga Forms New Government.**

Francesco Cossiga announced the formation of a new coalition government April 4 that included his own Christian Democrats, the Socialists and the Republican Party.

[2] The announcement ended a government crisis that began in mid-March when Cossiga, facing a vote-of-confidence defeat, resigned as premier.

[3] Unlike Cossiga's previous government, the new coalition would control a majority of the seats in the Chamber of Deputies, the lower house of parliament: 340 out of 630. The Christian Democrats, Italy's largest party, had 262 of these seats; the Socialists, the third-largest party, held 62 seats, and the Republicans had 16 seats.

[4] In deciding to join the coalition, Socialist Party leader Bettino Craxi abandoned his demand that the Communist Party be given a role in the government. Differences between the Socialist and the Christian Democrats over the Communists had led to Cossiga's resignation.

[5] **Cossiga Accused on Terrorists.** Premier Francesco Cossiga came under the threat of impeachment when charges surfaced May 29 that he had told fellow Christian Democratic Party official Carlo Donat-Cattin that his son, Marco Donat-Cattin, was wanted as a terrorist.

[6] The accusations against Cossiga were made in a confession by Roberto Sandalo, a recently arrested admitted member of the Front Line, an ultraleft terrorist group. Sandalo, a friend of Marco Donat-Cattin, said that he had served as a means of communication between the younger Donat-Cattin and his father over the past two years since Marco Donat-Cattin left the family home. Sandalo said that Carlo Donat-Cattin told him in late April to warn his son to leave the country immediately because the authorities were about to arrest him. Sandalo claimed that the father gave his warning on information from Cossiga.

[7] Sandalo's confession led to the convening of a special parliamentary commission to examine the charges. The commission May 31 exonerated Cossiga, ruling that there was a "manifest lack of grounds" to pursue the inquiry. This action did not bring the affair to a close, however, in part because the commission acquitted Cossiga by only an 11-9 vote. Had Cossiga won a four-fifths vote of the commission – 16 of its 20 members – then the case would have been officially closed. At is was, the Communists announced June 2 that they would seek a full-scale parliamentary investigation. (Carlo Donat-Cattin May 31 resigned his position as deputy leader of the Christian Democrats. His son was arrested in Paris Dec. 18, and his extradition was requested by the Italian authorities.)

[8] Cossiga was exonerated by parliament July 27, after four days of debate. The opposition Communist Party presented a motion that called for the case to be returned for further investigation to a parliamentary committee that had earlier cleared Cossiga. With both chambers of parliament meeting jointly on the matter, the motion was defeated by a vote of 507 to 416.

[9] **Government Resigns.** The three-party coalition government headed by Premier Francesco Cossiga resigned Sept. 27 after losing a vote on its economic plan by one vote.

[10] The economic plan – a major stabilization effort – had been introduced by the government in July by decree. While the government had experienced difficulty in getting parliament to approve its economic efforts, the defeat Sept. 27 came as a surprise. The economic plan was designed to shore up the value of the lira, assist troubled industries and control inflation, currently expected to total 17% for the year.

[11] The 298-297 defeat for the government came on a secret ballot, held just minutes after the government had won a vote of confidence in a public vote. Calculations taking into account ab-

sent members of parliament showed that at least 29 legislators who belonged to the three governing coalition parties – the Christian Democrats, the Socialists and the Republicans – had voted against the economic package. [See below]

[12] Former Foreign Minister Arnaldo Forlani, the president of the Christian Democratic Party, agreed Oct. 2 to President Sandro Pertini's request that he attempt to form a new government. It would be Italy's 40th administration since World War II.

[13] **Forlani Forms Four-Party Cabinet.** Arnaldo Forlani was sworn in as premier Oct. 18. He would head a four-party government that included the Socialists, Social Democrats and Republicans in addition to the Christian Democrats.

[14] Forlani's coalition was the same as that in Cossiga's government, except for the addition of the Social Democrats. The governing parties controlled 359 seats of the 630 in the Chamber of Deputies, giving Forlani a majority of about 90.

Arnaldo Forlani was sworn in as premier of Italy Oct. 18.

Economy

[15] **Government Package.** The government July 2 approved a package of measures designed to curb inflation, shore up Italy's currency, the lire, and lessen the international payments deficit.

[16] Various indirect taxes, including the second increase in the price for gasoline in a month, were approved with the aim of raising some $3 billion in revenue. A new effort to reduce tax evasion was seen as providing about $1.8 billion.

[17] The government also decided to assume responsibility for $4.3 billion in social benefits currently paid by employers. This move, it was estimated, might lower the cost of labor by up to 4% and was billed as an anti-inflation measure.

[18] About $3 billion was slated to aid development in Italy's depressed south, to assist troubled companies and to provide incentives for research and export. The government announced that 0.5% would be withheld from wages for at least a year, with the money going to an investment fund for the south.

[19] Plans to impose a partial freeze on the "scala mobile," the system that indexed wages to inflation, were dropped by the government in response to intense pressure from the unions, according to a report in the *Financial Times* (London) July 3. The scala mobile was viewed as highly inflationary.

[20] ***Unions, Communists Split on Economy.*** The deflationary economic package adopted by the government July 2 had resulted in a sharp split between the Communist Party (PCI) and the union movement, according to press reports July 8 and 10.

[21] The PCI had attacked the government's proposals, but the leadership of the three main union federations, including the Communist-dominated

CGIL, had endorsed the package in exchange for the governments promise not to touch the "scala mobile."

[22] **Fiat Layoffs.** The Fiat auto company, Italy's largest private employer, announced that 78,000 of its 114,000 car workers would be laid off for seven working days between June 13 and July 25, according to the May 20 issue of CCH's *Common Market Reports.*

[23] The announcement came as a surprise to the employees and the government, as Fiat had earlier said that it was having problems meeting demand. But Fiat said that slackening sales in Europe and America and competition from Japanese auto makers had prompted the move.

[24] Fiat announced Sept. 27 that is was deferring until early 1981 dismissal notices for about 14,500 workers which had been due to take effect within a few days. The unions had strongly resisted the move. (Fiat added that it would go ahead with temporary layoffs for 24,000 workers. The workers, however, would receive full benefits.)

[25] Fiat reached a tentative agreement with its unions Oct. 15 in an attempt to end job actions that had virtually paralyzed production at the company's Turin auto plant for over a month. Details of the accord were not released, but informed sources said the company had agreed to abandon its plan to dismiss some 14,000 workers.

[26] **Company Bars Mafia Payments.** A public works construction group, Salcos, let it be known publicly that is was refusing to pay $1.2 million demanded in protection to permit completion of a 25-mile (40 kilometer) superhighway across the tip of southern Italy, it was reported July 11.

[27] The Mafia had for the past 18 months been giving the company trouble in its efforts to build a highway from Gioisa Ionica on the Ionian coast to Rasarno in the Gioia Tauro plain in the west. Directors of Salcos sent a copy of a letter making the extortion demand to the government and asked for protection by the police or the military.

[28] Calabria, an impoverished region in the south, was considered a Mafia stronghold. The Communist Party had attempted to break the Mafia's grip on the region, with the result that two of the last 10 murders in Calabria were thought to be the work of the Mafia against local Communist representatives. A report published June 30 said that the frequency of murder in Calabria was presently three-and-a-half times the national average. The study, conducted at the University of Cosenza, said that the Mafia was thought to be responsible for about 27% of the region's murders in the 1970s; during the 1960s, by contrast, the Mafia's share was thought to be only about 13%.

[29] **Oil Tax Scandal.** Finance Minister Franco Reviglio told parliament that a special commission would investigate the Guardia di Finanza, the country's financial police, to determine the extent of its involvement in a tax evasion scheme regarding oil products, it was reported Nov. 5 and 6.

[30] Reviglio said that the lost tax revenue totaled at least $168 million, and this figure might be adjusted upward. Earlier press reports had estimated the lost revenue as high as $2.2 billion. The scheme, which apparently operated through much of the 1970s, involved the supplying of false documents so that petroleum products, such as gasoline, would be classified as other products and taxed at a lower rate.

[31] The scandal had actually been revealed several years earlier, but national attention had focused on it only recently, with the arrest of Raffaele Giudice, commander of the financial police between 1974 and 1978. The police announed Oct. 25 that Giudice had been arrested the day before. More than 80 persons had been arrested in the investigation, it was reported Nov. 5.

Terrorism

[32] **Sicilian Leader Murdered.** Piersanti Mattarella, president of the Sicilian Regional Council and Sicily's leading Christian Democratic politician, was murdered Jan. 6.

[33] Responsibility for the murder was claimed by both right and left-wing terrorist groups. Police also speculated that the Mafia might have been involved in the murder. Mattarella had favored a political alliance between the Christian Democrats and the Communists. He was killed as he was returning home from church.

[34] ***Six Policemen Slain***—Three policemen were killed in an ambush in Milan Jan. 8. The ultraleft Red Brigades terrorist group claimed responsibility in a telephone call to a Milan newspaper shortly afterward. Three carabinieri, members of the paramilitary police, were shot dead March 24 as they were riding on a bus outside Turin.

[35] **Magistrate Shot to Death.** A predominent judge and law professor, Vittorio Bachelet, was shot and killed Feb. 12 on the steps of the political science building of Rome University, where he had attended a conference on terrorism. The Red Brigades claimed responsibility. Bachelet was deputy chairman of the Higher Council of Magistrates, the judiciary's self-governing body, and had close ties with the Christian Democratic Party and the Vatican. Three magistrates were shot to death by ultra-leftist gunmen in Salerno, Rome and Milan between March 16 and 19.

[36] **Police Kill 4 Terrorists.** Four members of the ultraleft Red Brigades terrorist organization were killed when police raided an apartment in Genoa March 28. Other police raids on northern Italian cities led to the arrest of 19 persons.

[37] Italian authorities had arrested in recent days about 45 persons suspected of belonging to the Red Brigades, it was reported April 15. Many of the suspects were factory workers, some of whom had served as labor delegates. Others were university faculty members. The arrests took place mainly in Turin, Milan and Biella.

[38] Four members of the Red Brigades were captured in Naples May 19 after they had taken part in an attack in which a Christian Democratic politician was killed.

[39] Police in Turin announced July 5 that they had seized 21 suspected urban guerrillas in and around the city during the past week. Many of the suspects were said to belong to the Front Line, an ultraleft group with links to the Red Brigaes. In Paris, a series of raids July 7 and 8 netted seven suspects wanted in Italy on charges ranging from murder to kidnapping. All seven were believed to be members of Front Line.

[40] **Antiterrorist Official Slain.** Alfredo Albanese, head of the antiterrorist police unit for the Venice region, was shot to death May 12. Albanese was killed in an ambush in Mestre, the industrial city on the mainland opposite Venice. The Red Brigades claimed responsibility.

[41] In a separate development May 13, it became known that Marco Donat-Cattin, the youngest son of Christian Democratic Party Vice President Carlo Donat-Cattin, was being sought by the authorities as a suspected terrorist.

[42] **Reporter Slain in Milan.** An anonymous caller in Milan took credit on behalf of the Red Brigades for the shooting death there May 28 of Walter Tobagi, a reporter and commentator on *Corriere della Sera.* Tobagi specialized in the coverage of political terrorism.

[43] In another incident in Rome also on May 28, one policeman was killed and two were wounded in a terrorist attack. An anonymous caller said that the attack was the work of the Armed Revolutionary Nuclei, the neo-Fascist group.

[44] **Bologna Blast Kills 79.** An explosion in the crowded central train station of Bologna Aug. 2 killed 76 per-

sons and left about 160 people injured, many of them seriously. The number of dead rose Aug. 7 to 79 with the deaths of three of the injured.

[45] The city police chief said Aug. 3 that he was "95% or even more sure" that the explosion was the work of terrorists. Metal fragments thought to be part of a bomb were found near a crater in the floor of the second-class waiting room, where the explosion had presumably occurred. The blast tore through waiting rooms and a restaurant and caused the ceiling of an entire wing of the station to cave in. It came at a time when the station was particularly crowded—the first Saturday of August, when many people were starting their summer vacations.

[46] Suspicion centered on a neo-fascist terrorist group, the Armed Revolutionary Nuclei. A Rome newspaper received an anonymous telephone call claiming responsibility for the explosion for this group, and saying that the explosion was intended to honor a neo-fascist who was charged in connection with a 1974 train bombing. Other anonymous messages claiming to speak for the neo-fascists rejected responsibility for the blast. Nevertheless, they were considered the most likely suspects, since the explosion seemed to have the characteristics of earlier terrorist operations associated with the neo-fascists: a random bombing in a public place calculated to cause maximum terror.

[47] Police arrested 11 rightists in round-ups Sept. 22 and 23 in Rome and its vicinity in connection with the bombing. Arrests in the case now numbered over 40, but so far no individual had actually been accused of placing the bomb in the station.

[48] **Brigades Renew Attack.** The Red Brigades took responsibility for the murder of two business executives in Milan in November. The attacks followed a six-month period in which left-wing terrorists had not killed anyone.

[49] Manfredo Mazzanti, directly of a steel mill near Milan, was shot and killed Nov. 28. Earlier, on Nov. 12, two gunmen killed Renate Briano, a personnel director for an electrical equipment firm, on a Milan subway.

[50] **Carabinieri General Killed.** Two terrorists disguised as delivery boys fatally shot Enrico Calvaligi, a general in the paramilitary police (the Carabinieri), Dec. 31 as he was returning to his home in Rome.

See also Art [11-12]; Aviation [12]; Earthquakes [1-9]; Economy (International) [7]

J

JAMAICA

[1] **Seaga, JLP Win Election by Wide Margin.** Edward Phillip George Seaga, head of the Jamaican Labor Party, decisively defeated Prime Minister Michael Manley and his People's National Party in national elections Oct. 30.

[2] The JLP won 50 of the 60 seats in the House of Representatives, the elective branch of Jamaica's bicameral legislature, and 57% of the popular vote, the highest share in the party's history. Manley managed to retain his own seat in parliament by a small margin. In the last parliamentary elections, in 1976, the JPL had won only 12 of the 60 seats in the House. The results indicated widespread dissatisfaction with Manley's socialist policies. A U.S. State Department spokesman said Oct. 30 that though the U.S.had officially maintained a "strictly neutral stance in this election," the result was "warmly welcomed."

[3] The campaign had been especially violent with between 500 and 600 deaths recorded in 1980 as a result of political unrest. On election day, Seaga and members of his entourage had been involved in a shooting incident at a polling station. All told, five persons were killed during various outbreaks of violence on election day. Some 130 persons had been killed in the month preceding the election.

[4] Seaga was sworn in as prime minister Nov. 1. During his campaign, Seaga had promised more freedom for private enterprise and had said that he hoped to revive the economy by restoring business confidence and attracting foreign investment. As proof of that promise and hope, he announced that he was appointing himself minister of finance. He told the crowd gathered at his swearing in that the Bank of Jamaica had run out of foreign exchange the day before the election and that a last-minute $10 million loan from the government of Iraq secured by Manley's government would enable Jamaica to "make it through next Wednesday."

[5] Seaga, a Harvard-educated sociologist of Lebanese, Scottish and

Edward Seaga wins national elections in Jamaica Oct. 30.

Jamaican ancestry, was born May 28, 1930 in Boston of Jamaican parents. He went to Jamaica in 1958, joined the Jamaican Labor Party and was elected to parliament in 1962, the year Jamaica gained its independence from Great Britain. Seaga was minister of development and welfare from 1962 to 1967 and minister of finance and planning from 1967 to 1972. He developed a number of innovative financial institutions in Jamaica during that period and gained a reputation for financial prowness in the process.

Economy

[6] **Banks Turn Down Loan Request.** Representatives of eight major international banks April 7 turned down a request by Jamaican Finance Minister Ronald Hugh Small for emergency financial aid to keep the country's depressed economy going in 1980.

[7] The meeting came about as a result of Prime Minister Michael Manley's March 25 decision to halt negotiations with the International Monetary Fund for $180 million to help Jamaica repay $170 in interest and principal on previous loans. Manley had refused Jan. 15 to cut his government's budget by laying off 11,000 workers to satisfy the IMF's requirements for further financial aid.

[8] At the April 7 meeting in New York, the bankers refused to consider either Jamaica's request for a one-year deferral of principal payments on 12.5% of the country's outstanding commercial bank debt of over $400 million or proposals for a medium-term economic recovery program.

[9] Jamaica's net foreign debt over reserves of the government and private banking system in January stood at $658 million, three times what it was in 1977. Unemployment was at about 30% of the population of working age, and wages were only about 55% in real terms of what they had been in 1979. Inflation was running at a 20% annual rate.

[10] ***Tentative Accord***—Jamaica reached a tentative agreement with its major foreign credit banks April 15 that would avert default on $450 million in loans. The informal agreement called for Jamaica to continue to roll over about 90% of its foreign debt, subject to a monthly review.

[11] **Debt Refinancing Plan Advances.** Jamaica's faltering economy was given some hope of recovering June 4 when Prime Minister Manley announced that "good progress" had been made in securing short-term financing to deal with the country's expected foreign trade deficit in 1980.

Unrest

[12] **Five Slain at Political Event.** Five Jamaicans were killed and 10 wounded April 20 when gunmen stormed a fund-raising event for the opposition Labor Party (JLP), headed by Edward Seaga.

[13] **Soldiers Seized in Coup Attempt.** More than 20 members of the Jamaican Defense Force and at least one civilian were arrested in connection with an alleged plot to overthrow the government, Prime Minister Manley announced June 22.

[14] **Curfew Imposed in Kingston.** The Jamaican National Security Council decided July 18 to place troubled sections of Kingston under a nightly curfew to deter armed bands from circulating in the capital. In the week prior to the curfew, 25 persons were killed by gunmen. The total for the month was 70. In June, 60 persons were slain in violence related to the announcement by Manley of national elections.

[15] **Security Official Killed.** Roy McGann, assistant national security minister in the Jamaican government, was killed Oct. 14 during a clash between political factions in Kingston.

JAPAN

Economy

[1] **Record '79 Trade Deficit.** Japan

registered a record trade deficit of $7.5 billion (1.684 trillion yen) in 1979, according to figures released by the Finance Ministry Jan. 23. The deficit contrasted with the record trade surplus of $18.3 billion (3.828 trillion yen) in 1978.

[2] One result of Japan's overall trade deficit, the *Asian Wall Street Journal* reported Jan. 29, was a fading of U.S. complaints about its trade deficit with Japan. In 1978, President Carter had cautioned Japan that a reduction in Japan's bilateral surplus was a key condition for continued good relations between the two nations.

[3] **Japan Becomes No. 1 World Auto Maker.** Japan had overtaken the U.S. as the largest producer of cars and trucks in the world, the Japanese auto industry announced July 7.

[4] Industry officials said in Tokyo that statistics for the first six months of 1980 showed that Japan had produced 5.46 million vehicles, over a million more than the ailing U.S. auto industry.

Government & Politics

[5] **Ohira Loses Confidence Vote.** Premier Masayoshi Ohira's ruling Liberal Democratic Party (LDP) was defeated May 16 on a no-confidence motion in the House of Representatives. The lower chamber of the Diet (parliament) was dissolved May 19 to prepare for general elections.

[6] The LPD lost the no-confidence motion by a vote of 243 to 187, when 69 dissident Liberal Democrats abstained. The motion was introduced by the opposition Socialist Party, which had accused Ohira's government of failure to deal effectively with corruption and inflation.

[7] **Ohira Dies of Heart Attack.** Japanese Premier Masayoshi Ohira, 70, died of a heart attack in a Tokyo hospital June 12. He had been hospitalized since May 31, suffering from exhaustion and a heart ailment.

[8] The chief Cabinet secretary, Masayoshi Ito, became acting premier in accordance with Japan's Cabinet

Zenko Suzuki (center) rises to acknowledge applause of Diet following his election as premier of Japan July 17.

law. He was to retain the post pending parliamentary elections.

[9] **Liberal Democrats Win Election.** The ruling Liberal Democratic Party of the late Premier Masayoshi Ohira won firm majorities in both houses of the Diet (parliament) in national elections held June 22. In the previous Diet, the party had only slim working majorities with the aid of independents.

[10] **Suzuki Elected Premier.** Zenko Suzuki July 17 was elected premier of Japan, succeeding Ohira. Suzuki, 69, had helped form the ruling Liberal Democratic Party in 1955. He was appointed to his first Cabinet post in 1960 and subsequently to several Cabinet and party positions. His last position before being elected premier was that of chairman of the LDP's executive council.

Defense

[11] **Military Talks Held in Washington.** Japanese Foreign Minister Saburo Okita met with U.S. officials in Washington March 20 and 21 to discuss increasing Japan's defense expenditures.

[12] One concrete outcome of the talks appeared to be a commitment on the part of Japan to pay more of the cost of supporting the 46,000 U.S. troops stationed in Japan. Japanese Premier Masayoshi Ohira told government agencies March 24 to study ways of carrying this out.

[13] **Cabinet Backs Defense Increase.** The Japanese Cabinet July 29 approved a 9.7% defense budget increase over current spending.

[14] The larger defense budget would permit Japan to purchase more jet fighters, patrol planes and ships—mostly from the U.S.—for the coming year. The U.S. informed Tokyo that it considered the defense budget increase too small, it was reported Aug. 1.

See also Carter, Jimmy [12]; Economy (International) [8]; Energy [7]; Panama [1-3]; Space [16]

JORDAN JR., VERNON E.—*See* Civil Disorders [16-20]

JORDAN—*See* Iraq [25-26]

JUSTICE, Department of—*See* Carter, Billy [1-2, 8-9, 14, 19, 21-24]

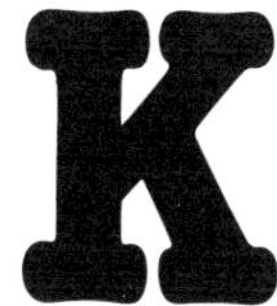

KIRKLAND, LANE—*See* Economy (U.S.) [34]

KISSINGER, HENRY A.—*See* Freedom of Information Act

KENNEDY, SEN. EDWARD M.—*See* Black Americans [6]; Elections [4, 8, 12, 14-15, 18-19, 42-51]

KENYA—*See* Defense (U.S.) [27]

KHOMEINI, AYATOLLAH RUHOLLAH—*See* Iran [3, 17, 33, 40-42, 46, 87-89, 93-94, 97, 103, 105, 119-20]; Iraq [3]

KOREA (North), People's Republic of

North-South Clashes

[1] **3 Infiltrators Killed; Spy Boat Sunk.** North and South Korean forces clashed March 23 and 25

[2] In the first engagement, South Korean troops March 23 shot and killed three heavily armed North Korean frogmen who had crossed the Han River near the Demilitarized Zone between the two countries. In the second clash, South Korean air and naval forces March 25 intercepted and sank a North Korean espionage boat off the southern port of Pohang, the government claimed. One South Korean sailor was killed and another wounded.

[3] **2 Die Along the DMZ.** A North Korean and a South Korean soldier were killed March 27 in an exchange of gunfire along the Demilitarized Zone, which divided the two countries.

[4] **North Korean Ship Sunk.** South Korean planes and ships June 21 sank a North Korean boat off the beach resort town of Taechon. Eight persons aboard the craft were killed and a ninth was captured, the South Korean Defense Ministry reported. The ship apparently had been attempting to land armed agents.

Other Developments

[5] **North-South Talks Canceled.** North Korea Sept. 25 canceled unity talks with South Korea after accusing Seoul of "trying to whip up a war atmosphere." Meetings which had begun Feb. 6 had been aimed at arranging discussions between the premiers of the two countries.

[6] In announcing Pyongyang's decision, North Korean President Kim Il Sung charged that the Panmunjom negotiations would only serve to legitimize South Korean President Chun Doo Hwan, whom he had accused of being "more vicious than the late Park Chung Hee."

[7] Meanwhile, the United Nations Command in Seoul Sept. 25 said it had received a protest from North Korea the previous day accusing South Korean forces of having fired across the demilitarized zone for the third time in four days.

[8] **Kim's Son Advances.** Kim Chong Il, son of President Kim Il Sung, made

political strides Oct. 10-14 at a conference of the ruling North Korean Worker's Party in Pyongyang.

[9] With the conclusion of the conference, the younger Kim ranked fourth in both the new standing committee of the Politburo and the Politburo itself, second only to his father in the Central Committee secretariat, and third in the party's Military Affairs Committee. Kim Chong Il had first gained public prominence in 1973 when he was named to lead the government drive to impose standards of technology, culture and ideology. (The younger Kim's age was variously reported as 38, 39 and 40.)

[10] At the opening session of the party conference, the first in 10 years, President Kim presented a 10-point program for reunification of North and South Korea. In a clarification of his proposals, Kim told the gathering Oct. 12 that the "military fascist" government in South Korea must first be overthrown before the two Koreas could unite. He also urged the demobilization of the armed forces of the two countries. South and North Korean armed forces currently totaled 615,000 and 510,000, respectively.

[11] South Korea Oct. 15 denounced North Korea's reunification plan.

See also Iraq [30]

KOREA (South) Republic of

[1] **Park Plotters Executed.** One of the seven men sentenced to death in connection with the October 1979 assassination of President Park Chung Hee was executed by firing squad March 6.

[2] Col. Pak Hung Ju was put to death after a military court rejected his appeal. Pak was chief bodyguard to former Korean Central Intelligence Agency (KCIA) Director Kim Jae Kyu, who was under sentence of death for shooting Park.

[3] South Korean authorities May 24 executed by hanging Kim Jae Kyu and four others convicted of being accomplices in the assassination.

[4] **Labor, Student Unrest.** South Korea was hit by widespread labor and student unrest in April and May.

[5] A report from Seoul April 30 told of strikes and sit-downs in at least 25 companies where workers demanded higher wages and the removal of union leaders regarded as pro-management. At least two disputes were marked by violence. About 1,000 steelworkers in the port city of Pusan clashed with police April 29 during a demonstration demanding a 40% wage boost. Coal miners in the central city of Sabuk the previous week had attacked a police station, killed one policeman, and destroyed several houses.

[6] Many of the antigovernment demonstrations staged by university students throughout the country May 1-10 were marked by violence. At Seoul National University May 2, several thousand students from 13 colleges around South Korea staged a rally demanding a quick end to martial law and the restoration of democracy. The protesters specifically called for the dismissal of Gen. Chon Too Hwan, who had become head of the KCIA in early April. The campus unrest had started March 19, when hundreds of students at Konkuk University in Seoul had forced its president to resign because of his close connections with the former government of President Park.

[7] **Total Martial Law Imposed.** South Korea May 18 imposed total martial law in an effort to quell widespread antigovernment demonstrations by students and others in Seoul and five other cities. The crisis deepened as the government of Premier Shin Hyon Hwack resigned May 20 "to take responsibility for failure to maintain domestic calm."

[8] The emergency rule was an extension of the limited martial law in effect since the assassination of President Park. It had applied only to the contiguous provinces of the country, with Cheju Island, off the south coast, exempted. The latest decress, widened to include Cheju, gave Gen. Lee Hi Song,

head of the Martial Law Command, virtually absolute rule to the country.
[9] Under the new martial law proclamation, universities were closed, political rallies and labor strikes were banned, and "slanderous statements" against either Park or President Choi Kyu Hah were prohibited. The issuance of the martial law decree was accompanied by the arrest of hundreds of dissidents, including prominent political leaders. Among them were former Premier Kim Jong Pil, head of the majority Democratic Republican Party; Kim Young Sam, leader of the opposition New Democratic Party, and Kim Dae Jung.

[10] The martial law decree was defied by thousands of persons who rioted May 19-20 in the provincial city of Kwangju, a stronghold of Kim Dae Jung. At least five persons were reported killed and 70 injured in clashes May 19 between demonstrators, mostly students and workers, and army troops that were rushed into the city. City police were said to have refused to assist the soldiers in quelling the rioters.

[11] Unrest continued in Kwangju May 20 as 30,000 demonstrators marched through the city, with some battling the troops. Some of the demonstrators set fire to a television and radio station. The attackers were said to have been angered by broadcast statements May 19 that there were no deaths or injuries in the Kwangju rioting. Seoul had been swept by violent demonstrations May 12-15. In the May 14 incident, more than 50,000 students protesting continued martial law clashed with thousands of policemen. More than 200 students were reported to have been seriously injured and 400 detained.

[12] **Troops Retake Kwangju.** Several thousand South Korean troops May 27 regained full control of Kwangju, the South Cholla province capital. Kwangju had been seized May 21 by

In Seoul, police vehicle sprays demonstrators with tear gas May 15.

antigovernment students and other rebel elements.

[13] The student takeover had followed three days of rioting that began May 18 in protest against the imposition of martial law. At least 100 persons were killed and many more injured in the period between the onset of the rioting and the retaking of the city by government troops. The dead included civilians, police and soldiers.

[14] **Chun Elected President.** Retired Gen. Chun Doo Hwan* was elected president of South Korea Aug. 27. He replaced Choi Kyu Hah, who had resigned Aug. 16. Chun, the sole candidate for the post, was endorsed by the National Conference of Unification (the electoral college), which gave him 2,524 out of 2,525 votes, with one ballot declared invalid.

*The preferred spelling of the new president's name in Roman letters was Chun Doo Hwan, not Chon Too Hwan, as previously reported in the Western press, it was announced Aug. 25.

[15] **Kim Sentenced to Death.** A four-member military court in Seoul Sept. 17 sentenced opposition leader Kim Dae Jung to death on charges of sedition. Twenty-three other defendants were given jail sentences ranging from three to 20 years. Kim's trial had started Aug. 14 and ended Sept. 13. Kim was accused by the government of having had "a direct, central and provable role in the May [antigovernment] student demonstrations . . . in Kwangju and a documented plan to take over the government through conspiratorial, revolutionary and violent means."

[16] The carrying out of the sentences was to be held in abeyance pending appeals to a second military court and then the Supreme Court.

[17] **Voters Back New Charter.** South Korean voters approved a new constitution in a referendum held Oct. 22. According to official results released Oct. 23, a total of 92% of the voting electorate cast affirmative ballots. The government said 95.5% of the 20.3 million eligible voters participated.

[18] The new charter replaced the one in effect since 1972. Among its major provisions:

- The president's powers were reduced. He would no longer appoint one-third of the National Assembly or name judges. His tenure would be limited to a single seven-year term.
- Human rights and habeas corpus were guaranteed, and forcible extraction of confession from political prisoners was forbidden.
- The National Assembly would be replaced by a Legislative Council to be appointed by the president in mid-1981.
- All existing political parties would be dissolved.

[19] **811 Politicians Purged.** The South Korean government Nov. 12 banned 811 politicians from running for office or conducting other political activities until June 1988.

See also Korean (North), People's Republic of [1-6, 10-11]

KOSYGIN, ALEXEI N.—*See* Union of Soviet Socialist Republics (U.S.S.R.) [1-5, 11-13]

KU KLUX KLAN (KKK)

[1] **Hoover Blocked Trial in '63 Bombing.** Former Federal Bureau of Investigation Director J. Edgar Hoover twice blocked prosecution of four Ku Klux Klansmen named by FBI agents as responsible for the 1963 Birmingham, Ala. church bombing that killed four black children, it was reported Feb. 18.

[2] According to a Justice Department report cited by the *New York Times,* Hoover rejected recommendations from his Birmingham field office that testimony identifying the suspects be forwarded by Justice Department prosecutors. It was not until 1977 that one of the suspected Klansmen, Robert Chambliss, was convicted of murder in the case on state charges. The other three Klansmen identified as accomplices were never indicted.

[3] **Ku Klux Klan Opens Toronto Office.** The Ku Klux Klan opened an office in Toronto as part of a cross-Canada membership drive aimed at informing Canadians of its message, Klan spokesman Wolfgang Droege said June 26.

[4] The Klan had had branches in Canada in the 1920s. In the 1960s, Canadian immigration rules were liberalized, allowing more nonwhites to emmigrate to Canada and leading to a resurgance of Klan activity.

[5] **Klan Rally in Connecticut.** Scuffling broke out near a Ku Klux Klan rally in Scotland, Conn. Sept. 13. About 400 people attended the rally at which a cross was burned.

[6] The fighting occurred as about 300 counterdemonstrators attempted to reach the rally site. A large contingent of state police was on hand and moved in quickly to quell the disturbance, in which six people were injured and eight arrested.

[7] Bill Wilkinson, the imperial wizard of the Invisible Empire, Knights of Ku Klux Klan, also showed up and another rally was called for Sept. 14. When Wilkinson arrived for this rally, police found a loaded pistol in the trunk of the car, a violation of state law. He was arrested but posted $1,000 bond and returned to the rally.

[8] ***Mississippi***—A Klan rally in Jackson, Miss. Oct. 4 drew about 300 sympathizers. The rally was held the same day 175 blacks staged a march to protest the shooting of a black by a white police officer.

[9] **Klansmen Acquitted in Slayings.** An all-white jury in Greensboro, N.C. Nov. 17 acquitted six Ku Klux Klansmen and Nazis of murder and of felonious rioting at an anti-Klan rally in Greensboro on Nov. 3, 1979.

[10] The dead included five Communist Workers Party demonstrators—four white men and one black woman—who were preparing for a "Death to the Klan" rally when a fight broke out with the Klansmen and Nazis. The defense contended that the Klansmen and Nazis had fired in self-defense out of fear for their lives. The prosecution attempted to show that the Klansmen and Nazis had initiated the shooting. Members of the Communist Workers Party and their sympathizers disrupted court proceedings at the outset of the trial Aug. 4 with protests that the trial was "a sham and a farce."

[11] The jury deliberated for seven days. Those acquitted were Ronald Wayne Wood, 35, and Jack Wilson Fowler, 28, of Winston-Salem, N.C.; Jerry Paul Smith, 33 of Maiden, N.C.; David Wayne Matthews, 25, of Newton, N.C. and Coleman Blair Pridmore, 37, and Lawrence Gene Morgan, 28, both of Lincolnton, N.C. Wood and Fowler identified themselves as members of the Nazi Party at the time of their arrest and admitted to previous membership in the Klan. The others were current or former members of the Klan.

See also Civil Disorders [12-14]

KUWAIT—*See* Carter, Jimmy [7]; Iraq [31-32]

L

LABOR

[1] **George Meany Dies.** George Meany, 85, a former plumber from New York City, pioneer leader in the U.S. labor union movement and president of the American Federation of Labor-Congress of Industrial Organizations for 25 years, died Jan. 10 of cardiac arrest in Washington, D.C.

[2] Meany had stepped down in November 1979 as head of the 13.5 million-member AFL-CIO. He had been the AFL-CIO's only president since its founding in 1955. As head of the AFL-CIO, Meany had preached labor unity and built the federation of 111 unions into a powerful political bloc on the American scene.

[3] Meany saw his basic goal as improving the economic welfare of union members through improved wages, working conditions, cash and fringe benefits. On the legislative front, he tried to promote higher minimum wages, public works, the right to organize and protection of the picket line. He also supported national health care projects, civil rights and proposals to limit economic concentration of corporation power.

[4] On foreign policy, Meany was often considered strongly conservative and anti-communist. He took a hawkish view on Vietman long after U.S. public opinion had turned against the war, condemned the initiatives toward China and attacked the policy of detente with the Soviet Union.

Court Actions

[5] **Hazardous Work Refusals Backed.** The Supreme Court ruled unanimously Feb. 26 that companies could not discipline workers who in good faith had refused to perform hazardous tasks or work in unsafe areas. The decision upheld a regulation of the Occupational Safety and Health Administration.

[6] The case, *Whirlpool Corp. v. Marshall*, concerned the refusal of a work assignment in 1974 by two employees of Whirlpool Corp.'s Marion, Ohio plant. The two had balked at stepping onto a screen, suspended 20 feet above the plant floor, to clear away parts that had fallen from an overhead conveyor belt. A worker at the same plant had fallen to his death earlier in the year while carring out a similar assignment.

[7] The two employees were dock six hours' pay each and were given written reprimands. They complained to the U.S. Labor Department which, in turn, sued Whirlpool for violating the OSHA regulation. A federal appeals court upheld the OSHA rule.

[8] Writing for the Supreme Court, Justice Potter Steward held that an employee could turn down a task if he "reasonably believes" the job created "imminent risk of death or serious bodily injury" and if there was "sufficient time or opportunity either to seek effective redress from his employer or to apprise OSHA of the danger." Steward noted that the regulation did not require companies to pay workers who refused dangerous assignments, but rather barred companies from discriminating against such workers through disciplinary actions.

[9] **Court Limits Children's Work.** The

U.S. Circuit Court of Appeals for the District of Columbia March 20 overturned Labor Department regulations that permitted the hiring of children 10 to 12 years old to pick crops where pesticides had been used.

[10] Under a 1977 amendment to the Fair Labor Standards Act, growers were permitted to hire children to harvest "short-season" crops, such as western strawberries or northeastern potatoes, as long as safety and other conditions were adequate.

[11] The Labor Department subsequently developed regulations allowing children to be hired if no pesticides had been used or if the pesticides used had been approved by the government. The government eventually compiled a list of approved pesticides. The list was challenged, however, by the Environmental Protection Agency. The court noted in its ruling that several pesticides on the approved list had been found to be either "high-risk or highly toxic." The ruling did not bar the hiring of children for work on fields where no pesticides had been used.

[12] **Child Labor Law Fines Upheld.** The Supreme Court ruled unanimously April 28 that the Department of Labor could fine violators of federal child labor laws. The case was *Marshall v. Jerrico.*

[13] The case dealt with a challenge to the Labor Department's practice of using money raised from such fines to reimburse its regional offices for the cost of child labor investigations. The U.S. Court of Appeals for the District of Columbia had held that the reimbursement practice created an impermissible conflict of interest and an undue motivation for seeking fines against alleged violators. The high court, led by Justice Thurgood Marshall, reversed the appeals court. Marshall opined that, since no Labor Department official stood to profit from the fines, there was no conflict of interest.

[14] **Registration of Itinerants Upset.** A local Louisiana law requiring registration of itinerant workers was ruled unconstitutional and invalid by federal appeals court Judge Gerald B. Tjoflat in New Orleans May 13. The statute, passed by St. Mary Parish in 1978, required itinerants to register at the parish police office for fingerprinting, photographs and interrogation on family background.

[15] The Supreme Court Oct. 20 affirmed the appeals court ruling without comment. The case was *Edwards v. Service Machine Corp.*

Strikes and Contracts

[16] **Dock Pact.** Agreement on a new three-year "master contract" for dockworkers at more than 30 Atlantic and Gulf Coast ports was reached May 27, more than four months before current contracts were scheduled to expire.

[17] The settlement, reached by negotiators for the shipping industry and the AFL-CIO International Longshoremen's Association, called for $4.85 an hour wage and benefit increases.

[18] The master pact set the terms of the money package. Other issues were to be negotiated at the various ports themselves. The money package called for wage increases of $1.20 an hour in each year of the contract. The raises would go on top of the current wage of $10.40 an hour. Employer contributions to the union's health and welfare funds, currently $1.50 an hour for each employee, would rise by 50¢—17¢ an hour each of the first two years and 16¢ the third year. The pension fund contributions by the employers, currently $2.25 an hour, would be increased 25¢ an hour each of the contract's three years. Negotiations were conducted in Miami Beach.

[19] **Aluminum Contract.** Agreement on a new basic contract between the aluminum industry and the AFL-CIO United Steelworkers of America was reached May 30 in Miami Beach.

[20] The settlement called for general

wage increases totaling 60 cents an hour over the three-year life of the contract (25 cents on June 1, 20 cents in June 1981 and 15 cents in June 1982). In the third year, workers also would receive cost-of-living adjustments under an improved formula that would provide an increase of one cent an hour for every .26 of a point rise in the consumer price index (instead of the current .3 of a point rise). Assuming an 11% annual inflation rate, the settlement amounted to a 42% total wage increase over three years.

[21] The settlement with the Big Three aluminum producers covered about 30,000 workers represented by the USW and another 20,000 represented by the St. Louis-based Aluminum Workers International Union, which coordinated its bargaining with the Steelworkers. The companies were Aluminum Co. of America, Reynolds Metal Co. and Kaiser Aluminum & Chemical Corp. The old contract expired May 31.

[22] **New York Unions Settle.** New York City and negotiators for its 42,000 uniformed employees reached agreement on terms of a new contract July 3. The settlement was reached only five hours before a threatened strike.

[23] The two-year settlement provided for wage increases of 9% in the first year and 8% in the second year. In addition, it made provision for increased allowances for uniforms plus another annual payment of $750 the city had been making in lieu of cost-of-living adjustments. Base pay of police officers and firemen would rise by the second year of the new contract to $22,769 a year. For sanitationmen, the base pay would go to $20,570 in the second year.

[24] The city had negotiated a similar settlement with its 200,000 nonuniformed employees June 19. These employees, including teachers, office workers and health-care employees, would receive 8% wage raises in each of the next two years.

[25] ***NYC Transit Workers Strike***—An 11-day, illegal strike by New York City transit workers ended April 11 with union leaders approving a new two-year contract. The settlement called for a 22% wage increase. However, the transit unions agreed to several productivity "givebacks" and had substantial fines levied against them.

[26] The walkout by 35,000 subway and bus workers had shutdown the nation's largest transit system; on a normal day, it carried 5.4 million riders.

[27] **Television, Film Actors Strike.** Members of the Screen Actors Guild and the American Federation of Television and Radio Artists walked off their jobs July 21 in a dispute with film studios and television networks. The strike ended Oct. 23 with approval of a three-year contract.

[28] The walkout halted filming of most feature films in the U.S. and production of nearly all prime-time television series being prepared for the fall season. It also idled some 20,000 nonstriking film craftsmen and technicians in the multi-billion-dollar movie and TV industry.

[29] The basic issue in the strike was how profits should be shared from Hollywood's emerging home video markets, which included pay TV, and video casettes and disks. The actors' unions in early talks had demanded 6% (originally 12%) of producers' gross profits from sales of original programming to pay TV and in the form of video disks and video casettes. Producers had countered with an offer of 3.6% on pay TV dramas, comedies and variety shows and 2% on talk and game shows after the programs had run for two years or had sold 100,000 casettes or disks.

[30] The new contract called for a 32.25% increase in minimum salaries for actors over a three-year period and a 4.5% share of revenue from programs made for pay TV. But actors would receive the 4.5% residual payments only after a program had

played for 10 days within a year on each pay-television system.

[31] **Stevens, Union Come to Terms.** J. P. Stevens & Co. and the AFL-CIO Amalgamated Clothing and Textile Workers Union announced a labor agreement Oct. 19 that would end their bitter 17-year fight over the union's attempt to organize the company's workers.

[32] Under the settlement, the company signed a 2½-year agreement with the union covering 10 plants where the union had already won representation. The ACTWU would represent about 3,200 workers, or about 10% of Stevens's hourly employees, in eight plants in North Carolina – seven of them in Roanoke Rapids – and factories in Alabama and South Carolina. Terms of the settlement also would be guaranteed for any of Stevens's 70 other plants if the union won representation rights within the next 1½ years.

[33] The Roanoke workers, who ratified the new contract Oct. 19, received an 8.5% pay increase plus retroactive pay for withheld wages. The retroactive payment, which amounted to about $1,000 per worker, was to compensate for the 8.5% pay increase that had been withheld since July 1979 from employees who had voted for union representation. Stevens also accepted a "check-off" provision for union dues to be deducted from paychecks, and agreed to refrain from any retribution against employees for union activity. For its part, the union agreed to end its boycott against Stevens products and to stop its campaign against businesses allied corporately with Stevens.

[34] **Copper Workers' Strike Drags on.** Employees of four of the nation's 11 major copper-mining companies remained on strike Oct. 24 despite earlier settlements by the two industry leaders.

[35] Kennecott Corp., the U.S.'s largest copper producer, had settled its strike Aug. 27, and Phelps Dodge Corp., the second largest producer, came to terms Oct. 8. The Kennecott settlement included a three-year contract providing wage and cost-of-living increases of 39% over the life of the contract. Phelps Dodge workers won a 35% wage and fringe benefits increase over three years.

[36] Executives in the four companies that had not settled said that one reason for their reluctance to settle was the low price of copper. The price of copper had fluctuated wildly in 1980. On February 12, the price of copper had reached a record $1.45 a pound. But by March 2, the price had dropped to $1.13 on the New York Commodity Exchange. When the copper strike started July 1, the price of copper, rather than advancing in expectation of possible shortages, actually dropped. Futures prices on the Comex were down 0.45 to 0.90 cents to 90.60 cents a pound. After the Kennecott agreement was announced, prices turned down again, with December contracts on the Comex selling at 89 cents a pound.

[37] A spokesman for the AFL-CIO United Steelworkers union Nov. 10 announced settlement of its labor dispute with Asarco Inc., the sixth largest U.S. copper producer. The settlement was the last of 11 agreements reached with copper companies in a 19-week dispute. The walkouts began July 1.

See also Baseball [7-10]; Steel [1-5]

LANCE, Thomas Bertram (Bert)

[1] **Lance Cleared on Misuse of Funds.** Former U.S. Budget Director Bert Lance was acquitted by a federal jury in Atlanta, Ga. April 30 of nine counts of bank fraud.

[2] A mistrial was declared on three remaining counts against Lance because the jury was unable to reach a verdict. The jury had deliberated for eight days. The acquittal came on charges that Lance had misused funds of two Georgia banks by making loans to family and friends with intent to defraud the banks. The jury dead-

locked on two counts that Lance lied on financial statements to obtain loans and one count of misapplication of bank funds.

[3] The jury delivered similar decisions on Lance's co-defendants. Thomas M. Mitchell, Lance's trustee when Lance took his federal position, was cleared of four charges of filing false financial statements for the benefit of Lance. Richard T. Carr, a former bank president, was cleared of three counts of bank fund misapplication. H. Jackson Mullins, a former druggist, was cleared of three charges of bank fund misapplication.

[4] U.S. District Judge Charles Moye of Atlanta June 9 dismissed remaining charges pending against Lance, Carr and Mullins. The justice department had asked for the dismissal on the ground that further prosecution would not be worth the expense.

LAW

Court Rulings

[1] **Testimony by Spouse.** The Supreme Court ruled unanimously Feb. 27 that a person could voluntarily testify against his or her spouse in federal criminal trials. The case was *Trammel v. U.S.*

[2] The decision amended the so-called "Hawkins Rule," established by the high court in 1958. The rule, based on English common law, held that a defendant-spouse could prevent his or her spouse from giving negative testimony in a criminal trial. The rule was based on the concept of preserving marital harmony.

[3] In the Trammel case, a man was convicted on federal charges of smuggling heroin into the U.S. His wife, who was a party to the action, testified against him after she was guaranteed lenient treatment by government prosecutors. The defendant sought to have his conviction overturned, citing the Hawkins Rule.

[4] The Supreme Court, led by Chief Justice Warren E. Burger, upheld the conviction and modified the testimony rule. The decision on whether or not to testify now rested with the witness, rather than the defendant-spouse. "The witness," Burger wrote for the court, "may neither be compelled to testify nor foreclosed from testifying." Burger maintained that the marital harmony rationale was outdated.

[5] The ruling did not apply to confidential communications between husband and wife, but did apply to actions observed by one or the other, as well as to discussions held in the presence of third parties. Also, the decision concerned only federal court cases. Many states had laws of their own governing the testimony of spouses.

[6] **Texas Habitual-Offender Law.** The Supreme Court voted, 5-4, March 18 to uphold the constitutionality of a Texas law that imposed an automatic life sentence on anyone convicted three times of committing a felony. The decision affirmed a mandatory life sentence for a Texas man found guilty of three crimes that had netted him a total of $229.11. The case was *Rummel v. Estelle.*

[7] **'Exclusionary Rule' Narrowed.** The Supreme Court ruled, 5-4, May 27 that illegally seized evidence could be used in a criminal trial to impeach the testimony of a defendant. The decision in *U.S. v. Havens* significantly narrowed the so-called "exclusionary rule" instituted in 1971.

[8] The exclusionary rule barred the use of illegal evidence to prove a person's guilt. As a result, such evidence had been automatically banned from trials.

[9] ***Power to Supress Evidence Curbed***—The Supreme Court ruled, 6-3, June 23 that federal judges could not suppress illegally seized evidence unless the seizure had directly violated the constitutional rights of a criminal defendant.

[10] The case, *U.S. v. Payner,* turned on the "supervisory power" of federal judges to bar tainted evidence from

trials. The power was used routinely, in accordance with the so-called "exclusionary rule," which generally meant that illegal evidence was inadmissable in courts of law. The defendant, Jack Payner, an Ohio businessman, was convicted of falsifyng a federal income tax return, based on a document obtained by the Internal Revenue Service through an illegal search. An IRS informant found the document–which revealed that Payner had a secret bank account in the Bahamas–while searching the briefcase of a Bahamian bank officer. Payner's conviction was overturned by a federal district court, using its supervisory power, on the ground that the evidence against him was tainted by the search. The U.S. 6th Circuit Court of Appeals agreed.

[11] The Supreme Court reversed the lower courts, holding that Payner's Fourth Amendment rights had not been abused. Writing for the majority, Justice Lewis F. Powell Jr. said that "the supervisory power does not authorize a federal court to suppress otherwise admissible evidence on the ground that it was seized unlawfully from a third party [the banker] not before the court." In dissent, Justice Thurgood Marshall criticized the majority for allowing the government to "invade one person's Fourth Amendment rights in order to obtain evidence against another person."

[12] **Use of Informers Restricted.** The Supreme Court June 16 voted to curb further the use of paid informers by law enforcement agencies. The vote was 6-3. In the case, *U.S. v. Henry,* the Federal Bureau of Investigation obtained evidence against a robbery suspect, Billy Gale Henry, through an informer planted in Henry's cell block. The Supreme Court affirmed a ruling by the U.S. 4th Circuit Court of Appeals overturning Henry's subsequent conviction.

[13] Chief Justice Warren E. Burger, writing for the majority, contended that the FBI was guilty of "impermissible interference" with Henry's Sixth Amendment right to counsel–that is, that the informer's conversations with the defendant constituted "interrogations" at which Henry's lawyer was not present. The decision extended a 1964 high court ruling that curbed the use of informants outside of jails.

[14] **Documents Secrecy Rule Takes Effect.** A procedural rule allowing federal judges to withhold pretrial documents from the public record took effect Aug. 1. The rule had been adopted by the U.S. Judicial Conference in June as a cost-saving measure. The conference, headed by Chief Justice Warren E. Burger, was the policy-making body of the federal court system.

[15] The rule concerned only the so-called "discovery" phase of pretrial activity in civil lawsuits. During this phase, lawyers for both sides exchanged data on the case in order to establish the facts and gather evidence. By tradition, this data was filed with the court and became part of the public record.

[16] Under the rule, judges were given the power to keep these documents secret, either upon recommendation of the parties in the suits, or upon their own discretion. The rule was backed by the American Bar Association but opposed by the press.

[17] **Lenient Sentence Appeal Backed.** The Supreme Court voted, 5-4, Dec. 9 to uphold a law that gave the federal government the right to appeal a criminal sentence it believed was too lenient. The court held that the law, the Organized Crime Control Act of 1970, did not violate the so-called "double jeopardy" clause of the Fifth Amendment. The case was *U.S. v. Di Francesco.*

See also Internal Revenue Service [1-3]; Police [1-3]

LEBANON—*See* Chad [3]; Human Rights [9]

LENNON, JOHN

[1] **Lennon Murdered.** Former Beatles

Jacket photo of John Lennon's last album, *Double Fantasy*, featuring Lennon and his wife, Yoko Ono. Dakota apartment house on Manhattan's West Side where he was shot and killed Dec. 8 is behind them.

rock musician and composer John Lennon was shot and killed Dec. 8 in New York City.

[2] Lennon, 40, was hit by bullets in the chest, back and left arm, outside his apartment building on New York's Upper West Side. He was pronounced dead on arrival at a nearby hospital. With Lennon when he was shot, but not hurt, was his Japanese-born wife, Yoko Ono.

[3] Police identified the alleged gunman as Mark David Chapman, 25, of Honolulu, a former security guard and Young Man's Christian Association youth worker. Chapman allegedly called out, "Mr. Lennon?" and then went into a "combat stance" and pumped five bullets into the singer with a Charter Arms .38-caliber handgun. Lennon, hit as he was stepping from a limousine into the archway of the Dakota apartment building, staggered up six steps into an office, cried out "I am shot" and collapsed on his face.

[4] Chapman, who had reportedly been in New York for a week and had been seen lingering outside the Dakota all weekend, was arraigned on charges of second-degree murder and criminal possession of a revolver, which he had purchased in Hawaii six weeks earlier for $169. After his arraignment, he was taken to Bellevue Hospital for psychiatric observation. Chapman was said to have been previously institutionalized in Honolulu after attempting suicide.

[5] According to some accounts, Chapman, when arrested, was carrying 14 hours of taped Beatles music and a copy of Lennon's latest record album, which Lennon had autographed for him only hours before the shooting. Immediately after the shooting, authorities said, Chapman dropped his gun and stood calmly, as building employees called the police.

[6] ***Mourning Fans Pay Tribute***—Word of Lennon's death brought an outpouring of grief and shock nationwide. In New York City, hundreds of persons began gathering in silent mourning outside the Dakota to pay last respects to the slain rock musician. Many of Lennon's fans, who brought flowers and candles, were weeping.

[7] All across the United States, radio stations began to play continuously Beatles music in tribute, interrupted only for news breaks and phone calls of bereavement from fans. Television networks rushed to provide on-the-spot coverage at the scene of the slaying and to produce instant specials on Lennon's life and work.

[8] News of Lennon's death set off a national buying spree of Beatles music as records were quickly bought up in record stores around the United States. Orders for almost one million of Lennon's last album, *Double Fantasy*, were reportedly received in a single day.

[9] Former Beatles Paul McCartney, George Harrison and Ringo Starr Dec. 9 reacted with shock and grief after hearing of Lennon's death. McCartney, reportedly pale and shaken, said in London: "I can't take it in at the moment; he was a great guy and is going to be missed by the whole world." Former lead guitarist George Harrison was reported too shocked to talk about the murder. A spokesman for Ringo Starr said that the drummer had boarded a plane for New York as soon as he had heard about the slaying.

[10] President-elect Ronald Reagan, who was visiting in New York City, Dec. 9 called the death "a great tragedy," adding that "we have to try to stop tragedies of this sort." President Carter Dec. 9 paid tribute to Lennon's music: "His spirit, the spirit of the Beatles – brash and earnest, ironic and idealistic all at once – became the spirit of a whole generation."

[11] ***Lennon's Background***—John Winston Lennon was born on Oct. 9, 1940 in England's northern industrial seaport of Liverpool, the son of a porter who abandoned the family to join the British Navy when Lennon was three. A poor student in high

school, Lennon's interest in music developed in his teens, listening to American rock and roll stars Elvis Presley, Little Richard and Jerry Lee Lewis.

[12] When Lennon was 17, he organized his first rock group, called the Quarrymen, and went on to enlist the services of Paul McCartney, George Harrison, and later, Ringo Starr. The music group, later known as the Beatles, gained success playing in such waterfront cities as Hamburg, West Germany and Liverpool.

[13] In 1964 the Beatles made their first concert tour of the United States and went on to enjoy an unbroken string of hit records that included *I Want to Hold Your Hand, Love Me Do,* and *She Loves Me.* The hit songs heralded the group's emergence as the leader of a worldwide rock movement that affected an entire generation and changed radically the course of popular music.

[14] As a lead singer, lyricist and composer, Lennon was thought to be the most intellectual and outspoken of the Beatles in their heyday and was responsible for writing many of their hit songs. He played a key role in getting the group to embrace influences that ranged from psychedelic drugs and the poetic innovations of folk singer Bob Dylan to the activist political protests of the late 1960s and early 1970s.

[15] Lennon made his last Beatles album, *Abbey Road,* in 1969. In 1970 after the group broke up, he continued writing songs and recording. But in 1975, he dropped out of the music business, saying that he wanted to be with his son Sean and his wife. In the summer of 1980, he returned to music, recording his 14-song album, *Double Fantasy.*

[16] At his death, Lennon had amassed a fortune worth nearly $235 million, with holdings that included luxury apartments, mansions, farms, purebred cattle, a twin-engine plane and a 62-foot yacht. He also owned 25% interest in Apple Records, which held copyrights to the Beatles' music, and had been receiving $12 million a year in royalties.

LETELIER CASE—*See* Chile [11-16]

LIBERIA

[1] **President Killed in Coup d'Etat.** Liberian President William R. Tolbert Jr., 66, and 27 others were slain April 12 in a coup d'etat staged by enlisted men in the Liberian army. Master Sgt. Samuel K. Doe, 28, assumed leadership of the government and vowed to end corruption.

[2] In a radio broadcast, Doe said the "rampant corruption and continuous failure by the government to effectively handle the affairs of the Liberian people left the enlisted men no alternative." One of his first official acts was to free Gabriel Baccus Matthews and other imprisoned members of the opposition Progressive People's Party.

[3] In a televised speech April 13, Doe introduced a 15-member Cabinet composed of five soldiers and 10 civilians. Matthews was named minister of foreign affairs. Doe promised to build a "new society" and run the government "without discrimination." The sergeant said that his government would maintain most of Liberia's policies, such as encouraging foreign investment, and respecting free enterprise and private property. He said former members of Tolbert's government would be tried for treason and corruption. (Liberia added April 15 that it would continue its shipping registration business, a major source of revenue. A large proportion of the world's ships flew Liberian flags of convenience, since Liberia's registration and safety requirements were less stringent than those of most other countries.)

[4] The U.S. said it expected its relations with Liberia to remain friendly. The coup was a surprise to most out-

side observers. Liberia had been regarded as a model of stability for Africa. Tolbert, president since 1971, was the son of a freed American slave who emigrated to Liberia. He had embarked on a program of wide-ranging reform in the country, but corruption and conflicts of interest still lingered among his government officials. Discontent was further heightened by the fact that the descendants of U.S. slaves, although less than 5% of the population, controlled the political and economic life of the country.

[5] **13 Executed, Constitution Suspended.** Liberia's 133-year-old Constitution was suspended April 25 by the country's military junta. Three days earlier, 13 of the former civilian government's highest-ranking officials had been executed for "high treason, rampant corruption and gross violation of human rights."

LIBYA

[1] **Libya, Syria Form One Nation.** Syria and Libya Sept. 10 announced the merger of their two countries into a single nation.

[2] A 14-point document proclaiming the event was issued in Tripoli and Damascus after the signing of an agreement in the Libyan capital by Syrian President Hafez al-Assad and Libyan head of state Col. Muammer el-Qaddafi. Both leaders had held discussions on the unity move Sept. 8-9.

[3] According to the proclamation, "This unified state will be the base and means of confronting the Zionist presence and a means of liberating Palestine." It denounced the U.S., Egypt and Israel for the Camp David peace agreements.

[4] While the proclamation did not specify how the new state would function, some details were provided in a separate statement issued jointly by the ruling bodies of the two countries – Syria's Baath Socialist Party and Libya's People's Congress. It said the single state would have one congress and one executive authority. The People's Congress and the Baath Socialist Party would meet in a joint congress.

[5] **Unity Delayed.** Libya and Syria delayed implementation of their proposed merger as their two leaders failed to reach agreement on details of the move at talks in Benghazi, Libya Dec. 16-18.

MAINE—*See* Civil & Constitutional Rights [2-4]; Indians, American [1-3]

MARITIME AFFAIRS

[1] **Draft Law of the Sea.** The ninth session of the United Nations Law of the Sea Conference ended Aug. 29 in Geneva with agreement on a wide range of issues. Delegates expressed optimism that the final text of a treaty would be written in the next session, scheduled to take place in March 1981.

[2] The session, which began July 28, followed six years of arduous negotiations involving more than 150 nations, as well as a number of nongovernmental groups, such as the Sierra Club. Depending on the issue, the countries had divided up in different ways: the question of seabed mining had pitted industrialized countries against developing nations, while fishing rights and other questions had resulted in the formation of different blocs.

[3]The major agreement reached in the ninth session dealt with the controversial issue of seabed mining. The industrialized nations had generally favored allowing private corporations to mine the ocean floor for profit. Third World nations had insisted that the mineral wealth of the ocean was the property of all countries, not just of those that had the technology to exploit it, and should be used to assist development.

[4] Under the draft agreement, an International Seabed Authority would be established to regulate deep-sea mining. The authority would control mining outside coastal nations' 200-mile (320-kilometer) economic zones. Private companies wishing to mine the seabed would apply to the authority for licenses; they would also be required to provide the authority with a mining site next to their own and sell the authority the technology to exploit the site. To meet the costs of mining itself, the authority would be granted a $1 billion loan by the industrialized nations.

[5] The draft accord incorporated more than 300 articles and eight annexes. Among the issues dealt with in addition to deep-sea mining:

[6] ***Boundaries***—A 12-mile (19.2-kilometer) territorial limit for coastal nations was approved. Coastal nations would also possess a 200-mile (320-kilometer) "exclusive economic zone" and, where the continental shelf extended past the 200-mile limit, the coastal nations would continue to have jurisdiction over marine resources. Coastal states would exercise complete control over fish in their economic zone.

[7] ***Environment***—Pollution by ships was outlawed, with violators subject to fines. Steps were taken to set up environmental controls, even against pollution emanating from inland waterways.

[8] ***Disputes***—The accord would establish a Law of the Sea Tribunal to adjudicate disputes.

[9] **Antarctic Fishing Pact.** Fifteen countries, including the U.S. and the Soviet Union, reached agreement in

Canberra, Australia May 20 on a pact designed to safeguard marine life in the Antarctic from overfishing.
[10] A two-week conference of the countries focused primarily on the increasing exploitation of krill, a crustacean that had a key role in the food chain. The countries established harvesting quotas for different forms of marine life. They also set up an international commission to recommend measures to protect marine and bird species in the Antarctic. The pact was signed Sept. 11.
See also Mexico [6-11]

MASSACHUSETTS—*See* Death Penalty [7]

MATHEMATICS

Finite Simple Groups. A number of mathematicians succeeded in putting together an extremely long proof showing that all finite simple groups were reducible to a known collection of finite simple groups, *Science News* reported Sept. 27. The proof had been a major goal of many mathematicians for at least 25 years. (Groups were sets of objects with a procedure for combining them that obeyed a few elementary rules. Groups were called simple if they could not be produced through a combination of other groups.)

MEANY, GEORGE—*See* Labor [1-4]

MEDICAID—*See* Abortion [1-3]

MEDICINE & HEALTH

Cancer

[1] **Rise in Lung Cancer Among Women.** Lung cancer among American women was increasing sharply, the U.S. surgeon general said Jan. 14. Within three years, it could become the leading cancer killer of women, exceeding breast cancer.
[2] The surgeon general's findings were contained in a 400-page report to Congress which pointed out that "the first signs of an epidemic of smoking-related disease among women are now appearing."
[3] Pregnant women who smoked ran increased risks of health problems, the surgeon general, Dr. Julius Richmond, also said. These problems could include spontaneous abortions, fetal and neonatal death and infants of less than average birth weight. The rate of fetal deaths and premature live births increased in direct proportion to maternal smoking levels, Richmond added.
[4] **Disease Fighting Protein Produced.** Human interferon, a natural disease-fighting protein believed to be greatly effective in curing a broad variety of viral diseases and some forms of cancer, had been produced in a laboratory by genetic engineering, it was announced Jan. 16. The announcement was made in Boston, Mass. by scientists and officers of Biogen, S.A., an international genetic research concern based in Geneva, Switzerland.
[5] ***Some Success Reported***—The first clinical tests in the United States of interferon showed some success in the treatment of bone and breast cancer, but none with lung cancer, scientists said May 28.
[6] Preliminary findings in a $5.4 million interferon research project showed the following effects of the antivirus protein:

- Among 14 patients treated for multiple myeloma or bone marrow cancer, four had reasonably good regressions. However, there were no cures or complete remissions.
- Against recurrent breast cancer, interferon produced a "partial response" in five of 16 patients. Two other patients showed tumor reduction, but not enough to qualify as a partial response.

[7] In the lung cancer studies, researchers for the Memorial Sloan-Kettering Cancer Center reported that

interferon showed no effect on the disease.

[8] **Cancer Deaths Increase Forecast in '80s.** Cancer deaths would claim the lives of at least 8.5 million Americans in the 1980s – at least 2 million more than in the 1970s, the American Cancer Society predicted April 28 in its annual report.

[9] According to the report, one reason for the expected rise in cancer deaths was that people were living longer and that cancer was now being regarded as a disease of aging.

[10] Said Lane W. Adams, the society's executive vice president: "In spite of solid progress in prevention . . . cancer will strike more people than ever.

[11] "The number of people who are living into the cancer-prone years is increasing. In 1976 the over-50 population was 50 million. By 1990, it will be 63 million." The accompanying chart, compiled from several sources, indicates the risk factors associated with various types of cancer.

[12] **Brain Cancer Found in Chemical Plant Workers.** An unusually high incidence of brain cancer cases had been found among workers at two Texas petrochemical plants, federal investigators reported July 24.

[13] Investigators found 43 cases of brain cancer, all but one fatal, among present and past employees at a Dow Chemical plant in Freeport and at a Union Carbide plant in Texas City. According to Gordon Reeve, an epidemiologist for the National Institute of Ocupational Safety and Health, the brain cancer rate at the Dow plant was twice the normal level in the general population and up to three times the normal level at the Union Carbide plant. Scientists from NIOSH and U.S. Occupational Safety and Health Administration had been studying the two plants since 1979.

[14] Higher-than-normal rates of brain, stomach, liver, pancreas, lung and skin cancers had also been reported among petrochemical workers along the Texas Gulf Coast in recent studies conducted by the National Cancer Institute.

[15] **U.S. Agencies Reject Nitrite Ban.** There was insufficient scientific evidence to justify banning the preservative sodium nitrite from food as a cancer-causing agent, the federal government said Aug. 19.

[16] In a joint statement, the Food and Drug Administration and the Department of Agriculture said that a 1978 study, which purportedly showed that nitrite caused animal cancer, had been found in various reviews to be inconclusive.

[17] However, the agencies acknowledged that in some cases nitrite could combine with other chemicals in cooking or digestion to form cancer-causing substances called nitrosamines. Therefore, they said they would try to have the amount of nitrite used in food reduced.

Agent Orange

[18] **Agent Orange Blamed in Birth Defects.** The children of former Australian servicemen who had been exposed to defoliant "Agent Orange" while in Vietnam were much more likely to suffer from birth defects than children in the general population, according to a study reported Jan. 3.

[19] The study covered 50 former servicemen who had various medical problems – such as a body rash and extreme nervousness – which they attributed to exposure to the toxic chemical defoliant. One in four of the men had fathered deformed children, the survey found. This contrasted with a national average of one seriously deformed child in every 1,000.

Toxic-Shock Syndrome

[20] **'Toxic-Shock Syndrome' Hits Women.** A baffling, recently discovered disease that frequently struck young women and could produce death within a few days had appeared in 13 states, killing seven women, medical scientists told a Senate Health subcommittee June 6.

[21] The disease, called toxic-shock syndrome, was characterized by such symptoms as high fever, vomiting, diarrhea, skin rash, a drop in blood pressure and malfunctioning of the kidney, liver or intestines or all three. The symptoms were believed to develop over a period of two days or more.

[22] Some of the victims died from shock, a condition that could result from a sharp drop in blood pressure, shutting off blood to the brain and other vital organs. Most of the victims were women who displayed symptoms in the first five days of their menstrual cycle. A bacterium, *Staphylococcus aureus,* was found in the mucus of nearly 75% of the patients.

[23] According to Dr. William Foege, director of the U.S. Center for Disease Control, 52 of the 55 reported cases were women with the average age of 25 for the patients. Foege also told the subcommittee that based on sampling of the cases, about 2,000 cases of the disease could be expected every year.

[24] **Tampon, 'Toxic-Shock' Linked.** A tampon product was ordered recalled Sept. 22 because federal studies had linked its use to increased risks of a serious and sometimes fatal disease called "toxic-shock syndrome." The disease to date had caused about 25 deaths.

[25] The recall was issued by Procter and Gamble Co., manufacturer of Rely tampons, after the U.S. Center for Disease Control Sept. 17 had identified the tampon brand as a contributing "risk factor" to toxic-shock syndrome. The center said that a review of women who had contacted the disease in July and August found that about 70% of them used the Rely tampons. The review also affirmed earlier findings by government studies that indicated a link between the syndrome and the use of tampons generally.

[26] The center said that studies had linked the disorder to a bacterium known as *Staphylococcus aureus.* The suspect bacteria, which could breed in the vaginal cavity, produced a toxin that entered the blood-stream, according to government research studies. Those organisms, thus far, had been found resistant to antibodies in the penicillin family. Preliminary theories, as yet unconfirmed, indicated that the Rely tampons' absorbency agent, carboxymethylcellulose, might act as a breeding agent for the bacteria because of the way it was located in the tampon. The substance was also used in other tampons, but not in the same way as in Rely.

[27] According to center studies, the chances of developing the disorder were greatest among women who used tampons continuously throughout their menstrual periods. Those who alternated tampons with sanitary napkins were believed less likely to develop the disorder.

Nutrition

[28] **U.S. Dietary Guidelines.** Dietary guidelines aimed at establishing a national nutrition policy and reshaping the American diet were issued Feb. 4 by the federal government.

[29] The guidelines offered jointly by the Departments of Agriculture and Health, Education and Welfare, recommended that Americans avoid excessive amounts of fat, cholesteral, sugar salt, and alcohol, which some researchers said contributed to heart disease, diabetes, tooth decay, high blood pressure and certain forms of cancer.

[30] The guidelines also recommended proper body weight and eating a variety of foods containing adequate amounts of starch and fiber. Among the foods recommended for daily consumption were: fruits; vegetables; whole grain and enriched breads, cereals and grain products; milk, cheese and yogurt; lean meats, poultry and fish; eggs, and legumes (dried peas and beans).

[31] The dietary guidelines had pro-

voked strong opposition from major sectors of the food industry, particularly from farm and cattle interests and also from the American Medical Association and some scientists. Opponents of the guidelines had argued that they were premature and not based on sufficient scientific fact.

[32] **Cholesterol Report Controversy.** A food and nutrition panel said in a controversial report May 27 that it had found no evidence to recommend that healthy persons reduce consumption of cholesterol or fat.

[33] The report, issued by the Food and Nutrition Board of the National Academy of Sciences, said that clinical studies had not shown any life-saving benefit from eating less fat and cholesterol. The board also said that it had not found any evidence linking fats and cholesterol as causes of heart disease and said it could not make any overall dietary recommendations aimed at reducing risks of heart disease. It did advise, however, a substantial reduction in salt intake to help prevent high blood pressure, and stressed the importance of maintaining normal body weight.

[34] The panel report was a sharp departure from recent dietary recommendations and came under heavy criticism from some nutrition and health experts, who assailed it as inaccurate, inadequate and misleading. Government officials expressed the following reservations about the Food and Nutrition Board members and the procedures:

■ The board had strong ties to the food industry. Two members were food company executives and some members from universities were serving as paid consultants to food companies, including egg producers. Also, the board's basic financial support came from the food industry.

■ Significant scientific data were disregarded by the board, particularly epidemiological or population studies that showed a link between a high-fat cholesterol diet and increased risks of heart attacks.

■ The board had no members who were epidemiologists, cardiologists or public health experts and consulted none for the study.

Drug Actions & Research

[35] **Anticholesterol Drug Risk.** A drug used by 25,000 people to lower cholesterol in the blood was reported Feb. 17 to have caused fatal heart abnormalities in monkeys on a high-cholesterol diet.

[36] The drug, called Lorelco or probucol, had been tested in a study in which eight monkeys were given the drug at three or more times the normal dose. The monkeys developed changes in electrocardiograms and dangerously irregular heartbeats. Four monkeys died.

[37] Dow Chemical Co., which manufactured the drug, was reported to have sent a letter at the request of the U.S. Food and Drug Administration to 115,000 doctors warning them to check for abnormal heart rhythms in patients receiving the drug. The letter also instructed the doctors to caution patients on a high cholesterol or fat diet against further use of Lorelco.

[38] Another cholesterol-lowering drug, Atromid-S, which was not chemically related to Lorelco, had also been criticized because of research indicating that it might cause cancer, liver tumors and gall bladder disease.

[39] **U.S. To Curb Darvon Production.** The U.S. Drug Enforcement Administration said April 24 that it would limit production of the active ingredient in Darvon as a result of action by a United Nations narcotics panel to reclassify the controversial pain-killer.

[40] The drug, manufactured by Eli Lilly & Co. of Indianapolis, had been prescribed by physicians as a mild analgesic. However, Darvon was also addictive, inducing euphoria and was said to have caused hundreds of deaths, accidental and suicidal. The U.N. action was taken in February,

when the Commission on Narcotic Drugs voted to place propoxyphene, Darvon's active ingredient, on its International Narcotics Schedule II. Under the 1961 drug convention agreement, this would require the United States and 109 other signatories to set tighter controls and production quotas for the substance.

[41] **Warnings on Tranquilizers.** The makers of Valium, Librium and other widely used tranquilizers were reported July 11 to have agreed to issue warnings to physicians that the drugs were not meant to relieve anxiety and tension "associated with the stress of everyday life."

[42] The agreement, which had been sought by the Food and Drug Administration, was aimed at reducing the overuse of tranquilizers. The tranquilizers, among the most widely prescribed drugs in the world, originally had been promoted as safe. However, they later were found to have a potential for physical and psychological addiction.

[43] The companies that agreed to the information change were: Hoffman-La Roche Inc., maker of Librium and Valium; Warner-Chilcott Laboratories Inc., maker of Verstran; Abbott Laboratories, maker of Traxene and Azene; Wyeth Laboratories Inc., maker of Serax and Ativan, and Parke-Davis & Co., maker of Centrax. Manufacturers of similar unbranded or generic tranquilizers were expected to comply with the agreement, the FDA said.

Genetic Research

[44] **Animal, Bacteria Gene Differences.** A discovery of basic differences in gene regulation in animals and bacteria was reported Jan. 23 by scientists who described the new finding as surprising and important.

[45] The discovery was said to mean that genetic studies would not be able to assume, as before, that evidence about gene regulation in bacteria would apply equally to cells in animals. Gene regulation was considered fundamental to the growth and development of all forms of life and also to knowledge of health and disease. Most scientific knowledge of how genes were regulated had been based on studies of bacteria largely because it had not been possible, until recently, to observe animal genetics in laboratory studies.

[46] It had been widely assumed that animal genes, while more complex than bacteria genetics, operated in the same fundamental way. The discovery of the animal and bacterial gene differences was reported by scientists of the Carnegie Institute of Washington. The details of discovery were described in two reports published in *Cell*, a scientific journal.

Other Developments

[47] **Little-Known VD at Epidemic Levels.** A sexually transmitted disease largely unknown a few years ago was reported Feb. 5 to have reached epidemic levels in the U.S. and other industrialized countries. The disease, called NGU or NSU, had reportedly become the most common venereal infection among young adults.

[48] Despite the rapid increase in the incidence of the disease, many physicians and public health authorities were said either to be unaware of the disease or unable to make the necessary diagnostic laboratory tests.

[49] NGU, nongonococcal urethritis, or NSU, for nonspecific urethritis, had also been connected recently to a broad variety of other illnesses in research studies by American, British and Swedish scientists. NGU had been linked to pelvic inflammatory disease (PID) in women and to epididymitis in men. The disease had also been found to be a possible cause of pneumonia and ear infections in children. Still other research studies had found evidence linking NGU to stillbirths and sudden deaths in infants, according to

Dr. King K. Holmes, an internationally recognized researcher in sexually transmitted diseases.

[50] Studies had shown NGU to be 10 times more common than gonorrhea among patients in student health clinics and in some hospitals. Venereal disease experts had found that NGU was also present as an infection in about 20% of gonorrhea cases in men and about 50% of gonorrhea cases in women. An estimated 2 million cases of NGU reportedly occurred in the U.S. every year. (U.S. physicians did not have to report cases of NGU to health authorities.) In England, where NGU was a reportable disease, it had shown a sharp increase to 98,606 cases in 1978 from 35,040 in 1968. By contrast during the same period, the number of gonorrhea cases had remained comparatively stable—43,922 in 1968 and 56,184 in 1978.

[51] **Airline Ozone Standards.** New ozone exposure standards were being implemented in the airline industry in the wake of a growing number of cases of ozone illness among high-altitude airline crews, it was reported Feb. 12.

[52] Previously, commercial jets had not flown high enough to enter the layer of the Earth's atmosphere containing ozone. But in recent years, to conserve increasingly expensive fuel, aircraft had begun flying more often in the ozone layer. Ozone illness includes such symptoms as a racking cough, difficulty in breathing, chest pains and occasionally eye irritation and bloody noses.

In response to the problem:

■ New Federal Aviation Administration regulations called for ozone levels averaging 0.1 for long-range flights, with peaks of less than 0.25.

■ Pan American World Airways, whose long-range overseas flights had had frequent ozone problems, was installing charcoal filters and catalytic converters on its jets to filter out the gas. The FAA estimated that 500 U.S. jets would need the filters.

[53] **Blinding Disease Spreads in Africa.** A viral disease that destroyed livestock and could cause blindness in human beings was reported March 2 to have spread widely across Africa.

[54] The disease, called Rift Valley Fever, was causing alarm to health officials who feared the disease might spread to other parts of the world. Health experts also were reported to have expressed fear that only inadequate steps had been taken to control the disease, that it could cause billions of dollars in damage to livestock and aggravate malnutrition problems in developing nations. The virus was carried by at least 18 different species of mosquitos.

[55] The disease had not been reported in the U.S. and federal law currently prohibited bringing the virus into the U.S., even for experimental purposes. Exceptions, however, had been made for government laboratories for the study of the virus as a biological warfare agent. The Army was the only source of a certified vaccine, but it had only enough doses available to immunize 100,000 persons, said Col. Gerald A. Eddy, chief virologist, U.S. Army Medical Research Institute, Frederick, Md.

[56] **FDA Approves New Rabies Vaccine.** The Food and Drug Administration announced approval June 9 of a safer, more efficient and less painful vaccine for people bitten by rabid animals.

[57] The new vaccine reportedly had to be administered only five times, rather than 23 as with the old. The injections could be given in the patient's arm rather than the abdomen. Moreover, the vaccine could be taken as a preventive measure by persons, such as veterinarians and animal trainers, who risked exposure to the disease. The new vaccine produced less frequent adverse reactions in patients than the old one, the FDA added.

[58] **AMA Adopts New Doctors' Ethics Code.** The American Medical Association July 22 adopted a revised code of medical ethics in a major policy change

that would permit doctors to advertise their fees and services and to refer patients to chiropractors. Endorsement of the new ethics code, the first revamping in 23 years, was voted by a heavy majority of the AMA's House of Delegates at the association's annual convention in Chicago.

[59] The new code came in the wake of intense legal and political pressure and debate over methods of medical practice and education. The AMA had been faced with a barrage of lawsuits filed by associations of chiropractors, charging that the old set of professional ethics had been used to isolate and deny them the opportunity to practice their healing art. The new code specifically permitted doctors to associate with chiropractors or other practitioners if they so chose. In addition, a Federal Trade Commission ruling had held that the AMA's old ban on patient solicitation had tended to restrain free competition among doctors.

[60] Overall, the lawsuits against the AMA were costing the association more than $1 million a year in legal bills and threatening it with possible bankruptcy. The association's problems were further complicated by a declining membership, leaving it on uncertain financial footing. In 1970, the AMA had 168,000 doctors as full dues-paying members, slightly more than half the 334,000 doctors in the U.S. at that time. However, by 1979, that number had dropped to 151,000, one-third of the nation's 453,000 doctors.

See also Abortion; Nobel Prizes [9-11]

MEXICO

[1] **Fighting Erupts over Land Dispute.** Fighting between landowners and landless peasants erupted May 31 in Mexico's southern Chiapas state near the Guatemalan border. The fighting came as a result of the expulsion by landowners of some 600 peasants who had invaded and occupied several small farms in the remote mountain region three weeks before.

[2] **Ford Plans $365-Million Engine Plant.** Ford Motor Co. June 12 said that it planned to begin construction this year on a $365-million engine plant in Mexico. To be built by Ford's Mexican affiliate, the plant would be Ford's fourth unit in Mexico and would produce four-cylinder engines for Ford cars sold in the U.S., Canada and Mexico beginning in the 1984 model year.

[3] **Drought Threatens Cattle, Crops.** Cattle and crops in Mexico's North and Northeast were threatened by the worst drought in 20 years, according to *Excelsior* June 13.

[4] Some 4.5 million head of cattle were affected, and newborn calves were being slaughtered before they died of hunger or thirst. The cotton crop, as well as the seasonal harvests of corn, sorghum and wheat, were in danger of being lost, making the shortage of basic food items in Mexico as serious as in 1979, when a prolonged drought in June of that year had been followed by an early fall frost.

[5] According to Mexican agricultural officials, the present drought would reduce Mexico's annual production of grain by about 30%. Since the first of the year, Mexico had had to import four million tons of grain, with 800,000 tons imported in the month of May – the largest amount of grain ever imported by Mexico in a single month. In addition, Mexico's federal electricity commission was forced to order a reduction in the use of domestic, commercial and industrial electricity because many reservoirs supplying hydroelectric plants had dried up.

[6] **U.S. Bans Tuna Imports over Dispute.** The U.S. July 14 halted imports of Mexican tuna because of Mexico's seizure of three U.S. tuna boats the week before.

[7] A 1976 U.S. law required the imposing of an embargo whenever a U.S. fishing vessel was seized because of a territorial claim that the U.S. did not recognize. On June 6, 1976, Mexico

had established a 200-mile (320-kilometer) offshore "economic zone," restricting fishing and mining off its Pacific and Gulf coasts and closing the Gulf of California to foreign fishermen. But the U.S. had never agreed to the Mexican law, claiming that while it recognized the right of countries to protect natural resources within 200 miles of their shores, migratory fish–like tuna–could not be included as residing within any country's jurisdiction. The U.S. recognized only a 12-mile (20-kilometer) limit for fish.

[8] U.S. fishermen continued to fish the waters off Baja California, while attempting to settle the dispute. But on July 8, a tuna boat operating out of San Diego was intercepted by the Mexican navy and taken to a naval base at Mazatlan. Again on July 10, two other large U.S. tuna boats were seized by Mexico. Mexican officials then fined the vessels the equivalent of $13,300 each for having violated Mexico's territory and confiscated their cargoes. The embargo on Mexico's tuna and tuna products followed. Imports to the U.S. of the fish products in 1979 had been worth about $20 million.

[9] ***Fishing Accords with U.S. Ended***—The Mexican government terminated its fishing accords with the U.S. Dec. 29 as a result of a continuing dispute between the two countries over fishing rights.

[10] Two treaties were revoked by Mexico. One was a 1976 agreement that set a quota for snapper and grouper caught by U.S. fishermen in the Gulf of Mexico and allowed smaller bait-boats to fish inside Mexico's 12-mile (19-kilometer) territorial waters in the Pacific. The other treaty was a 1977 agreement that allowed Mexico to apply for permits to fish for squid off the U.S.'s Eastern seaboard.

[11] Mexico's decision to renounce both treaties followed the U.S.'s refusal to grant Mexico squid fishing permits until a dispute over territorial waters was resolved. The two countries had been negotiating fishing rights and treaties for almost three years with no real results.

See also Environment [18-21]; United Nations [2]

MIAMI—*See* Civil Disorders [1-8]

MICHIGAN—*See* Weather [4-5]

MIDDLE EAST

[1] The Middle East continued to be a region of great turmoil in 1980 with the U.S. hostages still held by Iran [see Iran], the outbreak of war between Iraq and Iran [see Iraq], and fighting in southern Lebanon [see below]. The Palestinian, West Bank and Jerusalem issues remained volatile, marked by both controversial votes at the United Nations and incidents of violence. Meanwhile, Egypt and Israel took further steps towards "normalization" of their relations. Palestinian autonomy talks were held at intervals by Israel and Egypt; after reporting some progress, they were suspended near the end of the year, pending the assumption of office by U.S. President-elect Ronald Reagan.

Egyptian-Israeli Relations

[2] **Israel Ends 2d Sinai Pullout Phase.** Israel Jan. 25 completed withdrawal from two-thirds of the Sinai Peninsula. The move was followed Jan. 26 by the formal opening of the Israeli-Egyptian border in a further step toward the normalization of relations between the two countries.

[3] ***Egypt Terminates Economic Boycott***—A law terminating Egypt's participation in the Arab economic boycott of Israel was overwhelmingly approved Feb. 5 by the Egyptian People's Assembly (parliament). The Arab boycott, in effect since 1955, imposed sanctions against Israel and

companies that had dealings with it. Egypt had been observing an unofficial boycott before 1955.

[4] ***Envoys Exchanged***—Egypt and Israel exchanged ambassadors Feb. 26 in another step towards normalization.

[5] Eliahu Ben-Elissar, Israel's ambassador and former director general of Premier Menachem Begin's office, presented his credentials to Egyptian President Anwar Sadat in Cairo. In a simultaneous ceremony in Jerusalem, Egyptian Ambassador Saad Mortada, a career diplomat, presented his credentials to Israeli President Yitzhak Navon.

[6] **Normalization Speeded Up.** Egypt and Israel Oct. 29 agreed to speed up normalization of relations between the two countries. The agreement was announced at a joint news conference near Cairo by Sadat and visiting Israeli President Yitzhak Navon, who had been meeting with the Egyptian leader since his arrival Oct. 26.

[7] The normalization measures included the opening of a land route across the Sinai Peninsula to augment sea and air routes between the two countries already in use and people-to-people exchanges in many fields.

[8] **Reagan Backs Camp David Process.** President-elect Ronald Reagan had informed Egypt and Israel that he would continue the Camp David peace process and would approve of changes only if they agreed, it was reported Dec. 7.

[9] The disclosure was made by Sol Linowitz, President Carter's Middle East envoy. He said in an interview that he had been authorized Dec. 1 to convey Reagan's message to the two countries by Richard V. Allen, Reagan's foreign policy adviser.

Palestinian Automony Talks

[10] **Sadat, Begin Hold Summit Meeting.** Egyptian President Anwar Sadat and Israeli Premier Menachem Begin held a summit meeting in

In late December, former Secretary of State Henry J. Kissinger (left) toured countries of Middle East. Here, he confers with Egyptian President Anwar Sadat.

Aswan, Egypt Jan. 7-10 to discuss autonomy for Palestinian Arabs in the West Bank and Gaza Strip. It was the ninth such high-level meeting between the two leaders.

[11] **Egypt Opposes Autonomy Plan.** Egypt refused to discuss an Israeli plan for Palestinian autonomy during another round of negotiations in Cairo Jan. 17. The Egyptians said there was nothing new in the Israeli proposal to give limited administrative powers to Arabs in the West Bank and Gaza Strip.

[12] Interior Minister Yosef Burg, head of Israel's negotiating team, in turn rejected Egypt's counterproposal for a West Bank legislative assembly of 80-100 members, headed by an executive body of 10-15 members. Israel feared that a legislative body envisioned by Egypt could transform itself into a constitutional assembly and declare an independent Palestinian state. Burg also turned down Cairo's suggestion that East Jerusalem, which Egypt claimed was part of the West Bank, be included in the autonomy arrangement. Israel considered East Jerusalem a part of a unified Jerusalem under Israeli rule.

[13] ***Egypt Suspends Talks***—Egyptian President Sadat May 8 called for an indefinite delay in the Palestinian autonomy talks with Israel and the U.S., blaming Israel for the deadlock. His request followed another round of negotiations in Herzliya, Israel May 1-7.

[14] Sadat, however, announced a reversal of his decision May 14, following an appeal from President Carter the previous day. In yet another turnabout, Cairo said May 15 it would not resume stalled negotiations.

[15] Sadat sent a message to Israeli Prime Minister Begin Aug. 3 asking for a delay in the Palestinian autonomy talks with Israel and the U.S. The talks were to have resumed that day in Alexandria. Egypt called off the talks in protest against a new Israeli law declaring all of Jerusalem as Israel's capital.

[16] **Egypt, Israel To Resume Talks.** The U.S. announced Sept. 3 that Israel and Egypt had agreed to meet within a few weeks to resume Palestinian autonomy talks.

[17] The announcement was made in Alexandria, Egypt by Sol Linowitz, special U.S. envoy, following a meeting with Sadat. Linowitz had held similar discussions in Jerusalem Sept. 1-2 with Begin and other Israeli officials.

[18] ***Progress Reported***—Progress was reported at a renewed session of the U.S.-sponsored Palestinian autonomy talks in Washington Oct. 14-15.

[19] Special U.S. envoy Linowitz said Israel and Egypt had come up with new proposals moving them "closer to agreement" on self-rule for Arabs in the West Bank and Gaza Strip. Linowitz told a news conference that all three parties had agreed to resume negotiations Nov. 17.

[20] A summit meeting of the U.S., Egypt and Israel, tentatively scheduled for November, had been set back until December, or January 1981, it was announced.

[21] **Talks Postponed.** Israel and Egypt Dec. 4 agreed to postpone their negotiations on Palestinian autonomy pending the appointment of new American negotiators by the incoming Reagan administration. The decision was reached in talks held in Paris between Foreign Ministers Yitzhak Shamir of Israel and Butros Ghali of Egypt.

Palestinian Developments

[22] **U.S. vs. Palestinian State at U.N.** A U.N. Security Council resolution calling for the establishment of a Palestinian state was vetoed April 30 by the U.S.

[23] The U.S. cast the only negative vote. Ten nations, including the Soviet Union, China and East Germany, approved the resolution. France, Britain, Norway and Portugal abstained. The

principal section of the resolution affirmed that "the Palestinian people should be enabled to exercise its inalienable national right to self-determination, including the right to establish an independent state in Palestine."

[24] The United Nations General Assembly July 29 approved an Arab-sponsored resolution calling for the establishment of a Palestinian state and Israeli withdrawal from all the occupied lands, including East Jerusalem, by Nov. 15. If Israel refused to comply, the Security Council should consider economic sanctions against Israel, the document said.

[25] The vote was 112 to seven, with 24 abstentions and nine absent or not voting. The dissenting votes were cast by the U.S., Australia, Canada, Dominican Republic, Guatemala, Israel and Norway. All nine nations of the European Community abstained.

The resolution also:

■ Reaffirmed "the inalienable right of the Palestinians to return to their homes and property in Palestine, from which they had been displaced and uprooted. . . ."

■ Reaffirmed "the inalienable right of the Palestine Liberation Organization, the representative of the Palestinian people, to participate on an equal footing in all efforts, deliberations and conferences on the question of Palestine and the situation in the Middle East. . . ."

[26] The resolution omitted mention of Security Council Resolution 242, which guaranteed all states in the region, including Israel, the right to exist behind secure and recognized boundaries. Its absence from the adopted text was cited by West Europeans who abstained or voted against the resolution.

[27] **PLO Gains Support.** French President Valery Giscard d'Estaing toured the Persian Gulf states and Jordan March 1-10. In the course of the trip he issued a call for Palestinian "self-determination." Giscard also supported participation by the PLO in Middle East peace negotiations.

[28] Austrian Chancellor Bruno Kreisky announced March 13 that his government was extending "a new form of diplomatic recognition" to an official of the PLO in Austria. Kreisky said PLO diplomat Ghasi Hussain, who was accredited to Vienna-based United Nations agencies, would now be regarded also as a representative of his organization by the Austrian government.

[29] India March 26 extended full diplomatic relations to the PLO. The action was taken so that PLO leader Yasir Arafat could be greeted during his forthcoming two-day visit to India as a "head of government," Indian officials explained.

[30] Arafat was received in Managua, Nicaragua July 21. On July 22, Arafat took part in ceremonies officially opening diplomatic relations between the Nicaraguan government and the PLO.

[31] **Fatah Seeks Israel's Downfall.** Al Fatah, the main group of the PLO, June 1 called for the elimination of Israel.

[32] A published statement, issued at the conclusion of a 10-day conference in Damascus, said: "Fatah is an independent patriotic revolutionary movement and its aim is to completely liberate Palestine and liquidate the Zionist entity [Israel]. . . . Armed revolution is the only way to liberate Palestine and armed struggle is a strategic rather than a tactical goal."

[33] The conference May 31 had reelected Yasir Arafat as Fatah leader. He was to head a new 15-member Central Committee. The conference, which had started May 22, was the first held by Fatah in nine years and the fourth since its founding in 1969.

[34] **EC Backs PLO Peace Role.** The nine-member European Community June 13 urged full self-determination for the Palestinian people and suggested that the PLO be "associated with" negotiations for a peaceful settlement of the Arab-Israeli conflict. The views were contained in an 11-point

declaration issued by the EC at the end of a two-day summit in Venice.

[35] **Israeli Deputies Meet Arafat.** Two communist members of the Israeli Knesset (parliament)–Charlie Bitton and Tewfik Toubi–held talks in Sofia, Bulgaria Sept. 25 with Arafat.

[36] **Arab Summit.** The Arab League held its 11th summit meeting in Amman, Jordan Nov. 25-27 to draw up a new common policy against Israel and to discuss other regional matters. However, the parley occurred in a state of disarray as five of the organization's 21 members followed Syria's lead in boycotting the talks. The five were the PLO, Libya, Algeria, Lebanon and South Yemen.

[37] Syria had announced it boycott Nov. 22 because it felt the deteriorating relations among the Arabs over a number of issues, especially the Iranian-Iraqi war, would hamper the league's ability to attain major objectives. Asking for a postponement, Syrian Foreign Minister Abdel Halim Khaddam said, "There are a number of internal conflicts among Arab countries that should be resolved before any summit is held." The PLO announced its decision to shun the summit Nov. 24. The four others followed.

West Bank & Gaza Strip

[38] **Israel Approves Hebron Settlement.** The Israeli Cabinet Feb. 10 approved in principle the right of Israeli Jews to resettle in the Hebron, the exclusively Arab city in the West Bank. No date was set for implementing the ruling.

[39] Final approval would mark a radical departure from Israel's traditional practice of restricting Jewish settlements in the West Bank to vacant rural land, usually some distance from Arab cities. The Israeli Cabinet's decision on Hebron was in reaction to the fatal shooting Jan. 31 of a Jewish youth in the city's marketplace. A radical faction of the Palestine Liberation Organization took responsibility.

[40] The last Jewish settlement in Hebron was destroyed in Arab rioting in 1929. Residents of the Israeli outpost of Qiryat Arba, just outside of Hebron, said 56 buildings in the city were still registered to Jewish families. Twenty-eight of them were mostly houses that were abandoned. Since the spring of 1979, seven Jewish women had occupied an old Jewish medical clinic in one of the buildings. Hebron was held sacred by Jews and Moslems. The city was the site of the Jewish Tomb of Patriarchs and Hebron had served as King David's capital for seven years before Jerusalem.

[41] The U.S. Feb. 12 criticized the Israeli decision on Hebron, saying it could be "a step backwards in the peace process and could well have serious consequences" for the Israeli-Egyptian negotiations on autonomy for Arabs in the West Bank and Gaza Strip. The movement of Jews into Hebron, the State Department said, "raises a basic question of Israel's commitment to full autonomy."

[42] **U.N. Security Council Demands Israel Dismantle Settlements; U.S. Backs, Then Disavows Vote.** A resolution calling on Israel to dismantle its settlements in the West Bank and Gaza Strip was adopted March 1 by the U.N. Security Council. The vote was unanimous, with the U.S. joining the 14 other Council members in rebuking Israel.

[43] It was believed to be the first time that the U.S. had voted in the Council against Israel on the issue of settlements. However, in an extraordinary statement issued March 3, President Carter disavowed the American vote, saying it had been cast in error and had resulted from a communication failure between the U.S.'s delegation and the White House. The President's reversal created an international and domestic furor.

[44] The adopted resolution deplored Israel's decision "to officially support Israeli settlement in the Palestinian and other territories." It said Israeli

action in changing "the physical character, demographic composition, institutional structure or status of the Palestinians and other Arab territories, . . . , including Jerusalem, . . . have no legal validity. . . ."

[45] The following section of the resolution dealing with another facet of the Jerusalem problem had been deleted before passage because the U.S. had regarded it as too controversial: The Council called on Israel to comply with its previous resolutions regarding Jerusalem, "to respect and guarantee religious freedoms and practices [there] and other holy places in occupied Arab territories as well as the integrity of places of religious worship."

[46] After casting his vote, U.S. chief delegate Donald McHenry said, "We regard settlements in the occupied territories as illegal under international law, and we consider them to be an obstacle to the successful outcome to the current negotiations [between Israel and Egypt], which are aimed at a comprehensive, just and lasting peace in the Middle East."

[47] ***Carter Explains Stand***—In disavowing the U.S. vote in the Security Council, President Carter said March 3 that the action "does not represent a change in our position regarding the Israeli settlements . . . nor regarding the status of Jerusalem."

[48] While noting the long-standing U.S opposition to the settlements, Carter pointed out that the U.S. had "made strenuous efforts to eliminate the language with reference to the dismantling of the settlements in the resolution." To remove the existing Israeli outposts, he said, "was neither proper nor practical." As for the Security Council's reference to Jerusalem, the President reiterated his Administration's policy that the city "should be undivided with free access to the holy places for all faiths and that its status should be determined in the negotiations for a comprehensive peace settlement." The U.S. had approved the Security Council resolution "with the understanding that all references to Jerusalem would be deleted," Carter said. "The failure to communicate this clearly resulted in a vote in favor of the resolution rather than an abstention," he added.

[49] ***Vance Takes Blame***—A terse statement by the State Department March 4 said Secretary of State Cyrus Vance "accepts responsibility for the failure in communications" that led to U.S. approval of the Security Council resolution.

[50] According to official sources, Vance was said to have told Carter during the U.S. negotiations to draw up the resolution that a paragraph containing a negative reference to Jerusalem posed a problem. Both agreed that the paragraph should be deleted. Donald McHenry, at the U.N., was advised by the State Department Feb. 29 to seek a postponement of the vote until Vance could discuss the matter with Carter. McHenry succeeded in getting a delay and also in obtaining deletion of the paragraph on Jerusalem, but other references to the city remained. [See above]

[51] At a meeting Feb. 29, Carter and his advisers agreed that the U.S. should vote for the resolution provided that the paragraph on the Jerusalem problem and one other were taken out. Vance was said to have been under the impression that deletion of the paragraph satisfied Carter's concern about Jerusalem. The President, however, was reported to have understood that all references to Jerusalem in the Council statement had been removed. Carter gave the go-ahead for the U.S. vote after being further assured by Vance March 1 that references to the Jerusalem problem had been cleared up.

[52] Vance then informed McHenry to vote in favor of the resolution, but to express U.S. reservations about the paragraph calling on Israel to dismantle its 50 settlements in the West Bank and Gaza Strip. No such reservation was made when McHenry cast his

vote. McHenry March 5 conceded that the U.S. disavowal of his vote "doesn't help" his credibility at the U.N. "Obviously, my job is going to be made more difficult," he told a news conference.

[53] The Senate Foreign Relations Committee and the House Foreign Affairs Committee held separate hearings March 20 and 21 on U.S. support of the resolution and Carter's subsequent disavowal of the American vote. Vance defended the administration's position before both panels.

[54] ***Israel Criticizes U.S.***—The Israeli Cabinet March 4 denounced U.S. support of the U.N. Security Council resolution and President Carter's statement retracting the vote.

[55] During the Cabinet meeting, Premier Menachem Begin received a letter from Washington containing Carter's statement disavowing the American vote. Deputy Premier Simcha Ehrlich said he put more stock in the U.S. vote than in its later explanations. Another Cabinet member, Justice Minister Shmuel Tamir, said that despite Carter's explanation, "there is still a deep feeling of anxiety and dissatisfaction toward this strange and far-reaching attitude of the United States."

[56] ***Other International Reaction***—President Carter's reversal of the U.S. stand on its Security Council vote provoked a critical response from other countries and diplomats at the U.N.

[57] At the U.N., a Western diplomat March 4 said, "There is a credibility gap" in Washington. An East European called Carter's explanation "a gimmick." An Asian delegate friendly to the U.S. said, "It was domestic politics pure and simple. I don't believe the theory of communications." An envoy from an Arab nation said, "It shows how strong Zionist pressure is in the U.S."

[58] **PLO Kills 6 Jews in Hebron.** Palestinian terrorists using hand grenades and automatic rifles May 2 killed five Jewish settlers and wounded 17 in an attack in the West Bank city of Hebron. One of the wounded died later.

[59] The attack came as the settlers, members of the Gush Emunim, an Israeli ultranationalist group, were returning from Sabbath services. The assault took place near the former Jewish-owned Hadassah clinic, which had been occupied for the past year without official permission by Jewish women calling for Jewish resettlement in Hebron. Responsibility for the attack was claimed by Al Fatah, the main group of the PLO.

[60] The Israelis May 3 deported three prominent West Bank leaders to Lebanon—Hebron Mayor Fahad Kawasmeh, Mohammed Milhem, mayor of nearby Halhul, and Sheik Raja Bayud Tamimi, the Moslem judge of Hebron. The three were welcomed in Beirut, there they urged "all-out revolution" in Israeli-occupied territories.

[61] The attack in Hebron followed several weeks of heightened tensions on the West Bank, culminating in the fatal shooting May 1 of a 17-year-old Arab youth. The youth was shot by an Israeli army captain whom he had knocked to the ground with a stone, Israeli authorities said. The youth was trying to wrest the captain's automatic rifle from him, the authorities said. The incident took place in the village of Anabta, near Nablus. Following the shooting, Anabta was shut down by a general strike.

[62] Mayors Kawasmeh and Milhem, expelled by Israel in May, returned from exile Oct. 14 to appeal their deportation. Israel Dec. 5 deported them to Lebanon for the second time after the government rejected a Supreme Court recommendation that they be permitted to remain for at least a trial period.

[63] **Israel Uncovers Anti-Arab Plot.** Israel officials reported May 14 that small numbers of Israeli Jewish extremists were planning acts of ter-

rorism against Arabs. Defense Minister Ezer Weizman ordered the arrest and imprisonment without trial of Jewish suspects under emergency anti-terrorist laws aimed primarily at Arabs.

[64] Two suspects had been arrested May 13. They were U.S. Jewish Defense League leader Rabbi Meir Kahane and Baruch Ben-Yosef, another ultranationalist.

[65] **2 Mayors Wounded in Bomb Attacks.** Coordinated bombing attacks were carried out June 2 in four West Bank cities, seriously wounding two Arab mayors and injuring several other persons. Israeli Jewish extremists were believed responsible for the assaults.

[66] West Bank shopkeepers launched a general protest strike June 3 but Israeli soldiers June 4 forced the merchants to reopen their stores.

[67] The two seriously wounded mayors, strong supporters of the PLO, were Bassam Shaka of Nablus and Karim Khalef of Ramallah. Khalef lost part of his left foot and suffered injuries to his right leg when he pressed the clutch of his car, activating a bomb. Shaka lost both legs above the knees when a blast ripped through his car. A third mayor, Ibrahim Tawil of Bireh, escaped injury after having been warned by Israeli military officials to stay away from his car, which was parked in a neighbor's garage. But a bomb rigged to the garage door exploded in the face of an Israeli explosive expert, blinding him. In the fourth city, Hebron, a grenade was thrown into a crowd, injuring seven persons.

[68] ***U.N. Scores Israel for Bombings***—The U.N. Security Council June 5 approved a resolution condemning Israel for failing to protect Arab lives in the West Bank. The vote was 14-0, with the U.S. abstaining.

[69] The resolution assailed the attempt to assassinate the three West Bank mayors and called on Israel to compensate them. It also urged Israel "to end the prolonged occupation of Arab territories including Jerusalem."

[70] **U.S. Jewish Leaders Back Peace Move.** A group of 56 American Jewish leaders July 1 endorsed an Israeli peace group's proposals for territorial compromise on the West Bank.

[71] The Israeli group, Peace Now, released a statement May 19 criticizing alleged extremists in the government. The statement, signed by 250 prominent Israelis, criticized hardliners in the Israeli government and public who "advance the vicious cycle of extremism and violence, which nurture each other. Their way endangers and isolates Israel, undermining the ethical basis for our claims to a life of peace and security."

[72] **2 Arabs Die in Israeli Prison.** Two Arab prisoners participating in a protest hunger strike in an Israeli prison died July 23 and 24 after being force-fed by Israeli authorities. The two had been fasting with other inmates to protest alleged bad prison conditions. Their deaths touched off Arab demonstrations July 23-25 in East Jerusalem and Bethlehem.

[73] **Israeli Troops Fire on Rioters.** Israeli troops Nov. 18 fired at Palestinian student demonstrators in the West Bank towns of Ramallah and Bethlehem, wounding 11, one of them seriously.

[74] The soldiers began shooting when the students hurled stones during a demonstration against the closing Nov. 14 of the University of Bir Zeit, near Ramallah. Israeli military authorities had shut the school for a week on the grounds that its Palestine Week celebrations the previous day were marked by political speeches and songs anti-Israel in tone.

[75] In another incident, a Gaza Strip Arab official regarded as pro-Israel was fatally shot in his office Nov. 18. Mohammed Abu-Wardeh, chairman of the council of the Jabaliyeh refugee camp and a supporter of the Egyptian-Israeli peace treaty, was apparently

assassinated by Palestinian radicals, Israeli authorities said.

[76] Several hundred Palestinian students demonstrated Nov. 20 in several West Bank towns against the shooting of Arab youths Nov. 18. Many of the rioters hurled rocks at Israeli vehicles, blocked roads and attempted to set a school afire in Ramallah. The rioting spread to East Jerusalem, where young Arabs smashed shop windows and vandalized Arab stores that ignored a call for a general strike. Israeli authorities had demanded that the stores remain open.

Jerusalem

[77] **Begin to Move Office to E. Jerusalem.** The Israeli government announced June 22 that Prime Minister Menachem Begin would transfer his office and the Cabinet's conference room from West Jerusalem to East Jerusalem.

[78] The shift would underscore Israel's determination to retain the largely Arab sector of the city captured by the Israeli army in 1967.

[79] **U.N. Condemns Jerusalem Policies.** The United Nations Security Council appoved a resolution 14-0 June 30 opposing Israeli moves to make Jerusalem the capital of Israel. The United States abstained.

[80] The resolution, put forward by 39 members of the Islamic Conference and Egypt, repeated previous Security Council statements that all actions taken by Israel to alter the status of Jerusalem were legally invalid. The resolution specifically criticized a bill introduced in the Israeli Knesset (parliament) in June proposing that the whole of Jerusalem, including the eastern section, be made the country's capital.

[81] Donald F. McHenry, the U.S. ambassador to the U.N., said the Security Council resolution was largely consistent with U.S. policies. However, he explained that the U.S. abstained because Jerusalem's status could be determined "only in the give-and-take of negotiations."

[82] The United Nations Security Council approved, 14-0, Aug. 20 a resolution urging all nations not to recognize Israel's recent declaration that all Jerusalem was its undivided and eternal capital. The U.S. abstained. The resolution, introduced by the three Moslem states on the council, Tunisia, Niger and Bangladesh, originally sought economic and trade sanctions against Israel for its stand on Jerusalem. However, behind-the-scenes maneuvering led to a more moderate final version when it was apparent Western members would veto the stronger one. The final version did, however, embody a form of punishment, the first anti-Israel U.N. measure to do so. It called on the countries that maintained embassies in Jerusalem to remove them.

[83] **Israel Reaffirms Jerusalem Claim.** The Israeli Knesset (parlia-

Israeli Knesset July 30 reaffirmed all of Jerusalem as Israel's capital.

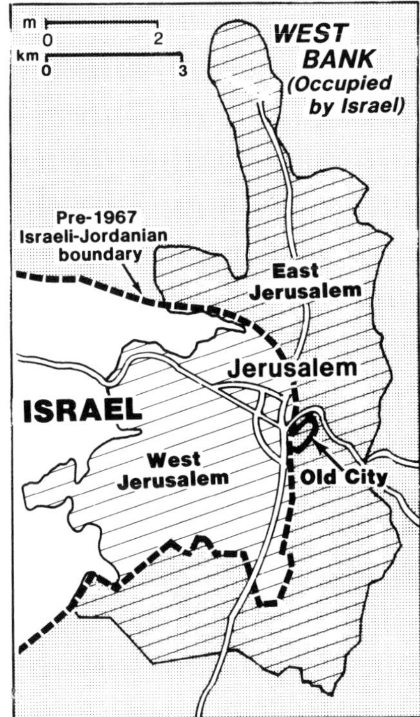

ment) July 30 adopted a law reaffirming all of Jerusalem as the capital of Israel. The vote on the bill, which had been introduced in May by ultranationalist member Geula Cohen, was approved by a 69-15 vote, with three abstentions.

[84] Egypt's Foreign Minister, Kamel Hassan Ali, said Aug. 3 that his country "totally rejected" Israel's law on Jerusalem and regarded it as "null and void."

[85] Following adoption of the law, five of the 13 nations with embassies in Jerusalem announced they would move their diplomatic missions to Tel Aviv in opposition to the change in the city's legal status. They were Venezuela, Uruguay, Ecuador, Chile and the Netherlands.

[86] **Fahd Urges 'Jihad.'** Crown Prince Fahd of Saudi Arabia Aug. 14 called for a *jihad* (holy war) by all Moslem nations against Israel because of its formal annexation of East Jerusalem.

[87] **Marchers Back Unified Jerusalem.** Thousands of Israelis and evangelical Christians from 25 countries Sept. 30 marched through Jerusalem in support of the city's status as Israel's unified capital.

Lebanon

[88] **Syria Announces, Then Delays Troop Pullout.** Syria announced Feb. 4 that it would pull its forces out of Beirut within 36 hours. The next day, Syrian President Hafez al-Assad said that his government would delay the withdrawal of Syria's estimated 5,000 troops from the Lebanese capital.

[89] The original directive raised fears of a renewal of civil strife between Lebanon's Christians and Moslems. It prompted Lebanese government leaders to go to Damascus to persuade Assad to change his plans. Assad agreed to delay the move to enable the Lebanese government to make preparations of its own. The president said he would wait "some time" before ordering his soldiers out of Beirut. He gave no specific date. Plans called for shifting the Syrian troops from Beirut to near the Syrian-Israeli border and in the Bekaa Valley, the entrance route to Damascus.

[90] Syria had decided to postpone indefinitely the withdrawal of its 8,000 troops from Beirut, Lebanese officials said Feb. 24. Instead, Syria would concentrate on what it called the threat of a possible Israeli military drive into southern Lebanon and Syria, it was said.

[91] ***Clashes Follow Announcement—*** At least 18 persons were killed in Beirut and in southern Lebanon following Syria's announcement Feb. 4 that it planned to shift its forces from the Lebanese capital to other parts of the country.

[92] The fighting was marked by a heavy exchange of artillery fire Feb. 10-12 between Lebanese-Palestinian militiamen. In one incident, four Christian civilians were killed and four others wounded Feb. 11 when bombs or booby traps blasted their home in the village of Deir Mimas, near the Israeli border. The attack, attributed to the Palestine Liberation Organization, triggered a five-hour exchange of artillery and mortar fire between the Christian militiamen and the PLO over the heads of members of the United Nations Interim Force in Lebanon (UNIFIL).

[93] At least 60 residents of the northern Lebanese village of Qnat were killed in six days of artillery clashes between Syrian troops and Christian Phalangist militiamen, it was reported Feb. 17. The Phalangists also were being attacked by a rival Christian group, followers of former President Suleiman Franjieh.

[94] In the south, artillery duels continued Feb. 13 between Palestinians and Israeli-supported Christian militiamen. The Christians fired at the Palestinian stronghold of Tyre.

[95] **Israelis Push into Southern Lebanon.** Israeli soldiers April 9 pushed five miles (eight kilometers)

into southern Lebanon in retaliation for a Palestinian terrorist attack on an Israeli kibbutz April 7. All five Palestinian raiders and three Israelis had been killed in the assault on the community of Misgav Am, near the Lebanese border. [See below]

[96] An estimated 300-350 Israeli soldiers, equipped with tanks and armored personnel carriers, encountered no opposition as they established positions near several Lebanese villages. They dug trenches, laid barbed wire around their positions and brought in reinforcements April 10.

[97] A United Nations spokesman said five Israeli personnel carriers had entered a zone patrolled by UNIFIL troops. One vehicle later withdrew, but four remained. UNIFIL lodged a strong protest against Israel.

[98] (One of the towns where the Israelis had taken up positions, Atiri, had been the scene of a gun battle April 7 between the Christian militiamen and Irish UNIFIL troops. The fighting broke out when the Christians moved into the UNIFIL-controlled town with the apparent intention of establishing a checkpoint. The Christians claimed the Irish permitted the Palestinians to set up bases in the area. One Irish soldier was wounded in the exchange of gunfire and nine were captured and brought to a nearby Christian enclave. The UNIFIL soldiers were freed April 8 after negotiations but another was wounded when the Christian militiamen fired at a vehicle carrying the released Irish soldiers.)

[99] ***Kibbutz Attacked***—The Arab Liberation Front (ALF), an Iraqi-supported group belonging to the Palestine Liberation Organization, claimed credit for the April 7 attack on Misgav Am.

[100] The five gunmen, passing UNIFIL-guarded areas in southern Lebanon, crossed the border into Israel and burst into a children's dormitory on the kibbutz. They came under immediate attack by armed members of the settlement. Israeli soldiers later arrived on the scene and stormed the building after several deadlines imposed by the terrorists had passed.

[101] During the nine-hour siege and attack, all five Palestinian raiders were killed, as were a two-and-a-half-year-old Israeli boy, a soldier and a kibbutz secretary. Eleven Israeli soldiers and four children were wounded. The ALF terrorists had taken the children hostage in a bid for the release of Palestinian guerrillas held in Israeli prisons. Israeli army officials said leaflets were found containing the names of 50 Palestinian prisoners.

[102] **Israeli Troops Withdrawn.** Israeli troops had withdrawn from southern Lebanon after a five-day occupation, an Israeli military official announced April 14.

[103] United Nations Secretary General Kurt Waldheim cited the Israeli pullout April 13 in a report to a private session of the Security Council. Waldheim also reported on recent attacks by Lebanese Christian militiamen on soldiers of UNIFIL. He expressed thanks to unnamed governments who were using good offices to "de-escalate the recent very dangerous developments" in southern Lebanon.

[104] The situation in southern Lebanon was discussed April 14 by Maj. Saad Haddad, head of the Christian militia, Maj. Gen. Emmanuel Erskine, UNIFIL commander, and Maj. Gen. Avigdor Ben-Gal, Israeli commander of the northern district. Haddad was said to have demanded the removal of UNIFIL's 600-man Irish battalion. Haddad April 11 had accused the Irish troops of being partial to guerrillas of the Palestine Liberation Organization. He said the Irish unit had provided tacit aid to the PLO by permitting them to pass through UNIFIL lines since Feb. 10, when Irish Foreign Minister Brian Lenihan said the Palestinians had a right to self-determination.

[105] In the latest incidents in southern Lebanon, UNIFIL troops April 12 threw back a Christian militia attempt to oc-

cupy the village of Atiri as Israeli troops and tanks pulled out of the area. A Fijian soldier and a militiaman were killed in the exchange of gunfire. The death of the Fijian brought to 38 the number of UNIFIL troops killed since their deployment in the region in 1978. UNIFIL's headquarters at Naqura came under Christian militia shelling April 12, a U.N. spokesman said. No casualties were reported but the firing damaged a number of buildings and three helicopters.

[106] More violence erupted in Lebanon April 18. An Israeli seaborne force raided a PLO base along the coast, and two irish soldiers of UNIFIL were slain in an ambush of a truck in the south.

[107] An Israeli army spokesman said the Israelis killed at least six Palestinian guerrillas in attacking what he described as a base near Sarafand used for training and carrying out assaults against Israel. Palestinian sources said 20 persons died in the attack, eight guerrillas and 12 Lebanese civilians.

[108] A UNIFIL spokesman said the two Irish soldiers were executed by a group of armed Lebanese after being kidnapped near Bint Jbail, not far from the Israeli border. A third Irish soldier was shot and wounded. Two other persons in the kidnapped party – a reporter and photographer for the Associated Press – were later released unharmed. A U.N. official said the two Irish soldiers were slain in reprisal for the death of two Lebanese Moslem youths in the clash April 12 between UNIFIL and Lebanese Christian militiamen at the village of Atiri.

[109] UNIFIL's Irish troops April 22 withdrew from their positions bordering the Christian enclave in southern Lebanon and were replaced by Norwegian soldiers.

[110] **Phalangists Defeat Rival Faction.** The Phalangist Party emerged as the dominant Christian faction in Lebanon when its militiamen decisively defeated the followers of its principal rival, the National Liberal Party, in fierce fighting in and around Beirut July 7-8. An estimated 320 persons were killed.

[111] The Phalangist victory climaxed months of military and political tension with the NLP, headed by former President Camille Chamoun. In the battle, the Phalangists seized positions and offices of the NLP in Christian East Beirut and in nearby coastal and mountain areas. The NLP militiamen surrendered their arms, leaving their areas in control of the Phalangists. The Phalangist militia was commanded by Bashir Gemayel, whose father, Pierre Gemayel was head of the party. Camille Chamoun's son, Dany, resigned as military commander of the NLP and said he was quitting political life.

[112] The Phalangist-controlled "Voice of Lebanon" radio announced July 9 that Camille Chamoun and Pierre Gemayel had agreed after two days of talks to allow the Phalangists to merge all private Christian militia groups in East Beirut into a single military unit to be called the National Home Guard. A Phalangist spokesman said July 10 that the National Home Guard would "liberate" Lebanon from "Palestinian occupation."

[113] **Israeli Raid in Lebanon Kills 40.** Israeli infantry and paratroop units attacked Palestine Liberation Organization military bases in southeastern Lebanon Aug. 19, reportedly killing at least 40 guerrillas in the two-hour battle, with three Israeli raiders killed.

[114] The PLO disputed the casualty figures put out by Israel, claiming it had lost only 12 dead while killing 30 Israelis. However, both sides agreed the Israeli raid was the largest since the Litani River invasion of March 1978.

[115] ***Israelis Down Syrian Jet***—Israeli fighter planes Aug. 24 downed a Syrian MiG-21 over southern Lebanon, the Israeli military command reported. It was the first Syrian jet downed by the Israelis since September 1979, and the aerial clash was the southernmost encounter ever

over Lebanon, 15 miles (24 kilometers) north of the Israeli border.

[116] The Israeli-Syrian encounter followed continued Israeli air and ground attacks Aug. 20-21 against Palestinian guerrilla bases in southern Lebanon. Also during the two-day period, Palestinian gunners shelled northern Israel. A major target of the Israeli attacks was Beaufort Castle, a 12th-century Crusader fortress commanding a hilltop overlooking the border region. In their major ground assault Aug. 19, Israeli forces had attempted to storm dug-in Palestinian postions at the castle.

[117] **Israelis Hit PLO Targets.** Israeli airborne troops Oct. 16 landed in southern Lebanon and attacked PLO targets, 14 miles (22 kilometers) north of the Israeli border.

[118] Israeli warplanes Nov. 7 struck at PLO positions in southern Lebanon, one day after missiles fired from Lebanese territory hit the Israeli border town of Qiryat Shmona.

[119] An Israeli seaborne force Dec. 3 attacked PLO targets about nine miles (14 kilometers) south of Beirut, killing two guerrillas and four Lebanese civilians.

[120] **Syrians Battle Christian Militia.** Syrian troops serving with the Arab League's cease-fire supervisory force in Lebanon fought Dec. 21-26 with militiamen of the Christian Phalangist Party in the town of Zahle, 30 miles (48 kilometers) east of Beirut.

See also Human Rights [9]; Libya [1-4]

MISSISSIPPI—*See* Ku Klux Klan (KKK) [8]

MONETARY DEVELOPMENTS (International)

[1] **Dollar Strengthens.** High interest rates improved the position of the dollar during 1980.

[2] The value of the U.S. dollar measured against 15 world currencies adjusted for their significance to U.S. trade strengthened March 17 to the highest level since April 20, 1978. The strong demand for dollars on foreign money exchanges resulted mainly from the promise of higher U.S. interest rates implicit in President Carter's anti-inflation program.

[3] In New York, the dollar gained 1.9% against the West German mark, rising to 1.87 marks to the dollar from 1.83. Against the Japanese yen, the dollar continued to show strength March 17. It was recorded in New York at 248.30 yen to the dollar.

[4] Japan had reached an agreement March 2 with the U.S., West Germany and Switzerland to boost the yen. Despite attempts March 17 by West Germany, Switzerland and Japan to intervene in the money markets to stop the dollar's advance, currency dealers noted that the dollar's momentum was strong. According to dealers March 17, West Germany's central bank sold more than $200 million in an attempt to slow the surge. The Swiss National Bank also intervened with heavy dollar sales, and the Bank of Japan unloaded more than $100 million to support its currency.

[5] Profit-taking March 9-20 slowed the dollar's March 17 rise on international markets, but dealers considered profit-taking inevitable and expected the U.S. currency to remain strong. One dealer summed up his feelings March 19: "The interest-rate constellation is still working in its [the dollar's] favor."

[6] The dollar gained strength against major European currencies Nov. 5, following the election of Ronald Reagan as U.S. President. The dollar closed at 1.9405 German marks to the dollar from the previous day's Frankfurt posting of 1.915. The dollar jumped to 1.7367 Swiss francs in New York from 1.7188. The value of the dollar against the mark was the highest since April 8, when the U.S. currency traded at a 2½-year high because of record U.S. interest rates.

[7] The dollar closed Dec. 31 at 2.3929

British pounds; 1.9640 German marks; 202.60 Japanese yen; 1.7675 Swiss francs to the dollar.

See also Canada [35-36]; Economy (International) [12-19]; Economy (U.S.); Gold; Silver [1-10]

MOROCCO—*See* Human Rights [9]

MOSLEMS—*See* United Nations [27]

MOTION PICTURES

[1] **Academy Awards.** The Academy of Motion Picture Arts and Sciences held its 52d annual awards ceremony April 14 in Los Angeles.

[2] *Kramer vs. Kramer,* the story of a divorced couple's child custody battle, won most of the major awards, including best picture of the year. *All That Jazz,* Broadway director Bob Fosse's musical autobiography, came in a strong second, dominating the craft awards.

[3] Other recipients were:

Best actor: Dustin Hoffman, *Kramer vs. Kramer;* **Best actress:** Sally Field, *Norma Rae;* **Best Supporting actor:** Melvyn Douglas, *Being There;* **Best Supporting actress:** Meryl Streep, *Kramer vs. Kramer;* **Best direction:** Robert Benton, *Kramer vs. Kramer;* **Best original song:** *It Goes Like It Goes,* from *Norma Rae,* music by David Shire, lyrics by Norman Gimbel; **Best original screenplay:** Steven Tesich, *Breaking Away;* **Best original score:** George Delerue, *A Little Romance;* **Best adaptation of an original score:** Ralph Burns, *All That Jazz.*

[4] **Best foreign-language film:** *The Tin Drum* (Germany); **Best Cinematography:** Vittorio Storaro, *Apocalypse Now;* **Best Sound:** Walter Murch, Mark Berger, Richard Beggs and Nat Boxer, *Apocalypse Now;* **Best art direction:** Philip Rosenberg, Tony Walton, Edward Stewart and Gary Brink, *All That Jazz;* **Costume Design:** Albert Wolsky, *All That Jazz;* **Best visual effects:** H. R. Giger, Carlo Rambaldi, Brian Johnson, Nick Allder and Denys Ayling, *Alien.*

[5] **Best documentary** (feature): *Best Boy,* Ira Wohl, producer; **Best documentary** (short subject): *Paul Robeson: Tribute to an Artist,* Janus Films Inc.,; **Best editing:** Alan Heim, *All That Jazz;* **Best achievements in short films:** Animated: *Every Child,* Derek Lamb, producer; Live action: *Board and Care,* Sarah Pillsbury and Ron Ellis, producers.

[6] **Motion Picture Revenues Soar.** U.S. motion picture theaters took in $2.821 billion in 1979, a 6.7% increase over 1978, the Motion Picture Association of America reported Jan. 31.

[7] The 1979 figure was a record for U.S. boxoffice receipts. The MPAA report noted that inflation had had an effect on boxoffices: ticket prices rose 7.43% in 1979, to an average of $2.51 per ticket.

[8] According to *Variety* Feb. 6, *Superman* was the runaway hit of 1979 in terms of domestic (U.S. and Canadian markets) rentals. Rentals were the revenues received by film distributors from theaters after those theaters had taken out an agreed share of the boxoffice revenues.

[9] The top rental films of 1979 were:

Superman—$81 million
Every Which Way But Loose—$48 million
Rocky II—$43.049 million
Alien—$40.086 million
The Amityville Horror—$35 million

[10] **'Heaven's Gate' Withdrawn by Studio.** United Artists Corp. Nov. 19 announced that it was withdrawing the motion picture *Heaven's Gate* from exhibition for the purpose of reediting.

Jimmy Stewart receives Life Achievement Award of American Film Institute in Beverly Hills, Calif. Feb. 28. He was honored as "one of world's most beloved actors."

The film had opened in New York City the same day as the announcement and had been scheduled to premiere in Los Angeles Nov. 21.

[11] *Heaven's Gate* was an epic Western directed by Michael Cimino, who had won an Academy Award in 1979 for his work in *The Deer Hunter.* The movie, which ran 220 minutes starred Kris Kristofferson. It depicted events in the so-called "Johnson County War," a conflict between cattlemen and immigrant farmers in Wyoming in the late 1880s. According to varying sources, *Heaven's Gate* cost between $36 million and $40 million. It was among the most expensive motion pictures ever made, and perhaps the most expensive.

[12] United Artists took its unprecendented action after the New York critics blasted the film upon seeing advance screenings. Vincent Canby of the *New York Times,* in a review printed Nov. 19, said *Heaven's Gate* was "something quite rare in movies these days–and unqualified disaster."

See also Great Britain [58-60]

MT. ST. HELENS—*See* Volcanos [1-15]

MUSIC

[1] **Grammy Awards.** The 22nd annual Grammy awards were presented Feb. 27 by the National Academy of Recording Arts and Sciences in Los Angeles.

[2] The big winners were the Doobie Brothers and Billy Joel. The Doobie Brothers won four Grammy's, including **best record** and **best song** of the year for *What a Fool Believes* and **best pop vocal performance by a duo, group or chorus** for the album, *Minute by Minute.* Billy Joel won the **best album of the year** and **best pop male vocal** Grammys for his album *52nd Street.*

[3] Donna Summer won the **best female rock vocal** performance for her single *Hot Stuff* and Gloria Gaynor won the **best disco award** for *I Will Survive.* Bob Dylan received an award for the **best male rock vocal performance** for *Gotta Serve Somebody,* his first Grammy.

[4] Paul Robeson, Bix Beiderbecke and Jelly Roll Morton were voted into the academy's hall of fame.

[5] Other Grammy award winners in 58 categories included: **Best Pop Vocal Performance, Female:** Dionne Warwick, *I'll Never Love This Way Again;* **Best Pop Vocal Instrumental Performance:** *Rise,* Herb Alpert; **Best Rock Vocal Performance by a Duo or Group:** *Heartache Tonight,* Eagles; **Best Rock Instrumental Performance:** *Rockestra Theme,* Wings. **Best Rhythm and Blues Vocal Performance, Female:** *Deja Vu,* Dionne Warwick; **Best R & B Vocal Performance, Male:** *Don't Stop 'Till You Get Enough,* Michael Jackson; **Best R & B Instrumental Performance:** *Boogie Wonderland,* Earth, Wind & Fire; **Best R & B Song:** *After The Love Has Gone,* David Foster, Jay Graydon, Bill Champlin, songwriters. **Best Country Vocal Performance, Female:** *Blue Kentucky Girl,* Emmylou Harris; **Best Country Vocal Performance, Male:** *The Gambler,* Kenny Rogers; **Best Country Vocal Performance by a Duo or Group:** *The Devil Went Down to Georgia,* Charlie Daniels Band; **Best Country Instrumental Performance:** *Big Sandy/Leather Britches,* Doc and Merle Watson; **Best Country Song:** *You Decorated My Life,* Bob Morrison, Debbie Hupp, songwriters. **Best Gospel Performance,**

John Williams conducts Boston Pops Orchestra April 29 at Symphony Hall. He succeeded Arthur Fiedler.

Contemporary or Inspirational: *Heed the Call,* Imperials; **Best Gospel Performance, Traditional:** *Lift Up The Name of Jesus,* the Blackwood Brothers; **Best Soul Gospel Performance, Contemporary:** *I'll Be Thinking of You,* Andrae Crouch; **Best Soul Gospel Performance, Traditional:** *Changing Times,* Mighty Clouds of Joy. **Best Jazz Vocal Performance:** *Fine and Mellow,* Ella Fitzgerald; **Best Jazz Instrumental Performance, Group:** *Duet,* Gary Burton and Chick Corea; **Best Jazz Instrumental Performance, Big Band:** *At Fargo, 1940,* Duke Ellington; **Best Jazz Fusion Performance, Vocal or Instrumental:** *8:30,* Weather Report. **Best Classical Album:** Brahms: *Symphonies Complete,* Sir Georg Solti, conductor, James Mallinson, producer; **Best Opera Recording:** Britten: *Peter Grimes,* Colin Davis, conductor; **Best Classical Orchestral Recording:** Brahms, *Symphonies Complete, Sir Georg Solti, conductor;* **Best Choral Performance, Classical (other than opera):** Brahms: *A German Requiem,* Sir Georg Solti, conductor; **Best Chamber Music Performance:** Copland: *Appalachian Spring,* Dennis Russel Davies, conducting the St. Paul Chamber Orchestra; **Best Classical Performance, Instrumental Soloist or Soloists:** *The Horowitz Concerts 1978/79,* Vladimir Horowitz; **Best Classical Vocal Soloist Performance:** *O Sole Mio,* Luciano Pavarotti. **Best Cast Show Album:** *Sweeney Todd,* Stephen Sondheim, composer, Thomas Z. Shepard, producer; **Best Ethnic or Traditional Recording:** *Muddy 'Mississippi' Waters Live,* Muddy Waters; **Best Comedy Recording:** *Reality . . . What A Concept,* Robin Williams; **Best Spoken Word Recording:** *Ages of Man,* (Readings from Shakespeare), Sir John Gielgud; **Best Original Score Written for a Motion Picture or a Television Special:** *Superman,* John Williams, Composer; **Best Latin Recording:** *Irakere,* Irakere; **Best Recording for Children:** *The Muppet Movie,* Jim Henson, creator, Paul Williams, producer.

[6] **Boston Pops Conductor Named.** John Williams, Academy Award-winning Hollywood composer and conductor, was named conductor of the Boston Pops Orchestra Jan. 10. Williams was celebrated as the composer of scores for such films as *Star Wars* and *Jaws.* His appointment ended a six-month search that began in 1979 following the death of Arthur Fiedler, who had conducted the Boston Pops for 50 years.

See also Lennon, John [1-17]

MUSKIE, EDMUND S.—*See* Defense (U.S.) [6]; Iran; United Nations [18-19]

N

NAZIS—*See* Germany, West [1-3]

NEBRASKA—*See* City & State Affairs [1-2]

NETHERLANDS

[1] **Beatrix Invested as Queen.** Princess Beatrix was invested April 20 as the Netherlands' sixth monarch. She succeeded her mother, Queen Juliana.

Princess Beatrix with her husband, Prince Claus, walks under canopy from palace to church for investiture as Queen of the Netherlands April 30.

[2] Queen Juliana had announced her plans to abdicate at the end of January, citing her age. The abdication ceremony, which was private, took place the morning of April 30, which was Juliana's 71st birthday. The investiture ceremony – no crown was placed on Beatrix's head, so it was not called a coronation – took place in the afternoon in the 15th-century Nieuwe Kerk (new church). Beatrix, 42, swore to "defend and preserve the territory of the state" and to "protect the general and specific freedoms and rights of all my subjects."

[3] Squatters in Amsterdam staged a protest to coincide with the ceremony, and fighting between the police and demonstrators left at least 125 persons injured. The squatters, despite Beatrix's expressed sympathy for their plight, had planned their protest with the slogan, "No housing, no coronation." Gangs of youths and leftists of various descriptions joined in the protest, which started in Waterloo Square but spread to the streets near the church where the investiture ceremony was held.

See also Chad [3] Economy (International) [6]

NEW HEBRIDES—*See* Vanatu

NEW JERSEY—*See* Census (U.S.) [4]; Environment [4, 6-7]; Weather [11-12]

NEW YORK—*See* Census (U.S.) [4]; City & State Affairs

[6]; Disasters & Accidents [16]; Education [1-2] Environment [2, 7-13]; Weather [11-12]

NICARAGUA

[1] **Somoza Assassinated.** Anastasio Somoza Debayle, the dictator of Nicaragua overthrown by rebels in 1979, was assassinated Sept. 17 in Asuncion, Paraguay. Somoza's driver and a business associate also were killed by gunmen firing machine guns and a bazooka.

[2] An alleged Argentine terrorist who was a suspect in the slaying was shot and killed by police Sept. 18.

[3] The ambush took place 10 blocks from where Somoza lived. Somoza was being driven to a bank when he was slain. A pickup truck pulled up behind Somoza's sedan and persons in the truck began shooting. Others on the street also began firing automatic weapons. Then from the front porch of a nearby house, a man with a rocket launcher fired a bazooka, that hit the car broadside.

[4] In Nicaragua, the Sandinista government Sept. 17 announced a day of celebration for Sept. 18 after hearing of Somoza's death.

Government & Politics

[5] **2 New Members of Junta Named.** Nicaragua's Sandinista leadership May 18 named two moderates to the five-member ruling junta.

[6] The new junta members were Arturo J. Cruz, former head of Nicaragua's central bank, and Supreme Court Justice Rafael Cordova Rivas. They replaced Violeta Barrios de Chamorro and Alfonso Robelo Callejas, who had resigned in April.

[7] It was hoped their appointments would persuade the country's private sector to participate in the Council of State, a governmental body formed to organize economic recovery. In his letter of resignation, Robelo had charged that the Sandinistas were loading the Council of State with their supporters, thus diminishing the chance for democracy in Nicaragua.

[8] Cordova, an opponent of the Somoza family since the 1940s and a member of the Democratic Conservative Party, was known to favor preserving the private sector and holding early elections.

[9] Cruz had taken a major role in helping the Sandinistas convince the business community that, despite Robelo's charges, the Sandinistas did not wish to impose a totalitarian form of government. Cruz had organized a series of talks between the Sandinista Popular Liberation Front's leaders and the private sector. As a result, the Sandinistas April 28 had announced an end to the state of emergency that had existed in Nicaragua since July 1979. They agreed to end the confiscation of lands and privately-owned companies and initiated laws giving individuals the right to appeal government actions in the courts.

[10] **Sandinistas Mark Anniversary.** Nicaragua's Sandinista government staged celebrations in Managua July 19 to mark the first anniversary of its victory over Anastasio Somoza Debayle in the 1979 civil war.

[11] **Junta Says No Elections Until 1985.** The Sandinista leadership said free elections could not be held in the country before 1985, it was reported Aug. 24.

[12] **Non-Sandinistas Boycott Council.** Non-Sandinista members of the Nicaraguan Council of State, an advisory body formed by the Sandinistas to create a forum for diverse political groups, walked out of a meeting of the council Nov. 12 to protest alleged repression by the Sandinista leadership.

[13] The incident followed an attack Nov. 10 on the offices of an independent political party in Managua, and the banning Nov. 9 of a rally in Managua that had been planned by Alfonso Robelo Callejas for his

National Democratic Movement. According to reports, the Sandinista National Revolutionary Front Directorate, the Marxist-dominated core of the Sandinista movement which controlled the real power in Nicaragua, had imposed censorship to prevent further protests over the incidents.

[14] **Security Forces Kill Business Leader.** Government security forces in Nicaragua Nov. 17 killed a politically prominent businessman in an armed confrontation at El Crucero, 12 miles (19 kilometers) outside Managua.

[15] Jorge Salazar Arguello, president of the Nicaraguan Coffee Grower's Association, was killed when he allegedly resisted arrest. Salazar's death shocked Nicaraguan business organizations, which had pressed political leaders for changes in government policies to allow private enterprises to operate without political interference. The Sandinista Directorate had stiffened its resistance to opposition from the business sector. According to the *New York Times* Nov. 18, several prominent business leaders had been arrested on charges of "counter-revolutionary" activity in the past few months.

Other Developments

[16] **$582 Million Debt Rescheduled.** After over nine months of negotiations with foreign creditors, the Nicaraguan government Sept. 5 agreed to repay $582 million of the foreign debt contracted by the Somoza regime.

[17] Under the agreement, drawn up by a 13-bank committee representing some 120 creditor banks and the Nicaraguan National Reconstruction Fund, past due interest and principal would be repaid over 12 years with a five-year grace period. The debt involved was $492 million in principal and $90 million in past-due interest payments.

[18] An unusual feature of the agreement was that the past-due interest was to be capitalized–that is, added to the principal and treated as part of the new loan being extended to Nicaragua. In most debt rescheduling, all past-due interest was paid at the time of the signing of the new loan agreement.

[19] Of the $582 million, 62% was owed to U.S. banks, with the remainder of the debt held by Canadian, British, European and Japanese banks. The major creditors included Citibank, $56 million; Bank of America, $30 million; Royal Bank of Canada, $24 million; First National Bank of Chicago, $19 million; Wells Fargo Bank, $18 million, and Swiss Bank Corp., $18 million.

[20] **U.S. Releases $75 Million Aid.** The U.S. Congress Sept. 12 released $75 million in aid for the Nicaraguan government that had been delayed by a requirement that President Carter certify that Nicaragua was not aiding acts of violence in other countries.

[21] The aid had been approved by Congress May 19 and release of the funds had been authorized by Congress May 31. The U.S. had already provided some $216 million in aid to Nicaragua since the Sandinistas had come to power in 1979. But those funds had been paid directly to private organizations and thus had not been contingent on Carter's certification.

NIGER—*See* United Nations [4]

NIXON, RICHARD M(ilhous)

Nixon Moves to New York. Former President Richard M. Nixon moved into his new home on Manhattan's Upper East Side Feb. 14. Nixon was accompanied by his wife, Pat, and daughter, Tricia Cox. The Nixons' four-story, 12-room townhouse, next door to the residence of banker David Rockefeller, cost $750,000.

See also Watergate [1-3]

NOBEL PRIZES

[1] The 1980 Nobel Prizes were an-

nounced by the Royal Swedish Academy in Stockholm for literature Oct. 9, medicine Oct. 10, chemistry and physics Oct. 14 and for economics Oct. 15. The cash value of each of the awards was about $212,000.

[2] The 1980 Nobel Peace Prize was announced Oct. 13 by the Nobel Committee of the Norwegian Parliament in Oslo. The value of the award was also about $212,000.

The awards listed by category:

[3] ***Peace***—The Nobel Peace Prize, was awarded to Adolfo Perez Esquivel, the leader of a human rights organization based in Buenos Aires. A former professor of architecture, Perez was jailed by the Argentine government in April 1977 and released more than a year later without having been charged with any crime. Perez had left his teaching post in 1974 to become the secretary general of *Servicio Paz y Justicia*, the rights organization which had been founded in Montevideo, Uruguay in 1966. In 1976, Perez began an international campaign to persuade the United Nations to establish a human rights commission. The following year he was arrested by the authorities in Argentina. In its citation, the five-member committee said that Perez' attempts to solve conflicts through nonviolence represented the same views as Soviet physicist Andrei D. Sakharov, who had been awarded the prize for peace in 1975.

[4] ***Literature***—The Nobel Prize for literature was given to Czeslaw Milosz, a self-exiled Polish writer and poet who lived in California. A teacher at the University of California at Berkeley, Milosz was a noted translator into Polish of Shakespeare, Eliot, Milton and other giants of English literature. He had also translated the work of some Polish poets into English. In addition, Milosz was said to have written poems imbued with the sense of loss that the exile feels and that derived much of their power from the intense personal point of view from which they were conceived. Among his works translated into English were *The Usurpers* (1955), *Selected Poems* (1973) and *Bells in Winter* (1978). A novel to be called *The Valley of Issa*, about Milosz' childhood in Eastern Europe, was scheduled for publication in 1981.

[5] ***Chemistry***—The Nobel Prize for chemistry was awarded to two Americans and an Englishman for the development of methods that made it possible to diagram in considerable detail the structure and function of DNA, the substance that determined the form and functions of the living cell.

[6] Half the prize went to Dr. Paul Berg, professor of biochemistry at Stanford University since 1959. The other half went jointly to Dr. Walter Gilbert, professor of molecular biology at Harvard University since 1968, and Dr. Frederick Sanger, professor of molecular biology at Cambridge University since 1961. Berg was considered the "father of genetic engineering" for his work involving the manipulation of gene structures. He was also one of the first genetic researchers to urge a moratorium on such activities, because of fear that the work could lead to the production of dangerous new forms of life. Gilbert and Sanger received the prize for their work on reading the fine details of the structure of DNA (deoxyribonucleic acid). The work had already been of use in deciphering genetic diseases and had led to cures.

[7] ***Physics***—The Nobel Prize for physics was awarded jointly to two Americans for discoveries concerning the symmetry of subatomic particles. The work was instrumental in the development of the "big bang" theory of the universe, the theory that the universe had been created 10 billion years ago with a gigantic explosion.

[8] The winners were Dr. James W. Cronin of the University of Chicago and Dr. Val L. Fitch of Princeton University. In 1963, Cronin and Fitch made the discovery that certain subatomic particles did not conform to

what physicists had long thought was an absolute principle of symmetry. The work involved a new type of elementary particles called K mesons. They discovered that K mesons, created in collisions of protons, switched back and forth from being particles to being antiparticles, which had the opposite charge as particles and were a form of antimatter. According to what had been the theory of absolute symmetry, the rate of the switch from particle to antiparticle should have been identical to the switch in the opposite direction. But Fitch and Cronin found the two rates to be measurably different and thus unaffected by the principle known as "symmetry under the reversal of time." This discovery represented a breakdown in a basic law of physics and led to an entirely new realm of scientific experimentation.

[9] ***Medicine***—The Nobel Prize for medicine was awarded to two Americans and a Frenchman for their discoveries on how genetic makeup determined the body's response to infection and to the development of cancer.

[10] The winners were Dr. Baruj Benacerraf, a Venezuelan-born American who was chairman of the pathology department at Harvard University, Dr. George Snell, senior staff scientist emeritus at the Jackson Laboratory in Bar Harbor, Maine, and Jean Dausset of St. Louis Hospital at the University of Paris. They were to share the award equally.

[11] All three, working independently but aware of each other's research, studied antigens, protein-carbohydrate complexes found on every cell membrane in the body. The work led to the development of rules for the transplantability of human organs, helped explain how the body's immunological system worked and led to the development of transplant immunology.

[12] ***Economics***—The Nobel Prize for economics was awarded to Lawrence R. Klein of the Wharton School of the University of Pennsylvania for the development of models for forecasting economic trends and the designing of policies to deal with them.

[13] Klein's work was called econometrics. The citation said that Klein's work dealing with "extremely complex and tedious material, involving thousands of equations and the collecting of enormous amounts of information" led to "a successful instrument for short-term forecasts." The citation noted that Klein had successfully concluded the early attempts at econometric analysis that Jan Tinbergen, the first Nobel economic laureate, had begun in the 1930s. Klein's econometric models had widespread use and were now found throughout the world at scientific institutions as well as in public administration, political organizations and large enterprises. The committee cited Klein for his role as the leader of LINK, a research project designed to coordinate econometric models in different countries, including those in socialist countries and the developing world.

NORTH ATLANTIC TREATY ORGANIZATION (NATO) & WARSAW PACT

[1] **NATO Reaffirms Nuclear Modernization.** Defense ministers of the North Atlantic Treaty Organization June 4 reaffirmed their intention to modernize nuclear forces in Western Europe at a meeting of the alliance's Nuclear Planning Group in Bodo, Norway.

[2] A communique issued by the 12-member group at the close of a two-day meeting said that recent developments had led it to believe NATO faced "an even larger Soviet superiority in theater nuclear forces in the mid-1980s than previously anticipated." British Defense Secretary Frances Pym said the Soviet superiority could be attributed to two factors: more rapid production and deployment

of its new mobile SS-20 long-range missile, and the retention of the older SS-4 and SS-5 missiles which the West had believed were to be dismantled.

[3] American officials June 3 had told the meeting that Britain and Italy would be the first European countries to receive American cruise missiles when the deployment of the weapons began at the end of 1983.

[4] **Warsaw Pact, NATO Maneuvers.** Thousands of soldiers from rival military blocs in Europe participated in separate war games throughout the continent in mid-September.

[5] The Warsaw Pact Sept. 11 ended four days of maneuvers in East Germany. More than 40,000 Soviet and allied troops took part in the exercise, code-named "Brotherhood in Arms '80." The war games, the largest Warsaw Pact maneuvers in 10 years, included contingents from the Soviet Union, East Germany, Hungary, Czechoslovakia and Bulgaria, as well as from strife-ridden Poland. The maneuvers, displayed Soviet equipment not previously seen in operation, including the swing-wing Backfire Bomber and a hover craft-type troop landing boat.

U.S. paratroopers drop from C142 Starlifter transport planes over Hildesheim, West Germany Sept. 18 in NATO "Autumn Forge" maneuvers.

[6] The North Atlantic Treaty Organization Sept. 1 began its own war games, code-named "Autumn Forge." Actually a series of separate maneuvers throughout the NATO area, the games involved more than 180,000 troops before they ended in late 1980.

[7] **Greece Rejoins NATO's Military Wing.** The Defense Planning Committee of the North Atlantic Treaty Organization unanimously approved Greece's re-entry into NATO's military wing Oct. 20. Greece had been absent from the alliance's military since 1974, when it left to protest the Turkish invasion of Cyprus.

See also Afghanistan [12]; Germany West [6]; Iceland; Poland [1,79-81]

NORTH CAROLINA—*See* City & State Affairs [5]; Ku Klux Klan (KKK) [9-11]

NORWAY—*See also* Disasters & Accidents [4]

NUCLEAR ENERGY

Three Mile Island

[1] **Another Accident.** The Three Mile Island nuclear power plant in Pennsylvania experienced another accident Feb. 11, when about 1,000 gallons (about 3,800 liters) of radioactive water leaked from the facility's primary cooling system into an auxiliary building. Three Mile Island had been shut down since March 28, 1979 after the worst accident in the history of commercial nuclear power.

[2] The leak lasted for 90 minutes and prompted the evacuation of 11 workers from the building. Traces of radioactive gas, probably krypton, were

released into the atmosphere. A spokesman for the Nuclear Regulatory Commission said that neither the water leak nor the released gas posed a threat to public health.

[3] In a related development, Bechtel Power Corp. disclosed Feb. 12 that it had been picked as the prime contractor for cleaning up and rehabilitating the damaged Three Mile Island reactor. Bechtel estimated that the job would take about four years and cost from $320 million to $400 million. (The cost did not include replacing the reactor core, which would cost up to $85 million more.) Revised estimates Aug. 9 suggested the clean up would require five years and cost $855 million.

[4] The first anniversary of the accident at Three Mile Island was marked by antinuclear protests March 28-31 around the nation. At 4 a.m. March 28, about 200 persons gathered near the front gate of the plant and held a candlelight vigil. Other antinuclear demonstrations were held in California, Connecticut, New Jersey, New York, Vermont, Virginia and Texas.

[5] ***GPU Sues Babcock and Wilcox***— General Public Utilities Corp. March 25 filed a $500 million lawsuit against Babcock and Wilcox Co., the manufacturer of the crippled Three Mile Island reactor.

[6] The suit, filed in U.S. District Court in New York City, charged the manufacturer with gross negligence in designing the reactor, breach of contract and failure to provide adequate training in emergency procedures to the reactor's operators. GPU was the parent company of Metropolitan Edison Co. which operated the plant.

[7] **Gas-Venting Plan Protested.** About 500 angry residents of the Middletown, Pa. area confronted officials of the Nuclear Regulatory Commission March 20 at a community meeting held in that city. The subject of the meeting was a proposal to vent radioactive gas from the containment building of the crippled reactor at the Three Mile Island nuclear facility.

[8] Before a cleanup could be initiated, the problem of radioactive krypton-85 gas trapped in the containment structure had to be dealt with. Krypton-85 was a highly radioactive gas, with a half-life of 11 years. The normal byproduct of nuclear fission, it was not easily filtered from the air. Under the proposal, recommended by the NRC staff March 12, about 24 million cubic feet of krypton-85 would be purged from the containment building in June. This would mean about 57,000 curies of radioactive krypton-85 gas would be released into the air. (About two million curies of xenon gas had been vented into the air during the 1979 accident, according to the government.)

[9] At the Middletown community meeting, residents assailed the NRC for disregarding their health and safety. The NRC officials present, when they were not shouted down by the crowd, attempted to allay the health fears of the community and explain the merits of the gas-venting proposal. Among other alternatives—all of which were more costly and time consuming—the gas might be liquefied, drawn off in vacuum bottles or absorbed with activated charcoal. Whichever method was tried, they said, the gas had to be removed before workers could clean up an estimated 700,000 gallons (2.64 million liters) of radioactive water spilled in the containment structure and reach the core of the damaged reactor.

[10] **Health Impact.** Pennsylvania health authorities said April 2 that they found no evidence that the Three Mile Island accident had caused increased birth defects or death during infancy.

[11] The Health Department findings came in the wake of continuing controversy over whether the reactor accident had cause health problems, particularly hypothyroidism and excess infant deaths. In recent months, some physicians and scientists in Pennsylvania had released data

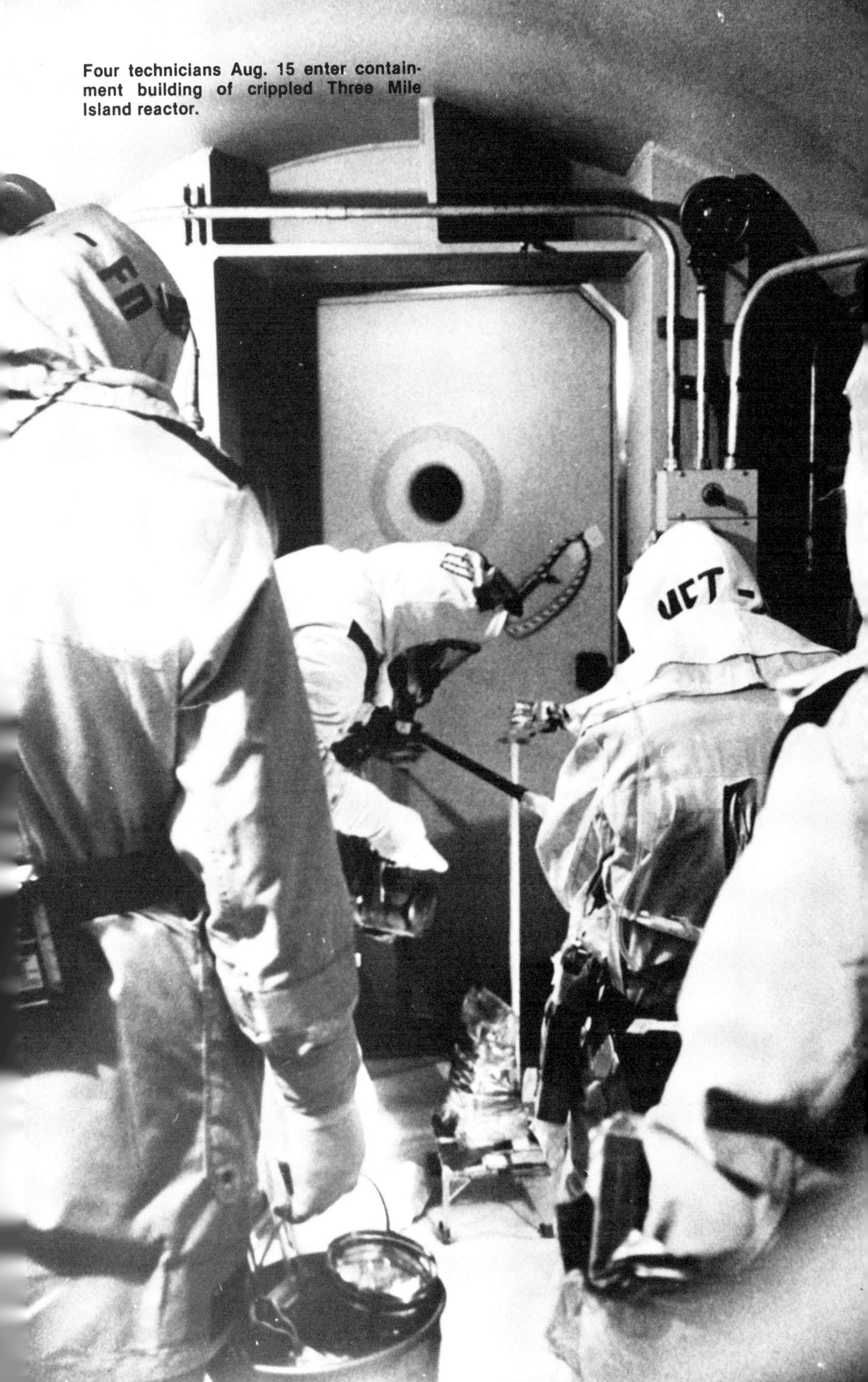

Four technicians Aug. 15 enter containment building of crippled Three Mile Island reactor.

suggesting a sharp increase in both areas.

[12] A Pennsylvania Health Department study reported April 17 that the accident had caused a persistence of anxiety among a large part of the population near the nuclear reactor. The study said that health effects of the accident had included a 113% increase in the number of persons using sleeping pills and an 88% increase in those using tranquilizers. Also, 14% of the residents used more alcohol and 32% smoked more cigarettes.

[13] **Gas Venting Approved.** The Nuclear Regulatory Commission June 10 voted unanimously to approve a plan to vent radioactive gas from the containment building of the reactor. The plan had received the unexpected support of the Union of Concerned Scientists, a group that was critical of nuclear power. Both the scientists group and the commission maintained that the gas venting posed less of a health threat than the contaminated water trapped in the containment structure. Two engineers, wearing protective clothing, had attempted to enter the structure May 20, but were frustrated by a jammed airlock door. This was the first effort to get into the building since the accident.

[14] The venting of 57,000 curies of krypton-85 gas began June 28 and was completed July 11. Despite assurances from the NRC and other agencies, hundreds of people in the central Pennsylvania region left their homes prior to the venting because they feared the gas might be a health hazard. Many did not return until after the venting.

[15] ***Engineers Enter Structure***—Two engineers were able to enter the containment structure July 23. They were the first persons to enter since the accident. They stayed inside for 20 minutes conducting tests for surface contamination, but did not approach the damaged reactor. A team of four technicians Aug. 15 conducted a more extensive examination of the damaged structure.

[16] **TMI Owner Seeks $4 Billion from NRC.** General Public Utilities Dec. 8 filed a damage claim with the Nuclear Regulatry Commission in Washington. GPU accused the NRC of regulatory negligence and asked for $4 billion compensation.

[17] The utility charged in its claims that the NRC "knew or should have know" that plants like Three Mile Island had "defects" in equipment and in the training of its operators.

Other Developments

[18] **Accident Shuts Down Florida A-Plant.** An unexplained power failure Feb. 26 triggered a series of events that caused the spillage of thousands of gallons of radioactive water onto the floor of the containment building of a nuclear power plant at Crystal River, Fla.

[19] It was the most serious accident at a nuclear plant since the mishap at the Three Mile Island unit in 1979. Both plants had been designed by Babcock and Wilcox Co.

[20] **Vienna Meeting Backs Plutonium Fuel.** A two-year study by nuclear experts concluded that the advantages of plutonium-based energy systems outweighed the risks of the proliferation of nuclear weapons. The study was announced Feb. 27 on the final day of the international Nuclear Fuel Cycle Evaluation conference in Vienna.

[21] A total of 46 nations and five international organizations took part in the study and the conference. The activities were initiated by the U.S. in an apparent effort to encourage other nations to find alternatives to plutonium-based atomic power. Reprocessing of the plutonium could provide the fissionable material required for nuclear weapons.

[22] However, the final report rebuffed the U.S. position by supporting the international use of fast-breeder reactors to produce plutonium. The conference warned that the industrialized nations would begin to run out of fuel for reactors by the end of the century unless

they switched to fast breeders or cut back plans for nuclear energy.

[23] **Canadian Vegetables Radioactive.** A study conducted by the Ontario Hydro energy corporation found that tomatoes and vegetables grown near the Pickering atomic energy station were 10 times more radioactive than other Ontario tomatoes and vegetables, it was reported May 22. The company maintained, however, that the tomatoes and vegetables were still safe.

[24] **Seabrook Protest.** Between 1,000 and 5,000 antinuclear demonstrators held a series of protests at the Seabrook nuclear power plant in New Hampshire May 24-26. Some 38 protesters were arrested during the three days, and at least 13 demonstrators and one state trooper were injured.

[25] In earlier antinuclear developments:

- About 10,000 demonstrators held a peaceful rally at the Rocky Flats plant near Golden, Colo. April 19-20. The facility is the country's only plant for plutonium components essential to nuclear weapons.
- An estimated 25,000 protesters gathered in Washington, D.C. April 26-28 in opposition to both the peacetime and military uses of atomic energy. Some 1,500 demonstrators marched on the Pentagon April 28, leading to more than 300 arrests for blocking entrances and defacing government property. It was the largest mass arrest of political demonstrators in the nation's capital since the Mayday anti-war rally in 1971.

[26] **Maine Votes to Keep A-Plant.** Voters in Maine Sept. 23 defeated a referendum proposal to shut down the state's only nuclear power plant, the Maine Yankee facility near Wiscasset.

[27] It was the first time U.S. voters ever had been asked to consider shutting down a nuclear plant already in operation. Maine Yankee, owned by a consortium of utilities headed by Central Maine Power Co., generated 840 megawatts and supplied about one-third of the state's electricity.

[28] **NRC Staff Backs Con Ed Fine.** The staff of the Nuclear Regulatory Commission Dec. 11 proposed a fine of $210,000 against Consolidated Edison Co. for failure promptly to report an accident at a nuclear power plant near Buchanan, N.Y.

[29] The mishap occurred at Con Ed's Indian Point 2 unit. On Oct. 17, workers discovered that an equipment failure in the reactor's secondary cooling system had allowed 100,000 gallons (378,500 liters) of river water to leak onto the floor of the unit's containment building. The NRC said that it had not received a report on the accident from Con Ed until Oct. 20. The agency ordered the unit indefinitely shut down Oct. 23, pending an investigation.

[30] The mishap was marked by controversy. Con Ed did not issue a public statement on the accident until Oct. 21, and the statement itself was sketchy. The NRC contended that preliminary evidence showed that the leak might have begun as early as Oct. 7 and had been either ignored or overlooked by the unit's operators. The NRC also faulted Con Ed for attempting to restart the reactor after it was initially closed down on Oct. 17, without checking to see if the water had damaged the reactor vessel.

[31] ***2d Leak at Indian Point 2***—Consolidated Edison's Indian Point 2 unit suffered another water leak on Nov. 3. About 8,000 gallons (30,280 liters) of water spilled into the reactor containment building as workers "pressure-tested part of a river water system," according to the utility.

See also Armaments (International) [1-5]; Defense (U.S.) [1-15]; Energy; European Community [5]; France [14, 25-27]; Great Britain [42-52]; India [29-35]; Israel [14] Sweden [1-6, 9-10];

NUCLEAR REGULATORY COMMISSION (NRC)—*See* India [30-32]; Nuclear Energy [2, 10-11]

O

OBITUARIES

Joy Adamson. *See* Crime [26-8]

Andrei A. AMALRIK, 42, Soviet human rights activist and political exile who was a leader in the movement for intellectual and political freedom in the U.S.S.R.; a dissident writer, historian and polemicist, he gained worldwide attention for his unrelenting criticism of repression and backwardness in Soviet society; he was the first dissident to seek out American correspondents in Moscow in the mid-1960s, which foreshadowed a link between Soviet political dissidents and Western journalists; he endured university expulsion, police harassment and Siberian exile for his beliefs and in 1976 was pressured to leave the U.S.S.R.; among his major writings were *Will the Soviet Union Survive Until 1984?* and *Involuntary Journey to Siberia;* Nov. 11 in an automobile accident near Guadalajara, Spain en route to the Helsinki accords review conference in Madrid.

Roland BARTHES, 64, French philosopher, writer and social critic; he was one of the most influential French intellectuals and wrote on such subjects as popular cultural phenomena, classical literary figures and the esoteric science of semiology, the formal study of signs and symbols; March 25 after injuries suffered in an automobile accident in Paris.

Cecil BEATON, 76, English author, designer and portrait photographer; he was know for his sartorial style and became the favorite photographer of the British royal family and of rich, famous and fashionable figures in the theater, films and literature; he conceived the stage sets and costumes for some two dozen shows and won two Academy Awards for his work on the motion pictures *Gigi* (1959) and *My Fair Lady* (1965); his many books included collections of photographs and selected diaries; Jan 18 of a heart attack near Salisbury, England.

Harold E. CLURMAN, 78, theater director, drama critic, author and teacher whose stage productions and scholarly erudition influenced the American theater for nearly 50 years; he founded the Group Theater in 1931, which became known for landmark stage productions in the 1930s that included *Awake* and *Sing* and *Golden Boy;* he also directed numerous other plays, including *The Member of the Wedding* and *The Waltz of the Torreadors;* he served as drama critic for *The Nation* magazine and wrote several books, including an autobiography, *All People Are Famous;* Sept. 9 of cancer in New York City.

Jacqueline COCHRAN, age reported as 70 or 74, pioneer pilot, businesswoman, writer and the first women to fly faster than the speed of sound; she set more than 200 aviation records in her career and held more speed, distance and altitude records than any other flyer of her era; she also served as the director of the Women's Air Force Service Pilots in World War II, a program that trained more than 1,200 women; Aug. 8 of a heart attack in Indio, Calif.

Steward CORT, 69, former president and chairman of the Bethlehem Steel

Corporation; he was associated for 40 years with the company, and considered one of the industry's most aggressive leaders in the early 1970s; May 25 in Bethlehem, Pa.

Lt. Gen. Willis D. CRITTENBERGER (ret.), 89, World War II commander of Allied troops in Italy who accepted the first surrender of German Army there; as commander of the IV Corps, he directed infantry and armored divisions in 326 days of continuous combat, freed more than 600 cities and towns and accepted the unconditional surrender of the German Ligurian Army, which marked the imminent collapse of German resistance in Italy; a former cavalry officer, he was credited with setting up the Army's first armored forces in the late 1930s and early 1940s; Aug. 4 of chronic brain syndrome in Chevy Chase, Md.

Dorothy, DAY,83, Catholic social activist who founded many homes for the poor and homeless and was a leader for more than 50 years in numerous battles for social justice; a founder of the Catholic Worker Movement in 1933, she played a seminal role in influencing the thinking of a generation of American priests, intellectuals and laymen; she was a devout Roman Catholic as well as nonviolent social radical who embraced a philosophy of voluntary poverty and care for the destitute through direct involvement; however, her philosophy looked to the person rather than to mass action to transform society; Nov. 29 of congestive heart failure in New York City.

Karl DOENITZ, 89, former German grand admiral who succeeded Adolf Hitler and presided over Nazi Germany's unconditional surrender in World War II; he was also the architect and commander of Germany's submarine campaign against Allied shipping; he served 10 years in Berlin's Spandau Prison after his conviction for war crimes at the Nuremberg trials in 1947; Dec. 24 of a heart attack near Hamburg.

William O(rville) Douglas. *See* Supreme Court [7-10]

Jimmy (Schnozzola) DURANTE, 86, vaudeville, night-club and film comedian whose uproarious antics and raffish humor won him millions of fans worldwide for more than a half-century; he was known for his bulbous nose, raspy voice, battered hat, penguin strut, butchered diction and honky-tonk piano playing; he gained national popularity in the 1920s in a song-and-dance vaudeville trio, Clayton, Jackson and Durante, performing in Prohibition-era speakeasies; he later appeared in Broadway stage and MGM musicals in the 1930s; he extended his fame in the mid-1940s on radio and later on television, ending his program appearances with his celebrated sign-off, "Goodnight, Mrs. Calabash, wherever you are"; Jan. 29 of pneumonitis, a form of pneumonia, in Santa Monica, Calif.

Erich FROMM, 79, German-born psychoanalyst, social philospher and humanist; he wrote widely influential works on the theories of Karl Marx and Sigmund Freud, the religious precepts of Judaism and Christianity, the Cold War and the alienation of the individual in a technological society and a nuclear world; schooled in traditional Freudian psychoanalysis, he later developed his own eclectic theories that stressed social and economic factors, not just unconscious drives, in explaining human behavior, he emigrated from Nazi Germany to the United States in 1934, lectured at Columbia, Yale and other universities and wrote 20 books, including *Escape From Freedom, The Sane Society* and *The Art of Loving;* March 18 of a heart attack in Muralto, Switzerland.

Sanjay Gandhi. *See* India [10-12]

Alfred HITCHCOCK, 80, British-born film director regarded as a master of cinematic technique and screen suspense; he was among the most celebrated film makers for a half-century; Hitchcock directed scores of psychological thrillers, nightmares of menace and the macabre that became film classics; he first won international acclaim in the 1930s for his pacesetting spy thrillers that included *The Man Who Knew Too Much, The 39 Steps* and *The Lady Vanishes;* he moved to Hollywod in 1939 and went on to make such melodramas and shockers as *Rebecca, Suspicion, Notorious, North by Northwest* and *Psycho;* he was nominated for five Academy Awards and won a directorial Oscar for *Rebecca* (1940); he was also noted for his sardonic pronouncements in two popular weekly television series, *Alfred Hitchcock Presents* and the *Alfred Hitchcock Hour,* which he hosted in the late 1950s and early 1960s; April 29 of kidney failure in Los Angeles.

Seretse Khama. *See* Botswana

Oskar KOKOSCHKA, 93, Austrian painter and a major figure in the expressionist art movement; he became known for his intense, penetrating portraits that evoked psychological and emotional depth by means of a nervous tense line and an expressive use of distortion; a painter, writer, graphic artist, illustrator, teacher and humanist, he first gained fame in the cultural ferment of pre-World War I Vienna; Feb. 22 of a heart seizure in Montreux, Switzerland.

John Lennon. *See* John Lennon

Willard F. LIBBY, 71, chemist who won a Nobel Prize in 1960 for his pioneering work in developing the carbon-14 object-dating technique; the technique which greatly aided in the study of ancient man, grew from his discovery in the mid-1940s that radioactive carbon decayed at a predictable rate and thus could be used to date dead organic archaeological and geological remains; he also participated in the World War II Manhattan Project, helping to develop the gaseous-diffusion method of separating uranium isotopes; he later servedon the Atomic Energy Commission (1954-59); Sept. 8 of a blood clot in Los Angeles.

Alice Roosevelt LONGWORTH, 96, the elder daughter and last surviving child of President Theodore Roosevelt and widow of Nicholas Longworth, who was speaker of the House of Representatives (1925-31); she was a leading figure of Washington, D.C. society for nearly 80 years and was renowned for her beauty, charm, acerbic wit and influential political connections; sometimes called Washington's other monument, she was acquainted with and held outspoken opinions about nearly every important political figure from President Benjamin Harrison (1889-93) to Gerald Ford; Feb. 20 of bronchial pneumonia in Washington, D.C.

Bjoern LUNDVALL, 60, Swedish industrialist; chairman of the multinational telecommunications firm L. M. Ericsson and also board chairman of Saab-Scania, the aircraft, car and truck manufacturer; reported dead Sept. 22 of injuries in a car accident in Valdemarsvik, Sweden.

Yakov A(leksandrovich) MALIK, 73, Soviet diplomat, United Nations ambassador (1948-52, 1968-76) and deputy foreign minister; he was best remembered for the decision to boycott the U.N. Security Council in 1950; the U.S. used his absence when the Korean War broke out to persuade the Council to send U.N. forces to South Korea; he proposed a year later a Korean truce that touched off talks that led to a cease-fire in 1953; he was regarded as one of the country's leading experts on the West and played a key role in negotiating the terms that ended the Berlin Blockade in 1949; Feb. 11 after a long illness in Moscow.

Katharina MANN, 97, widow of Thomas Mann, the German novelist; she published a book of her reflections entitled *Unwritten Memories* a few years before her death and also suggested much of the detail and atmosphere of her husband's classic 1924 novel, *The Magic Mountain;* April 18 near Zurich, Switzerland.

John W. MAUCHLY, 72, co-inventor

of the first electronic computer; with J. Presper Eckert Jr., he built ENIAC (Electronic Numerical Integrator and Computer) for the U.S. War Department in 1946; the computer took up 15,000 square feet (about 1,600 square meters) and applied electronic speed for the first time to mathematical tasks; the two later designed the more advanced general-purpose UNIVAC I computer; Jan. 8 while undergoing heart surgery near Ambler, Pa.

Herbert Marshall McLUHAN, 69, Canadian-born communications theorist, professor and author who gained international fame in the 1960s for his studies on the effect of the electronic media on mass culture; considered by some as an oracle of the electronic age, he contended that the electronic media, especially television, were transforming the world technologically into a global electronic village in which books would become obsolete; his often quoted maxim, "the medium is the message," expressed one of his key ideas, that the way people acquired information affected them more than the information itself; among his major studies were *The Gutenberg Galaxy, Understanding Media: The Extensions of Man* and *The Medium Is the Massage;* Dec. 31 in Toronto.

Carey McWILLIAMS, 74, editor of *The Nation* magazine (1955-75) and a long-time crusader for the rights of the underprivileged; originally schooled in law, he turned to journalism in the 1930s in outrage over injustices to migrant workers and others during the Depression and afterward; June 27 of cancer in New York City.

George Meany, *See* Labor [1-4]

Henry MILLER, 88, controversial American novelist and essayist who gained fame for his Bohemian writings, vigorous individualism and advocacy of hedonism; his bawdy, widely acclaimed 1934 autobiographical novel, *Tropic of Cancer,* was banned in the United States until 1964 as obscene for its explicit depiction of sex; his writings contained a strong element of eclectic anarchism and opposition to establishment morality and exerted a great philosophical influence on members of the Beat Generation; among his best known novels, travel books and collections of essays and letters were *Tropic of Capricorn, Sexus, Plexus, Nexus, The Colossus of Maroussi* and *The Air Conditioned Nightmare;* June 7 of circulatory ailments in Pacific Palisades, Calif.

Pietro NENNI, 88, Italian socialist leader whose political career spanned seven decades; he led the Socialist party from 1949-69, helped found the postwar Italian republic and served in its first government as deputy prime minister and foreign minister; his political alliance with the Communist Party and opposition to the North Atlantic Treaty Organization earned him a Stalin Peace Prize in 1952, but he broke with the Communists and repudiated the award after the Soviet intervention in Hungary in 1956; in 1962, he allied his party with the Christian Democrats in a coalition that ruled Italy until 1976; he was a strong opponent of Fascism and suffered exile and many imprisonments for his political activism; Jan. 1 after a heart attack in Rome.

Bob NOLAN, 72, Western songwriter, baritone singer and one of the original members of the Sons of the Pioneers musical group; he was among the foremost Western songwriters of his time and composed some 1,000 Western, gospel and country songs, including the classic *Cool Water* and *Tumbling Tumbleweeds;* the group dominated Western music in the 1930s and the 1940s and appeared in 153 Western movies that starred another of its original members Roy Rogers; June 16 of a heart attack in Costa Mesa, Calif.

Jesse OWENS, 66, black track and field star, hero of the 1936 Berlin Olympics games and among the greatest athletes in the history of track competition; he achieved fame as a sprinter, hurdler and long-jumper of surpassing grace; as a college sophomore, he broke five world records and equalled a sixth all within 45 minutes; he was best known for his memorable performance at the Berlin Olympic Games, when he won four gold medals at a time when Adolf Hitler was proclaiming Aryan racial superiority and mocking America's black athletes as an inferior race; after his career as an amateur runner, he became a public speaker and operated his own public relations and marketing firms; March 31 of lung cancer in Tuscon, Ariz.

Joe PAGE, 62, ace relief pitcher for baseball's New York Yankees in the 1940s; he was a hard-throwing left-hander who turned relief pitching into an honored craft by saving scores of games and helping the Yankees to win two World Series; he pitched 278 games for the Yankees between 1944 and 1950, recording 57 victories, 49 defeats and 76 saves; April 21 of heart failure in Latrobe, Pa.

William A. PATTERSON, 80, pioneer in the commercial aviation industry and retired president of United Airlines (1934-66); he was the first president of United and helped build the company into the world's largest private airline; he made United the first airline to commit itself to jet travel and was also credited with introducing the use of female flight attendants and guaranteed monthly pay for pilots; June 13 after a prolonged illness in Glenview, Ill.

Stanley F. REED, 95, retired U.S. Supreme Court justice (1938-57) who was noted for his support of New Deal legislation and his restrained view of civil liberties; he was named to the Supreme Court by President Franklin D. Roosevelt and wrote more than 300 opinions along a broad range of issues, including social welfare, civil rights and the regulatory power of the federal government; Reed's decisions often defied prediction; April 3 following a stroke in Huntington, N.Y.

Francisco Sa Carneiro. *See* Portugal [11-12]

Jean-Paul SARTRE, 74, French existentialist philosopher whose novels, plays, biographies, essays and political treatises profoundly influenced the social consciousness of the post-World War II generation; he was known for his leftward political commitments and lent his name to manifestoes and protests on behalf of oppressed groups in Greece, Chile and Spain; he also stirred controversy in his support of the Algerian nationalists in their struggle with France and was an active member of the French Resistance in World War II; he helped found the influential review *Les Temps Modernes* in 1945, which published many of his writings, and he turned down the Nobel Prize for literature in 1964; his existential writings, which expressed the widespread disillusionment in post-war Europe, was credited with influencing the development of the anti-novel, the anti-hero, the New Wave cinema and the notion of modern man's anguished consciousness amid moral doubt; Sartre was also noted for his relationship with the feminist writer and philosopher Simon de Beauvoir, his companion of 50 years; among his more than 20 literary and philosophical works were *No Exit, Nausea, Being and Nothingness, The Words* and *Situations;* April 15, of edema of the lung in Paris.

Peter SELLERS, 54, British comedian known for his zany film roles, farcical humor and mastery of impersonation; among Britain's foremost comedians, he gained international acclaim for his versatile portrayals of a wide array of comical characters; he was best known for his portrayal of the bumbling "Inspector Clouseau" in the boxoffice success *The Pink Panther* and its four sequels; among his other films were *Dr. Strangelove or: How I Learned to Stop Worrying and Love the Bomb, The Mouse That Roared, A Shot in the Dark, I'm All Right, Jack, What's New Pussycat?* and *Being*

There; July 24 of a heart attack in London.

Gen. Anastasio Somoza Debayle. *See* Nicaragua [1-4]

Clyfford STILL, 75, American abstract painter; he was considered among the foremost American painters of the 20th century and known for his uncompromising attitudes toward artistic matters; among the founders of the Abstract Expressionist school of painting, he believed in developing a unique American art form that was free from European artistic traditions; June 23 of cancer in Baltimore.

Josip Broz Tito. *See* Yugoslavia

John Van VLECK, 81, Nobel Prize-winning physicist who was recognized for his pioneering work on magnetism; a Harvard University professor emeritus, he was best known for creating the modern theory of magnetism based on quantum mechanics; much of his research was done in the 1930s when he published the book, *Electric and Magnetic Susceptibilities;* Oct. 27 in Cambridge, Mass.

Vladimir Vysotsky. *See* Union of Soviet Socialist Republics [58-59]

Mae WEST, 87, stage, film and nightclub star who reigned as a legendary sex queen for more than 60 years; she epitomized burlesqued sex and was known for her hourglass figure, impeccable blondness, diamond-studded, skin-tight gowns, garish furs and sultry innuendos that evoked the raucous laughter of the bawdyhouse and the honky-tonk; her heyday spanned the 1920s and the 1930s when as "Diamond Lil," the Bowery saloon vamp, she devised her own legend in films and on stage; her suggestive invitation to "come up'n see me sometime," became one of the most often repeated phrases of its day; among her film credits were *My Little Chickadee, I'm No Angel, Belle of the Nineties* and *She Done Him Wrong;* Nov. 22 in Hollywood, Calif.

OIL

Supplies

[1] **U.S. Oil Supplies At Record High.** U.S. crude oil inventories reached record levels during the week ending March 7, according to the American Petroleum Institute March 12. The nation's stock of crude oil rose to 356.3 million barrels March 7, nearly 40 million barrels above stocks on hand for the same period in 1979.

[2] A spokesman for the institute said that sluggish demand for gasoline, due in part to rising prices at the pump, had resulted in an 8.6% drop in domestic deliveries of gasoline in February. Total deliveries were 6.6 million barrels a day. (The API calculated petroleum demand on the basis of deliveries during a given period.)

[3] For all petroleum products, the API reported the largest year-to-year decline ever in domestic deliveries into primary storage in a given month. Total deliveries in February 1980 were 18.4 million barrels a day, compared with about 21.2 million barrels a day in February 1979. This was a drop in demand of 13%.

[4] **Gasohol: Food Versus Fuel?** World–watch, a nonprofit independent research organization, warned March 15 that uncontrolled production of gasohol fuel could sent food prices soaring and limit grain supplies for the world's poor and hungry.

[5] Lester R. Brown, director of the Washington-based group, said, "The alcohol fuel program is unfolding at a time when the world is losing momentum in food production." Brown emphasized that the push for alcohol fuel would divert investment capital, water, fertilizer, and management services away from food production.

[6] One possible way to alleviate the problem might be to "double-crop the land with a winter food grain, such as wheat or barley, and a summer energy

crop, such as sweet sorghum," Brown said. A ban on automatic transmissions for most new U.S. cars would save as much gasoline as the President's gasohol program was designed to yield, he pointed out.

[7] As a part of his July 15, 1979 speech outlining a new U.S. energy program, President Carter had committed the U.S. to gasohol production as one in a series of moves to reduce U.S. dependence on imported oil. Carter's proposal called for the production of 2 billion gallons of ethanol (grain alcohol) by 1985 for use as fuel. This would require 800 million bushels of corn or its equivalent, and could cut U.S. grain exports by as much as 20%.

[8] **Standby Gas Rationing Plan Submitted.** President Carter June 12 submitted to Congress a standby gasoline rationing plan that would go into effect if the nation's crude oil imports were drastically reduced by suppliers.

[9] The President submitted the plan as required by a provision of a standby gas rationing bill he had signed into law in 1979. Under the plan, gasoline rationing would begin if a 20% shorage of oil supplies existed, or was likely to exist, for 30 days. However, the President would have to get further congressional approval before he could actually institute rationing.

[10] The proposal called for the government to distribute ration coupons to states on the basis of historical gasoline use, rather than on the number of motor vehicles registered in each state. Drivers of registered vehicles in each state would receive special ration checks in the mail every three months during a gasoline shortage. These checks could be exchanged for ration coupons at banks and other points.

[11] **Venice Summit Vows to End Reliance on Oil.** The leaders of the seven major industrial democracies met in Venice June 22-23 and pledged to develop their coal reserves and other alternatives to oil.

[12] In a communique, the leaders of the U.S., West Germany, Japan, Great Britain, Canada, France and Italy vowed to break "the existing link between economic growth and consumption of oil." Oil prices should reflect the need to conserve oil, they said. The use of alternative energy sources had to be increased: the potential was seen for increasing production from these sources by the equivalent of 15 million-20 million barrels of oil a day by 1990.

[13] A number of goals set by the 21-nation International Energy Agency were ratified at the summit. These mandated: cutting the overall oil import target for IEA members in 1985 to about 22 million barrels a day from 26.2 million (imports in 1979 averaged about 23 million barrels a day); cutting oil's share in total IEA energy consumption to 40% by 1990 from the present level of 53%; and improving energy efficiency so that a 1% increase in economic output would require only a 0.6% hike in energy use, down from the current 0.85%

[14] **Oil Companies Absolved in '79 Shortage.** U.S. oil companies did not conspire to cause or deepen the 1979 gasoline shortage, according to separate reports made public July 17 by the Justice Department and the Energy Department. The reports reiterated the conclusion of preliminary studies issued by the departments in August 1979.

[15] As in 1979, the new studies basically held that the shortages in the spring and summer of 1979 were caused by the sharp cutback in crude oil production in Iran.

[16] **White House Assured on U.S. Needs.** U.S. oil companies had assured the Carter Administration that they could meet domestic demand for gasoline, heating oil and other petroleum products for several months in the event of worldwide fuel shortages, the White House said Oct. 3.

[17] The Administration received the assurances in the wake of the war between Iraq and Iran. Western Europe and Japan, but not the U.S., depended

heavily on oil from the warring countries. In the event of a complete cutoff of oil from the combatants, the Administration planned to divert some of its crude imports—mainly from Saudi Arabia and Nigeria—to its allies. To do this, the Administration had to be certain that the oil companies could avoid a crisis in the U.S. by supplying enough petroleum to make up for an import shortfall. (The U.S. strategic reserve contained only about two weeks' worth of imported oil.)

[18] Thirty-three oil companies had informed the White House that they had enough stockpiles of gasoline and other petroleum derivatives to meet U.S. needs without the federal government having to fill the strategic reserve. Crude oil inventories had hit a record high at the end of August, it was reported Sept. 5. According to the American Petroleum Institute, the inventories had reached 391.4 million barrels by Aug. 29. This compared with 323.1 billion barrels during the same period in 1979.

[19] ***Oil Reserve Being Filled Quietly***—The Carter Administration was quietly proceeding with its plan to increase the U.S. strategic petroleum reserve. According to the *Wall Street Journal* Oct. 27, the U.S. had concluded agreements to acquire about two thirds of the 36.5 million barrels of oil that it hoped to add to the reserve in fiscal 1981.

[20] The *Journal* noted that the decision to go ahead with the plan had been difficult as it jeopardized U.S. relations with the Organization of Petroleum Exporting Countries, which opposed U.S. stockpiling.

Other Developments

[21] **Windfall Profits Tax.** President Carter April 2 signed the Crude Oil Windfall Profit Tax Act of 1980, calling his action "a victory for every American citizen."

[22] The Senate had passed the compromise conference committee version of the bill on March 27 by a 66-31 vote. The House March 13 endorsed the final version by a 302-107 vote.

[23] The legislation, proposed by President Carter to complement the decontrol of oil prices, was expected to bring the government more than $227 billion in revenues by 1990. Decontrol by allowing American prices to rise to world levels was expected to bring producers an extra $1 trillion by the end of the decade.

[24] Although it was called a "windfall profits" tax, the legislation actually applied to price increases above the 1979 controlled levels, not to profits. Of the $1 trillion, other federal state and local taxes and royalties would take about $552 billion, which coupled with the more than $227 billion collected by the "windfall profits" measure, would leave producers with $221 billion.

[25] Passage of the tax was seen as a major domestic triumph for Carter, even though Congress had trimmed the President's original proposal for a $294 billion tax. The "windfall profits" tax was part of Carter's energy package introduced in April 1979. The two other major elements, an energy mobilization board and a synfuels development program, were still being shaped in House-Senate conferences.

[26] **Congress Bars Oil Import Fee.** Congress gave President Carter one of the worst setbacks of his presidency by overwhelmingly overriding his veto of a resolution blocking the oil import fee. The Carter-proposed fee would have imposed a 10-cent-a-gallon duty at the gasoline pump to discourage energy consumption.

[27] The House voted June 5 shortly after the casting of the veto and overrode Carter's action, 335-34, easily exceeding the two-thirds majority required. The Senate overrode the Carter veto the next morning, June 6, by a 68-10 vote, making the bill law. It was the first override of a Democratic president's veto since 1952, when Harry S. Truman was president. Congress had overridden Truman's veto of the

Walter-McCarran Immigration Act.
See also Budget [21]; Canada [4-5, 25]; Disasters & Accidents [4-6]; Economy (International) [10-11]; Energy [3, 7]; Environment [17-21]; Iran [143]; Iraq [31-32]; Israel [16]; Organization of Petroleum Exporting Countries (OPEC); Solar Energy; Trade & Tariffs [2]; Union of Soviet Socialist Republics [15]

OLYMPICS

[1] **Winter Olympics Held at Lake Placid.** The XIII Winter Olympic Games were held at Lake Placid, N.Y. Feb. 12-24. About 1,600 athletes from 38 nations competed for gold, silver and bronze metals.

[2] The 150-member U.S. contingent won a total of 12 medals – six gold, four silver and two bronze. The East Germans topped all countries with 23 metals, with the Soviet Union taking second place in total medals, with 22. The U.S.S.R. won 10 gold medals, more than any other nation.

[3] As in past Olympics, political controversies competed with athletics for public attention. The major political issue of the 1980 games was the absence of the team from Taiwan [See below] Another political issue, the mounting movement to boycott the 1980 Summer Olympics in Moscow, had little effect on the Lake Placid competition. The U.S.S.R. contingent competed without interference.

[4] The outstanding individual performer of the games was speed skater Eric Heiden. However, Heiden's five gold medals were not as much a surprise as the astonishing triumph of the U.S. ice hockey team. [See below] U.S. hopes for a gold medal in the ice skating pairs competition were dashed Feb. 15, when the world champion team of Tai Babilonia and Randy Gardner had to withdraw from the event because of injuries Gardner had sustained in practice.

Winter Games Final Medal Standing

	Gold	Silver	Bronze	Total
East Germany	9	7	7	23
Soviet Union	10	6	6	22
United States	6	4	2	12
Norway	1	3	6	10
Finland	1	5	3	9
Austria	3	2	2	7
West Germany	0	2	3	5
Switzerland	1	1	3	5
Liechtenstein	2	2	0	4
Netherlands	1	2	1	4
Sweden	3	0	1	4
Italy	0	2	0	2
Canada	0	1	1	2
Britain	1	0	0	1
Hungary	0	1	0	1
Japan	0	1	0	1
Bulgaria	0	0	1	1
Czechoslovakia	0	0	1	1
France	0	0	1	1

[5] ***Taiwan Does Not Compete***— Taiwan, barred from competing in the Winter Olympics under the name, flag and anthem of the Republic of China, decided Feb. 13 not to participate in the games and asked the International Olympics Committee for an excused absence.

[6] The IOC had imposed the restrictions on Taiwan in 1979 at the same time it decided to permit the People's Republic of China to compete in the Olympics for the first time since the Communist takeover.

[7] ***Five Gold Medals for Heiden***— Speed skater Eric Heiden of the U.S. became the first athlete ever to win five gold medals for individual events during the course of a single Olympics. He accomplished the feat Feb. 15-23 by taking all five men's speed skating competitions in record times.

[8] Heiden, 21, surpassed the achievement of Soviet speed skater Lidiya Skoblikova, who had won four gold medals at the 1964 Winter Olympics. (Mark Spitz, a U.S. swimmer, had grabbed a total of seven gold medals at the 1972 Summer Olympics. However, three of Spitz's medals were for relay events.)

[9] Heiden established new Olympic records in all of his races and set a new world record in the 10,000 meters as

well. His epic feat began Feb. 15, when he skated the 500-meter race in 38.03 seconds – 1.14 seconds better than the previous Olympic mark. On Feb. 16, he took the 5,000 meters in 7 minutes 2.09 seconds, or 22.19 seconds better than the old mark. Heiden skated the 1,000 meters Feb. 19 in 1 minute 15.18 seconds – 4.14 seconds under the previous record. He won the 1,500-meter race Feb. 21 in 1 minute 55.44 seconds, or an improvement of 3.94 seconds on the old record. Heiden conquered his greatest test, the grueling 10,000 meters, Feb. 23 in the spectacular time of 14 minutes 28.13 seconds – 22.46 seconds better than the previous Olympic record and 6.2 seconds under the previous world record.

[10] Heiden's sister, Beth, did not fare as well in the women's speed skating events. Beth, 20, finished seventh in the 1,500 meters, seventh in the 500 meters and fifth in the 1,000 meters, before winning a bronze medal in the 3,000 meters Feb. 20.

[11] ***U.S. Wins Ice Hockey Championship***—The United States ice hockey team beat Finland, 4-2, Feb. 24 to clinch the Olympic gold medal in that event. The victory touched off a wave of jubilation across the U.S. that rivaled the national euphoria of Feb. 22, when the U.S. upset the Soviet Union.

[12] The U.S. squad was composed of collegians and amateur minor league players. Assembled in August 1979 by coach Herb Brooks of the University of Minnesota, the team was ranked seventh among the 12 Olympic ice hockey entrants and was not expected to challenge for the gold medal. The team surprised everyone by going undefeated in the opening round. After tying Sweden, 2-2, in their first game, the Americans beat Czechoslovakia (7-3), Norway (5-1), Rumania (7-2) and West Germany (4-2).

[13] The Americans stunned the world Feb. 22 by knocking off the Soviets, 4-3. The Soviets were the reigning world and Olympic ice hockey champions and were thought to be unbeatable. The last time the U.S.S.R. had failed to win a gold medal in the sport was 1960, when another underdog U.S. team won the Olympic title. The unlikely triumph prompted patriotic celebrations that carried through to the final win over the Finns Feb. 24.

Winter Games, Gold Medal Winners (Asterisk denotes new Olympic record; double asterisk new world record)

Alpine Skiing

Men's Downhill (Feb. 14) Leonard Stock, Austria 1:45.50
Men's Giant Slalom (Feb. 19) Ingemar Stenmark, Sweden 2:40.74 (two runs)
Men's Slalom (Feb. 22) Ingemar Stenmark, Sweden 1:44.26
Women's Downhill (Feb. 17) Annemarie Proell Moser, Austria 1:37.52
Women's Giant Slalom (Feb. 21) Hanni Wenzel, Liechtenstein 2:41.66 (two runs)
Women's Slalom (Feb. 23) Hanni Wenzel, Liechtenstein 1:25.09

Nordic Skiing

Men's 30-kilometer cross country (Feb. 14) Nikolai Zimyatov, U.S.S.R. 1:27:02.8
Men's 15-kilometer cross country (Feb. 17) Thomas Wassberg, Sweden 41:57.63
Men's Nordic combined (Feb. 19) Ulrich Wehling, East Germany 432.200 points
Men's 40-kilometer relay (Feb. 20) U.S.S.R. 1:57:03.46
Men's 50-kilometer cross country (Feb. 23) Nikolai Zimyatov, U.S.S.R. 2:27:24.60
Women's 5-kilometer cross country (Feb. 15) Raisa Smetanina, U.S.S.R. 15:06.92
Women's 10-kilometer cross country (Feb. 18) Barbara Petzold, East Germany 30:31.54
Women's 20-kilometer relay (Feb. 21) East Germany 1:02:11.10

Ski Jumping

70-meter jump (Feb. 17) Anton Innauer, Austria 266.3 points
90-meter jump (Feb. 23) Jouko Tormanen, Finland 114.5 and 117 meters

Biathlon

Individual 20 kilometers (Feb. 16) Anatoly Alabyev, U.S.S.R. 1:08:16.31
Individual 10 kilometers (Feb. 19) Frank Ulrich, East Germany 32:10.69
30-kilometer relay (Feb. 22) U.S.S.R. 1:34:03.27

Ice Hockey

U.S. 6 wins, 0 losses, 1 tie

Figure Skating

Men's (Feb. 19) Robin Cousins, Great Britain 189.48 points
Women's (Feb. 23) Anett Poetzsch, East Germany 189 points
Pairs (Feb. 17) Irina Rodnina and Alexander Zaitsev, U.S.S.R. 147.26 points
Ice Dancing (Feb. 17) Natalia Linichuk and Gennadi Karponosov, U.S.S.R. 101.28 points

Speed Skating

Men's 500 meters (Feb. 15) Eric Heiden, U.S. 38.03 seconds*
Men's 5,000 meters (Feb. 16) Eric Heiden, U.S. 7:02.29*
Men's 1,000 meters (Feb. 19) Eric Heiden, U.S. 1:15.18*

Men's 1,500 meters (Feb. 21) Eric Heiden, U.S. 1:55.44*
Men's 10,000 meters (Feb. 23) Eric Heiden, U.S. 14:28.13* **
Women's 1,500 meters (Feb. 14) Anne Borckink, Netherlands 2:10.95*
Women's 500 meters (Feb. 14) Karin Enke, East Germany 41.78 seconds*
Women's 1,000 meters (Feb. 17) Natalya Petruseva, U.S.S.R. 1:24.10*
Women's 3,000 meters (Feb. 20) Bjoerg Eva Jensen, Norway 4:32.13*

Luge

Men's singles (Feb. 16) Bernhard Glass, E. Germany 2:54.79 (four runs)
Men's doubles (Feb. 19) East Germany 1:19.33 (two runs)
Women's singles (Feb. 17) Vera Zozulya, U.S.S.R. 2:36.53 (four runs)

Bobsled

Two-man (Feb. 16) Switzerland II 4:09.36 (four runs)
Four-man (Feb. 24) East Germany I 3:59.92 (four runs)

[14] **Moscow Summer Olympics.** The XXII Olympic Games were held in Moscow July 19 to Aug. 3. It was the first Olympics ever staged in a communist nation.

[15] As in all recent Olympics, controversy drew as much world attention as the games themselves. The central controversy at Moscow was the U.S.-led boycott in protest of the Soviet invasion of Afghanistan. A total of 81 countries took part in the Moscow Olympics. Some 65 nations did not participate. About 55 of the nonparticipants, including West Germany, Japan, China, and Kenya, stayed away expressly because of Afghanistan. Other nonparticipants had given other reasons, such as lack of financial resources or the inability to field world-class athletes. The boycott reduced the number of athletes to about 6,000 from the anticipated 10,000. Likewise, the number of foreign tourists who attended the games came to about 100,000. The U.S.S.R. had made plans to accommodate 300,000 tourists.

[16] Other controversies included the ultratight security around the games, the Soviet crackdown on the foreign press, the visit of Yasir Arafat—head of the Palestine Liberation Organization—to the games, and charges that Soviet officials blatantly favored Soviet athletes in many events.

[17] In terms of competition, the boycott clearly benefited the communist-bloc nations in general and the Soviet Union in particular. Of the 12 nations that finished with 10 or more total medals, eight were communist. Six of the top 10 medal-winning nations were communist. The Soviet Union won more gold medals (80) and more total medals (197) than any other nation in the history of the Olympics. The U.S.S.R. also captured 70 silver medals, denoting second-place in finishes, and 47 bronze medals, denoting third-place finishes. The U.S.S.R.'s only real competition in the medals race was East Germany (47 gold, 36 silver and 43 bronze).

Summer Games
Final Medal Standing

(Duplicate medals awarded in some events)

	Gold	Silver	Bronze	Total
Soviet Union	80	70	47	197
East Germany	47	36	43	126
Bulgaria	8	16	16	40
Hungary	7	10	15	32
Poland	3	14	14	31
Rumania	6	6	13	25
Great Britain	5	7	9	21
Cuba	8	7	5	20
Italy	8	3	4	15
France	6	5	3	14
Czechoslovakia	2	2	9	13
Sweden	3	3	6	12
Australia	2	2	5	9
Yugoslavia	2	3	4	9
Finland	3	1	4	8
Spain	1	3	2	6
Denmark	2	1	2	5
Austria	1	3	1	5
North Korea	0	3	2	5
Brazil	2	0	2	4
Ethiopia	2	0	2	4
Mongolia	0	2	2	4
Netherlands	0	1	3	4
Mexico	0	1	3	4
Greece	1	0	2	3
Jamaica	0	0	3	3
Switzerland	2	0	0	2
Tanzania	0	2	0	2
Ireland	0	1	1	2
Belgium	1	0	0	1
India	1	0	0	1
Zimbabwe	1	0	0	1
Venezuela	1	0	0	1
Uganda	0	1	0	1
Guyana	0	0	1	1
Lebanon	0	0	1	1

Source: *New York Times* Aug. 4

[18] ***Eight Medals for Dityatin***— Alexandr Dityatin collected his eighth medal of the Moscow games July 25, when he won the still rings competition and assured the Soviets of a first place

in men's gymnastics. The rings gold gave Dityatin (previously transliterated as Ditiatin) more medals than any other athlete had ever won at a single modern Olympics.

[19] In the Moscow Olympics, Dityatin captured three gold medals (team title, all-around and still rings), four silver medals (horizontal bar, side horse, vaulting and parallel bars) and one bronze medal (floor exercises). Only two other Olympic athletes had gathered as many as seven medals at one time. They were Soviet gymnast Nikolai Adrianov in 1976 and U.S. swimmer Mark Spitz in 1972.

[20] Numerous other record-breaking and outstanding performances took place in Moscow, including those by:

■ Barbara Krause of East Germany, who set a world's record in women's 100-meter freestyle – 54.98 seconds – in a heat July 20. She smashed her own record the next day, by swimming a 54.79-second race for the gold medal.

■ Vladimir Salnikov of the Soviet Union, who swam the punishing 1,500-meter freestyle in an astounding 14 minutes 58.27 seconds July 22. Salnikov was the first swimmer ever to break the 15-minute barrier in the 1,500 meters. (The barrier had been considered roughly equivalent to the four-minute mile in running.) Salnikov won two other gold medals: July 23 as part of the winning Soviet 800-meter freestyle relay team, and July 24, by swimming an Olympic record 3:51.31 in the 400-meter freestyle.

■ Daley Thompson of Great Britain, who garnered the coveted decathlon championship July 26, with 8,495 points. Thompson, 21, was the youngest man to win a decathlon title since 21-year-old Bob Mathias of the U.S. in 1952.

■ Wladyslaw Kozakiewicz of Poland, who set a world record in the pole vault – 18 feet 11½ inches – July 30, despite the whistles and jeers of the pro-Soviet crowd. Five other pole vaulters in the competition also exceeded the former Olympic record of 18'½".

■ Teofilo Stevenson of Cuba, who won an unprecedented third Olympic heavyweight boxing crown Aug. 2. Stevenson, the Olympic heavyweight champion in 1972 and 1976, grabbed his third gold medal by decisioning Pyotr Zaev of the Soviet Union.

[21] ***Coe vs. Ovett***—Much of the drama of the Moscow Olympics centered on the long-awaited confrontation between two British middle-distance runners, Sebastian Coe and Steve Ovett. The two battled in the 800-meter final July 26 and the 1,000-meter final Aug. 1.

[22] Coe, 23, had established himself as a track superstar in 1979, when he set world records in the 800 meters (42.33 seconds), 1,500 meters (3 minutes 32.1 seconds) and the mile (3 minutes 49 seconds). He was the first man ever to hold all three marks at the same time. On July 1, 1980, Coe added a fourth world record to his achievements. At an international meet in Oslo, he captured the 1,000 meters in 2:13.4. However, Coe's jubilation was short-lived that day. About 55 minutes after he set the 1,000-meter mark, Ovett, who was also at the Norway meet, broke Coe's mile record. Ovett ran a 3:48.8 mile – two-tenths of a second better than Coe's 1979 mark.

[23] Ovett won the gold medal in the 800 meters July 26. He took the lead about 80 meters from the finish and used his fabled kick to sprint in at 1:45.4, three seconds off Coe's world mark. Coe was second. Coe avenged his defeat Aug. 1, by winning the 1,500-meter final. Grabbing the lead about 180 meters from the finish, Coe virtually glided to victory in 3:38.4, more than six seconds off the world mark he and Ovett shared. Ovett ended up third, behind Jurgen Straub of East Germany.

[24] ***Disputes Mar Women's Gymnastics***—In a competition marked by drama and controversy, the Soviet

Steve Ovett of Great Britain wins 800-meter race July 26. Sebastian Coe (right) finished second. Ovett's time was 1:45.4.

team dominated women's gymnastics July 21-25.

[25] The Soviet women July 23 easily captured the team gold medal for the eighth consecutive Olympics, but the victory of the Soviet Union's Yelena Davydova over Nadia Comaneci of Rumania July 24 for the all-around gold medal was hotly contested by Bela Karolyi, the Rumanian coach.

[26] Karolyi charged that Helen Berger, the East German chairman of the gymnastics federation, had lowered Comaneci's score on the balance beam to 9.85 in "an arrangement" to assure Soviet victory. Berger denied the charge. A Soviet spokesman explained that the 30 minute lapse between the end of Comaneci's performance and the posting of her score was due to the refusal of Rumanian head judge, Maria Simionescu, to accept the score. A jury reviewed the dispute, he said, and upheld the judges' decision.

[27] Therefore, Comaneci, the marvel who had won the all-around in Montreal in 1976 after gaining seven perfect scores, tied with Maxi Gnauck of East Germany for the silver medal. Comaneci July 23 had shocked the Moscow crowd by falling from the uneven parallel bars in the optional program. She recovered and finished the routine, but dropped to fourth place until her comeback in the final round of the all-around competition.

[28] The individual apparatus competition July 25 was marred by further discord when Simionescu protested the 9.85 score awarded Natalya Shaposhnikova of the Soviet Union for her balance beam routine. She was overruled again. Comaneci won the event, Davydova got the silver and Shaposhnikova, the bronze.

[29] ***Killanin Steps Down, Rips Boycott***—The International Olympic Committee, meeting in Moscow, July 16 elected Juan Antonio Samaranch of Spain to succeed Lord Killanin as president. Killanin one month earlier had announced he would not stand for reelection. Samaranch, 60, was a former Barcelona industrialist and was

Spain's ambassador to the Soviet Union at the time of his election. He indicated he would resign the diplomatic post. Louis Gurandou-N'Diaye, an Ivory Coast diplomat, was elected IOC vice president.

[30] At a press conference July 18 in Moscow, Killanin criticized the Olympic boycott and accused President Carter and his advisers of being ignorant on matters of international sports. "They did not understand how sport is organized in the world," he said. "They did not understand how national Olympic committees work. They did not understand the workings of the International Olympic committee. . . . To my mind, they had virtually no knowledge other than about American football and baseball, which if they had been Olympic games, perhaps we wouldn't have had the boycott." Killanin added: "I only hope that some of the heads of state I've met, and some of the governments I've met, are better advised on important matters than they are on sport. Because if they are not, God help us all."

Summer Games, Gold Medal Winners (Asterisk denotes new Olympic record; double asterisk new world record)

Archery

Men's (Aug. 2) Tomi Poikolainin, Finland 2,455 pts.
Women's (Aug. 2) Keto Losaberidze, U.S.S.R., 2,491 pts.

Basketball

Men's (July 30) Yugoslavia
Women's (July 30) U.S.S.R.

Boxing

Light Flyweight (106 pounds) (Aug. 2) Shamil Sabyrov, U.S.S.R.
Flyweight (112 pounds) (Aug. 2) Petar Lessov, Bulgaria
Bantamweight (119 pounds) (Aug. 2) Juan Hernandez, Cuba
Featherweight (126 pounds) (Aug. 2) Rudi Fink, East Germany
Lightweight (132 pounds) (Aug. 2) Angel Herrera, Cuba
Light Welterweight (140 pounds) (Aug. 2) Patrizio Oliva, Italy
Welterweight (148 pounds) (Aug. 2) Andres Aldama, Cuba
Light Middleweight (157 pounds) (Aug. 2) Armando Martinez, Cuba
Middleweight (165 pounds) (Aug. 2) Jose Gomez, Cuba
Light Heavyweight (179 pounds) (Aug. 2) Slobodan Kacar, Yugoslavia
Heavyweight (over 179 pounds) (Aug. 2) Teofilo Stevenson, Cuba

Men's Canoeing

500-Meter Kayak Singles (Aug. 1) Vladimir Postrekhin, U.S.S.R. 1:43.43
500-Meter Canoe Singles (Aug. 1) Sergei Postrkhin, U.S.S.R. 1:53.37
500-Meter Kayak Pairs (Aug. 1) U.S.S.R. 1:32.38
500-Meter Canoe Pairs (Aug. 1) Hungary 1:43.39
1,000-Meter Kayak Singles (Aug. 2) Rudiger Helm, East Germany 3:48.77
1,000-Meter Canoe Singles (Aug. 2) Lubomir Lubenov, Bulgaria 4:12.38
1,000-Meter Kayak Pairs (Aug. 2) U.S.S.R. 3:26.72
1,000-Meter Canoe Pairs (Aug. 2) Rumania 3:47.65
1,000-Meter Kayak Fours (Aug. 2) East Germany 3:13.76

Women's Canoeing

500-Meter Kayak Singles (Aug. 1) Brigit Fischer, East Germany 1:57.96
500-Meter Kayak Pairs (Aug. 1) East Germany 1:46.91

Cycling

100-Kilometer Team Road Race (July 20) U.S.S.R. 2 hrs, 2:21.70
1,000-Meter Time Trial (July 22) Lothar Thoms, East Germany 1:02.95*
Individual Pursuit (July 24) Robert Dill-Bundi, Switzerland 4:35.66
Team Pursuit (July 26) U.S.S.R. 4:15.70
Road Race (July 28) Sergei Soukhoroutchenkov, U.S.S.R. 4:48.28

Equestrian

Individual 3-Day Event (July 27) Federico Euro Roman, Italy 108.6 pts.
Team 3-Day Event (July 27) U.S.S.R. 457.00 pts.
Individual Jumping (Aug. 3) Jan Kowalczyk, Poland 8.00 penalty pts.
Team Dressage (July 31) U.S.S.R. 4383.0
Individual Dressage (Aug. 1) Elisabeth Theurer, Austria 1,370
Team Jumping (July 29) U.S.S.R. 20.25 penalty pts.

Men's Fencing

Individual Foil (July 23) Vladimir Smirnov, U.S.S.R.
Individual Saber (July 25) Viktor Krovopuskov, U.S.S.R.
Individual Epee (July 28) Johan Harmenberg, Sweden
Team Foil (July 26) France
Team Saber (July 29) U.S.S.R.
Team Epee (July 31) France

Women's Fencing

Individual Foil (July 24) Pascale Trinquet, France
Team Foil (July 27) France

Field Hockey

Men's Team Championship (July 29) India
Women's Team Championship (July 31) Zimbabwe

Men's Gymnastics

Team Competition (July 22) U.S.S.R. 589.60 pts.
All Around (July 24) Alexandr Dityatin, U.S.S.R. 118.65
Floor Exercises (July 25) Roland Bruckner, East Germany 19.750
Horizontal Bars (July 25) Stoyan Delchev, Bulgaria 19.825
Pommel Horse (July 25) Zoltan Magyar, Hungary 19.925
Parallel Bars (July 25) Alexandr Tkachyov, U.S.S.R. 19.775
Rings (July 25) Alexandr Dityatin, U.S.S.R. 19.875
Vault (July 25) Nikolai Andrianov, U.S.S.R. 19.825

Women's Gymnastics

Team Competition (July 23) U.S.S.R. 394.90 pts.
All Around (July 24) Yelena Davydova, U.S.S.R. 79.150 pts.
Balance Beam (July 25) Nadia Comaneci, Rumania 19.800
Floor Exercises (July 25) (tie) Nelli Kim, U.S.S.R.; Nadia Comaneci, Rumania 19.875
Vault (July 25) Natalya Shaposhnikova, U.S.S.R. 19.725
Uneven Bars (July 25) Maxi Gnauck, East Germany 19.875

Team Handball

Men's Championship (July 30) East Germany
Women's Championship (July 29) U.S.S.R.

Judo

132-Pound Class (Aug. 1) Thierry Rey, France
143-Pound Class (July 31) Nikolay Solodukhin, U.S.S.R.
157-Pound Class (July 25) Ezio Gamba, Italy

172-Pound Class (July 29) Shota Khabareli, U.S.S.R.
190-Pound Class (July 28) Juerg Roethlisberger, Switzerland
209-Pound Class (July 27) Robert Van De Walle, Belgium
Heavyweight (July 27) Angelo Parisi, France
Open (Aug. 2) Dietmar Lorenz, East Germany

Modern Pentathlon

Individual (July 24) Anatoly Starostin, U.S.S.R. 5,568 pts.
Team (July 24) U.S.S.R. 16,126

Men's Rowing

Coxed Pairs (July 27) East Germany 7:02.54
Coxless Pairs (July 27) East Germany 6:48.01
Coxed Fours (July 27) East Germany 6:14.51
Coxless Fours (July 27) East Germany 6:08.17
Single Sculls (July 27) Pertti Karppinen, Finland 7:09.61
Double Sculls (July 27) East Germany 6:24.33
Quadruple Sculls (July 27) East Germany 5:49.81
Eights (July 27) East Germany 5:49.05

Women's Rowing

Coxless Pairs (July 26) East Germany 3:30.49
Coxed Fours (July 26) East Germany 3:19.27
Single Sculls (July 26) Sanda Toma, Rumania 3:40.68
Double Sculls (July 26) U.S.S.R. 3:16.27
Quadruple Sculls (July 26) East Germany 3:15.32
Eights (July 26) East Germany 3:03.32

Shooting

Free Pistol (July 20) Aleksandr Melentev, U.S.S.R. 581**
Small-Bore Rifle, Prone Position (July 21) Karoly Varga, Hungary 599
Trap (July 22) Luciano Giovanetti, Italy
Small-Bore Rifle, 3 Positions (July 23) Viktor Vlasov, U.S.S.R. 1,173**
Running Boar Target (July 24) Igor Sokolov, U.S.S.R. 589**
Rapid-Fire Pistol (July 25) Corneliu Ion, Rumania 596
Skeet (July 26) Hans Kjeld Rasmussen, Denmark 196

Soccer

Team Championship (Aug. 2) Czechoslovakia

Men's Swimming

100-Meter Backstroke (July 21) Bengt Baron, Sweden 56.53 seconds
200-Meter Backstroke (July 26) Sandor Wladar, Hungary 2:01.93
100-Meter Breaststroke (July 22) Duncan Goodhew, Great Britain 1:03.34
200-Meter Breaststroke (July 26) Robertas Zulpa, U.S.S.R. 2:15.85
100-Meter Butterfly (July 23) Par Arvidsson, Sweden 54.92
200-Meter Butterfly (July 20) Sergei Fesenko, U.S.S.R. 1:59.76
100-Meter Freestyle (July 27) Jorge Woithe, East Germany 50.40
200-Meter Freestyle (July 21) Sergei Kopliakov, U.S.S.R. 1:49.81*
400-Meter Freestyle (July 24) Vladimir Salnikov, U.S.S.R. 3:51.31*
1,500-Meter Freestyle (July 22) Vladimir Salnikov, U.S.S.R. 14:58.27**
800-Meter Freestyle Relay (July 23) U.S.S.R. 7:23.50
400-Meter Individual Medley (July 27) Aleksandr Sidorenko, U.S.S.R. 4:22.89*
400-Meter Relay (July 24) Australia 3:45.70

Women's Swimming

100-Meter Backstroke (July 23) Rica Reinisch, East Germany 1:00.86**
200-Meter Backstroke (July 27) Rica Reinisch, East Germany 2:11.77**
100-Meter Breaststroke (July 26) Ute Geweniger, East Germany 1:10.22*
200-Meter Breaststroke (July 23) Lina Kachushite, U.S.S.R. 2:29.54*
100-Meter Butterfly (July 24) Caren Metschuck, East Germany 1:00.42
200-Meter Butterfly (July 21) Ines Geissler, East Germany 2:10.44*
100-Meter Freestyle (July 21) Barbara Krause, East Germany 54.79**
200-Meter Freestyle (July 24) Barbara Krause, East Germany 1:58.33*
400-Meter Freestyle (July 22) Ines Diers, East Germany 4:08.76*
800-Meter Freestyle (July 27) Michelle Ford, Australia 8:28.90*
400-Meter Freestyle Relay (July 27) East Germany 3:42.71
400-Meter Individual Medley (July 26) Petra Schneider, East Germany 4:36.29**
400-Meter Medley Relay (July 20) East Germany 4:06.67**

Men's Diving

Springboard (July 23) Aleksandr Portnov, U.S.S.R. 905.02 pts.
Platform (July 28) Falk Hoffmann, East Germany 835.65

Women's Diving

Springboard (July 21) Irina Kalinina, U.S.S.R. 725.91 pts.
Platform (July 26) Martina Jaschke, East Germany 596.25

Men's Track & Field

20-Kilometer Walk (July 24) Maurizio Damilano, Italy 1 hr, 23:35*
100-Meter Dash (July 25) Allan Wells, Great Britain 10.25
Triple Jump (July 25) Jaak Uudmae, U.S.S.R. 56' 11 1/8"
400-Meter Hurdles (July 26) Volker Beck, East Germany 48.70
800-Meter Run (July 26) Steve Ovett, Great Britain 1:45.40
Decathlon (July 26) Daley Thompson, Great Britain 8,495 pts.
110-Meter Hurdles (July 27) Thomas Munkelt, East Germany 13.39
10,000-Meter Run (July 27) Miruts Yifter, Ethiopia 27:42.7
Javelin (July 27) Dainis Kula, U.S.S.R. 229' 2 3/8"
200-Meter Dash (July 28) Pietro Mennea, Italy 20.19
Long Jump (July 28) Lutz Dombrowski, East Germany 28' 1/4"
Discus (July 28) Viktor Rashchupkin, U.S.S.R. 218' 8"
50-Kilometer Walk (July 30) Hartwig Gauder, East Germany 3:49:24.0
400-Meter Dash (July 30) Viktor Markin, U.S.S.R. 44.60
Pole Vault (July 30) Wladyslaw Kozakiewicz, Poland 18' 11 1/2"**
Shot Put (July 30) Vladimir Kiselyov, U.S.S.R. 70' 1/2"
3,000-Meter Steeplechase (July 31) Bronislaw Malinowski, Poland 8:09.7
Hammer Throw (July 31) Yuri Sedykh, U.S.S.R. 268' 4"*
1,500-Meter Run (Aug. 1) Sebastian Coe, Great Britain 3:38.4
5,000-Meter Run (Aug. 1) Miruts Yifter, Ethiopia 13:21.0*
Marathon (Aug. 1) Waldemar Cierpinki, East Germany 2:11:03.0
400-Meter Relay (Aug. 1) U.S.S.R. 38.26
1,600-Meter Relay (Aug. 1) U.S.S.R. 3:01.1
High Jump (Aug. 1) Gerd Wessig, East Germany 7' 8 3/4"**

Women's Track & Field

Pentathlon (July 24) Nadezhda Tkachenko, U.S.S.R. 5,083 pts**
Shot Put (July 24) Ilona Slupianek, East Germany 22.41 meters*
Javelin (July 25) Maria Colon, Cuba 224' 4 3/4"*
100-Meter Dash (July 26) Lyudmilla Kondratyeva, U.S.S.R. 11.06
High Jump (July 26) Sara Simeoni, Italy 6' 5 1/2"*
800-Meter Run (July 27) Nadezhda Olizarenko, U.S.S.R. 1:53.5**
100-Meter Hurdles (July 28) Vera Komisova, U.S.S.R. 12.56
400-Meter Dash (July 28) Marita Koch, East Germany 48.88

200-Meter Dash (July 30) Barbel Wockel, East Germany 22.03*
Long Jump (July 31) Tatiana Kolpakova, U.S.S.R. 23' 2"
1,500-Meter Run (Aug. 1) Tatyana Kazankina, U.S.S.R. 3:56.6
400-Meter Relay (Aug. 1) East Germany 41.60**
1,600-Meter Relay (Aug. 1) U.S.S.R. 3:20.2
Discus (Aug. 1) Evelin Jahl, East Germany 229' 6"

Volleyball

Men's (Aug. 1) U.S.S.R.
Women's (July 29) U.S.S.R.

Water Polo

Team Championship (July 29) U.S.S.R.

Weight Lifting

115-Pound Group (July 20) Kanibek Osmanoliev, U.S.S.R. 539 lbs*
123-Pound Group (July 21) Daniel Nunez, Cuba 606.2 lbs**
132-Pound Group (July 22) Viktor Mazin, U.S.S.R. 639.3 lbs**
149-Pound Group (July 23) Yanko Roussev, Bulgaria 755 lbs**
165-Pound Group (July 24) Assen Zlatev, Bulgaria 792 lbs**
182-Pound Group (July 26) Yusik Vardanyan, U.S.S.R. 881.3 lbs**
198-Pound Group (July 27) Peter Baczako, Hungary 832.2 lbs
220-Pound Group (July 28) Ota Zaremba, Czechoslovakia 870.8 lbs
242-Pound Group (July 29) Leonid Taranenko, U.S.S.R. 931.4 lbs
Super Heavyweight (July 30) Sultan Rakhmanov, U.S.S.R. 970 lbs

Greco Roman Wrestling

106-Pound Class (July 22) Zaksylik Ushkempirov, U.S.S.R.
114-Pound Class (July 23) Vakhtang Blagidze, U.S.S.R.
125-Pound Class (July 24) Shamil Serikov, U.S.S.R.
136 Pound Class (July 22) Stilianos Migiakis, Greece
150-Pound Class (July 24) Stefan Rusu, Rumania
163-Pound Class (July 23) Ferenc Kocsis, Hungary
180-Pound Class (July 24) Gennady Korban, U.S.S.R.
198-Pound Class (July 22) Norbert Nottny, Hungary
220-Pound Class (July 23) Gheorghi Ralkov, Bulgaria
Super Heavyweight (July 24) Aleksandr Kolchinsky, U.S.S.R.

Free-Style Wrestling

106-Pound Class (July 29) Claudio Pollio, Italy
115-Pound Class (July 30) Anatoly Beloglazov, U.S.S.R.
126-Pound Class (July 31) Sergei Beloglazov, U.S.S.R.
137-Pound Class (July 29) Magomedgasan Abushev, U.S.S.R.
150-Pound Class (July 31) Saipulla Absaldov, U.S.S.R.
163-Pound Class (July 30) Valentin Raitchev, Bulgaria
181-Pound Class (July 31) Ismail Abilov, Bulgaria
198-Pound Class (July 29) Sanasar Oganesyan, U.S.S.R.
220-Pound Class (July 30) Ilya Mate, U.S.S.R.
Super Heavyweight (July 31) Sosian Andiev, U.S.S.R.

Yachting

Soling Class (July 29) Denmark 23 pts.
Tornado Class (July 29) Brazil 21.4
Flying Dutchman Class (July 29) Spain 19
Star Class (July 29) U.S.S.R. 24.7
470 Class (July 29) Brazil 36.4
Finn Class (July 29) Finland 36.7

See also Afghanistan [17-18, 20-25, 65]

OMAN—*See* Defense (U.S.) [27]

ORGANIZATION OF AFRICAN UNITY (OAU)—*See* Africa [1-4]; Chad [10]

ORGANIZATION OF AMERICAN STATES (OAS)—*See* Human Rights [15-18]

ORGANIZATION OF PETROLEUM EXPORTING COUNTRIES (OPEC) (Algeria, Ecuador, Gabon, Indonesia, Iran, Iraq, Kuwait, Libya, Nigeria, Quatar, Saudi Arabia, United Arab Emirates, Venezuela)

[1] **Base Price Set at $32 a Barrel.** The Organization of Petroleum Exporting Countries set a theoretical base price for crude oil at $32 a barrel and a ceiling price of $37 a barrel at the end of a two-day ministerial meeting in Algiers June 9-10. The floor price was to be used as the basis from which a unified pricing system would be applied.

[2] The base price was not agreed to by all of OPEC's 13 members. Saudi Arabia, and the United Arab Emirates voted against the price base, finding it excessive. Sheik Ahmed Zaki Yamani, Saudi Arabia's oil minister, said June 10, "I am not raising my price." The Saudis May 14 had lifted the price of their petroleum an average of 8% from $26 to $28 a barrel in an effort to narrow the gap between their oil and that of the other 12 OPEC countries. But several OPEC members had then raised their prices, negating the Saudi attempt to bring unity to OPEC's pricing, and costing oil consumers an additional $20 billion a year.

[3] The idea of a pricing formula was to prevent further price "leapfrogging" in OPEC. The top ceiling of $37 would apply to the African countries—Libya, Nigeria and Algeria—which had been the most hawkish on prices because of

the quality of their light-grade crude oil and demand for it among oil consuming countries.

[4] On June 11, Kuwait, Venezuela, Iraq and Qatar announced plans to raise their oil prices by as much as $2 a barrel in July. Algeria and Libya said that they would raise their prices by less than a dollar by July 1. But oil ministers from other OPEC countries said that they would study the oil market before raising their prices. If all of the OPEC countries were to raise their prices as much as they could under the new formula, including a $4-a-barrel increase by Saudi Arabia, the impact on oil consumers would be enormous. However, there was nothing binding in the new agreement, and present prices could stand if the producers so chose.

[5] **Oil Price Compromise.** OPEC Sept. 18 achieved a partial compromise aimed at resolving pricing differences.

[6] The agreement on pricing, reached on the final day of an OPEC meeting in Vienna Sept. 15-18, hinged on Saudi Arabia's promise of an immediate $2 increase in the price of its benchmark light crude oil to $30 a barrel. In exchange, the other OPEC members agreed to freeze their prices until the end of 1980.

[7] The proposal that led to the agreement was offered by Kuwait's oil minister, Ali Khalifa al-Sabah, and seconded by Abdul Aziz al-Turki, Saudi Arabia's deputy oil minister. The compromise on the part of the Saudis was taken, according to Aziz, "to reach a unified price" among OPEC's 13 members.

[8] **OPEC Postpones Parley.** OPEC Oct. 8 indefinitely postponed its scheduled meeting in Baghdad, Iraq because of the conflict between Iran and Iraq, both OPEC members.

[9] The development announced from the Iraqi Embassy in Vienna, Austria, where OPEC had its headquarters, cast doubts on the ability of OPEC members to reach agreement on pricing and marketing policies at a time when world oil supplies were threatened by the conflict in the Persian Gulf. Oil experts had hoped that the meeting in Baghdad, which had been intended as a celebration of the 20th anniversary of the oil producers' cartel, would have settled the issue of pricing.

[10] **Abu Dhabi Lifts Oil Price $2.** Abu Dhabi, the largest oil producer in the United Arab Emirates, lifted the price of its crude oil by $2, retroactive to Sept. 1, according to reports reaching Western oil companies Oct. 15.

[11] The price increase was the first substantial rise in oil prices by a member of OPEC since the Sept. 18 agreement reached in Vienna. Abu Dhabi produced about 1.4 million barrels of oil a day. It now charged $33.56 a barrel for its highest quality Murban 39 oil.

[12] Saudi Arabia, Kuwait, the UAE and Qatar had agreed Oct. 5 to raise their oil production to make up for the 2.9 million barrel-a-day shortfall in oil supplies caused by the cutoff of exports from Iran and Iraq. In a move that hinted at possible price increases from other OPEC nations, an oil official in Kuwait said Oct. 15, "There will have to be an incentive for these exporters to boost their oil production."

[13] **OPEC Output at 5-Year Low.** Oil production by members of OPEC sank to 25.44 million barrels a day in September, a five-year low, according to *Petroleum Intelligence Weekly* Nov. 23.

[14] OPEC's September output was 20.7% lower than it had been in September 1979 because the Persian Gulf war had cut off 3.2 million barrels a day of oil exported from Iraq and 500,000 barrels a day from Iran. The cutoff of supplies from the Persian Gulf had resulted in a sharp increase in the price of oil on the spot market. Since the outbreak of hostilities Sept. 22, the price of oil had surged to over $40 a barrel.

[15] **OPEC Hikes Price Ceiling to $41.** The OPEC oil ministers Dec. 16 agreed to raise oil prices as high as $41 a barrel. The decision was announced at the

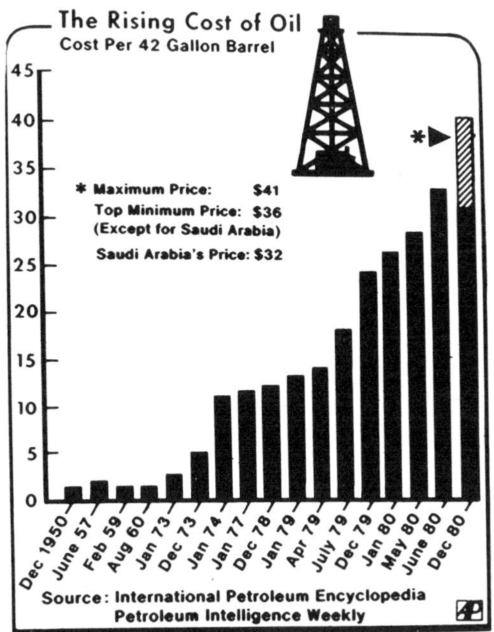

end of a two-day meeting on the Indonesian island of Bali.

[16] The pricing agreement, which gave a great deal of flexibility to each OPEC country, was a compromise designed to satisfy exporters, particularly the Persian Gulf states, that wanted a price freeze or little increase, and more hawkish producers, such as the African members of the cartel, that wanted more dramatic raises.

[17] The Saudis, who accounted for more than 40% of OPEC production, made the agreement possible by consenting Dec. 15 to raise the price of their Arabian light crude by $2 a barrel to the $32 per barrel reference price that had been used by other OPEC members. The increase was made retroactive to Nov. 1. (The reference price was the base from which all other oil prices were calculated, depending on the quality of the product.)

[18] Once the Saudis had agreed to the $32 price, which applied only to them, the OPEC members forged a "broad agreement" for raising the benchmark price of oil by $4 to $36 a barrel and for setting a maximum ceiling at $41 per barrel, an additional $4 per barrel increase.

P

PAHLEVI, Shah Mohammed Riza—*See* Iran [29, 129-139]

PAKISTAN

[1] **U.S. vows Assistance.** The U.S. had assured Pakistan that it could depend on American forces to come to its assistance in the event of any large-scale Soviet attack threatening its independence and security, U.S. and Pakistani officials announced Feb. 3.
[2] The pledge was made during two days of talks between Pakistani officials and a visiting U.S. military and diplomatic mission to Islamabad. The delegation, headed by National Security Adviser Zbigniew Brzezinski, was sent to discuss regional security in light of the Soviet invasion of neighboring Afghanistan. A member of the delegation said that President Muhammad Zia ul-Haq had been told at the meetings that the U.S. expected Pakistan to defend itself against any border skirmishes with Soviet forces but that if the Soviets launched a major assault the U.S. would invoke its 1959 security treaty with Pakistan.
[3] Zia told a news conference Feb. 3 that the U.S. mission had given "new life" to the 1959 accord. Any doubts about the U.S. commitment to Pakistan, Zia added, had now been resolved.
[4] Brzezinski said that the Carter Administration would delay requesting congressional approval of $400 million in economic and military aid to Pakistan. Submission of the aid package would be deferred to permit further U.S.-Pakistani military talks and formation of a wider group of aid donors to Pakistan, the security adviser said. The $400 million, Brzezinski said, was "only the beginning of the United States response to the threat" posed by Soviet troops in Afghanistan.
[5] Zia Jan. 17 had dismissed the proposed $400 million aid program as "peanuts," saying the amount was "terribly disappointing" and would not "buy" security for Pakistan. In his latest remarks, Zia said he was longer concerned about the size of the aid package because of the renewed American commitment.
[6] Agha Shahi, Pakistan's Foreign Minister, said March 5 that Pakistan had "officially conveyed to the United States that we are not interested in the aid package as proposed." U.S. foreign policy officials said March 6 that the Carter Administration was suspending its plans to seek congressional approval of the package.
[7] **IMF Approves $1.7 Billion Loan.** The International Monetary Fund Nov. 25 approved a $1.7 billion loan to Pakistan. The IMF said the three-year assistance package, the largest ever given to a developing nation, would help Pakistan's efforts to "promote economic growth in a stable environment."
See also Afghanistan [29-32]; Human Rights [7]

PALEONTOLOGY

[1] **Earliest Ape-Human Link Discovered.** Fossils found in Egypt

over the past three years demonstrated the existence of a monkey-like primate, about the size of a house cat, which lived 30 million years ago and was the common ancestor of man and ape.

[2] The primate, called *Aegyptopithecus,* apparently was a vegetarian and had a complex social structure. The animal was the earliest evolutionary link so far found between apes and humans. The findings were described in a news conference at Duke University, reported in the *New York Times* Feb. 7.

PALESTINIAN LIBERATION ORGANIZATION (PLO)—*See*

Carter, Jimmy [8]; Middle East [25, 27-37, 58-59, 92, 99, 106-107, 113-114, 117-119]

PARAGUAY—*See* Human Rights [18]

PATENTS

[1] **Patents on Life Forms Upheld.** The Supreme Court ruled, 5-4, June 16 that biological organisms could be patented under federal law. The decision in *Diamond v. Chakrabarty* (formerly *Diamond v. Bergey)* was regarded as one of the most important handed down by the high court in recent years.

[2] The case involved an attempt by General Electric Co. to gain a patent for a laboratory created bacterium that broke down crude oil and therefore could be used to clean up oil spills.

[3] The new bacterium, *Pseudomoma Originosa,* had been created by crossbreeding four existing strains of bacteria. The process had been perfected by a scientist working for GE, Ananda M. Chakrabarty. (Chakrabarty had since left for a faculty post at the University of Illinois.) GE, joined by Upjohn Co., had been frustrated in repeated attempts to patent the microorganism. The U.S. Court of Customs and Patent Appeals finally rule in their favor. Upjohn dropped out of the case in January 1980.

[4] The Supreme Court upheld the patent appeals court and drew a distinction between the GE bacterium and "laws of nature, physical phenomena and abstract ideas," which were not patentable. Chief Justice Warren E. Burger, writing for the majority, held that Chakrabarty's invention had "markedly different characteristics from any found in nature," and therefore could not be considered "nature's handiwork" but the result of the "human ingenuity and research" of the scientist. Burger stressed that the high court was not delving into the broad issues raised by genetic engineering, but was addressing the narrow question of whether current patent laws demonstrated an intent by Congress to deny patents to life forms.

[5] Justice William J. Brennan Jr. wrote the dissenting opinion. He was joined by Justices Lewis F. Powell Jr., Bryon R. White and Thurgood Marshall. Brennan noted that on two occasions, in 1930 and again in 1970, Congress had permitted some types of plants to be patented. Those laws, he said were "evidence of a congressional limitation that excludes bacteria from patentability. . . . It is the role of Congress, not this court, to broaden or narrow the reach of the patent laws. This is especially true where, as here, the composition sought to be patented uniquely implicates matters of public concern."

[6] There were more than 100 applications for patents on microorganisms pending with the U.S. Patent and Trademark Office. Legal experts believed that the Supreme Court ruling would affect most of those claims.

[7] ***Reaction***—Reaction June 16 to the decision in *Diamond v. Chakrabarty* was deeply polarized – an indication of the controversy surrounding biological engineering research.

[8] A spokesman for one vocal opponent of such research, the People's

Business Commission, a nonprofit educational foundation, contended that the ruling "lays the groundwork for corporations to own the processes of life in the centuries to come . . . and gives the green light to begin engineering the gene pool. . . . The Brave New World that Aldous Huxley warned of is now here." (*Brave New World*, a Huxley novel first published in 1932, presented a nightmarish vision of a future society that controlled behavior through genetic manipulation and drugs.)

[9] On the other end of the argument, a spokesman for Genentech Corp., one of several companies involved in genetic research, praised the high court for assuring "the country's technology future."

PENNSYLVANIA—*See* Weather [11-12]

PERSIAN GULF—*See* Carter, Jimmy [1-2, 6-15]

PERU

[1] **Belaunde Reelected President.** Fernando Belaunde Terry, who was overthrown in a military coup Oct. 3, 1968, was elected president of Peru May 18.

[2] Belaunde captured 43% of the vote in a contest with 14 other candidates. Armando Villaneuva del Campo, the candidate of the American Popular Revolutionary Alliance (APRA), received 27% of the vote, and Luis Bedoya Reyes, the former mayor of Lima, who represented the Popular Christian Party, won 11% of the vote.

[3] Belaunde's strong showing in the presidential race was not matched by his Popular Action Party in the vote for Congress. Eighteen parties had registered lists of 3,284 candidates for the 60 Senate seats and 180 seats in the Chamber of Deputies. While the 6.4 million voters apparently found in Belaunde's candidacy a clear-cut means of registering their strong distaste for the military junta that had overthrown him, the multitude of congressional choices left Belaunde without a majority in Congress.

[4] As a result, it was apparent that Belaunde would have to make alliances with other parties in order to obtain legislative support for his programs. The easiest alliance was expected to be with Bedoya, whose support among Lima's business and upper classes was likely to accomodate Belaunde, the scion of an old, aristocratic family that had played an important part in Peru's political history. A more important alliance for Belaunde, were it possible, would be with Vallanueva's APRA, the anticommunist labor party founded by Victor Raul Haya de la Torre, who died Aug. 2, 1979. With at least 20% of Peru's labor force unemployed, agricultural production reduced because of droughts and inflation running near 70%, Belaunde would need the support of labor to achieve success during his presidency.

[5] Belaunde was inaugurated as president July 28.

PHILADELPHIA—*See* Census (U.S.) [4]; Weather [11-12]

PHILIPPINES

[1] **Aquino Released from Detention.** Former Sen. Benigno S. Aquino Jr. was released May 8 from seven and a half years of detention. The opposition leader then flew to the U.S. for medical treatment.

[2] **Anti-Marcos Group Formed.** Eight political opposition groups Aug. 29 announced the formation of a coalition to unseat President Ferdinand E. Marcos.

[3] Seventy-two leaders of the organizations signed a document, called Covenant for Freedom, in which they pledged peaceful means to end martial law and restore democratic freedoms.

[4] **Bombings Kill More than 20.** More than 20 persons were killed and at least 120 were wounded in antigovernment bombing attacks between Sept. 20 and 26. Most of the bombings were carried out in southern Mindanao Island by the rebel Moslem Moro National Liberation Front, which was fighting for automony.
[5] Antigovernment terrorists Oct. 19 set off a bomb at the opening of a convention in Manila of the American Society of Travel Agents. Twenty persons, including seven Americans, were injured, none seriously.
See also United Nations [4]

PHYSICS

[1] **Neutrino Mass.** Recent experiments indicated that the subatomic particle known as the "neutrino" appeared to have mass, physicist Frederick Reines of the University of California at Irvine told a meeting of the American Physical Society in Washington April 30.
[2] When originally posited, the neutrino was conceived as having neither mass nor charge. However, Reines said, experiments by his group of researchers suggested that the neutrino oscillated between different states, an instability that was associated, in theory, with mass.
[3] Experiments by other scientists had also given support to the notion that the particle had mass. If it did, the mass was quite small: on the order of 10 to 50 electron-volts. This was 50,000 times less than the mass of an electron, and 100 million times less than that of a proton or neutron. However, neutrinos were thought to be so numerous that assuming that they had mass would have profound consequences for cosmology. In particular, giving mass to neutrinos might mean that there was enough matter in the universe for gravitation attraction to eventually end the universe's expansion and cause it to fall back and collapse on itself.
[4] **Tokamak Fusion Advance Reported.** Experiments at Culham Laboratory in Britain showed that the use of "neutral beam" heating might enable tokamak fusion machines to operate in a steady-state, rather than pulsed, mode, the *New Scientist* reported July 17. (Tokamaks were devices that used magnetic fields to confine charged particles to a tire-shaped area; if these particles could be heated sufficiently at the right density, they would fuse and provide energy in the same reaction that fueled the Sun. "Neutral beam" techniques injected a stream of fast-moving hydrogen atoms into the tokamak's plasma; some of the energy from this beam was transferred from the plasma, heating it.) Most tokamaks currently were operated in pulses. Making them into steady-state or continuously operating machines would simplify the engineering of the power generators that might eventually be developed from tokamaks.
See also Nobel Prizes [7-8]

POLAND

[1] A workers' revolt swept Poland in 1980. Hundreds of thousands went on strike. They demanded and eventually gained the right to organize free trade unions. Polish government leaders were ousted, the Communist Party apparatus – Politburo and Central Committee – purged. The U.S. and the North Atlantic Treaty Organization warned the Soviet Union against military intervention. Plans to strengthen the country's severely troubled economy were announced.
[2] **Meat Price Increases Cause Unrest.** Meat price increases of up to 100% triggered sporadic work stoppages that idled 30 industrial facilities, according to the dissident Social Self Defense Committee (KOR). Workers demanded wage hikes to compensate for the price increases, which took effect July 1.
[3] In a television broadcast July 9,

Polish officials announced that there would be less meat and butter for the year because of a poor 1979 grain harvest and the suspension of butter imports from the Common Market as part of an attempt to eliminate a large trade deficit.

[4] Edward Gierek, Polish Communist Party leader, promised wage increases for low-paid workers and pensioners, but said that most workers would have to absorb some of the consequences of inflation by holding back wage demands. Nevertheless, after a July 11 meeting, Polish authorities advised plant managers threatened with strike action to be conciliatory in response to wage demands.

[5] Strikes took place around the country in July and the first weeks of August. Among the developments:

■ Railroad workers in Lublin walked out July 16 in a demand for higher wages to compensate for the increased meat prices. Locomotives and other cars were parked to block the lines, and on July 18 soldiers and police were used to deliver food to the city. The strikers had blockaded the railway station. Bus drivers and deliverymen joined the strike, virtually shutting down the city. A government statement July 18 warned that the situation could "awaken concern among Poland's friends," which was generally interpreted as an allusion to the possibility of provoking Soviet intervention. A commission, headed by Politburo member Mieczyslaw Jagielski, was appointed that day to look into workers' grievances. On July 19 workers in Lublin said that were suspending their strike action and would accept a compromise pay offer providing raises of $13-$20 a month ($43 a month had been sought).

■ Workers in a ball-bearing plant in Kransnik struck July 19, and a walkout was also reported to have started over the July 19-20 weekend at a steelworks in Stalowa Wola.

■ Tram drivers in Baltic port cities won a 10% pay rise after a 30-minute strike, it was reported July 31, and a strike at an electrical works at Wroclaw was also reported the same day.

■ Garbagemen in Warsaw ended a six-day strike Aug. 9 after winning pay increases of about $33 a month (their salaries had been in the $115-150 a month range). Bus drivers in Warsaw went on strike Aug. 12 but returned to work the next day after winning a substantial pay increase.

[6] **120,000 Workers Strike Baltic Region.** Labor unrest in Poland intensified Aug. 14 when 17,000 workers at the Lenin Shipyard in Gdansk went on strike and took over the shipyard. Strikes spread throughout the region, and by Aug. 22 a strikers' committee representing 120,000 workers from northern Poland presented the government with a list of far-reaching demands, including an unprecedented call for political reform. The crisis appeared to pose the most serious threat to the government since riots by

workers in Gdansk in 1970 toppled Wladyslaw Gomulka's administration.

[7] The shipyard walkout was distinct from earlier labor unrest because of its political overtones. Aside from the economic demands spawned by the July 1 meat price increases that triggered the strike, workers demanded that a monument be built to honor the workers killed by police in the 1970 riots. Gdansk authorities agreed to that, and also reinstated three workers who had been previously dismissed, but the authorities refused to consider the principal demand that the official party-controlled trade unions be replaced by independent unions run by the workers.

[8] In a gesture of solidarity, Gdansk bus drivers Aug. 15 walked off their jobs and brought municipal transportation to a halt. That night Premier Edward Babiuch appealed to the workers in a television broadcast. He asked them to go back to their jobs and acknowledged that "many changes will have to take place in the management of the economy." However, he reiterated an earlier government refusal to roll back the July 1 meat price increases.

[9] By Aug. 16 Gdansk bakers and factory workers in the nearby ports of Gdynia and Sopot had joined the strike, despite an official press agency claim that the strike had been settled. Strike committees reportedly urged the estimated 80,000 strikers to avoid clashes with the police. Nevertheless, few police had been seen on the streets in strikebound cities, it was reported.

[10] Striking workers in the tri-city area of Gdansk, Gdynia and Sopot Aug. 17 formed a strike committee called the Interfactory Strike Committee to consolidate the striker's demands and strengthen their bargaining position with the government. The committee then issued a list of 16 demands, including a guaranteed right to strike, the release of political prisoners, the abolition of government

Crowd outside Lenin Shipyard in Gdansk, Poland Aug. 19 demonstrates support for striking workers. Polish flag and portrait of Pope John Paul II are attached to fence.

censorship and free access for all religious groups to the mass media.

[11] The government responded by establishing a special committee to investigate the workers' complaints. The government committee Aug. 18 began negotiating with the strike committee, but the strikers then raised the number of their demands to 21. After an emergency meeting with the ruling Politburo of the Communist Party, party leader Edward Gierek Aug. 18 made promises of pay increases in a television speech but flatly rejected the demands for political reform.

[12] Gierek, who had cut short a vacation in the Soviet Union and postponed a state visit to West Germany, added: "It is our duty to state that no activity that strikes at the political order of Poland can be tolerated. On this fundamental problem, no compromise is possible."

[13] Dissident sources Aug. 19 said that the strikes had spread to 174 factories and enterprises in the tri-city industrial region, in what was considered a blatant disregard of Gierek's order to abandon the protest. Throughout the day, delegates from factories in the region arrived in the Gdansk shipyard, which was serving as strike headquarters. Twenty-four leaders of the Social Self Defense Committee (KOR), the dissident group that had supported the strikes and was reportedly behind the political demands, were arrested Aug. 20-21. Jacek Kuron, a leader of the group and a primary source of information on the strikes for the foreign press, was arrested in the round-up.

[14] ***U.S.S.R. Cites Gierek Speech—*** The Soviet news agency Tass Aug. 19 gave the first Soviet report on the Polish labor unrest, quoting lengthy excerpts from Polish leader Edward Gierek's Aug. 18 broadcast to the striking workers.

[15] Tass referred to the Polish strikes as "work stoppages," but otherwise did not comment on the extent of the troubles or the issues involved. The Soviets quoted Gierek's criticism of the strikers, who he said had attempted to exploit the stoppages for "hostile political aims."

[16] ***Official U.S. Reaction Low-Key—*** The U.S. State Department Aug. 21 limited its first comment on the turmoil in Poland to a statement that it hoped arrested Polish dissidents would be released soon.

[17] **Premier Ousted; Strikes Continue.** The labor crisis in Poland was marked by the ouster Aug. 24 of Premier Edward Babiuch as part of a shakeup of the Communist Party's leadership, major government concessions to the workers and a plea from the Polish Roman Catholic Church. Despite these developments, the labor unrest spread outside the Baltic region to involve more than 300,000 workers.

[18] In a move to quell the labor unrest that threatened his leadership, party leader Edward Gierek Aug. 24 announced the dismissal of Premier Edward Babiuch, three other Politburo members, and 11 other top officials. He also promised free elections for new leadership of the official labor unions.

[19] Although Gierek managed to retain leadership of the party, his authority was somewhat diminished by the inclusion of rivals in the Politburo. Former Foreign Minister Stefan Olszowski, a critic of Gierek's policies who had been "banished" to East Germany as ambassador five months earlier, was restored to the Politburo as a national party secretary. Babiuch, another of Gierek's allies, was replaced by Josef Pinkowski, the secretary of the Central Committee. Politburo hardliners Jerzy Lukaszewicz, Tadeusz Pyka, and Zdzislaw Zandarowski were ousted, along with Jan Szydlak, the official union leader.

[20] In reaction to the personnel shift, Lech Walesa, chairman of the strikers' committee which had its headquarters at the Lenin Shipyard in Gdansk, said, "Our main problem is free trade unions, and it is not important for us who will meet with us." Walesa hailed the changes in the trade union as a "victory

Polish strike leader Lech Walesa.

for the workers" but added, "We'll go on striking."

[21] The first major concession in the dispute came Aug. 23 when the government reversed its previous stand and agreed to negotiate directly with the strikers' representatives. The government also dropped the anti-strike campaign that had been launched Aug. 21 in the state-controlled media.

[22] It was reported Aug. 25 that the strike committee was being advised for the first time by a group of seven dissidents. Another 18 dissidents arrested Aug. 20 were reportedly still being held. Because of a Polish law that prohibited detention for more than 48 hours without a formal charge, the dissidents were released and rearrested every two days.

[23] As the strike continued to spread outside the Baltic region and negotiations with government officials resumed in Gdansk, both the Roman Catholic church and the state Aug. 26 appealed to the workers to call a halt to the work stoppage for the sake of the nation. Stefan Cardinal Wyszynski, the Roman Catholic primate, urged "peace, calm, reason, prudence and responsibility for the Polish nation" in a 45-minute televised address. The broadcast of Wyszynski's speech was a highly unusual development that reflected the depth of official concern over the strike. Wyszynski had pressed for church access to television for many years, but had always been refused.

[24] As negotiations continued Aug. 27, the strikes spread further. Work stoppages reported by dissident sources included: an auto factory in Bielsko-Biala; the Cegielski heavy machinery plant in the western city of Poznan, and a new section of the steel mill in Nowa Huta, where a list of 41 demands was drawn up. Other labor disruptions included: 30 factories in Wroclaw, where the municipal transportation system was also shut down; a ship equipment plant in Torun where the platform of the Gdansk workers was adopted; a tire factory in Olsztyn; a fire-proofing equipment plant in Koscian, and bus transportation in Cracow.

[25] ***Soviets Score Strikers***—The Soviet Union Aug. 27 made its first direct criticism of the striking Polish workers, charging that "antisocialist forces" sought to subvert Poland's socialist system. The Tass news agency made the charge after strike leaders in Gdansk rejected Polish leader Edward Gierek's concessions. Earlier, the Soviets had accused the West of interfering verbally to exploit the unrest in the country.

[26] Tass Aug. 26 blamed the situation on "mistakes in the economic policy and many objective factors." Soviet Foreign Ministry officials Aug. 26 said the political crisis in Poland was "completely the internal affair of that state."

[27] ***East European Reaction***—Apparently reflecting growing concern among the countries of Eastern Europe about the labor troubles in

Poland, press reaction in the Communist bloc continued to vary.

[28] Without referring to the situation in Poland, the Czechoslovak Communist Party newspaper Aug. 25 warned factory committees to pay closer attention to the interests of workers. The newspaper, *Rude Pravo,* specifically warned that problems on the job, shortages in stores, and complaints about public transportation should be closely monitored. East German television broadcast Gierek's Aug. 25 speech live, with simultaneous German translation. The country's newspapers omitted all references in the speech to trade union elections. The Hungarian newspaper *Esti Hirlap* Aug. 25 reported the Polish Cabinet changes and singled out the problems of trade unions, which were ignored by most of the other Eastern European media. The Yugoslav newspaper *Politika* Aug. 25 said the ousted Polish leaders had been "pro-Stalinists," out of step with the workers' problems.

[29] ***Major Western Loans***—A consortium of Western banks Aug. 22 granted Poland a $325 million loan, despite the spreading labor troubles in the country. The seven-year, multicurrency credit was signed by Poland's Bank Handlowy and was coordinated by the Bank of America International Group.

[30] Another consortium of Western banks, including four major West German institutions, agreed Aug. 12 to give Poland a credit of more than $650 million.

[31] **Right to Form Trade Unions Granted.** The right to form free, independent trade unions was granted Aug. 30 by the government, and most of Poland's striking workers were back on their jobs by Sept. 3. Trade unions independent of the Communist Party had not existed in Poland since the end of World War II, and did not exist anywhere else in Eastern Europe. The government went to great lengths to assure the Soviet Union that concessions to the workers did not dilute Poland's commitment to socialism and to its Soviet-dominated alliance.

[32] The labor crisis had spread Aug. 29 to the important mining and industrial region of Silesia in southern Poland. More than 20,000 coal miners initiated a walkout in the region, centering on Katowice, an area that produced much of the country's chief export, coal, and which had been the political base of Poland's Communist Party chief, Edward Gierek.

[33] The Polish government and strike committees in the Baltic centers Aug. 30 reached agreement on the question of free trade unions. Polish television announced the Communist Party Central Committee had approved an agreement reached by Deputy Premier Mieczyslaw Jagielski and strike leader Walesa in Gdansk and a similar one concluded by negotiators in Szczecin.

[34] Both agreements provided for "independent, self-governing trade unions." The government also agreed to pay strikers their full salaries for the period of the walkout, and promised that supplies of meat and other basic commodities would be increased and distributed in all stores without favoritism. The agreements stated that censorship would be limited to state and military secrets, hostile propaganda against the government, and pornography. Wages were increased, compensated maternity leave extended to three years, and reemployment of workers who had lost jobs because of strike activity between 1970 and 1980 was promised, as was a reduction in waiting time for housing.

[35] State television and radio Aug. 31 gave full coverage to the emotional session at which strike leaders and government negotiators formally concluded the far-reaching agreements. Lech Walesa, who had overcome resistance within the strikers' ranks to loyalty pledges by the new unions to Poland's communist system, said the workers had "gotten all that's possible in the current situation. It's what we

Chronology of the Polish crisis

July 1 – Government increases meat prices.
July 2 – Workers in Warsaw, protesting higher meat prices, demand pay raise.
July 9 – Communist Party leader Edward Gierek warns higher wages are inflationary.
July 15-17 – Protests spread to Lublin.
July 20 – Strikers accept compromise pay offer.
Aug. 8-13 – Warsaw municipal workers strike.
Aug. 14 – Workers take over Lenin Shipyard in Gdansk. National radio admits for the first time that strikes are occurring.
Aug. 15 – Strikes spread throughout the Baltic industrial region.
Aug. 16 – Telephone lines to Gdansk are cut by authorities. Interfactory Strike Committee is formed.
Aug. 17-18 – Strikers' committee makes first political demands, including the right to form free trade unions and the abolition of censorship. Authorities say they will not negotiate with the committee.
Aug. 20 – Warsaw police detain dissident leader Jacek Kuron and 17 other members of the Committee for Social Self-Defense. Soviet Union commences jamming of Western broadcasts.
Aug. 22 – West German Chancellor Helmut Schmidt cancels trip to East Germany because of Polish unrest.
Aug. 23 – Polish Deputy Premier Mieczyslaw Jagielski meets with Gdansk strikers for the first time. Authorities agree to restore telephone links to Gdansk as precondition for negotiating.
Aug. 24 – Polish Premier Edward Babiuch and three other members of the Politburo are dismissed in major purge of party and government officials; 300,000 workers strike.
Aug. 26 – Negotiations begin. Soviets, in first comment on situation, describe events as "completely internal affair." Stefan Cardinal Wyszynski calls for peace and calm.
Aug. 29 – Strikes spread to mining region of Silesia and elsewhere. Dissidents estimate that 350,000 industrial and transport workers are on strike.
Aug. 30 – Government negotiators and strike representatives in Gdansk and Szczecin agree on formation of independent trade unions. Communist Party Central Committee approves agreement.
Aug. 31 – Strike leaders and government negotiators formally sign agreement for Baltic area workers.
Sept. 1 – Silesian workers remain on strike, while Baltic workers return to their jobs. Soviet press reports the end of strikes in the Baltic region. Dissidents released by authorities.
Sept. 2 – Government negotiators reach accord with most Silesian strikers.
Sept. 3 – Approximately 200,000 Silesian miners return to work; 15,000 remain out. Polish goverment announces Soviets will lend it hard currency.
Sept. 4 – Polish govenment reaffirms its ties to alliance with Soviet Union.
Sept. 6 – Party Secretary Edward Gierek is ousted.
Sept. 17 – Free trade unions register as federation, "Solidarity."
Oct. 6 – Eight members of Polish Central Committee are purged.
Nov. 19 – Government announces economic crisis moves.
Dec. 2 – U.S. warns Soviet Union against military intervention in Poland.

wanted and dreamed of—we've got independent trade unions."

[36] Silesian coal miners Sept. 1 remained off the job while Baltic coast strikers returned to work. The miners demanded assurances they would be covered by the agreements reached in Gdansk and Szczecin, but they were also protesting local working conditions. Most of the arrested dissidents, including their leader Jacek Kuron, were released from jail.

[37] A government commission headed by Deputy Premier Aleksander Kopec reached agreement Sept. 2 with most of the Silesian strikers, which conflicting reports numbered at between 30,000 and 300,000. Miners in Silesia, generally satisfied that their demands had been met, returned to work Sept. 3. However, 15,000 miners remained out in an effort to force changes in local management personnel.

[38] Meanwhile, the Polish government announced the Soviet Union had granted it a major loan. The official news agency said Moscow had issued a hard currency loan for the purchase of raw materials for the country's chemical and steel industries.

[39] The Soviet news media responded slowly to the conclusion of the Polish labor crisis, delaying its reporting of the end of the strike in the Baltic region for 24 hours until Sept. 1. When on Sept. 2 the Soviets finally described the proposals for liberalization, they said changes were being forced on Poland in order to impose Western notions of freedom and rights. On Sept. 3 the Soviets continued their criticism of the Polish settlement, saying anti-socialist forces in the country "do not cease their subversive activity."

[40] ***Carter Urges Aid for Poland***—President Carter Aug. 29 sent letters to government leaders in Western Europe to urge that the major Western nations respond positively to anticipated requests by Poland for

Coal miners on strike near Katowice in Silesia.

substantial economic aid once the workers' unrest subsided, Carter Administration officials said Sept. 2.

[41] U.S. unions had provided cash and other help to the striking Polish workers, according to statements by U.S. labor figures. Douglas Fraser, president of the United Auto Workers, said Aug. 31 that his union and other labor groups had contributed "cash to the Polish cause." Fraser, who was appearing on CBS News' *Face the Nation* program, said the money was channeled through the International Federation of Metal Workers in Switzerland. A spokesman for the International Metal Workers group said Aug. 31 that the organization had given the Poles about $120,000, in contributions from U.S., British and French unions.

[42] **Gierek Replaced.** Ailing Communist Party Secretary Edward Gierek Sept. 6 was replaced by Stanislaw Kania, who pledged to honor the agreements Polish authorities made with striking workers the previous week.

[43] Gierek, who had not been seen in public since a government shakeup in late August, was officially reported Sept. 5 to have suffered "serious" heart trouble requiring hospitalization. The party Central Committee met in emergency session, and Sept. 6 replaced Gierek with the 53-year-old Kania, a little-known party official.

[44] Kania, a party member for 35 years who had joined the Politburo in 1975, played an inconspicuous but crucial role during the strikes. He reportedly persuaded hardline local party officials in Gdansk that only mediation and political methods could solve the crisis. His chief areas of responsibility had previously been relations with the Roman Catholic Chruch in Poland and management of the police, army and internal security forces.

[45] **U.S. Gives $670 Million Grain Credit.** President Carter Sept. 12 announced the approval of $670 million in government credit guarantees for the purchase of U.S. grain by Poland.

[46] **New Unions Form Federation.** The organizers of the country's new independent trade unions Sept. 17 decided to form a national federation and register the entire movement as one union, "Solidarity."

[47] Representatives from workers' groups throughout the country met in Gdansk to discuss for the first time the form of inter-union cooperation. Workers from areas where government controlled unions were still strong wanted a strong central federation of independent unions. However, delegates from regions where the independent movement was powerful, such as Silesia and the Baltic, favored loosely related union groups, with only a consultative commission at the top of the national structure. Lech Walesa, a leader of the Baltic strikes, argued that a national federation would be more vulnerable to direct pressure from the government. Walesa and his supporters also believed that regional organizations would be more responsive to workers' needs than a national body.

[48] The assembled delegates voted a compromise that established in Gdansk a national commission that was primarily consultative and advisory. However, all the new unions would adopt the same by-laws and would register as a single group. The union organizers Sept. 18 announced that 3 million workers from 3,500 factories and institutions throughout Poland had pledged to join the new union groups. The membership figure the unions claimed gave them equal size with the the Polish Communist Party.

[49] ***Strikes Continue***—Labor trouble continued in at least 16 locations across the country, it was reported Sept. 19.

[50] Polish television reported that strikes persisted in Silesia, where transport was halted throughout the region, and in work places elsewhere.

[51] State radio Sept. 21 broadcast a Roman Catholic Sunday mass, keeping an agreement made with striking Baltic workers in August. The government had pledged that the broadcast masses would be a regular Sunday event.

[52] **Eight Party Leaders Purged.** The Polish Communist Party Central Committee Oct. 6 ended three days of bitter debate during which eight of its members were purged.

[53] The meeting began one day after a one-hour work stoppage called and led by Solidarity, the independent trade union federation. The stoppage protested the goverment's delay in implementing promised wage increases. It involved hundreds of thousands of workers nationwide.

[54] The expulsion of the eight party officials, including former Premier Edward Babiuch, was considered mild in view of the sweeping reforms demanded by many party members following the country's labor troubles. There were no major changes in the Politburo, the party's decision-making body. Besides Babiuch, five officials who had held responsibility for economic planning and labor management were ousted. Two other committee members, including the former head of radio and television, Maciej Szczepanski, were dismissed in particular disgrace. They were under criminal investigation for corruption and embezzlement.

[55] **Allies' Criticism, Warnings Increase.** Rumanian President Nicolae Ceausescu had strongly criticized the leadership of Poland's Communist Party and claimed that antisocialist forces had instigated the recent troubles in that country, it was reported Oct. 21. Ceausescu's remarks capped a recent spate of stepped-up criticism and warnings to the Poles by Eastern European communist leaders.

[56] **Registration Conditions Anger Union.** Polish authorities Oct. 24 conferred legal status on the country's new independent trade union federation, Solidarity, but imposed registration conditions unacceptable to the group's leaders.

[57] Zdzislaw Koscielniak, president of the three-judge Warsaw court that had reviewed Solidarity's charter, made the announcement granting legal status to the union group. Koscielniak then unilaterally attached a provision to the charter stipulating that it must acknowledge the "leading role" that the Polish Communist Party played in national affairs. The stipulation also required an explicit endorsement of socialism as the foundation of Polish society and a statement of respect for the country's international alliances and commitments.

[58] After the court's decision was announced, Solidarity leader Lech Walesa said the unilateral changes in the charter had "unlawfully crippled" the union bylaws. Walesa pledged to appeal the decision to the country's Supreme Court.

[59] ***High Court Backs Union***—The Polish Supreme Court Nov. 10 ruled that the charter of Solidarity was not required to assert the supremacy of the Communist Party.

[60] The high court decision, reversing the judgment of a lower court, averted the threat of a major strike the unions had called for Nov. 12 if the ruling had gone against them.

[61] **Major Economic Overhaul Planned.** The Polish government Nov. 19 announced plans for strengthening the country's failing economy and said that investment cutbacks, decentralization of the economic decision-making process, and food rationing were likely for the beginning of 1981.

[62] Polish government officials Nov. 12 revealed the precise extent of the problems besetting the country's economy. Deputy Premier Aleksander Kopec said that industrial production was far behind anticipated targets. He said that coal production was almost 6 million tons less than the planned 206 million tons, steel output was over 400,000 tons short and that cement

production was down by nearly one million tons.

[63] Premier Josef Pinkowski told party members in Lodz that the poor 1980 grain harvest meant that the country would have to import more than 10 million tons in the next year. Approximately 50% of the country's potato crop, more than 20 million tons, had been lost. It was predicted, in addition, that the country's meat supply would be 100,000 tons short despite imports of more than 50,000 tons. A disastrous sugar beet harvest would leave the Poles with a 300,000-ton deficit despite imports of over 100,000 tons.

[64] **Threats of Intervention.** The Communist Party's Central Committee Dec. 4 said Poland's continuing labor problems had put "the fate of the nation and the country in the balance." The statement, issued two days after a major party purge, came against a backdrop of increasing threats of Soviet military intervention.

[65] The latest crisis began Nov. 21 after police arrested two sympathizers of the independent trade union federation, Solidarity, and charged them with having stolen and duplicated a secret government document. The government paper was reportedly a two-part directive detailing the activities of dissident groups and outlining possible measures for use against the groups.

[66] More than 16,000 workers at the main assembly plant of the Ursus tractor factory in Warsaw stopped work Nov. 24 and demanded the men's release. Solidarity leaders in Warsaw Nov. 25 called for a general strike in the capital if the two men, Jan Narozniak and Piotr Sapielo, were not freed. Several other plants in Warsaw went on strike the same day. Narozniak and Sapielo were released Nov. 27 as the government attempted to defuse the tension that was building in the country.

[67] ***Further Shakeups***—A new wave of government and Communist Party leadership shuffles began Nov. 21 after a session of the Sejm (parliament), when four Cabinet ministers lost their jobs and a prominent Roman Catholic layman was named as one of the country's six deputy premiers.

[68] Jerzy Ozdowski, an independent member of parliament, was named to the deputy premiership with special responsibility for family and social affairs. His appointment, reportedly made with the approval of Poland's Stefan Cardinal Wyszynski, was the first time a politician publicly affiliated with the church had achieved such a prominent position anywhere in Eastern Europe.

[69] On the same day, Labor Minister Maria Milczarek, Health and Social Welfare Minister Marian Sliwinski, Construction Minister Edward Barszcz, and Maciej Wirowski, a Cabinet member with no portfolio, lost their jobs.

[70] A second purge began Dec. 2 when, after two days of meetings in a crisis atmosphere generated by rumors of Soviet military maneuvers, the Polish Communist Party Central Committee announced it had dismissed four members of the Politburo, the party's decision-making body. The committee also announced that Gen. Mieczyslaw Moczar, a former Politburo member, had been reelected to it.

[71] The four men who were removed from the Politburo were regarded as members of a conservative faction that had resisted cooperation with the trade union movement. Wladyslaw Kruczek, Stanislaw Kowalcyk, a former interior minister with close ties to deposed party leader Edward Gierek, former Warsaw party chief Alojzy Karkoszka, and party ideologist Andrezj Wreblan lost their Politburo membership.

[72] Gen. Moczar, an opponent of Gierek's who had been disgraced, had formerly been considered a hard-liner and an outspoken anti-Semite. However, recent speeches of his had indicated a more balanced attitude. A former interior minister, he had been

the mentor of party leader Stanislaw Kania and of Stefan Olszowksi, the influential Politburo member in charge of economic reforms.

[73] ***U.S. Cautions Soviets***—President Carter Dec. 2 issued a statement through his press secretary, Jody Powell, that warned the Soviets of the consequences of military intervention in Poland.

[74] Powell said that such an action "would be most serious and adverse for East-West relationships in general and particularly relations between the United States and the Soviet Union."

[75] **Moscow Summit; New Invasion Fears.** The leaders of the Soviet Union and its Eastern European allies met in Moscow Dec. 5 for a summit conference to discuss the problems in Poland. They expressed confidence in the Poles' ability to overcome their crisis in accordance with "the socialist path." However, their countries subsequently continued press attacks on the Polish labor movement.

[76] The holding of the Moscow conference, coupled with reports of troop movements and the calling up of reservists of some communist states, intensified U.S. fears of a possible invasion of Poland.

[77] Until Dec. 7, U.S. officials had maintained that Warsaw Pact military intervention in Poland was "neither imminent or inevitable." However, U.S. officials that day told reporters they could no longer say a Soviet military move was not imminent. A White House statement said "preparation for possible Soviet intervention in Poland appears to have been completed." The U.S. officials said, however, they had no evidence of a definite Soviet decision to intervene in Poland.

[78] The U.S. Dec. 9 ordered the dispatch of four radar warning aircraft to monitor Soviet troop movement in Eastern Europe. The Airborne Warning and Control Systems aircraft operating in West Germany would be able to give Western military intelligence a detailed picture of Warsaw Pact military activity in East Germany, one of several potential launching points for an invasion of Poland.

[79] **NATO Warns Soviets.** The foreign ministers of the North Atlantic Treaty Organization Dec. 12 warned the Soviet Union that military intervention in Poland would wreck East-West detente.

[80] The ministers in a communique issued at the conclusion of a two-day meeting, said that if the Soviets intervened militarily, the NATO countries "would be compelled to react in the manner which the gravity of this development would require."

[81] No firm package of retaliatory actions had been agreed on. However, proposals were being studied that included halting loan credits to the Soviet Union and Poland and the end of the Western cooperation in major Soviet industrial and technological projects such as the multibillion-dollar natural gas pipeline to Western Europe.

[82] **Church Warns Dissidents.** The leadership of the country's Roman Catholic Church Dec. 12 condemned acts by political dissidents and extremists that it claimed "could raise the danger of a threat to the freedom and statehood of the fatherhood."

[83] ***Unity Appeal***—Government, church and labor union officials joined together in an appeal for national unity at the Dec. 16 Gdansk memorial service to shipyard workers killed by government forces in 1970.

[84] **Austerity Plan.** An austerity plan, announced in parliament Dec. 19, projected layoffs of 5,000 government workers, cutbacks on the number of automobiles used by government employees, suspension of $30 million in construction projects, a $3 billion reduction in investment spending and meat and butter rationing.

See also Aviation [7-9]

POL POT—*See* United Nations [28]

POLICE

Supreme Court Rulings

[1] **Warrantless Home Arrests Curbed.** The Supreme Court ruled, 6-3, April 15 that in most cases, police had to obtain a warrant before entering the home of a suspect to make an arrest.

[2] The decision upset laws in 24 states that permitted police to make routine home arrests without a warrant. The cases, consolidated for judgment, were *Payton v. New York* and *Riddick v. New York.*

[3] **Illegal Search Protection Narrowed.** The Supreme Court ruled, 7-2, June 25 in two cases that persons charged with illegal possession (in one case, of stolen checks, and in the other, of drugs) did not have the automatic right to challenge police searches. The cases were *U.S. v. Salvucci* and *Kentucky v. Rawlings.*

POLITICS

[1] **Government Political Firings Barred.** The Supreme Court March 31 ruled, 6-3, that public employees could not be normally fired solely on the basis of political affiliation. The case was *Branti v. Finkel.*

[2] The ruling broadened the high court's decision in *Elrod v. Burns* (1976). In that case, the Supreme Court held that lower-level government workers could not be fired because of their political beliefs.

[3] The Branti case concerned two Rockland County, N.Y. assistant public defenders, both Republicans, who were threatened with firing by a newly appointed public defender, who was a Democrat. A Circuit Court of Appeals each found that the two could not be discharged simply because they belonged to the "wrong" party.

[4] The Supreme Court upheld the lower courts. Justice John Paul Stevens wrote in his majority opinion that political firings were illegal unless it could be shown that membership in a particular party was "essential to the discharge of the employee's governmental responsibilities." Examples of this exemption, Stevens said, would be the key aides to a governor. These aides, he said, must "share [the governor's] political beliefs and party commitments." The 1976 decision had applied only to public employees who were not in policy-making or confidential advisory positions.

[5] **Mitchell Named to Muskie Seat.** U.S. District Judge George J. Mitchell, a political protege of Edmund S. Muskie, was appointed May 8 to serve the remaining 31 months of Muskie's Senate term.

[6] Mitchell, 46, whose mother was a Lebanese immigrant and father a son of immigrants, was a lawyer from South Portland. Maine Gov. Joseph E. Brennan (D) made the appointment shortly after Muskie resigned the seat to take up his new post as secretary of state.

PORTUGAL

[1] **Sa Carneiro's Cabinet Sworn In.** The 15-member Cabinet of Portuguese Premier Francisco Sa Carneiro was sworn in Jan. 3. For the first time since the 1974 military coup that restored democracy to Portugal, no military officials were appointed to Cabinet posts.

[2] Sa Carneiro's Cabinet was center-right. It included nine members of his own Democratic Alliance, five Christian Democrats and one independent. Most of the new ministers were noted as experts in their fields, rather than politicians.

[3] **Sa Carneiro, Eanes Clash.** Premier Sa Carneiro and President Gen. Antonio Ramalho Eanes had repeatedly clashed on issues of political ideology since Sa Carneiro's victory in general elections Dec. 2, 1979. The crucial issue that divided them, according to reports April 1, was the question of whether the military should continue to hold the real power in Portugal.

[4] Sa Carneiro had begun to push hard for measures designed to open up the economy to the private sector, thus reducing the power of the military men. Reports in three leading right-wing newspapers March 4 claimed that members of Portugal's military Council of the Revolution had discussed the possibility of forcing Premier Sa Carneiro to resign. Eanes angrily denied the paper reports.

[5] The dispute between the president and the premier was heightened by Sa Carneiro's austerity budget, proposed April 2. Tax reductions and an increase in the public's purchasing power were designed to encourage economic expansion, stimulate private investment and curb inflation.

[6] **Eanes Vetoes New Economic Laws.** President Eanes April 11 vetoed economic laws that were essential to the 1980 budget proposed by Premier Sa Carneiro April 2.

[7] The veto of the laws was supported by the Council of the Revolution. Significantly, the veto coincided with the announcement that Sa Carneiro's Democratic Alliance had finally settled on a presidential candidate to oppose Eanes in elections scheduled for January 1981. Antonio Soares Carneiro, a general who had held a high office under the Salazar regime, was picked by the AD after opinion polls showed that Sa Carneiro would lose to Eanes in a presidential race.

[8] The choice of Gen. Soares came as a surprise to most politicians in Portugal, who had expected the AD to run a civilian candidate against Gen. Eanes. On April 19, thousands of leftists staged demonstrations throughout Portugal in protest against the right's choice of a general as its presidential candidate. The rallies were the biggest antigovernment demonstrations since the AD came to power Jan. 3.

[9] **Rightists Gain in Assembly Election.** The Democratic Alliance increased its majority in the National Assembly, winning a decisive victory in parliamentary elections Oct. 5.

[10] The AD won 47.3% of the popular vote and raised its majority in the 250-seat Assembly to 136 seats, up 8 seats and 2.3 percentage points over the majority the AD had gained in the Assembly elections of December 1979. The big losers were the Communists, led by Alvaro Cunhal. They won only 16.7% of the vote, down from 19%, and 40 seats down from 47.

[11] **Sa Carneiro Dies in Plane Crash.** Premier Francisco Manuel Lumbrales de Sa Carneiro and Defense Minister Adelino Amaro da Costa were killed Dec. 4 when their light plane plunged into a house after taking off from Lisbon Airport.

[12] Also killed in the crash were Sa Carneiro's companion, Scandinavian-born Snu Abecassis, Amaro da Costa's wife, an aide, Antonio Patricio Gouveia, and his wife, and the two pilots. An unidentified man was killed on the ground when the plane's wing struck his car.

[13] **Eanes Wins Landslide Reelection.** President Eanes won a striking victory in Portugal's presidential election Dec. 7. Eanes received 57% of the popular vote compared with the 40% won by Gen. Antonio Soares Carneiro, candidate of the ruling Democratic Alliance Coalition.

[14] Soares' candidacy appeared to have been irrevocably damaged by the death Dec. 4 of the AD's leader Premier Sa Carneiro. Eanes was supported by Socialists and Communists as well as independents. He swamped his opponent in Lisbon and in Oporto, which had been the base of Sa Carneiro's support.

[15] Eanes Dec. 8 labeled his reelection victory "nobody's defeat" and promised to resign as chief of the armed forces, thus subordinating the military to civilian rule. He also promised to abolish the Military Council of the Revolution, the military's watchdog body, which had held the real power in Portugal following the coup in 1975.

PRESS

[1] **Open Criminal Trials Upheld.** The Supreme Court ruled, 7-1, July 2 that "absent an overriding interest," judges were forbidden from barring the public and press from criminal trials.

[2] The case, *Richmond Newspapers v. Virginia,* coincidentally was decided exactly one year after the high court's controversial ruling in *Gannett Co. v. DePasquale.*

[3] In the Gannett decision, the Supreme Court held that judges could close pretrial criminal hearings to the public and press. The court found that the Sixth Amendment, which guaranteed a "speedy and public trial" was the personal right of the accused and could not be used by outsiders to gain access to pretrial hearings. The Gannett ruling triggered heated debate over whether it could be extended to close full-scale criminal trials. Since the 1979 decision, judges in more than 30 cases had used Gannett to ban either the press or the public, or both, from criminal trials.

[4] The Supreme Court backed the right to attend criminal trials. Although the decision did not supersede Gannett, it put some aspects of the earlier ruling in doubt. The high court specifically overturned a decision by the Virginia Supreme Court barring reporters from papers owned by Richmond Newspapers Inc. from a murder trial in 1979. In doing so, seven of the eight participating justices issued opinions. Justice Lewis F. Powell Jr., a Virginian, did not take part in the ruling.

[5] Chief Justice Warren E. Burger, author of the controlling opinion, maintained that access to criminal trials was guaranteed in the First Amendment, which protected freedom of speech and freedom of the press, and the Fourteenth Amendment, which made the First Amendment binding on all states. Burger indicated that judges could close criminal trials, but only under extraordinary circumstances, which he did not specify. The lone dissenter was Justice William H. Rehnquist, who chided the majority for interfering in the actions of a state judiciary.

[6] **Idaho TV Station Raided by Police.** A Boise, Idaho television station July 26 was raided by sheriff's deputies and representatives of the Ada Country prosecutor's office armed with a search warrant. The law enforcement officials seized two video tapes after rifling desks and file cabinets.

[7] The tapes had been made by the station, KBCI-TV, during a two-day riot at the Idaho State Penitentiary a few days before the raid. A KBCI reporter, accompanied by a cameraman, had been allowed inside the prison at a time when inmates controlled the prison yard and held two corrections officers hostage. The newsmen toured the facility and filmed interviews with some of the inmates. The county prosecutor wanted the tapes to establish the identities of those inmates who took part in the riot. He justified his action by citing a 1978 Supreme Court decision that permitted police to use a search warrant, rather than a subpoena, to obtain evidence from news organizations.

[8] Ada County Prosecutor James Harris was sued Aug. 1 by KBCI in state court over the seizure of the tapes.

[9] The station sought no monetary damages, but asked for a declaratory judgment that the action violated KBCI's First Amendment (free speech) and Fourth Amendment (illegal search and seizure) protections.

[10] The Idaho raid was the second such incident to occur during 1980. In May, police in Flint, Mich. had used a warrant to search a printing shop for information related to an article published in the Flint *Voice,* a small local newspaper. The article was based on a report by the city's ombudsman that was critical of Mayor James W. Rutherford.

[11] **Bill Curbing Newsroom Searches OK'd.** President Carter Oct. 14 signed

the Privacy Protection Act, a bill limiting the power of federal, state and local law enforcement officials to carry out surprise searches of newsrooms.

[12] The bill stemmed from White House and congressional opposition to a 1978 decision by the Supreme Court. The ruling upheld the authority of Palo Alto, Calif. police, armed with a search warrant, to raid a Stanford University newspaper in search of evidence.

[13] The Privacy Protection Act required law enforcement officials seeking evidence from news gatherers to obtain a subpoena, rather than a search warrant, under most circumstances. A subpoena gave news gatherers notice and an opportunity to challenge in court the right of the police to the material in question. The law protected such documentary material as reporter's notes, films, audio and video tapes and photographs. It shielded members of the news media, plus authors and scholars, as long as they themselves were not suspects in a crime.

[14] Surprise searches, backed by court-ordered warrants, would be permitted under three circumstances:

- If there was reason to believe that the news gatherers were directly involved in a criminal act, including the possession of classified national security documents.
- If there was reason to believe that the news gatherers might destroy or alter the material in question.
- If immediate seizure of the material was necessary to prevent the death or serious injury of someone related to the case.

[15] Also, lawyers, physicians, psychiatrists and other such professionals did directly come under the law and therefore were not immune from having their records seized. The legislation had been given final approval in the Senate by voice vote Sept. 24 and in the House, 357-2, Oct. 1.

[16] **UNESCO: New World Information Order.** A resolution calling for the establishment of a new world information order was adopted unanimously Oct. 25 by delegates to the 21st general conference of the U.S. Educational, Scientific and Cultural Organization. The conference met Sept. 23 through Oct. 28 in Belgrade, Yugoslavia.

[17] The concept of a world information order was a controversial one, with the industrialized Western democracies on one side of the issue and Third World and Soviet bloc countries on the other. The developed Western countries were concerned that the new "order" could be used to curb press freedom, while the Third World nations saw it as a way of reducing the dominant role of Western news organizations.

[18] The Third World countries complained that the Western news services offered a distorted account of developing countries by concentrating on natural disasters, political instability and corruption. They also maintained that a new information order would enable governments to assist economic development and promote national identity through the handling of news dissemination. One section of the resolution said that news organizations could be employed to promote "development strategies." This passage was criticized by the Western nations, which saw it as a threat to the independence of the news media.

[19] Another passage of the resolution stated that journalists should be responsible. This was interpreted by some nations as authorizing UNESCO to draw up codes of journalistic conduct. Once again, the Western nations voiced concern that this could lead to an infringement of the freedom of the press.

[20] The Western nations nevertheless, with the exception of Switzerland, decided not to oppose the resolution on the grounds that it did include various statements affirming press freedom. U.S. negotiator William Haley observed Oct. 25 that the resolution "affirms a number of principles of freedom

and diversity to which we subscribe." He added that it also "contains some points—and many more than we like—which are exceedingly troublesome." (The Swiss delegation absented itself from the conference room when the resolution was adopted by consensus. Switzerland had termed the resolution unacceptable, saying that it was an "attempt to reconcile the irreconcilable.")

Sales, Mergers & Shutdowns

[21] **UPI Financing Plan Fails.** A plan to sell limited partnerships in United Press International to subscribers had fallen short of its necessary goal, the press agency announced Jan. 31.

[22] Under the plan, UPI which projected a pretax loss of $6 million for 1979 hoped to sell 45 limited partnerships, each with a 2% share of ownership, to the news media. By Jan. 30, only two-thirds of the needed partnerhips had been sold. UPI was 95% owned by E. W. Scripps Co. and 5% owned by Hearst Corp.

[23] **Atlantic Monthly Sold.** The *Atlantic Monthly* had been sold to Morton Zuckerman, a Boston real estate developer, it was reported March 1.

[24] Atlantic Monthly Co., which included the magazine and a small book division, was sold by Marion D. Campbell for an undisclosed sum. Campbell's family had owned the company since 1938. The magazine, founded in 1857, had a high reputation for the quality of its fiction, poetry, essays and political writings. Its circulation at the time of the sale was about 339,000.

In other developments:

■ News Group Publications Inc., headed by Australian publisher Rupert Murdoch, had agreed to purchase *Cue New York* magazine, it was reported March 4. News Group published *Cue New York's* chief competitor, *New York* magazine. Both magazines covered entertainment and lifestyles in New York City. *Cue*, a bimonthly, was owned by North American Publishing Co. of Philadelphia. Sources close to the deal said that News Group would pay about $3 million to acquire *Cue.*

■ MacFadden Group Inc. had bought *Us* magazine from New York Times Co., it was reported March 7. *Us*, which was devoted to celebrity profiles, had lost about $2 million in 1979 while competing with Time Inc.'s popular *People* magazine. MacFadden, a New York City-based publisher of such magazines as *True Romance* and *Photoplay*, said it had acquired *Us* for "a modest amount of cash" and also assumed the magazine's subscription liabilities of $4 million.

■ United Features Syndicate Feb. 29 disbanded the North American Newspaper Alliance and replaced it March 3 with a new service, the Independent News Alliance. NANA had been founded as a cooperative news service in 1922 and went on to number, at its peak, more than 150 major newspaper subscribers in the U.S., Canada and abroad. A companion cooperative, the Women's News Service, founded in 1946, also was discontinued in the move.

[25] ***Saturday Review* Sold.** *Saturday Review*, a biweekly literary magazine, was sold May 20 to an investment magazine, *Financial World*. The purchase price was not made public.

[26] ***Berkeley Barb* Folds.** The *Berkeley Barb*, the prototype for the "counterculture" newspapers of the 1960s, had ceased publication, it was reported July 3.

[27] The *Barb*, a weekly paper founded in Berkeley, Calif. in 1965, had its best year in 1969, when its readership topped 90,000. It reported and advocated the activities of the anti-Vietnam war movement, the drug culture and campus radicals. Its circulation had dropped to about 2,500 by 1980.

[28] ***Harper's* Magazine Retrieved.** *Harper's* magazine was bought by two philanthropic organizations July 9, saving it from extinction. Minneapolis Star and Tribune Co., the magazine's previous owner, had announced in

June that *Harper's* was ceasing publication.

[29] *Harper's* was purchased by the John D. and Catherine T. MacArthur Foundation of Chicago and the Atlantic Richfield Foundation. The MacArthur Foundation was based on the fortune of insurance billionaire John D. MacArthur, who died in 1978. The Richfield Foundation had been established by Atlantic Richfield, Co., a California-based petroleum company. The two foundations were to operate *Harper's* as a nonprofit enterprise. They were reported to have paid only about $250,000 for the magazine, which had long-term liabilities of more than $3 million.

[30] **Times Mirror Co. to Buy Denver *Post*.** Times Mirror Co., a Los Angeles-based publishing and broadcasting conglomerate, Oct. 22 agreed to purchase the Denver *Post* for $95 million.

See also Central Intelligence Agency [11-12]; Crime [18]; France [43-44]; Freedom of Information Act [1-6]; Great Britain [61-2]; Haiti [1]; Pulitzer Prizes [1-2, 4-5]; Spain [7-9]

PRISONS

[1] **33 Die in New Mexico Riot.** Inmates at the New Mexico state penitentiary in Santa Fe, N.M. rioted Feb. 2-3 in a 36-hour rampage of murder and vandalism in one of the worst prison uprisings in U.S. history.

[2] By Feb. 10 the death toll was 33 dead and 89 hospitalized. All of the dead were prison inmates. The majority of the dead and wounded were victims of violence by other prisoners. There were also victims of drug overdoses and smoke inhalation from fires ignited by inmates during the rioting.

[3] Convicts reportedly told of terror and murder by inmates during the uprising. Said one convict: "They killed, they butchered. It was horrible."

Guards in tower watch over prisoners who surrendered after rioting Feb. 2-3 at New Mexico state penitentiary. View is from office gutted by fire.

Witnesses said that an execution squad of prisoners armed with blowtorches and axes had tortured and murdered fellow prisoners. Other prisoners were reportedly beheaded, doused with flammable liquid and set afire, slashed and beaten and thrown from buildings.

[4] State officials estimated damages and other costs associated with the riot at $82.5 million, making it the costliest prison uprising to date. Prison officials cited indiscriminate use of drugs from the prison dispensary, racial conflict, personal vendettas and intense hatred of informers as factors contributing to the murder and destruction.

[5] More than 250 state police and National Guardsmen Feb. 3 recaptured the prison without firing a shot. The inmates offered no resistance.

[6] ***Conditions Had been Challenged***—The state prison had been the subject of previous controversies. A class action lawsuit filed by the American Civil Liberties Union two years earlier had charged that overcrowding in the maximum security prison—it held one-third more prisoners than it was designed for—had promoted general violence and homosexual rape. The suit also challenged the prison's mail policies, food service, visitation privileges and disciplinary procedures.

[7] Conditions at the prison had also drawn criticism just weeks earlier in investigations by state and local authorities. The state attorney general in a special investigation had said that the prison had poorly trained guards and too few of them, faulty intelligence processing and inadequate security procedures. A Santa Fe County grand jury, which had concurred with these findings, also charged that nepotism had been the basis for hiring and promoting prison guards.

PUERTO RICO

[1] **Lower Welfare Aid Backed.** The Supreme Court ruled, 6-3, May 27 that the equal protection rights of Puerto Ricans were not violated when the federal government provided a level of reimbursement for the island's welfare program that was lower than it provided for any of the 50 states. The case was *Harris v. Rosario.*

[2] Reversing the U.S. Court of Appeals for the District of Columbia, the high court held that residents of the commonwealth in the Aid to Families with Dependent Children program were not entitled to the same levels of benefits accorded to AFDC recipients residing in the states.

[3] In an unsigned opinion, the majority cited three factors in its stance:

- Puerto Rican residents, although U.S. citizens, did not pay federal income tax.
- The cost of treating Puerto Rico as a state under the current public assistant laws would be prohibitive.
- Higher welfare benefits could disrupt the island's economy.

Justices Thurgood Marshall, William J. Brennan Jr. and Harry A. Blackmun dissented.

[4] **Suspects Found Murdered.** Two men suspected of having been involved in the Dec. 3, 1979 attack on a U.S. Navy bus in Puerto Rico had been found murdered, and a third was missing, it was reported Sept. 19. All three were on the Federal Bureau of Investigation list of 23 suspects in the case, and they were to have appeared before a grand jury investigating the attack.

[5] One of the victims, Jose Juan Adorno Maldonado, was shot to death in front of his home Aug. 11 in a suburb of San Juan. The second man, Jorge Zayan Candal, was found shot to death on an isolated road in the outskirts of San Juan Sept. 11. The third man, Luis Colon Osorio, had been reported missing Sept. 8.

[6] **Romero Declared Election Victor.** Gov. Carlos Romero Barcelo was declared the winner of Puerto Rico's gubernatorial election Dec. 18, six weeks after the Nov. 4 election. The

results were so close that Romero's main opponent, Rafael Hernandez Colon, had initially been named the winner.

[7] The final totals gave Romero 759,540 votes, 47.4% of the more than 1.5 million votes cast. Hernandez received 756,037 votes, 47.2% of the total.

See also Immigration

PULITZER PRIZES

[1] **Pulitzer Prizes.** Columbia University, acting on the recommendation of the advisory board on the Pulitzer Prizes, presented the 64th annual Pulitzer awards in New York April 14.

[2] In journalism, the Gannett News Service won the public service gold medal for exposing mismanagement of gifts and contributions to the Pauline Fathers, a Roman Catholic religious community. The Philadelphia *Inquirer* won a prize for the sixth consecutive year. The Boston *Globe* won three prizes, the second time this had happened in the 64-year history of the awards.

[3] An Off Broadway comedy that made its way to Broadway, *Talley's Folly,* by Lanford Wilson, won the drama award. Normal Mailer won the fiction prize for *The Executioner's Song,* the novelistic story of the life and execution of Utah murderer Gary Gilmore. The award was Mailer's second Pulitzer Prize.

[4] A photograph, *Firing Squad in Iran,* submitted by United Press International on behalf of an unidentified freelance photographer, won the prize for spot news photography. UPI said that it had withheld the photographer's name because the "present unrest in Iran" could endanger him.

[5] A record 1,550 entries had been submitted, including 1,082 in journalism. The names of finalists in jury screening for the 19 categories were made public for the first time. Winners of the prizes were:

ARTS AND LETTERS

Fiction: Norman Mailer for *The Executioner's Song;* **Drama:** Lanford Wilson for *Talley's Folly;* **History:** Leon F. Litwack for *Been in the Storm So Long: The Aftermath of Slavery;* **Biography:** Edmund Morris for *The Rise of Theodore Roosevelt;* **Poetry:** Donald R. Justice for *Selected Poems;* **General Nonfiction:** Douglas R. Hofstadter for *Godel, Escher and Bach: An Eternal Golden Braid;* **Music:** David Del Tredici for *In Memory of a Summer Day.*

JOURNALISM

Public Service: The Gannett News Service for its investigative series on mismanagement of gifts and contributions to the Pauline Fathers; **General Local Reporting:** the Philadelphia *Inquirer* for coverage of the Three Mile Island nuclear reactor accident near Harrisburg, Pa.; **Special Local Reporting:** Nils J. Bruzelius, Alexander B. Hawes Jr., Stephen A. Kurkjian and Joan Vennochi of the Boston *Globe* for an investigation of mismanagement in the transit system; **National Reporting:** Bette Swenson Orsini and Charles Stafford of the St. Petersburg, (Fla.) *Times* for an investigation of the Church of Scientology; **International Reporting:** Joel Brinkley, reporter, and Jay Mather, photographer, of the Louisville *Courier-Journal* for their stories on Cambodia; **Editorial Writing:** Robert L. Bartley of the *Wall Street Journal;* **Feature Photography:** Erwin H. Hagler of the Dallas *Times-Herald;* **Editorial Cartooning:** Don Wright of the Miami *News;* **Commentary:** Ellen H. Goodman of the Boston *Globe* for her columns; **Feature Writing:** Madeleine Blais of the Miami *Herald;* **Criticism:** William A. Henry 3d, television critic of the Boston *Globe.*

QADDAFI, Muammer el—*See* Iraq [29]

QATAR

Qatar Buys French Warplanes. French military officials announced Dec. 5 that Qatar had ordered 14 French Mirage F-1 fighter-bombers, Reuters reported. The cost, including spare parts, was $200 million.

RADICALS

[1] **Fugitive Ex-Yippie Surrenders.** Abbie Hoffman, ex-Yippie leader, antiwar activist and counterculture figure of the 1960s surrendered to authorities Sept. 4 in New York. He had been sought by authorities since he jumped bail in 1974 on a cocaine possession charge.

[2] Hoffman, 43, founder of the Youth International Party, better known as the Yippies, disclosed that he had been hiding in Fineview, N.Y., a small community on Wellesley Island in the St. Lawrence River near the U.S.-Canadian border.

[3] He also said that he had undergone plastic surgery in 1974 to alter his appearance and had been posing as a freelance television writer under the alias Barry Freed. Under his alias, Hoffman said, he had become an environmental activist and led a successful battle in Upstate New York to keep the St. Lawrence River from being dredged to permit winter navigation.

[4] Hoffman said that as "Barry Freed" he had appeared on television, given newspaper interviews, spoken to chambers of commerce and Rotary Clubs, testified before a Senate subcommittee presided over by Sen. Daniel P. Moynihan (D, N.Y.) and received a letter of commendation for his environmental crusade from New York Gov. Hugh L. Carey. As Barry Freed, he also had been appointed to a federal commission in 1979.

[5] Hoffman's surrender, which came amid extensive media coverage, including an interview Sept. 2 with ABC News correspondent Barbara Walters, coincided with the publication of his sixth book, an autobiography, titled *Soon to Be a Major Motion Picture.*

[6] **Radical Leader Surrenders.** A former leader of the Weather Underground, a radical political group linked to terrorist activity and bombings during the Vietnam War, surrendered to authorities Dec. 3 in Chicago after 11 years in hiding.

[7] Bernadine Dohrn, sought in connection with the 1969 "Days of Rage" antiwar demonstrations in Chicago, turned herself in at the Cook County Criminal Court. Dohrn, who was accompanied by William Ayers, another radical leader, father of her two children and companion in flight, was arraigned on charges of mob action, flight to avoid prosecution and assault in allegedly kicking a policeman in the groin and striking another with a club.

[8] After arraignment and release on $25,000 bond, Dohrn read a statement in which she declared her renewed dedication to the causes for which she had fought in the late 1960s. Said Dohrn: "I remain committed to the struggle ahead. I regret not at all our efforts to side with the forces of liberation. The nature of the system has not changed." Dohrn, who at one time had appeared on the Federal Bureau of Investigation's list of 10 Most Wanted Criminals, had been living under an assumed name in New York City, where she had worked as a waitress.

[9] ***Radical Leader Sentenced—*** Cathlyn Platt Wilkerson, another former Weather Underground leader,

who had pleaded guilty in July to charges stemming from a 1970 bomb explosion that accidentally killed three persons in New York, was sentenced Oct. 28 to three years in prison on charges of illegal possession of dynamite and criminally negligent homicide.

RAILROADS

[1] **Carter Signs Deregulation Bill.** President Carter Oct. 14 signed the Staggers Rail Act of 1980, a bill substantially deregulating the operations of the nation's railroads.
[2] The bill, named after House Commerce Committee Chairman Harley O. Staggers (D, W.Va.), gave railroads more flexibility to set their own rates without interference from the Interstate Commerce Commission.
[3] The following were among the provisions of the bill:

■ The ICC could determine rate reasonableness when a railroad had market dominance and when the rate exceeded 160% of the railroad's variable, or out-of-pocket, costs. The percentage would rise five points per year until Oct. 1, 1984. (The ICC could not review rates below those percentages.)

■ A "zone of flexibility" would be created whereby railroads could raise rates by 6% a year, plus an amount equalling their cost increases from inflation, until Sept. 30, 1984. After that time, only rail carriers not receiving adequate revenues could raise rates by 4% plus inflation.

■ Most of the railroad carriers' current immunity from antitrust laws was removed.

■ New federal financial assistance to beleaguered railroads was provided. In particular, the bill authorized another $329 million for Consolidated Rail Corp. operations in fiscal 1981 and doubled to $1.4 billion the money available to aid other financially troubled railroads. The bill also revised the labor protection plan for Conrail employees to close unintended costly loopholes.

[4] The House Sept. 30 approved the bill by voice vote. The Senate passed the bill Oct. 1 by a vote of 61 to eight.

REAGAN, RONALD WILSON

[1] **Reagan Goes to Washington.** President-elect Ronald Reagan arrived in Washington Nov. 17 for visits and conferences with federal officials in the legislative, judicial and executive branches of government, including President Carter.
[2] ***Two Key Posts Filled***—Reagan Nov. 14 had named two of his top White House aides.
[3] James A. Baker 3rd, 50, of Houston, an attorney, was named White House chief of staff. Edwin Meese 3rd, 49, of San Diego, an attorney, was named counselor to the President with Cabinet rank.
[4] Meese was to be responsible for Cabinet administration, the domestic policy staff of the White House and staff operations of the National Security Council. He had been Reagan's chief of staff during governorship of California.
[5] Baker was a relative newcomer to the Reagan ranks who had earned high marks for his handling of negotiations for the presidential campaign debates. Before that he had worked as President Ford's campaign manager in 1976 and had managed Bush's presidential campaign earlier in the year against Reagan.
[6] **Eight Cabinet Posts Filled.** President-elect Ronald Reagan announced eight Cabinet-level appointments Dec. 11. The choices were:

Secretary of the Treasury—Donald T. Regan, 61, chairman and chief executive officer of Merrill Lynch & Co., the New York City-based brokerage and investment giant.

Secretary of Defense—Caspar W. Weinberger, 63, vice president and general counsel of the Bechtel Group, a former secretary of health, education and welfare and a former director of the Office of Management and Budget.

Secretary of Commerce—Malcolm Baldrige, 58, chairman and chief executive of Scovill Inc. of Waterbury, Conn., a diversified manufacturing company.

Director of the Office of Management and Budget—Rep. David A. Stockman (R, Mich.), 34, who served two terms in the House. Before that he had served as executive director of the House Republican Conference. He was not trained as an economist. He studied at Harvard University's Institute of Politics.

Secretary of Health and Human Services—Sen. Richard S. Schweiker (R, Pa.), 54, who was retiring from the Senate after two terms. He served four terms in the House before that.

Secretary of Transportation—Andrew L. (Drew) Lewis Jr., 49, a management consultant in the Philadelphia area and deputy chairman of the Republican national committee.

Attorney General—William French Smith, 63, a Los Angeles attorney, Reagan's personal lawyer.

Director of Central Intelligence—William J. Casey, 67, a New York tax lawyer and former chairman of the Securities and Exchange Commission. He served as chairman of Reagan's election campaign.

[7] **Haig Named Secretary of State.** Alexander M. Haig Jr. was named by President-elect Ronald Reagan Dec. 16 as his choice for secretary of state.

[8] Haig had been White House chief of staff for President Richard M. Nixon in the final year of his presidency at the climax of the Watergate scandals. A retired four-star general who currently was president of United Technologies Corp., Haig also was a former commander of the North Atlantic Treaty Organization forces.

[9] His nomination, aroused controversy. The appointment "should not have been made," Sen. Alan Cranston (D, Calif.), the Democratic whip, asserted Dec. 16. Sen. Edward M. Kennedy (D, Mass.) said the choice raised "serious questions" that had to be answered.

[10] ***Donovan Picked for Labor Post***—Raymond J. Donovan, a construction company executive of New Jersey, was chosen by Reagan Dec. 16 to be secretary of labor.

[11] Donovan, 50, was executive vice president of Schiavonne Construction Co., a company based in Secaucus. Its primary work was building tunnels and highways. Donovan handled its labor relations.

[12] **More Cabinet Selections.** President-elect Reagan announced more selections to Cabinet-level positions Dec. 22. Among them were the first woman and the first black to be named to the Reagan Cabinet.

[13] The black was Samuel R. Pierce Jr., 58, a New York City lawyer and former judge, who was named secretary of housing and urban development. The woman was Jeane J. Kirkpatrick, 54, a Georgetown University political scientist and resident scholar at the American Enterprise Institute. She was chosen to be United States representative to the United Nations. The post was to be kept at the Cabinet level. She was the first Democrat to be named by Reagan to his Cabinet. The other selections were James G. Watt, 42, of Colorado as secretary of interior and James B. Edwards, 53, former governor of South Carolina, as secretary of energy.

[14] Reagan's choice of John R. Block as his secretary of agriculture was announced Dec. 23. Block, 45, a farmer, was director of the Illinois Department of Agriculture. He owned and managed with his father a prosperous hog-and-grain farm near Galesburg, Ill. of 3,000 acres (1,215 hectares) and 6,000 swine.

[15] ***Teamster Aide's Role Queried***—The Reagan transition office announced Dec. 15 that Jackie Presser, a vice president of the Teamsters union, would be senior adviser to the economic affairs transition panel. The

announcement led to persistent queries from the press.

[16] Presser, 54, of Cleveland, was allegedly tied to organized crime. Only a week prior to the announcement, a state police detective testified before the New Jersey Commission of Investigation that Presser was a contact for the approval of union loans to mobsters. In addition, Presser had been a member of the board of trustees of the Teamster's central states pension fund before the board was reorganized in 1977 under federal pressure. The fund had been under scrutiny for years because of its investment practices, which included loans to businesses indentified with organized crime.

See also Black Americans [6]; Christians, Evangelical [16-18]; Defense (U.S.) [36]; Economy (U.S.) [35]; Elections [1, 3-7, 9, 11, 13-15, 20, 32-35, 38-40, 52-53, 59-62, 65-74, 76, 83-85]; Iran [99-101]

REFUGEES

[1] **Refugee Immigration Law.** Legislation revising refugee immigration law was signed March 17 by President Carter.

[2] In the first major overhaul of immigration law since 1965, the legislation established new procedures for admitting refugees and for resettling them in the U.S. It raised the number of refugees and immigrants allowed to enter the U.S. from any part of the world to 320,000 from 290,000 a year.

[3] Also raised in number was the limit on refugees, to 50,000 from 17,400. Congress would review the 50,000 limit in three years. Under the law, the president was allowed to authorize the admission of more than 50,000 refugees annually prior to each year in consultation with Congress. The president was also allowed to admit refugees of "grave humanitarian concern," on an emergency basis, in consultation with Congress, for up to one year.

[4] The bill provided a new definition of refugee, including for the first time persons from any part of the world, not just those fleeing communist countries or displaced in the Middle East, as under the law being superseded. That definition specifically excluded anyone who ordered, incited or otherwise participated in the persecution of any person on account of race, creed or politics.

[5] The bill also created the office of U.S. Coordinator for Refugee Affairs, appointed by the president with the Senate's consent, with the rank of ambassador at large, to consult with and advise foreign and local officials. The House adopted the bill March 4 by a 207-192 vote. Senate passage came Feb. 25 by voice vote.

[6] **Federal Aid to States Provided.** President Carter Oct. 10 signed a bill providing federal grants to states to educate and offer social services to Cuban, Haitian and Indochinese refugee children.

[7] The government had estimated that about 155,000 Cubans and Haitians had fled to the U.S. in 1980, and that by the end of 1981, some 405,000 Indochinese refugees would have entered the U.S. About 20% of the first group and 40% of the latter were school-age children.

[8] The education aid portion of the bill was expected to cost between \$90 million and \$127 million. Social services provided by the bill were expected to cost \$100 million. The bill had cleared the House Oct. 1 and the Senate Sept. 25.

See also Crime [46]; Cuba

RELIGION

Roman Catholics

[1] **Pope Visits Six African Nations.** Pope John Paul II set forth May 2 on an 11-day pilgrimage to six African nations.

[2] The declared objective of the

pilgrimage, the fifth international tour of John Paul's papacy, was "to pay homage to the whole of Africa" and to encourage the growth of Catholicism. It was the second visit by a Roman Catholic pontiff to a continent where there were some 50 million Catholics and where Christianity as a whole was growing at a faster rate than anywhere else in the world.

[3] The 11,200-mile (17,900 kilometer) trip took the Pope by plane, river barge, limousine and Land-Rover to Zaire May 2-6, the Congo May 5, Kenya May 6-8, Ghana May 8-10, Upper Volta May 10 and the Ivory Coast May 10-12. The Pope directed most of his speeches to defining Vatican policy on Christianity's social role in Africa, and addressing the dramatic cultural changes in the African Catholic Church. Among the controversial issues facing the pontiff was the movement to "Africanize" church liturgy and sacraments in which tribal customs and folk religion were adapted to Catholicism.

[4] The Pope arrived May 2 in Zaire, the most Catholic of the countries on his itinerary, where he declared that his mission was to "confirm the faith" among that country's 12.4 million Catholics. In Kinshasa, the capital, the pontiff was greeted by large and exuberant crowds that included spear-carrying tribal dancers clad in striped costumes, bands, military honor guards, government officials and Zairian clergymen.

[5] In Zaire, the pontiff urged unity and discipline within the church and declared that Roman Catholics must adhere to the universal doctrines of monogamy, chastity, and clerical celibacy as well as the papal ban on contraception. Celibacy and polygamy had both been sensitive issues in which the African church had been unsuccessful in overcoming well-established social customs. Marriage among African priests and nuns was widespread and polygamy was also common among priests and bishops.

[6] On the third day of his tour, the Pope held and open-air mass in Kinshasa, where he issued greetings in four local languages, consecrated seven new bishops and shared a platform with Zaire's President Mobuto Sese Seko. The mass was marred, however, by the deaths of seven women and two children who were trampled and by injuries to dozens of others as they attempted to get into a cordoned area to see the mass.

[7] The Pope made a one-day visit May 5 to the Congo, the only socialist state on his schedule. He was greeted by hundreds of thousands of Congolese, chanting and waving crosses and flags when he arrived by river barge from Zaire. The Pope moved on to Kenya May 6, and there delivered the principal speech of his trip. In an address before a gathering of diplomats in Nairobi, he attacked "aetheistic ideology" (an apparent reference to Marxism), abuse of governmental authority, racism, terrorism, the exploitation of weaker classes by the strong. He celebrated an outdoor mass in Nairobi May 7 before more than a million people.

[8] Arriving in Ghana May 8, the Pope met in Accra with President Hilla Limann and later issued a call to the people to work together and raise agricultural production. The Pope's statement was an apparent reference to political factionalism in Ghana and its low production of cocoa, the economic mainstay of the country. On May 10, the Pope stopped briefly in Upper Volta, a drought-stricken region and one of the world's poorest countries. He issued an appeal for world aid for drought victims. Said the Pope: "I launch this appeal to everyone. Do not wait for the drought to come back, appalling and devastating. Do not wait again for the sand to bring death."

[9] ***John Paul II in France***—Pope John Paul II arrived in France May 30 for a four-day pilgrimage. The Pontiff's visit was the first by a Roman Catholic Pope to that country since 1814.

[10] The Pope's trip came amid reports of a widespread decline of influence in French Catholicism, dispirited leadership and dissidence within the French hierarchy. Church statistics had shown that although 85% of all French citizens had been baptized as Catholics, only about 15% regularly attended church as compared with 35% twenty years earlier.

[11] The Pontiff's major theme was the "spiritual fatigue" of the French church. He visited Paris and the shrine of St. Therese in Lisieux, Normandy.

[12] ***Brazilian Pilgrimage***—Pope John Paul II arrived June 30 in Brazil for a 12-day pilgrimage.

[13] The pilgrimage, the longest papal trip outside Italy in modern times, was also the first visit by a Pope to Brazil, the world's most populous Catholic country. The pontiff's 17,500-mile (28,000-kilometer), journey took him to: Brasilia June 30, Belo Horizonte July 1, Rio de Janeiro July 1-2, Sao Paulo July 3, Aparecida do Norte July 4, Sao Jose dos Campos July 4, Porto Alegre July 5, Curitiba July 5, Salvador (Bahia) July 6, Recife July 7, Teresina July 8, Belem July 8, Fortaleza July 9 and Manaus July 10-11.

[14] The Pope's trip came amid mounting controversy over alleged political repression by Brazil's military regime and sharp economic inequities between the wealthy and poor. A key issue was the role of the Brazilian church: its advocacy of liberation theology and its growing militancy in defense of labor unions, the urban poor, landless peasants and Indians.

[15] In recent years, the activist clergy had come under frequent attack from conservatives. A number of priests and nuns had been jailed, tortured and killed or threatened with violence by the military and vigilante groups.

[16] Although the pontiff had declared that his mission to Brazil was "purely religious and pastoral," he directed many of his addresses to the deep economic and social divisions within Brazilian society. Overall, the Pope reaffirmed the Roman Catholic Church's commitment to seek non-violent social change, to fight political repression of human rights by dictatorial regimes of the right or left and to denounce political and economic injustice. On the liberation theology issue, the pontiff endorsed the work of the activist clergy in behalf of the poor, but he cautioned that the liberation of the poor and the oppressed must be without class violence and in accordance with Christian, not Marxist concepts.

[17] ***Pope Visits West Germany***—Pope John Paul II arrived in West Germany Nov. 15 for a five-day pilgrimage.

[18] The stated objective of the pilgrimage, the eighth of John Paul's papacy, was to strengthen the Roman Catholic Church there and to improve its ties with Protestant churches. The Pope said that although his visit to West Germany was "pastoral" and "religious," he had come to honor the "entire German nation" and its close

Arriving in West Germany on pilgrimage, Pope John Paul II waves to crowd at Cologne airport Nov. 15.

links with the history of Christianity.

[19] The pontiff's pilgrimage was the first papal visit since 1782 to the homeland of Martin Luther, the German theologian, who started the 16th-century Protestant Reformation, which split Catholicism in Europe. The Pope's visit came amid reports that the West German Catholic Church, among the world's wealthiest, was shaken by declining membership, strained political relations with the government and a revival of conservatism that was alienating many of its intellectuals.

[20] The Pope's trip was also buffeted by controversy stemming from a booklet issued for the visit by German bishops, which contained attacks on Martin Luther, referring to him as a "church-splitter" and "heretic." Furthermore, a group of some 130 West German religious and literary figures, including dissident theologian Hans Kung and novelist Heinrich Boll, had petitioned the Pope a week earlier in an open letter to respond to a series of issues from world hunger to arms reduction.

[21] **Pope's Comments on Lust Stir Debate.** Pope John Paul II said Oct. 8 that a man was guilty of "adultery in his heart" if he looked at his wife in a lustful manner.

[22] The Pope made the statement, which stirred considerable controversy, in a homily delivered at his regular weekly audience in St. Peter's Square for tourists and pilgrims. The Pope said: "Adultery in the heart is committed not only because a man looks in a certain way at a woman who is not his wife, but precisely because he is looking at a woman that way. Even if he were to look that way at the woman who is his wife, he would be committing the same adultery in the heart."

[23] A Rome newspaper, *Il Messaggero,* commented Oct. 11 that the statement indicated that the Pope "insists on squeezing ever tighter the limits of what is 'lawful' in sexual relations. It is another chapter in the tormented history of the church's ideas on sexual matters." Another Italian newspaper said that the Pontiff was "confusing eroticism with hedonism."

[24] The Pope later tried to explain his statement in remarks to a Vatican audience on Oct. 22. He said that his original statement that a man was guilty of adultery if he lusted after his own wife did not mean that sex should be restricted to the act of procreation. He added: "The correct interpretation and understanding of these words are important for us. They do not contain a comdemnation or an accusation against the body. Rather they subject the human heart to critical examination. The judgment against lust, which these words enunciate, is an affirmation of the body, not a negation."

[25] **Dutch Bishops Affirm Traditional Catholic Doctrine.** Dutch bishops of the Roman Catholic Church affirmed Jan. 31 traditional Catholic doctrine, ending a special synod called at the Vatican by Pope Paul II.

[26] The synod, unprecendented in modern church history, had been convened Jan. 14 in an effort to reconcile disagreements between liberals and conservatives in the Dutch Catholic hierarchy. The synod at its close issued a document designed to curtail liberal tendencies in the Dutch church. It contained the following decisions:

- Strict enforcement of the celibacy rule for priests and other clergy.
- A return to traditional seminary training of priests instead of education at lay universities.
- Careful restrictions on lay pastoral workers who had been allowed to perform priestly functions, including the administration of sacraments and other tasks reserved by canon law for ordained priests.
- A ban on the practice of intercommunion with Protestants.
- A return to the Roman missal and liturgy, which had been replaced in many areas by local liturgies, and a return to the practice of individual con-

fession, which had been replaced by group absolution.

[27] Adoption of the decisions by the synod was seen as part of Pope John Paul II's drive to curtail liturgical experimentation and reassert greater unity within the Catholic Church along conservative lines. The pontiff's decision to sponsor the synod came in the wake of long-standing doctrinal differences within the Dutch Catholic hierarchy that had intermittently threatened to become an open schism.

[28] **Kung Accepts Compromise.** The Rev. Hans Kung, the liberal Roman Catholic theologian who was censured by the Vatican in 1979 and banned from teaching as a Catholic theologian, agreed on a compromise April 10 in the dispute over his university teaching post.

[29] The settlement, announced by Father Kung and the president of Tubingen University, Adolf Theiss, would allow Kung to remain as a professor of theology and as director of the university's Institute for Ecumenical Research. However, Kung and the institute would both be detached from the university's Catholic theological faculty and placed under the authority of the university's Senate. Kung would be able to teach, write and conduct research, but his classes would not be recognized by the Catholic Theological Faculty.

[30] Kung had been censured by the Vatican for his writings that questioned the doctrine of papal infallibility, the divinity of Christ and the dogma of the Virgin Mary. The Vatican forbade Kung to teach Catholic theology and called for his replacement at the university's Institute of Ecumenical Research.

[31]Kung's censure had prompted an international controversy involving church-state issues, the unity of the Catholic Church, the direction of papal leadership under John Paul II and freedom of theological research. The University of Tubingen, where Kung held his post, was maintained as a secular university by the German state of Wurttemberg-Baden. But under a 1933 church-state agreement, the Catholic church was accorded the right to veto members of the school's Catholic theological faculty.

[32] **Catholic Priests Barred from Politics.** Pope John Paul II had apparently issued a directive banning all Roman Catholic priests from serving in public office, a reaffirmation of existing canon law, it was reported May 4. While the order affected some U.S. priests active in elective politics, it was unclear what impact the new papal policy would have on Roman Catholic clerics in Latin America, many of whom were deeply involved in political and social movements.

[33] The directive caused the withdrawal from politics of Father Robert F. Drinan, the only Catholic priest in the U.S. Congress. On May 5, Rep. Drinan (D, Mass.), a Jesuit priest who had served in the House 10 years, said he would not seek reelection in the fall.

Other Developments

[34] **Protestants Approve Common Ministry.** A proposal for a common ministry for a projected united church was approved Jan. 24 by delegates from 10 Protestant denominations seeking church unity.

[35] Approval of the proposal, which drew unanimous support from the 100 delegates, came at the end of a three-day meeting of the Consultation on Church Union (COCU) in Cincinnati. The proposal envisioned a common ministry that would include bishops, presbyters (pastors) and deacons or recognized lay ministers. The agreement was considered a major step toward ending the divisions that had existed between Protestant denominations for centuries. The new church would be known as the Church of Christ Uniting.

[36] The draft proposal called for the member denominations of COCU to re-

spond to the plan by the end of 1981. In all 20 million Protestants belonged to the participating churches in the COCU. Member denominations included: the African Methodist Episcopal Church, the African Methodist Episcopal Zion Church, the Christian Church (Disciples of Christ), the Christian Methodist Episcopal Church, the Episcopal Church, the National Council of Community Churches, the Presbyterian Church in the U.S., the United Church of Christ, the United Methodist Church and the United Presbyterian Church in the U.S.A.

[37] **Mass. School Prayer Law Controversy.** A new Massachusetts state law requiring a period of voluntary prayer in public schools went into effect Feb. 5, setting off a renewed church-state legal controversy.

[38] The state law required teachers in public schools to invite student volunteers to lead their class in prayer. Under the measure, children who did not wish to participate were allowed to leave the classroom. The law replaced an older state statute that permitted a minute of silence at the start of the school day.

[39] Opponents of the new law charged that it violated the constitutional provision on the free exercise of religion. The Civil Liberties Union of Massachusetts, the American Jewish Committee and other organizations sought a preliminary injunction to bar enforcement of the law, but it was denied Feb. 13 by a state Supreme Court justice. The justice said that opponents had failed to prove that the law would irreparably harm students.

[40] Massachusetts was one of nine states to require either spoken prayer or silent meditation in public schools since the U.S. Supreme Court's 1963 decision that recitation of prayers and Bible readings violated the Constitution. The other states were Connecticut, Florida, Maryland, Mississippi, Nevada, New Hampshire, New Jersey and Texas.

[41] ***10 Commandments School Law Upset***—The Supreme Court ruled, 5-4, Nov. 17 that a Kentucky law requiring public schools to post a copy of the Ten Commandments in every classroom violated the First Amendment. The case was *Stone v. Graham.*

S

SADAT, ANWAR—*See* Egypt [1-4]; Iran [131]; Middle East [5-6, 10, 13-15]

SAHARA, WESTERN—*See* Africa [1-2]

ST. PAUL, MINN.—*See* City & State Affairs [5]

SARASOTA, FLA.—*See* City & State Affairs [5]

SAUDI ARABIA

[1] **Mosque Raiders Executed.** Sixty-three persons who took part in the November 1979 raid on the Grand Mosque in Mecca were executed Jan. 9 by Saudi Arabia. The executions were carried out in public squares in Riyadh, Medina and four other cities. All were beheaded.
[2] **Stricter Law Enforcement Seen.** The Saudi government had tightened enforcement of Islamic law in an attempt to solidify its grip on the country, the *Washington Post* reported Feb. 5.
[3] One aspect of the tighter enforcement was the greater attention being paid by newspapers to banning the use of photographs of women. Interior Ministry officials had also stepped up opposition to the employment of women, even by foreign companies. Police also were reported to be cracking down on shopkeepers who defied rules requiring them to close their shops for the five daily times of prayer.
[4] At the same time, the Saudi royal family had taken several political actions to try to forestall further unrest. The tradition of dispensing royal gifts to tribal leaders had been continued on a more lavish scale, the *Post* reported, and old promises about creating a "consultative assembly" had been revived.
See also Aviation [13]; Carter, Jimmy [9]; Great Britain [58-60]; Human Rights [9]; Iraq [31-32]

SCHMIDT, HELMUT—*See* Germany, West [5-6, 8-12, 17-20]

SCIENCE—*See* Budget [8]; Congress (U.S.) [8]; Nobel Prizes [1, 5-11]; Oceanography; Paleontology [1-2]; Patents [1-9]; Physics [1-4]

SEAGA, EDWARD—*See* Jamaica [1, 3-5, 12]

SIERRA LEONE—*See* Chad [10]

SILVER

[1] **Hunt Group Sets Silver-Backed Bonds.** A group of five powerful and wealthy men, led by Texas billionaire Nelson Bunker Hunt, March 26 announced a joint venture to market bonds backed by $3.5 billion in silver bullion that the men owned or controlled.
[2] Hunt had been buying large quan-

tities of silver and silver futures options in 1979. His activities had helped to drive the price of silver from about $6 and ounce to a peak of more than $50 dollars an ounce. A rumor that Hunt would call for actual delivery of silver he controlled through his position on the New York Commodity Exchange (Comex) had forced the Comex Jan. 8 to limit trading in silver in an effort to avoid chaos in the market.

[3] Hunt and his partners were said to control 200 million ounces of silver, worth $15.80 an ounce in New York March 26. A substantial portion of the silver would be used to back the bonds, which were to be distributed through a Swiss bank. Analysts in New York said that the purpose of the bond sales would be to help finance the group's position in silver, which had declined in value by some 70% since hitting its all-time high price of $50.35 an ounce January 21. In addition, the bonds could yield funds to the group at rates significantly lower than the 20% or so that banks charged for commercial loans.

[4] The participants in the plan, other than Hunt, were identified as Prince Faisal ibn Adbullah Al Saud, Mahmoud Fustok and Shiek Mohammed al-Amoudi, all from Saudi Arabia, and Naji Nahas of Brazil. The project, according to one metals trading expert, could cause some changes in the money markets because it came close to "remonetizing" precious metals. Andrew Racz, president of Racz International, said March 26:

[5] "The Hunt group, in effect, would be printing their own money. More important, they could be paying 4% for West Germany mark and Swiss francs, dollars, or whatever credit they want, while the [U.S.] Treasury is being forced to borrow for 17.5% in today's money market."

[6] Other sources said that the Hunt bonds would be offered "offshore" and would not be available to U.S. citizens. This would make it possible for the groups to avoid registering with the Securities & Exchange Commission.

[7] ***Price Plunge Generates Huge Losses***—The price of silver plunged $5 to $10.80 March 27, generating huge losses for speculators and causing turmoil on the commodity and financial markets. It was the 15th consecutive day that silver prices had declined, a record.

[8] A flurry of margin calls from brokerage houses March 26 forced investors who had bought silver on credit to sell off their silver holdings at a loss or put up more collateral to maintain their equity positions. Hardest hit by the margin calls were the Hunt brothers. The Hunts and their Arab associates had been told March 25 by their New York brokers, Bache Halsey Stuart Shields Inc., that they needed to put up $100 million to cover their position in silver futures. When the Hunt group either refused or was unable to pay, Bache began to sell out the Hunts' silver-futures and stock positions March 26. Evidence that the Hunts needed cash had surfaced that day when they announced the plan to issue silver-backed bonds. [See above]

[9] The sell-off sent the price of silver down sharply and caused turmoil in the stock market March 27 that reflected investors' fears about what the Hunts' troubles might lead to. The Dow Jones industrial average was down 25.43 points a half hour before the close of trading, but it then staged a remarkable recovery when rumors circulated that the Hunts would probably be able to cover their margin calls. The Dow ended the day at 759.98, down 2.14 points, on trading of 63.7 million shares, the seventh heaviest volume on record. The American Stock Exchange index failed to stage a last minute recovery March 27 and posted a record loss of 16.23 points, closing at 215.69.

[10] Caught in the midst of the upheaval was Bache itself. Not only did the Hunts own 450,000 shares in Bache's parent company – 5.6% of the

total—but the brokerage unit had borrowed heavily from its parent to finance its silver operations. At 2:14 p.m. March 27, the Securities and Exchange Commission ordered a halt in trading in Bache Group Inc., which was at $8, down $1.25. The New York Stock Exchange also halted trading in the shares of two other brokerage houses—Shearson Loeb Rhoades Inc. and Dean Witter Reynolds—as well as Louisiana Land and Exploration, an energy company owned in part by the Hunts.

[11] **Hunts Use Oil Assets to Pay Debt.** Nelson Bunker Hunt and W. Herbert Hunt signed a preliminary agreement March 31 to cover $400 million in losses that resulted from their silver trading activities.

[12] The brothers agreed to turn over Canadian oil and gas properties and 8.5 million ounces of silver to Engelhard Minerals and Chemicals Corp. in exchange for Engelhard's agreeing to let the Hunts out of a contract to buy 19 million ounces of silver at $35 an ounce. The contract came due March 31, but silver that day had closed in New York at $14.20, and the Hunts had asked to renegotiate. The contract would have required the Hunts to pay $665 million for silver worth $269.8 million March 31.

[13] The oil and gas properties in Canada used to pay Engelhard included what were described as "significant interests in the Beaufort Sea." The value of the Canadian assets was placed at about $500 million by Canadian oil executives.

[14] **Rescue Plan.** Members of the House commerce, consumer and monetary affairs subcommittee investigating the March 27 collapse of the silver market heard Federal Reserve Chairman Paul A. Volcker May 2 give his approval to a $1.1 billion plan to bail out billionaires Nelson Bunker Hunt and W. Herbert Hunt.

[15] Under Volcker's guidance, a group of the U.S.'s largest banks—including Morgan Guarantee Trust Co. and First National Bank of Dallas—had agreed to extend a line of credit worth $1.1 billion to the Hunt-owned Placid Oil Co. to help pay off the Hunt's estimated $900 million loss in the silver market.

[16] ***Hunts Mortgage $3.2 Billion of Assets***—As part of the $1.1 billion bail out of the Hunt brothers by 13 major U.S. banks, the Hunts had had to mortgage $3.2 billion of assets for use as collateral.

[17] The collateral included the Hunts' oil and gas properties, real estate and even personal items such as Lamar Hunt's private automobile, his Rolex watch and his wife's mink coat. A partial list of some of the Hunts' mortgaged assets was published May 28 in the *Asian Wall Street Journal*. It included the following:

- Personal items: all household items in Lamar's Dallas home and all furnishings in Nelson's Kentucky horse farm. Nelson also put up his collection of rare Boehm bird statues. Herbert Hunt had mortgaged 20 bags of U.S. silver dollars worth about $20,000.
- Real estate: Bunker had mortgaged 250,000 square feet (23,000 square meters) of property in downtown Anchorage, Alaska. He had also mortgaged cotton plantations in Mississippi and Louisiana.
- Agriculture: the Hunts had mortgaged 16.7 million pounds (7.6 million kilograms) of grain stored in silos across Texas and 75,000 head of cattle grazing on ranch land around the U.S. Nelson had also mortgaged his farms and ranches in Texas, Oklahoma, Colorado, California, Montana, Kentucky, Mississippi and Australia.
- Stock: the Hunts had interests in dozens of major corporations and companies around the world.
- Art objects: Herbert's list of mortgaged art included "one bronze statuette of a sphinx from West Greece, c. 530 B.C.," and "one Hellenistic bronze dancing girl in

perfect state of preservation found at Tarentum, c. 200 B.C."

■ Sports: Nelson's sporting assets included more than 500 thoroughbred race-horses—considered one of the largest stables in the world. He had mortgaged his interest in 47 syndicated horses, including former greats like Nashua, Bold Forbes, Canonero II and Dust Commander.

See also Commodities [3]

SKATING

[1] **Heiden Loses World Speed Title.** Eric Heiden, three-time world champion and winner of five gold medals at the 1980 Winter Olympics, lost the world speed skating championship March 2 at Heerenveen, the Netherlands.

[2] Heiden, 21, won only one of the four events in the competition, the 500 meter race, and finished second in the cumulative standings, behind Herbert van der Duim of the Netherlands. Heiden placed sixth in two events, the 5,000- and 10,000-meter races, his worst showings in championship skating in three years, and second in the 1,500-meter race. Heiden was the world champion for three consecutive years, from 1977 to 1979.

[3] **Petruseva Wins Women's Cup.** Natalya Petruseva of the Soviet Union took the women's speed-skating championship Jan. 13 in Hamar, Norway. Petruseva beat the 1979 champion, Beth Heiden, by posting winning times in three of four races the 500-, 1,000-, and 1,500-meter competitions.

[4] **E. Germans, Soviets Take Figure Crowns.** Jan Hoffmann and Anett Poetzsch of East Germany took the men's and women's individual championships, and Marina Chersekova and Sergei Shakhrai of the Soviet Union won the pairs title at the 1980 World Figure Skating Championships in Dortmund, West Germany in March.

See also Olympics

SKIING

[1] **Wenzels Win World Cup.** Andreas and Hanni Wenzel, a brother and sister from Liechtenstein, won the overall men's and women's 1980 World Cup Skiing championships in March.

Andreas, 23, won his title March 11, after Hanni, also 23, clinched hers March 2. Andreas took the lead in Cup competition late in the season, overtaking Sweden's Ingemar Stenmark, the double gold medalist in the 1980 Winter Olympics, who placed second in the Cup race.

SOCCER

[1] **Cosmos Win Soccer Bowl '80.** The Cosmos whipped the Fort Lauderdale Strikers, 3-0, Sept. 21 to capture Soccer Bowl '80, the championship of the North American Soccer League. The contest was played before 50,768 fans in RFK Stadium in Washington, D.C.

[2] The Cosmos had reached the final by eliminating Tulsa, Dallas and Los Angeles in the playoffs. The Strikers had downed California, Edmonton and San Diego to gain the Soccer Bowl.

[3] The Cosmos had never lost an NASL title game, winning championships in 1972, 1977 and 1978. The Strikers had lost their two previous attempts at titles—in 1970, when the team was known as the Washington Darts, and in 1974, when it was the Miami Toros.

[4] ***West Germany Wins European Crown***—The West German national team edged Belgium, 2-1, June 22 to win the European Soccer Championship. The final took place in Rome's Olympic Stadium before 47,864 fans.

SOCIAL SECURITY SYSTEM—

See Budget [16-18]

SOLAR ENERGY

[1] **Oil Industry Solar Monopoly Denied.** A report by the American

Petroleum Institute had denied that U.S. petroleum companies exercised a monopoly over solar energy development and business, it was reported May 5.

[2] The report by the institute, the petroleum industry lobbying group, said that oil companies had not and could not seize control of the solar energy industry, despite fears of some solar and consumer advocates that petroleum company involvement could be detrimental to solar energy development.

[3] The report confirmed that oil companies had invested almost $100 million in solar energy research and development. However, the API contended, "Because oil companies have only a minor share of total sales (no more than 10%), and because entry is unrestricted and capital requirements for entry are not high (in the range of a few million dollars), monopolistic behavior by oil firms in this market is virtually impossible."

[4] Summarizing oil company involvement in solar energy, the report said only three major companies–Exxon, Atlantic Richfield, and Shell Oil–were commercially producing solar devices. It listed eight major oil companies conducting solar research in the U.S., and named nine others that had been awarded solar-related patents or used solar technology.

See also Space [12-13]

SOMALIA—*See* Defense (U.S.) [27-28]; Ethiopia [1-3]

SOUTH AFRICA

Unrest

[1] **5 Die in South Africa Bank Siege.** Three black nationalists held 25 persons hostage Jan. 25 in a bank in a white suburb of Pretoria to demand freedom for imprisoned black activists. In a shoot-out with police several hours later, they were killed along with one white hostage. Another white hostage died the next day of injuries.

[2] **Report on '76 Soweto Riots.** A government-commissioned inquiry into the outbreak of black violence in 1976 concluded that hostility to the *apartheid* system was the root cause of the unrest. The report was prepared by Petrus M. Cillie, chief justice of the Transvaal Supreme Court, and presented to Parliament Feb. 29.

[3] The 1,200-page report was compiled after several months of hearings that ended in July 1977. It covered the period from June 1976 to February 1977.

[4] The immediate spark that set off the riots, Cillie said, was student protests in black schools in Soweto, the main black township of Johannesburg. However, he wrote, the climate of "frustration, resentment and resistance" to *apartheid* helped spread the protests throughout South Africa.

[5] **2 Petroleum Plants Bombed.** Two synthetic fuel plants in the Johannesburg area were bombed June 1, culminating a two-week wave of anti-government protests and rioting by non-whites.

[6] Urban guerrillas attacked the two plants, as well as a related refinery, owned by the South African Oil, Coal and Gas Corporation (SASOL), and caused more than $7 million worth of damage. The raids at Sasolburg and Secunda were the largest and most successful ever staged by groups protesting the government's *apartheid* policies. The London-based African National Congress, a black nationalist group banned in South Africa, claimed responsibility.

[7] **30 Die in Capetown Riots.** At least 30 persons were killed and 174 injured in clashes June 16-18 on the outskirts of Capetown, South Africa between police and mixed-race demonstrators. The violence climaxed two months of unrest which had started with a student boycott protesting alleged racial discrimination in the school system.

[8] **Johannesburg Strike Broken.** A

Victim of Cape Town unrest Frederick Jansen sits at side of road Aug. 11 minutes after his vehicle was stoned, overturned and set afire. Jansen suffered severe burns, and died the next day.

series of walkouts by municipal workers in Johannesburg ended Aug. 1, when more than 1,200 black strikers were deported to their homeland settlements. The strikers, who originally went out July 24 and who numbered more than 10,000 at one point, had demanded recognition for their union and equal pay with whites for comparable work. The strike was said by the *Times* (London) Aug. 2 to be the largest stoppage against a single employer in the country's history.

[9] **Blacks, Police Clash in Soweto.** Police fought Oct. 15 with over 3,000 black rioters, capping a day of violent protest against rent increases in Soweto and the conferral of honorary citizenship in the black community on South Africa's race relations minister who was white.

[10] Earlier in the day more than 150,000 commuters were left stranded when bomb damage led to the suspension of rail service between Soweto and Johannesburg. Groups of stone-throwing youths also disrupted bus service between the two communities.

Apartheid

[11] **Johannesburg Stores Integrate.** The major department stores of Johannesburg announced Feb. 15 that they would no longer forbid blacks to use their cafeterias. The stores added their restaurants to the list of at least 68 in Johannesburg that had decided to apply for integrated status.

[12] The integration of department-store restaurants was expected, since blacks accounted for some 40% of sales in the downtown Johannesburg stores. "It makes good sense and it is long overdue," remarked a spokesman for one department store chain, OK Bazaars. OK Bazaars planned to desegregate its restaurants in Cape Town, Durban and Port Elizabeth, he added.

[13] In other developments concerning race relations:

■ Pieter Koornhof, minister of plural relations and development, was reported Feb. 7 to have announced an easing of restrictions on blacks who visited two South African cities. As an experiment, he said, blacks would no longer be limited to a visiting period of 72 hours in Pretoria and Bloemfontein.

■ Ford Motor Co. in Port Elizabeth was criticized for its race relations policies. In a report issued Feb. 27, a race-relations group charged that the company, a subsidiary of Ford Motor Co. in the U.S., still paid blacks much less than whites. Black and colored (mixed race) workers received from $130-184 a month, which was below the South African subsistence level, the report charged. Ford was praised, however, for its efforts to integrate company facilities and to train blacks for higher positions. The report added that the company had done well in health care and in recognizing black unions.

[14] **Botha Survives Rightist Challenge.** South African Prime Minister Pieter W. Botha March 12 survived a factional challenge in his ruling National Party over his willingness to change some of the country's *apartheid* policies. The challenge to his leadership was led by Andries Treurnicht, minister of public works and a powerful opponent of racial integration.

[15] **New Broederbond Head Chosen.** Carel Boshoff had been chosen leader of the *Broederbond,* the secret Afrikaner society influential in shaping government policy, it was reported Sept. 26.

[16] Boshoff, chairman of a right-wing research organization called the South African Bureau of Racial Affairs, was selected to replace Gerrit Viljoen, who had been named minister of national (white) education.

[17] **Botha Names Multiracial Council.** Prime Minister Pieter W. Botha Oct. 2 named 54 men and women to the new, multiracial President's Council on constitutional change. All major non-white South African groups except

blacks were represented on the council, which was strictly advisory in function.

[18] The council, which included whites as well as coloreds (mixed race), Indians and Chinese, was the first multiracial political organization established in South Africa since the National Party came to power in 1948. However, the group had only 15 nonwhite members, partly due to the boycott by several colored and Indian political organizations because of the exclusion of blacks. The white opposition Progressive Federal Party also boycotted the council. Botha had planned to establish a separate black advisory council, but abandoned the idea because of opposition by several black leaders.

[19] **Apartheid Alterations Proposed.** Pieter G. Koornhof, minister of plural relations and development, Oct. 30 introduced legislative proposals aimed at streamlining the South African system of *apartheid.*

[20] The proposals were intended to increase the mobility of black workers within predominantly white urban areas while at the same time tightening the enforcement of limits on black emigration to the cities. Other provisions would allow qualified blacks to be joined for the first time by their families if suitable accommodation was available. Curfews would be lifted, the "pass," or internal passport for blacks, would be replaced in favor of an identity card similar to that carried by white South Africans, and the time limits for unqualified blacks to remain in white areas would be lengthened.

[21] Koornhof said the proposals, which would involve the repeal or amendment of 58 currently existing laws, would be considered by the country's all-white parliament in 1981. Koornhof, considered by many as one of the *verligte,* or enlightened, members of the ruling National Party, said the package showed the government's intention to "think anew and act anew."

[22] **Radical Black Union Recognized.** The South African Allied Workers' Union Nov. 5 became the first unregistered black trade union in the country to be recognized by a major company.

[23] Chloride Holdings recognized the union after a referendum was held among the workers at its battery factory in East London to determine if the SAAWU had majority support among the 500-strong black work force. The South African government had long argued that it could not permit two industrial relations systems, one involving registered trade unions and the other composed of unregistered groups, to coexist.

Other Developments

[24] **Rhoodie Conviction Reversed.** South Africa's Appeals Court Sept. 29 struck down the 1979 fraud conviction of former information official Eschel Rhoodie.

[25] Rhoodie had been sentenced to six years in prison for misappropriating 63,000 Rand ($76,230) from a slush fund he had controlled. The former director of South Africa's Department of Information had headed a multimillion dollar secret government effort to influence world opinion. He had been free on bail pending his appeal.

[26] **Business Worried by Import Rise.** Many South African businessmen were worried about the massive increase in the country's imports since the beginning of the year, it was reported Oct. 15.

[27] The value of imports during the first eight months of 1980 totaled 9.2 billion Rand (approximately US$12.2 billion), a 57% increase over the same period in 1979. Import controls had been relaxed in March. South Africa's booming economy, projected to grow by 7% in 1980, had encouraged the demand for foreign-made capital and consumer goods.

See also Africa [3]; Disasters & Accidents [2-3, 11]

SOUTH-WEST AFRICA (Namibia)

[1] **Namibia Clashes Intensify.** South African troops and guerrillas of the South-West Africa People's Organization engaged in several major clashes during February. Military officials in Windhoek, the Namibian capital, said SWAPO had intensified its actions against South African troops to strengthen its bargaining position in the United Nations-sponsored peace process.

[2] In the most serious clash, four South Africans and six SWAPO guerrillas were killed Feb. 3 near the Angolan border. Military headquarters reported the clash Feb. 6 and said the South Africans had been ambushed as they chased the guerrillas, some of whom escaped over the border.

[3] **Pretoria Delays New Talks.** The South African government told the United Nations May 12 that it was still interested in granting independence to Namibia. However, Pretoria asked the U.N. for more assurances that the South-West Africa People's Organization would abide by the terms of any agreement between the U.N. and Pretoria.

[4] Foreign Minister Roelof Botha told U.N. Secretary General Kurt Waldheim that Pretoria was committed to solving the Namibian problem. However, Botha said the South African government was still skeptical of the U.N.'s commitment to impartial elections.

[5] Further details of the U.N. cease-fire plan had been presented to South Africa earlier in the year. The demilitarized zone envisaged under the plan would extend for 31 miles (52 kilometers) on either side of Namibia's border with Angola and Zambia. SWAPO guerrillas would not be permitted to cross the zone and would have to stay in seven bases in Angola and Zambia. South Africa wanted 20 bases for its troops inside Namibia.

[6] Meanwhile, in the fighting, SWAPO switched its tactics from clashes with South African troops to sabotage. Two explosions April 16 and 20 wrecked a hydroelectric power line and threw Windhoek, the capital, and most of the country into total darkness. South African military reports March 24 said 21 South African soldiers, 22 civilians and 195 guerrillas had been killed since the beginning of the year.

[7] **Guerrilla Bases Raided.** South African air and ground troops raided Namibian guerrilla bases in southern Angola, killing more than 200 insurgents and destroying their operational headquarters, Prime Minister Pieter Botha disclosed June 13.

[8] The attack, launched from bases in Namibia, left 16 government troops dead and secured 100 tons of equipment for the raiders. The South African casualties were the highest in any single reported operation in 14 years of fighting.

[9] It was feared that the South African attack would imperil the United Nations plan for a cease-fire and elections for Namibia, which South Africa had tentatively accepted. The black African nations backing the guerrillas had held a summit in Zambia June 2 at which they reiterated their support for the U.N. efforts. Following the attack, Sam Nujoma, the leader of SWAPO, indicated that he might retreat from his earlier endorsement of the U.N. initiatives.

[10] **U.N. Fairness on Namibia Questioned.** South Africa Aug. 29 accused the United Nations and U.N. Secretary General Kurt Waldheim of being too prejudiced to supervise free elections in Namibia.

[11] U.S. Ambassador to the U.N. Donald McHenry Sept. 9 defended the U.N. and its top official against the South African accusations. He called the charges "distorted" and "unjustified." McHenry indicated South Africa had demanded that the U.N. General Assembly retract its recognition of SWAPO as the "sole legitimate

representative" of the Namibian people. He said South Africa sought to "extract a major concession without commiting itself to an agreement." McHenry, testifying before the U.S. House of Representatives Foreign Affairs subcommittee on Africa, said the U.N. Security Council, which could be in charge of the Namibian elections, had never recognized the guerrilla group. The diplomat insisted that U.N. peacekeeping operations throughout the world were impartial.

[12] United Nations and South African officials held talks in Pretoria Oct. 20-24 without reaching an agreed date for a cease-fire in Namibia.

[13] The U.N. delegation, led by Under Secretary General for Special Political Affairs Brian E. Urquhart, had gone to South Africa in an attempt to overcome Pretoria's reluctance to implement the terms of a 1978 settlement for a cease-fire and election in the disputed territory.

[14] **Turnhalle Alliance Parties Lose.** The governing multi-racial Democratic Turnhalle Alliance suffered important political setbacks when its major ethnic components lost in racially differentiated elections in mid-November.

[15] The Republican Party, the DTA's white member-party, Nov. 14 lost to the right-wing National Party in elections for the white legislative assembly. The Nationalists won 56% of the 52,000 white votes taking at least 10 of the 18 seats in the assembly. The 100,000 whites in the country constituted its second largest group.

[16] The South West Africa People's Damara United Front took only 16 of the 39 seats in the Damara Legislative Assembly. A black nationalist group took the remaining 23. The Damaras, who numbered approximately 90,000 persons, were the third largest ethnic group in the country. No elections were held among the Ovambo tribe, the nation's largest single ethnic group with 46% of the population, because of the guerrilla war between the South African-led forces in Namibia and SWAPO, which the Ovambos supported. The DTA defeats damaged South Africa's claim that the multiracial group had the support of the majority of Namibians and was therefore entitled to international recognition.

[17] **Talks, Cease-fire Linked.** The United Nations announced Nov. 24 that South Africa had conditionally agreed to a March 1981 cease-fire in the disputed territory of Namibia if it were linked to an earlier meeting of all the participants in the Namibian independence process.

[18] U.N. Secretary General Kurt Waldheim reported to the Security Council that South Africa had committed itself for the first time to a specific date for commencing the U.N.-supervised process that could lead to independence for the territory. Namibia had been ruled by South Africa under a 1920 mandate from the League of Nations. The U.N. revoked the mandate in 1966.

[19] The U.N. plan called for the March 1 stationing of a 7,500-man peacekeeping force in Namibia and a 60-mile (96 kilometer) wide demilitarized zone to monitor internal and external guerrilla activity. SWAPO, the major black nationalist group fighting South African rule in Namibia, used bases in neighboring Angola and Zambia. The cease-fire would be followed by a U.N.-supervised election. The winning parties would form a constitutional assembly.

[20] Before the U.N. operation began, SWAPO, the multiracial Democratic Turnhalle Alliance, which governed the territory for the South Africans, various local Namibian parties and South Africans would meet for a "pre-implementation" conference opening Jan. 7, 1981 in Geneva. The "front line" African nations (Mozambique, Botswana, Angola, Tanzania and Zambia) and Western "contact group" (U.S. U.K., France, West Germany and Canada) would also attend the meeting, which would be held to "dispel

the acute mutual distrust" of the directly involved parties.

SPACE

[1] **Voyager 1 Flies by Saturn.** The unmanned U.S. spacecraft Voyager 1 flew by Saturn Nov. 12, gathering information about the giant planet, its complicated ring structure and its varied collection of moons.

[2] Another American spacecraft–Pioneer 11–had flown by Saturn in 1979, but the one-ton Voyager 1, with its more sophisticated equipment, amassed far more data. Voyager 2, a twin to Voyager 1, was scheduled to pass by Saturn in the summer of 1981.

[3] At its closest approach, Voyager 1 came within 78,000 miles (125,000 kilometers) of Saturn's cloud tops. It came much closer to Titan, Saturn's largest moon and the only planetary satellite in the solar system known to have a substantial atmosphere. The spacecraft skimmed within about 2,800 miles (4,500 kilometers) of Titan.

[4] Titan's clouds prevented Voyager from observing the moon's surface. But spectometer and radio-wave analysis afforded much new information. The atmosphere turned out to be mainly molecular nitrogen, together with atomic and ionized nitrogen. Methane, which had been observed from Earth, apparently made up less than 1% of the atmosphere. Atmospheric pressure was much higher than expected: 1.5 times that of Earth at one level in the atmosphere, and possibly twice or three times that of Earth at the moon's surface.

[5] Titan's atmosphere appeared similar to that of the inner planets–Earth, Venus and Mercury–at an early stage in their evolution. The cold temperatures on the moon had blocked the development that occurred on Earth and presumably made it impossible for life to evolve.

[6] Saturn's other moons were markedly smaller that Titan. They were half rock, half ice, according to scientists involved in the Voyager mission, and in this respect resembled the nuclei of comets. Most of them showed extensive signs of cratering; an exception to this was the moon Enceladus, which appeared smooth. Scientists speculated that tidal forces set in motion in Enceladus by the gravitational attraction of other moons could have heated up the satellite and erased the craters.

[7] Voyager discovered three new moons as it approached Saturn, raising the known number of satellites circling the planet to 15. Another discovery made as the spacecraft approached Saturn was a vast cloud of hydrogen gas circling the planet. The tenuous cloud was distributed in Saturn's equatorial plane and apparently ranged from 300,000 to 940,000 miles (480,000 to 1.5 million kilometers) out from the planet.

[8] ***The Rings***—The most surprising and apparently inexplicable findings of Voyager 1 dealt with the rings that circled Saturn.

[9] Previous observations had indicated that there were six rings, or possible a few more. As Voyager produced more and more detailed photographs, scientists increased their estimates of the number of rings, at one point counting 95 and later figuring that there were several hundred. This was not the result of observing new material circling Saturn. Rather, the previously observed broad rings, under closer examination, proved to be made up of numerous finer rings. Narrow rings were also discovered in the Cassini Division, a gap (as viewed from Earth) between two of the broad ring structures.

[10] It was not just the number of rings that was surprising. Previously, it had been thought that Saturn's rings were held in place by a pattern of gravitational resonances from the moons. While the gravitational force of the moons obviously played a role in the shaping of the ring system, the struc-

Composite of images of Saturnian system taken from Voyager I during November 1980. Dione is in forefront, Saturn rises behind, with Tethys and Mimas fading in distance to right. Enceladus and Rhea are off Saturn's right at left and Titan is in distant orbit at top.

ture of the rings appeared to be too complicated for that to be the only effect responsible.

[11] One of the features noted by Voyager was the presence of dark spokes in the rings, directed radially outward from the planet. These spokes appeared to be gaps when Voyager viewed them from above the plane of the rings, but when the spacecraft dipped below the ring plane they were seen as bright. This meant, scientists said, that the spokes held particles that scattered sunlight forward instead of reflecting it back. This in turn meant that the particles were small in size—in the range of the wavelength of light. As Voyager came nearer, it discovered that several rings were eccentric—that is, they were not circular, as were the other rings around Saturn. Then it was discovered that two rings appeared to be braided: they crossed over each other like threads in a rope.

Space shuttle *Columbia* Dec. 29 heads toward pad at Kennedy Space Center, Fla. Launch was scheduled for 1981.

Mission scientists said that other forces besides gravity might have to be invoked to explain these effects.

[12] **Solar Study Satellite Launched.** The U.S. Feb. 14 launched an unmanned Delta rocket that lofted into orbit a 5,100-pound (2,300-kilogram) satellite called the Solar Maximum Mission Observatory.

[13] The satellite was intended to study solar flares, which were expected to peak in the next few months in accordance with their 11-year cycle. Different instruments on the craft would record such data as X-rays, gamma rays and ultraviolet rays. An official of the National Aeronautics and Space Administration said that flares were "probably the most energetic manifestation of changes in the sun that we know about. It's very important for us to understand the physics of the solar flare and to understand how flares come about." The satellite was the first launched by the U.S. to be equipped so that it could be retrieved from orbit by the space shuttle.

[14] **Increased U.S. Spending Urged.** An increase in U.S. spending for research on manufacturing in space was urged Feb. 16 by the General Accounting Office, the investigative arm of Congress. Otherwise, the U.S. might lose it pre-eminence in space technology, the GAO warned.

[15] The GAO said that it was too early to determine what materials could successfully be processed in space, or what their economic potential was. Consequently, research into this area "receives little visibility or support from Congress or by the Administration, and correspondingly, low priority and funding by the National Aeronautics and Space Administration."

[16] The Soviet Union, Japan and several European nations had strong programs to investigate the industrial possibilities of space, the GAO cautioned. Simply to keep up with these countries, the U.S. should double or treble its current budget of $20 million.

The Soviet Union had 350 top scientists working on space-related topics, the GAO noted, and Japan was advancing with research that could lead to improvements in glasses, optics and semi-conductors.

[17] **Cosmonauts End Record Flight.** Soviet cosmonauts Leonid Popov and Valery Ryumin returned safely to Earth Oct. 11 after setting a new space endurance record. The two men had spent 185 days in space, 10 days more than the previous record.

[18] Ryumin and Popov appeared on television several hours after they landed. The two men, who had spent six months in weightless conditions, were seated in reclining chairs, but they talked easily and appeared to be in good condition. A statement by the official Soviet news agency, Tass, said that the cosmonauts on board the orbiting Salyut space station had carried out observations of the Earth, experimented on the formation of crystals and metal alloys under weightless conditions, and studied various biological questions.

See also Astronomy [1-4]

SPAIN

[1] **Basques, Catalans Become Autonomous.** The Basque country and Catalonia formally became autonomous regions within Spain Jan. 11.

[2] Statutes granting the regions automony had been approved in referendums held Oct. 25, 1979. The statutes gave the two industrial regions power to elect their own parliaments and to control taxation, police, education and broadcasting within their territory.

[3] **Unemployment Highest in Europe.** Government statistics showed that unemployment had increased 23% during 1979, giving Spain the highest rate of unemployment in Europe, it was reported March 5.

[4] In 1979, the level of unemployment had risen to 1.33 million from 1.08 million while the total workforce remained more or less constant at 13.15 million persons. The percentage of unemployed had passed 10%. The greatest percentage of unemployed persons continued to be those seeking jobs for the first time. They represented 40% of the total unemployed. The only sector of the Spanish economy where unemployment remained unchanged was agriculture. All other sectors recorded sharp increases in unemployment.

[5] ***Hunger Strikes Hit Jobless Andalusia***—A hunger strike that started Aug. 14 in the rural village of Marinaleda spread to other towns in Spain's southern Andalusia region Aug. 19. Local government officials and political groups joined the strike to protest the Madrid government's failure to alleviate unemployment in the depressed area. The strike ended Aug. 22 with a government promise of public works projects.

[6] In Andalusia, which had the highest unemployment rate in Spain, 2.5% of the population owned 64% of the land.

[7] **Editor Sentenced for 'Insults.'** Juan Luis Cebrian, the editor of the independent daily newspaper *El Pais,* was sentenced May 9 to a suspended three-month jail term and fined $750 by the Spanish Supreme Court.

[8] Cebrian's conviction was the result of an editorial he had published in 1978 entitled "Press and Democracy," which accused the government of hindering freedom of the press in Spain through antiquated press laws. The Supreme Court's 6-5 vote against Cebrian came at a time when several editors and journalists were being called before civilian and military courts. Cebrian said that "there is a great deal of activity by the courts against journalists."

[9] The editorial that led to Cebrian's troubles had singled out the case of one editor who had been prohibited from practicing journalism for 32 years for having published photographs of nudes. The editorial had lamented that in a time of a pornographic "boom" in

Spain, the harsh punishment of the banned editor "recalls the worst times of Nazism or the time of [Idi] Amin Dada today."

[10] **Cabinet Shuffle.** Premier Adolfo Suarez replaced his foreign minister and made other major changes in his Cabinet Sept. 8 in an effort to restore public confidence in his government's ability to handle Spain's economic problems and give his Union of the Democratic Center Party broader backing in parliament.

Unrest

[11] **6 Police Killed in Ambush.** Six Spanish Civil Guards were ambushed and killed Feb. 1 on a coastal road outside Bilbao.

[12] **Basque Bomb Kills Guard, Injures 34.** A bomb planted on a Spanish Civil Guard bus near the Basque region exploded July 22, killing one guardsman and seriously injuring 34 others. The bombing was believed to be the work of the militant Basque ETA terrorist group.

[13] **Marques and Wife Slain.** Manuel de la Sierra Torres, the Marques de Urquijo, and his wife, members of one of Spain's wealthiest families, were found murdered in their homes near Madrid Aug. 1, apparently the victims of Basque terrorists.

[14] **Terrorists Slay General.** Gunmen thought to be members of the shadowy October First Revolutionary Anti-Fascist Group (GRAPO) ambushed the car of Gen. Enrique Briz Armengol Sept. 2 as he was being driven to work in Barcelona. The general was killed instantly, and his body guard and driver were seriously wounded.

[15] The assassination was an apparent revenge killing motivated by the death in Madrid Aug. 29 of a founder of the terrorist group. Abelardo Collazo Araujo had been shot to death by plainclothes police as he was entering a Madrid subway.

[16] **ETA Attacks Spawn Rightist Backlash.** Political violence in the Basque region had produced a backlash from rightists who felt that a stronger military presence in the region was the only solution to the problem.

[17] Persons opposed to political terrorism had become increasingly vocal in their views, and demonstrations in support of the police and the military were attracting large crowds. On Nov. 23, tens of thousands of rightists gathered in Madrid's Plaza de Oriente to mark the death of Generalissimo Francisco Franco Nov. 20, 1975.

[18] In the weeks leading up to the event, hardly a day had passed without news of another assassination or terrorist act attributed to the Basque terrorist group ETA. On Nov. 21, ETA terrorists struck down two Civil Guards in San Sebastian after the police had stopped the terrorists for a routine identity check. To date in 1980, ETA had been linked to at least 85 deaths.

[19] **ETA Chief slain in France.** Jose Martin Sargardia, a leader of the Basque separatist organization ETA, was assassinated Dec. 30 in the town of Biarritz in southern France. A bomb attached to the accelerator of Sagardia's car exploded when he started it.

See also France [3-4]; Guatemala [1-5]

SPORTS—*See* Auto Racing [1-6]; Baseball [1-15]; Basketball [1-3]; Boxing [1-9]; Cycling; Football; Golf; Hockey [1-6]; Horse Racing [1-9]; Olympics; Skating; Soccer; Track & Field [1-12]; Yachting

STEEL

[1] **Plant Closing Blocked.** An order temporarily restraining U.S. Steel Corp. from closing two steel mills in Youngstown, Ohio was issued Feb. 28 by Judge Thomas Lambros of the U.S. District Court in Cleveland.

[2] The order was requested by four locals of the United Steelworkers union

who alleged that U.S. Steel had broken a promise to keep the plants open as long as they remained profitable. The steelworkers' suit contended the plants were making money when U.S. Steel announced in 1979 that it would close them as part of a retrenchment program. Judge Lambros said at a pretrial hearing that the suit had widespread implications since "we're deciding the economic survival of a large segment of this state."

[3] ***Closings Upheld***—A federal appeals court July 25 ruled that U.S. Steel Corp. had the right to close two Ohio steel plants, but ordered a trial on the question of whether the company's refusal to sell the plants to workers was an antitrust violation.

[4] In Cincinnati, the U.S. Sixth Circuit Court of Appeals upheld a federal district court ruling that the company could close the Youngstown, Ohio-area plants. The 3,500 employees who stood to lose their jobs had sued in district court, basing part of their case on a contract agreement the company had made to keep the plants open as long as they were profitable.

[5] However, the appellate court differed with the lower court on the question of the workers' other charges. The employees alleged U.S. Steel's refusal to sell them the plants was a violation of antitrust laws. The district court had dismissed the workers' contention; the appeals court panel said the allegations "should be the subject of briefing, argument and trial court decision."

[6] **Bethlehem Pleads Guilty in Bribery.** Bethlehem Steel Corp. July 24 pleaded guilty to charges it had paid more than $400,000 in bribes between 1972 and 1976 to obtain ship repair business. The bribes were part of a scheme involving nearly $2 million Bethlehem had overcharged customers to furnish the funds for the bribes.

[7] According to the charges, filed in the federal district court in New York, Bethlehem made secret cash payments to representatives of U.S. and foreign ship-owners to induce them to use Bethlehem's shipyards for maintenance. Bethlehem, the nation's second largest steelmaker, pleaded guilty as a corporation. Under the terms of the plea agreement, no individuals were named in the charges. Nor were the payoff recipients of the payoffs identified.

[8] **New Trigger Price Mechanism.** President Carter set forth a package of proposals Sept. 30 to aid the steel industry.

[9] The key proposals were to reestablish a "trigger price" mechanism to prevent dumping of foreign steel on the American market and to delay deadlines for meeting air-quality standards. On the environmental deadlines, Carter said he would ask Congress to allow the Environmental Protection Agency to extend deadlines for steel companies on a "discretionary, case-by-case" basis.

[10] The trigger prices would be set 12% higher than their levels in March, when they had been suspended for investigation of a dumping complaint. At that time, they had averaged $358 a ton. The higher levels reflected the increase in Japanese prices. The trigger price, or minimum price for steel imports, was pegged to Japanese steel products because they were considered the most efficiently produced in the world. When imports fell below the trigger price, an investigation was begun to determine if penalty duties were necessary to curb dumping.

See also European Community (EC) [6-7]; Union of Soviet Socialist Republics [15]

STOCKS, Bonds & Securities

[1] **'Insider' Trading Conviction Voided.** The Supreme Court voted, 6-3, March 18 to overturn the criminal conviction of a financial printer who had profited from inside knowledge of impending stock transactions. In doing so, the high court limited the definition of corporate "insiders" subject to pro-

secution under the antifraud provisions of federal securities law.

[2] The case, *Chiarella v. U.S.*, concerned the activities of Anthony F. Chiarella, an employee of Pandick Press of New York City. Chiarella had used confidential information on four upcoming takeover bids and one merger to make $30,000 by buying stock in the target companies and selling the shares as soon as the transactions were made public.

[3] Chiarella's actions were investigated by the Securities and Exchange Commission and he was successfully prosecuted under a federal law requiring corporate insiders to disclose any knowledge of impending transactions to stock sellers. He was sentenced to one year in prison, with 11 months suspended. Chiarella's conviction was upheld by the U.S. 2d Circuit Court of Appeals. The high court reversed the appeals court and held that Chiarella was not a corporate insider and therefore had no fiduciary duty to reveal his knowledge to those that sold him stock. (Federal securities laws did not mention or define "insiders," but the term traditionally applied to corporation officers, directors and majority shareholders.)

[4] **SEC Must Prove Intent to Defraud.** The Supreme Court ruled, 6-3, June 2 that in some civil enforcement actions, the Securities and Exchange Commission had to prove that stock fraud was intentional, rather than the result of negligent conduct. The case was *Aaron v.* SEC.

[5] Until the high court's action, lower courts had generally supported the SEC's contention that proof of fraudulent intent was not necessary to enforce key provisions of the Securities Act of 1933 and the Securities Exchange Act of 1934.

[6] **Market Developments.** The stock market moved up strongly during 1980. It closed at 824.57 Jan. 2, and ended at 963.99 Dec. 31. Its low for the years was 759.13 April 21, its high 1,000.17 Nov. 20.

[7] From its low point, the market climbed to 817.06 April 30, and then rose more or less steadily from 850.85 May 30 to 924.49 Oct. 31.

[8] The election of Ronald Reagan as president sent the market sharply upward Nov. 5, with defense, oil and technology stocks leading the surge. The market climbed 27.31 points in the first two hours of trading before settling at 953.16, up 15.96 points for the day. Over 84 million shares changed hands, a record.

[9] The market's highest level for the year, 1,000.17 Nov. 20, was the highest since Dec. 31, 1976, when the indicator closed at 1,004.65.

See also Commodities

SUPREME COURT

[1] **Case-By-Case Rulings Cause Confusion.** The Supreme Court ended its 1979-80 term July 2. As in recent terms, the court continued to defy ideological labels, with no identifiable trend in its "liberal" and "conservative" judgments.

[2] The high court decided 136 cases during the 1979-80 term and issued opinions in 129 of those cases. Of the 136, a total of 36 were decided by unanimous vote and 15 with only one dissenting vote. Twenty-seven cases were decided by a 5-4 vote.

[3] The lack of a consistent ideology on the court brought forth apparent contradictions in many areas. In criminal justice rulings during 1979-80, the court restricted warrantless searches in the home, permitted prison inmates or their families to sue directly under the Constitution and curbed the use of jailhouse police informants. However, the court also expanded the role of illegal evidence in trials and held that a casual remark by a police officer did not necessarily constitute an "interrogation," even if the remark prompted a suspect to make self-incriminating statements.

WILLIAM O. DOUGLAS

[4] Critics charged that the Supreme Court was leaving lower courts and state and federal officials without needed judicial guidance. "Whole categories of the law are in shambles," asserted Bruce Fein, a high court analyst with the American Enterprise Institute. "Judges are saying, 'Oh my God, what does this mean?' The court's approach can only be described as 'benign neglect' of the law."

[5] Jesse H. Choper, a University of California law professor, contended that the Burger Court was radically different from its predecessor, the Warren Court, in the manner in which cases were decided. "The Warren Court," he said, "operated on the basis of broad, fundamental principles. [The Burger Court] operates on a case-by-case basis paying close attention to the facts, drawing extremely fine distinctions from one case to another."

[6] One professor of constitutional law, Gerald Gunther of Stanford University, defended the high court's avoidance of sweeping decisions. "There is something to be said for dealing with a set of issues again and again," he argued. "There are a lot of competing interests and complicated issues at stake in these cases. In complicated areas, I am suspicious of simple solutions."

[7] **Justice Douglas Dies.** William O. Douglas, 81, who served on the U.S. Supreme Court longer than any other justice, died Jan. 19 in Washington, D.C.

[8] A towering figure in the nation's judicial history, Douglas had written more than 1,200 opinions during his record 36-year tenure on the high court. A liberal in outlook, he staunchly defended civil liberties, the right to dissent, the right against self-incrimination, the protection from search and seizure and from intrusions against privacy and due process.

[9] Douglas' liberalism on the court often made him a target of controversy. He survived several impeachment attempts and his writings were denounced by some as subversive. During the McCarthy era in the early 1950s, he wrote strong dissents condemning government loyalty oaths and security actions as encroachments on individual liberities. He came under attack when he granted a stay of execution in 1953 for Julius and Ethel Rosenberg, convicted of stealing atomic secrets for the Soviet Union. Twenty years later during the war in Vietnam, he ordered the U.S. government to stop bombing Cambodia. He was overruled by the full court in both cases.

[10] Douglas was born Oct. 16, 1898 in Maine, Minn. He came east in 1922 virtually penniless and entered Columbia University Law School, graduating in 1925 second in his class. He taught law at Columbia and later at Yale University. He became recognized as one of the nation's legal experts in corporate finance and was appointed in 1936 to the Securities and Exchange Commission. He became its chairman in 1937. Two years later, at the age of 40, he was named to the Supreme Court by President Franklin D. Roosevelt. Ill health forced his retirement from the court in 1975.

See also Abortion [1-3]; Antitrust Actions [7-8]; Business [13-15]; Census (U.S.) [7]; Central Intelligence Agency [1-4]; Citizenship [1-2]; Civil & Constitutional Rights [1-8]; Death Penalty [2-4, 6-7] Draft Registration [1, 11-13]; Education [1-3]; Environment [5, 14, 17]; Freedom of Information Act; Indians, American [4-7]; Labor [5-8, 12-13, 15]; Law [1-17]; Patents [1-9]; Police [1-3]; Politics [1-6]; Press [1-5] Puerto Rico [1-3]; Stocks, Bonds & Securities [1-5]; Water [1-3]

SWEDEN

[1] **Referendum Backs A-Power.** Swedish voters gave qualified support to continuing use of nuclear power in a nonbinding referendum March 23. Premier Thorbjorn Falldin said he would respect the wishes of the voters.

[2] The referendum allowed voters to state one of three preferences regarding nuclear energy. One proposal, backed by opponents of nuclear energy, called for dismantling the country's six operating reactors over the next 10 years. That proposal was endorsed by 38.6% of the voters. (About 75% of Sweden's 6.3 million voters took part in the referendum.)

[3] The two proposals that backed continued use of nuclear power jointly won 58.1% of the vote. One called for operating at most 12 nuclear power plants, and phasing out nuclear power after 25 years. This option won 39.4% of the vote. The other pro-nuclear proposal backed the use of 12 power plants for 25 years—their estimated service life—without specifying what nuclear policy Sweden would follow later.

[4] Nuclear power had been one of the most controversial issues in Sweden for over a year. Disagreements over nuclear power had made it difficult for the various political parties to join and form a workable coalition. So the referendum had been seen as a way of resolving a conflict that was blocking normal political activity.

[5] Falldin's own Center Party had been joined by the Communists in opposing nuclear power. The Liberal Party along with the Social Democrats favored the referendum proposal that called for continued use of nuclear power but a phase-out after 25 years. The Moderates—who were politically on the right in Sweden—backed continued use of nuclear power without prejudging whether it should be eventually abandoned. This position was also favored by Swedish industry.

[6] Sweden currently obtained 25% of its electricity from nuclear energy. In addition to its six operational power plants, four more nuclear facilities were near completion and two others were in the early stages of construction. The 12 plants, if completed, were intended to provide 40% of Sweden's electricity needs.

[7] **Lockout, Strikes Halt Industry.** Much of Sweden's industry and transportation was shut down in early May as a result of lockouts and strikes affecting about 900,000 private-sector workers and another 26,000 employees in the public sector. The last comparable labor dispute took place in 1909. A wage agreement proposed by government mediators ended the strife May 11. The agreement provided wage increases of about 7%.

[8] The unrest started April 25 with a strike by 14,000 public-sector workers and the lockout of another 12,000. The action shut down airports and Stockholm subways, halted most freight traffic through the west coast ports and reduced hospital services. The private-sector stoppage began May 1, when the employers association, the SAF, locked out about 770,000 workers. The employers took the action after the country's main union federation, the LO, refused to call off wildcat strikes or end a ban on overtime work. The LO responded by ordering strikes involving more than 100,000 workers. The combined actions shut down all heavy industry and most international transportation.

[9] The dispute centered on wages. The LO had rejected a 2.3% increase proposed by government-appointed mediators, calling for a hike of 11.3%. Management claimed that Sweden could not afford to continue increasing labor costs substantially without damaging the competitiveness of Swedish industry on world markets.

[10] **Government Wins Confidence Vote.** The center-right coalition government headed by Premier Thorbjorn Falldin won a no confidence vote, the first ever held in Sweden, by one vote Oct. 22. The vote was 175-174, with the Communists joining the opposition Social Democrats in an attempt to oust Falldin.

[11] The vote was on economic policy. The opposition charged that the government had fallen away from Sweden's traditional full employment

policies, and also had broken commitments to pensioners. Falldin insisted he would stand by his plans to curb public spending.
See also Economy (International) [6]

SWITZERLAND

[1] **Church-State Separation Rejected.** Voters in a national referendum March 2 rejected a proposal to bar all ties between church and state.
[2] In most of the country's 26 cantons, the government provided money directly or indirectly to local Catholic and Protestant churches. The sponsors of the referendum objected that this practice was unfair to nonbelievers and adherents of other religions.
[3] **Youths Riot in Zurich.** Police arrested 124 persons during 12 hours of skirmishes in Zurich July 12-13. More than 50 people were treated for injuries.
[4] The disturbance began with a meeting calling for the dismissal of charges against youths involved in unrest at the end of May. The meeting was held at an abandoned factory occupied two weeks earlier by youth groups ranging from anarchists to punks and rockers. The May rioting followed a decision by authorities to refurbish an old city opera house. The youth groups called for funds to fix up the factory as a center for "alternative culture."
[5] More than 300 youths were arrested in Zurich as fighting broke out Sept. 6 when police moved in to break up a demonstration protesting the shutdown of a youth center in an unused factory. The police had closed the center Sept. 4.
[6] **Currency Curbs Abandoned.** The Finance Ministry and the central bank announced Aug. 27 that the last remaining restrictions on nonresident foreigners making Swiss franc-denominated deposits in Swiss banks would be eliminated as of Aug. 31.
[7] The move, observers said, aimed to prevent the Swiss franc from losing value too rapidly against the U.S. dollar. High interest rates in the U.S. had pushed up the value of the dollar against the Swiss currency recently. The restrictions had originally been put into effect to halt speculation in the Swiss currency.
[8] **Longest Road Tunnel Opened.** The longest underground highway tunnel in the world was formally opened Sept. 5, linking Goschenen in Uri Canton to Airolo in Ticino Canton through the St. Gothard Massif. The 10.1 mile (16.2 kilometer) two-lane tunnel cost $415 million and took over 10 years to build.
[9] **U.S. A-Export Protest Rejected.** The Swiss government Sept. 22 announced it was not prepared to unilaterally limit exports of sensitive nuclear technology despite a request from the United States.
[10] The U.S. had protested to the Swiss several times about sales of equipment to Pakistan that the U.S. believed was being used to construct an atomic bomb. The Swiss contended the sales violated no national laws or international guidelines.
See also Economy (International) [7, 8]; Espionage [5-6]

SYRIA

[1] **Brezhnev, Assad Sign Accord.** The Soviet Union and Syria Oct. 8 signed a 20-year friendship pact in Moscow.
[2] The accord, signed by Presidents Leonid Brezhnev and Hafez al-Assad, provided for continued "cooperation in the military field" between the two nations. Other articles of the agreement provided for cooperation in the political, economic, scientific, technological and cultural spheres.
[3] **Syria, Jordan Mass Troops.** Syrian soldiers and tanks had begun massing on the border of Jordan, Arab officials and Western diplomats in Amman reported Nov. 26. Jordan responded by placing its armed forces on the alert and dispatching troops and tanks to the Syrian frontier. Syrian forces to-

taled abut 35,000 men and more than 1,000 tanks, while Jordan had massed about 24,000 soldiers.

[4] Syria's action was believed related to its differences with Jordan over the Iranian-Iraqi war and its boycott of the Arab League summit in Amman Nov. 25-27.

[5] Syria's first public statement on the situation appeared Nov. 29 in a government newspaper, which reiterated the frequent charge that Jordan was behind the terrorist activities of the Moslem Brotherhood in Syria, a charge often denied by Jordan.

[6] Syria Dec. 2 submitted a list of 21 demands to King Hussein as conditions for the withdrawal of Syrian troops from their common border. Among other things, the Syrians called on Jordan to pledge to continue to recognize the PLO as the sole legitimate representative of the Palestinian people and that it state in writing that it was not assisting the Moslem Brotherhood. Jordan rejected the Syrian demands.

[7] By Dec. 3, tensions between the two countries were said to have eased as a result of mediation efforts by Saudi Arabia.

See also Human Rights [9]; Iraq [27-28]; Libya [1-4]

T

TANZANIA

Nyerere Wins New Term. Julius K. Nyerere Oct. 26 was elected unopposed to his fourth consecutive five-year term as president of the east African nation.

TAXES (U.S.)

[1] **Congressional Body Recommends Cut.** Arguing that government economic policies were "too contradictory," the Joint Economic Committee of Congress Feb. 28 recommended a winding down of federal spending and a tax cut.

[2] In its annual report, the committee proposed a tax reduction of about $25 billion a year, enacted by the summer of 1981. About half of that cut would benefit individuals, the other half would help business. The committee suggested, as "supply-side" economists had propounded, that policies promoting investment and improved productivity could lead to economic growth great enough to offset soaring energy costs and stave off a decline in purchasing power.

[3] Data Resources Inc., an economic forecasting firm, was hired by the committee to develop a "supply-side" model. Data Resources concluded that policies of fiscal and monetary restraint, such as those implemented by the Carter Administration, would have to produce a 7.5% unemployment rate for five years to reduce the "core" inflation rate (estimated at 9% by the Administration) by one percentage point. A $10 billion reduction in business taxes, Data Resources found, could bring the inflation rate down by 1% without an alteration of the unemployment rate.

[4] **Dems, GOP Back Cut.** Support for a tax reduction in 1981 was solidified at a White House breakfast with Democratic congressional leaders July 1. "There's no question at all in our mind that there's going to be a tax cut in 1981," House Speaker Thomas P. O'Neill (D, Mass.) reported after the meeting. O'Neill said the question was whether to act on the legislation "this year or next year."

[5] The flurry of Democratic discussion on tax reduction followed unveiling of a Republican tax-cut plan by presidential candidate Ronald Reagan on June 25. His plan called for a 10% reduction in individual income tax rates in 1981 and accelerated tax write-offs for business on assets. Senate Republicans attempted to attach the Reagan plan to a bill extending some airway taxes June 30, but the Democrats banded together to rebuff the effort, 52 to 33. It was the second time within a week that the Republicans had forced the Democrats to vote against a tax reduction. On that day, White House Press Secretary Jody Powell insisted that the Administration had no plans to submit a tax-cut proposal to Congress this session. The President was "skeptical" of the possibility of getting "responsible action" on reducing taxes in the current congressional session, he said. But the Administration would be "talking and working with the Congress" on the subject, he said.

See also Books [9-11]; Budget [21]; Canada [45-46]; Elections [100-101]; Internal Revenue Service [1-5]

TELEVISION & RADIO

[1] **RKO General Loses 3 TV Licenses.** The Federal Communications Commission voted, 4-3, Jan. 24 not to renew the licenses of three television stations run by RKO General Inc., a subsidiary of General Tire and Rubber Co.

[2] The stations were WNAC-TV, an affiliate station of CBS Inc. in Boston, WOR-TV in New York City and KHJ-TV in Los Angeles. The latter two stations were independent. The FCC action stemmed from challenges to RKO General's WNAC license. The licenses of the other two stations were also under challenge, and the commission had linked those challenges to the outcome in the WNAC case.

[3] The commission lifted the licenses because of RKO General's relationship with its parent company. The Securities and Exchange Commission had tied General Tire to illegal foreign and domestic payoffs from 1971 to 1976.

[4] RKO General had repeatedly denied any complicity in the alleged actions of General Tire. However, the FCC noted that the two concerns operated under a unified management structure. The commission further accused the concerns of attempting to "pressure companies into placing advertising with RKO stations as a condition of doing business with General Tire." As a result, the FCC said it "could not be assured that RKO could be trusted in the future to operate [its stations] in a manner consistent with FCC standards."

[5] **Rather Succeeds Cronkite.** CBS news correspondent Dan Rather Feb. 15 was named to succeed Walter Cronkite in 1981 as anchorman and managing editor of the *CBS Evening News*. Rather, 48, a correspondent for the CBS-TV magazine program, *60 Minutes*, was reported to have signed a five-year contract valued at $8 million. Cronkite, 63, had been asking for almost two years to be relieved of the "day-to-day grind" to concentrate on hard news, special assignments and to work on a new occasional science series, *Universe*.

[6] **Cost of TV Advertising Soaring.** Rising costs were causing most television advertisers to either raise their budgets or shun prime-time programs, the *Wall Street Journal* said April 4.

[7] According to the *Journal*, TV advertising costs since 1975 had increased 75% for network time and 58% for spot time. A 30-second spot on a top-rated program cost about $116,000 in 1980 and was expected to cost about $342,000 by 1990.

Top 10 TV Advertisers in 1979

Company	Amount Spent (in millions)	Increase from 1978
1. Procter & Gamble Co.	$463.4	10%
2. General Foods Corp.	$291.3	18%
3. American Home Products	$165.1	10%
4. General Motors Corp.	$147.2	11%
5. General Mills Inc.	$141.7	5%
6. Bristol-Myers Co.	$140.6	10%
7. McDonald's Corp.	$137.8	20%
8. Ford Motor Co.	$127.9	15%
9. Pepsico Inc.	$119.2	29%
10. Lever Brothers Co.	$112.1	13%

Sources: Television Bureau of Advertising Inc., Broadcasting Advertisers Reports Inc.

[8] **Protected AM Radio Signals Limited.** The Federal Communications Commission May 29 voted to narrow the protection from signal interference enjoyed by the nation's 25 so-called "clear-channel" AM radio stations. The move paved the way for as many as 125 new AM stations in 37 U.S. cities.

[9] **Cable-TV News Network Debuts.** The nation's first all-news cable television network began broadcasting at 6 p.m. (EST) June 1. The Cable News Network, based in Atlanta, had been con-

ceived by Ted Turner, the controversial communications magnate and sports impresario.

[10] Turner, a critic of commercial network TV news, was reported to have spent $40 million on CNN. The operation had 300 employees in bureaus in nine cities, including London and Rome. CNN operated 24 hours a day. It was available to more than two million viewers through cable outlets in 30 states.

[11] ***Cable-TV Restrictions Lifted—*** The Federal Communications Commission July 22 made a significant move to deregulate the cable television industry. The commission voted, 4-3, to remove two major restrictions on cable-TV's access to programs carried by commercial broadcasters.

[12] One rule that was eliminated had prevented cable systems from electronically "importing" distant broadcasts, or those outside a cable system's designated market. The second, and more controversial, rule abolished had kept cable systems from showing syndicated programs that were being broadcast by a local commercial TV station in the same area. Both regulations had been adopted by the FCC in 1972 to prevent cable encroachment on broadcast television, particularly local independent or network-affiliated stations.

[13] **Emmy Awards.** The 32nd annual Emmy Awards were presented Sept. 7 by the Academy of Television Arts and Sciences in Los Angeles.

[14] Many Emmy winners boycotted the awards presentation because of an actors' strike against film studios and television networks. Members of the Screen Actors Guild and the American Federation of Television and Radio Artists had been on strike since July 21.

[15] The winner for the 1979-80 season were:

Dramatic series: actor–Ed Asner, in *Lou Grant;* **Actress**–Barbara Bel Geddes in *Dallas;* **Supporting Actor**–Stuart Margolin, in *The Rockford Files;* **Supporting actress**–Nancy Marchand, in *Lou Grant;* **Best series**–*Lou Grant;* **Directing**–Roger Grant for *Lou Grant;* **Writing**–Seth Freeman for *Lou Grant.*

Comedy series: actor– Richard Mulligan, in *Soap;* **Actress**–Cathryn Damon, in *Soap;* **Supporting actor**–Harry Morgan, in *M*A*S*H;* **Supporting actress**–Loretta Swit, in *M*A*S*H;* **Best series**–*Taxi;* **Directing**–James Burrows, for *Taxi;* **Writing**–Bob Colleary, for *Barney Miller.*

Limited series or special: actor–Powers Boothe, in *Guyana Tragedy: The story of Jim Jones;* **Actress**–Patty Duke Astin, in *The Miracle Worker;* **Supporting actor**–George Grizzard, in *The Oldest Living Graduate;* **Supporting actress**–Mare Winningham, in *Amber Waves;* **Directing**–Marvin Chomsky, for *Attica;* **Writing**–David Chase, for *Off the Minnesota Strip;* **Best series**–*Edward and Mrs. Simpson.*

Best drama special–*The Mircle Worker.*

Best information program–*The Body Human: the Magic Sense.*

Variety or Music Program–*Baryshnikov on Broadway.*

Classical Program in the Performing Arts–*Live From Studio 8H: A Tribute to Toscanini.*

[16] **FCC Backs Vast TV Station Expansion.** The Federal Communications Commission, in separate actions Sept. 9 and Sept. 18, proposed sweeping rule changes that would allow the creation of a large number of new television stations.

[17] On Sept. 9, the commission voted, 7-0, to approve tentatively the establishment of new TV stations on the UHF (ultra-high frequency) band through the use of so-called "translators," or low-cost, low-power transmitters.

[18] On Sept. 18, the commission voted, 4-3, to approve tentatively the addition of up to 140 new TV stations in the top 100 markets of the VHF (very high frequency) band by allowing the newcomers to broadcast in areas previously allotted to existing stations. The proposals were subject to a period of public comment and amendment. Final action on either was not expected until 1981.

[19] **Westinghouse to Acquire Teleprompter.** Westinghouse Electric Corp. Oct. 15 announced that it had reached agreement to acquire Teleprompter Corp., the nation's largest cable television company. Teleprompter's cable-TV systems had 1.3 million subscribers in 32 states. In addition, the company also operated Muzak, the pre-recorded music supplier.

[20] **'Dallas' Episode Sets Viewing Mark.** An episode of the CBS television

series *Dallas,* aired Nov. 21, was viewed by more people in the U.S. than any other TV program in history.

[21] According to A. C. Nielsen Co. Nov. 25 the program achieved a rating of 53.3 and a 76% share. That meant that well over half of the nation's households with televisions were tuned to the show and that during its time-slot (10-11 p.m. Eastern standard time) more than three-quarter of the viewing audience watched the program. A total of 83 million people saw the episode.

[22] The record setting *Dallas* episode answered the question "Who shot J.R.?" It was J.R.'s sister-in-law and former mistress, Kristin Shephard, played by actress Mary Crosby.

See also Great Britain [7-9]; Labor [27-30]

TENNIS

[1] **Borg, Goolagong Win Wimbledon.** Bjorn Borg of Sweden defeated John McEnroe of the U.S. July 6 for his fifth consecutive men's singles title at the All England lawn tennis championships at Wimbledon. On July 4, Australia's Evonne Goolagong had downed Chris Evert Lloyd in the women's singles final. Borg was the first man to win five straight Wimbledon titles since Britain's Lawrie Doherty accomplished the feat from 1902 to 1906.

[2] The final between Borg and McEnroe was regarded by many observers as the best singles match ever played at Wimbledon. Borg took 3 hours 53 minutes to win the contest, with McEnroe fighting him every minute of the way. Borg lost the first set, 1-6, but came back to take the next two, 7-5 and 6-3. McEnroe's finest moments came in a 22-minute, 34-point tie-breaker in the fourth set. The New Yorker saved five match points to win, 18-16, and take the set, 7-6. Borg rebounded to grab the fifth set, 8-6, and with it, the match. In the record 55th game, he hit a backhand crosscourt past McEnroe for the victory.

[3] Goolagong beat Evert Lloyd in 1 hour 33 minutes with a dazzling variety of shots–lobs, smashes, backhands, slices. The Australian took the first set, 6-1, and second set, 7-6, on a 7-4 tie breaker. This was the first Wimbledon title ever decided on a tie-breaker.

[4] ***Borg, Lloyd Capture French Open***—Sweden's Bjorn Borg June 8 became the first man ever to win the French Open singles title three years in a row and five times in a career. Borg accomplished the feat with a victory over Vitas Gerulaitis of the U.S. in the Paris tournament, 6-4, 6-1, 6-2.

[5] On June 7, Chris Evert Lloyd defeated Rumania's Virginia Ruzici in the final of the women's singles event, 6-0, 6-3.

[6] ***McEnroe, Lloyd Win U.S. Open***—John McEnroe beat Bjorn Borg in five sets Sept. 7 to win his second consecutive United States Open singles title, and Chris Evert Lloyd defeated Hana Mandlikova Sept. 6 for her fifth women's singles crown. The U.S. Open was played in Flushing Meadow, New York.

[7] Like Wimbledon, the U.S. Open men's finals saw the sport's top two players battle for over four hours until McEnroe finally won in the 55th game, the same number of total games played at Wimbledon. The final score was 7-6, 6-1, 6-7, 5-7, 6-4.

[8] In the women's final, 25-year-old Evert Lloyd demonstrated more patience and skill than her teen-aged opponent from Czechoslovakia. Mandlikova beat Evert Lloyd in the first set, 7-5. But Evert Lloyd controlled the tempo in the second and third sets, winning both by identical 6-1 scores.

[9] **Vilas, Jordan Win Australian Open.** Guillermo Vilas of Argentina won his second consecutive Australian Open men's singles title Jan. 2, when he defeated John Sadri of the U.S., 7-6, 6-3, 6-2. Barbara Jordan had downed fellow American Sharon Walsh, 6-3, 6-3, Jan. 1 in the women's singles final.

The tournament was held in Melbourne.

[10] **Czechs Win Davis Cup.** Czechoslovakia Dec. 7 became the first Eastern European country to win the Davis Cup with a 4-1 victory over Italy. The Cup finals were held in Prague Dec. 5-7.

TERRITORIAL Waters—*See* Mexico [6-8]

TERRITORIES (U.S.)

[1] **3 Pacific Islands Sign Self-Rule Pacts.** Officials of the Pacific island groups of the Marshall Islands and the Federated States of Micronesia Oct. 31 initialed agreements providing for future self-government. On Nov. 17, the Republic of Palau signed a similar agreement.

[2] The three island groups, together with the Northern Mariana Islands, which had voted to become a U.S. Commonwealth in 1978 but lost the status in March, made up the Trust Territory of the Pacific Islands, also called Micronesia, which had been administered by the U.S. for the United Nations since 1947.

[3] Under the agreement, the four states would be independent of one another, and would manage their internal and foreign affairs separately. The U.S. would only take responsibility for the defense and security of the area and would be responsible for determining what constituted a threat to the security of the islands. In return for military concessions granting the U.S. the right to construct military bases in strategic areas, the U.S. would provide an economic support program worth about $100 million for the 120,000 islanders for an initial period of 15 years.

TERRORISTS

[1] **11 FALN Suspects Seized.** Eleven suspected members of the Armed Forces of National Liberation (FALN), the nationalist Puerto Rican terrorist organization responsible for 11 bombings in the U.S. since 1974, were apprehended April 4 in Evanston, Ill. by agents of the Federal Bureau of Investigation.

[2] Among those arrested was Carlos Torres, whose name had gone to the top of the FBI's list of 10 most-wanted fugitives because of his alleged part in several bombings, including the 1975 bombing of Fraunces Tavern in New York City. In that blast, four persons were killed and 53 injured. The arrests were made when police received a tip that a "suspicious looking" group of joggers was making repeated visits to a parked van. Law enforcement agents went to the scene where they arrested nine persons inside the van. Two others were apprehended later.

[3] Eight of those arrested were convicted July 30 in Chicago of conspiracy to commit armed robbery and illegal possession of weapons. They were Torres, Adolfo Matos, Elixzan Escobar, Freddie Mendez, Carmen Valentine, Dickie Jimenez, Ida Luz Rodriguez and Dylcia Noemi Pagan. Two others, Alycia Rodriguez and Luis Rosa, had been convicted of robbery and were sentenced Aug. 4 to 30 years in prison. The 11th suspect, Marie Hayde Torres, had been extradited to New York and convicted of a fatal bombing. She was currently serving a life sentence.

See also France [28-42]; Germany, West [13-16]; Great Britain [53-57]; Guatemala [1-5, 12]; Ireland, Northern [13-15]; Italy [32-49]; Middle East [58-59, 65-67]; Spain [11-18]

THAILAND

[1] **Vietnamese Troops Attack.** Vietnamese forces in Cambodia June 23 crossed the border into Thailand and clashed with Thai troops. More than 30 Thai soldiers were reported killed and another 100 wounded, according to

Bangkok. Fighting continued the following day.

[2] An unspecified number of Cambodian refugees and Thai civilians were killed and refugee centers were set afire in the initial attack which occurred around the village of Non Mak Mun. Two other Thai villages were shelled. Hanoi said the attack was provoked by Thailand's support of guerrillas of Cambodia's ousted Pol Pot government operating along the Thai-Cambodian border.

[3] **U.S. Orders Weapons Airlift.** President Carter July 1 ordered an airlift of weapons to Thailand following incursions into that country by Vietnamese forces.

[4] Carter made the decision in response to a June 25 request from the Thai government. State Department officials July 1 listed the equipment for immediate shipment to Thailand, including 1,000 M-16 rifles, 38 106-millimeter recoilless rifles, 18 105-millimeter howitzers and "significant amounts" of ammunition. The equipment was estimated to be worth $3 million, and the transportation effort cost an additional $1 million.

[5] **Waldheim in Peace Mission.** United Nations Secretary General Kurt Waldheim met with Thai and Vietnamese officials in Hanoi and Bangkok Aug. 2-5 in an effort to reduce tensions along the Thai-Cambodian border. Waldheim was said to have made no progress in bridging Thai-Vietnamese differences stemming from Vietnam's invasion of Cambodia and Vietnamese incursions into Thailand in June.

[6] In the discussions, the Vietnamese proposed establishment of a demilitarized zone on both sides of the Thai-Cambodian border under international control and a halt to the flow of international relief assistance from the Thai side to forces of former Cambodian Premier Pol Pot and other combatants fighting the Vietnamese in Cambodia.

[7] Waldheim was told by Bangkok officials that any plan that required the pullback of Thai troops from the frontier would be an infringement of Thai sovereignty. The Thais also said that their basic disagreement with Vietnam was related to its refusal to accept a United Nations General Assembly resolution of Nov. 14, 1979 calling for the withdrawal of the 200,000 Vietnamese troops in Cambodia.

[8] The Thais instead proposed the formation of U.N.-supervised demilitarized zones inside Cambodia to assure the safety and feeding of Cambodian refugees now astride both sides of the frontier. The Vietnamese leaders rejected the Thai proposal and reiterated their belief to Waldheim that the Thais were actively supporting the Pol Pot forces.

See also Cambodia [3, 8-9, 11]

THATCHER, Margaret—*See* European Community [1]; Great Britain [25, 39, 41]; Ireland, Northern [22-23]

THEATER

[1] **Tony Awards.** The League of New York Theaters and Producers presented the 34th annual Antoinette Perry (Tony) Awards June 8 in New York.

[2] *Evita*, about Argentina's Eva Peron, was named best musical of the 1979-80 theater season. In addition, the show won six other awards in the category of musicals. Patti LuPone received the best actress award for her title role in the show. Harold Prince won the award for best direction. Tim Rice received the award for best book, Andrew Lloyd Weber won for best score, Mandy Pitinkin won for best performance by a featured actor and David Hersey won for best lighting designer.

[3] A drama, *Children of a Lesser God*, a play about the relationship of a deaf woman and her teacher, was named best play. In addition, the play won

two other Tony awards. John Rubinstein won the best actor award, Phyllis Frelich won the best actress award.
[4] Other Tony recipients were:

Best actor in a musical: Jim Dale, *Barnum;* **Best featured actor in a play:** David Rounds, *Morning's at Seven;* **Best featured actress in a play:** Dinah Manoff, *I Ought to Be in Pictures;* **Best featured actress in a musical:** Priscilla Lopez, *A Day in Hollywood/A Night in the Ukraine;* **Best director of a play:** Vivian Matalon, *Morning's at Seven;* **Best scenic designer:** John Lee Beatty, *Talley's Folly,* tied with David Mitchell, *Barnum;* **Best costume designer:** Theoni V. Aldredge, *Barnum;* **Best choreographer:** Tommy Tune and Thommie Walsh, *A Day in Hollywood/A Night in the Ukraine;* **Best revival of a play or musical:** *Morning's at Seven.*

[5] Special awards were given to the Actors Theater of Louisville (Ky.) and the Goodspeed Opera House, of East Haddam, Conn. The Lawrence Langner Award for Distinguished Lifetime Achievement was given to Helen Hayes. Theater Award '80 went to Hobe Morrison, *Variety* magazine's theater editor, and to Richard Fitzgerald of Sound Associations. Mary Tyler Moore, in appreciation of her Broadway debut, in *Whose Life Is It Anyway?* received a special Tony award for the appearance in live theater of a major television star.

TRACK & FIELD

[1] **National Indoor Championships.** The U.S. national indoor track and field championships were held Feb. 29 through March 1 at Madison Square Garden in New York City. The meet had formerly been the Amateur Athletic Union indoor championships, but was now sponsored by the Athletics Congress.
[2] Rosalyn Bryant Feb. 29 set an electronically timed world record in the 440-yard dash, with a 54.31 seconds performance in a qualifying heat.
[3] Merlene Ottey of the University of Nebraska also set a world mark Feb. 29. She sprinted through the 220-yard dash in an electronically timed 23.69, breaking the record set by Chandra Cheeseborough at the AAU indoor championships in 1979.
[4] The Los Angeles Naturite's team flashed through the 640-yard relay in 1:10.7 for another world record Feb. 29. The team members were Jeanette Bolden, Alice Brown, Jodi Anderson and Jackie Washington.
[5] The Philadelphia Pioneers sprint medley relay team (Tony Darden, Steve Riddick, Herman Frazier and Bill Collins) set a world mark in that event Feb. 29, with a time of 2:01.
[6] ***National Outdoor Championships***—The U.S. national outdoor track and field championships were held at Walnut, Calif. June 13-16. They also were sponsored by the Athletics Congress.
[7] Maren Sidler, a shot-putter, June 14 equaled a record for most career victories in one event in the national championships by winning the women's shot put for the 11th time. Her winning throw was 59 feet 1 inch, more than three feet short of the American record.
[8] Madeline Manning, 32, won her fifth national outdoor title June 15 in the women's 800-yard run. Manning turned in a time of 1 minute 58.75 seconds, about eight-tenths of a second off her own American record, set in 1976.
[9] **Rodgers Wins Boston Marathon.** Bill Rodgers won his third straight Boston Marathon April 21. It was the fourth victory overall in the event for the 32-year-old Boston-area native. Rodgers' time for the 26 mile, 385 yard race was 2 hours, 12 minutes and 11 seconds. He set the event record of 2:09.27 in 1979.
[10] ***Ruiz Victory Ruled Invalid***—Rosie Ruiz of New York was the apparent women's winner of the Boston Marathon with a time of 2:31.56. But, marathon officials April 29 invalidated her victory and awarded the race to Jacqueline Garreau of Canada, who had crossed the finish line second in 2:34.26. Ruiz's victory was disputed almost as soon as the race was concluded. Many race officials and runners claimed she could not have run the race. Few spectators and no runners said they actually saw her during the course of the race.
[11] Her earlier win in the October 1979 New York City Marathon, was invalidated April 25. New York officials reviewed evidence from the 1979 race after the Boston controversy broke out. Their decision was based on

videotape pictures of the race (which did not show Ruiz), reports from officials and other runners, and the account of a woman who said she had ridden to the finish line with Ruiz on the subway.

[12] **Ovett Breaks 1,500-Meter Mark.** Great Britain's Steve Ovett Aug. 27 set a world record in the 1,500-meter run at a track meet in Koblenz, West Germany.

[13] Ovett ran the race in 3 minutes 31.4 seconds. It was seven-tenths of a second under the previous mark held jointly by Ovett and fellow Briton Sebastian Coe.

TRADE & TARIFFS

[1] **'79 Trade Deficit Down.** The U.S. deficit on merchandise trade fell in 1979 by $3.7 billion to $24.7 billion, according to the Commerce Department Jan. 29. Imports rose 20%, to a record $206.3 billion. Exports were up 27%, to $181.6 billion. The U.S. paid a record $56.7 billion for petroleum in 1979, up 44% from $39.5 billion in 1978. The price of crude oil averaged $18.72 a barrel, compared with the 1978 average of $13.30 a barrel. But oil imports in 1979 were 150 million barrels fewer than the 3.18 billion barrels imported in 1977. President Carter had pledged that the U.S. would never again use more foreign oil than it did in 1977.

[2] ***Trade Gap Wider***—The U.S. deficit in its balance of merchandise trade account totaled a seasonally adjusted $1.86 billion in October, according to the Commerce Department Nov. 28. The monthly trade gap raised the cumulative deficit for the first 10 months of 1980 to $28.01 billion. The February deficit of $5.57 billion was the largest monthly trade deficit in U.S. history. During the same 10-month period of 1979, the U.S. trade deficit had been $20.07 billion.

[3] **Soviet Bloc Debt Increases.** The Soviet bloc grew more indebted to the West during 1979, according to an annual report released April 1 by the United Nations Economic Commission in Europe. The total deficit on current account was estimated at $57 billion, up $6 billion from a revised 1978 total of $51 billion.

[4] The Soviet bloc's debt was offset partially by a decline in its trade deficit with the West to $3.8 billion from $6.6 billion in 1978. This was achieved because exports from the U.S.S.R. and Eastern Europe, mostly raw materials, rose 23% in value in 1979. Imports from the West grew by only half that amount, the U.N. commission said.

[5] In an effort to limit the growth of its debt, the Soviet bloc began to increase its use of barter deals. Also called compensation agreements, the deals involved an exchange of technology for goods. For example, a Western European country would agree to construct a plant in an Eastern European country in exchange for a certain percentage of the plant's output once it was finished.

See also China [24, 39-40]; Coffee; El Salvador [7]; Germany, East [1]; Iran [17-20, 74-76]; Japan [1-2]; Union of Soviet Socialist Republics [14-19]

TRUCKING

[1] **Truck-Decontrol Bill Cleared.** Congress cleared a bill that substantially deregulated the trucking industry. The House passed the complex legislation June 19 by a 367-13 vote. The Senate approved the House version June 20 by a voice vote. President Carter signed the bill July 1.

[2] Like the airline and banking deregulation bills already enacted, the trucking bill was designed to introduce more competition into a sector of the economy that had been heavily regulated by the Interstate Commerce Commission. The legislation would make the entry of new companies into trucking easier, and would remove and ease regulations that restricted service. Further, the bill gave trucking

companies more freedom to raise or lower rates (10% a year without ICC approval and 5% more annually if the ICC didn't object), and gradually ended the antitrust immunity that trucking companies had in setting rates.

TRUDEAU, Pierre Elliot—*See* Canada [1-2, 5-6, 8-7, 19, 21-22, 40-41]

TUNISIA—*See* United Nations [4]

TURKEY

[1] The Turkish government, beset by economic difficulties and terrorist violence, was overthrown by the armed forces in 1980. A military council took control of the country; thousands of persons were arrested; parliament was dissolved and the constitution suspended.

[2] **Military Issues Warning.** The top leaders of the armed forces sent a letter to Turkey's President, Fahri Koruturk, Jan. 2 in which they criticized the political parties for failing to deal with Turkey's severe economic problems and its widespread political violence.

[3] The letter called upon the political parties to abandon their "sterile arguments" and unite in order to deal with Turkey's internal unrest and the dangers posed by recent external developments. The military leaders said that "the developments in the region are such that they could turn into a war in the Middle East. The anarchists and the separatists are making a rehearsal for a general uprising all over the country."

[4] Koruturk gave copies of the letter to Premier Suleyman Demirel and to Bulent Ecevit, head of th chief opposition party, the Republican People's Party. The letter was later broadcast on radio and television.

[5] The letter, which was signed by Gen. Kenan Evren, chief of the general staff, and by the heads of the separate armed services, raised concern about the possibility of a military takeover. However, sources close to the generals cited in the *New York Times* Jan. 3 said they did not believe a military coup was imminent. They noted that the military leaders had described their message as a "warning," not as an ultimatum.

[6] **Armed Forces Overthrow Government.** The armed forces took control of the country Sept. 12 in an apparently bloodless coup.

[7] Gen. Kenan Evren, chief of staff of the Turkish military, announced the coup and said that the parliament was being dissolved. The privileges of members of parliament were being revoked and the Constitution suspended, Evren said. In Washington, a U.S. State Department spokesman said, "We understand from our embassy there that there was no violence and no danger to Americans."

In Istanbul, soldier guards bridge entrance Sept. 14, two days after military coup.

[8] The coup followed a number of warnings by the military that the political parties in the country were failing to deal with Turkey's economic problems and extensive political unrest. Political violence had reportedly cost 1,800 lives so far in 1980, and had seriously fragmented the country, as left-wing and right-wing extremists took control of city neighborhoods and villages. The violence had accelerated in recent weeks: for August, the death toll was thought to be 400, and some 220 persons died from political conflicts in the first 11 days of September.

[9] Ousted Premier Suleyman Demirel had been hamstrung in his effort to deal with the country's problems by a lack of a parliamentary majority. Demirel, leader of the Justice Party, had been forced to rely upon the uncertain cooperation of a smaller pro-Islamic party to stay in power.

[10] A State Department statement Sept. 12 said that the U.S. "must be concerned about the seizure of power from any democratically elected government," but went on to "note that in taking power the Turkish military have stated that they do so to restore a functioning democratic government." U.S. aid to Turkey would continue, the statement said.

[11] **Junta Sworn In.** Members of a six-man military junta headed by Gen. Kenan Evren, swore themselves in as the country's rulers Sept. 18, reaffirming their commitment to human rights and democratic principles.

[12] The junta had apparently not experienced any major difficulties in consolidating its power. Immediately upon taking power the military rulers rounded up about 100 members of parliament, including leaders of three major parties: Justice Party leader Suleyman Demirel (the ousted premier), Republican People's Party head Bulent Ecevit (a former premier), and National Salvation Party leader Necmettin Erbakan.

[13] Alpaslan Turkes, leaders of the far-right Nationalist Action Party, surrendered to the military authorities Sept. 14 after evading the initial round-up. The Nationalist Action Party was believed to be behind much of Turkey's widespread political violence.

[14] In a television and radio broadcast Sept. 12 explaining why the coup had been launched, Evren said the military had acted because "the state with its main organs was totally immobilized." Political violence, Evren said, had cost more than 5,000 lives, not the 1,700 that was reported by the Demirel government. The economy was also in dire trouble, despite emergency efforts. Partisan politics, he maintained, had absorbed the attention of the politicians, preventing serious efforts to solve Turkey's problems.

[15] The junta Sept. 20 appointed retired Admiral Bulent Ulusu, as premier. Ulusu Sept. 21 announced the formation of a 27-member Cabinet that included seven retired officers in addition to himself.

[16] The junta Sept. 21 announced a number of changes in the martial law code, in particular tightening censorship rules. The decree stated that people who "intentionally propagate erroneous, unfounded or exaggerated information in a manner to create alarm or excitement among the public" would be subject to jail terms of six months to two years. If an offense were committed in collusion with a foreigner the jail sentence would be a minimum of one year; if it involved the media the penalty would be doubled. The decree also tightened control over union and labor activities, and stipulated that prison sentences of up to three years would not be subject to appeal. It set a limit of 30 days to the period of detention before arrest.

[17] Suleyman Demirel and Bulent Ecevit were freed by the military authorities Oct. 11. Some 60 other legislators also were released. The military rulers still held an estimated 20,000 persons under arrest, most of them reportedly belonging to groups of the extreme right and left. Among

those under detention were legislators, union heads and student leaders.

[18] Turkey's ruling military junta affirmed its powers Oct. 27 by approving a new law that in effect superseded the country's constitution. It stipulated that "any statements, decisions and laws of the National Security Council [the ruling junta] that do not conform to the 1961 constitution will be regarded as constitutional changes and those that do not conform to the laws in force will be considered legal changes." The head of the council, Gen. Evren, would exercise the powers of the presidency, the new law said.

Other Developments

[19] **U.S. Bases, Aid Accord.** An agreement allowing the U.S. continued use of 12 military bases in Turkey in exchange for economic and military aid was signed March 29 in Ankara by U.S. Ambassador to Turkey James W. Spain and Turkish Foreign Minister Hayrettin Erkmen.

[20] Erkmen told reporters after signing that there was "no fixed figure" for the amount of American aid. "The important thing," he continued, "is the equipment and arms that they would provide."

[21] The 12 installations covered by the accord were an air base, four intelligence-gathering facilities and seven communications bases. Two of the intelligence bases were located on the Black Sea and considered of prime importance for keeping track of Soviet troop movements and atomic tests. The air base, at Incirlik on the Mediterranean, was also seen as a key part of the U.S.'s system of bases.

[22] A statement by the Turkish Foreign Ministry said that the agreement provided for U.S. use of the bases "only within the NATO [North Atlantic Treaty Organization] framework." This language was included to prevent the U.S. from using the facilities in support of operations against any countries in the Middle East, such as Iran.

[23] A supplementary accord also announced March 29 covered military-industrial cooperation. The projects that would get U.S. support were not officially announced, but they reportedly included construction of a frigate, an ammunition factory and a plant to make antiaircraft artillery.

[24] **IMF OKs $1.6 Billion Loan.** The International Monetary Fund granted a $1.6 billion, three-year loan to Turkey June 18. It was the larget loan ever approved by the IMF.

[25] The loan was part of a broad international aid effort to rescue Turkey's struggling economy, and was conditional upon Turkey's acceptance of various austerity measures and proposals to reduce government regulation of its economy.

See also Cyprus

U

UGANDA

[1] **Army Group Seizes Power.** President Godfrey Binaisa was eased out of power May 11 as soldiers loyal to Chief of Staff Brig. Gen. David Oyite Ojok seized control of the radio station and post office in Kampala. The takeover was apparently completed by May 14, although Binaisa continued to insist that he ruled Uganda.

[2] Binaisa was held incommunicado at his official residence in Entebbe, 20 miles (35 kilometers) from Kampala but issued statements through a spokesman. Meanwhile, a six-member Military Commission led by Labor Minister Paulo Muwanga, a civilian, criticized the deposed president for corruption and incompetence.

[3] (Binaisa had dismissed Muwanga from the Cabinet in February, but Tanzania had persuaded him to bring Muwanga back as labor minister. Tanzania which had helped to overthrow Idi Amin in 1979 still had 10,000 troops in Uganda.)

[4] The coup was triggered by Binaisa's dismissal of Ojok May 10 from the National Consultative Council, the country's interim ruling body. Ojok refused to accept his dismissal, and soldiers launched the coup the next day. Ojok was considered a close associate of ousted President Milton Obote, who lived in exile in Tanzania. Obote was deposed by Amin in 1971.

[5] **Obote Returns.** Former President Obote returned to Uganda May 27 from Tanzania. His remarks upon arriving appeared to mark the beginning of his campaign to regain the presidency.

[6] Obote flew from the Tanzanian capital of Dar es Salaam in a Tanzanian air force plane and landed first in the southwestern town of Mbarara. He addressed a political rally attended by 10,000 people, where he was greeted by former political associates and friends, including Paulo Muwanga, chairman of the military commission that overthrew President Binaisa.

[7] Obote's return came at a time of mounting violence, which the post-Amin governments had been unable to curb. Moreover, famine in northern Uganda was reportedly causing the deaths of hundreds of persons each week.

[8] ***Amin Wants to Return***—Former President Idi Amin said, in a British television interview broadcast June 3, he wanted to return to Uganda. Amin was interviewed by BBC reporter Brian Barron in an unspecified Middle East country, where he reportedly lived with 2 wives and 24 children who accompanied him when he fled Uganda.

[9] **Obote Party Ousts Cabinet Rivals.** The Uganda People's Congress, led by former President Obote, Sept. 17 took full control of the country's political institutions when Cabinet members outside the party were ordered to resign or be dismissed.

[10] Paulo Muwanga, chairman of the governing military commission, made public the order expelling all non-UPC members. Supporters of rival political parties then boycotted the sessions of the interim parliament, the National Consultative Council.

[11] **Amin Forces Invade, Are Routed.** Forces loyal to deposed dictator Idi Amin had invaded Uganda from the neighboring countries of Zaire and Sudan, Obote said Oct. 7.
[12] Government officials did not confirm Obote's assertions until Oct. 10. Foreign Minister Erifasi Otema Alimadi said the raiders had invaded the West Nile region of the country, taking control of the city of Arua. He did not identify the invaders, who he said had destroyed a unit of government troops near Koboko before seizing contol of that town. Koboko was Amin's home town.
[13] Troops reportedly loyal to Amin had been put to flight, it was reported Oct. 15. Government troops previously driven back by the invaders had retaken areas around Koboko and Arua with the support of Tanzanian soldiers. Ugandan officials charged that the Saudi Arabian government had financed the expedition. Saudi Arabia denied the charge.
[14] **Election Outcome Uncertain.** The Democratic Party, headed by Paul Ssemogerere, apparently won an upset victory in national parliamentary elections Dec. 10 and 11, but it was not clear whether the party would be permitted to take power.
[15] Paulo Muwanga, the chairman of the six-member Military Commission that ruled Uganda, issued an order Dec. 11 banning publication of the election results and stating that Muwanga, not the electoral commission, would decide whether the elections were fair and whether the winners were entitled to a place in the 126-seat parliament. Muwanga, together with a majority of the Military Commission, had supported former President Obote at the polls.

UNEMPLOYMENT (U.S.)

[1] **Jobless Rate Up.** The nation's unemployment rate rose from 5.9% in December 1979, representing 6.1 million jobless workers, to 7.5% the following November, representing a total of 7.9 million unemployed, the Labor Department reported. There was a total labor pool of about 104 million persons.
[2] The jobless rate increased from 6.2% in January to a high of 7.8% in July and then declined slightly.
[3] In November, the unemployment rate for adult males dropped to 6.3% from 6.4% in October; for adult women the rate fell to 6.7% from 6.8%; for teenagers the rate increased to 18.7% from 18.4% in October; for blacks the rate dropped to 14% from 14.3%, and for Hispanics the rate declined to 10.1% from 10.9%.
See also Black Americans [4]; Great Britain [15-6]

UNION OF SOVIET SOCIALIST REPUBLICS (U.S.S.R.)

Government & Politics

[1] **Premier Kosygin Resigns.** Premier Alexei N. Kosygin Oct. 23 resigned as head of the Soviet government on the grounds of ill health. He was succeeded by his first deputy, Nikolai A. Tikhonov, a 75-year-old economic planner from the Ukraine and long-time associate of Soviet President Leonid Brezhnev.
[2] Kosygin's resignation, the most significant leadership change in the Soviet Union in 16 years, was announced after three days of speeches before party and government officials telling them of the disappointing recent performance of the Soviet economy and the severe agricultural problems facing the nation.
[3] President Brezhnev Oct. 23 told the 1,500 delegates of the country's parliament, the Supreme Soviet, he had received a letter from the 76-year-old Kosygin asking to be relieved from his position because of bad health, "which has been worsening lately." Brezhnev also revealed Kosygin's request to be

relieved of his membership in the Politburo, the decision-making body of the Soviet Communist Party Central Committee.

[4] Kosygin, who rose to power with Brezhnev in 1964 when former Soviet leader Nikita Khruschev was ousted, had reportedly suffered a severe heart attack in 1979 and had been plagued by relapses. He had not been seen in public in two months. Kosygin was the first Soviet premier to completely resign from official life while still apparently in favor with his senior Communist Party colleagues. Vyacheslav Molotov had resigned as premier in 1941 but had remained foreign minister. The last voluntary resignation from the Politburo was Anastas Mikoyan's in 1965.

[5] Tikhonov, a metallurgical engineer associated with economic planning in the country's heavy industries, was thought to be personally loyal to Brezhnev. His early career had been spent in the Dniepropetrovsk area of the Ukraine, where many another of Brezhnev's senior aides had begun their political careers. Tikhonov had worked in factories and party posts in the Ukraine until 1955, when he went to Moscow as a deputy minister. In 1963 he became deputy chairman of the State Planning Commission. In 1965, soon after Brezhnev became party secretary, Tikhonov was named a deputy premier with responsibility for the Soviet steel industry. He was also made a member of the party Central Committee. When Kosygin had his first heart attack in 1976, Tikhonov was made first deputy premier, although he did not receive until 1978 Politburo membership, a traditional accompaniment to that post. He became a full member of the Politburo in 1979.

[6] Ivan Arkhipov Oct. 27 was named first deputy to Tikhonov. The 73-year-old Arkhipov, a native of the Russian Soviet Federated Socialist Republic, had been named a deputy premier in 1974. Prior to that he had been first deputy chairman of the State Committee for Foreign Economic Relations for 15 years.

[7] ***Agricultural Problems***—Brezhnev, addressing an Oct. 21 plenary session of the Communist Party Central Committee, enumerated the problems facing Soviet agriculture. He acknowledged that food shortages were reaching serious proportions and that 1980 had produced the second poor grain harvest in a row.

[8] The Soviet president did say that in some places agricultural productivity had recently increased. However, he pointed out that in certain areas where much time and many resources had been invested, "output actually had not grown over a number of years." He said that Soviet authorities still encountered difficulties in supplying many nonagricultural areas, such as cities and industrial centers, with foodstuffs such as meat and milk.

[9] Brezhnev also hinted at poor 1980 grain crop results. He did not provide an exact figure but alluded to a five-year average that indicated as much as a 30% shortfall from the year's target. The Soviet leader said that only two of the previous five years, 1976 and 1978, "can be regarded as relatively good for agriculture." But, adverse weather conditions were only partly to blame, according to Brezhnev. In addition, Soviet output and design of farm equipment were inadequate. The president announced that a separate department for farm machinery was being set up within the central party committee.

[10] The leadership's concern with the poor state of the country's agriculture was reflected in the Oct. 21 election of a 49-year-old agricultural specialist, Mikhail Gorbachov, to full membership in the Politburo. Gorbachov became the youngest member of the party's decision-making body.

[11] **Kosygin Dies.** Former Premier Kosygin, 76, who resigned earlier in the year because of ill health, had died, it was reported Dec. 19.

[12] The Soviet leadership did not issue immediate official confirmation of

Kosygin's death, which was first disclosed by dilopmatic and unofficial Soviet sources. Observers in Moscow said that Soviet President Leonid Brezhnev celebrated his 74th birthday the same day and that officials feared divulging the information would mar any celebration.

[13] The government announced Kosygin's death Dec. 21, two days after he had died.

Economy

[14] **Economy Lagged in 1979.** The Soviet report of its 1979 economic performance, published Jan. 25, revealed that 1979 was one of the worst years for the country since World War II. The economy had failed to reach its targets in almost every critical sector.

[15] National income, the closest measure of Soviet gross national product, had risen by 2%. Soviet economic planners had called for a 4.3% growth rate. Overall industrial production grew by 3.4% instead of 5.7% as planned. In individual sectors, the growth rates were (planned rates in parentheses):

■ Heavy industry [machinery, steel, chemicals and similar products]–3.5% (5.8%)

■ Consumer goods–3.3% (4.6%)

■ Industrial labor productivity–2.4% (4.7%)

■ Steel production fell below the 1978 level to 149 million metric tons, from 151 million metric tons in 1978.

■ Oil production increased 2.4% to 586 million metric tons (11.7 million barrels a day) instead of the planned 593 million metric tons. (A metric ton is 2,204.6 pounds, or approximately 6.6 barrels of oil.)

[16] Other products that failed to fulfill the plan were: machine tools, cement, fertilizer, ferrous metals, meat and milk. Labor productivity in agriculture was down 4% as a result of the country's poor grain harvest of 179 million metric tons. Housing construction also was down 4%. The average monthly wage increased by 2.2% to reach 163.50 rubles ($253.50 at the official exchange rate). The labor force was put at 110.6 million, and the total population at 264.5 million.

[17] **Trade with U.S.** Soviet trade with the U.S. in 1979 was even higher than in the record year of 1978, the U.S. Embassy in Moscow reported Feb. 20. According to the embassy's trade figures, total two-way trade in 1979 was $4.48 billion, more than 50% higher than in 1978.

[18] As usual, the U.S. exported more to the U.S.S.R. than it imported. The U.S. surplus in 1979 was $2.73 billion. Grain made up the bulk of the U.S. exports. Imports from the Soviet Union also went up, in large part because of the rise in the price of gold, which the Soviet Union exported to the U.S.

[19] The value of U.S.-Soviet trade for the first six months of 1980 had declined by 50% compared with the same period in 1979, the U.S. Commerce Department reported Aug. 20. The large drop reflected the impact of trade sanctions the U.S. had imposed on the Soviets after they invaded Afghanistan.

U.S. Relations

[20] **Biological Weapons Mishap Suspected.** Reports of an anthrax epidemic in the Ural Mountains city of Sverdlovsk in April 1979 prompted the U.S. to question the Soviet Union's adherence to the 1972 ban on biological weapons. The U.S. State Department said March 18 that it had asked the U.S.S.R. for an official explanation of what happened in Sverdlovsk.

[21] The Soviet Union March 20 admitted that there had been an outbreak of anthrax in Sverdlovsk, but said the epidemic was caused by tainted meat. (Anthrax, which affects cattle, could be transmitted to humans through the air or through infected meat.)

[22] The U.S. House Intelligence oversight subcommittee June 29 accused the Soviet Union of covering up the

real cause of the deaths of an estimated 40 to 1,000 persons in an anthrax epidemic. The committee said that the anthrax epidemic had been caused by an explosion at Military Compound 19, a facility in Sverdlovsk long suspected by U.S. intelligence of germ warfare activity. The explosion was said to have released lethal anthrax spores into the atmosphere. Subcommittee Chairman Les Aspin (D, Wis.) said that "all arms control conventions" were threatened by the Sverdlovsk cover-up.

[23] An article in a Soviet legal journal,*Man and the Law,* reported Sept. 25 that two persons had been tried and punished for selling anthrax-infected meat during a 1979 outbreak of the disease in the city of Sverdlovsk.

[24] **U.S. Cites Chemical Weapons Use.** The State Department Aug. 7 released a collection of reports that claimed internationally banned chemical weapons were being used by the Soviet Union or Soviet-backed governments.

[25] The 124-page survey offered evidence supporting allegations that chemical agents were used to combat opposition groups in Afghanistan and Laos. The survey claimed chemical weapons were used in Cambodia but had little substantial evidence to verify the charge. It indicated that the U.S. had received "fragmentary reports" that chemical warfare had been waged in Ethiopia.

[26] The survey said the U.S. regarded "as highly likely that the Soviet forces have used some form of chemical agent to suppress Afghan resistance." The U.S. based the allegations on reports from refugees.

[27] ***Soviet Poison Gas Use Disputed***—A State Department report claiming it was "highly likely" that the Soviet Union had employed chemical weapons against Afghan rebels was disputed by an unnamed U.S. official. An article in the *New Scientist* Aug. 21 cited an anonymous U.S. official as questioning the State Department report. The official said that in most of the accounts of alleged use of chemical weapons, the symptoms displayed by the victims were those characteristic of non-lethal chemicals, not of nerve gases.

[28] **U.S. Complains of Nuclear Violation.** The United States Sept. 15 complained to Soviet officials about an underground nuclear test conducted in the Soviet Union that the U.S. believed had exceeded limits laid down by a 1974 agreement.

[29] State Department officials said that on Sept. 14 the Soviet had carried out their largest underground test of nuclear device in recent years. Reports put the size of the weapon between 160 and 650 kilotons. (One kiloton was equivalent to 1,000 tons of TNT.) In 1974 the U.S. and the Soviets had signed the threshold test ban treaty, which prohibited underground tests of nuclear weapons with yields greater than 150 kilotons. Both countries announced in 1976 they would abide by the terms of the agreement although it had not been ratified by the U.S. Senate.

[30] **More Accurate ICBMs Said Deployed.** The International Institute for Strategic Studies Sept. 18 said the Soviets were deploying "significantly more accurate" intercontinental ballistic missiles that threatened the United States' land-based missile force.

[31] The London-based international study group said the deployment of the new Soviet missiles had increased the vulnerability of the fixed silo U.S. ICBMS, Minuteman and Titan. In its annual survey *The Military Balance 1980-81,* the IISS said the increased vulnerability of the U.S. missiles did not necessarily render U.S. deterrence to nuclear war less credible. However, the study's authors remarked that the improved accuracy of the Soviet ICBMS exacerbated the "unwelcome uncertainty" of the U.S.-Soviet nuclear balance. The IISS reported that more than half of the Soviet's ICBMS were less than 10 years old while the U.S. Minuteman II and Minuteman III

missiles, the bulk of the U.S. land-based force, were 10 and 15 years old, respectively.

[32] **Brezhnev Urges Resumed Talks.** Soviet President Leonid Brezhnev Oct. 14 called on the U.S. to resume bilateral arms negotiations "before it is too late."

[33] Brezhnev was quoted by U.S. businessman Armand Hammer, who had met for 90 minutes that day with the Soviet leader. The chairman of Occidental Petroleum Corp., in Moscow to press a fertilizer deal with the Soviets, said Brezhnev asserted the U.S.S.R. "will do everything to assure its security" and will not permit the U.S. to achieve military superiority.

Dissidents

[34] **Sakharov Seized & Expelled from Moscow.** Soviet authorities detained Nobel laureate Andrei Sakhorov Jan. 22 and sent him and his wife, Yelena Bonner, into internal exile in Gorky, an industrial city 250 miles (400 kilometers) east of Moscow. A decree from the Presidium of the Supreme Soviet, the country's figure head parliament, declared the 58-year-old scientist stripped of all his honors.

[35] Sakharov, a pioneer in the development of the Soviet Union's hydrogen bomb, was the country's most respected spokesman for human rights. On Jan. 2 he had called for international pressure to force a Soviet withdrawal from Afghanistan. He also had come out in support of boycotting the summer Olympic Games slated for Moscow.

[36] Western governments and organizations expressed shock over Sakharov's arrest. The U.S. Jan. 22 issued a statement saying: "All those who value freedom will deplore this official act of repression against a man who has struggled valiantly for human rights in the Soviet Union." Great Britain and the Netherlands declared their concern. Other protests were heard from Amnesty International, the French Socialist Party and the Italian Communist Party.

[37] (On the same day of Sakharov's exile, Tass announced the resignation "at his own request" of Vladimir Kirillin from his government posts. Kirillin was deputy chairman of the Council of Ministers and chairman of the State Committee for Science and Technology. He was believed to favor increased contact with the West and was thought to have defended Sakharov in the past.)

[38] The European Community delivered a joint protest Jan. 24 to Moscow. Western European Communist parties expressed varying degrees of disapproval over the Soviet action Jan. 22-24. The Italian Communist Party, generally the leader in criticizing Moscow, printed a strong denunciation Jan. 23 in its newspaper, *L'Unita.* The French and Spanish Communist parties issued milder expressions of protests Jan. 22 and 24, respectively.

[39] Within the Soviet Union, protests were heard from persons normally not identified with the dissident movement. Bella Akhmadulina, a noted poet, issued a protest verse Jan. 31 in Sakharov's defense. A statement issued Jan. 29 said Moscow's accusations of subversion against Sakharov were "a blasphemous lie." Signers of the statement included Vasily Aksyonov, one of the Soviet Union's leading contemporary authors.

[40] Sakharov remained a member of the Soviet Academy of Sciences, despite having been refused permission to attend its March 4-6 annual meeting. The possibility of his ouster from the group was not discussed by its 230 full members, according to a spokesman. The Academy of Sciences, founded in 1724, had a history of independence from political control over its membership.

[41] **Other Dissidents Held**—Sakharov Jan. 14 reported the arrest the week before of Vitaldas Skuodis, a Lithuanian nationalist in Vilnius, the capital

of the Lithuanian republic. Skuodis was one of a group of Lithuanians who had called for independence for the Baltic republics of Lithuania, Latvia and Estonia, Sakharov said.

[42] The arrest of Father Dmitri Dudko, a Russion Orthodox priest, was reported Jan. 15 by his wife. Dudko had been dismissed from his Moscow parish in 1974 for his outspoken sermons on political and social topics.

[43] A Soviet court June 13 sentenced Viktor Nekipelov, a member of the Moscow watch group that monitored Soviet compliance with the 1975 Helsinki accords on human rights, to seven years in a labor camp plus five additional years' internal exile.

[44] **Soviet Authors Emigrate.** Vladimir Voinovich and Vasily Aksyonov, two of the U.S.S.R.'s leading writers, announced in April that they had applied to emigrate. Both men had come under official pressure to leave the country, although neither wanted to go.

[45] Aksyonov was a favorite author among young people in the Soviet Union. He ran into trouble at the end of 1979 when he supported a group of authors who wanted to publish a collection of prohibited works. Voinovich was the author of two satirical books that were not published in the Soviet Union but were successful in the West.

[46] Aksyonov left the Soviet Union to live in the U.S. July 22. Voinovich left for Munich Dec. 21.

[47] **Amnesty Reports on U.S.S.R.** A report that charged the Soviet Union with having imprisoned more than 400 dissidents between 1975 and 1979 was issued April 29 by Amnesty International.

[48] The 200-page document was a comprehensive study of Soviet dissidence based on information from activists in the Soviet Union and published material. The London-based organization concluded that "abuses have continued" since its last report on the Soviet Union in 1975. At least 100 dissidents had been imprisoned in psychiatric hospitals, AI reported. The organization had received "much recent evidence of the abuse of psychiatry for political purposes."

[49] "There are many more prisoners of conscience than those of whom we know," the report added. "The real number is veiled by official censorship, secrecy and the threat of retaliation against those who speak out against political imprisonment."

[50] **Soviet Youth Gets Political Asylum.** A 12-year-old Ukrainian boy, Walter Polovchak, who was unwilling to return to the Soviet Union from the U.S. with his parents was granted political asylum by the U.S. Immigration and Naturalization Service July 21.

[51] Polovchak had fled his Chicago home July 19 when he heard that his parents wanted to return to the Soviet Union. The Polovchaks had emigrated with their three children in January, but were dissatisfied with American life.

Jewish Developments

[52] **'79 Jewish Emigration Sets Record.** The total number of Jews who left the Soviet Union reached 51,320 in 1979, according to figures reported Jan. 11 by the National Conference on Soviet Jewry, a U.S. organization. It was the largest number of Jews permitted to leave since Soviet emigration restrictions had been eased.

[53] **Soviet Jews Hold Science Conference.** More than 60 Soviet and foreign scientists crowded into a Moscow apartment April 13-15 for an unofficial scientific conference. The meeting, called the Fourth International Conference on Collective Phenomena, was organized by Soviet Jewish scientists who had lost their jobs for trying to emigrate.

[54] Twenty-four foreign scientists attended, the largest number since the first unofficial seminar was held in 1974. Four came from the U.S., nine

from France, five from Great Britain, three from Sweden, two from Norway and one from Mexico. The conference took place in the apartment of Viktor Brailovsky, a cybernetics expert and Jewish activist.

Other Developments

[55] **Philby Given Award.** Kim Philby, the double agent who had risen high in British intelligence in the 1940s before defecting to Moscow in 1963, was awarded a top Soviet honor, the newspaper *Izvestia* reported July 15.
[56] The article, reviewing Philby's autobiography, which had just been published in Russian, said that he had received the Order of People's Friendship for "more than 40 years of difficult but honorable work." Earlier he had been awarded the Order of the Red Banner and the Order of Lenin. Philby's autobiography, *My Secret War,* was published in Britain in 1968.
[57] Philby was the "third man," who in 1951 had warned two fellow agents, Guy Burgess and Donald Maclean, that they were about to be arrested. The two escaped safely to Moscow. The *Izvestia* article added that Philby, "as before, holds a battle post."
[58] **Thousands at Balladeer's Funeral.** Thousands of Moscow residents gathered at a city square July 28 to pay tribute to Vladimir Vysotsky, 46, a popular actor and underground balladeer who had died July 24 of a heart attack.
[59] The demonstration of spontaneous sentiment witnessed people climbing on top of buses, kiosks, and rooftops to view the theater where Vysotsky was being eulogized in an unannounced private service. The crowd was said to have numbered 10,000-30,000. When 20 mounted police arrived to disperse the demonstration, the crowd jeered at them. Many of Vysotsky's ballads, which were circulated privately because of their anti-government content, described life in the labor camps where he had spent part of his youth.

See also Afghanistan; Armaments (International) [1, 5]; Astronomy [3]; Australia [5]; Carter, Jimmy [1-5, 10-15]; China [26-40]; Defense (U.S.) [1-5, 7, 9-10, 24-25]; Disarmament [4-10]; Espionage [1, 3-10]; Germany, West [8-12]; Grain [1]; Helsinki Review Conference; Human Rights [1-5, 13]; Iran [25, 79]; Iraq [12]; Olympics; Poland [14-15, 25-26, 75-77]; Skating [3-4]; Space [16-18]; Syria [1-2]; Trade & Tariffs [3-5]; Yemen, People's Democratic Republic of [1-3]

UNITED NATIONS

[1] **U.N. Membership.** The 154 member states were:

Afghanistan
Albania
Algeria
Angola
Argentina
Australia
Austria
Bahamas
Bahrain
Bangladesh
Barbados
Belgium
Benin
Bhutan
Bolivia
Botswana
Brazil
Bulgaria
Burma
Burundi
Byelorussia
Cambodia
Cameroon
Canada
Cape Verde
Central African Empire
Chad
Chile
China
Colombia
Comoro Islands
Congo Republic
Costa Rica
Cuba
Cyprus
Czechoslovakia
Denmark
Djibouti
Dominica
Dominican Republic
Ecuador
Egypt
El Salvador
Equatorial Guinea
Ethiopia
Fiji
Finland
Liberia
Libya
Luxembourg
Malagasy Republic (Madagascar)
Malawi
Malaysia
Maldives
Mali
Malta
Mauritania
Mauritius
Mexico
Mongolia
Morocco
Mozambique
Nepal
Netherlands
New Zealand
Nicaragua
Niger
Nigeria
Norway
Oman
Pakistan
Panama
Papua New Guinea
Paraguay
Peru
Philippines
Poland
Portugal
Qatar
Rumania
Rwanda
St. Lucia
St. Vincent and Grenadines
Sao Tome e Principe
Saudi Arabia
Senegal
Seychelles
Sierra Leone
Singapore
Solomon Islands
Somali Republic (Somalia)

France
Gabon
Gambia
German Democratic Rep.
Germany, Federal Rep. of
Ghana
Greece
Grenada
Guatemala
Guinea
Guinea-Bissau
Guyana
Haiti
Honduras
Hungary
Iceland
India
Indonesia
Iran
Iraq
Ireland
Israel
Italy
Ivory Coast
Jamaica
Japan
Jordan
Kenya
Kuwait
Laos
Lebanon
Lesotho
South Africa
Spain
Sri Lanka
Sudan
Swaziland
Sweden
Syria
Tanzania
Thailand
Togo
Trinidad and Tobago
Tunisia
Turkey
Uganda
Ukraine
Union of Soviet Socialist Republics
United Arab Emirates
United Kingdom
United States
Upper Volta
Uruguay
Venezuela
Vietnam
Western Samoa
Yemen Arab Rep.
Yemen, People's Democratic Rep. of
Yugoslavia
Zaire
Zambia
Zimbabwe

[2] **Mexico Elected to Security Council.** Mexico was elected Jan. 7 to a seat on the U.N. Security Council by the General Assembly.

[3] Cuba and Colombia had been competing for the seat since balloting had started Oct. 26, 1979. Since neither country could muster the necessary two-thirds majority, both agreed at a meeting of Latin American delegates to withdraw. Latin America was entitled to one seat on the Security Council. In the final General Assembly balloting for the seat being vacated by Bolivia, the vote was Mexico 133 and Cuba three; eight abstained.

[4] The other four nations elected to the Security Council Oct. 26, 1979–Tunisia, Niger, East Germany and the Philippines–took their seats Jan. 1. They replaced Kuwait, Gabon, Czechoslovakia and Nigeria, whose two-year terms expired Dec. 31.

[5] **Development Meeting Ends in Discord.** A general conference of the United Nations Industrial Development Organization ended in discord Feb. 9 in New Delhi, India, when the industrialized Western nations lined up against a proposal by poorer developing countries to create an international fund to assist the developing nations.

[6] The so-called Group of 77, made up of many of the world's developing nations, called for establishment of a global fund with resources of $300 billion by the year 2000. The richer countries would support the fund by contributions.

[7] John W. McDonald, the head of the U.S. delegation, argued that the fund was unnecessary because it would duplicate the efforts of the International Monetary Fund and the World Bank. He also objected to certain specific proposals for administering the funds.

[8] The fund proposal was voted on the last day of the conference and was approved by a margin of 83 to 22. Of the 23 countries in the Organization for Economic Cooperation and Development–a grouping of noncommunist industrialized countries–all but Turkey voted against the proposal. A large number of developing countries–including many of the smaller African nations–abstained or were absent from the final vote. Joining the Group of 77 countries in support of the resolution were China, the Soviet Union and other communist nations.

[9] **U.S. Rejoins ILO.** The U.S. Feb. 18 rejoined the International Labor Organization. The U.S. had withdrawn from the U.N. agency in November 1977 after protesting that it had become politicized and was thus endangering its stated policy of improving the welfare of workers. The Carter Administration was now convinced that the majority of the ILO's membership was "intent on assuring that the organization will live up to its principles and promises," Secretary of State Cyrus Vance said.

[10] **Poland Sentences U.N. Worker.** Alicia Wesolowska, an employee of the United Nations Development Plan, was sentenced March 7 in Poland to seven years' imprisonment. Wesolowska was charged with spying

for an unnamed member of the North Atlantic Treaty Organization.

[11] ***UNESCO Aide Sentenced as Spy***—Percy Stulz, an East German official of the United Nations Educational, Scientific and Cultural Organization was sentenced Sept. 6 by an East German court to three years in prison after having been convicted of spying for West Germany.

[12] East German authorities had disclosed June 10 that Stulz, head of UNESCO's Cultural Heritage Division, had been arrested during a March visit to East Berlin.

[13] **Women's Parley in Copenhagen.** About 1,000 delegates from more than 100 countries met in Copenhagen July 14-30 for the second world conference of the United Nations Decade for Women.

[14] The first conference had been held in Mexico City in 1975. The Copenhagen meeting was intended to assess progress made since the Mexico meeting and to map out strategies for the second half of the women's decade. (In addition to the main conference, there was a parallel gathering—called the Nongovernmental Organization Forum—being held elsewhere in Copenhagen for women's organizations not sponsored by member nations of the U.N.)

[15] In addition to such topics as health, education and employment, the agenda of the main conference provided for discussion of women refugees around the world and the impact upon women of apartheid in South Africa and the Israeli occupation of Arab territories. The controversy surrounding these topics, particularly the Arab-Israeli dispute, absorbed much of the delegates' attention and prompted complaints that extraneous political issues with little connection to women were dominating the conference.

[16] The U.S. and 52 other nations July 17 signed a 30-article agreement, the U.N. Convention on the Elimination of All Forms of Discrimination Against Women. The accord had been approved by the U.N. General Assembly in 1979 and had already been signed by a dozen nations before the Copenhagen ceremony. As in the case of a treaty, U.S. ratification of the convention would require a two-thirds majority in the Senate.

[17] The conference July 30 adopted a five-year plan that incorporated a number of politically controversial sections. They included measures equating Zionism with racism and providing future U.N. aid to Palestinian women in consultation with the PLO. The vote was 94 to 4, with 22 abstentions. Voting against were the U.S., Canada, Australia and Israel. Other sections urged that the U.N. increase its budget for women's projects, that all nations recognize their responsibilities with regard to the increasing number of refugee women and children, and that new emphasis be given to women's health and welfare.

[18] **Muskie Addresses Special Session.** U.S. Secretary of State Edmund Muskie Aug. 25 told the 11th Special Session of the General Assembly the U.S. would "participate constructively" in a new round of international economic discussions scheduled to begin in January 1981. The session was devoted to the discussion of aid by industrialized countries to poor Third World nations.

[19] Cautioning the assembled delegates that they must be realistic, Muskie presented a list of proposals the U.S. was prepared to discuss. He said the U.S. supported programs for funding the search for oil and other energy sources in the Third World, help for food producers, a bigger voice for the Third World countries in international economic institutions such as the International Monetary Fund and the World Bank, and the expansion of preferential tariffs on some products from the developing world.

[20] Indian Foreign Minister P. V. Narasimha Rao presented Third World demands for economic aid. Rao called for a doubling of foreign aid from rich

countries to poorer ones, easing of barriers in industrialized countries to exports from developing ones, and increased prices for raw materials produced by the third World. (See below [26])

[21] ***Zimbabwe Becomes Member***— Zimbabwe Aug. 25 became the 153rd member of the United Nations. The country's prime minister, Robert Mugabe, was present when the Zimbabwean delegation took its seat in the General Assembly.

[22] **Cuban U.N. Diplomat Assassinated.** Felix Garcia Rodriguez, an attache with the Cuban mission to the United Nations, was shot and killed Sept. 11 while driving in the New York borough of Queens. He was the first U.N. official to have been assassinated in New York since the founding of the organization in 1945.

[23] A short time after the murder, callers to news organizations claimed responsibility for the act on behalf of Omega 7, an anti-Castro terrorist group.

General Assembly

[24] **35th General Assembly Opens.** The 35th United Nations General Assembly convened at U.N. headquarters in New York Sept. 16.

[25] The Assembly elected by acclamation its first president from West Germany – Baron Rudiger von Wechmar, who succeeded Salim Ahmed Salim of Tanzania. It also admitted St. Vincent and the Grenadines as the U.N.'s 154th member.

[26] In his inaugural address, von Wechmar criticized the failure of the wealthy nations to agree on a new international economic order, noting that they gave less than seven-tenths of one per cent of their output in foreign aid to Third World nations. Von Wechmar's remarks were especially directed at his own country, which had joined the U.S. and Britain in refusing to back Third World-supported guidelines under which the industrialized states would provide poor nations with billions of dollars in goods

Four persons were injured Oct. 12 in bomb explosion outside Turkish center near headquarters of United Nations in New York. Reponsibility for blast was claimed by "Justice Commandos of Armenian Genocide."

and services. A three-week special U.N. session on economic cooperation and development had ended Sept. 15 with no agreement.

[27] **Moslems Drop Plan to Oust Israel.** The chairman of the Conference of Islamic States announced Oct. 9 that his group had dropped plans, at least for the present, to seek Israel's ouster from the General Assembly.

[28] ***Pol Pot Government Keeps Seat***—The General Assembly Oct. 13 voted, 74 to 35 with 32 abstentions, to defeat a motion to unseat the representative of the deposed Cambodian government of former Premier Pol Pot. The Assembly had defeated a similar move in 1979.

[29] **5 Security Council Members Chosen.** The U.N. General Assembly Nov. 13 completed the selection of five new nonpermanent members of the 15-member Security Council.

[30] Panama, which would replace Jamaica for a two-year term, was chosen by a 111-24 vote, after Costa Rica had withdrawn from the race Nov. 12. Cuba Oct. 20 also had given up its efforts to attain a Security Council seat for the second year in a row. (The other four new members elected (replacements in parentheses) to a two-year term starting Jan. 1, 1981: Japan (Bangladesh); Ireland (Norway); Spain (Portugal), and Uganda (Zambia).

[31] **Assembly Urges Sanctions Against Israel.** The U.N. General Asembly Dec. 15 approved a resolution calling on the Security Council to sever trade relations with Israel unless it withdrew from Arab lands occupied since 1967. The vote was 98-16, with 32 abstaining. Among those voting against were the U.S. and eight of the nine Common Market countries. France abstained.

Another resolution, condemning the Camp David agreements, which had established peace between Israel and Egypt, was approved, 86 to 22, with 40 abstentions. In a third action, the Assembly adopted a document censuring Israel for annexing East Jerusalem. The vote was 143 to one, with four abstentions, including the one cast by the U.S. Only Israel voted against.

See also Afghanistan [13-16, 30, 66]; Cambodia [1-7, 10-11, 15-16]; Cyprus; Iran [23-26, 28-47]; Iraq [12, 20-22, 38-41]; Maritime Affairs [1-8]; Middle East [22-26, 42-57, 68, 79-82]; South Africa [3-5, 9-13]; South-West Africa (Namibia) [1, 3-5, 9-13, 17-20]; Thailand [5-8]

URUGUAY

[1] **Proposed Constitution Voted Down.** A proposal to adopt a new constitution that would have extended the military's power in the government permanently was defeated Nov. 30 in nationwide balloting.

[2] Some 880,000 voters, or 58% of those who cast ballots, opposed the constitution. About 642,000 votes were cast in favor of the constitution. The bulk of the support for the constitution was reported to have come from voters who were lower-middle class, rural, female and over 50 years of age. Voters opposed were said to be younger, urban, better educated and wealthier.

[3] Casting his vote, President Aparicio Mendez Manfredini said, "I feel satisfied for having fulfilled by civic duty." Later after the results had become clear, Interior Minister Gen. Manuel Nunez said the defeat of the government's proposed constitution "is not important to us." The military power in Uruguay rested in a council of 28 generals and admirals who ruled through Mendez, a civilian figure-head president.

See also Human Rights [18]

VANCE, CYRUS—*See*

Afghanistan [11, 17]; Disarmament [8-9]; Iran [1-2, 68-70, 73]; United Nations [9]

VANUATU (New Hebrides)

[1] **Independence Declared.** The joint rule of Britain and France over the New Hebrides, a group of some 70 islands in the South Pacific, came to an end at midnight July 29 as independence ceremonies marked the birth of a new nation, to be called Vanuatu. Walter Lini, an Anglican minister, was installed as the country's first prime minister.

[2] The island group had a population of 112,000. Independence was granted despite a movement on Espiritu Santo, the largest island of the group, seeking autonomy from the rest of the island group. A 200-man force of British and French troops had landed on Espiritu Santo July 24 in an attempt to restore the rule of the overall island government. The soldiers were welcomed with flowers by the natives of the island and there was no fighting, but it was not clear that the separatist movement had been suppressed. Jimmy Stevens, who had led the separatist agitation, was not arrested and neither were other separatist leaders.

[3] **Island Rebellion Put Down.** About a hundred troops from Papua New Guinea Aug. 31 quelled a secessionist movement on Espiritu Santo, arresting some 70 rebels, including the leader of the movement, Jimmy Stevens. The troops from Papua New Guinea, invited by the Vanatu goverment, replaced a British and French force.

[4] Stevens was sentenced Nov. 21 to 14 years and six months in prison by Vanatu's Supreme Court.

VETERANS' AFFAIRS (U.S.)

[1] **WWII WAACs Gain Veterans Status.** The Defense Department April 2 extended full military veteran status to thousands of women who served in the Women's Army Auxiliary Corps (WAAC) during World War II. The move awarded veteran status to some 16,000 women who joined the auxiliary corps but did not remain on duty with its successor, the Women's Army Corps, which was part of the Army. The WAAC functioned for just 15 months, starting in May 1942.

[2] **Vet Aid Bill Signed by Carter.** President Carter Oct. 17 signed a veterns' education bill.

[3] The House Sept. 25 approved a compromise agreement by voice vote, and the Senate passed it Sept. 26. The final bill contained provisions from half a dozen other bills that cleared either the House or Senate. The measure provided a 10% cost-of-living increase for veterans receiving GI Bill education assistance. It also increased by 17% living allowances for disabled veterans enrolled in vocational rehabilitation programs.

[4] One controversial issue was the proposed extension of educational benefits, which was to provide an additional three years during which low-income Vietnam-era veterans could use their GI Bill benefits for appren-

ticeships, on-the-job training or secondary education programs. President Carter had supported this proposal, which the Senate accepted in a modified form. But the House rejected the extension and successfully moved to omit it from the final version of the bill. The House argued that extension of the benefits would violate the principle of "equal benefits for equal service" by giving Vietnam-era veterans a longer period of benefits than earlier veterans had received.

[5] In addition, the bill expanded the available vocational rehabilitation services for veterans with service-related disabilities to include training in skills not directly necessary for employment, but essential to independent living. The bill would cost $152.5 million in fiscal 1981.

VIETNAM, Socialist Republic of

[1] **Cabinet Shakeup.** In a government shakeup announced Feb. 7, Vo Nguyen Giap was replaced as defense minister by Gen. Van Tien Dung, and Foreign Minister Nguyen Duy Trinh was succeeded by Nguyen Co Thach, who had served as minister of state for foreign affairs. Both Giap and Trinh were still referred to as deputy premiers.

[2] **Vietnam Quits China Peace Talks.** Deputy Foreign Minister Dinh Nho Liem, Vietnam's representative at the Sino-Vietnamese peace talks in Peking, left China Feb. 8. His return to Hanoi signified an indefinite halt to the peace talks.

[3] The conference had failed to produce an agenda for settling the dispute between the two countries. China had insisted that the talks include Vietnam's invasion of Cambodia, which Vietnam refused to discuss.

[4] China told Vietnam March 6 that it was suspending the peace talks between the two countries. China accused the Vietnamese of "redoubling their activities of opposition and hostility to China" and of "intensifying their war of aggression in Cambodia and threatening the peace and security of Thailand and Southeast Asia." Chinese Premier Hua Kuo-feng March 9 promised his country's full support for Cambodian guerrillas fighting the Vietnamese-supported Cambodian government forces.

[5] **China, Vietnam Trade Charges.** China and Vietnam accused each other of armed border violations.

[6] A Chinese protest note sent to Hanoi July 5 accused Vietnam of "incessant armed provocations" along the frontier. It claimed that Vietnamese troops had intruded into China or fired across the border on five separate occasions between July 1 and 3. China claimed the attacks were intended to divert attention from Vietnamese raids into Thailand and to "lighten the pressure on world opinion for a Soviet troop withdrawal" from Afghanistan.

[7] Vietnam July 4 had accused China of shelling Vietnam territory earlier in the week, causing many deaths and heavy property damage. Vietnamese Foreign Minister Nguyen Co Thach said July 7 that China had moved three new divisions to the border with Vietnam.

See also Cambodia [3, 7, 9-13]

VOLCANOS

[1] **Mt. St. Helens Erupts in Washington.** A long-dormant volcano in Washington state, Mt. St. Helens, erupted March 26, hurling a plume of volcanic ash and gases 15,000 feet (about 4,600 meters) into the air and setting off mudslides and avalanches.

[2] Mt. St. Helens, dormant since 1857, was the first volcano to erupt in the contiguous United States since Mt. Lassen erupted in northern California in 1917.

[3] Officials said that volcanic steam and ash had been billowing from two crescent shaped faults across the summit of the 9,677-foot (2,950-meter)

Mt. St. Helens erupts May 18.

mountain, one three miles (five kilometers) long, the other about a mile (1.6 kilometers). The steaming crater was reported to have widened from 1,000 to 6,000 yards (900 to 5,500 meters) during the eruptions, which continued regularly through April 1.

[4] The eruption of the volcano had followed a week-long series of earthquakes and smaller explosions of smoke and ash. The quakes had been registering an average of 4.0 on the Richter scale and were occurring at the rate of about one per hour, according to the U.S. Geological Survey and University of Washington scientists. But by March 25 the quakes had increased in frequency to more than 60 an hour before returning to two or three per hour a day later.

[5] The volcano was located about 100 miles (160 kilometers) south of Seattle and 25 miles (40 kilometers) north of Portland in the Cascade mountain range in southwestern Washington.

[6] Mt. St. Helens erupted May 18 in a giant blast that hurled a plume of ash and steam some 60,000 feet (18,000 meters) into the sky, set off mudslides and floods and ignited lightning storms and huge forest fires. Nineteen persons had been confirmed dead by May 23 as a result of the eruption and at least 77 persons were reported to be missing.

[7] Dark clouds of volcanic ash and dust from the explosion blotted out the sun over eastern Washington, turning the day into night more than 160 miles (260 kilometers) away and creating problems of fallout in areas 500 miles (800 kilometers) downwind. The eruption triggered flows of super-heated rock and gas that swept down the volcano's slopes flattening every tree in a 120-square-mile (310-square-kilometer) area. Later, massive mudflows from ash and melted snow sent walls of churning mud, water and debris down the Toutle River on the volcano's north side. The mudflows destroyed a sawmill, dozens of houses and cabins and at least 10 bridges.

[8] Many communities in eastern Washington, northern Idaho and western Montana were virtually closed, blanketed by drifting volcanic ash up to seven inches (18 centimeters) deep. In Walla Walla, Wash., 160 miles (260 kilometers) to the east of the volcano, drifting ash blackened the sky, triggering automatic street lighting as if dusk had come. Near-zero visibility forced the closing of highways and airports. Schools closed and public offices operated on curtailed schedules. Ash clogged roads, stranding motorists in many area where ash drifts were reported three to four feet high.

[9] The volcanic blast blew off the mountain's 9,677-foot (2,949.5 meter) summit, reducing it to an elevation of between 8,000 and 8,300 feet (2,438 and 2,528 meters). The blast also opened a crater more than a mile (1.6 kilometers) long and about 1,700 feet (500 meters) deep.

[10] President Carter declared Washington state a major disaster area May 21, which would permit the use of federal funds in disaster relief and recovery efforts. He flew to the Pacific Northwest to inspect the devastation and to meet with federal experts and local and state officials.

[11] Further eruptions of Mt. St. Helens occurred May 25 and June 12. Twenty-five persons were confirmed dead by July 4, authorities reported. At least 40 persons were still missing and believed dead.

[12] The destruction from the eruptions covered some 150 square miles (390 square kilometers) with forests laid flat, thousands of miles of roads blocked, bridges destroyed, fish and game killed, crops destroyed and damaged.

[13] In Yakima, Spokane and smaller cities in central Washington, northern Idaho, Oregon and Montana, choking clouds of volcanic ash blocked streets, crippled automobiles, clogged sewers and streets and brought life to a virtual standstill in some instances. The dust

Tall fir trees toppled like toothpicks by force of Mt. St. Helens eruption May 18.

drifted some 200 miles (320 kilometers) northward over British Columbia, dusting the northern population centers of Puget Sound in Washington state. In Portland, Ore., ash descended on the city in a fine, gritty film, turning leaves and lawns a dull gray and forcing the closing May 25 and June 13 of the Portland International Airport.

[14] The economic damage to the region from the Mt. St. Helens eruptions was reported June 10 to have been set at $2.7 billion. Losses in felled and seared timber on federal lands alone were reported May 24 at $500 million. The cost of reforestation and the estimated loss of wildlife and fish were expected to add at least $300 million. Agricultural losses in wheat and other crops were expected to reach $260 million.

[15] Volcanic debris clogged the Columbia River. At leat 33 ships were reported June 30 trapped upriver and the U.S. Army Corps of Engineers had mobilized some 300 men and six dredges in a $44 million operation to reopen the river.

VOLCKER, PAUL A.—*See* Federal Reserve System

WATER

[1] **Imperial Valley Water Rights Upheld.** The Supreme Court June 16 ruled unanimously that the owners of farms in California's Imperial Valley could continue to receive federally subsidized irrigation water regardless of the size of their farms. The cases, consolidated for judgment, were *Bryant v. Yellen, California v. Yellen,* and *Imperial Irrigation District v. Yellen.*

[2] The high court overturned a 1977 ruling by the U.S. 9th Circuit Court of Appeals and upset the effort of Interior Secretary Cecil D. Andrus to enforce a provision of the Reclamation Act of 1902. The provision limited the size of the farms receiving federal water to 160 acres (64 hectares). According to papers filed with the Supreme Court, about 233,000 acres (93,200 hectares) of the Imperial Valley were held by large landowners, including major corporations.
[3] The high court held that under the Boulder Canyon Project Act, which implemented the Reclamation Act in the Imperial Valley in 1929, the farms in the valley were exempt from the acreage restriction. Led by Justice Byron R. White, the court noted that a large number of acres in the valley had been under private irrigation before 1929, and concluded that Washington, through the project act, had not intended farmers to relinquish land that already had a vested right to Colorado River waters. The decision concerned only the Imperial Valley and did not appear to be applicable to more than one million acres of federally irrigated land in other Western states.

WATERGATE

[1] **Tapes Made Public.** The Watergate tape recordings were opened to the public for the first time at the National Archives in Washington May 28.
[2] The tapes were being played in a series of sessions, which would continue as long as there was demand. Some 31 tapes were being made public, only 12½ hours of the 6,000 hours of conversations secretly recorded by former President Richard M. Nixon in the White House and other presidential offices. They had all been heard before in courts and transcripts from them had been published. Nixon was pursuing court action to bar public access to the other tapes.
[3] **Nixon Impeachment Lawyer Sentenced.** The attorney who argued against the impeachment of President Nixon was sentenced June 10 to a year and a day in prison for embezzling $46,000 from a client.
[4] Samuel A. Garrison, 38, had been charged with embezzling the funds while serving as a court-appointed trustee of A&U Mobile Homes of Georgia. The sentence was handed down by U.S. District Judge James Turk in Roanoke, Va. Under its terms, Garrison would be eligible for parole one day after he reported to the minimum security prison at Maxwell Air Force Base in Alabama. Once released, he would be placed on probation for three years.

[5] As special counsel to the Republicans on the House Judiciary committee, Garrison unsuccessfully sought to convince the committee's members to vote against impeaching Nixon. Garrison also served as chief counsel and legislative liaison for Vice President Spiro Agnew before his resignation.

WATER POLLUTION—*See* Environment [1-5]

WELFARE—*See* Civil & Constitutional Rights [2-4]

WEATHER

[1] **Pacific Storms Lash Calif., Ariz.** Pacific storms struck southern California Feb. 13-22 with torrential rains, gale-force winds and flash-flooding that left at least 26 dead and thousands homeless in dozens of communities.

[2] The ocean storms dumped nearly 13 inches (33 centimeters) of rain on the region in a nine-day onslaught that flooded streets and highways, damaged hundreds of homes, turned valleys into oozing mud and debris and broke river levees. The Pacific storms struck as far east as Phoenix Feb. 14-17, bringing the worst floods in 40 years. Floodwaters from the Salt River covered many low-lying communities and washed out roads and bridges; some 6,000 families were forced to evacuate their homes.

[3] President Carter declared six California counties (Feb. 21) and three Arizona counties (Feb. 20) federal disaster areas. The California counties were Los Angeles, Ventura, Orange, San Diego, Santa Barbara and Riverside. The Arizona counties were Gila, Maricopa and Yauapai.

[4] **Tornadoes Hit Kalamazoo, Mich.**

Deluge breaks over Everett, Wash. early April 28. Electrical circuits were cut, thousands startled out of their sleep. Photo is 12-second exposure.

& Grand Island, Neb. Tornadoes struck Kalamazoo, Mich. May 13 killing at least seven persons, injuring dozens of others, destroying some 400 buildings and leaving more than 1,200 persons homeless.

[5] A series of seven tornadoes June 3 struck Grand Island, Neb., killing four persons and injuring nearly 200. More than 550 buildings were destroyed in the central Nebraska city. The twisters swept through the city of 40,000 for three hours, causing a six-block-wide swath of damage.

[6] **Drought & Heat Wave in Midwest, South.** A summer-long drought and record-breaking heat wave hit the United States June 23-Aug. 15, causing an agricultural disaster to farm crops and livestock and more than a month of 100-degree Fahrenheit temperatures. By Aug. 15, the heat wave had left 1,265 persons dead in 20 states.

[7] The heat wave blanketed states in the mid-Mississippi Valley, the Southwest and the South with the hottest weather in decades, causing particularly high death tolls in Texas, Arkansas, Oklahoma, Missouri, Kansas and Louisiana. In Dallas and Fort Worth, Texas, where the temperature hit 100 degrees or more for 33 consecutive days, the heat wave drove up energy comsumption to record highs, strained electric utility service, dried up reservoirs and caused highways to buckle. On July 16, President Carter ordered that nearly $7 million in emergency funds be made available to Texas, Oklahoma, Missouri, Kansas and Louisiana to aid heat sufferers.

[8] The drought, considered the worst since the Dust Bowl years of the 1930s, caused extensive agricultural damage, withering crops, destroying livestock and poultry, scorching range grass and aggravating forest fires. Overall, losses were expected to exceed $12 billion. Among the hardest-hit by the high temperatures and drought were the poultry farmers and cattle ranchers in the South and Southwest and wheat farmers in the northern Great Plains. Other farm crops badly damaged by the drought included corn, cotton, fruits, hay, grain, peanuts, soybeans, tobacco and vegetables.

[9] The drought also triggered forest fires in Arizona, where thousands of acres of woodlands were burning out of control June 29. In Colorado, the state's worst forest fire on record destroyed nearly 10,050 acres (40.66 square kilometers) in the White River National Forest. The meteorological cause of the drought and heat wave was basically a high-pressure system that had held in place over the Texas, Oklahoma and Arkansas region. The system had kept away cloud-bearing, low-pressure systems, which thus increased the heat hitting the ground below.

[10] **'Allen' Rips Caribbean, Texas Gulf Coast.** Hurricane Allen, the second-strongest Atlantic storm of the century, tore a path of destruction Aug. 4-11 across the eastern Caribbean, Mexico's Yucatan Peninsula and the Texas Gulf Coast in a 1,200-mile (1,920-kilometer) rampage that demolished thousands of homes, destroyed millions of dollars in crops and left at least 272 persons dead.

[11] **Water Shortages Hit Northeast.** The four-state commission that regulated public use of drinking water in the New York-Philadelphia metropolitan region warned residents Dec. 1 to begin conserving water in the wake of the worst drought to hit the area since the mid-1960s.

[12] The warning, issued by the Delaware River Basin Commission, said that the water levels in Delaware, New Jersey, New York and Pennsylvania were "substantially below normal as a result of rainfall deficiencies . . . and that severe drought conditions could develop in 1981 if these trends continue."

WICHITA, KAN.—*See* Civil Disorders [15]

From Peking, playful giant pandas. Ling-Ling nuzzles Hsing-Hsing at Washington's National Zoo May 16.

WILDLIFE

[1] **Alaska Lands Bill Signed.** The Alaska lands bill was signed into law by President Carter Dec. 2.

[2] The new law designated more than 104 million acres of national parks, wildlife refuges and wilderness areas. By so doing, the law doubled the size of the nation's national park and refuge system, tripled the size of the country's wilderness areas and doubled the size of the federal wild and scenic rivers system.

[3] **Law Protects Non-Game Wildlife.** The Fish and Wildlife Conservation Act of 1980 was signed into law by President Carter Sept. 29.

[4] The goal of the legislation was to provide protection for non-game animals, or those that were not hunted for sport, food, fur or pelt. Legislation already existed for protection of game animals.

[5] The law called for inventories of non-game animals by states. A determination would be made of the status of each species. Grants were authorized for the implementation of conservation plans, once approved. The act provided $5 million a year over a four-year period.

WOMEN'S RIGHTS

[1] **U.S. Bars Sexual Harassment at Work.** The Equal Employment Opportunity Commission April 11 issued regulations prohibiting sexual harassment of workers by their supervisors whether in government or in private business.

[2] The regulations, published in the *Federal Register,* would apply to federal, state and local government agencies and to private employers with 15 or more employees. The federal rules stated that employers would have an "affirmative duty" to prevent and eliminate sexual harassment on the job, whether "physical or verbal in nature."

[3] The commission set forth three

criteria for determining whether an action constituted unlawful sexual harassment. "Unwelcome sexual advances" were defined as illegal if the employee's submission were made an explicit or implicit condition of employment; if the employee's response were made a basis for employment decisions or if the advances hindered a workers' performance, creating a hostile or "offensive" environment.

[4] To enforce the regulations, the commission was empowered to ask for an award of back pay, reinstatement of an employee, promotion or other types of redress available under Title VII of the Civil Rights Act of 1964. If an employer declined to settle a complaint through conciliation, the commission could take action in a federal court for the same types of legal relief.

[5] Eleanor Holmes Norton, chairman of the commission, said that "prevalence of sexual harassment is well known to be great." However, statistics were not available on the extent of the problem, because female employees were often hesitant to make formal complaints, fearing embarrassment or retaliation, Norton said. Norton also said that the new regulations would apply in the same way to complaints filed by male employees.

[6] **Chicago Settles Strip Search Cases.** The city of Chicago agreed March 26 to pay $69,500 in damages to 191 women who were stripped and searched for minor offenses ranging from traffic violations to smoking on the subway.

[7] The agreement, announced by the U.S. Justice Department, was filed in U.S. District Court in Chicago and, if approved by the court, would settle a lawsuit brought against the Chicago Police Department by the American Civil Liberties Union on behalf of the women.

[8] **Firefighter Wins Breast-Feeding Case.** An Iowa City, Iowa firefighter, who had been suspended for breast-feeding her baby at the firehouse, March 20 was awarded $2,000 in damages and $26,400 in lawyer's fees by the Iowa Civil Rights Commission.

[9] Linda Eaton, 27, the city's first female firefighter, had waged a year-long legal battle to retain her job and win the right to nurse her son, while on 24-hour shifts at the fire station. She had been sent home from work for nursing her child during unassigned work time in a women's locker room. Later suspended from her post, she filed a sex-discrimination suit, citing an unwritten fire department policy banning "regularly scheduled family visits."

[10] **Chicagoan Indicted in ERA Bribe Probe.** A volunteer for the National Organization for Women was indicted June 5 by a Sangamon County, Ill. grand jury in Springfield on charges of offering a $1,000 bribe to an Illinois lawmaker to vote for the proposed federal Equal Rights Amendment.

[11] The indictment charged Wanda Brandstetter of Chicago with bribery and solicitation in offering a $1,000 campaign contribution to State Rep. Nord L. Swanstrom, a Republican, in exchange for a 'yes' vote on the ERA.

[12] A major effort to win ERA ratification had been aimed at Illinois, the only major northern industrial state that had not approved the proposed constitutional amendment. (The amendment to ban sex discrimination had been ratified to date in 35 of the 38 states needed to win passage. Five states had rescinded their approval, but the legality of those actions was being challenged in court.)

[13] Brandstetter Nov. 7 was fined $500 and ordered to perform 150 hours of public service work following her conviction on the bribery charge.

[14] ***Narrow Defeat in Illinois***—The Illinois House of Representatives June 18 failed to ratify the proposed Equal Rights Amendment to the U.S. Constitution, for the seventh time in eight years.

[15] After two hours of sometimes heated debate, the vote was 102 in favor to 71 against, five votes short of

the majority of 107 needed for approval. Since 1972, the Illinois House had defeated the ERA six times and the Senate four. The amendment had been approved by each legislative chamber once, but not in the same year, as required by law.

[16] **Excommunication of Mormon Feminist Upheld.** The excommunication of Mormon feminist Sonia Johnson was upheld by the highest authority in the Church of Jesus Christ of Latter-day Saints, it was reported July 1. Mormon leaders meeting in Salt Lake City urged Johnson to repent before seeking reinstatement. She had been expelled in 1979 for being an Equal Rights Amendment activist. The Mormon Church opposed the ERA on the ground that it was a threat to the family.

See also Congress (U.S.) [8]; United Nations [13-17]

WORLD BANK—*See* Appointments & Resignations [4]; Economy (International) [9-10, 16-18]

YACHTING

[1] ***Freedom* Retains America's Cup.** The U.S. 12-meter yacht *Freedom* Sept. 25 completed the 24th consecutive successful defense of the America's Cup. *Freedom* defeated the 12-meter yacht *Australia*, four races to one, in the best-of-seven competition. This was the 129th year of the triennial event.

[2] *Freedom*, skippered by Dennis Conner, had been chosen to defend the cup Aug. 29, after winning 43 of the 47 trial races. *Freedom's* toughest competition in the trials had been the yacht *Clipper*, which finished with a won-lost record of 13-32. The 1974 and 1977 America's Cup victor, *Courageous*, skippered by Ted Turner, had been eliminated in the trials Aug. 25, after winning only seven of 34 races.

[4] *Australia*, skippered by Jim Hardy, had won the right to challenge for the 1980 cup Sept. 5, after ousting *France 3* in the trials. It was the yacht's second straight appearance as the cup challenger. All of the trials and the America's Cup races were held on a 24.3-mile (38.8-kilometer) course off Newport, R.I.

YEMEN ARAB REPUBLIC (North Yemen)

[1] **Guerrilla War.** Fighting between the North Yemen army and opposition guerrillas backed by South Yemen increased in May, it was reported June 1. The escalation of hostilities ironically came at a time when relations between the governments of the two Yemens had significantly improved.

[2] The clashes were described as the most extensive in the area since the March 1979 border war that prompted President Carter to send an emergency arms shipment to North Yemen.

[3] The fighting escalated after Abdel Fattah Ismail was replaced as President of South Yemen by Ali Nasser Mohammed Al-Hasani April 23. Hasani reportedly tried to increase his control over the southern-based guerrillas, who then fled in large numbers back to North Yemen, which led to several clashes with North Yemeni regular forces, as well as with local tribes.

YEMEN, PEOPLE'S DEMOCRATIC REPUBLIC OF (South Yemen)

[1] **Soviet, Cuban, East German Activity Grows.** The Soviet Union stepped up its military presence in South Yemen during the first part of 1980, it was reported June 9. Cuban and East German military activity also increased in the country.

[2] Diplomatic and official sources in South Yemen said that Soviets turned the country into a "military warehouse" after the Soviet invasion of Afghanistan in December 1979. Western intelligence reports estimated that the number of Soviet military advisers had grown from 500 in 1977 to more than 1,000 in 1980.

[3] South Yemeni officials were quoted as saying that over 4,000 Cuban military instructors were in the country, twice the number that were there in 1978. The East Germans in South Yemen reportedly ran the internal security system, the external intelligence network and the immigration section.

YUGOSLAVIA

[1] **President Tito Dies.** Josip Broz Tito, president of Yugoslavia and leader of the League of Communists, its ruling party, died May 4 after being hospitalized since January. The last of World War II's major figures died three days before his 88th birthday.

[2] Stevan Doronjski replaced Tito as League of Communists chairman. Vice President Lazar Kolisevski was named interim president of the State Presidency, an eight-member collective presidency made up of representatives from Yugoslavia's six republics and two autonomous provinces. Kolisevski was replaced later in May by Cvijetin Mijatovic, who would serve a one-year rotating term.

JOSIP BROZ TITO

[3] Tributes to Tito poured into Yugoslavia from around the world, U.S. President Carter called him "a towering figure on the world stage. . . ." The U.S.S.R., which had expelled Tito from the international communist movement in 1948, praised the Yugoslav leader. Moscow did not mention the stormy course of Soviet-Yugoslav relations since 1948.

[4] Josip Broz was born May 7, 1892 in the village of Kumrovec in Croatia. He left home at age 15 to work in Vienna and enlisted in the Austro-Hungarian army when World War I broke out. Wounded and captured by the Russians, he joined the Communists when the October Revolution erupted in 1917.

[5] Broz left Russia in 1920 to work for the Yugoslav Communist Party, which had been organized the year before. He took the alias Tito after the party was outlawed in 1921. Tito rose rapidly, but was arrested in 1927 and again in 1929. Released in 1934, he worked underground inside Yugoslavia and abroad. He was named Communist Party leader in 1937 by the Comintern, the international communist organization.

[6] In 1938, Tito returned to Yugoslavia. When World War II started, he organized his League of Communists into the Partisan guerrilla army. They soon became the strongest anti-Nazi fighters in Yugoslavia and received some Allied support. A coalition between Tito and the Yugoslav government in exile collapsed soon after the war, and the League of Communists emerged as the sole power in Yugoslavia. Tito consolidated his control by brutally suppressing opponents, including Gen. Draja Mihailovic, who was executed, and

Aloysius Cardinal Stepinac, who was imprisoned until 1951.

[7] Although Tito was a dedicated follower of Stalin, he quarreled with the Soviets in 1948 over Soviet economic assistance. Moscow demanded that Yugoslavia concentrate on raw materials and light industry. Tito wanted to develop the country's heavy industry sector. The conflict escalated into a question of whether a communist country must follow Moscow's orders or whether it should place its own interests first. Yugoslavia was expelled from the Cominform, the organization that replaced the Comintern after World War II. Relations with the U.S.S.R. varied from hostile to cordial after Stalin's death, but Yugoslavia never rejoined the Soviet bloc.

[8] Instead, Tito sought to steer a foreign policy course that was distant from both the Soviets and the West. His nonaligned policy took concrete shape in 1961 at the first conference of nonaligned nations in Belgrade. Domestically, Tito's policies progressed from extreme repression to increasing openness. Major economic reforms began in 1965 and turned Yugoslavia into a mixed economy, with elements of private enterprise combined with central control. Among the principal features were factory management by workers' councils, less media censorship and fewer limits on travel abroad than in most other communist countries.

[9] **New Party Chief Chosen.** Lazar Mojsov Oct. 20 was elected president of the collective leadership of the country's ruling communist party.

[10] Mojsov, a 59-year-old Macedonian, succeeded Stevan Doronjski, from the autonomous province of Vojvodina, who had assumed temporary duties as party chief at the death of Tito. A lawyer and former director of the party newspaper *Borba*, Mojsov also had held diplomatic posts. He had been a Yugoslav delegate to the United Nations and served as president of the U.N. General Assembly in 1977-78.

Z

ZAIRE

[1] **Corruption Found in U.S. Aid.** U.S. aid officials told Congress Feb. 28 that much of the food and military aid sent to Zaire was diverted from its intended recipients. American officials conceded that "corruption and black marketeering" were widespread and beyond U.S. control in Zaire.

[2] U.S. investigations concluded that about 13% of all aid shipments was diverted to personal use by Zairian government officials. They admitted that they did not know if the rest of the aid reached the general population.

[3] **Students Boycott Classes, Riot.** University students in Kinshasa, the capital, rampaged through the streets April 16-17, burning buses and cars in a protest against the high cost of public transportation. They ignored a warning April 15 by President Mobutu Sese Seko to end a boycott of their classes, which had begun in the middle of March.

[4] **Debt Rescheduling Agreed.** The government of Zaire reached agreement April 23 to reschedule $400 million in debts owed to more than 130 foreign banks. The debt would be repaid over the next 10 years, with strict timing on when each portion of the total debt was due. The banks involved were U.S., Western European and Japanese.

[5] Zaire's total foreign debt was put at almost $4 billion, according to a report April 24 in the *Journal of Commerce.*

ZIMBABWE (formerly Rhodesia)

[1] Zimbabwe became independent in 1980. Former guerrilla leader Robert Mugabe and his party won the elections, and Mugabe was named prime minister. The U.S. congratulated Mugabe on his victory. The prime minister later visited the U.S., and in New York, described his Marxist election campaign statements as "propaganda." Meanwhile, Zimbabwe broke diplomatic relations with South Africa.

[2] **Mugabe Wins Election.** Robert Mugabe, who for six years fought the white minority Rhodesian government as leader of the Zimbabwe African National Union guerrilla force, won the election for a new black government in Zimbabwe Rhodesia. The results were announced March 4 after three days of voting Feb. 27-29.

[3] Mugabe's party received 62.9% of the popular vote. It captured 57 of the 80 seats reserved for blacks in the future 100-member parliament and was assured of an unchallenged majority.

[4] The rest of the results were: 20 seats and 24.1% of the vote for Joshua Nkomo, Mugabe's former guerrilla colleague and head of the Zimbabwe African People's Union-Patriotic Front, and three seats and 8.2% of vote for Bishop Abel Muzorewa, prime minister of the former black-led government. (Whites voted separately Feb. 14 for the 20 parliamentary seats reserved for them. The Rhodesian

Front, led by former Prime Minister Ian Smith, won all seats.)

[5] In a news briefing March 4, Mugabe held out the possibility of including some of his former rivals in his government despite his majority. He said, "Our theme is one of reconciliation. We want to insure a sense of security on the part of everyone. . . ." An avowed Marxist, Mugabe nevertheless assured the whites that their interests would be taken into account. "There is no intention on our part to use the advantage of the majority we have secured to victimize the minority," he declared. "That will not happen. We will ensure that there is a place for everybody in this country."

[6] "We recognize that the economic structure is based on capitalism and that whatever ideas we have must build on that," he continued. "We are not going to interfere with private property, whether it be farms or whether it be the mining sector or the industrial sector. The modifications can only take place in a gradual way." Moderation was evident also in Mugabe's reference to his foreign policy intentions, especially with regard to South Africa. "The reality is that we have to coexist with them," he commented at his news conference. He added that "we should pledge ourselves . . . to noninterference in South African affairs and they to noninterference in our affairs."

[7] ***Domestic Reactions***—Nkomo accepted the results March 4 with grace and indicated that he would accept a position in Mugabe's Cabinet if it were offered. Muzorewa at first pledged "absolute commitment to cooperate," but later charged that the elections were "absolutely unfree and unfair" because of intimidation by Mugabe's supporters.

[8] Whites generally were disheartened by the results of Mugabe's reputation as a doctrinaire Marxist. But Ian Smith indicated that his attitude had softened somewhat. "I learned in London that Mr. Mugabe is a far different

A boat on Zimbabwe's Kariba Lake is polling station Feb. 27. British bobby shows woman how to cast ballot as others wait their turn.

person from the Marxist doctrines that surrounded his people," he said "He is a pragmatist."

[9] ***Foreign Reactions***—The U.S. March 4 congratulated Mugabe on his "resounding victory" and said that it looked forward to working with the new government. A British government statement expressed satisfaction that the elections had gone smoothly considering the history of hostility in the country. South African Prime Minister Pieter Botha had no direct comment on Mugabe's victory except to warn that "any neighbor which allows its territory to be used for attacks on . . . South Africa and its security will have to face the full force of the republic's strength." (On stock markets March 4, Rhodesian government bonds and shares in companies with Rhodesian interests fell sharply.)

[10] ***Vote Called Fair***—A Commonwealth observation team March 2 concluded that the election had been basically free and fair. The team was composed of 63 members from 11 Commonwealth nations and had been sent to monitor Britain's handling of the election.

[11] **Independence Gained.** Zimbabwe Rhodesia officially became the independent nation of Zimbabwe midnight April 17 as the British flag was lowered over Salisbury.

[12] Prince Charles of Britain presided at the ceremonies. He gave the country's charter of independence to President-elect Rev. Canaan Banana. Immediately afterward, Banana took the oath of office. Next was the swearing-in of Robert Mugabe as prime minister, ending 90 years of white rule.

[13] The 21 ministers in Mugabe's Cabinet were sworn in April 19 as independence celebrations continued. The next day, Finance Minister Enos Nkala issued a budget, the government's first official action. Nkala said priority would go to easing the burden on Zimbabwe's poor blacks. The sales tax was reduced to 10% from 15% on many items. It was eliminated completely on staple foods such as margarine, cooking oil, sugar and tea. Prices for luxuries, especially liquor, were increased an average of 35%. A 10% price increase was decreed on tobacco and beer.

[14] The U.S. and Britain had quickly announced their intentions to aid Zimbabwe. The U.S. April 14 offered $15 million in aid to help rebuild the country's rural areas, which were shattered by years of guerrilla war. Britain April 15 announced that it would give Zimbabwe $165 million between 1981-83. Part of the money would go to train civil servants and the Zmibabwean army.

[15] **Ties to South Africa Are Ended.** Zimbabwe severed diplomatic relations with South Africa June 26.

[16] **White Army Chief Resigns.** Lt. Gen. Peter Walls, the white chief of Zimbabwe's joint Military High Command, planned to leave his post July 29, the Defense Ministry announced July 17. Walls had commanded the Rhodesian army in the seven-year war against the black nationalist guerrillas.

[17] **Cabinet Minister Charged with Murder.** Edgar Z. Tekere, a senior Zimbabwe Cabinet minister and a powerful figure in Prime Minister Mugabe's ruling party, Aug. 6 was arrested and charged with the Aug. 4 murder of an elderly white farmer.

[18] Tekere, considered the most radical member of the Cabinet, was the minister of manpower, planning and development.

[19] ***Tekere Freed***—A Salisbury court Dec. 8 freed Manpower, Planning and Development Minister Edgar Z. Tekere along with one of his bodyguards even though it had determined that Tekere had murdered white farmer Gerald Adams Aug. 4.

[20] Judge John Pittman, a South African-born white, said he had not found that Tekere and his men had acted "in good faith" as required by the 1975 Indemnity and Compensation Act, which shielded government of-

ficials from criminal charges resulting from antiterrorist activities. However, the two court assessors, whose function in determining the issues of fact in the case was similar to a jury's, disagreed with Pittman. Peter Nemapara, a black, and Chris Greenland, a colored (person of mixed race), were both Zimbabwean magistrates temporarily serving as assessors. Their decisions carried equal weight with the judge's.

[21] **Mugabe, in the U.S., Praises Carter.** Prime Minister Mugabe Aug. 27 praised President Carter for his role in helping settle Zimbabwe's civil war.

[22] Mugabe's praise came during a week-long trip to the U.S., which earlier had taken him to New York City, where he had taken Zimbabwe's new seat at the U.N., visited Harlem, encouraged businessmen to invest in his country and called the Marxist statements of his election campaign "propaganda."

[23] **Press Curbs.** The government Oct. 24 reimposed controls on foreign journalists similar to those enforced by former Rhodesian authorities under minority rule.

[24] The controls required foreign journalists to obtain temporary employment permits. The temporary permits, which the Rhodesians had issued on a monthly basis, would allow the government to deny facilities to "irresponsible and undesirable" journalists.

[25] **43 Killed in Guerrilla Clashes.** At least 43 persons were killed and 300 injured in fighting Nov. 10-11 between Zimbabwean rival guerrilla factions.

[26] Supporters of Prime Minister Mugabe and of his chief rival, Home Affairs Minister Joshua Nkomo, clashed near Bulawayo, the country's second largest city, where more than 3,000 former guerrilla soldiers from both factions had been resettled. Only six of the dead were former guerrilla soldiers. The rest were black civilians caught in the crossfire of mortar, rocket, and machine gun attacks.

[27] ***Nkomo Supporters Arrested***— Nine prominent supporters of Home Affairs Minister Nkomo were arrested Nov. 21 as tensions between rival factions in Prime Minister Mugabe's coalition government continued to rise.

[28] Violence continued the next day during weekend municipal elections. Two persons were killed and 18 injured Nov. 22 when a hand grenade was thrown into a beerhall in a black township near Salisbury. The attack brought to 92 the number of persons killed in factional violence since Zimbabwe achieved independence in April.

[29] Incomplete returns from the elections reported Nov. 23 reflected the tribal divisions of the ruling coalition. Mugabe's ZANU had won the votes of the country's majority Shona tribesmen while ZAPU-PF, led by Nkomo, won among the minority Ndebeles.

See also United Nations [21]